The Syndicalist

The Syndicalist

**Reproduced in facsimile
with an introduction by
Geoff Brown**

Spokesman

First published in 1975 by Spokesman

This edition published in 2011 by
Spokesman
Russell House, Bulwell Lane
Nottingham NG6 0BT
England

Phone 0115 9708318
Fax 0115 9420433
elfeuro@compuserve.com
www.spokesmanbooks.com

Printed by the Russell Press Ltd (www.russellpress.com)

Contents

1912
VOLUME ONE

1913
VOLUME TWO

1914
VOLUME THREE

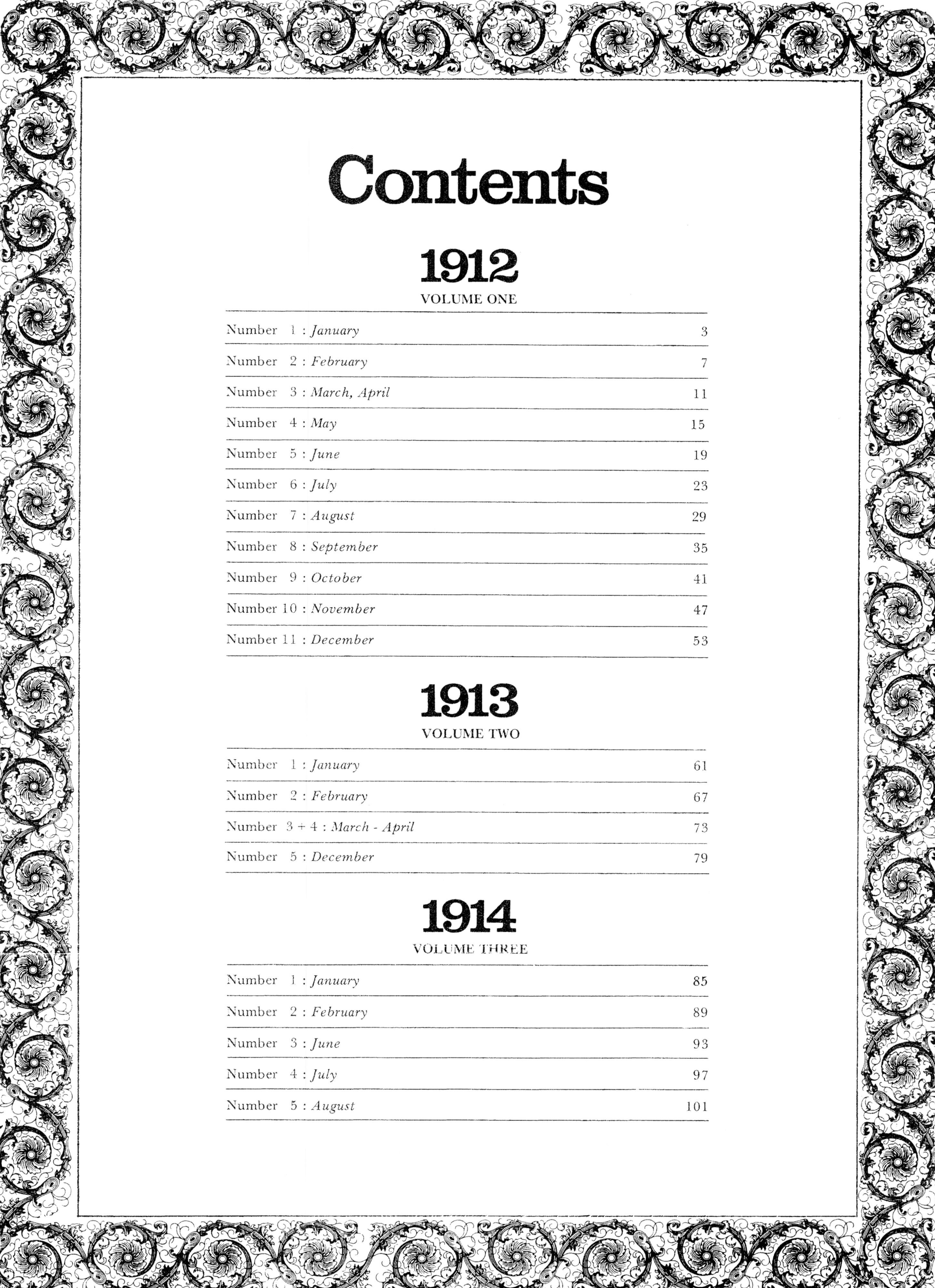

Introduction

In a long article, "Syndicalism in England. Its Origin and History", in *The Times* of April 16, 1912, it was stated with considerable confidence that "The existence of a strong Syndicalist movement in this country can no longer be denied, though attempts have been made up till quite recently to deny it." One of the reasons for putting forward this claim was the belief that the successful wave of transport workers' strikes in the summer of 1911 had been organised "under Syndicalist influence". This is not entirely true. The leaders of the main unions involved, Havelock Wilson of the National Sailors' and Firemen's Union, and Ben Tillett and James Sexton of the London and Liverpool based dockers' unions respectively, were not, and did not claim to be, syndicalists. But in the summer of 1911 they seemed to act as if they were — they stressed the importance of thorough preparatory organisation, of solidarity actions and sympathetic strikes. Tom Mann, the leading syndicalist in Britain, had worked extremely closely with Tillett and Wilson in particular and was closely involved in both the preparations for the seamen's strike and in the conduct of the strike itself. Mann had been assigned by the NSFU to lead the strike in Liverpool — where as elsewhere the original seamen's strike quickly broadened to include dockers and other waterside workers, and indeed in August 1911 strike action in Liverpool widened even further to include railwaymen and to constitute the beginnings of the national strike of railwaymen. The events in Liverpool had an exceptionally dramatic nature — with deployment of troops and police against the strikers, and gunboats in the Mersey with their guns trained on the town.[1] The three month long strike seemed to observers like the father of Margaret Cole to signify "the beginning of the end of the world."[2] Lord Derby similarly wrote to Winston Churchill at the Home Office to tell him that he had had an earnest phone call from the Lord Mayor of Liverpool complaining that people in London did not realise that the Liverpool strike was no ordinary strike but that "a revolution was in progress". The King telegraphed Churchill in similar vein: "Accounts from Liverpool show that the situation there more like a revolution than a strike . . ."[3] The hostile press dubbed Tom Mann "the dictator of Liverpool".

Mann had been away from Britain from the end of 1901 to the spring of 1910. His experiences in Australia and New Zealand had led him to attach far more importance to industrial action than to political activities. Confirmed in this by what he learnt of the progress of revolutionary syndicalism in France, Mann and Guy Bowman (at the time a member of the Social Democratic Party and the translator of Gustave Hervé's *Leur Patrie* into English) began to issue a monthly magazine from July 1910. The *Industrial Syndicalist* provided Mann and his colleagues with an important platform for the dissemination of their syndicalist ideas. The last issue of the *Industrial Syndicalist* appeared in May 1911. That issue, apart from a couple of pages of introductory matter by Mann, was devoted to a long essay on the railway industry, "Conciliation or Emancipation", by the Chesterfield railway signalman Charles Watkins.[4] A further issue of the *Industrial Syndicalist* had been planned but it never appeared, probably due to Mann's deep involvement in the seamen's strike which began in June 1911. During the last few weeks of the transport workers' strike in Liverpool Mann began to issue a new publication from there, *The Transport Worker* this ran for eight issues between August 1911 and March 1912. Meanwhile in London, Mann's associate Guy Bowman started to publish a further paper; *The Syndicalist Railwayman* which had Charles Watkins as its editor, from October 1911. This publication was short-lived, lasting only for three months. Mann's comments on it were: "This organ, whose title conveyed the impression that it was a trade paper, had its title altered to that of *The Syndicalist* in January 1912."[5]

The Syndicalist was, as its masthead makes clear, "Edited under the auspices of the Industrial Syndicalist Education League". The ISEL had been formed on the initiative of Mann and Bowman at the end of November 1910 to propagate the views on trade unionism that Mann had advocated with great force and considerable success since his return to Britain in May 1910. As can be seen from Mann's front page article, "What We Syndicalists Are After", in the first issue of *The Syndicalist,* the purpose of the ISEL was "to popularise Syndicalist principles amongst Trade Unionists with a view to the realisation of the Industrial Commonwealth." Mann continues later on in the same article, with considerable truth, that "1911 opened the eyes of many as to a few things that can be done when Solidarity is in the saddle"[6] and he predicted that "1912 will show this in a much larger degree." Events in the early part of 1912 seemed to bear Mann out. 1912 did prove to be a year of great industrial militancy. Over 40 million days were lost due to industrial disputes — many of them on account of the national coal strike of the first part of the year. Syndicalists were frequently blamed for the strikes, particularly after the prosecution in March 1912 of the editor of *The Syndicalist*, Guy Bowman; its printers the Brothers Buck; and Tom Mann as president of the Industrial Syndicalist Education League. The prosecution of these people was the result of the publication in the January 1912 issue of *The Syndicalist* of the famous "Open Letter to British Soldiers" -- the "Don't Shoot" letter, calling on soldiers mobilised during strikes not to fire on their fellow members of the working class. The letter had been published anonymously; but it was in fact written by the Liverpool stonemason Fred Bower and had originally appeared in James Larkin's *Irish Worker*. Strikers in Liverpool had got hold of the letter and reproduced it as a leaflet. Fred Bower recalled later that:

> "Unknown to me, a newspaper just started called *The Syndicalist*, got hold of a copy, and printed it in its first issue. The outcome of it was that the editor of that paper (Guy Bowman), the printers (two brothers named Buck), Tom Mann (the Secretary), and a young zealot named Fred Crowsley (who got hold of one of the leaflets, and thought so much of it that, at his own expense, he had some hundreds of it reprinted, which he himself distributed), all got gaoled, from one to six months. I had offered to give myself up, but Tom Mann would not hear of it. 'It will only mean one more victim for them,' he said, 'so why do it?'"[7]

The prosecutions and imprisonments caused a great deal of uproar. The case was discussed widely in the national press, and was raised in Parliament. Its most important effects were to make "syndicalism" a household world, to boost the sales of *The Syndicalist* from around 5,000 to about 20,000 copies, and to strengthen the commonly held view that the "Labour Unrest" was entirely caused by syndicalist agitators.[8] Bowman and Mann were only out of action for a short time. Mann was released after serving only seven weeks of his six months sentence on June 23, 1912. The wealthy American socialist turned syndicalist Gaylord Wiltshire had taken over the responsibility for editing *The Syndicalist*'s issue of March — April 1912.[9] Bowman quickly returned to the job of editing *The Syndicalist,* and Mann after only a short break once again immersed himself in his speaking campaign. Mann had been released from prison only a few days before the London dock strike of 1912 went down to an ignominious defeat. The National Transport Workers' Federation had, on June 10, called upon transport workers in the provinces to strike in sympathy with the London dockers. The response, however, was poor. Only the provincial branches of the London based dockers' union joined the strike — and this support was not sufficient to prevent the collapse of the strike in London on July 27.[10] None of the elaborate preparation work that had gone into the 1911 strike had gone into the 1912 strike, and the constituent unions of the National Transport Workers' Federation were not sufficiently altruistic to strike when their own interests did not seem to be involved. In short, solidarity was no longer "in the saddle".

Mann, however, was not dismayed. For him the failure of the 1912 strike merely proved his point negatively about the value of solidarity actions. The 1911 strike, he pointed out, had been a success because "for the first time in the history of such fights unity had characterised the men." Even late in the 1912 strike when defeat was imminent, Mann urged united action. "I blame none," he wrote, "and raise no quibble, but I put in my plea for solidarity."[11] Mann's suggestions were not taken up — and Mann felt obliged to draw the larger, long term lessons from the failure of the strike. Speaking to transport workers in Southampton on August 1, Mann argued strongly that the time had come for the transport workers' unions to take their unity one step further, and to replace the National Transport Workers' Federation with an amalgamation of all the unions in the transport industry. In a letter to the *Daily Herald* he wrote that the chief lesson of the defeat of the strike was that the "most rational and effective system" was to form "one big Union". "Federation," he continued, "has advanced the movement a stage, but this is a case where Amalgamation is distinctly better, and for this we must be ready to drop individual and Union identity to secure the well-being of the whole."[12] But Mann's proposals by now were falling on deaf ears. This fact, however, only seemed to increase his determination. Mann threw himself with great vigour into a speaking tour of Lancashire and Yorkshire, where he restated his point of view with considerable force. Writing from Featherstone towards the end of August 1912 he commented that he was disappointed that the miners there seemed to be "solaced with trifling monetary concessions" and that the railwaymen were "smoothed over with paltry wage increases through conciliation boards." It was vital, he felt, that the workers came to see the "omnipotence of real industrial solidarity." This would not be achieved immediately — there would be an educative process of strikes, "every one leading to the great one, when the working class shall triumph, that will be the general strike . . . This, of course, will be the revolution; it will be achieved by the conscious action of the workers refusing to allow their lives and their destiny to be longer thwarted by a ruling hostile class . . ."[13]

Mann had decided that "a vigorous and extensive educational campaign" for syndicalism should be launched. He called for local groups of syndicalists to convene conferences in addition to the bigger conferences that were arranged to take place in Manchester and London in November 1912. Further he suggested that a thousand speakers were needed to carry the campaign into the trade unions. His opinion was that a couple of years' "solid educational work" would create the body of opinion necessary for "definite action."[14] The Industrial Syndicalist Education League also decided around this time to set its organisation on sounder lines. At the end of August, E.J.B. Allen (who had been a leading figure in the Industrialist League and the author of the pamphlet *Revolutionary Unionism* in 1909) was appointed full-time assistant secretary of the ISEL, and F.J. Passmore was appointed as part-time organiser in London.

The 1912 meeting of the Trades Union Congress proved to be a great test of to what extent syndicalist ideas has been accepted in the official trade union movement. Will Thorne, the gas workers' leader and president of the TUC for 1912, was asked on the eve of the Congress what he thought would be the subject most likely to arouse controversy during the Congress proceedings. Thorne expected that it would be the Parliamentary Committee's resolution reaffirming the necessity of political action. This, he pointed out, might be regarded in some quarters "as a direct challenge to the supporters of Syndicalism and anti-Parliamentarianism generally."[15] This turned out to be so. The syndicalists were implicitly challenged — and beaten. The Parliamentary Committee's resolution was carried by 1,693,000 to 48,000 votes — though only after a long debate in which Noah Ablett and Jack Wills made hard-hitting speeches in support of the "syndicalist" case. Earlier in the Congress there had been another setback for the syndicalists when Jack Wills, a leading campaigner for industrial unionism in the building industry, had moved a resolution to re-affirm the TUC's support (in principle) for industrial unionism.[16] Wills' resolution also called on the Parliamentary Committee to set in motion an educational campaign in support of amalgamation of trade unions on industrial lines. A delegate from the Liverpool based National Union of Dock Labourers (one of the unions which had not struck in sympathy with the London dockers earlier that year) moved an amendment deleting any commitment by the TUC to industrial unionism. The amendment was carried by 1,123,000 to 573,000 votes. It is instructive to see that the N.U.D.L. delegate drew completely the opposite conclusion on the failure of the 1912 Dock strike to the one that Mann drew. The N.U.D.L. delegate said:

> "The mistake our friends are making is in assuming that at any time the workers of the country ought to be prepared to 'down tools' whenever someone makes a call. No more dangerous policy could be imagined than that . . . And more than that. This resolution is based on the assumption that a great national strike is bound to be successful. I venture to say that if we had had a national transport strike in recent months, we should have been beaten and smashed and sent back to work, and the organisation work of twenty years would have been lost."[17]

Mann had been in Scandinavia at the time of the TUC, but Sam Brierley, the circulation manager of *The Syndicalist,* had been at Newport and had sold copies of the paper outside the Congress hall and at "fringe" meetings. Brierley had often accompanied Mann on the latter's speaking tours, and noticed that without him things did not go so well. "I have not been able," commented Brierley, "to get the same sales as when I was with him at meetings."[18] But after his return from Scandinavia Mann observed that the TUC leadership had done its best to disparage syndicalism at the Congress "when there was not one Syndicalist present at the Conference", although there were several who believed in industrial solidarity *and* parliamentary action. But Mann was not one to complain — he merely announced that he and his colleagues would continue to work inside the existing unions and would "definitely and systematically work to convert them to Syndicalism."[19]

After the fairly serious rebuff at the TUC the Industrial Syndicalist Education League turned its attention increasingly to the various unofficial amalgamation movements that had developed. It was as if the two years of "spreadshot" propaganda that had gone on since the formation of the ISEL now had to be replaced by more concentrated and systematic efforts in specific industries in which there were existing groups working for amalgamation. At the London conference held by the ISEL in November 1912 there was considerable representation from such groups, and a resolution was carried at the conference which committed the ISEL to action which would lead to the formation of a National Federation of Amalgamation Committees.[20] A conference of Amalgamation Committees was convened by the ISEL in London on November 24, 1912, at which such a Federation was formed. Representatives of existing amalgamation committees in the building, transport, and engineering industries were at the forefront at the conference. Not all those who were active in amalgamation committees were keen on syndicalist ideas. Some of the amalgamationists it is clear were suspicious of the ISEL's motives in convening the conference. It was to allay such suspicions that Guy Bowman, who presided during the initial stages of the conference, quickly vacated the chair to Jack Wills of the building workers. When he vacated the chair Bowman told the conference that the syndicalists had "no desire to interfere with the work of the Amalgamation Committees in any way. They were simply calling the meeting to give effect to the resolution referred to."[21] But although the ISEL had no direct control over the amalgamation committees it did provide considerable servicing for the new federation. Many individual members of the ISEL spoke at Amalgamation Committee meetings, and *The Syndicalist* began to carry a considerable amount of news of the movement. This latter function was regarded by the ISEL as being so important that it was decided to change the name of the paper to *The Syndicalist and Amalgamation News.* To some amalgamationists this action only seemed to confirm the opinion that the ISEL was out to capture the Amalgamation Committees Federation.[22]

In the first issue of *The Syndicalist and Amalgamation News* in January 1913, Tom Mann once again made a review of the past year and an assessment of the prospects for the coming year. According to Mann Syndicalism had grown "out of all proportion to any other phase of the revolutionary propaganda during the past year." He acknowledged that this success was greatly helped by the Government's "absurd action" over the "Open Letter to British Soldiers" which brought *The Syndicalist* a great deal of publicity. But he made it clear to his readers that no such windfall could be guaranteed in 1913, and that the syndicalists would need to "undertake with greater definiteness and vigour — if that is possible — to conduct a systematic propagandist campaign amongst the Trade Union branch members." But Mann made it clear that he did not think that this entailed making the Industrial Syndicalist Education League a mass-membership organisation. The key to success, he felt, was to influence the conscious minority of trade unionists. "It is of more importance to the revolutionary movement," he continued, "that the active one million of trade unionists shall be influenced aright than six times that number of others . . . The ISEL need not strive to obtain an enormous membership, but it must be equal to reaching the rank and file of the trade unionists, and every advocate must himself or herself be a trade unionist." Before long, however, the ISEL was in no shape to mount such a campaign. It is clear that, in the early days of 1913, the ISEL experienced a considerable internal split. The crucial figure of Mann detached himself from the London-based organisation. Mann wrote in January 1913: "For myself, I feel strongly the necessity for centring my energies more than I have done the last few years, so I give this information that from now on I intend to make Manchester my centre, and shall confine my efforts within a radius of some eighty miles or so of that industrial centre."

There is a possibility that Mann was opposed to an attempt on Bowman's part to turn the ISEL into a more tightly directed organisation. Another article in the January 1913 issue lends support to this suggestion. George Simpson, the ex-treasurer of the British Socialist Party and a convert to syndicalism, pointed out that the ISEL had up to then existed to spread the ideas of syndicalism but that it had not attempted to organise effectively the existing syndicalists. The ISEL was made up only of "a small number of loosely organised groups and a large number of individuals scattered all over the country." Simpson considered that the time had come for a strong national syndicalist organisation. Readers of *The Syndicalist* were asked to send their comments on this suggestion to Guy Bowman. Between the appearance of the January and February issues it had been decided to call a General Meeting of the ISEL. Bowman, equating increased centralisation with democracy (with much justification in this case), stated that at this meeting the League would be "definitely organised as a democratic body . . . Up to now the League has been more or less an amorphous organisation owing to the method of its inception.

There were but few comrades who started it, and the need for a definite constitution, rules, and so forth was not felt. We were all personal friends, and we just selected a committee of five and appointed a general secretary and a president without giving definite duties to either, and let them get on with the work of spreading Syndicalist propaganda." All this was to be changed — and it seemed to cause a serious fraction fight. It was not long before E.J.B. Allen announced that he was emigrating to New Zealand,[23] and before 1913 was out a rival "syndicalist" organisation, the Industrial Democracy League, had been formed by the dissidents.[24] The damage was done. After this the ISEL seemed to lose coherence — in spite of changes designed to increase that very quality — and *The Syndicalist and Amalgamation News* appeared only sporadically. The next issue was a joint one for the months of March and April 1913, and it was December 1913 before a further issue appeared. That issue contained these uncompromising words from Bowman: "It is time we realised and acknowledged that there is no Syndicalist movement at all."

Having said that, Bowman and his colleagues found their second wind. Further numbers of the paper were published in January and February 1914 — and, after another break, three issues were issued in June, July and August 1914. The January 1914 issue had taken on a sectarian tone which had been entirely absent from the paper during Mann's period of association with it. The editorial criticised Guild Socialism, Daily Heraldism, and Larkinism as all being simply "the 'two arm' policy of the SLP" and the editorial board stooped sufficiently low to reprint an anti-Syndicalist article from Frank H. Rose (with whom Mann had debated in 1910) in which Mann was referred to as "probably the most bumptious of the whole conclave of bumptious charlatans."

Arthur D. Lewis, who in his book on Syndicalism published in 1912 had stated that "Tom Mann is Syndicalism in England",[25] was by this time a leading member of the editorial board of *The Syndicalist and Amalgamation News.* The corollary to Lewis's statement came increasingly true. Syndicalism in England lost its effectiveness with great rapidity after Mann's disassociation from the ISEL and its paper. Mann's allegiance had, in fact, moved elsewhere. In the first few weeks after his removal to Manchester early in 1913 Mann was true to his word and undertook only fairly local speaking engagements. But early in February 1913 Mann broadened the field of his activities. Ben Tillett, George Lansbury, and Victor Grayson were all, for a variety of reasons, temporarily out of action. These three men were at the time the principal speakers for the *Daily Herald* League. The *Daily Herald* League was a politically broadly based organisation (reflecting the admirable and effective non-sectarianism of the *Herald* itself), its main purposes being to increase the sales of the *Daily Herald* and to promote the principles it stood for. Since the *Daily Herald* had a sympathetic attitude towards "all degrees of revolutionary thought",[26] the League could unite on the same platform representatives of all these "degrees" — suffragist, social democrat, Christian socialist, and syndicalist. The loss of Tillett, Lansbury, and Grayson — all of them great crowd pullers — to the League and its 150 or so local branches was a great one, and it looked as if the publicity for the *Herald* might begin to suffer. On February 6, 1913, however, the League's organiser W.F. Rean allayed that fear with the announcement that "the redoubtable Tom Mann has stepped into the breach, by kindly agreeing to speak for the HERALD LEAGUE whenever possible."[27] Mann spoke for the League on numerous occasions after this, which often involved his going outside his self-imposed limits. But he did set in motion an important Manchester based campaign against low wages amongst engineering labourers. There were, he estimated, about 40,000 engineering labourers in the Manchester area earning between 17 shillings and 21 shillings a week.[28] Mann soon broadened his campaign to cover the many low paid, less skilled workers all over the country, especially in the Black Country and also in Cornwall. Much of this work was done on behalf of the Workers' Union, of which he was vice president.[29]

In the early months of 1913 Mann did not often use the word "syndicalism" in his platform speeches. He concentrated largely on advocating what he regarded as its main principles to workers involved in actual struggles — most notably amongst the low paid workers the Workers' Union was endeavouring to organise. He was, though, saying basically the same things as he had said when he was closely involved with Bowman and the ISEL, but now he was taking a less dogmatic attitude when urging workers to organise and to act. When he chose to put a name to what he was saying he preferred to talk about "Greater Unionism" rather than "syndicalism".[30] Mann spent most of the summer of 1913 out of Britain, travelling extensively in the United States and raising an intense debate inside the Industrial Workers of the World about the merits of "boring from within" the existing unions and the demerits of the IWW's "dual unionism".[31] On his return to Britain he affiliated himself to the Industrial Democracy League and its "monthly journal of Militant Trade Unionism", *Solidarity,* which first appeared in September 1913. The Industrial Democracy League and *Solidarity,* rather than the Industrial Syndicalist Education League and *The Syndicalist and Amalgamation News,* were the new centres of the syndicalist "tradition" that Mann had pioneered. Most of the most significant names in the militant trade union movement now attached themselves to the Industrial Democracy League, which was created out of the Amalgamation Committees' Federation.[32] The building workers Jack Wills and George Hicks; the engineers Jack Tanner and W.F. Watson; the secretary of the National Transport Workers' Federation Robert Williams; the stonemason and author of the "Open Letter to British Soldiers" Fred Bower; the railwayman and leading figure in the *Plebs* League W.W. Craik; W.F. Hay, one of the authors of *The Miners' Next Step;* the wealthy American socialist turned syndicalist Gaylord Wilshire – all wrote articles for *Solidarity.* Tom Mann, too, was a regular contributor. In his articles he was still showing a sensitivity to, and an optimism about, the actual struggles (warts and all) which were then proceeding — unlike his old comrades on *The Syndicalist and Amalgamation News* who, in the months before the first world war, were in a profoundly pessimistic mood and were only issuing their paper to expound the "pure" syndicalist doctrine. Mann's finest article in *Solidarity,* "The Path to Power" in the March 1914 issue, epitomises his qualities. The article opened as follows:

"The one word above all others that is understood in practically all languages by those who know nothing but their mother tongues, is SOLIDARITY. Many a struggle of a sectional character will be necessary before the workers are able to resort to common action for the final overthrow of the wages system; education of the economically class-conscious variety receives its best stimulus by means of a strike for better conditions. If we could, as a class, reason out the economic problem completely, and proceed in a logical fashion to achieve emancipation, there would be no necessity for repeated efforts on a comparatively small scale; but the forces at work in society are such, that it is impossible to achieve full emancipation until more educational work is done, which, as already stated, can be best done by and through demands for reduced hours and higher wages.

"Those who determine simply to theorise and to argue interminably as to the most logical method, get left high and dry by the workers' movement which takes its own course."[33]

That last sentence of Manns' might serve as an epitaph for the Industrial Syndicalist Education League.

Geoff Brown
December 1973

1. See H.R. Hikins "The Liverpool General Transport Strike, 1911" in *Transactions of the Historic Society of Lancashire and Cheshire,* 1961, pp. 169-195; see also *Tom Mann's Memoirs* (London 1967 edn.) Chapters 18 and 19; and Bob Holton's fine article "Syndicalism and Labour on Merseyside, 1906-1914" in *Building the Union: studies on the growth of the workers' movement: Merseyside, 1756-1967,* ed. H.R. Hikins (Liverpool 1973).
2. Margaret I. Cole *Growing Up Into Revolution* (London 1949) p. 34.
3. Randolph S. Churchill *Winston S. Churchill* Vol. 2, 1901-1914 (London 1967) pp. 381-383.
4. Watkins had been a student at Ruskin College, and was one of the group of ex-Ruskin students who did much to establish branches of the *Plebs* League, devoted to independent working class education: see W.W. Craik *The Central Labour College* (London 1964) p. 86. Watkins was one of the leading militants in the Chesterfield/Sheffield area during the 1911 railway strike: see Rowland Kenney "The Brains Behind the Labour Revolt" in *The English Review* March 1912.
5. Tom Mann *From Single Tax to Syndicalism* (Walthamstow 1913) p. 76.
6. Even the "Lib-Lab" Havelock Wilson, who had struggled for years to get legislative improvement for seamen, acknowledged that the 1911 strike had achieved in weeks what twenty years of "strenuous work" had failed to achieve. He told the 17th Annual Conference of the NSFU that "Whatever improvements had been achieved in the amelioration of the condition of the Seafarers has been due to direct action."
7. Fred Bower *Rolling Stonemason* (London 1936) p. 182. See also *Tom Mann's Memoirs* Chapter 20. Cowsley was a railwayman who distributed the leaflets to soldiers in Aldershot.
8. See *The Syndicalist* March-April 1912, and *Bulletin International du Mouvement Syndicaliste* May 5 1912.
9. Wilshire was assisted by Upton Sinclair: see *The Autobiography of Upton Sinclair* (New York 1962) p. 178 and also the magazine *Wilshire's* May 1912.
10. John Lovell *Stevedores and Dockers* (London 1969) p. 201.
11. *Daily Herald* July 22, 1912.
12. *Daily Herald* August 3, 1912.
13. Tom Mann, "Revolution" in *Daily Herald* August 27, 1912.
14. *The Syndicalist* July 1912.
15. *Daily Herald* September 2, 1912.
16. A resolution to this effect had been passed at the 1910 Congress.
17. NUDL delegate at 1912 TUC, quoted in B.C. Roberts *The Trades Union Congress,* 1868-1921 (London 1958) p. 253.
18. S. Brierley, "Circulation Notes" in *The Syndicalist* October, 1912.
19. Tom Mann, "Syndicalism in Sweden and Denmark" in *The Syndicalist* October 1912.
20. See the report in *The Syndicalist* December 1912.
21. *Daily Herald* November 27, 1912, see also *The Syndicalist* December 1912. Branco Pribicevic has wrongly suggested that "It is very likely that Tom Mann and the ISEL wanted to have more direct control of the Federation.": *The Shop Stewards' Movement and Workers' Control, 1910-1922,* (Oxford 1959) p. 69.
22. This attitude is best exemplified in the attitude of Charles Woodward, the secretary of the Printing Workers' Amalgamation Committee which had refused to be represented at the November 24 conference because it wanted nothing to do with the syndicalists. Woodward further thought that the appearance of *The Syndicalist* as *The Syndicalist and Amalgamation News* confirmed the fear that the ISEL was out to capture the amalgamation movement: see Woodward's letter in *Daily Herald* February 1, 1913.
23. *The Syndicalist and Amalgamation News,* February 1913. Allen was later active in the Guild Socialist movement in New Zealand, and in 1936 contributed a message to the *Daily Worker's* issue of April 15 in honour of Mann's 80th birthday.
24. Some information on this can be found in an article by the American IWW member George H. Swasey in *Solidarity* (USA) October 25, 1913. A British Administration of the IWW (with which Swasey was intimately connected) was another product of the split. See also B. Pribicevic *The Shop Stewards' Movement and Workers' Control, 1910-1922* (Oxford 1959) pp. 69-70.
25. Arthur D. Lewis *Syndicalism and the General Strike* (London 1912) p. 199.
26. George Lansbury in *Daily Herald* February 7, 1913.
27. *Daily Herald* February 6, 1913. The *Daily Herald* had, of course, a full coverage of national and international news as well as items about the labour movement. It also carried photographs, sports news, brilliant cartoons by Will Dyson — and it had the services of many top class writers. Raymond Postgate in his *Life of George Lansbury* (London 1951) p. 136 states that the average sales of the paper fluctuated between 50,000 and 100,000. See also R. Holton "The *Daily Herald* and the Labour Unrest" in *Bulletin of the Society for the Study of Labour History,* No. 25, pp. 27-28; and for the origins of the *Daily Herald* League see W.F.K. Rean "As I Remember: An Epitome of the English Labour Movement" in Amalgamated Engineering Union *Monthly Journal* January 1921, pp. 84-93.
28. See Tom Mann "Manchester Labourers' Move" in *Daily Herald* February 17, 1913, and his pamphlet *The Labourers' Minimum Wage: a demand for 25/- a week* (Manchester 1913). It should be noted that Seebohm Rowntree in his enquiries into poverty in York had estimated that in 1899 the minimum weekly expenditure upon which physical efficiency could be maintained for a family of father, mother, and three children was 21s. 8d.: see Asa Briggs *Social Thought and Social Action. A Study of the Work of Seebohm Rowntree* (London 1961) p. 38. Between 1899 and 1913 prices had risen considerably.
29. See Richard Hyman *The Workers' Union* (Oxford 1971) Chapter 3. The membership of the Workers' Union grew dramatically in the years of the Labour Unrest. Membership rose from around 5,000 in 1910 to about 40,000 in May 1913. In some places the accession of membership was particularly striking: "In Cardiff alone, in one week, over 2,300 members joined the Workers' Union." — *Workers' Union 13th Annual Report and Statement of Accounts,* January 1 — December 31, 1911, p. 5.
30. Tom Mann "The Greater Unionism" in *Daily Herald* March 24, 1913.
31. P.S. Foner *History of the Labor Movement in the United States,* vol. 4, "The I.W.W. 1905-1917" (New York 1965) pp. 430-433; Joseph R. Conlin *Bread and Roses Too* (Westport, Conn. 1969) Chap. 1.
32. See *Solidarity* September 1913.
33. Tom Mann "The Path to Power" in *Solidarity* March 1914. Mann left for a tour of South Africa at the beginning of March. He did not return to Britain until a few days after the outbreak of war.

1912

The Syndicalist

Edited under the auspices of the Industrial Syndicalist Education League

Vol. I. No. 1.　　　JANUARY, 1912.　　　MONTHLY, One Penny.

What we Syndicalists are after.

The Industrial Syndicalist Education League has come into being for a specific purpose. That purpose is to popularise Syndicalist principles amongst Trade Unionists with a view to the realisation of the Industrial Commonwealth.

We are not wishful, however, to bring into existence some organisation or society to take the place of the existing Trade Union Movement; we simply wish to facilitate its development towards real Solidarity and Direct Action lines. True, the present Unions are sectional and lacking in proper appreciation of Direct Action Methods, but we are confident that our efforts will make them appreciate the necessity of Federating, in many cases of amalgamating, and of resorting to the methods of Industrial Solidarity for all grades and industries. We of the League, being members of the existing old-line unions, seek by visits to Union Branches and Lodges, Trades Councils, Working Man's Clubs, etc., to stimulate discussion on Syndicalist principles and methods.

We are ourselves non-parliamentarians; but we do not worry over the fact that many attach importance to the political action which we have discarded. Our concern is that the Trade Unionist Movement, as the chief agency of working-class activity, should be made as perfect as may be for fighting the class war, and shall eliminate for ever the sectional and racial animosities that have hitherto checked our advance.

We lay special stress upon the urgency of the necessity for a substantial reduction of working hours in all industries. We are therefore favourable to, and earnest advocates of, a maximum eight hour day, though we consider that miners, chemical workers, and all those working in specially dangerous trades, ought not to work more than six hours a day.

But we hasten to say that neither an eight hour day, a seven, or a six hour day, can cure unemployment. The cure for unemployment is to be found in the proper regulation of working hours; and this will be done when the industrial organisations undertake to regulate working hours themselves, in each industry, to the complete absorption of all available workers, and to follow up with further reductions as rapidly as capitalists apply labour-saving devices. When, under this system, the price of trade goes below the normal, we Syndicalists would reduce the hours of all, and keep all at work, instead of allowing a percentage to be thrown out of work to starve, and when abnormal activity comes about, working hours would be added to, in order to meet requirements. This would give the workers the power to fix wages, because it would remove competition for employment amongst the workers.

The orthodox declare this cannot be done; but 1911 opened the eyes of many as to a few things that can be done when Solidarity is in the saddle. 1912 will show this in a much larger degree, and when the capitalists get tired of running industries, the workers will cheerfully invite them to abdicate, and through and by their industrial organisations, will run the industries themselves in the interests of the whole community.

We know the advantage of achieving results with the least expenditure of energy, and will, therefore always discourage unnecessary strikes; but we also know that the strike is the chief weapon of the working class. It is all-powerful when wisely conducted over a sufficiently extensive area. We therefore most certainly favour strikes; we shall always do our best to help strikes to be successful, and shall prepare the way as rapidly as possible for THE GENERAL STRIKE of international proportions. This will be the actual Social and Industrial Revolution. The workers will refuse to any longer manipulate the machinery of production in the interest of the capitalist class, and there will be no power on earth able to compel them to work when they thus refuse.

Into it, then, Fellow Workers! No longer hesitate! Into your Unions by the million! No arbitration! No compromise! But straight out definite slogging for our children, our women, and the whole working class!　　TOM MANN.

THE RAILWAYS TO THE RAILWAYMEN.

Striking Demonstration by Italian Railwaymen of the ability of the Workers to Organize their own Work.

The following report, by our friend Odon Por, on the progress of the Italian Railway industry is of tremendous importance as illustrating the wide separation between the practical talent, developed by the working class in the performance of really useful toil, and the inefficiency that results from lives spent only in schemes for the conquering of political power, or for the acquiring of title to what the real workers have produced.

" By far the most revolutionary organisation of European railroad men is the Union of Italian Railroaders. I have been lately in Milan at the headquarters of this Union for the purpose of studying its history, organisation and tendencies, and will try to give here the rough outlines of my investigation.

After many sterile struggles for improving their material conditions, the various craft Unions of the Italian railroaders came to the conclusion that only a strong and unified movement could be victorious. So they called a joint congress in 1904, where, burying the petty craft jealousies, they laid down the lines of future united action.

Giving the Doctor his own Medicine.

Soon after this the Italian Government announced its intention to take over the railroads from the private companies, and amongst the new laws before Parliament was one proposing to deprive the railroad workers of their right to strike. As soon as this law came to the knowledge of the various organisations their joint agitation committee called a passive resistance strike, which consisted in obedience to the letter of all the rules of service, with the effect that the dispatching of passenger trains and their arrival was greatly retarded and freight trains were everywhere entirely tied up. Neither the railroad companies nor the Government was able to suppress this new formidable but legal method of action. Finally the Government yielded and the " obstruction " was called off. The next Cabinet introduced the same law in an attenuated form, whereupon a general strike was called on the 16th April, 1905. During this strike the Italian Parliament voted the State ownership of the railroads and the law which made " public officials " of all railroad men, i.e., practically deprived them of their right to strike. There was nothing left but to call off the general strike and face the new situation. The railroad men were defeated, but the experiences gathered in these two great movements gave them courage to continue the struggle.

In 1906 the various craft Unions of the railroad men merged into one industrial Union. This new organisation went out in 1907 on a general strike in sympathy with some strikers who were shot down by the soldiers. The State punished the strikers most severely, and public opinion was decidedly against them. More than 20,000 strikers were punished, some were discharged, some put in jail, and the rest fined and degraded. This terribly defeat naturally caused much dissatisfaction and friction within the young organisation. Two factions faced each other : the revolutionists who proposed direct economic action for the revindication of the rights of the railroad men and the realization of better wages, and the reformists, who wanted to realize the same with the aid of the various Radical Parliamentary groups. After the complete defeat of the latter method the organization has become since 1908 thoroughly revolutionary, and has worked out a revolutionary method of action which distinguishes it from all similar organizations.

Organisation Methods improved through experience.

This Union, embracing practically the entire 60,000 Italian railroad men, has the following inner structure.

All skilled and unskilled male and female railroad workers, belonging to any category, may become members of the Union. The functions of the Union are divided amongst the following bodies : the Congress of the Delegates, the General Committee, the Central Executive Committee (C.E.C.), the Sections, the Groups, the Commissions of Categories, the Auditors, the Arbitrators, and the members voting by referendum.

Decisions of the Congress are obligatory on all members. The Congress discusses the questions on the order of the day and passes judgment upon the yearly reports of the officials. Its delegates are elected by referendum vote of the membership. The General Committee is the deliberative body of the Union; it is composed of five members from the C.E.C. and the secretaries of the Commissions of Categories. Its chief duty is to examine national, accepted or proposed laws that refer to railroads or railroadmen; it studies the rules of the service and the conditions of the workers, and publishes the results of its investigations in the official paper of the Union. It further decides upon the reports of the Commissions of the Categories and of the C.E.C.

The C.E.C. is composed of 15 members, elected by referendum. It reports the desires of the individual members and of the sections, and prepares the annual financial report and the report on the activity of the Union; it edits and publishes the official paper of the Union, organises the propaganda and the movements for the defence of the acquired rights and for the conquering of other rights. It executes the decisions of the Congress and the General Committee and those passed by referendum vote of the rank and file. It co-ordinates the functions of the Sections and Groups and transmits all special technical and craft questions to the Commission of Categories; it keeps in touch with the national and international Labour organisations, and finally attends to all work necessary for the advancement of the Union.

Local Autonomy Conceded.

Every locality with at least 150 members constitutes a Section. The Sections handle internal affairs affecting their members and the propositions which they desire to submit to the C.E.C. or other bodies of the Union. They execute the orders of the C.E.C. and attend to the local propaganda. Their functions are regulated by internal rules. Their expenses of administration and propaganda are paid by the Union. The members of each Section divide into Trade-Groups. Each group elects its chief, who receives the requests for admission to the Union, collects the dues and distributes the official paper of the union among the members free of charge. The trade-groups communicate on craft questions with the Commission of Categories. These latter are consultative technical bodies. They study all the problems that concern their members in their professional faculty, and pass their reports for approval or rejection, through the C.E.C., to the General Committee. There are eight Commissions of Categories within the Union, each representing a group of the various crafts. Every such Commission is composed of six members and has a secretary; its expenses are covered by the Union, and it regulates its functions by inner rules. Controversies between these Commissions and the C.E.C. are settled by the General Committee.

A referendum is ordered in case of important and immediate action to be taken by the organization and for the election of the various officers. The five auditors examine the books of the Union and control the work of the C.E.C. They have the right to call a Congress. The three Arbitrators settle the conflicts between the various bodies and their members.

Industrial Team-Work.

Through this organic and comprehensive system of organization, with its subdivisions determined by the necessities of propaganda and the technical nature of the various crafts, all members are forced to co-operate for the good of the whole organization as well as for the good of the single categories or the single sections. Within its fold the scabbing of one craft upon another, or the using by the State of one craft against the other is impossible. The various subdivisions are so organized and the statutory duties of the members so formulated that the problems of the whole organization are not merely kept before the mind of each member, but he has to continually give his personal view and vote on every occasion. Further, every railroad-man, by force of the statutes, has to affiliate with the local Labour Exchanges, which latter are the central organizations of all workers in a given district. This abolishing of all craft distinctions, this uniting into one class-organization, has co-ordinated the relations between the various categories of the railroad man, educated them to solidarity, and excited and intensified their interest in the problems of their own organization and of the whole working class. We can set it down as a law of all Labour organizations that as soon as craft unionism is replaced by genuine industrial unionism larger revolutionary issues will inevitably come into play.

Triumphant Class-Consciousness.

That the problem of industrially organizing the railroad man was successfully solved in Italy is attested by the fact that this organization, conscious of its collective efficiency and power, has set for itself a revolutionary scope, " The Railroads for the Railroad Men."

This revolutionary object was inspired not only by the Socialist ideal predominant amongst the Italian workers, but also by the actual conditions of the railroad system. The State, which took over the railroads from the private corporations in 1905 at a tremendous cost (graft), in order to give better and cheaper service, has proved its utter incapacity for managing railroads. The technical incompetency and deficiency of the bureaucratic administration called to run the enterprise has demoralised the whole passenger and freight traffic and caused a growing deficit in the treasury of the State. While the State has created thousands of new sinecures and highly paid offices, it has utterly neglected the technical part of the system. For instance, it failed to increase the number of trackmen, and has increased instead, to an unbearable degree, the work of all the railroad men. The politicians in-charge of technical duties have bought useless and antiquated material, causing besides a great financial loss and even greater confusion of the service, so that, at present, experts declare the State railroad system quite impossible to continue.

Proven Ability of Workers to be their own Managers.

On the other hand, the industrially organised railroad men have learned, through continuous discussion of the details of the system, the principles of organizing, managing and combining its factors. Their constructive and analytic criticism disclosed all the flaws of the railroad administration, proved that the State is an uneconomic institution, and demonstrated all the details necessary to a successful reorganisation of the railroads.

They indicated that they must get back, above all, their whole liberty, and that in order to secure from the railroads greater benefits for the public, they must become personally interested in the enterprise. They demonstrated that this can be attained only by leasing the State railroads to the Union of the Italian railroad men. This measure would allow them to organise the administration with more liberty and with economic instead of bureaucratic criterions. They would be free of all political obligation and could therefore suppress the thousands of useless clerical jobs and increase the number of productive employees, securing thus a prompter, safer and cheaper service, while their duty would be to pay a certain rent to the State and to guarantee a regular service. The State would retain for itself, in some simple form, the right of supervising the administration of the railroad system, without, however, directly interfering with the administration itself. The workers would draw a certain minimum wage, would participate in the net profits of the enterprise and subscribe the necessary cash for its running expenses.

Liberty of Initiative.

By this system every employee would realize that the more conscientiously he applied his energies, the better would the system work and the larger would be his personal income. This state of things would awaken in the employees the liveliest sense of responsibility and would at the same time give them liberty of initiative, which is the most important psychological factor of production.

While a few years ago the Italian railroad men met from all sides with opposition, and their enslavement to the State was greeted by the majority of the nation with great rejoicing; to-day, in view of the fact that the State has not made good, and especially because the railroad men have proved their technical efficiency, moral seriousness and social consciousness, in short, because they proved responsible enough to be entrusted with the most important industry of a nation,—to-day public opinion is largely on their side. And even conservative economists of great fame, and experts in the matter like Vilfredo Pareto, have publicly declared that: the only possible practical solution of the situation —inasmuch as private ownership of the railroads is a public nuisance and the State enterprise a veritable disaster—is the giving up of the State railroads to the co-operative enterprise of the organized railroad men; and that with some sense and prudence this could be realised at a small risk and surely with no such financial loss as that menacing the country at present. And Mr. Ferraris, ex-Minister of Commerce, a universally recognised authority in the matter, went even so far as stating that not only the railroads, but all State services, including the postal and telegraph service, could be safely entrusted to the organised workers and employees of these services.

Economic Determinism displaces Capitalism.

Through concentrated technical experience and discussion and reciprocal moral education, possible only within a great industrial organisation that eliminates all secondary problems, the Italian railroad men have created within the organizaton itself a force that logically drove them upon the road of practical, essentially economic, revolutionary action. Thus the proletarian organization, arriving at the summit of its perfection, demonstrates its profound economic nature and social usefulness, and proves itself capable to succeed the bourgeois private and statal institutions of production and exchange. " The Railroads for the Railroad Men," this utopia of yesterday, has become a practical, realizable demand.

" The Social Revolution is about to become a practical problem."

The Syndicalist

EDITED UNDER THE AUSPICES OF

The Industrial Syndicalist Education League

Offices—
4, MAUDE TERRACE, WALTHAMSTOW, LONDON, E.

MONTHLY - ONE PENNY.

Subscription—
Great Britain or Abroad ... 12 months 1s. 6d.
Orders for Subscriptions, Copies of the Paper, and Advertisements, should be sent to the Publisher GUY BOWMAN, 4, Maude Terrace, Walthamstow, London, E., who will also receive payment for same.

The receipt of a Sample Copy of this Paper is an invitation to you to become a Subscriber.

JANUARY, 1912.

THE

Legacy of 1911 to 1912

AT this season—when reviewing and forecasting seems to be the order of the day—it is noticeable that, one after another, the imitative scribes of the capitalistic press come to the front with a special title which they have dug up from monkish records for the characterizing of the year that has just expired.

"Annus Mirabilis" is the description which they have thus engraved upon the coffin-plate of old 1911; and presumably they mean by this that last year was a great time for the shaking up of the dry bones!

From the view-point of Labour, the title has not been so badly chosen. 1911 has been a year of shaking up, and also of shaking down;—a shaking up of values and distinctions as between man and man and between men and things, and a shaking down of many a time-honoured superstitious belief that had passed current simply because no one had had the courage to demand its credentials and compel it to fight for its life.

One of the antique idols that has thus fallen from its pedestal is the belief so long entertained by the British working man in the efficiency of the talk-shop at Westminster as a means of securing the annulment of those numerous special privileges which the secret bosses of that talk-shop have brought into action, or continued in action, as instruments for the taking from the workers of the surplus value produced by their toil.

After centuries of laudation of the mere external shell of Parliament—regardless of its stuffing of squires and squireens—as a glorious contrast to the feudalism of the old nobility; and then after decades of further talk about what Labour would achieve if only it would put Labour officials in the talk-shop in place of the squirearchy; and now, after actually accomplishing that aim to the extent of conquering for Labour a balance of power in the talk-shop—it has at last been demonstrated by the events of 1911 that the whole thing is a sham and a delusion, an institution which gives to scoundrels an opportunity to give national scope to their scoundrelism, and which so ties the hands and gags the mouths of honest men that they are actually made to appear as consenting parties to the scoundrelism.

And while all this has been proven and re-proven by the attitude of Parliament toward the great happenings of the year; by the shocked surprise and panic of so-called Labour members no less than by the intrigue and brutality of the confessedly bourgeois representatives; the achievements which have occasioned all this surprise and panic and intrigue and brutality have at least opened the eyes of the workers of England and of the whole world to the fact that Labour needs only to get disgusted with this capitalistic stalking-horse called Parliament to find itself master of the situation through that direct action which as a result of that disgust is inevitably let loose.

For it is to be noted that it is this automatic and inevitable sequence of direct action to the abandonment of Parliamentarianism that is the significant thing. Direct action, or Syndicalism as it has come to be called, is not an academic theory invented and put forward as an experimental nostrum for the ills of Labour, but comes rather from within the forces of life and nature. It is the necessary and natural action of human beings moving toward the satisfying of their wants along the straightest possible road as soon as the obstructions that have been set up by special privileges, and buttressed by such influences as Parliamentarianism, have been removed by the ignoring of privilege and Parliamentarianism.

It is this alignment of the principles of Syndicalism with the elemental forces of human nature that accounts for the tremendous success of the *Industrial Syndicalist Education League.* Deriving its birth from the instinctive demand of the workers for methods possessing inherent promise of the relief which they at length were perceiving the parliamentarian policy to be not only opposed to granting but incapable of granting, the *League* has already demonstrated itself to be the one ark of safety on the storm-tossed sea of industrial troubles—the one vessel which can always be depended on to answer its helm and steer a straight course toward a fruitful shore.

Its rousing meeting at Stratford Town Hall was a fitting climax to a year in which direct action had proven to both a delighted proletariat and a panic-stricken bourgeoisie that Syndicalism was militant; and its New Year's symposium at Anderton's Hotel has enthusiastically opened a campaign which, as 1912 advances, will prove that the militant Syndicalism of 1911 was only the prelude to a Syndicalism triumphant in 1912. The studying and propagating of Syndicalism is everywhere being undertaken by the wide awake trade unionists of Britain; and the proof of this that will be afforded by the Battersea meeting of January 14th will be duplicated many times over by similar demonstrations in other districts that have hitherto been dominated by Parliamentarianism.

The Receipt of a Sample Copy of this Paper is an Invitation to you to become a Subscriber.
Yearly Subscription, 1/6 post free.

Jottings.

The article on "The Railways to the Railwaymen" which appears on our front page is a most interesting one for Syndicalists and Socialists alike. We invite correspondence on the subject.

The duty of every Syndicalist is to make this paper known by pushing it at every meeting, be it a Socialist, Trade Union, Co-operative, or any other meeting, or by getting subscribers for it.

The following are the names and addresses of our wholesale and retail newsagents, from whom the "Syndicalist" may be had:—

London.—The National Labour Press, 23, Bride Street, E.C.
   ,,   J. Jaques, 191, Old Street, E.C.
   ,,   W. Tarbart, 316, Kentish Town Road, N.W.
   ,,   E. Denton, 427, High Road, Willesden, N.W.

Birmingham—The National Labour Press, 100, John Bright Street

Manchester.—Sam Brierley, 328, Hyde Road, Ardwick.
    Abel Heywood, 56 & 58, Oldham Street.

Glasgow.—David G. Lindsay, 139, West Nile Street, and 132, Gairbraid Street, Maryhill.

Bristol.—John Flynn, 19, Horsefair.

Peeping Abroad.

FRANCE
The Female Garment Makers' Strike

Since the end of last November the women workers of one of the greatest ready-made tailoring firms of Paris are on strike. The boss, a man named Esders, refuses to pay any attention to the just claims of his employees.

The situation lasting too long, the Paris Trades Council has resolved to force the hand of the man Esders. In the first place a subscription has been opened so that the comrades out of work should not starve. Then, demonstrations were organised in front of Mr. Esder's premises, so as to boycott the sale, *i.e.*, to prevent customers doing their shopping.

Otherwise the demonstrators are most pacific; the crowd contents itself with hissing the ferocious tradesman, but the howls and the agitation are such that he was compelled last Sunday and again on Wednesday to close his premises and to call for the police. And until Esders yields, the demonstration will go on.

To attack the finance of a shameless boss in such a way, without violence, without brutality, this is nothing but direct action, which will have for its result the smoothing down of recalcitrant exploiters.

Syndicalist Demonstrations

In order to protest against the prosecution of three militants of the Building Trades Federation, and to get them out of the clutches of the Government, our comrades Vian, Dumont and Baritaud, who have already been detained for the last six months, the Syndical Councils had decided upon a 24 hours strike last Wednesday.

The previous night, nine important meetings organised by the C.G.T. had taken place in different quarters of Paris. The Building Trades Federation had launched to all its members the following appeal:—

"Comrades,—Vian, Dumont and Baritaud after six months' detention are to appear to-morrow before the Correctional Court in pursuance of the exceptional laws of 1893—1894. You cannot allow these three comrades to be sentenced. You have but one order to obey, that of your workingman's conscience, which will tell you: To-morrow, yards and sheds will be deserted; I shall not go to work: I shall go to the meeting; I will take part in the demonstration; All up against the exceptional laws."

Ever since the morning of the 10th instant 40,000 proletarians have shouted their reprobation of the oppressors and their solidarity towards the victims. They did so at 2 o'clock in the afternoon around the Law Courts, and all the evening from 5 o'clock at the meeting places.

Judgment being adjourned till Jan. 19th the workers of Paris are preparing for that day another demonstration which promises to be still more imposing provided they promise to be 100,000 strong.

AUSTRALIA
War against War

Anti-militarism is developing everywhere more and more. Men of heart and sense have had enough of fratricidal wars which are the shame of civilised nations.

At Adelaide an Anti-militarist League has just been formed with the object of promoting peace and opposing militarism in any shape or form.

NEW ZEALAND
No Compulsory Military Training

Last October a journal bearing the title *The Anti-Militarist* was created at Christchurch. It is the official organ of the National Peace and Anti-Militarist Council of N.Z. for the Repeal of the Compulsory Training Clauses of the Defence Act, and the inculcation of the principles of peace and goodwill among the peoples; the advocacy of Arbitration instead of War as a means of settling international disputes.

In a short article entitled, "Worthy of Special Notice," *The Anti-Militarist* says "Citizens of New Zealand remember this: *Remember that under the Defence Act all the youths and young men of the country are brought under military law in time of peace, and do not rest until the Act is repealed!*"

WELLINGTON
Anti-Militarist Conference

At a session of the Anti-Militarist Conference the following remits were passed:—

"Brooklyn.—That this Conference expresses its great pleasure at the 'War upon War' efforts being made by peace organisations in many countries, assures them that the New Zealand workers stand for international fellowship and peace, and sends to the workers of Britain, France and Germany, and other countries fraternal greetings; it deplores the constant menace to the peace of Europe created by vested interests, both on the Home and foreign markets, and pledges itself to place every obstacle in the way of these interests leading to war."

"Wellington.—That all educational authorities be asked to delete from school books matters appertaining to the glorification of war."

"Wellington.—That lessons be inserted in school journals re matters of peace and the brotherhood of man."

"Runanga.—That this conference considers the advisability of interviewing the executive of the New Zealand Federation of Labour, and kindred organisations, asking them for their moral support in the event of the Ward Government continuing to prosecute the boys for non-registration."

The League of Anti-militarists recently formed had grown to 11,000 strong, with sympathisers in every town and village of the Dominion. They had already accomplished something. Sir Joseph Ward had promised that military drill would be abolished in the schools. Junior cadets would no longer drill with guns and bayonets.

HOLLAND.
Women and Child Labour.

We learn that Holland has reduced the legal hours of labour for women employed in factories and workshops to 10 per day, instead of the 11 per day which has ruled hitherto. No child under the age of 13 is to be employed in an industrial establishment.

GERMANY.
Reduction of hours.

The recent metal trades dispute in Leipzig, was settled after lasting for 16 weeks. The men asked for an increase of 10% in wages. This they obtained, the workmen with the lowest wage receiving a larger increase than the more highly paid workmen. That is to say, while the average increase was 10%, the individual increases ranged from 6% to 15% (1s. to 3s. in the £). Hours of labour were reduced to 56, which, it will be observed, is over 9 hours a day, including Saturday. Overtime rates were increased from 25% to 50%. The agreement is not considered very satisfactory by the men, and is only to hold good until 1st April, 1913.

Sparks.

Profit is the the amount the worker pays for the privilege of earning his own wages.

Power, not rhetoric, is what the worker should cultivate. "There is little benefit or dignity," so Austin Lewis says, " in shaking one's fist and shouting a fact."

They are either maudlin sentimentalists or downright humbugs who prate of race suicide. Are the workers continually to rear children for the masters to murder by slow degrees in their industrial hells and stinking slums?

The master class always strives to appear religious so as to set an example to its slaves who cannot be successfully robbed of surplus value unless their minds are befogged with superstitious ideas.

The co-operative commonwealth will be realised, not by preaching the merits of collectivism, but by building up a fighting organisation of the working class.

Our only fault with the workers is that their methods of class warfare have hitherto been too feeble.

Socialism may be the worker's dream, but it is undoubtedly the master's nightmare.

A working man with a capitalist conscience is a traitor to himself, his family, and his class.

Correspondence.

Bulvan, Pear Tree Corner,
Guy Bowman.   Romford, Essex,
Dear Comrade,   Jan. 9th, 1912.

Please enrol me as a member of the I.S.E.L. I enclose 1/- for this year's subscription and I am sorry not to be able to give more.

I was' at your Conversazione on the 1st, and I was delighted to see and hear you all, and it was with very great regret I had to come away in the middle of the evening to catch my train, especially as that was before Tom Mann's address. I have had the pleasure of hearing him only once before, 14 years ago, at Brighton.

I am afraid I must confess that I have not altogether lost all belief in Parliamentary action, and two years ago my belief in Syndicalism was very small; but the industrial events of 1911, and *especially the action of the Government with regard to those events*, have shown me very plainly the need of direct action by the people, without which Parliament is not only futile but dangerous. So you see that I still retain a little of the Parliamentary orthodoxy. I am afraid I cannot hope to be a very useful member of the League, as I do not belong to any organised industry and my own small business (growing and selling) keeps me very much involved in the struggle for enough to live on. However, the class that my last ten years has been spent among should present an interesting problem to the Syndicalist. They are practically unorganised, and seem to be almost without "industrial" consciousness (I do not like the word "class") and so form a constant recruiting ground of the worst nature for other industries, particularly railwaymen, carmen and drivers, and the police force.

I have written the above to put you in touch with a new member, but please do not, in the midst of all the business which must come to you, trouble to reply.

With all good wishes, Yours fraternally,
THOS. M. READ-ANDREWS.

A Hopeful Start.

Enthusiastic Syndicalist Leaguers open the campaign of 1912, with a happy combination of frolic and zeal.

NEW Year's Eve was celebrated by the Industrial Syndicalist Education League by a " Feu de Joie " in the big hall of Anderton's Hotel on Fleet Street. The brightly illuminated room was filled with an assemblage of comrades famous in the annals of England's working class struggle; and the occasion furnished an enthusiasm that will last far into the coming months.

The Chairman of the evening was George Lansbury, M.P., who had magnanimously consented to become the visible representative of that Parliamentarian bull the baiting of which is a very natural recreation at Syndicalist love-feasts.

Probably Bro. Lansbury's risking of himself in the hands of his jovial tormentors was due to his rightful good conscience as the one Labour M.P. who had shown the courage to " sit into council " with the Transport Workers in their great general strike at Liverpool — a record which naturally offsets to some extent such reflection upon his general sanity as might arise from his having become an inmate of Parliament.

After a musical and literary prelude contributed to the pleased satisfaction of all present by Mrs. Tom Mann and Miss Dorothy Needs, and by Bros. Corum and Rouse and Jimmy Barnes, the speaking part of the programme was inaugurated with a graceful introductory speech by Chairman Lansbury in which he paid a glowing tribute to the quick fire executive ability which with his own eyes he had seen evinced by Tom Mann and the Transport Workers' local Executive Committee in the recent Liverpool strike. It had been his good fortune, as he expressed it, to have occupied a chair in the councils of the workers in that exceedingly strenuous affair ; and he coyly admitted that what he had there seen of the native ability of the working class had " almost persuaded " him to quit Parliament and become a Syndicalist apostle !

The theme of Syndicalism in its general aspects was then ably dealt with by Bros. Walters and Barnes, and Secretary Bowman. It was announced that it was no part of the policy of the League to attack persons. All ,the time and ability possessed by its speakers and writers would be fully needed for the crowding labour involved in the spreading of the doctrine itself among the workers eagerly reaching out for it. The programme mapped out for systematically attending to the wants of these enquirers was dealt with by Secretary Bowman in an exposition of the League's new appeal card —which in itself was evidently a very important and interesting document.

President Tom Mann followed with a vivid and most instructive narrative of the Liverpool fight—using its various phases as illustrations of the way in which to meet problems coming up suddenly for solution in the heat of conflict, and proving from the course of events how futile were the expectations of those who were still looking to the cobwebbed halls of Westminster for remedies that could only be discovered and applied by men whose brains were clear of mental fog, and accustomed to meet the crises produced by action itself in conjunction with other men —the kind of brains in short that were naturally developed by the performing of the everyday duties of usefully productive life. (Continued applause.)

After another contribution of song and story from the " group on entertainment," reinforced this time by Bro. Tom Mann himself, Comrade Malatesta of Italy congratulated the League on its libertarian ideals, and Bro. John Turner of the Shop Assistants' Union declared that Syndicalism was giving to progressives a much needed opportunity to translate their theories into action.

As the closing speaker Bro. Mann called upon Comrade Honoré Jaxon of America, who spoke briefly on direct action in Mexico as an example to the workers of Europe to make similarly short work of law-created special privilege, and then called attention to the privileges of members of Parliament—and the exemption of modern legislators, as of ancient ones, from real responsibility to the people —as conclusive proofs that these modern legislators were merely heirs to the kingcraft of the past, and not by any means a genuine outcome of modern democracy.

The final scene of the gathering was a general jollification in which the Carmagnole, spiritedly led by Guy Bowman and Dorothy Needs, was sung by all present in a manner that would never have suggested to Bernard Shaw " the funeral of a fried eel " ; and so the comrades finally parted, with high hopes and brimming enthusiasm for continued propaganda.

Open Letter to British Soldiers.

Men ! Comrades ! Brothers !

YOU are in the army.

So are WE. YOU, in the army of Destruction. WE, in the Industrial, or army of Construction.

WE work at mine, mill, forge, factory, or dock, etc., producing and transporting all the goods, clothing, stuffs, etc., which make it possible for people to live.

YOU ARE WORKINGMEN'S SONS.

WHEN WE go on·Strike to better OUR lot, which is the lot also of YOUR FATHERS, MOTHERS, BROTHERS and SISTERS, YOU are called upon by your officers to MURDER US.

Don't do it !

You know how it happens. Always has happened.

We stand out as long as we can. Then one of our (and your) irrepressible Brothers, goaded by the sight and thought of his and his loved ones' misery and hunger, commits a crime on property. Immediately YOU are ordered to MURDER US, as YOU did at Mitchellstown, at Featherstone, at Belfast.

Don't YOU know, that when YOU are out of the colours and become a « Civy » again that YOU, like US, may be on Strike, and YOU, like US, be liable to be MURDERED by other soldiers ?

Boys, DON'T DO IT !

« THOU SHALT NOT KILL,» says the Book.

DON'T FORGET THAT !

It does not·say, « unless you have a uniform on.»

No! MURDER IS MURDER, whether committed in the heat of anger on one who has wronged a loved one or by pipe-clayed Tommies with rifles.

Boys, DON'T DO IT !

ACT THE MAN ! ACT THE BROTHER ! ACT THE HUMAN BEING !

Property can be replaced ! Human life, never !

The Idle Rich Class, who own and order you about, own and order us about also. They and their friends own the land and means of life of Britain.

YOU DON'T. WE DON'T.

When WE kick they order YOU to MURDER US.

When YOU kick YOU get court-martialled and cells.

YOUR fight is OUR fight. Instead of fighting AGAINST each other WE should be fighting WITH each other.

Out of OUR loins, OUR lives, OUR homes, YOU came.

Don't disgrace YOUR PARENTS, YOUR CLASS, by being the willing tools any longer of the MASTER CLASS.

YOU, like US, are of the SLAVE CLASS. When WE rise YOU rise, when WE fall, even by your bullets, YE fall also.

England, with its fertile valleys and dells, its mineral resources, its sea harvests, is the heritage of ages to us.

YOU, no doubt, joined the Army out of poverty.

WE work long hours for small wages at hard work because of OUR poverty. And both YOUR poverty and OURS arises from the fact that, Britain, with its resources, belongs to only a few people. These few, owning Britain, own OUR jobs. Owning OUR jobs, they own OUR very LIVES. Comrades, have WE called in vain ? Think things out and refuse any longer to MURDER YOUR KINDRED. Help US to win back BRITAIN for the BRITISH and the WORLD for the WORKERS !

THE COTTON LOCK-OUT

Read this Pamphlet :

THE COTTON RING, AND A TWO-FOLD WARNING

BY TOM MANN

Price : ONE PENNY : Usual discount to Branches, Socialist Societies, etc.

From The Publisher, GUY BOWMAN, 4, Maude Terrace, Walthamstow,
ABEL HEYWOOD, 56 & 58, Oldham St., Manchester.   London, E.
SAM BRIERLEY, 528, Hyde Road, Ardwick, Manchester.

Cuttings.

The British mining death roll for 1910 is staggering. As many as 1,902 persons were killed in our mines and quarries last year, an increase of 325 as compared with 1909. In addition, 165,113 persons were injured by accidents which disabled them for more than seven days. Also fully as many more were injured by accidents which disabled them for less than seven days. Let the reader imagine what a sensation would be caused by the fighting of a British battle in which 1,902 soldiers were killed, 165,113 were seriously injured, and some 150,000 others slightly wounded. Poets would be moved to the writing of epics ; monuments would be erected in every city in the country to the memory of the fallen, and we should mark in our history books a great day.

When I was a young man, and a Fabian, we were all trying to put the blessings of Socialism (i.e., of State and legislative action) in the strongest possible light, and the unassisted trade union movement, with the strike as its chief or solitary weapon, somewhat in the shade. Whether we were right or no, our efforts did tend to the impulse towards ameliorative law and administrative action. We desired, indeed, to keep the two tendencies going together. We thought the eight hours day could best be obtained by State action. But we supported strikes for shorter hours, as well as for better wages and conditions of work. What we never imagined was that our fight for more social intervention in economic matters was an incitement to social anarchy, and, in fact, it had no such effect.

Enter Syndicalism.

What has now happened in the labour world is something new and startling.. It is that at last the more Socialistic movement among the workmen has slackened down, but that its place has been taken not so much by a reversion to the old trade union method, as by the new development called Syndicalism. Syndicalism, I need not say, had its birth-place in France, where the legitimate trade union movement has always been discouraged by the State, both under the Imperialist and the Republican form. The result has been the birth of the " C.G.T.," or the General Federation of Labour. This is nominally a federation of trade unions. But neither its weapons nor its spirit are those of British trade unionism. It has undoubtedly encouraged "sabotage," or the destruction of machinery and plant. And its favourate idea is that of the general strike, run on very slight reserves of funds, and aiming more or less vaguely at the paralysing of industrial society, and so of the State itself.

Now this idea of the general strike, which has not had a very brilliant success in France, has undeniably caught on here. It is not Socialistic. It has indeed outrun the Socialistic movement in France, and forced it into a series of difficult compromises. And it is bound to interfere with the settlements of local disputes by the method of collective bargaining. Probably it represents more than anything else the impatience of the younger generation at the slowness of social progress. What are we to say to it ? Is "Syndicalism " good or evil ? Well, it is obviously an answer and a menace to the increasing luxury of our time. It is a reminder to the plutocrat class that their character and habits are known, and watched with no friendly eyes by masses of men who have the power to arrest, for some period at least, the processes of State life, and the machinery under which wealth is accumulated and distributed.

" Honourable Contracts."

But no one, I think, can maintain that unbridled Syndicalism can lead to good. It is too thoughtless, too impulsive, to last. Here and there it may achieve a signal and a most desirable victory. The autumn strikes for " recognition " and for better wages in the transport trades were generally of this character. The national conscience was rudely shaken, and it had nothing to say in defence when the case was put by the workmen in this rough challenging fashion.

Sabotage.

The term "Sabotage," which a few years ago was an " unknown quantity " among people of modesty and good manners, has become so universal in France, that it is almost impossible to conceive how people got along without it in the past. One cannot think of any dialogue between ministers, farmers, home-guards, schoolchildren or workers in which the term would not be used in some of its manifold meanings. A newspaper in which it did not appear at least twice in each column would be an impossibility —yes, it would really be a result of " Sabotage." It is not alone in everyone's speech, but it is a dominant factor in every phase of French life, and, on the other side of the boundary, its use is preferred to illustrate the general characteristics of French decadence.

But, looking from a greater elevation, it is very probable that Nietzsche would have been delighted with the term, because it signifies, basically, the most energetic rebellion of the autonomic individual against laws, capitalists, boards of examiners—in short, against all yokes with which the State harnesses the individual.

Yet to portray " Sabotage " in order to· have a clearer and better understanding of the term it will be necessary to give some concrete examples which are more tangible than analytical illustrations. Here are· some of them :

Between the 30th of October, 1910, adn the 30th of June, 1911, 2,967 railroad signal wires were cut—by former and present employees—to purposely block communication and transportation, and to create a pressure upon the State and railroad companies which would coerce them to comply with demands for better conditions.

During the uprising in the Province Champagne—the aim of which was to abolish a law restricting the name " Champagne " to the wine from the vicinity of Reims—the participants demolished more than two million bottles of " Fizz " ; emptied innumerable hogsheads of wine into the streets ; battered and burned a large number of wine presses, and destroyed entirely several large vineyards.

During an alteration in the tremendous track system connected with the largest railroad station in Paris a section of track only 67 feet long had to be changed, and to avoid any delay in the traffic, etc., this had to be accomplished on a certain night and at a certain time. But, here comes " Sabotage ! " The work was carried on so leisurely that at the expired time nothing was in readiness for the resumption of traffic. More than a hundred trains were delayed for hours—some of them had to wait in tunnels. A hundred thousand of the bourgois and judiciary had their day's work spoiled.

A few weeks ago, during the baccalaureate examinations at the Sorbonne (otherwise known as the University of Paris) one of the tests was a verbal translation from the Latin of Cicero, and because of the absurdity and difficulty of the text, the hundred and fifty students arose simultaneously, tore the note books to pieces, smashed the desks and broke the windows of the Auditorium. They addressed the professor with such uncomplimentary epithets that his holy person hurriedly disappeared, which possibly saved him from coming into more personal contact with " Sabotage."

A lighthouse on the coast of Corsica failed in its function. It was discovered that the reflector was broken to pieces and the lamp taken apart.

The " Lightning Express,." which runs between Havre and Paris, ran off the track a short distance from a bridge. Instead of going into the river it turned over. Without much trouble the tools with which the job was done were found. Also —to avoid mistakes, as it were, about the occasion of this " accident "—a number of revolutionary pamphlets were discovered with the tools ; these strongly advocated ' Sabotage ' as a means to the liberation of humanity!"—*Wholstand Fur Alle.*

The Syndicalist

Edited under the auspices of the Industrial Syndicalist Education League.

President—Tom Mann   Secretary—Guy Bowman

Vol. 1. No. 2.   FEBRUARY, 1912,   MONTHLY, One Penny.

Now for the Fight.

The principles of Syndicalism are rapidly in the ascendant in Britain. Without exception, wherever the Syndicalist gospel of Industrial Solidarity and Direct Action is preached—not as a supplementary effort backing up Parliamentarianism, but as the one sound method that will secure substantial improvements immediately, and rapidly lead on to the Social Revolution—it is accepted with hearty enthusiasm.

1912 is the year that should witness an enormous advance in the condition of the workers. This is the year entirely favourable, as regards "the state of trade," to call for vigorous and courageous action. More and more we must realise that the workers *must* become the deciding factors in controlling industrial conditions. Hitherto the capitalists have had it nearly all their own way, modified here and there by trade union effort; and because the capitalists always and everywhere run industry for their own profit, poverty has been imposed on the workers.

Now the workers are about to step in and have a voice in the deciding of the conditions under which work shall be done, and the first important step to take is the REDUCTION OF WORKING HOURS, and this will be done this year. Later on we shall regulate the hours in each industry, on the basis of absorbing *all* in the ranks of the *regularly employed*. We can and will wipe out unemployment, but that requires more perfect organisation than we have at present. But we can and must *demand and get* the 48-hour week for all trades and occupations where they work more than that number, and proportionately less in dangerous occupations.

We cannot say which union or which body of workers will take the initiative in conducting the struggle, but it will be done. This time last year very few persons expected to see the great fight in the Transport Industry, but it came off, and it has demonstrated the power of Direct Action more effectively than ten thousand articles in papers, because the workmen *themselves* achieved a triumph almost universally thought to be impossible.

It has been frequently said since that this triumph was accidental and unexpected, and will not take place again. On the contrary, it was most carefully calculated and deliberately arranged for, and this year's work must put last year's entirely in the shade.

We must bear in mind *this year is the boom year in trade*. It cannot last over next year. British shipping has increased enormously; every vessel fit to go to sea is in use; shipbuilders and marine engineers are busier than ever: but by the end of the year, for a certainty, there will be a plethora of boats. Such an enormous tonnage as that now possessed and in course of construction, for an absolute certainty means an excess of tonnage in a year's time. That means shipbuilding will begin to decline, freights will go down, and owners will prepare to attack wages, etc.

As sensible men we must on no account miss our chance *this year*, and be prepared to effectively resist encroachments of the capitalists when they begin to show their teeth.

Nothing on earth can so well entrench the workers as the reduction of working hours. By this means higher wages become possible, unemployment ceases, and leisure to think and time to act is secured.

Let every trade unionist in the militant ranks get to work at once. Working hours must be reduced this year of 1912. It is not a *Right to Work Bill* we want, it is the application of the power of industrial organisation to the complete absorption in the workers' ranks of every one ready for work, and this, not occasionally, but constantly.

Get at it Fellow Workers! Reduce the Hours and secure Leisure and Pleasure for our class.

Tom Mann.

A NATIONAL FEDERATION OF OUR TRADES COUNCILS.

To take the place of the Municipal Councils of to-day, and form the Industrial Councils of the future.

I have often asked myself the question: "What good purpose is being fulfilled by the Trades Councils of England?" In answer to this question I have been compelled to admit to myself that in reality they serve no purpose of noticeable prominence.

In other words, it seems to me they have not yet perceived the full scope of their possible mission. They have not grasped the far-reaching tendencies of their undertakings, nor have they measured with one sweep of the eye the career which lies open to their activities.

Asleep at the Post.

The reason for our Trades Councils being thus asleep at the post is not to be traced to criminal neglect on the part of their individual officials, for the latter are themselves the victims of the mistakes of the rank and file. The trouble is that the workers do not know each other enough personally, and, therefore, do not as yet respect each others individual talents—much less comprehend the resistless power which would belong to them as a class if they would only act unitedly as a class.

Moreover, they have had it constantly dinned into their ears by the Parliamentary doctors that it will be impossible to effect any social transformation without first making conquest of the political power, and when they begin to doubt the accuracy of these political judgments their ears catch next the preachments of those other doctrinaires who insist that the "redeeming catastrophe" must first clear the ground before any Socialist structure can be erected thereon.

In the midst of these conflicting counsels from partisan advocates of competing medicines the workers have naturally become distrustful of their own judgment and have limited their activity to attending to what seemed to be the necessity of the immediate moment.

The Word of March.

Observing that the workers have fallen into this habit of awaiting the turn of events, the capitalist class has not failed to perceive that such a hesitating policy makes it possible for themselves to really give the word of march to the workers. This opportunity, therefore, they have industriously followed up, and by dictating these governing events and bringing them on the stage of action at times and by methods suitable to their own interest the capitalists have at all times been enabled to choose the time and place of battle. Hence the repeated defeats and embarassments by which the movements of the workers have been retarded and hence the continuing of this incoherence of their institutions that has opened the way for their set-backs. Truly a vicious circle from which it is insistently necessary that the workers shall deliver themselves!

A Legitimate Field of Action.

To succeed in breaking away from this vicious circle in which bad policy and defeat are successively the causes of each other it is necessary first of all that the workers shall recognise that these Trades Councils have a legitimate field of action in which they may themselves set the pace, without waiting for capitalism to take the initiative—and, therefore, with the further advantage of causing the capitalists to be confused and unprepared, instead of Labour being saddled with these handicaps.

This field of action is indicated by the fact that at present these councils form the only ground on which the general problems of Labour may be discussed without the narrowness of view which in the individual unions is apt to permit only the immediate selfish interest of each craft to be discussed.

They, therefore, provide in their respective local districts a forum in which, from that local point of view, the general interests of Labour in that locality may be actively furthered. In other words, they are substantially an Industrial Council for each district, and need only to perform their part of bringing about the social revolution to take the place of the Municipal Councils of to-day.

In like manner, from the national point of view, it may be unhesitatingly declared that in the event of such direct and united industrial action the National Trades Council that may be formed by the co-ordinating of these district Trades Councils will in its turn be acknowledged as part of the National Council of the society of the future, and will thus partly take the place of the Parliament of to-day.

Our Friends Abroad.

Already this truth of the future has been declared by the workers of the United States in their memorable declaration by which they chastised the United States President Roosevelt when he attacked the principle of the union shop in connection with the "Miller case" of 1903. Addressing President Roosevelt, they said:—

"The flag of Labour will yet be planted upon the battlements of a success which shall include all within its walls; and in this program of justice and triumph you are invited to take part. As President of the United States and as the head of what will some day be the central Labour body of the United States, you are in a position to act in some large degree as an umpire during that part of the transitional period which shall be covered by your presidency. In your performance of this function of umpireship we ask you to hold the balance with an even hand."

Testimony to similar effect is furnished by our fellow workers of France. For example, in discussing the future of the Trades Councils of France, Pelloutier—formerly General Secretary of the Federation of Trades Councils of France and the Colonies—expresses himself as follows:—

"The Trades Councils reflect the state of the soul of the working-men's groups; and upon these groups they in their turn react. They give body to the secret desire of the workers to shake off all tutelage and to henceforth draw from themselves the elements of their emancipation."

True Functions.

This truth, then being recognised by the workers, it remains for them to put it into effect. What they have got to do is to augment the functions of these Trades Councils, which are thus seen to be the natural discussion ground for Labour in its general interests. Not only must the tactics adopted by the capitalist class—in the district covered by each of these Councils—be thoroughly discussed by the members who assemble in them, but there must also be carried on a systematic and intelligent campaign for the constant reinforcement of the workers in both their trade struggles and their individual struggles with these local capitalists. The spirit of comradeship must be constantly appealed to and constantly manifested. All problems of individual and trade unemployment must especially be made the subject of solicitous, brotherly consideration, and the principle of solidarity thereby presented to the minds of the workers as a vital force, bringing instant betterment wherever it is permitted to come into play, in even a partial way, and, therefore, promising immeasurable results when acted on universally.

Towards the Revolution

In this connection should be noted the desirability of the workers keeping constantly in mind the maxim that, in their endeavours to do away with the evils of unemployment, they must never commit themselves to any fixed minimum of the hours of labour. They will, on the contray, boldly and insistently proclaim the doctrine that in each industry, and at all times, the hours of labour shall be regulated wholly and solely with a view to the giving of employment, on a good living scale of recompense, to every worker dependent upon such industry. This rule of action will in itself compel the employers to perceive the futility of their ordinary policy of flooding a disaffected district with extra unemployed men in order to keep down the wages of those who do find employment.

In fact, this is the revolution itself! For on that very day on which this policy is universally put in force by the workers thus boldly taking into their own hands this function of regulation which through all the ages has belonged to them but has always been denied them—on that same day, and through that very act, the domination of the masters has crumbled to the ground!

A First Start.

Towards this assumption by the Trades Councils of their proper functions an important start has already been made. There are at present four federations of existing Trades Councils—the North-Eastern Federation, the Yorkshire Federation, the Lancashire and Cheshire Federation and the South-Western Federation. The fact that in the London territory there is no such federation—although in this metropolitan district there are not less than a score of scattered Trades Councils—has always appealed to my mind as proof that the systematic co-ordinating of the Trades Councils for effective action was being sadly neglected in this country; and, accordingly, when on November 9th, 1910, I delivered, by request, an address on Syndicalism to the Trades Council of Walthamstow I took advantage of the opportunity to expound succinctly the views which have above been expressed. This bore immediate fruit in the fact that to the first Industrial Syndicalist Conference—held at Manchester on November 26th, 1910—this same Walthamstow Trades Council sent a delegate in the person of Brother A. G. Tufton, who, as stenographically reported in the December, 1910, number of the *Industrial Syndicalist*, made an able speech setting forth the views which I had pressed upon the attention of the Walthamstow Trades Council a fortnight previously.

Get to Work at Once.

The general favour with which these views were received has made it clear to my mind that it would be a grave mistake to longer delay the forming of a national federation of Trades Councils in this country, and it is to be hoped that each local Trades Council will take the matter up in discussion and adopt resolutions which will express their position as favourable to such action and so serve as a basis for the consummating of the action.

For the sake of securing democracy of administration and promptness of response to the wishes of the rank-and-file members it is important that each Trades Council should be connected directly with this proposed national body rather than through some intermediary organisation of District Trades Councils, since it is evident that in the latter case the officers of the national body would be further removed from ready control by the workers.

The events of the last year have furnished unanswerable evidence on one hand that the occasion itself will always develop among the rank-and-file members, the initiative and executive ability to deal with the occasion, and, on the other hand, that officers too far removed from ready control by those whose interests they are supposed to serve, become only too readily forgetful of the fact that they are servants and so fall an easy prey to cowardice in the face of danger or unexpected responsibility, or to the personal vanity of leadership when approached with that subtle flattery which the ruling classes of this country are so shrewdly capable of employing when cunning rather than brutal violence promises to serve their purpose.

We will Help You.

Trades Council officers and delegates desiring to take some form of action in accordance with these suggestions are cordially invited to send in to *The Syndicalist* their views on the subject and also the news of their respective organisations.

And, in any other way that they may desire, the Trades Councils are invited to make use of the friendly offices of the *Industrial Syndicalist Education League.*

Guy Bowman

The Syndicalist

EDITED UNDER THE AUSPICES OF

The Industrial Syndicalist Education League

Offices—
4, MAUDE TERRACE, WALTHAMSTOW, LONDON, E.

MONTHLY - ONE PENNY.

Subscription—
Great Britain or Abroad ... 12 months 1s. 6d.

Orders for Subscriptions, Copies of the Paper, and Advertisements, should be sent to the Publisher GUY BOWMAN, 4, Maude Terrace, Walthamstow, London, E., who will also receive payment for same.

The receipt of a Sample Copy of this Paper is an invitation to you to become a Subscriber.

FEBRUARY, 1912.

No Compromise of Truth

From various quarters of the world the success of the tactics of Syndicalism is being proven by offers of compromise from our once exclusively political action friends and by a correspondingly significant toning down of editorial utterance in their journalistic attitude towards our movement.

When Syndicalism first demonstrated the courage of its convictions by boldly breaking loose from the parliamentary program, the editors of the politically inclined Labour Press attempted to rule the new departure out of court entirely as being " hopelessly unpractical."

Now that Syndicalism has given proofs of its being the eminently practical movement that it is, and has, therefore, established itself as the coming force in the Trades Union field, these editors are making overtures which show that our politically inclined brothers are anxious to save for themselves the half loaf rather than find themselves with no bread.

In other words, they are now expressing a chastened admiration for Syndicalist tactics and a willingness to lend kindly editorial support to struggles in which those tactics are employed, provided that we Syndicalists shall on our part abstain entirely from editorial criticisms of Parliamentarianism, and shall also keep close under hatches those of our oratorically gifted comrades who have formed the habit of castigating the political game.

Much as we Syndicalists would like to be governed by our desire to give full rein to those personal friendships which we feel for the many politically inclined brothers whom we belive to be sincere in their intentions, we nevertheless feel that to accept the proposed compromise would be treason to the proletarian cause; and, therefore, with the best of good feeling for individual opponents, we must go steadfastly forward in that part of our work which consists in the exposing of Parliamentarianism as one of the most subtle and, therefore, most dangerous ambuscades that have been laid out by the master class for the confusing and entrapping of the workers.

For the fact is that this compromise in favour of Parliamentarianism which we are now asked to make with our politically inclined Socialist friends is simply a repetition of the compromise which they themselves have accepted with the common enemy —a compromise by means of which the master class, which formerly ruled by open force, now manages to keep on ruling through the employment of cunning and trickery instead.

For thanks to this compromise, the masters have the tremendous advantage of possessing as a field for the use of this trickery a territory with whose every mountain range and valley and jungle, so to speak, they themselves are thoroughly familiar, but a territory in which the workers are hindered and embarrassed by ignorance of its strategic positions and by lack of experience in use of the cunning necessary to the taking of advantage of such positions even if they were acquainted with the swamps and by-passes of Parliamentary action.

That Parliament is simply the bourgeois successor and substitute for the openly practised King rule and Baron rule which preceded it is shown by

those privileges and honours, the enacting of which proves members of legislatures to be, not the " servants " of the people, as they hypocritically pretend to be before elections, but rather the masters whose rôle they boldly assume the day after election. As an exceptionally straightforward candidate once said to a gathering of voters whom he had induced to leave their work for a " five-minute " hearing of his claims:—

" To-day I have come here to kiss your feet. The day after election you may kiss *mine*."

Thus it happens that when the workers have once permitted themselves to be coaxed away from the industrial field in which their work lies —the field which they, therefore, understand in every detail, in which they can instantaneously detect both an act of treason and the traitor who commits it, and in which they are, therefore, able to readily unite for positive and direct action regardless of differences of race or creed as any other occasion of prejudice—they find themselves entangled, in this jungle of Parliamentarianism, in a series of skilfully placed obstructions which may be roughly catalogued as follows:—

1.—The temptations to discord created by the innate tendency of individuals to seek honours and salaries in competition with each other and by their consequent resort to trickery and back-biting and other measures incompatible with brotherhood and comradeship.

2.—The action of the political managers of the master class in accentuating this natural temptation to internal strife by deliberately sending their hirelings here and there among the workers to spy out all natural rivalries among those of the workers who are susceptible to political ambition, and then providing the initial incentive and, if necessary, the financial means for the dividing of the politically inclined workers into as many mutually neutralising factions as there may be rival political leaders capable of attracting partisan followers.

3.—The action of the Master class, inside Parliament, in blocking for years the recognition of Labour representatives, even when after those previous years of repeated disappointments, through such red herring diversions as those just mentioned, the workers have at last obtained a foothold inside the " talk-shop."

4.—The further action of the master class in still further postponing real action by plying with subtle flattery the few working class speakers who finally conquer recognition in the " talk-shop "—so that for all purposes of real betterment these " applauded persons " become even worse than useless!

5.—A whole battery of Master Class weapons which the Master Class have already got ready for use whenever that long promised day of the " Capture of Parliament " shall really arrive.

No! Brothers of the political Socialist School! We Syndicalists must decline to trot in double harness with you! Life is too short to take all these chances against the success of the present generation of working class fighters, while meanwhile another generation is growing up under the discouraging and enslaving influence of these repeated postponements and repeated disappointments! We desire rather to advance to the inspiring music of our Direct Action and of the prompt and fruitful victories by which Direct Action makes the Master Class weary of the task of holding the reins. To you the dull round of double-faced diplomacy-deceiving and being deceived! To us the clash of real battle! *Vive le son du canon!*

The Receipt of a Sample Copy of this Paper is an Invitation to you to become a Subscriber.

Yearly Subscription, 1/6 post free.

Syndicalist Journalists, Printers, Clerks, and others who are willing to take a hand in bringing the newspaper-producing trades into line, please communicate with WILLIAM H. SEED, Emerson Club, Buckingham Street, W.C.

Politicians and the General Strike.

By E. J. B. ALLEN.

All the old Labour Party politicians were opposed to the General Strike, except a few who admitted its utility for the purpose of hindering or preventing war. The newly-formed British Socialist Party have not made up their mind about it yet—officially, that is.

Thousands of the members of the B.S.P. believe in the General Strike. They propagate it orally. Some, like A. Barton, of Sheffield, write in its favour, whilst supporting Parliamentary politics.

Some of them understand the General Strike in its revolutionary sense for the direct and forcible expropriation of the capitalists—the sense in which the Syndicalists understand it.

But politicians, even those rareties—honest men—are apt to have strange kinks in their reasoning faculties where the General Strike is concerned.

Writing in the *Clarion* of January 12th, in an article entitled the " Dawn of Hope," Mr. Tom Groom argued:—

Moreover, the General Strike will not be given the field free to itself. Already the employing class has taken care to minimise the power of the General Strike; and though, for the present, one is bound to recognise the irresistible power of the workers, should they decide to stand together, yet it may be taken for granted that a Capitalist Party, having Parliamentary powers, will not rest content until they have passed such measures as shall destroy the effectiveness of combined action.

In another column this week we include a criticism, by example, of the dangers—to the Working Class—of such an ill-advised measure as the Conciliation Bill. That such a measure will be forced through Parliament, should the General Strike prove successful ,may be taken as certain, and the only place where that measure can be successfully defeated is in Parliament itself.

Now, this is wrong. The place where Parliamentary measures, to prevent strikes, must be combatted is in the mills, mines, railways, and other places where strikes take place. The reply to laws against a General Strike is for a General Strike to take place. The work of production of useful articles is not carried on at Westminster. Laws against a General Strike would have no value inside the places of production; and if the workers were wise they would have no value elsewhere.

Besides, if our rulers, by Parliament, can prevent a General Strike, so equally can they take measures to prevent a Parliamentary Socialist victory. A redistribution of seats, accomplished in a proper manner, may chop up a number of industrial centres and make them part of some constituencies with suburban or agricultural areas added, thus lowering the average of political thought. After all is said and done, it is the more thickly populated parts which generate the most progressive thought.

Even proportional representation can easily mean the perpetual lack of a majority.

Germany has not yet solved the problem by the ballot box, nor will it be solved in that manner.

Where " Labour Governments " are in power the workers are still wage-slaves. They are still exploited. Direct Action will have to carry the victory ultimately. There is no solution for the abolition of the wage system of slavery other than expropriation. Political action may give us State and Municipal ownership—which is simply the confirmation of the right of someone to rob the workers by extracting profit, rent and interest from them, through the medium of the local or national authorities. Co-operation, which is purely voluntary, only benefits those who already possess something. It creates nothing except small capitalists. Four per cent. is the usual interest on shares. Excellent thing for those who possess some wealth and for those who endure to practise the sacred bourgeois virtue of thrift and deny themselves pleasure and leisure in order to save. Co-operation, at present, does not help the " have-nots."

Does it ever strike the politicians that if capitalist politics can be used to tie up the workers' industrial revolt how still more easily can they be used to tie up, deceive, or cajole the workers politically?

The base of the matter is to be found in the formulable error of thinking that the workers can emancipate themselves with the *permission* of their rulers.

Grotesque mistake! The workers will have to *take their* freedom *sans cérémonie*. It will not be by obeying laws that we can overthrow the existing system, but by breaking them.

The whole of history bears eloquent testimony to the fact that when a class has emancipated itself, the object has been achieved first and legalised after. The thefts of the common lands were accomplished in this manner. If we want precedents from the workers' side the history of Trade Unionism furnishes ample supply. The Unions were formed and organised in spite of laws prohibiting them. Strikes were indulged in, though illegal. Determination and tenacity, on the part of our grandfathers and great grandfathers, compelled the capitalists of this country to legally sanction that which existed in spite of their opposition.

The General Strike cannot be combatted by laws if the workers are determined to resort to it. A few orators, a few writers, a few organisers may be imprisoned, but that would not break the strike. To imprison the strikers in large numbers would be expensive and dangerous and of itself would assist the general stoppage.

Practically every argument that Socialist or Labour politicans can bring to show how a General Strike might be broken because of legal enactments can be used with equal force against the likelihood of success through Parliament.

The strike is a movement of revolt, of defiance. Fortunately, it tends also to rouse a spirit of rebellion and activity in the strikers that exceeds that of their leaders and carries the mass beyond them. Every man or woman on strike feels a direct personal responsibility in the matter. It is a

movement of the rank and file. Every one is brought into the firing line. Quite the reverse holds true in politics. It is delegation; and, still more, delegation of all power and responsibility. It is " Get our man in! " Then one man is supposed to shoulder the responsibility and activity of three or four thousand electors—a clearly impossible task even with the most honest and energetic man. Besides, Parliamentary oratory will never engender that mass psychology that the action of the strike movement of 1911 did.

We have no quarrel with the B.S.P. as such, but we do advocate the General Strike, Direct Action, Anti-Militarism, and all those forms of activity which are necessary for the workers to accomplish their emancipation from the wage system. I believe the B.S.P. to have been a necessity. A Socialist Party can serve a useful purpose as an organisation for propaganda; but when that stage is left and attempts are made at legislation the most obtained by Parliamentary means is a modified form of the capitalist system—all its evil essentials untouched.

The State or Municipality may be the exploiting party instead of an individual, company, or trust; but the slavery is still there. We Syndicalists object to be skinned under any form, no matter how polite or democratic it may be. It is the abolition of the wage system, of slavery, that we are after; that is what we mean to get by means of the Revolutionary General Strike for the expropriation of the capitalists.

Hark from the Tomb.

Among the unpleasant stenches that rise from the decaying body of private capitalism must be reckoned the malodorous conduct of those intellectual prostitutes who, in every struggle between the masters and the workers attempt to win favour with the parasites by dealing out slander against the victims of parasitism.

The struggle for fairer conditions now contemplated by our mining brothers has naturally created a great panic and stir among all members of the parasite class, and it is, therefore, not surprising that in a graphic publication, of wide circulation in parasitic quarters, there has recently appeared a lengthy deliverance purporting to show cause why the support and sympathy of the dear " public " should be denied to the miners.

With naïve confidence in private capitalism's control of the public Press, the article advances, as its chief ground of attack upon the miner's cause the absurd statement that the miners know nothing of economics or of class relationships, and that, in their struggle for betterment they are moved chiefly by a desire for tawdry luxury and for drink and other " vulgar gratifications of carnal sense."

That such stale and untruthful allegations as these should be relied on to establish the case of the workers furnishes striking and convincing proof, not only of the injustice of the capitalistic cause, but also of the decadence of the society of to-day. Such statements convince nobody and are believed by nobody.

Least of all are they believed by the men who utter them and repeat them. They are simply the whistling of private capital to keep up its courage as it stumbles through its own graveyard on its unwilling journey towards its own tomb!

A DETECTIVE

By WILLIAM D. HAYWOOD.

A detective is the lowest, meanest, most contemptible thing that either creeps or crawls, a thing to loath and despise.

A detective has the soul of a craven, the heart of a hyena. He will barter the virtue of a pure woman or the character of an honest man. He will go into the labour unions, the political party, the fraternal society, the business house, the church. He will drag his slimy length into the sacred precincts of the family, there to create discord and cause unhappiness. He breeds and thrives on the troubles of his own making. He is a maggot of his own corruption.

That you may know how small a detective is, you can take a hair and pinch the pith out of it and in the hollow hair you can put the hearts and souls of 40,000 detectives and they will still rattle. You can pour them out on the surface of your thumb nail and the skin of a gnat will make an umbrella for them.

When a detective dies he goes so low he has to climb up a ladder to get into hell, and he is not a welcome guest there. When his Satanic Majesty sees him coming, he says to his imps, " Go get a big bucket of pitch and a lot of sulphur, give them to that fellow and put him outside. Let him start a little hell of his own, we don't want him in here starting trouble."

There is not room enough in hades for a detective. —*Int. Soc. Review.*

Jottings.

All journals which pioneer the way for advancement and, therefore, go ahead of the established thought of the day—"the old-time truth that has now become a be"—are necessarily published at a loss for a long period after they are founded, and should, therefore, be pushed forward by the shoulder-to-shoulder efforts of those upon whose vision has dawned the forecast of the ultimate triumph of the ideas which such journals propagate.

The *Syndicalist* is no exception to this general rule, and, in addition to the more generally perceived expenditure for paper and composition, must be reckoned the large amount expended at each issue of the paper in paying postage on free copies sent to all parts of the world to keep workers elsewhere in touch with what the workers of England are doing on this the fighting line of working-class action.

To help sustain the paper in this important work some of the comrades have conceived the idea of starting a

PUBLICITY FUND,

and contributions to this fund have already begun to come in. Any of the comrades who find themselves temporarily in funds and at the same time inclined to "help the good work along" can materially assist in pushing the circulation of our paper by occasionally giving a friendly lift to this fund. Feed the baby!

Mrs. A. V. Montgomery .. £0 10 0

Towards the same ends a great advancement will be made if our "colporteur" friends will incorporate as much system as possible into their branch of work by keeping constantly handy for reference a list not only of the working class meetings which occur at regular intervals in their respective neighbourhoods, but also all special meetings of the working class.

In this connection the

LEAGUE MAINTENANCE FUND

should also be remembered. It should be steadily borne in mind that upon the Funds that may be placed at its disposal depends very largely the activity of the League's propaganda, and the consequent volume of the aid which it will render to the working-class struggle. Subscriptions to this fund have already commenced in a small way.

George Davison ... £1 1 0

Of each of the four numbers of the *Syndicalist Railwayman* there is a limited number of extra copies that may as well be put to work in conveying the idea of Syndicalism to the minds of new chums. Comrades can have bundles of these free of charge by paying "carriage forward" on the same. Send in your requests for these back numbers.

Finally, a notable "boat" will be given to the propaganda of Syndicalism if the comrades will *never fail* to make it a point to pointedly ask their local news-agents for copies of each new issue of the *Syndicalist* as it becomes due (at the middle of each month). Each time a newsagent realises that he has missed a sale by not having the *Syndicalist* on hand he is propelled one step nearer to the point where he will keep it on hand.

The following are the names and addresses of our wholesale and retail news-agents, from whom the "Syndicalist" may be had:—

London.—The National Labour Press, 23, Bride Street, E.C.
,, J. Jaques, 191, Old Street, E.C.
,, W. Tarbart, 316, Kentish Town Road, N.W.
,, E. Denton, 427, High Road, Willesden, N.W.
,, G. Baker, 24, Netherwood St., West Hampstead.

Birmingham—The National Labour Press, 100, John Bright Street

Manchester.—Sam Brierley, 328, Hyde Road, Ardwick.
,, Abel Heywood, 56 & 58, Oldham Street.

Glasgow.—David G. Lindsay, 139, West Nile Street, and 132, Gairbraid Street, Maryhill.

Bristol.—John Flynn, 19, Horsefair.

BATTERSEA

Populous south side Working Class District hails with crowded and enthusiastic Meeting the opportunity to hear the truths of Syndicalism expounded by Tom Mann.

As might have been expected from the general ineffectiveness of the old-time methods relied upon for the relief of the undeserved poverty of the working class, the meeting of the Industrial Syndicalist Education League at Latchmere Baths, in Battersea, was packed to overflowing by a crowd of workers anxious to learn if Syndicalism had something better to offer.

Among those who thus came frankly in search of information was the Chairman of the meeting, Brother Dennis Hird, Warden of the Central Labour College.

In opening the proceedings, Mr. Hird announced that he had come for three reasons: First, having been a curate here twenty-five years ago he wanted to see whether things here had improved or not. Second, having acted as chairman for Tom Mann at Battersea meetings of twenty-five years ago, he wanted to see how much Tom Mann had improved—(laughter)—and thirdly, because he wanted to hear about Syndicalism from one of its leading exponents. (Applause.)

The revolution that we are out for, continued Mr. Hird, must be one that will not fail. It must shake the very foundations of society and give us a new social order based on justice, and not on bayonets tied into bundles with red tape. (Applause.) Welfare based on human misery must be swept away and the present beneficiaries of that sort of welfare must be taught that the real citizens of the country are those who produce the welfare.

We are tired of the gruesome game of blanks and prizes—mostly blanks, since our society is one in which success is an anti-social crime.

The glory of every aristocracy is reared on the corpses of the proletariat and decorated with famine. The luxuries of the rich are the funeral trappings of the poor.

The crumbs which fall from the tables of the rich are so many telegraph messages sent by folly to humanity. We are learning to interpret these messages, and a new science is flashing new messages of hope to mankind.

We know that modern fiscality is a new name for ancient rascality. We know that the glories of Western civilisation are moth-eaten, and that a "great nation" is an ugly weed growing in a crack of that tombstone which conceals the bones of the buried proletariat. We *know* all this, but we do not *act*. We *contradict* where we ought to *construct*. We *dream* when we ought to do.

But we cannot act, we cannot construct, unless we have unity. If Syndicalism means unity, then Syndicalism means triumph. Let us listen to Tom Mann that we may learn more clearly what Syndicalism means.

TOM MANN was received with the boisterous welcome befitting the return of a long-absent warrior and plunged into his subject by stating that he also remembered Dennis Hird and had often wondered how much advancement the passing years were conferring on Dennis. (Laughter.) In his opinion action would congratulate the other on having learned a great deal—(laughter)—and it on this occasion Brother Dennis had come to learn what Brother Tom had learned, why that was so much to the credit of the compelling force of Syndicalism. (Applause.)

Many of his old comrades of Battersea were present, he perceived, and he was glad to greet them, not only for old friendship sake, but also because they would be good witnesses for him, as the meeting progressed, that, under the old-time methods of fighting Labour's battles, progress in Battersea had been like that of a crab. (Laughter.)

As a card carrying member of the Battersea branch of the Engineers' Union he had been very active in Battersea a quarter of a century ago, and in conjunction with his then associates had been forced to the conclusion that the Trades Union Movement, as then conducted, was "deadly dull." (Laughter.) As "young men in a hurry" they were especially impressed by the fact that while as Trade Unionists the workers acted against the capitalist class, yet, when it came to voting, they nearly always supported some individual member of the capitalist class. To them, in their youth and inexperience, it had seemed to be the right thing to try and get this subject discussed in the Trades Unions and to suggest as a remedy that the workers should not only work for eight hours, but should also vote for someone belonging to the working class. They had not then learned that the thing that was wrong was the voting itself—a method worked out by the capitalist class for the benefit of the capitalist class—and that, very often, to elevate a worker through the voting method into a position of prominence was in reality to lower him to the sad position of a worker forgetful of his class. (Applause.) The present conditions in Battersea—conditions even worse than they were twenty-five years ago—showed very plainly the futility of the political method of fighting working class battles. (Applause.) And this general retrogression of working class conditions in England had taken place in spite of the fact that many honest and capable working class men had been elected to political office—thus proving that it was the system and not the individual that was wrong.

Some who had not yet had their eyes opened to the futility of trying to fight the capitalist class on its own chosen ground, the political battlefield, might say that the trouble was that the political method had not yet been given a fair trial in England—that the workers had not yet elected a sufficient number of working class representatives. Very well! Let that end of the discussion be taken up—with himself as a witness, and with the course of events in the great British Commonwealth on the other side of the world as evidence. (Applause.)

Taking up this line of testimony, Brother Mann went on to say that Fate had sent him to the Australasian world about ten years ago, possessed of a strong initial prejudice in favour of political methods, but in that land, where the workers had in many states achieved a complete conquest of political power—a conquest such as they could not hope to achieve in England for many years to come, even if all the workers were to throw themselves with full zeal and vigour into a continuance of the political method —his hopes for working class success from political methods had suffered a rude and killing shock. This conclusion he stated thus frankly and positively after nearly nine years of constant observation and study—with opportunities for observation and study such as had come to no one else in that country with whom he, at any rate, was personally acquainted.

Proceeding to narrate specific episodes as the ground of this loss of confidence in Parliamentary methods, Brother Mann piled up a tremendous mass of evidence that left his hearers more and more doubtful of the probability of any real benefit being likely to come from the injecting of the working class members into the talk-shop at Westminster.

In New Zealand the small plutocrats had simply stolen the name of the Democracy and were posing as a working class Government. As a matter of fact, there never was even a Labour group pure and simple in the New Zealand Parliament, and that country was, therefore, out of the evidence as much as England was.

In Australia, however, a great strike had turned the attention of the workers, nearly a dozen years ago, to the fact that the politicians were firing at them in the interest of capital; and being captivated by the idea that the thing to do was to abandon their frontal attack made by industrial methods and go after the capture of this side fort, they had succeeded in getting possession of the fort—only to find that capital's main fortress held the really dominating position by virtue of its occupancy of the economic field.

That nothing was gained by all these political so-called victories was proved not only by the capitalist minds developed by many Labour members, and even Labour legislatures as a whole, but still more convincingly by the material conditions of life—the pay the workers received, the conditions under which they had to labour, and the purchasing power of their pay as revealed by the quality of food and clothing they consumed, the houses they lived in, the joy of life at their command in the way of recreation.

All these tests gave crushing evidence as to the utter incapacity of politicians—no matter what party name—to remedy the conditions of Labour.

These conditions could only be remedied by the working class itself taking action on the industrial field—by the workers in each industry determining what the conditions in that industry should be, and then enforcing those conditions by Direct Action methods calculated to render impossible any other method of carrying on the industry. (Loud applause.)

It might be asked how it was going to be possible to get all, or even a majority, of the workers organised for industrial action? This would be accomplished by steadfastly continuing to call the workers' attention to the meaning of the circumstances which from day to day were exposing the weakness of those so-called Labour leaders who were in the habit of insidiously claiming to be in favour of industrial action, but who were at the same time advocating the capture of that glorious old "Mother of Parliaments." (Laughter.) These fellows constituted the really dangerous element because of the plausibility of their pretence of friendship for industrial methods, while their real love was reserved for the political method whose tendency was to confuse the workers and thereby prevent them from intelligently uniting their efforts on the field where all their trouble really arises—the field of actual productive industry. (Applause.)

Would this industrial action mean strikes? Possibly yes; but only when striking was necessary, and when organisation had been perfected to the point when striking would prove quickly victorious.

Of course it would be pleaded by the masters and their friends that the strike is "barbarous." That might be; but there was something that was still more barbarous, and that was the rotten, stinking poverty and degradation that was everywhere forced upon the workers and their wives and families. The workers would change all this by the working class revolution—the "right kind of revolution" that Brother Hird had spoken for. (Applause.)

This would bring far readier and more satisfactory results than that policy of "peace, sweet, sweet peace!"—(laughter)—which would delude us into waiting years to get our men into Parliament ,then further years of endeavour, on the part of those representatives, to "catch the Speaker's eye"—(laughter)—and finally the winning of permission to make a speech that after all would be received with empty plaudits— that would be followed by no action!

The stirring events of the recent year had taught the workers the truth as to their real power. The workers were now fighting directly for the abolition of poverty, and a few old frumps would no longer be able to head them off by drawing bogey pictures of the horrors of revolution and that "strength of the military" which the workers had now found out to be powerless and ridiculous when pitted against united and intelligent working class action.

"Fired with the zeal of our fathers, we will use our opportunities to remove all stumbling blocks and to leave to our children not a fight, but a victory—the achievement of peace and plenty, and the glory of a world redeemed from poverty." (Hearty and continued applause.)

After the ovation to Brother Mann had died down, Chairman Hird called for questions, and in answer to the many that were propounded Brother Mann explained in still greater detail that Syndicalism means:—

1.—That the workers who manipulate the tools shall regulate the conditions under which the tools shall be used.

2.—That there shall be no class above the workers to dictate to them.

3.—That the tools of each industry shall be owned by the workers in connection with the rest of the community.

Cuttings.

MARXIAN SOCIALISM.

From **The Philistine,** (New York).

Marxian Socialism is the apotheosis of the weak —the exaltation of the defeated—the enthronement of the inefficient—the survival of the unfittest.

COALOWNER'S CYNICAL STATEMENT.

From **The Morning Leader** (London).

"A well-known Midland coalowner" is reported to have made the following extraordinary statement on hearing the official figures of the ballot:
"It will be a God-send to the collieries if the men will strike. There were many thousands of tons of coal in stock before the minimum wage was discussed. Now there are none at the collieries. They are cleared, and stocks are on the railways, in works and factories.

Seven or eight weeks' stoppage will wipe these out, and we should have a glorious summer with good prices. If the miners stop they could not have arranged it better for coal owners than they have done. It will be a fine holiday for the men, the distribution of union funds, the much-required rest in the colliery world, considering the present output."

COUNTRY WOULD BECOME DEAD.

From **The Daily Mirror** (London).

The Times, in a leading article, draws a graphic picture of the state of Britain in the throes of a national coal strike:—

Let no one suppose that it would be like previous coal strikes and other sectional disputes, or that it would stop with the miners. If it continued even for a few weeks coal would not only become excessively dear, but would be unprocurable.

Gradually industries would cease to be carried on, works and mills would be closed, railways would leave off running, ships would be laid up, gas, electric light and power would fail.

Most employments would cease, the country would become dead, and the sufferings of the poor would be intense. We should have to rely for locomotion on petrol and horses, for light and warmth on oil.

Nor would that be all..

From the beginning efforts would be made to procure coal from abroad, and commercial activity in this direction would be intensely stimulated,

But the next step would be that the transport workers, whose organisation and temper were sufficiently proved last summer, would refuse to handle cargoes, and there would be riots, probably in every port in the kingdom.

Then, as the pinch of cold and hunger began to be felt, the mob would proceed to pillage. The military would be called out everywhere and a state of civil war would exist.
"In short, the general strike, of which so much has been heard—the true revolutionary general strike—would be realised."

Mr. MANN IN HYSTERICS.

From **The Newcastle Chronicle.**

The ridiculous outburst of vulgar profanity in which Mr. Tom Mann indulged at Glasgow last evening is hardly the sort of thing to help the cause of labour. The root of Mr. Mann's grievance appears to be his belief that the Government will endeavour, by all the means in its power, to preserve order if the threatened troubles in the labour world should develop to such an extent and in such a manner as to threaten the peace of the community, and as Mr. Mann's methods consist chiefly in inciting the more impressionable class of the workers to deeds of violence, his resentment is easily understood. He knows, of course, that he is perfectly safe in these exhibitions of impropriety for the excellent reason that the authorities are not sufficiently foolish to indulge his passion for cheap notoriety by helping him to pose as a martyr. But it is a lamentable thing that any class of workers should take hysterical nonsense of this kind seriously.

From **The Bleachers' Journal** (Bolton),
To the Editor of the Bleachers' Journal.

Sir.—The only way to keep the peace, said Lord Roberts, is to be prepared for war, and the only way to prevent strikes is when Industrial Unionism is strong enough. The workers must organise upon the basis of their class. The principle of industrial unionism is to conduct the class struggle on non-parliamentary lines. It is to the interest of the master class to get their labour as cheap as possible, and it is to the interest of the working class to sell their labour as dearly as possible.

If we look back before the Industrial Revolution we shall find that the workers were better off than they are to-day. Although the workers had little chance of becoming rich, they had still less chance of ending their days in the workhouse, and their struggle for existence was not so keen as it is at present, because there were no millionaires and pauperism was almost unknown. But to-day we have the two extremes—the millionaire and the pauper.

We are beginning to understand the real meaning of Industrial Solidarity. Here we have no less than seven unions in Glasgow agreed to take common action in sympathy with the carters and dockers if the disputes in which they are engaged lead to a strike. Our grand old battle cry of Industrial Solidarity shall become increasingly forceful, and we shall realise fully the true meaning of direct action. For the day of sectionalism is over, and the Bolton Amalgamation membership is open to all men and women in the trade, whether skilled or unskilled. All together is our motto, up with wages and down with the hours.

Yours fraternally

Wm. MUTTER.

Mr. TOM MANN AT MERTHYR.

From **The Merthyr Express.**

Mr. Tom Mann, at a meeting held at the Drill Hall, Merthyr, last night under the auspices of the Workers' Union, spoke on effective industrial organisation. However indifferent colliery workers might be in other parts, they in South Wales were, he said, sturdy, and knew exactly what they desired, and they ought not to allow any negotiation to proceed that did not include a minimum wage for all sections. Mr. Matt Giles, the organiser of the Union, who presided, urged the workers to make their Trades Union an "approved society" under the Insurance Act.

Peeping Abroad.

NORWAY.

The Syndicalist Movement.

CHRISTIANIA.—Until last year. Syndicalism was almost unknown in Norway, but during these last few months, a very important change has taken place, and the movement is shaping definitely. A particularity of the new current is that, without absolutely discarding parliamentarism, it wants to apply in the trade union struggle, sabotage and all other methods advocated by Syndicalism. This movement disposes of a few very intelligent agitators who have already gained much influence.

ITALY.

Syndicalism won't Die.

PIOMBINO.—After the recent strike which took place here in the metallurgic centre, the masters and the police thought they had destroyed any vestige of Syndicalism, but the workers have not allowed themselves to be demoralised by their failure. The unions that were dissolved are being reconstituted one after the other.

The same thing is taking place in the isle of Elba, where the miners' organisations announce the coming resurrection of Syndicalism.

Women Trade Unionists.

ROME.—From information provided by the Trades Councils, the Italian C.G.T. has been enabled to publish a statistic of the number of women Trade Unionists in Italy up to the end of 1911. The number is 62,543 or 13 per cent. of the total number of Trade Unionists. The province of Emilia heads all Italian regions for the organisation of women workers ; about 30,000 women are organised.

SWITZERLAND.

International Trade Union Conference.

BERNE.—The Executive of the Swiss Trade Union Centre (the *Gewerkschaftsbund*) has decided to accept the organisation of the International Conference of Trade Union Centres in 1913.

It may be pointed out that there is no question here of an international congress of Trade Unions or Federations. The parliamentary majority in the international trade union movement does not want to hear anything about real international trade union congresses : this evidently out of fear that these congresses might be detrimental to the international congresses of social-democratic politicians where trade unions are also admitted . . . on condition, however, that they be faithful worshippers at the social-democratic Church.

Switzerland, in 1913, will but witness a simple international conference of Trade Union Centres' secretaries of different countries. Great Britain will probably be again represented by Allan Gee and Bro. Appleton, secretary of the General Federation of Trade Unions.

TURKEY.

Turkish Unions.

SALONIKA.—It is very interesting to see that trade unions are now being started in Turkey. At Constantinople a union has been formed by the cabinet makers, by the tailors, and the railway workers of Anatolia.

At Broussa a union of silk weavers, at Smyrna a union of shop assistants, and a society of mutual aid among railwaymen. The chief centre of the movement is Salonika, the most modern town of Turkey. The local union of tobacco workers was recently on strike and gained a victory. There exists also a society of mutual aid among the tobacco workers of the Regie, a union of male and female cotton weavers (the fact that men and women are together in one union for the same purpose is important in Turkey.

Reviews.

"The Universal Strike." By Alf. Barton; B.S.P. Rooms, 57, Arundel Street, Sheffield. Price 1d.

This pamphlet is another evidence of the new spirit. The idea of the General Strike is well expounded. It is a good sign to find such an admirable booklet written by a Britisher and dealing with British conditions. It contains a brief history of the General Strike movement abroad, and deals with its development in Great Britain. The recent strike movement amongst the Transport Workers is well noticed. The new relations of the Socialist political movement and the revolutionary unionist agitation are dealt with. If the ideas that Mr. Barton so clearly advocates are held in common by the rest of his fellow members of the B.S.P. a welcome change has really come over the Socialist movement. Mr. Barton, whilst seeing the desirability of a certain number of Socialist members in Parliament, does not by any means intend to let the obtaining of Socialist members of Parliament outweigh the urgency of the General Strike. He argues from the expression of working class solidarity that has manifested itself this year that it is possible for a Universal Strike to be carried through to its logical conclusion of the expropriation of the landlord and capitalist class long before a Socialist Revolutionary majority could be obtained. His careful analysis of Parliament and of the Parliamentary method is worthy of the attention of every intelligent worker. Whilst the keen fighting spirit and cheery optimism in which his brochure is written tells its own story of the author's enthusiasm. It is a pamphlet to read and recommend.

The Soldier's Creed, The Rifle,

AND

The Territorials.

THE SOLDIER'S CREED.

"Captain, what do you think?" I asked,
  Of the part your soldiers play ? "
But the captain answered, "I do not think;
  I do not think, I obey !"

" Do you think you would shoot a patriot
  Or help a tyrant slay ? "   [down,
But the captain answered, "I do not think;
  I do not think, I obey !"

"Do you think your conscience was meant
  And your brain to rot away ? " [to die,
But the captain answered, "I do not think ;
  I do not think, I obey !"

"Then if this is your soldier's creed," I
  "You're a mean, unmanly crew ; [cried,
And for all your feathers and gilt and braid,
  I am more of a man than you !"

" For whatever my place in life may be,
  And whether I swim or sink,
I can say with pride, " I do not obey ;
  I do not obey, I think !"

    The Anti-Militarist (Christchurch)

THE RIFLE.

I serve both parties—the party which enslaves and the party which delivers from bondage.

I have no preference. With the same fury, the same force I send forth the bullet which kills the defender of liberty and the bullet which lays low the myrmidon of tyranny.

I was made by workingmen to kill workingmen.

I am the rifle, the liberticide when I serve the masters, the emancipator weapon when I serve the slaves. Without me no man would be able to say: " I am more than you." And, without me, no slaves would be able to shout: " Down with tyranny !"

The tyrant class calls me " Supporter of institutions."

The free man pats me with love and calls me " Instrument of redemption." I am the same thing, and meanwhile I serve to oppress as much as to set free. I am at the same time murderer and avenger, according to the hands which control me.

I am able to tell into whose hands I have fallen. Do they shiver ? They are without question the hands of myrmidons. Is the pulse firm ? I say without hesitation: " These are the hands of a lover of freedom."

It is not necessary for me to hear the pass words to know to which party I belong. It is sufficient to hear the chattering of the teeth to know that I am being handled by oppressors. Wrong is cowardly ; Right is valiant. When the ruffian places me on his breast to make me throw up the death confined in the cartridge I notice how his heart beats with violence. It is because he realises his crime; he does not know whom he has to kill. They have given him orders to ' shoot to kill," and he shoots to kill ; and perhaps the bullet will pierce the heart of his father, his brother, or his son, whom Honour had summoned to revolt.

I shall exist as long as there shall exist on this earth a stupid humanity divided into two classes: the rich and the poor, those who enjoy life and those who suffer.

When the last bourgeois shall have disappeared, when the shadow of Authority shall have vanished, then will I, in my turn, disappear also, and then will the material of which I am constructed be made into ploughs and into thousands of other instruments which men, at last become brothers, will handle with the enthusiasm of love for their brothers.

    RICARDO FLORES MAGON.

THE TERRITORIALS.

" Reader, are you taking your fair share in the protection of *your* country ? It is not anybody's business to safeguard *our* shores—but *everybody's*. Compulsion is a hard, unpleasant word, and there is no compulsion in the Territorial Army. There need never be any if only you and your friends will bear *your* share of the very light burden it lays on you. The duties of citizenship of this mighty Empire demand something more of you than mere " looking on." At present the State is satisfied with a very little service. If that service cannot be obtained willingly and voluntarily, then you may be sure it will be got compulsorily. . . .

" You don't want to see that day come—nor do we. But there is only one way to prevent it, and that is for you, and all of us who are young and healthy, to cheerfully don the King's uniform, and play a manly part by doing a man's work in defence of all an Englishman holds dear —*his* King, Home and Country.

" Will you come *now*, and show your patriotism by helping us fill our ranks ? "

How many officers and men belonging to this regiment have laid down their lives that you might be free ? Will you be untrue to the great traditions of our mighty Empire by refusing to stand by ? . . .

    Leaflet issued by one of the London Territorial Battalions.

Brothers, ten minutes' reasoning should be ample for you to see the scoundrelism and hypocrisy that lies behind all such appeals as that quoted above.

Your country, *your* empire! How much of this precious island or of this glorious empire do *you* own? You know if you be true to yourselves how much of it you own. Nothing! Not one ten-millionth part of a square inch. Why are you called the proletarian class by the economists of all schools and all countries?

Because the word proletariat means the dispossessed and those that are foolish enough to provide the flesh for the cannon the capitalists want.

In the face of that, are you willing to fight for, and defend, nothing ? Is it not obvious and patent to you that all these appeals are merely the tricks of the master class to keep you under the iron heel of repression? Does it not occur to you that by this means they lead the workers of one country to believe they have a grievance against the workers of another or every other country; that by this means they always have a large body of hired murderers at their disposal, ready at all moments to perpetuate any filthy deed in the interest of their plunderous cause—capitalism?

They tell you that men have died on the battlefield in order that you, the working-class, might be free.

Free? Yes, free to starve and die of starvation. You are about as free as a rat is with a ferret at one end of its hole and a fox-terrier at the other.

Free to work for as many hours as the masters tell you to work.

Free to live in just such dwellings or hovels that your masters let you live in.

Free to eat just as wholesome or as unwholesome food as the masters say you shall eat.

Free to wear just the kind of garments that the masters say you shall wear.

This is the freedom that was gained for you on the bloody battlefields that the patriots prate to you about. These are the results of the glorious deeds of a bygone day. What a cause to fight for! The maintenance of a system that means starvation, consumption, syphilis, suicide, and all the attendant evils of the rottenest state of society the world has ever seen.

Brothers, forswear it!

Let the creature who make these appeals to you know, by all the means at your disposal, that you have discovered them, and that you will have no more of them.

Tell them that when you *have* a country you *will* fight for it. But that while the country is *theirs* you are going to fight *them* for it.

Tell them also that if military service " will be got compulsorily " and they put a rifle into your hands you will use it as an " Instrument of Redemption."

Tell them finally that the army you are going to join is not the Territorial Army, but the Syndicalist Army: the army that stands for the organisation of the workers to fight their own great battle against the capitalist class upon the Industrial Field ; the army that means the General Strike and the World for the Workers.

    COUNTRYLESS.

Syndicalist Activity.

Our Syndicalist friends are specially requested to send in reports of their respective Trade Union branch meetings at which Syndicalism is discussed, or a Syndicalist resolution moved.

Such reports to reach the office before, or by the 10th of each month.

WEST HAM TRADES COUNCIL.—A special meeting of delegates and friends was held on December 14th, to hear and discuss an address on "Industrial Syndicalism" by Guy Bowman, Secretary Industrial Syndicalist Education League.

Brother O'Malley, who was in the chair, said he had known Guy Bowman for several years, and could assure the Council that they were going to listen to a thorough revolutionary who was in dead earnest.

Guy Bowman then proceeded to outline the world-wide organisation of the working class; he showed how "trade" unions were, and had to evolve into "industrial" unions, which in their turn were also organised internationally; he described the International Bureau of Trade Union Centres, and gave a picture of what its functions would be in future Society. Continuing, he drew a parallel between the basis of Socialism and that of Syndicalism, showing how the former was leading to Stateism and centralisation, and the latter towards federalism and the destruction of the State. He showed how Direct Action could be applied against Capitalism, against the State, and against Society. Finally, he dealt with the General Strike, its meaning, and its purpose. Questions and discussion followed, in which Councillor Shreeve took part, his remarks being rather friendly towards the theories expounded by the speaker of the evening.

The meeting had apparently been called in order that the members might understand the aim and methods of Syndicalism before deciding upon the Council's affiliation to the proposed London Federation of Trades Councils. The impression created seems to be favourable, and it is most likely the Council will adhere to the new scheme.—ARTHUR JONES.

STRATFORD CARPENTERS AND JOINERS.—As a sequel to an address on Syndicalism delivered to the West Ham Trades Council by the Secretary of the Industrial Syndicalist Education League, Guy Bowman was asked to address this branch on January 30th. He dealt with Direct Action as applied to the Building Industry, and gave a few examples of what had been gained by such method in France and other countries. He also dealt with that moral prejudice called "patriotism," which was only used by the capitalists to get the workers of one country to throw themselves at the throats of the workers of other countries, when they (the capitalists) had to settle a quarrel amongst themselves. He said the workers had no country, and consequently no country to defend. All they ought to be concerned about was to get hold of the tools of production all over the world and work these collectively for the benefit of all.

Honore Jaxon of America, who was also present, said that a quarter of a century ago he happened to be the secretary of the General Council of the Carpenters and Joiners of Chicago. He gave a vivid picture of the Direct Action methods they then employed to obtain the eight-hour day which they had maintained up to the present time.

There were a number of questions, but there was no opposition ; the members heartily thanked both lecturers, and seemed to be very much in agreement with the new methods of action.
    CARPENTER.

HACKNEY SHOP-ASSISTANTS.—On the last day of January this branch, for the first time, had a lecture delivered to it. The subject was Syndicalism, and the lecturer Guy Bowman, who dealt with the subject in its relation to the Distributing Industry. He said that all those in any way connected with distribution would have to amalgamate, or at least federate, into one solid fighting body in order that they might get hold of that industry itself, and manage it themselves for the benefit of the whole community. Proceeding, he went on to describe sabotage, the pearl strike, anti-militarism, and the General Strike, all means of direct action the workers would have to make use of if they wanted to become emancipated. Brother Legg, in opposing, said that the more he heard about Syndicalism and its methods the less he was inclined towards it. There was something much better than direct action, and that was "law and order," which everybody respected, and was therefore much more efficacious. All the workers had to do was to alter the law, and the rest would take care of itself. Guy Bowman, in his reply, said that no change had taken place, anywhere in the world existed, without it being brought about against "law and order," and recited numerous examples of history to substantiate his arguments. The meeting closed at midnight, and our members gained their homes with plenty of food for thought.—JOHN WERRY.

BRIXTON CLERKS (N.U.O.C.)—At the monthly meeting of the above branch, held at the end of 1911, the following resolution was moved by Comrade J. Lloyd :—" That in the opinion of this branch the time has arrived when definite steps should be taken to unify the industrial movement on the basis of organisation by industry." The motion was seconded by Comrade William Archer.

In moving this resolution Comrade Lloyd stated the Syndicalist position, laying particular stress on the thoroughness of organisation by industries, comparing it with the crazy conditions which were existent in the orthodox Trade Union movement. It was Revolutionary Unionism we wanted, he said. The temper displayed by the Transport Workers last August needed fostering. Solidarity, of the kind which was expressed in London, Liverpool, and in other great ports at that time, was essential. Against such tactics Parliament and its institutions were utterly impotent. Let only this spirit be imitated in the other great industries and the Industrial Revolution would be an accomplished fact. This revolutionary spirit, he said, must be imparted by all who believed in Syndicalism to those who were, though Trade Unionists, not released from the bonds of Trade Union orthodoxy.

After considerable discussion, in which T. J. Fisher took up the most hostile position, the resolution was put to the meeting and, on a show of hands, was carried with two dissentients. About 22 members were present.—J. CHARLES.

Printed by BUCK BROS. (T.U.), Stainforth-road, and published by GUY BOWMAN, at 4, Maude-terrace, Walthamstow

The Syndicalist

Edited under the auspices of the Industrial Syndicalist Education League.

VOL. 1. NO. 3.   MARCH-APRIL, 1912.   MONTHLY, ONE PENNY.

SOCIAL CREATION THROUGH CONQUEST.

BY ODON POR.

SYNDICALISM, or revolutionary unionism, is not merely a reaction against the poor success of Socialist and Labour politics, nor is it merely a reaction against the inefficiency of trade unionism. Its roots reach far deeper.

As the industrial consciousness and efficiency of the modern capitalists have resulted in more definite actions through the evolution of their economic functions, so has the industrial consciousness and efficiency of the workers evolved, and is still evolving, through the process of building up their industrial movement.

Through the effort to realise the object of their trade organisations, the workers have been forced not merely to make of them large, militant bodies, but individually to concern themselves with the technical problems of production upon which the conditions of their labour rest.

The more active the workers' organisations have been, or, in other words, the more thoroughly they wanted to control the conditions of their labour, the more intense their technical insight has necessarily become, and the more opportunities have they created for themselves to utilise their new knowledge.

When the workers fully understand the technical nature and possibilities of their labour, they must inevitably turn their attention to the problems of organising production and distribution, of improving and co-ordinating the machine process of saving labour and material, of organising the economic process in the interest of the collectivity.

The very fact of acquiring an exact knowledge of these problems makes them desirous of applying it, through their industrial organisations, upon the industries concerned. They have become conscious of their capacity to manage their own affairs, and because the formation of their own efficiency had been determined by the activities of their own industrial organisations, they must logically conclude that these same organisations are destined in the future to operate the industries.

Thus, when labour organisations make a special collective effort to improve labour conditions, they simultaneously call out in the individual worker a desire to reorganise labour in all details. This desire when intensified leads to an intensified action not only for better, but for entirely new conditions of labour. When the workers feel themselves capable of working better under certain new conditions, when they become fully conscious of their capacities, then will they fight most energetically for a change. The battles of fit and capable workers, conscious of their power, are substantially different in quality and scope from the struggles of workers unawakened and unconscious.

The very fact of being a better producer, or even the mere prospect of becoming a more efficient worker, increases the exigencies of the individual, and he inevitably finds himself impelled to struggle for conditions wherein his greater efficiency may be brought into play.

But this struggle will be a collective struggle, inasmuch as the broadened knowledge of labour and of the social organisation of industries has become the common property of numberless workers, and has merged itself into a collective force of sufficient dynamic potency to urge the whole working class towards social industrialism.

Through their industrial organisations, engaged in creative action, a new conception of labour has already arisen among the workers. A sense of social responsibility fills them. Labour is becoming with them a social profession, a civic duty. They no longer regard their labour merely as a means of getting daily bread. They consider their work organically in relation to all problems of life. They insist on being free producers, on applying their creative faculties to their full capacities by co-ordinating them in their organisations to the work of their fellow-workers. The degree of intensity of this to the professional consciousness in the apersons determines the various manifestations of the Syndicalist movement both

within and without the sphere of the industries and the unions.

The limitless importance of Syndicalism is that in the last analysis it creates, develops, focusses, and sets to work the productive and moral energies of man.

As this new tendency has crystallised into a definite social action, so it has expressed itself in a definite social attitude, a new social philosophy.

Through collective action the workers have learned how to assume new functions. They have acquired a positive knowledge of how social progress has been made and how it can be made. They have learned a new social law—namely, that we may consciously determine upon a substantially new form of society, if its vital tendencies are already living within us—and that we may consciously work out, adopt, and furnish the means necessary for its realisation.

They have learned that this conscious adoption of means puts them in possession of the hidden source of the spiritual power necessary to social progress. They have discovered those forms of organisation by which progress can be evolved, enforced, and called into action. They now know how to act in order to develop a social organisation and its proper social spirit. Social evolution is now a conscious process to them.

In short, they have found that the problems of evolution and social revolution reduce themselves to problems of organisation, the laws of which can be controlled. Nay, more, they make of these problems real activities, the outcome of which is entirely dependent upon the intensity of their work of organisation.

Feeling a new reality grow in and around them through their own action, they have realised that their combined efforts will engender the new society. They are convinced that economic and technical progress already offers the material to build the new society, the only work left to do is to actually build it. They conceive the revolutionary process as entirely dependent upon them, and by placing themselves within the process itself they are pushing it on. Their philosophy is but a spiritual precipitate of their collective action, and therefore is a philosophy of conscious creation.

Progress does not operate above us and in spite of us, but it is by virtue of our conscious desire and organised action. Progress towards the ideal social will be realised by the organised will of the working-class.

So a new philosophy is being worked out, the philosophy of social creation through conquest. In order to have social progress it is not necessary for the workers to wait for anything to happen, to wait for either an industrial crisis or a period of prosperity, nor for the introduction of new methods of production, nor for a favourable political situation or combination. If they want progress the workers must themselves propose certain problems for solution, as expedients for action. They must themselves raise new issues and create the platforms for their struggles.

The workers no longer consider themselves as passive and inert material, movable only by outside force, but as an active force capable of producing great effects by its own inherent energy.

Thus enters with the conscious volition of the new workers their determination to create. A new will is emerging from the soul of men, emanating from their collective experiences and operating as a socially formative factor through the medium of their organisations. Knowing that this will has been acquired by organised action, they will be impelled to develop its formation in other workers by drawing them into the sphere of their social and industrial activity.

A social will, independent of the pseudo-social laws, is springing into life by which men will overcome the tendency to depend on others and will act on their own account.

This will to create independently, and the modes of action through which it has

WHAT IS SYNDICALISM?

IS IT THE FUTURE CREED OF LABOUR?

THE essence of Syndicalism is the control by the workers themselves of the conditions of their work.

The growth of the machine process has divorced the worker from the control he formerly exercised by his individual ownership of the tools of production.

To-day the Capitalist owns and controls the tools formerly owned by the worker, with the result that the worker is practically his slave.

Syndicalism proposes that this control of the technical processes now exercised by the Capitalist shall pass to the various groups of organised workers of the various industries. The product which is now the property of the Capitalist would become under Syndicalism the property of the community.

The Syndicalist looks to the future organisation of human society to be an Industrial Society, as opposed to the present Capitalist State.

The present Capitalist State is represented by a Parliament composed of representatives from certain territories, from geographical sections of the country, whereas the future Industrial Society will have its National Committee composed of delegates from the various organised industries.

The present political organisation of society is anarchical, inasmuch as the representatives in Parliament are not representative of men as organisations, but of unorganised individuals—or, at least, organised in no natural, vital, industrial organisation.

We look upon the present State as moribund, as a relict of an order of society fast passing away, and, therefore, we do not think Parliament as at present composed can ever do much of anything toward preparing the way for the future Industrial Society. Hence the Syndicalist thinks the energy and strength of the workers should be mainly directed toward industrial organisation rather than to political action.

We set our faces toward the future rather than the past. We look forward to humanity organised in a world-wide Industrial Society, where the means of production and distribution are owned and controlled by the workers.

Syndicalism has no thought of arranging industry upon the basis of each group of workers in each industry holding up the community to the full extent of its economic power in order to extract the greatest amount of reward for its particular form of labour.

The remuneration of the worker will be determined either by deeds, or by needs as may hereafter be decided, but most certainly not upon the basis of allowing him a reward according to the importance of his industrial product to the community, for that would be merely changing the present system, with its small number of Capitalist exploiters, to a worse system, with a myriad of exploiting workers.

We think that the workers, by combining their forces in the various industries, will have it in their power to determine for themselves the future course of society. We think the example of what the British coal-miners with their great strike have done is proof of our theory.

We think the craft unions have their

place in Syndicalism, but only as they are united with other craft unions, to form a solid organisation, controlling completely the whole industry of which they are a part.

A union to be really powerful must be a union of all the workers in the industry affected, and a strike to be effective must be wide enough spread to not only seriously curtail the profits of the employers, but must also be a menace to the community itself through the stoppage of supplies.

With the workers properly organised there is nothing that they may not successfully demand from the Capitalists by means of a general strike.

We part company with the Socialists in thinking that the effectiveness of sending men to a moribund Parliament of a moribund State can in any manner of way compare with the effectiveness of organising men into all-powerful industrial unions.

Both Syndicalism and Socialism look to a world-wide democratic organisation of the workers for co-operative production and distribution. But whereas Socialism looks to social organisation, proceeding from the present Capitalist State downward to the workers, the Syndicalist looks to the evolution proceeding upward from the workers to organised society.

Instead of the community giving industrial control to the workers, as the Socialists fondly hope, the Syndicalists look to the workers taking such control and giving it to the community.

Syndicalism is inverted Socialism. The difference between Syndicalism and Socialism is the difference between a man and a machine. The man himself controls his own activities; the machine is controlled from without.

The Socialist imagines that he can assemble the parts of the future society as a watchmaker assembles the wheels of a watch; whereas the Syndicalist insists that future society must follow the natural lines of growth like a plant or an animal. Syndicalist philosophy is deductive, whereas Socialist is inductive.

Syndicalists look upon the new industrial unions of to-day as direct progenitors of the organisation of the future industrial community.

We think that the practical test of experience shows plainly that whereas it is a comparatively easy thing to get men to go out on a strike for the success of their unions, to face starvation for a principle, it is paradoxically almost impossible to get them to vote for a revolutionary candidate, to give a vote which costs them neither trouble nor pain, merely thought. The worker is guided more by his feelings than his thoughts.

We think the explanation of this phenomenon exists in the workers' understanding, sub-consciously, perhaps, that in striking for their union they are working for a living organism of which they are an integral part; whereas in sending their man to Parliament they are forcing him into a decaying organisation which nothing can successfully galvanise into renewed life.

However, to the extent that political action does not distract the workers from industrial unionism we have no quarrel with those who thus employ themselves.

During the transition period there can be no doubt but that a group of revolutionary Socialists in Parliament has some value to the workers. Especially in the control of local conditions, there can be no question but that the election of Labour and Socialist Members to Boards of Guardians, of Aldermen, &c., is a distinct advantage. But to those Socialists who look for a social transformation to come about by the election of a Socialist majority to the House of Commons we can but extend our pity.

We think the evolution of the social organism follows the law of the living organism; the development is from the extremity to the centre rather than the contrary.

The future Industrial Society will normally take a valid possession of its tools of production in any certain industry, first through the gaining of the control by the workers in that industry, rather than through the control first passing to the present Capitalist State.

Even when the present State does nationalise an industry, as it has already, for instance, taken over the Post Office, and as it will no doubt take over the railways and mines, this may be really of little, if any, benefit to the workers concerned in those industries, as, indeed, it is not always of any certain benefit to present society.

An industry will never become an integral part of the future Industrial Society until it is under the control of its workers, and worked for the joint benefit of those workers and the community. Such a condition is practically impossible under the present Capitalist State. Hence, Syndicalists view with more or less indifference nationalisation by the Capitalist State. In fact, it is not difficult to foresee a condition in which the superior power of the State over the Capitalist might even be turned against the workers in an industry that has become nationalised.

There can be no denial that the State has not in all instances been a model employer. What may be said in regard to nationalisation applies with even greater strength to the fixing of a minimum wage by the State.

The workers can have no guarantee when they have not only to struggle with the Capitalist but also with the State, controlled by Capitalists, that they will be in any better condition to insist upon a fair wage than they are to-day. True, they will be protected against lowering of the minimum, but there is no guarantee that the minimum fixed will not become a practically unalterable maximum, and a maximum which may not allow the necessaries of life.

The present Minimum Wage Bill is especially obnoxious, as its district boards tend to divide the Labour forces in the next contest.

Syndicalists refuse to be drawn aside by red herrings of any sort, and declare that the main object to-day in life for the workers is so to perfect their industrial unionism that they may have complete control of their own destinies.

In union there is strength, and in the just and proper exercise of strength lies happiness. In Syndicalism man will attain racial manhood; he will at last know his own soul.

---

been developed and called forth prove more conclusively than any theory that economic forces are far from being the only determinants in revolutionary action, that in the last analysis the questions before the working-class are really psychological and moral, and that the vital problem is to discover and develop those forms of organisation which create a revolutionary consciousness in the individual worker.

Even during the first stages of the formation of this consciousness the desire for power will express itself in revolutionary action. The will to conquer in the individual worker is the solvent and progenitor of revolutionary mass action and mass consciousness.

What the organised working-class thinks, what it wills, is of supreme importance, but what it wills depends on its con-

sciousness of power. And this realisation comes as the direct result of its collective activity.

If the organisations fail to enlarge themselves into vast industrial bodies so as to give opportunities for a superior and continuous working-class action in which the workers may conceive and intensify their power, if they fail to concentrate all the attention and all the passion of the workers on the complex economic and ethical problems of labour, then they are doomed to be forces of conservation and, ultimately, of reaction.

It is this new mentality, this concentration on the creation of new forces and capacities within and through the organisations, that gives to Syndicalism a universal importance.

Hitherto we have only been theorising

Now we know that all the problems of social revolution are problems of organisation, volition, force and creation, that life itself can be transformed and developed only by the force of a higher life.

The structure of the future society distinctly emerges upon the basis of those working men's institutions which exclude the exploitation of the members by individuals. We know now that upon such we are to build the society of the future.

We know now how to prepare ourselves materially, spiritually, and morally for the new social order. We know how the right men and means can be created for it. We know now that man is capable of establishing a just system of distributing wealth on the basis of a new method of production, seeking his salvation through the salvation of his own class and of the collectivity.

The Syndicalist

EDITED UNDER THE AUSPICES OF

The Industrial Syndicalist Education League

Offices—

12, RED LION COURT, FLEET STREET, E.C.

MONTHLY · ONE PENNY.

Subscription—

Great Britain or Abroad ... 12 months 1s. 6d.

The receipt of a Sample Copy of this Paper is an invitation to you to become a Subscriber.

MARCH-APRIL, 1912.

TO THE PUBLIC.

THIS number of the SYNDICALIST appears under circumstances which make an apology necessary. Our printers are in gaol for one month; our editor, Guy Bowman, is in gaol for six months; at the time of going to press, Tom Mann, the president of our publication society, is awaiting trial. Under such circumstances the editing and publishing of our paper recall the saying of Dr. Johnson about a woman preaching: "It is like a dog dancing on two legs; it is not well done, but one is surprised that it is done at all."

Yet, you will observe that the paper is published; you may take our word for it that its succeeding issues will be published. Behind this paper there drives the mightiest impulse, before it there looms the most glorious vision that has ever yet thrilled mankind. We had supposed that the British ruling classes had learned one lesson—but apparently they have not yet learned it, and once more we propose to teach it to them—that you cannot suppress ideas by putting men into gaol.

We were taught in childhood that the blood of the martyrs was the seed of the Church; our posterity will be taught that the same was true of the new religion of humanity and justice, which it is our mission to teach.

Two or three weeks ago the Editor of the SYNDICALIST was an unknown man; his paper was an obscure little sheet; a few hundred copies of which were struck off and distributed by hand. To-day the SYNDICALIST is the most-talked-of publication in Great Britain, the subject of daily debates in Parliament. Extracts from it have been printed in every daily newspaper we have seen, and its message has been discussed in hundreds of editorials. So once more our ruling classes have impressed upon them that "important lesson" that you cannot suppress ideas by putting men into gaol.

It is not a pleasant thing to leave one's wife and little ones to struggle with want and go to prison—especially in such prisons as British capitalists maintain for the terrifying of their victims. But when we face the fact that our going has been the means of stamping our message into the minds of tens of millions of men and women, we welcome our fate with a song of joy. There are plenty more of us ready to go on those terms.

You may not call yourself a "Syndicalist"; until a few weeks ago you probably did not know that such a kind of person existed. But, at least, you know what freedom of speech and discussion is; you know the ideal for which through six centuries the finest spirits of England have fought and suffered, have died on the scaffold and at the stake. In their name and with their voices we call upon you in this new crisis in our country's affairs.

We are not asking just now that you become a "Syndicalist." We content ourselves with asking that you protect us in the right to teach you what Syndicalism is. We ask that you assert your own right to learn what Syndicalism is. We demand the right to teach the British people what Syndicalism is. And note that we demand the right to teach it to the *whole* people. You will say, perhaps, that this is a precedent, an extension of the liberty of teaching; but we assert it, and we are ready to maintain it—if need be—by the time-honoured method of going to gaol for it. That which we know, all humanity will know before another generation is past; and on the walls of the prison-cell from which we send our message men will inscribe the words of one of the greatest of English poets:

Eternal spirit of the chainless mind!
Brightest in dungeons, Liberty, thou art . . .
And when thy sons to fetters are confin'd,
To fetters and the damp vault's dayless gloom,
Their country conquers with their martyrdom,
And Freedom's fame finds wings on every wind.

RELEASE THEM NOW!

As the SYNDICALIST goes to press the newspapers are announcing that the sentences passed on the two Buck brothers have been reduced from six months' hard labour each to one month without hard labour, and that the sentence of nine months' hard labour on Guy Bowman has been reduced to six months' without hard labour.

If we were properly meek and lowly we would doubtless bow the knee and give thanks to the clemency of the powers that be. Being simple lovers of justice, we raise our voice with others of our kind and demand the RELEASE of these men who are in prison. It is not enough to reduce outrageous sentences; they must be abrogated.

From all over the country Labour is calling upon the Government to release Bowman and the Bucks. Nor are threats lacking. Let us hope the Government will have the foresight to avoid the results that the execution of these threats would entail.

The treatment of Tom Mann has brought forth the following from an official of the London Carmen's Trade Union: "If Tom Mann is sent to prison, even if it be for one day, the transport workers of the country will lay down their tools." And if the Government refuse the release of Bowman and the Bucks the protests and resolutions from bodies of workers and advocates of free speech, throughout England, Scotland, and Wales may well be expected to take a more militant tone.

MR. STEPHEN WALSH, M.P.

No doubt Mr. Walsh thinks he is cutting a great figure now before the public with his platitudes about citizenship being higher than trade unionism, which is merely his way of intimating that the blackleg is the better citizen.

We quote the following from the "Daily Mail" of March 30:

Mr. Stephen Walsh, M.P., addressing a miners' meeting at Hindley, near Wigan, yesterday said:

"I dare say you have heard of Syndicalism. It represents a phase of thought which says: 'Oh, never mind the law, never mind the Government, come out in a body, break laws, take no notice, but bring down ruin upon everybody.' Well, if I have to forfeit every position I hold I will never agree to such a doctrine."

Mr. Walsh is not the first man who has gained the approbation of the "Daily Mail" by setting up a man of straw and then performing a war dance upon him.

The men who sent him to Parliament decided to "come out in a body," and now Mr. Walsh says this is equal to crying, "Never mind the law."

Perhaps Mr. Walsh is looking to a higher sphere in the political world where he will be enabled to help make the act of "coming out in a body" against the law?

What is it in the Minimum Bill, we ask, that Mr. Walsh finds so excellent? The miners went out to get higher wages, and they are now asked to return to work upon a promise that their wages will most probably not be reduced. Mr. Walsh throws his cap in the air and hails it as a triumph of the citizen over the trade unionist.

As to whether the miners should or should not go back, we would say that it in no way a question of the value of the Bill, but a question of whether they shall risk defeat by starvation through sticking out for the original schedule of wages they asked for.

The Bill in our estimation is nothing; it is the exchequer of the miners that is important.

The next time the miners "come out in a body," provided meanwhile Mr. Walsh has not made it illegal to come out, there will not only be a better exchequer, but there will be no giving of three months' warning enabling the owners to actually make money out of the stoppage rather than lose.

The next coal strike will come without warning, and with the miners will come out the railwaymen and the transport workers.

"EYE" vs. "I"

TYRANNY OF THE MINORITY.

Ever have something in your eye? Insistent thing an eye for such a small body, is it not? When it won't work you have to stop work yourself and humour it, don't you?

You don't call out the troops and shoot it when it goes on strike, do you?

You don't try to crush it by a majority vote of the rest of your members. On the contrary, you give it every consideration. You make every effort to find out its grievance and try to remedy it.

You don't tell it that you are never, never going to submit to it being in control of such a vital function as sight, and using that control to control you. You know that it is in such control and will remain there and that your best policy is to treat it reasonably and rely on being treated reasonably in turn. You cannot coerce your eye, and you know it will not coerce you as long as you treat it decently.

It wants neither too much attention nor too little, and it is its own judge of what it wants. You must give it what it calls for and rely upon its good sense to take what it wants for itself to give its services to the rest of the body when needed.

The coal mines give sight to the nation, give light by night, and the miners working them must be treated decently or else they will suffer and fail in energy, and if they suffer you suffer.

If they refuse to work you know you cannot force them to work any more than you can force your eye to see when it is much inflamed.

The eye was the first Syndicalist. When you think of the miners bear in mind the courage of the eye when it is ill-treated.

TRADE UNIONS AMALGAMATING INTO INDUSTRIAL UNIONS.

From the Syndicalist view point any tendency to create big industrial organisations is of great importance, inasmuch as it prospects great industrial fights in the future, fights that not merely make the possibility of gaining immediate advantages almost a certainty, but also call out the revolutionary spirit of the workers.

The following scheme of amalgamating the various trades in the clothing industry is welcomed by us especially, because the clothing trades belong to the most sweated ones of this country.

At a national Conference convened by the General Federation of Trade Unions the preliminary scheme for amalgamating the Trade Unions catering for the clothing trades into one huge national organisation was unanimously approved by delegates representing the Amalgamated Society of Tailors and Tailoresses, Amalgamated Union of Clothiers' Operatives, Jewish Tailors and Tailoresses (Leeds), the London and Provincial Clothiers' Cutters' Trade Union, London Society of Tailors and Tailoresses, East London Waistcoat Makers, Garment Workers' Trade Union, Military Uniform Tailors, Birmingham International Tailors (Machinists and Pressers), Scottish Operatives' Tailors and Tailoresses, Independent Pressers' and Machinists' Trade Union. The new amalgamation is to be known as the United Garment Workers' Trade Union. Its objects are to promote and consolidate the interests of all workers engaged in the trades and occupations connected with the clothing industry. It was decided that the minimum contribution for male workers should be 4d. per week, for women workers 2d., and for girls under eighteen years of age 1½d. per week. A sub-Committee was appointed to propose scales of benefits and draft model rules.

(We propose to publish regularly in the SYNDICALIST, under the above heading, all the news concerning the amalgamation and federating of trade unions, and will be grateful for copy from trade unionists.)

DON'T SHOOT, BOYS!

Inasmuch as the case of Tom Mann is *sub judice*, and as we have not too great a surplus of SYNDICALIST editors to risk letting any more go to gaol, we will refrain from any pointed comments upon the matter.

We may, however, say that the question of whether British troops shall or shall not fire upon their British brothers is not of such moment from the economic and political standpoint to Syndicalists as some would think.

The " violence " that Syndicalists advocate is a strike of men united in such a powerful and solid Industrial Union that there are no scabs for the troops to protect. No scabs, no violence! And it is the business of Syndicalists to see that there are no workers not in the Union.

True enough, the SYNDICALIST proposes that the workers shall take the control of industry to themselves, but we might suggest that a mine is of no value to the Capitalist when he can find no miners, so that he would be losing nothing.

We think that nothing will conduce to a peaceful transfer of Capital from the Capitalists to the Community as the realisation on the part of the Capitalists that the Syndicalists have it in their power to annihilate their profits by withdrawing the workers.

What can be more fatuous for the Capitalists of this country to think that their property rights hang upon the suppression of appeal to the soldiers not to shoot strikers?

In the days when the soldiers were uneducated either by books or by a growing class-consciousness there is no doubt but that keeping them as ignorant as possible was good Capitalist policy. But to-day in a democratic country the only real dependence for their allegiance to the community that can be placed on soldiers is the fact that they have full knowledge of why they are asked to shoot, and with this full knowledge they think it right and proper to shoot. Events will educate the soldiers far more than SYNDICALIST editors.

Certainly if there were any real validity to the appeal to soldiers which we published, then the re-publication of the essentials of this appeal in every paper in this country which gave an account of the Bowman trial should have made a mutineer of every British soldier.

If the Appeal is really so dangerous is it not obvious that the law should have prevented re-publication under any pretence?

On the other hand, if the Appeal, admittedly, had no import, then the Government put Bowman and the Bucks in gaol, not on account of the " Appeal," but on account of Syndicalism.

THE ASSAULT ON THE LIBERTY OF THE PRESS.

Of course, we know well enough that the Government feels it has made a fool of itself in the sending to gaol of our editor and printers. It did not take the outburst of the Recorder to the Grand Jury to inform one that it was Syndicalism for which Bowman was to be tried and not for inciting troops to mutiny.

It is not that the Government feels regret at committing such a contemptible act under the cloak of enforcing an obsolete law that no one knew existed, but that it realises that it has produced exactly the contrary effect to that intended.

The intent was to discredit Syndicalism and by locking up its leaders to prevent its truths becoming further known to the public.

But what idiocy? Syndicalism was not to become known to the public through the medium of an obscure sheet like this but through the actual event of the miners' great strike.

Syndicalism is ringing throughout England not on account of the efforts of conscious Syndicalists—for unfortunately they are only too few in number—but on account of the greatest strike in history being conducted upon Syndicalist theories, a fact which is being trumpeted by every Member of Parliament and editor who rises to denounce Syndicalism, at the same time explaining that he is not in sympathy with Syndicalism.

True, the miners' leaders themselves say they are not Syndicalists, and it is also true that there was once a man who was astonished to discover that he had been talking prose all his life.

But the editors of the daily Press are perfectly right in saying that the strike is a Syndicalist Strike, and the fact that the miners' leaders refuse the label merely means that the editors are naturally enough in possession of the more accurate vocabulary. It's their trade, words.

True enough, the miners had little or no thought when they came out on their concerted strike that they were going to hurt the consuming public far more than they would the mine owners.

They were shortsighted enough to consider the strike as being merely a personal quarrel with the owners about the question of a shilling or so a day extra wages.

And, in fact, the owners also looked upon it merely as a matter of their profits being somewhat concerned.

And why should masters and men not have taken such a shortsighted view of the matter? The coal industry to-day is carried on not that the community may have coal nor the miners wages, but that the owners may have profits.

There is a great outcry being made throughout the land that the miners propose to take the mines away from the owners and then hold up the community for an exorbitant price of coal. It seems to be quite forgotten that the owners to-day are doing exactly the same thing to the full extent of their ability. We ask what difference it makes to the community whether they are robbed by a handful of owners or one million miners?

However, while it is perfectly true that the Syndicalists do advise the miners to use all their efforts to obtain the control over the mines now exercised by the owners, yet it is far from our idea that this control shall be, when obtained, used as the owners frankly try to use it. To-day the mines are primarily worked for the benefit of the owners. The Syndicalist urges that the miners should control them and work them for the benefit of the community of which they themselves are so large a part.

There is nothing new or novel in this theory that the control of the mines should pass from the present owners to the workers for the benefit of the community. The only thing new about it is the startling fact that the coal strike has shown us that this transition is within measurable distance.

When the only people who talked about expropriation were the Socialists and when it was known that the day set for expropriation was when there was a majority of Socialists in the House of Commons, the Capitalist Class were as much alarmed about the imminence of danger as they were about the last day of judgment.

However, once the coal strike came into being and its inner meaning was explained by the Syndicalists, then there was a panic, and quite rightly too.

Expropriation has been reduced from abstract theory to a concrete fact, and it takes an exceedingly blind man not to see that the days of Capitalist ownership of industry are fast drawing to a close.

Balfour is reinstated as the Leader of the Tories in the House and makes a speech wherein he admits that he returns to find the country in the " political grip " of the Syndicalists. Of course, Balfour exaggerates, but, nevertheless, we have yet to hear of him ever having expressed the remotest thought that the country was ever to fall into the "political grip" of the Socialists. Yet Socialists have been working to that end for twenty-five years, whereas we Syndicalists have not been in evidence that many weeks.

No; we are not surprised that we should see our Editor in gaol, when we reflect that while gaol is no answer to our arguments, yet we admit that there is no other answer to be made unless it is the scaffold.

We are not anxious to pose as martyrs, and while we know that there is no better advertisement of our views than to have Tom Mann and Guy Bowman in gaol, nevertheless we feel that now we have had the advertisement we would like to have them out.

We notice that the Government has practically promised that some clemency is to be extended.

Clemency in certain instances may be depended upon, but, after all, the safety that Syndicalists must depend upon in the future lies in their ability to command justice, not clemency.

We venture to say that with the growth of Syndicalism in this country and with the prospect of a General Strike being called, when the next Syndicalist editor is thrown into gaol Sir Rufus Isaacs will not be so eager to vindicate the necessity of a British soldier to shoot down his British brother.

FROM THE AUTHOR OF "THE JUNGLE."

(To the Editor of the SYNDICALIST.)

I am in receipt of your letter asking me to discuss the case of Bowman and Mann. No, I am not in the least afraid the authorities will lock me up for it, and I am always willing to say what I think about a public wrong. I am, however, in a rather delicate position in this case, as I have come as a visitor to England, and I cannot be sure how far the British people will welcome a discussion of the proceedings of their Government from a stranger. I have known mothers to express themselves freely as to the shortcomings of their own children, but become excited when the same things are said by another.

However, it is, indeed, a serious thing that a man-should be sent to prison for advocating the ideas of Christ in a Christian country, And I personally have an especial reason for sympathy with men who have gone to gaol for the violating of a forgotten law, having myself been sent to prison for playing tennis on Sunday, which has been an offence in the pious State of Delaware since 1794. I do not know how bad your English gaols may be, but I hope that they are not as bad as the one to which I was consigned.

It is impossible for us lazy and comfortable fellows who are out of gaol to say anything to you fellows who are in it, without that thing sounding smug and presumptuous. But this one thing I will venture; it is the function of editors and publishers to impress ideas, and the Editor and the publisher of the SYNDICALIST, who are in gaol are impressing ideas more effectively than all the company of the editors and publishers of England who are out of gaol.

No, I do not call myself a Syndicalist, if you use the word in the sense of a man who rejects political action altogether. I do not see why the working-man should not both vote and strike. But I must confess that I greatly underrated the power of the industrial organisation for the forcing of revolutionary changes in society, and that the events of the last few weeks in England have taught me a lesson—along with all the rest of the world. It seems to me that we are witnessing in England to-day the beginning of the greatest social event that the world has ever seen, and I go my way singing hymns of joy for it.

It marks the beginning of a social deliverance, for which I have waited with sickness of heart. In my own country I have seen, in the soft-coal mining country of West Virginia, villages which were like mediæval fortresses, with high stockades about them and chains across the entrance road. In these places everything belongs to the companies, including the bodies and souls of the men. I met a poor woman who, because of the fear of competition with the company-store, was not allowed to keep a cow to furnish milk for her own children; a country doctor who had to get a pass before he could enter the village to attend a patient at night. In such places, needless to say, there was no room for agitators; there were no unions and no politics among those wretched representatives of a score of nations, whose labour furnished the wealth by which one of our millionaire senators bought his way into office. I could see no hope in life for these modern slaves; I can see it now, in this marvellous lesson of solidarity which the British miners have set before the working-class of the world.

UPTON SINCLAIR.

For fifty years the capitalists have accused the Socialists of wanting to " divide up." Now the Socialists, in their turn, accuse the Syndicalists of wishing each group of workers to seize their own industry in order to exploit public.

PROTESTS AGAINST THE PROSECUTIONS.

LORD RUSSELL PROTESTS.

I am invited to contribute to a number of the SYNDICALIST, and I feel that I am rather rash in accepting this invitation. I do not know what a Syndicalist is, and I am fairly sure that I am not one myself. I have never read a number of the paper, and indeed, I never heard of it until the Attorney-General thought fit to inform the whole world of its existence and its opinions by prosecuting the Editor and the printers. But I have an inherited passion for justice and free speech, and therefore I feel no reluctance in making one or two remarks.

First, as to the actual words for which sentences of hard labour were imposed, and which were published in full in the *Times* without any fear of prosecution. They do not strike me as very terrible, but my Tory friends and the majority of my Liberal friends say that that is due to my having an irresponsible and anarchical mind. The first statement, that soldiers are called upon to murder men who go on strike, is simply untrue, and I don't suppose any soldier or workman would believe it. It is, of course, sometimes true that soldiers are ordered to fire on a riotous mob who are destroying property with violence. Once matters have reached that stage civilised government may fairly be said to be at an end, and the occurrence of such an incident reflects no credit upon either the workmen or the Government. It is perfectly true that in the last resort the safety of life and property in a civilised community depends upon force at the moment, but it is quite as true, and more often lost sight of, that if it depends upon force only it is not a civilised community, but a martial tyranny. Force which has not got the moral sense of the community behind it has no real value as an instrument of law and order in a modern State. A policeman who arrests a pickpocket in the Strand and takes him to the police-station, generally without resistance, does not do so by virtue of the fact that he is bigger and stronger than the pickpocket, still less by virtue of the fact that he carries a bâton, but because he has the whole moral sense of the community behind him; and the pickpocket knows the moment an outlaw outside the pale of the community's protection. If guns were not so every arrest would be a street fight, and its result would depend upon the preponderance of physical strength on the side of the policemen or the criminals. A mob of riotous workmen intent upon doing physical injury to any workman who is not a unionist, or intent upon wrecking other people's property, are equally outside the pale of the community, and however much justice there may be in the demands of labour which they are seeking in a rough-and-ready way to enforce, they do as much harm to their cause as the Government that has to use bayonets against them does to the cause of law and order.

All the same, if I were one of the class likely to be shot by soldiers, it would not seem to me unnatural to appeal to them not to shoot me, and I think the prominence given to this appeal by the Government prosecution has done far more harm than ever the appeal itself could do, and has inevitably embittered and hardened class feeling. A wise Government does not assume that people take to extreme measures without extreme provocation, and seeks rather for the cause of the unrest than a mere suppression of its symptoms. The running sores of the body politic are not to be cured by being hidden under sticking-plaster, but by seeking the internal cause that produces them. A certain portion of our population have votes and the opportunity of using them at the ballot-box. I could wish that all adults had them. They have in this way a power to make their grievances felt even in Parliament, and to compel Governments to remedy them. They have also the terrible weapon of the general strike. If the capitalist class remain deaf to argument and obdurate to temperate appeals, these more forcible appeals can be used without any breach of law and order. But in the industrial fight that I see coming upon us it would be a fatal thing if it should come to be thought that the police and soldiers are tools of one class, to be used only against another, and are not looked upon, as they should be, as merely the instruments of the community as a whole for preserving the safety of life and property for every individual from the highest to the lowest. It is for this reason above all that I deprecate the recent prosecutions, whatever technical justification there may have been for them, particularly while Sir Edward Carson is allowed to remain at large.

All good Socialists ought to be grateful to the Syndicalists for providing the newspapers with something worse than Socialism

A NOTABLE PROTEST.

(To the Editor of THE TIMES.)

SIR,—We, the undersigned, have read with the gravest alarm the reports of the trial of the editor and printers of the SYNDICALIST newspaper, and the sentences passed upon them. The offence was that the newspaper contained as one of its articles an " Open Letter to British Soldiers," of which the most incriminating sentences ran as follows :

" When we go on strike to better our lot, which is the lot of your fathers, mothers, brothers, and sisters, you are called upon by your officers to murder us. Don't do it. . . . Boys, don't do it. ' Thou shalt not kill,' says the Book. Don't forget that. It does not say unless you have a uniform on. No ; murder is murder, whether committed in the heat of anger on one who has wronged a loved one or by pipeclayed Tommies with rifles."

For publishing and printing this letter in his newspaper the editor, Mr. Bowman, was sentenced to nine months' hard labour, and the printers, the brothers Buck, to six months' hard labour. The printers, by their counsel, " contended that they were merely the printers of the paper and had nothing to do with the article, the views of which they did not share." This was not denied, but they had the same measure meted out to them as the little printers and booksellers who supplied the public with Paine's works during the anti-Jacobin terror in England. The sentences the brothers Buck are now undergoing are cruelly severe, as well as impolitic.

These proceedings against the SYNDICALIST were taken under an Act of 1797, under which there has been no prosecution since 1804. The Act was passed in the year of the mutiny at the Nore, when the loyalty of the armed forces of the Crown was most seriously in question, in time of a dangerous European war. To-day we have peace abroad, and at the date of the trial the strike had been remarkably orderly at home. The troops were nowhere in collision with the strikers or the mob. Above all, the loyalty of Army and Navy was never less in question than it is to-day. What soldier cared about the SYNDICALIST and how many had heard of it before this ill-advised prosecution ?

Now, as the first result of these proceedings, there is perhaps not a soldier but has heard that it is a moot question under what circumstances he is justified in refusing to fire on a mob. And the civilian population has been set on to discuss the question with heat and mutual recrimination. In this way the prosecution has done, on a mild calculation, about ten thousand times as much to advertise the question as the SYNDICALIST could have done by itself. It has, moreover, compelled many who completely disagree with the SYNDICALIST to stand up at its side for the right of free speech.

If the Government adopts the course of prosecuting everyone who expresses publicly the view that the soldiers should not fire on a mob of their fellow-citizens they will be issuing a challenge to the leaders of working-class opinion to take up that attitude. The opinion that soldiers should refuse to shoot their fellow-citizens, whether true or not, is very prevalent and will not be put down by State prosecutions, but only fostered a hundredfold. If the expression of this opinion is persecuted, it will become more and more the shibboleth of the whole Labour movement. The view was held not only by the Quakers in old time, but in our own day was taught to all Europe by Tolstoy in works of his which have been broadly circulated in translation and highly honoured by all classes and parties in this island, however much they may disagree with him.

There is another serious aspect of the matter—namely, the very different treatment accorded to the rich and powerful men who incite the Protestants of Ulster to prepare for armed rebellion, and who by threats of violence have actually prevented a meeting from being held in a certain hall in Belfast. To Liberals and Conservatives in the House of Commons this is a subject of good-natured banter, but in the working-man who sees one of his own class thrown into prison for six months' hard for doing less, as he imagines, than some highly-placed politicians feelings of fierce indignation against injustice are aroused. This is not an era when we can afford to have one law for the rich and another for the poor in political cases.

The methods by which Pitt crushed the premature Radicalism of his day will not serve to crush the Labour movement now, but they may serve to render it revolutionary and to enlist it under the banners of the more extreme leaders. These methods of State prosecution will certainly embitter the social strife which it is the object of all of us, whatever view we take of the questions at issue, to keep within peaceful channels.

We are, &c.,
SAMUEL A. BARNETT.
H. A. L. FISHER.
JOHN MASEFIELD.
PHILIP MORRELL.
ARTHUR PONSONBY.
JOSEPH ROWNTREE.
BERTRAND RUSSELL.
G. M. TREVELYAN.
J. C. WEDGWOOD.
RALPH VAUGHAN WILLIAMS.
J. H. WHITEHOUSE.
ISRAEL ZANGWILL.
House of Commons, March 26.

CABLE FROM VANCOUVER.

Monster protest meeting against your imprisonment.—Riley, sec., 322, I.W.W.

MR. WEDGWOOD, M.P.

(To the Editor of THE DAILY NEWS.)

SIR,—This country seems to me to be threatened with a danger so serious as to call for a public remonstrance.

Three men have been imprisoned and two are awaiting trial for taking part in disseminating an opinion with which numbers of men of all politics and religions sympathise. One is under remand for handing to soldiers a leaflet urging them not to fire on their fellow-countrymen ; one is sentenced to nine months' hard labour and two small printers to six months' hard labour for printing the same appeal ; the fourth, for publicly declaring that he agrees with them, is awaiting trial.

These men are five, but who knows how many will be in prison before the " crusade " is over, and how many thousand more would be so, too, if they were not cowed into silence ? . . . .

These men are prosecuted technically for inciting soldiers to disobey orders (orders not yet given). Technically that is their offence. In reality their offence is that they have ventured to question one of the accepted ideas of comfortable society. It is foolish to pretend that their real crime is inciting to mutiny. Unless you forbid soldiers to read and talk you cannot keep them isolated away from such ideas. The trials alone of Crowsley, Bowman and the Bucks must have made the British Army think, more than any letter in a paper they probably never see, or a leaflet handed to them by a modest railway worker on a Sunday morning.

The mediæval States were wise in suppressing by similar means the circulation in the vulgar tongue of the New Testament. In it, too, men are bidden not to kill.

These leaflets, letter, speech, expressed ideas which are also approved by most non-resisters and by many ordinary citizens, who, recalling horrors of past English history, know that the intervention of the military in industrial disputes leads to the futile barbarities of Peterloo. But supposing this Open Letter had contained something glaringly wrong, is that a reason in England for checking the liberty of the Press and of public speech? Who knows what other doctrines may next be called in question! May we only think and speak freely so long as our beliefs tally with the opinion of the authorities? Are we to be bound in a political creed as particular and circumscribed as any 39 Articles of Religion?

The Crown lawyers imagine that they are suppressing agitation by these " Treason Trials." In reality, they are creating revolutionaries. For every man who is sentenced under this obsolete Act of 1797 ten men spring up fired with indignation and with fanatical hatred of Government methods.

Those who believe that freedom of speech and writing are vital to any country's health and far outweigh all danger that can come from the utterance of wrong opinion—as well as those who believe that in appealing to soldiers not to shoot working-men the prisoners were right—must regard this action of a Liberal Government with something of shame and dismay.

JOSIAH C. WEDGWOOD.
House of Commons, March 23.

M.P.'S AND MR. TOM MANN.

At a meeting of the newly formed Free Speech Defence Committee, held at the House of Commons on March 25, the following resolution was passed :

" That this meeting records its protest against the action of the Government in instituting criminal proceedings against Messrs. Tom Mann, Guy Bowman, and others for the free expression of their opinions with regard to the use of the military in Labour disputes, and demands the release of those convicted and accused and the repeal of the Act of 1797, under which they were charged."

The members present at the meeting were Messrs. Philip Morrell (in the chair), T. Richardson, H. A. Watt, Will Thorne, A. M. Scott, F. W. Jowett, J. Keir Hardie, J. Wedgwood, F. Neilson, J. Grady, and G. Lansbury. It is proposed to hold a public meeting at an early date. A fund for the defence of the prisoners and for other purposes in connection with the protest is being raised, Mr. Lansbury, M.P., acting as the treasurer. £330 have been raised to date.

TOM MANN DEFENCE FUND.

We want money to fight the Tom Mann case to a finish, and we expect the readers of this paper to contribute generously.

The attack on Tom Mann is a menace to Free Speech, and every lover of liberty should do his share.

Contributions may be sent to George Lansbury, M.P., Treasurer, House of Commons.

PROTEST BY FRENCH WORKERS.

The " Journal " states that the workmen at the Toulon arsenals and the National Dockers' League of France have published a general order protesting against the arrest of Tom Mann.—Central News.

British politics is a system of compromise. Therefore, if you want to get Socialist legislation advocate Syndicalism.

SYNDICALISM AT WORK.
BY TOM MANN.
(Written in Salford Gaol.)

The exceptional trade union activity, the increase in volume and variety of the various phases of " Labour Unrest," and the recent application of " Syndicalist " principles and methods in the industrial world, is simply so much evidence that the efforts of the working-class to obtain improved conditions are not flagging, but multiplying, and all who recognise the existence of the " Social Problem " have cause for satisfaction, that this stimulating force is apparently in the ascendency and destined to produce great results in the near future.

Syndicalism means the control of industry by " Syndicates," of Unions of Workers, in the interest of the entire community ; this necessarily pre-supposes the relatively perfect industrial organisation of all who work, and the right relationship to each other of every section. Robert Owen, over eighty years ago, advocated the necessity for such a method of organisation, and made a very good start at putting it into practice ; but, as it proved, the workers were not equal to resorting to such relatively highly-trained methods ; and the workers have had to spend twice forty years in the industrial wilderness because they were neither mentally nor physically qualified to enter the " promised land." Several other methods have been resorted to by the workers to escape from their industrial bondage since Owen's time, but none of them have proved really effective, Parliamentary action least of all.

In Robert Owen's vigorous days the workers of England had no political " rights," and it would appear that Owen set small store by the possession of any such " rights." He saw and taught that the workers' difficulties arose as a consequence of their industrial subjugation to the Capitalist class—in other words, that the Employing class had no concern for the working class, except to control and exploit their labour force for the specific purpose of using them as profit-making machines for themselves.

The Syndicalist of to-day has learned that all-important fact, and so refuses to play at attempts at social reform through and by means of Parliaments, these institutions being entirely under the control of the plutocracy, and never tolerating any modification of conditions in the interest of the working class, save with the ulterior motive of the more firmly entrenching themselves as the ruling class.

All this is admitted by most Socialists as regards the motive and object of the capitalist class, but the typical Socialist retains an abiding faith in the " wisdom and power " of Parliament, and seeks to achieve revolutionary changes by means of Parliament. And yet he also fully admits that all the really serious grievances of the workers are economic or industrial, and not political in character. Many of them can also see clearly enough that Parliament cannot manage or control an industry, or really rectify industrial wrongs, but still the glamour of this imposing bourgeoise institution commands their obeisance and subjection.

The Syndicalist, that is, the trade and labour unionist of the revolutionary type, recognises not only that all changes favourable to the workers must be brought about by the workers, but also that the only correct method of doing this is through and by the workers' own industrial organisations. Organised labour means the control of labour power by the labourers organised, and this means the control of wealth production to the extent to which Labour is organised.

It is only whilst Labour is partially organised that recourse to strikes is necessary ; not even the general strike will be necessary when Labour is universally organised. Universal organisation must carry with it industrial solidarity—i.e., universal agreement upon the object to be attained, or otherwise the capitalists will still triumph ; but with solidarity on the industrial field the workers become all-powerful.

There is nothing but a little reflection wanted to enable anyone to see that such is really the case. All students of social economics, who recognise the operation of the law of wages, know that, irrespective of what the worker produces, all that the worker on the average receives is the subsistence wage ; but we also know that, in order to get that subsistence wage, there are some who work but six hours a day, whilst others work twice and even three times as long. The most effective means of securing social betterment is by reducing the working hours. It is better to get the subsistence wage for relatively few than for many hours of work.

This Syndicalism will do, and by so doing will solve the problem of unemployment, and by the same means will kill excessive working hours ; and by the same methods will wipe out all low wages, and a further application of the same principle will secure to the workers the full reward of their labour. All will come in a perfectly natural manner as the direct outcome of *industrial solidarity*, guided intelligently and applied courageously.

The State Socialist, confronted with the unemployed problem, admits the necessity for trying to cure the evil, and proposes a " Right to Work " Bill. This proposal has been in the forefront of the State Socialists' programme for fully twenty years, and it has never yet reached the stage of serious discussion—that is, it has not yet been considered of sufficiently urgent importance to be classed by the average Parliamentarian as being within the region of practical politics. Nor is there any valid reason for supposing it is likely to be seriously dealt with by those who claim to attach importance to it.

The Syndicalist says, " Apply direct action and reduce working hours up to the point of absorbing all available workers in the ranks of the actively employed, and quite as rapidly as labour-saving devices are applied still further reduce working hours, so that there will never be any unemployed."

" But," says the Parliamentarian, " in order to reduce hours we must have an Act of Parliament." The Syndicalist says, " Such reductions of working hours can be far better brought about by industrial organisation. Nothing is wanted but the organisation of the workers and agreement to use the organisation for such a purpose."

The trade unionists themselves, having had their minds so fully occupied with the idea that Parliament is the all-important institution, and never having even hoped to see all workers organised industrially, have failed to realise what enormous power lies in industrial solidarity.

The nearest approach to any one industry exhibiting solidarity was that of the late great strike of the miners in March, 1912 ; but even here it was not complete, for many colliery enginemen and others did not give in their notices at the same time as the colliers, and no arrangement at all was made with other organised workers to secure their co-operation in an active and warlike manner.

The arm-chair discussions that took place for several weeks before the miners' notices expired ; the ready acceptance of the intervention of the Government, all showed how childishly simple were many of those responsible on the men's side. As a fact they did not view it as a national battle to be fought by the organised workers engaged in the " class struggle." Unfortunately, a large percentage of the " miners' leaders " had no conception that there was or that there is a " class struggle," and, indeed, they had done their utmost to prevent the national claim for a minimum wage coming along as forcefully as it did.

Some of the Capitalist papers charged these same leaders with being " Syndicalists " !! The fact being many of them had never pronounced the word in their lives, and not five per cent. of them knew what the term meant. But they made an excellent fight, and were truer Syndicalists in fact than in theory. Nevertheless, if the Syndicalist principle of brotherly solidarity in all industries had been understood and resorted to, the whole pressure of the transport workers, including railwaymen, would have been applied at the end of the first week, and no power on earth could have prevailed against them.

Once again, the object aimed at by the Syndicalists is the control of each industry by those engaged in it in the interests of the entire community. This will be followed by the ownership of the tools and other means of production and transportation jointly by the industrial community. Strikes are mere incidents in the march towards control of industry and ownership of the tools of production. " Sabotage," " Ca' Canny," and irritation strikes are mere incidentals in the progress onwards. The master key to the entire problem is INDUSTRIAL SOLIDARITY.

Naturally, much absurd criticism has been directed to " Syndicalism," and quite a host of Labour men have hastened to declare that not only are they " not 'Syndicalists,' but, indeed, they have pronounced opinions against it "—which, upon analysis, amounts to this : they are obsessed with the plutocratic institution of Parliament and are also fearful lest identification with the workers' real movement should bar them in sharing in the contents of the Egyptian fleshpots ; but they need not fear, timid souls ; they may still propitiate plutocratic opinion by disclaiming identification with the virile fighting force that is already lifting the working class out of the bogs and quagmires of mugwumpish Parliamentarianism.

The watchwords are INDUSTRIAL SOLIDARITY and DIRECT ACTION. By these means we can and will solve unemployment, cure poverty, and secure to the worker *the full reward of his labour*.

THE LIBERAL (?) BILL.

BY A SOUTH WALES MINER.

The great coal strike, which will be a landmark in the Industrial History of Great Britain, entered into its final stage on Wednesday morning with the passing of the third reading of the Bill. The battlefield has now been removed from Westminster to the coalfields; from the Government and the workmen's leaders to the workmen themselves.

The miners will have to say, through the medium of the ballot, not whether they will consent to work under the Bill—that has been decided for them both by the Government and the Miners' Conference—not that, but whether they will resume work, pending the construction of the machinery provided for in the Bill, and the final decision of the figures that are to become the legal minimum wage for at least fifteen months. Such being the situation, it will surely be very appropriate at this juncture to examine the Bill in relation to (1) the original demands of the miners; (2) the working conditions obtaining before the strike; and (3) to the bargaining powers of the combatants.

The first fact worthy of notice in this historic dispute is that all the negotiations have been conducted by the Government on the one hand and the workmen's leaders on the other. The part played by the coalowners has been very small and mainly confined to saying, No! No! No!

The Higgling of the Market.

The curious drama we are about to unfold has its *dramatis personæ*. On the one hand, the M.F.G.B. Executive, the chief spokesmen of whom are Mr. Enoch Edwards, "Bob" Smillie, George Barker, and Vernon Hartshorne, all of whom, until recently, were obscure persons trudging along in the local trade unions dealing with the almost infinite minutiæ of the trade union world of negotiation and conciliation; on the other hand, by the Prime Minister, Mr. Lloyd George, Sir Edward Grey, and Mr. Sydney Buxton, all of them "intellectuals" trained to governing class service in the miry channels of political intrigue, with all its bribery and sleight of hand. Behind the miners' leaders was the M.F.G.B. Conference with its influence over the rank and file. Behind the Government officials was Parliament with its anxiety to settle this strike, and all future strikes, even if it meant settling the miners at the same time.

The Government, like skilled antagonists, struck the first blow. They listened to both sides and very rapidly struck a "bargain." This is as easy as a sum to a politician and is a pure process of arithmetic. They laid down four proposals :

(i.) To the miners they granted the *principle of a reasonable* minimum wage.

(ii.) To the owners they gave safeguards that said reasonable wage should only be a minimum wage with qualifications.

(iii.) To both parties they offered to provide machinery to decide the equivalent in money of the reasonable minimum wage.

(iv.) In case of failure they agreed to cut the Gordian knot themselves.

In putting forward these proposals Mr. Asquith made a pathetic speech, full of compliments to the miners, urging them to realise the importance of the concession of the great *principle*. Not a word did he say about the other three proposals, as everyone who has read his *great* speech can see for themselves.

The Miners' Reply.

Let it be known, to the credit of the miners, they were not taken in by his *great* speech. They said, and Mr. Asquith agreed, that there could be *no negotiations* with the owners until the schedule rates—i.e., colliers, daymen, and boys—were accepted. Immediately these were accepted they were prepared to negotiate the intermediate rates with the coalowners. As to Nos. iii. and iv. of the Government proposals, they considered they were irrelevant points and were such as committed the miners to principles which the Labour Movement of England had rejected for nigh sixty years. Now, then, the bargaining commenced. The miners had put forward their three points as rates they had, as a whole, revised, and they were therefore irreducible. Then the Government replied. How?

Government's Reply.

The Government let matters hang as they were for nearly a week—no doubt in the belief that the workmen would concede the points contained in Nos. iii. and iv. by that time. The Government's reply of "do nothing" had this effect:—On March 11 the miners agreed to meet the coalowners on *all the points in dispute*

except the principle of the minimum wage. On March 13 they again expressed themselves as "willing to enter into negotiations at once with the mineowners in the various districts for the purpose of securing a settlement of all *points in dispute* at the earliest possible moment." On March 14 they went still further. Then they agreed to allow that "some neutral person might attend to help to guide the discussion to facilitate an agreement." It will be seen now that three out of the four points submitted to the Government are agreed to by the miners. How to get agreement on the fourth point? The Government continued negotiating with the miners and on March 15 issued an ultimatum to the miners that a Bill would be introduced on the lines of the Government's proposals. The miners' reply was that they would not commence work until they saw the final shape of the Bill. That was indeed a concession. It told the Government that they had "struck oil." The Government were by no means slow to take advantage. Indeed, they need have no qualms, as the miners actually left some persons in London to help Government to draft the Bill. The Bill was read and printed on March 19. When Conference saw the Bill their indignation knew no bounds, but before March 22 they had agreed that while two of their three irreducible demands—viz., 5s. and 2s.—were indispensable, the third—i.e., hewers' rates—was entrusted to a pious amendment by the Labour Party. The Government replied by asking for a guarantee for a resumption of work in case the "5 and 2" were conceded. On the failure of the guarantee they refused to insert the "5 and 2." The pretext was that the mineowners might themselves agree to this insertion, and an abortive conference was actually arranged for this by-play. Of course the owners refused to agree, and then—the Government passed the Bill, including the obnoxious No. iv. The miners, gaining a little spirit, asked the Labour Party to move the rejection of the Bill. This was done, but by 213 to 48 the Bill passed the third reading. The miners met and agreed to the following : (1) That a ballot vote be taken as to the opinion of the miners in the following terms:—(2) "Are you in favour of resuming work pending the fixing of the minimum wage rates by the joint boards?" Then the Bill was accepted after all !

The Next Step.

That was the result of twenty-seven days of bargaining. The Government carried their four points. But they neglected one thing—the rank and file. The obnoxious point—No. iv.—in the Bill is actually submitted to the decision of the workmen. If they say "No!" (the coalowners' word) in sufficient numbers they may yet accomplish what their leaders failed to achieve—viz., the defeat of the Government on No. iv. Before we elaborate this point let us briefly examine the Bill itself that the *Miners' Conference* has already agreed to accept.

The Bill.

The Bill provides (1) that in every contract the underground workman shall receive "wages at not less than the minimum rate settled under this Act"; (2) in order to determine what these rates shall be a joint board is set up which "in the opinion of the Board of Trade *fairly and adequately* represents the workmen . . . and employers in the district"; (3) "the chairman of which is an independent person" agreed to by both sides, or in default appointed "by the Board of Trade"; (4) there will be twenty-two of these joint boards formed, and if the joint board agrees, each district may be subdivided "ad infinitum"; (5) these boards will have power to do three things —(a) to settle minimum rates; (b) to form rules under which they shall be paid; (c) to revise these rates after fifteen months, on application by either side— (6) these boards may increase *or lower* wages now received, but any custom or rate of wages now prevailing shall not be considered as a hindrance to the *increase* of wages or the *betterment* of customs (that is a good point which we advise the miners to make the most of); (7) the boards shall have power to isolate groups of mines or any individual mine from the operation of the district minimum, and may increase or decrease that district minimum, as the circumstances dictate; (8) the Act shall continue in force for three years unless *Parliament shall determine otherwise*. So much for the minimum rates. But now for the rules: (1) they exclude aged and infirm workmen, also workmen partially disabled by illness or accident (here is a concession, if you can please!). (2) The rules shall have regard to the "regularity and efficiency of the work to be performed." What! Yes; these are the actual words in an Act dated

1912. What has the regularity of work to do with a minimum wage? The workmen's side are quite ignorant of any reference to this point until it appears in the Bill. Is there not a mediæval flavour about this—a sort of schoolmaster spanking the unruly schoolboy-touch? In any case, what does it want in a Minimum Wage Bill? As to the question of efficiency, it must be remembered that for nearly twelve months the miners debated as to whether they would strike on an "abnormal places question" or on a minimum wage question. The supporters of a minimum wage easily carried the day because it could not be demonstrated in any given case whether it was the man or place that was abnormal. Well, in this Bill, nicknamed a Minimum Wage Bill, that very difficulty is replaced with the authority of law behind it, and so call it what one may, it is not a Minimum Wage Bill. (3) The Bill can be prolonged by Parliament as they think fit. That means not merely compulsory arbitration in this case, but also in any other trouble that may arise, as far as the miners are concerned.

What We Advise.

It must surely now be clear to the most dense that the miners' leaders have shown themselves quite incompetent to bargain with the Government. They have obtained the whole of their four points. We have not obtained one. That is, the miners' leaders have not obtained one of their points. But whatever may be said of the impossibility of the ultimate aim of Syndicalism, we have never been guilty of crying over spilt milk. We are not referring to the present partial defeat to dishearten the miners. On the contrary, we wish to point out to them a way by which they can minimise the errors and incompetencies of their leaders. The position now is that the figureless Bill is accepted with all its obnoxious machinery. There are three courses open to the miners—viz : (1) They can tamely surrender to every proposal of the Government and vote for a resumption of work. (2) They can defeat the Government on their proposals by remaining idle until the figures are actually fixed and the obnoxious rules made known. (3) They can in the last resort if figures and rules are unsatisfactory appeal to the railwaymen and transport workers to come out with them with the object of compelling the Government to withdraw the Bill and compelling the owners to accede to their demands. The first course is not to be thought of. The third can wait a while in reserve, where it will be a strong influence. But the second we heartily advise the miners to adopt. The miners' leaders were defeated by the Government in bargaining. Do the workmen desire to condemn them? Then they must vote for No 2, or be guilty of even worse errors. *Is it sensible; is it reasonable to expect so good a bargain when in the mine and the board sitting, as when on strike at the very time the shortage of coal is beginning to be felt?* You have now been on strike nearly a month and the governing classes are only now beginning to feel the pinch. *Every day ADDS to your power and weakens the other side.* If you are out for another fortnight or three weeks, or more, it may mean an immediate loss and perhaps suffering to you, but what is that in comparison to *years and years of higher wages.* What your leaders failed to see was that they were *bargaining* with a wily set of men; they took words on their face value. A fisherwoman or onionseller would know a good deal better than that. *Don't make the same mistake.* By stopping out until the figures and rules are known you are not disobeying the law and you are obtaining the demands your leaders failed to achieve. Workmen, stand fast and you will win easily.

Lessons of the Strike.

This strike has taught us that any conflict of this magnitude must not reckon only on direct employers as the enemy, but also the forces of the Government. It has shown that even the M.F.G.B. is only a sectional union. True, its power has been modified by the policy of the fossils who adhere to the ridiculous custom of giving long notices to the detriment of the community and the ruin of the workmen. Yet, in spite of all the defects, a victory is yet possible for the miners if they will only believe in themselves enough. You are weak as you are stronger than all your enemies. Hold fast and win, not only for yourselves but for the working-class.

Bernard Shaw almost made us hope that we might have an article from his pen in this issue, but at the last moment he writes "Impossible; I haven't time; the post goes early to-day. Besides, why waste two bullets on one discharge? Russell will carry you through."

WHAT THE MINIMUM WAGE BILL MEANS.

There is only one point of view from which the Syndicalists can scrutinise the Coal Mines Minimum Wages Bill. It is the point of view of organisation. The only question they can ask is : Does the Bill clear the ground for revolutionary industrial mass action; does this Bill make for solidarity between the workers without putting new shackles upon them?

What are the tendencies of modern capitalism in the basic industries? Concentration of capital, centralisation of management, scientific organisation on a national and international scale for the exploitation of the workers.

What are the means by which the workers strive to oppose these tendencies of modern capitalism? By industrial unionism, the combining and amalgamating of the different trade unions within the same industry into big organisations capable of acting simultaneously over all the territory in which the industry operates.

Now, the Minimum Wage Bill not only does not curtail the efforts of the capitalists to bring about a more perfect co-operation, but will practically paralyse the tendency of the labour organisations to establish themselves as industrial organisations capable of successfully meeting the organised capitalists.

The Bill is nothing else than an exceptionally cunning device to put the miners' organisations back to where they were before the Miners' Federation attained a practical monopoly of the labour force of miners. It is an attempt to break up organisation and to make it almost impossible for it to reorganise itself.

Let us analyse the Bill. We see that it provides only for the workers employed "underground" in coal mines. Anybody with a practical knowledge of the problems of organisation will know that through the exclusion of the various categories of the surface workers in the mining industry from the operations of the Bill, which the workers must consider henceforth in all their disputes with the mining corporations, a thorough amalgamation of these different categories into one fighting body is practically made impossible. For while the underground workmen must go with their demands before the Joint District Boards, provided for in this Bill, the surface workers' demands, if represented by the Miners' Federation, must be thrashed out between the employers and the employees directly. This evidently would gravely complicate both the regular routine of the Federation and its greater strike movements.

One of the factors that has attributed to the present defeat is the position of surface workers in relation to the Federation. They came out with the miners, to be sure, but some categories amongst them kept in operation certain machines, the stoppage of which would have brought the mineowners to terms in a very short time. On the other hand, the federation, not demanding the revision of the schedule for the surface-workers and not demanding a minimum wage for them either from the employers or from Parliament has naturally raised their just discontent. The miners have realised their mistake, and they will now try to take the surface-workers into the Federation. But the Minimum Wage Bill will render this amalgamation immensely difficult, if not impossible.

The Bill, by establishing twenty-one Joint District Boards and by giving them the power of appointing as many sub-Joint District Boards as they wish, will certainly tend to break up the yet incomplete, but already powerful, unity of the Federation and to defeat the intention of the miners to bring about a complete and organic unity of all the workers in the mining industry. Hitherto the districts operated too independently; there was little regular communication between them. The first and most important work before the miners after this strike was to reorganise the Federation's machinery so as to work out a less complicated and therefore more rapid means for collective action.

Of course, sooner or later this must be realised; but the Joint District Boards, with the feature of permanency in them, localise the movement, isolate the districts, and by dividing the workers cater to local interests, local egotisms, and limit the spirit of industrial solidarity.

The Joint District Boards will be a permanent machine for arranging compromises and fostering the spirit of compromise on all issues.

We do not go into the details of how the Joint District Boards will be appointed to represent "fairly and adequately" the workers and the employers and how they are to fix the schedules and the district rules and how they are to decide in the future the disputes that will come before them. We will discuss this side of the new situation created by the Bill in a later issue.

But just let us ask ourselves what the

Bill means when it says that the district rules shall "lay down conditions with respect to the regularity and efficiency of the work to be performed by the workmen and provide that a workman shall forfeit the right to wages at the minimum rate if he does not comply with those conditions, except in cases where the failure to comply with the conditions is due to some cause over which he has no control." This sounds well, but, inasmuch as the workers have no direct control over the decisions of the Joint District Board as to the conditions in question, and inasmuch as it is practically impossible to bring every case in which the workers think they have lost control over the conditions of their labour before these Boards and to have them settled quickly, their efficiency will be continually questioned by the employers and their right to the minimum wage continually threatened.

Several big labour organisations have already expressed their intention to insist on a Minimum Wage Bill for their industries. Let them beware ! They should study this Bill brought for the enslavement of the miners and convince themselves that a great danger to their growth and social action lies in such a law.

Let the workers realise, once for all, that the forces which lead them towards their entire liberation from the yoke of Capitalism are not to be worked out by a society entirely opposed to their liberation. That must be created within their own labour organisation.

The Bill has not changed the situation for the better as far as the workers are concerned. It enforces Capitalism, and there is no way of dodging this unpalatable fact.

The only force that can change the position in favour of the workers is their compact force of resistance, as created by their industrial organisation. This Bill, and all other Bills on similar lines, render the industrial organisation of the workers very difficult, and therefore impair their industrial action of resistance.

In the last analysis, Capitalism as represented by Parliament has set up in this Bill a machine by which the formation of the revolutionary spirit of solidarity may be checked.

Let the workers beware !

"SYNDIC."

"THE SYNDICALIST" CASH-BOX.

This paper has hitherto been run at a loss; and while we hope that the free advertising given us by the Attorney-General and the two Houses of Parliament will turn our deficit into a profit, we have no guarantee of it. If you wish to help us carry on our propaganda then send what you can to the SYNDICALIST Cash-Box, care of our publishing office address. All contributions will be acknowledged in our next number.

If you can't send cash, then send us a pat on the back with a postal card.—Yours,

THE SUB-EDITOR,
who is "still out of gaol."

THE SYNDICALIST,
12, Red Lion Court, Fleet Street, E.C.

ANSWER TO THE "DAILY MAIL"

BECAUSE "WE" ARE NOT SYNDICALISTS.

If anything more is wanted as conclusive proof that the Government has put our Editor in gaol under an absurd pretence, the following from the "Daily Mail" of April 2 is quite sufficient :

The "Open Letter to British Soldiers," for the publication of which Guy Bowman, journalist; Benjamin Edward Buck, printer; and Charles Ernest Buck, printer, are now undergoing punishment, was published in the SYNDICALIST of January 15, 1912. In connection with the same publication Mr. Tom Mann now stands committed for trial.

The question at issue in both these prosecutions is the question of publication. No evidence has been forthcoming as to the identity of the writer.

We find that the same "Open Letter" was published in the *Irish Worker* (a paper printed in Dublin, and bearing on the title-page the words, "Edited by Jim Larkin") on Saturday, July 29, 1911, about six months before it appeared in the SYNDICALIST, and it was reprinted in the *Irish Worker* of Saturday, March 2, 1912. In both cases the article is signed "Right Bower," but no information is given as to the name of the writer.

In the *Irish Worker* for March 2 the questions are asked, "Why is Fred Crowsley arrested for repeating what was said by us eight months ago? Why are we not charged?"

We return the same suggestion to the "Irish Worker" and to Victor Grayson. If they really wish to get into a British gaol then let them announce themselves as Syndicalists and republish the ten commandments, especially including the sixth.

Both Bowman and Mann were arrested long after the "Irish Worker's" challenge of March 2.

Printed and Published by the INDUSTRIAL SYNDICALIST EDUCATION LEAGUE, 12, Red Lion Court, Fleet Street, E.C.

The Syndicalist

VOL. 1. NO. 4.   LONDON, MAY, 1912.   MONTHLY, ONE PENNY.

SYNDICALISM: THE REFORMATION OF SOCIALISM.

By FREDERICK VAN EEDEN.
Author of "The Quest."

SYNDICALISM is for Socialism what the Reformation was for the Christian Religion.

It took fourteen centuries of blundering and aberration to convince a few honest people that existing Christianity was not what Christ had really meant, and that the Roman Catholic Church was not the sort of establishment He had in mind as a result worth being crucified for.

Things move now at a more rapid rate. Socialism has been a great movement for somewhat over a century. We have seen it split up in Communism, Collectivism, Anarchism, and Social Democracy, or Political Socialism.

None of these have brought us what we hoped for.

Social Democracy, or Political Socialism, though winning millions of voters, has lost the old glory of revolutionary Socialism of fifty years ago. It has become merely an opposition party. It has lost its genuine Socialistic tendencies; it is for patching up the old order. And it was bound to come to that end, because of the erroneous conceptions and ideas on which it started.

It confused the political state — the organised system of exploitation based on violence—with the true commonwealth, which has no borders of nationality. It expected from legislation what only the action of life could bring about. It was founded on the materialistic philosophy of the last century, which was to make place for a deeper insight.

And now, at last, we have Syndicalism! Hurran! What is in a name? And we so wanted a new word, to indicate another course.

I never used the word before, but I have been preaching Syndicalism for over twenty years in Holland, in the face of Social Democrats and Anarchists who called me many names and said that I was misleading the labourer.

I told the labourers that if they objected to work for the benefit of a master, and to be exploited by idle people, they had only to follow this simple rule: *Workers, do not work for the parasite, work for workers only.*

This sounded very simple and convincing. Yet as a matter of practice it is not so easy nor so simple. The whole of Syndicalism is in it when you come to bring the rule into execution.

Because, when I want to work for those poor Russians, or Indians, or Chinamen, who raise the wheat or the rice that I find on my table, or who work to provide me with shoes and clothes and whatever I want, I find them out of my reach, hopelessly remote, and I see no chance to do anything for them in return, to satisfy my feeling of social duty. They are not living in my land, nor can I have any influence on their fate by legislation, nor by any social effort in my own country. I do not know them, I have no social relation to them, and I find between them and me a host of merchants and dealers and business men, of whose activity I have no notion, and about whose ways and means I may have very serious misgivings.

In the true commonwealth of the future—the state of things that true Socialism is aiming at—all workers who provide me with the necessities of life will have to belong to one organised concern, and will stand in commercial relation with one another, on the basis of fair dealing and honest exchange. This can only be possible in a gigantic trust, or syndicate, or company, that is not confined to any national area. And here we see the essential feature of Syndicalism in opposition to Social Democracy.

The State, in its present form, is necessarily and essentially national. It was created to defend and bring prosperity to a definite area of land and people, and with a tendency to enrich itself at the cost of all other national groups. This means simply Capitalism—the gospel of exploitation—transferred to groups or States instead of individuals. The State is Capitalistic in its deepest essence. It was started for the sake of exploitation, and the best governed State must always remain Capitalistic, because its attitude to other States is either hostile or indifferent.

Therefore, when Socialists look to the State as the true commonwealth and want

the State to take possession of the sources of wealth and to abolish the abuses of monopoly or exploitation, they will necessarily drift into Nationalism—as we see it happen in Germany and France—and thereby lose their true Socialistic character.

This was felt by the leaders of Anarchism—when the great schism between Bakonism and Marx took place. But Anarchism, as understood by the Russian mind, neglected the immense importance of organisation, and supposed the workers to be capable without leadership, without discipline, to achieve the tremendous task of creating a well-organised commonwealth. This was indeed Utopian in its worst sense. It jumped long periods of slow and difficult education. It did not teach the workers the terrible strength of their opponents, the exploiters. It did not realise how the intricate structure of modern society demanded great organising capacities, scientific knowledge, economical insight, first-rate leadership, and strict discipline, in order to replace the old order by a new and a better one. So Anarchism was soon paralysed and left behind in the struggle. It could strike, but not conquer. It proved to be destructive, not constructive. It withered for want of successful deeds, and Social Democracy, having all the advantage of bringing action, deeds, success, won the day.

Yet the victory of Social Democracy was only apparent. The best way to kill it—and this is a gratis advice to the German Kaiser—would be to bring it into power. Make a Social Democrat Prime Minister, and he will have to support the Capitalistic régime just like his predecessors, and the great party will melt like snow or split up into harmless groups.

They will consolidate Capitalism by making it tolerable. They will create, under fine labour laws, grateful workers with contented and servile minds, far more easy to exploit. The fetters of the slaves will be cushioned and the old order will remain unchanged.

We do not want, however, a sort of mitigated and patched-up Capitalism. We want a new and better commonwealth. We want a deep and thorough regeneration. The sores and evils must be radically removed, not plastered up under humanitarian foments and unguents. It is not sufficient for a dirty person to perfume his clothes; he ought to be stripped and cleansed.

With the deepest sympathy, therefore, I see the revival of the old revolutionary spirit under the newly-coined word of Syndicalism; revolutionary in the sense of rooting up the old evil thoroughly—not revolutionary with the idea of cutting of heads and burning down palaces and museums.

Peace is all right, but not at the cost of great ideals. And peace on the basis of nationalism will always mean war, and a long series of wars.

The fight we want is an economic fight, a fight between honest labour and exploitation, between fair means and deceit. And that fight ought to be fought relentlessly, without compromise, to the bitter end.

And it is, in my view, the new and hopeful feature of Syndicalism that it begins to see what is wanted to wage this great war. For, if anything, Syndicalism ought to be constructive; it ought not, or not only, to destroy, but to create.

I will try to indicate in my next article what arms it has and what strategical plans of attack it may follow.

WORKERS OF THE WORLD, UNITE!

MAY DAY, 1912.

SYNDICALISTS celebrate May Day as the symbol that Labour looks forward to a profound, yet rapid, metamorphosis of social life from that of the present Capitalistic Society to a future Industrial Democracy.

Being evolutionists, albeit revolutionists, and looking upon Society as a living organism, we would be the last to urge that force can bring about an organic change in social life. And by the same token we deny that force can prevent that change when the time is ripe for it.

The change will come only when the workers evince sufficient Solidarity to make the change possible. A Parliamentary majority is no sign that this Solidarity has been effected, nor, on the other hand, is the lack of a Parliamentary majority any sign that it has not been effected.

Parliament is merely the organ of the existing Capitalist Class, and with the inevitable decay and passing away of that class as a class Parliament itself must also wither and decay with it. Nay, not only that, but as Capitalism approaches its end and gives forth the unmistakable signs of its early dissolution, so, too, will Parliament show signs of a lost vitality and no longer be properly responsive to the needs of existing society.

This, in fact, is already the condition of Parliament. It is an organism which, having fulfilled its mission in life, is now naturally withering and passing away before our eyes. Outwardly, it makes a show of its pristine strength ; inwardly, it is already fetid with decay.

Quite outside it, and far beyond its grasp and power, is silently and swiftly forming the Industrial Organisation of the Workers which is destined to supersede Parliament by a process that will be normally accomplished by the two natural processes of elimination and absorption.

It is the mission of SYNDICALISM to interpret to the workers the full meaning of their organic tendency to Industrial Solidarity, to sound the tocsin when the process has proceeded to the point where Direct Action on both a National and International scale must inevitably be crowned with success.

Never before in the history of Capitalism has the movement of Labour throughout the world toward Solidarity been so pronounced as it is on this May Day, 1912. Never before were the hopes of Labour so high, and never before were there so many happy auguries of the near approach of the Emancipation of Man.

Hail, Comrades ; the dawn of a New Day is at hand ! Let us but have confidence in each other and the fruits of Victory are ours for all mankind to share.

Let no petty feelings of jealousy and distrust separate us. Let Solidarity be our watchword and the day is ours !

We require neither strike funds nor a complicated labour union organisation to win our battle. Let us stand together, one to the other, firm and true as steel, and the world is ours. Solidarity is our Capital.

Although ill-considered and badly organised the strike of the miners showed us what a tremendous force lies latent in Human Solidarity. It astonished the whole world, and probably the miners themselves were the most astonished part of it. It took that strike to make the workers have some small conception of the God-like power that lies in Solidarity.

Let us, then, organise with the full knowledge of our potential strength when we are all united into one great Industrial Union. Organising with this conception and with the Emancipation of Man as our aim, the enthusiasm we will mutually inspire in each other will be all-compelling and make obstacles that now seem insurmountable disappear as by magic.

The Solidarity of Labour will in itself dissolve all opposition.

Workers, Arouse, Unite, the World is ours to Command.

Let the all-compelling words, Solidarity of Labour, resound from Nation to Nation till all the World responds !

Working-men of the World, Unite; you have a World to gain, you have but your chains to lose !

GREAT SYNDICALIST VICTORY IN LAWRENCE, MASS.

The great strike lasting for over two months and affecting over 2,000 workers in the mills of the American Woollen Co. in Lawrence, Massachusetts, culminated in a great victory for the workers.

It is a triumph for the principle of Syndicalism Unionism as against the old-style craft Trade Unionism.

If the strikers had attempted to carry on the strike with disunited craft trade unions they would have been doomed to a quick and certain defeat, but united into one great Industrial Union they have won the greatest victory ever accomplished by Labour in the United States.

A victory won by the way in spite of the jealous opposition of the old style craft union leaders.

The winning of the Lawrence strike has been followed up by a general rise of wages throughout other mills in the United States.

ENGINEERS' QUESTION FOR THE ATTORNEY-GENERAL.

The York branch of the Associated Society of Locomotive Engineers, Firemen, and Cleaners recently passed a resolution which will be sent to the Attorney-General asking him whether he has taken proceedings against Lord Londonderry and Sir Edward Carson for the same offence as that for which Mr. Tom Mann is awaiting trial. A considerable sum of money was collected for the Mann Defence Fund.

Syndicalists not proposing a Utopia from above are therefore happily relieved from feeling called upon to solve either the marriage problem or how we shall apportion the products of labour.

LONG LIVE SYNDICALISM !

By EDWARD CARPENTER.
(Author of "The Drama of Love and Death.")

SUCCESS to the Syndicalist movement, and hearty congratulations on what has already been done ! We are at last beginning to see a way out of the old jungle of commercialism— a light in the distance through the trees. Socialism has certainly taken us a long way in the right direction. It has taught us that the industrial life of the nation must in the future be carried on collectively for the benefit of the mass-peoples, and not for the greedy profits of the few. But we are now beginning to see that its path is in danger of winding through some ugly swamps of bureaucracy, officialism, and over-government (even the Capitalist classes themselves are crying out against Socialism on that score !) and that it may be difficult to get safely through along that line. So the Syndicalists are branching into a new route. They are adopting the entirely sensible scheme of getting the workers in each industry to organise that industry and its conditions of production for themselves.

The splendid thing about the present movement is the rapidity with which the workers themselves are grasping the new idea. The strike of the miners and the way in which the rank and file of them are laying down and deciding on their own conditions of labour is full of promise. And similar movements in the other trades, combined with the success and spread of the " Don't shoot " propaganda among the military, are opening up the way to a new era in our industrial life.

Of course, our opponents say that each trade is going to organise its industry for its own advantage, and " hold up " its own produce at a monopoly price against the rest of the nation, we shall only have exchanged exploitation on its present scale for exploitation on a much larger scale, and abandoned the petty competition of Capitalists for warfare of a much more serious character among the unions. But such people are only speaking from their own experience and ideals of life. No one who knows the masses of the workers or the present tendencies of the unions could make such a foolish mistake as to suppose that this is really the direction in which they are moving or wishing to move. On the contrary, the immense and growing Federations of the trades and the continual conferences and congresses of sections point most distinctly towards the ultimate harmonising of the various interests in one great scheme.

As I have said, the well-to-do classes have been in terror hitherto at the prospect of possible government by a " cast-iron " bureaucratic Socialism. It only remains for them now to cordially welcome the arrival of an anti-governmental Syndicalism and of a free and voluntary co-operation of workers (all workers, of course, whether manual, clerical, artistic, or what not) in countless guilds, which shall be self-determining as to their own conditions, but federated together in a great whole for the reasonable exchange of their products. For many years now folk have pointed out what a splendid work the old English Craft Guilds did, how they organised the workers of that period and gave them substantial position and comparative affluence in face of the tyranny of the great landholders and barons; how they laid the foundations of England's industrial greatness; what fine and artistic things they produced—what metal-work, wood-work, architecture, and so forth—out of their free and self-determining organisations, and such folk turn with pride to this page in our history. But to-day Syndicalism is going to restore just these very guilds in a form suited to modern conditions, and every one who values what may be called real culture and the restoration of beauty and joy in daily life must surely welcome the movement and lend, as far as he can, a helping hand.

It is true that the movement will ultimately bring to an end the mean and futile social life of the dividend-drawing classes. And a good thing, too ! The more one sees of that life the more one sees of its futility and essential wretchedness, and the less one sees that is worth preserving. Even for the sake of these classes themselves one may sincerely say, Long live Syndicalism !

The Syndicalist

EDITED UNDER THE AUSPICES OF

The Industrial Syndicalist Education League

Offices—

12, RED LION COURT, FLEET STREET,
LONDON, E.C.

MONTHLY . ONE PENNY.

Post Paid Subscription—

Great Britain or Abroad ... 12 mon.hs 1s. 6d.

Bundle Rates—

1s. 4d. per quire, Carriage Prepaid

The receipt of a Sample Copy is an invitation to Subscribe.

Where to Buy "The Syndicalist."

The following are the names and addresses of our wholesale and retail newsagents from whom the SYNDICALIST may be had :—

London.—The National Labour Press, 23, Bride Street, E.C.

,,   London and Suburban Publishing Co., 9, St. Bride's Avenue, E.C.

,,   E. Lilyan, 103, Bolsover Street, W.

,,   J. Jaques, 191, Old Street, E.C.

,,   W. Tarbart, 316, Kentish Town Road, N.W.

,,   E. Denton, 427, High Road, Willesden, N.W.

Birmingham.—The National Labour Press, 100, John Bright Street.

Manchester.—Sam Brierley, 328, Hyde Road, Ardwick.

,,   Abel Heywood, 56 and 58, Oldham Street.

Glasgow.—David G. Lindsay, 139, West Nile Street, and 132, Gairbraid Street, Maryhill.

Bristol.—John Flynn, 19, Horsefair.

Sheffield.—A. M. Barton, 46, Stannington Road.

P.S.—If any of our friends can get their local newsagents to agree to handle the SYNDICALIST at 1s. 4d. per quire delivered we would be glad to get their names. Back numbers, except the last number, are out of stock.

MAY, 1912.

THE TITANIC DISASTER.

One of the striking things about the Titanic disaster was the evidence of the stupidity of the Capitalist Class, as exhibited in every capacity.

What shall it profit a man to live if he fail to take a chance of making an extra dividend, when to do it merely means risking the life of others, or, indeed, even his own life, seems to be the motto of the Twentieth Century Capitalist.

Everyone who is the least conversant with ocean travelling knows, and has known for years, that not one of the big trans-Atlantic steamers carries lifeboats sufficient for half the people aboard.

It needed no Rider Haggard a quarter of a century ago to teach us this.

It was obvious to every observing man who has sailed on a liner. It is impossible that Colonel J. J. Astor, a man who had crossed more times than he had years, a man who, himself, owned a steam yacht almost as large as a liner, did not know perfectly well that the Titanic was short of lifeboats.

Mr. Bruce Ismay, the President of the Company, of course, knew it only too well as he stepped into the last boat and left 1,600 of his fellow-passengers behind to their fate.

It is impossible to think that Mr. Guggenheim and Mr. C. M. Hays, and all the other millionaires did not also know the risk they were taking. But it may be said that they thought the Titanic was unsinkable. If this be so, then why did the law require her to carry any lifeboats at all? Why did the Titanic augment the legal requirement?

Why was Colonel Astor quite willing to pay £870 for a special cabin for himself and yet not insist that he should have a certain percentage of his fare applied to securing him a seat in a lifeboat as well as at the dinner table.

He would not think of going to a theatre without a seat engaged, where the lack of it would simply mean discomfort, yet he takes a ticket year after year on an Atlantic liner where the lack of a place in a lifeboat means the loss of his life.

And yet the workers are called upon to look upon the Astors and Guggenheim class as being of such a superior intellectual mould that commerce and industry would be unable to continue were it not at the helm to guide.

As for the loss of the crew and the third-class, that was only to be expected. No one looks to the Capitalist Class to provide safety accommodations for suchlike trash. But it has hitherto been the theory that it did have sense enough to look after itself, even if at the expense of profits.

With Colonel Astor perished another illusion.

WAR ON SYNDICALISM IN SAN DIEGO.

San Diego is a peculiar place to see a volcanic manifestation of the revolutionary spirit which is now hovering over all the world, but nevertheless there it is.

The town is in the extreme southern part of California, not far from the Mexican border; the inhabitants, however, about 30,000, are purely American. There is little of either commerce or industry, the climate is the chief and only asset. Naturally, with climatic conditions attracting the unemployed and commercial conditions not affording any chance of their employment, the unemployment problem is chronic and difficult of solution. The inhabitants, realising that unemployment is considerably a result of outside importation rather than home growth, are strongly inclined to try and make artificial conditions so offset the natural that there will be little temptation for anyone to remain in San Diego who has no visible means of support.

These energetic methods have been developing for the last year or so with rapidity, and in opposition the unemployed and revolutionists have been holding large meetings to denounce the ferocity of the police and the inhumanity of the city administration.

In turn the city council has passed fiercer and fiercer laws to prohibit free speech and the right of public meeting and the methods of enforcement by the police have been inconceivably brutal.

Hundreds were arrested, and the town gaol, crowded to suffocation, has become a pest-house, rivalling the Black Hole of Calcutta. Men and women have been clubbed for merely being spectators of a free speech meeting. So extreme has been the brutality of the police that the attention of all America is centreing upon San Diego. It has become a crime to even sell the local *Daily Herald* or the San Francisco *Bulletin* upon the streets, merely because these papers have dared to give a plain recital of the events which have led up to the conversion of an American city into an inferno like unto some Russian village given over to a pogrom.

The brunt of the fight for free speech has largely fallen upon the industrial workers of the world, an organisation which has a strongly Syndicalist basis. But the various trade unions and the Socialists have united with the I.W.W., and all are making determined resistance. There is a movement now being made to direct a march of all the unemployed of America upon San Diego, in order to convince the city that America is not quite Russia—at least, not yet.

A call for help is being sent out by California Free Speech League. Contributions may be sent to Kasper Bauer, secretary, Union Building, San Diego, California.

Merely to show solidarity, the SYNDICALIST will remit a small amount. We hope our readers will follow suit.

TOM MANN'S TRIAL.

Tom Mann will be tried in Salford on May 6. We hope he will get a jury that will refuse to send a man to gaol for merely assisting to suggest that Britishers should refuse to shoot their brother Britishers, no matter what an obsolete and forgotten law made by a long dead and rotten aristocracy may command.

We would, however, again remind our readers that if the workers of this country had sufficient Industrial Solidarity there would be no reason for any misgiving about the trial.

With Solidarity, the workers not only have it in their power to take the lead out of the soldiers' rifles, but, what is more important, the bread out of their baskets.

Napoleon well said that an Army travels on its Stomach. He might have added that the Stomach of an Army travels on the Backs of the Workers.

A QUARREL AND A WELCOME.
By H. HALLIDAY SPARLING.

I quarrel with Syndicalism, as I have hitherto understood it, on several grounds, but welcome its arrival in England on quite as many, if not more. In so far as it is offered as a complete, or even approximately complete, solution of the social problem, my attitude towards it is and must be critical, so strongly critical as to be practically hostile. But if, and in so far as it is put forward as a strategical method as a means of intensifying and utilising the solidarity of the workers along the line of greatest efficiency, I am ready to welcome and work for it.

We in England have a way of adopting a foreign name for some new phase of a perfectly native thing and serenely disregarding any implications or "principles" that the name might be supposed to carry with it. I can only hope that this is the case with "Syndicalism." As I have known it in France these last few years, I could feel no friendship either for the word or the teachings that went with

MY VERSION OF "SYNDICALISM."
By LEONARD HALL.

IT is most amusing, and not less edifying, to see the little crowd of dried Tories who have for years been labelling themselves "Socialists"—even "Revolutionary Socialists"—with the capital "R" tumbling over each other since the "Mutiny" prosecutions to disclaim and repudiate any connection or even sympathy with that disreputable and unholy thing "Syndicalism."

I confess myself as not particularly in love with the name, but since the invaluable lift and free advertisement given it by the Government through the Attorney-General, it is quite clear the word is to stick, and that it will do just as well as any other to connote a certain policy for Labour and a definite attitude of mind towards the State and social change.

It now remains for that already strong and rapidly growing body of social revolutionaries who are convinced that the essential basis of any real movement towards social and industrial democracy must be a highly developed and socially conscious organisation of the workers on the industrial plane—for these, it now remains to carefully think out and elucidate not only the militant tactics to be employed as well as reconstructive lines and practical proposals.

On the constructive and positive side the Syndicalists are admittedly still a little nebulous and indeterminate, and their first business is to build up a coherent programme to free Labour from the bondage of privateering Capitalism as well as the equally obnoxious bondage of Governmental bureaucracy.

Syndicalism is essentially Socialism, but is against "State" Socialism or bureaucratic collectivism, the conception and aim of many of the prominent advocates of "Socialism" in this country, the friends of the enslaving Insurance Act, Poor Law Minority Report scheme, Miners' Minimum Wage Act, and so forth.

Syndicalism, in short, pits the ideal of industrial *democracy* against the present rapid tendency towards Social bureaucracy, and—on its militant side—declares that the only effective answer to the syndicating (or pooling) of capital by the exploiters will be the syndicating of labour by the exploited.

In the last issue the SYNDICALIST said : "To the extent that political (meaning Parliamentary, &c.) action *does not distract the workers from industrial unionism* we have no quarrel with those who thus employ themselves. [Italics mine.] During the transition period there can be no doubt that a group of revolutionary Socialists in Parliament has some value to the workers," and especially in the control of the local administrative councils the presence of Socialist members "is a distinct advantage."

The solution of the debate now waxing hot between the ultra-Parliamentarist Socialists and the Industrial Unionist Socialists, in my opinion, is to be found in the words I have above italicised.

The working-class, in its struggle for existence against Capitalism and in its forward movement towards Socialism, possesses or can possess two weapons of defence and offence—viz.: (1) Direct action, including the *general or combined* industrial strike, the boycott, and constructive co-operative movements; and (2) Electoral action, or the voting into Parliament and local governing councils of social-revolutionary delegates with a view to capturing for the workers (or, failing that, to paralysing) the executive powers of the country.

Now, these two methods of revolutionary activity need not be inconsistent with each other. On the contrary, it is precisely our business to make them supplementary and complementary of each other. Militant industrialist action by the workers operating in the labour market, and militant political action by the workers operating through the ballot-box, are in the relationship of the hammer to the beaten iron.

Meanwhile, it is imperative to realise that, pending the establishment of fighting forces of Socialist delegates in Parliament and the local bodies, Industrial Unionism (the national union of all the Labour unions for common action with a common object in the industrial sphere) is the only effective instrument of self-defence and self-assertion in the workers' possession at all; and that even for mere purposes of attack upon the Capitalist governmental system, upon its marionette parties and their opportunist manœuvres, we can never hope to have a reliable or effective Parliamentary Socialist-Labour movement unless such movement be the reflex and be kept the instrument of a wide-awake social-revolutionary public opinion and a powerful and aggressive industrialist organisation outside. These would act as at once the driving and directing force of the men and measures inside, and the political agents of Socialism would be fortified by the weapons of the general strike and boycott—or the standing threat of and readiness to use these potent weapons—in the sense of our heavy industrialist artillery covering and supporting our political cavalry. It is, however, as well to realise that nothing seems more certain than that the least real danger of the Socialist working-class "capturing Political power" will be the signal for the Capitalist class to forsake all pretence of representative government and resort to force of arms.

(To be continued.)

[Whilst welcoming expressions of opinion like those given by Leonard Hall, it must be understood that Syndicalism *requires* no revolutionary advocates in Parliament. The economic emancipation of the workers can be and will be brought about by and through industrial organisation. It matters not to us what the politicians may do or attempt, we need have no regard whatever for their opinions or their deeds. Whatever they do we can cope with it on the industrial field, and no special pleaders are wanted or wished for in legislative institutions.—Note by T. M.]

---

it. As a philosophy it was too hopelessly out of touch with the trend of modern science and much too irregular in its reasoning. As a social synthesis it left too many elements outside, too many factors unaccounted for. But it may have suffered a sea-change, and in England have come to mean little more than the revival of militant trade unionism on a higher plane, made possible by the growth of Socialist thought and enthusiasm.

Even if it has not, it can do little harm under existing conditions, and, indeed, can hardly fail to do a great deal of good.

As a reaction against over-reliance upon Parliamentary action, something of the kind was inevitable. The more men know and feel, the more keenly they desire to be doing something useful. You cannot expect, and surely should not hope, that they will mark time between elections or waste years of work on the problematic chance of being "represented" by somebody who is just as much interested in Temperance, Disestablishment, or Free Trade as he is in the claims of Labour. Syndicalism—as it is preached by Tom Mann, at any rate—gives them something tangible to do and something quite as tangible to work for. They can readily understand what they are after, as well as how they are to get it. It isolates and emphasises their position in the modern state: acting through their Unions in the industrial field, they are freed from the confusing forces and traditions which divide, distract, and so largely nullify their strength in the political field.

At the least and lowest, it has a right to be heard, and even if I were less in sympathy with its teachings and tactics than I am, I should be on its side until it has been fully and freely discussed, and had its fair chance of survival.

AN APPEAL TO SOLDIERS.
By GEORGE LANSBURY, M.P.

It might help the House of Commons to remember that James Russell Lowell, who was American Ambassador here, held these views which I hold. I am proud to be a follower of his. He was laughed at for a time, but later on we were proud to welcome him as one of the most distinguished Ambassadors who ever came to St. James's. Here is what he says :

Ez for war, I call it murder—
   There you hev it plain an' flat ;
I don't want to go no furder
   Than my Testyment fer that.
God hez said so plump an' fairly
   It's ez long ez it is broad,
An' you've gut to git up airly
   Ef you want to take in God.

'Taint your eppylettes an' feathers
   Make the thing a grain more right ;
'Taint a-follerin' your bell-wethers
   Will excuse ye in His sight.
Ef you take a sword an' dror it,
   An' go stick a feller thru,
Guv'ment aint to answer for it—
   God'll send the bill to you.

Tell ye jest the cend I've come to,
   Arter cipherin' plaguey smart,
An' it makes a handy sum, tu,
   Any gump could larn by heart :
Labourin' man an' labourin' woman
   Hev one glory an' one shame,
Ev'ry thing thet's done inhuman
   Injers all on 'em the same.

Those are the sentiments I stand by in the House of Commons. You call upon one set of the working classes to murder another set of the working classes, for the soldiers are drawn from the working classes. If you set out to shoot down their fathers and their mothers you know perfectly well that you are calling upon them to murder their loved ones. It is nothing else.

KEIR HARDIE ON SYNDICALISM.

"THE RIGHTS OF THE COMMON PEOPLE."

(From THE TIMES.)

Mr. Keir Hardie, M.P., speaking in Bradford, referred to the Syndicalist cases, and said that if the prosecutions in this country spread, others would take the places of those who were sent to prison. He had no desire to be put under lock and key, but he was prepared to go to prison, or even the scaffold, in advance of what he believed to be the rights and liberties of the common people.

When the Syndicalist said that every trade union should be merged into one union he was preaching the same theory as the Socialists. They differed with the Syndicalists when they said that the mines should belong to the miners and the railways to the railwaymen, and so on. That was a debatable point on which he need not enter. The final goal of the Syndicalist was not essentially different from that of the Socialist. He did not want the colliers to own the pits or the factory workers the mills ; he wanted the community as a whole to own them so that they could be worked for the good of the community. He would defend to the utmost any attempt to cause antagonism between Syndicalism and Socialism, as they were both trying to put some backbone and determination into the working-classes. Both were equally anxious for the overthrow of the existing state of society and the creation of a newer and better state in which there should be freedom in the widest and broadest sense of the term. (Cheers.)

[Hardie is mistaken in saying that Syndicalists propose that the miners should belong to the miners as opposed to community ownership.—ED. SYNDICALIST.]

HOW TO FEDERATE.

To THE SYNDICALIST.

SIR,—I am sure you are advocating the right line of action for abolishing the present order of society—that is, that it is necessary to federate the Trade Unions so that they may act in conjunction with one another, and that every producer must recognise (what the investor knows by instinct) that the interests of those who live by work are directly opposed to the interests of those who live by idle ownership.

By acting on right principles we must get right results, but as yet it is not easy to tell what they will be. You say the "control of the technical processes now exercised by the Capitalist shall pass to the various groups of organised workers of the various industries." This might, I think, take place in two different ways (we are, of course, discussing the ultimate form of a new society) :

1. Either the whole of an industry could be managed by the workers in that industry—"the mines for the miners" is the common formula—the products being distributed in conjunction with the total product from all the other industries. This involves the idea of great, centralised Unions as permanent institutions, though, of course, when once Capitalism is dead and done for, with very different functions from what they now have.

2. Or in each small district (or commune) a Trades Council, representing all the Trade Unions of the district (or all the producers as all producers would then be in their Unions) would work out the needs of the district, and how best to supply them. The apparent complexity of many great undertakings is only apparent—being due to the adding together of a large number of locally solved problems (each not so complicated in itself) with a little adjustment where necessary. Thus you can take the train from Paris to Constantinople across many countries with no common railway centre or capital ; each district works out its own needs and adjusts them a little to allow for the necessities of more far-reaching needs. This second, uncentralised, idea is certainly the common idea of French revolutionary Syndicalism. I am inclined to prefer it to the first idea, and venture to suggest it to your consideration.—Yours sincerely,

April 6, 1912.   ARTHUR D. LEWIS.

FROM AN OLD WARRIOR.

Dear Mr. Bowman.—Should I congratulate you, or condole with you, on the offence you have given to law and order? I really can't say; but I have every confidence that the Syndicalist "cause," with which, as you know, I entirely sympathise—methods apart —will take no detriment from your presentation of its tenets. And that is the great, nay, greatest, matter.

As you may be aware, I am personally a "Passive Resister," but even at that I can discover in the incriminated matter almost nothing *morally* reprehensible. Nor, speaking as a barrister, do I think the grounds of prosecution other than *legally* flimsy and gratuitous on the part of the Liberal Government.

I am too infirm to venture down to the Old Bailey to-morrow, as I would have liked to do; but you will take the wish for the deed, I am sure.

Tom Mann is, indeed, a man of men, and I wish I could aid him in any way. We have been warm friends for many years; but I am getting old, infirm, and poor, and have little but good wishes left to contribute to the "cause" which you and he and I have so much at heart.

Howbeit, I am satisfied that all is for the best, and have no regrets for the past or fears for the future. You are young. Be of good cheer and you will, peradventure, help to celebrate the epiphany of the universal co-operative commonwealth, the revolution of revolutions. *Deus tecum!*—Ever fraternally, J. MORRISON DAVIDSON.

SYNDICALISM IN ENGLAND.

ITS ORIGIN AND HISTORY.

(THE TIMES, April 16.)

THE existence of a strong Syndicalist movement in this country can no longer be denied, though attempts have been made up till quite recently to deny it. Revelations in connexion with the coal strike and the prosecutions for inciting soldiers to mutiny have opened the eyes of all to an agitation which was only half seen last year during the strikes in the transport trades, and was ridiculed in some quarters. Its rapid development has taken every one by surprise, including both the older trade unionists, who have of late years been dominated by Socialists, and the Socialists who have dominated them. Even careful observers, who have made some study of Syndicalism abroad, were unprepared. It was thought that England, like Germany, offered a very unfavourable soil for doctrines which grew naturally in France and might be successfully transplanted to Italy, but were uncongenial to the calmer Teutonic temperament. Professor Sombart has given currency to this view in his "Socialism and the Social Movement" (Dent). The fact that the new movement arose in France and has only taken root in Italy is, he says, not accidental.

On closer observation we shall see that Syndicalism is something specially Franco-Italian, or perhaps more exactly French, and that it could not have developed in any other land. There is some ground for this opinion. Direct action and revolution appeal with exceptional force to the French, who have more reason than most peoples to distrust political methods and to attach small importance to forms of Government, because they have tried them all.

PREDISPOSING INFLUENCES.

For several years the ground has been preparing for Syndicalism under the influence of separate but simultaneous and gradually accumulating forces. The first of these is the advent of a younger generation of men, who have grown up since the series of great industrial conflicts which led to the flourishing period of conciliation and mutual agreement, the zenith of collective bargaining. These younger men have the inexperience, the irresponsibility, and the fighting spirit proper to youth; they have more education, more ambition, and a higher standard of needs than the older generation. A certain number of the most intelligent and ambitious have undergone a special intellectual training at Ruskin College, which seems to have been applied largely to turning out agitators. Its offshoot, the Central Labour College, the result of a revolt against authority and University influence, carried out chiefly by students from South Wales, has avowedly assumed that function. The second influence at work is illustrated by this institution; it is the active, systematic, and ceaseless dissemination of Socialistic doctrines—anti-capitalism, the class war, the right to the whole produce of labour, and so forth. In November, 1910, a conference on Industrial Syndicalism was held in Manchester at the Coal Exchange. According to the report it was attended by 198 delegates, representing between 70 and 80 trade unions and societies, 16 trades councils, and about 60,000 persons. The industrial groups most largely represented were building, engineering, transport, and mining. The textile unions held aloof; and, though several of the cotton towns round Manchester were represented by their trades councils, the largest were not. Discussion at this conference was devoted almost entirely to the subject of organising labour on the new lines previously explained, and a resolution was passed in that sense. Very little was said about the methods of Syndicalism and "direct action." Subsequent conferences have been held in London and elsewhere; but the propaganda is mainly carried on by district work. It has been so actively taken up that by last summer there was a standing list of some fifty speakers available in twenty different centres from Southampton to Glasgow, and from Bristol to Newcastle. They represent a great variety of trades, including clerks, shop assistants, and postmen; but miners and railwaymen are most numerous. Their names are not known to the public; they are not candidates for Parliament or trade union "leaders." Indeed, one of the marks of the movement is objection to "leaders"; it professes to do without them. But it would be a great mistake to despise these Syndicalist missionaries because they are unknown to fame. There are very capable men among them, who can more than hold their own with the ablest and most influential of known trade unionists.

THE PROPAGANDA.

The means of carrying on the propaganda here are the usual ones—cheap publications, both periodicals and pamphlets, lectures, meetings, and discussions. Of the publications the earliest was the "Industrial Syndicalist," started by Mr. Mann in 1910, nearly two years ago. It was a sort of monthly pamphlet, sold for a penny, in which the principles were expounded and direct appeal was made to particular industries. No. 2, for instance, which appeared in August, 1910, was addressed to the transport workers; No. 8, issued more than a year ago, to the miners; No. 10, to the cotton trade; No. 11, issued last May, to the railwaymen. Twelve numbers of this publication were issued. In September last a monthly penny paper especially for railwaymen was started under the name of the *Syndicalist Railwayman.* After four numbers it was apparently transformed into the *Syndicalist,* which began its career in January last as the mouthpiece of the Industrial Syndicalist Education League, an organisation founded in Manchester towards the end of 1910. The object of the League, of which Mr. Mann is the president, is :

To carry on among trade unionists and the workers generally a campaign of education in the principles of Syndicalism—which may be described as revolutionary trade unionism, since its immediate purpose is to conduct a scientific class war against capitalism—such war having as its objective or ultimate aim the capture of the industrial system and its management by the workers themselves for the benefit of the whole community.

As a general definition of the aim and character of the movement, the foregoing statement is admirably clear and concise. The League seems to be the only definitely Syndicalist organisation as yet formed, though there are some local bodies of a revolutionary character and similar aims. Its mission is to convert the trade unions and perfect their organisation on the lines indicated above in preparation for the grand attack. Unlike the American Syndicalists, Mr. Mann and his friends have not sought to form a new set of trade unions; they have taken the far wiser course of adapting the old. The SYNDICALIST explains that the object of the League is not to displace the existing trade-union movement, but to "facilitate its development towards real solidarity and direct action lines." They are themselves members of the old trade unions and they aim at reform from within. To this end they "visit union branches, trades councils, working-men's clubs, &c., to stimulate discussion on Syndicalist principles and methods." The campaign appears to be conducted with marked ability and adroitness. The Syndicalists do not denounce the old trade unionism or oppose the Parliamentary movement, though they do not believe in it. They strive rather to persuade and convince. They also eschew personal abuse, and exercise a restraint in controversy which compares very favourably with the practice of old-fashioned Socialists, whose arrogance, invective, and laboured sarcasms make them intolerably tedious.

CONCLUSION.

Syndicalism is a banner which attracts the youthful and pugnacious and those who are tired alike of the older trade unionism, with its conciliation agreements, and of the older Socialism, with its politics. Syndicalism enlists the spirit of the one by advocating more complete organisation and greater solidarity, and that of the other by preaching the class war with the promise of a more speedy and vigorous campaign fought with the weapon so forged. The banner is borne with particular enthusiasm by a new class of trade unionists, young men who have received special training. They are being turned out by the Central Labour College. The connexion of this institution with the movement is shown by the fact that it is supported chiefly by South Wales miners and railwaymen, among whom Syndicalism has made most progress. This is due rather to the influence of individuals than to any conditions rendering those industrial sections specially receptive. Similar influences exerted in other directions must be expected to produce similar impressions; and they are now active in the building, printing, shipbuilding, and engineering trades, and among clerks and shop assistants. The curious revival of fierce intolerance against non-unionists lately exhibited in Lancashire both among cotton weavers and miners suggests the influence of the new doctrine.

All who march under the banner are not necessarily devotees of the cause or convinced believers in all or any of the doctrines it represents. Most of them are rather willing to give it a trial. Its hold is, therefore, indefinite and hard to gauge; but for the same reason its potentialities are great. Their reality was demonstrated to the eye by the strikes in the transport trades last year, which were organised under Syndicalist influence.

SEVEN SHILLINGS FOR A SIX-HOUR DAY.

By TOM MANN.

COMRADES,—This year 1912 should witness the obtaining of substantial reductions of working hours and actual increases in the real wages received.

If we believed the day had arrived for the actual taking over by the workers of the entire control of the Industry, and the ownership of the means of production, we would shape our course accordingly, but we know that we must secure much more perfect solidarity amongst the workers before that can be possible. To hasten that solidarity and to fit the working class to actually become the absolute controllers of the industries in which they work it is essential that we should, without delay, get out of and away from the accursed poverty that Capitalism has imposed upon us. If we cannot at once solve the industrial problem and secure our economic emancipation, we can at least so direct our energies as to secure work for all by reducing working hours in each occupation until no one is out of work.

Syndicalism, to the extent of the workers in each industry deciding what the working hours shall be in that industry, could be applied and ought to be applied now.

If the organised workers could realise the enormous power they have in Industrial Solidarity they would refuse to turn to Parliament to achieve the change desired. But solidarity must first exist and function between each industry.

The Miners showed solidarity amongst themselves, but that was not sufficient; the other requirements of Labour should have been brought up to have forced the fight hot and strong till victory crowned their efforts.

This would certainly have happened in the second week of the coal strike had there been such fighting, instead of mere talking, resorted to.

The demand now is for *reduced hours of work.* It may be that all cannot expect a six-hour day this year. The actual number of hours is less important than the *absorption of all in useful employment.* Not by attempts at a "Right to Work Bill," but each industry, in addition to fixing upon the right scale for itself, shall be ready to co-operate with each and every other industry.

If the Trades Councils were really fulfilling their proper rôle they would by this time have had every industry linked up in each town and district, and each of these districts connected with the others throughout the country. The ideas are abroad all right, and there is nothing like a healthy struggle for spreading ideas further and bringing the ideas into a realised fact.

The unemployed question can be settled for ever by *direct action* through industrial solidarity. Fluctuations are met to-day by variation in the number of persons employed. The Capitalist class is the deciding factor. We workers intend now hereafter to become the deciding factor, and therefore shall never allow any unemployed to exist. All must have work. Fluctuations will be met by variations in working hours—not men. As rapidly as new labour-saving appliances are introduced the working hours shall be further lessened.

We demand a six-hour day as the normal working day, and not less than a wage of seven shillings a day, or a minimum of two guineas a week.

In some occupations our first demand will probably be for an eight-hour day and an all-round increase of 20 per cent. in wages, but, whatever the particular demand in a given industry or trade, the immediate aim must be the complete and permanent absorption of all unemployed.

Every student of the industrial problem knows that it is the existence of unemployed workers struggling against starvation for work at any price that gives power to the Capitalist. It is our work to transfer power from the Capitalist class to the working class. In doing this we secure the means of life for those who have been deprived of comforts and of necessaries. If the reader will ponder over the stupendous effects that must follow upon a bold policy of Direct Action in the matter of reduction of hours, he will see that it is precisely the way to raise wages also, because low wages are the accompaniment and consequence of unemployment. We shall raise the standard of life by shortening the hours of labour, and the workers, having both leisure and means, will become the better qualified for further fights. No need for committees to secure starving children a few meals; we will destroy the cause of poverty. There shall be no starving children, no need to talk of Parliament securing a minimum wage, the minimum wage will be secured by the organised workers systematically adjusting conditions in each department of industry: the ultimate aim is the Co-operative Commonwealth. The only people qualified to actually realise such a Commonwealth are those mental and manual workers engaged in the various industries and occupations. No Parliament, as we know it, can organise and regularly conduct industry. This must be done by industrial experts formed by, and found in, the industries themselves.

Comrades, do not for a moment forget the millions of children in this country ill-fed, ill-clad, shamefully housed, and horribly neglected. Keep in mind the hundreds of thousands of young women working excessive hours and never getting a sufficiency to keep themselves in health. The talking has been done, The time for action has come. No Crusaders of old had a cause half so worthy as ours. We are out for the regeneration of the whole working class. We are challenging Capitalist civilisation. We shall be confronted with the Capitalist forces. Be it so. Absolutely self-reliant, we march forward. Victory after victory, till Capitalism falls and Justice prevails.

SYNDICALISM IN ACTION.

IMPORTANT MOVE OF THE BUILDING TRADE UNIONS IN LONDON.

(From THE MANCHESTER GUARDIAN, April 19.)

The first step in an important movement towards the grouping of trade unions in the various industries was taken to-day at the national conference attended by delegates from the unions in the building trade, held in Essex Hall, Strand. The meeting was private, and it was stated afterwards that the following two resolutions were carried almost unanimously:

1. "(a) That this conference expresses its adherence to the resolutions passed by the last two Trade Unions Congresses embodying the principle of amalgamating the present trade unions in the various industries, and therefore we, the representatives of the building trade unions, consider the time is now opportune to put that principle into operation in our industry; (b) that a committee be appointed, to consist of one member from each society represented, to draw up a scheme to give effect to the previous resolution, such scheme to be submitted to the next conference."

2. "That the time has arrived when all those who work in the building trade, mechanics and labourers alike, should form one great union for the betterment of all concerned and be able to resist employers, as they are one body."

Mr. Will Thorne, M.P., chairman of the Parliamentary Committee, presided, and among those present were Mr. C. W. Bowerman, M.P., and Mr. John Ward, M.P. There was no difference of opinion as to the policy of amalgamating the unions, and the discussion centred upon various practical difficulties. The following are some of the societies represented at the conference, with the approximate membership of each :—

Amalgamated Carpenters and Joiners, 60,000; Gasworkers and General Labourers, 60,000; Amalgamated Union of Labour, 38,000; Operative Bricklayers, 25,000; House and Ship Painters, 21,000; Plumbers' Association, 11,000; General Union of Carpenters and Joiners, 6,500; United Builders' Labourers, 6,000; Scottish Painters, 3,500; Builders' Labourers, 3,500; Manchester Unity of Operative Bricklayers, 2,800; Street Masons and Paviors, 1,500; Slaters and Tilers, 1,200; Engine-drivers, Crane-drivers, Hydraulic and Boiler Attendants, 1,200; Operative Stonemasons, 1,200; French Polishers, 1,200; General Labourers, 1,200. The Operative Plasterers, the Wood-cutting Societies, the Mosaic and Tile-fixers' Society, and the Navvies were also represented.

After the committee is appointed it will meet in Manchester on May 23, when schemes will be presented and the lines upon which the amalgamation will proceed will be laid down. The report of the committee will be presented to a further conference to be held probably in London, after which the scheme will be submitted for final endorsement to the executives of the various unions.

The building trade unions are thus the first to put into practical effect the resolution in favour of amalgamation which has been passed at the two last Trade Unions Congresses. The resolution last year was brought forward by the Bricklayers' Society. It instructed the Parliamentary Committee to call conferences of the different industries with a view to amalgamation, adding: "Recognising the increased power of the Capitalists in closing up their ranks and their adoption of improved methods, we deplore the lack of similar consolidation among the workers." "Their proposal," said the mover, Mr. E. Morris, "was in the direction of amalgamation, not federation, for they believed that in the past federations had not achieved the objects they were intended to accomplish. In their view federation of trades at the present time was simply a federation of officials. They wanted, on the contrary, a federation or amalgamation of the rank and file. The Parliamentary Committee could get the various societies together and act as arbitrator between them." Another delegate said : "There are still too many unions in one industry, and we still find isolated unions being created. . . . we are still disunited and bringing failure, absolute and certain, upon our cause."

£70,000 BONUS DECLINED.

VIRUS OF SYNDICALISM.

The offer of the directors of the North-Eastern Railway Company to distribute a large sum of money in the form of bonuses among the lower-paid workers has been rejected by the branches of the Amalgamated Society of Railway Servants.

The proposal was to distribute £70,000 in the form of bonuses. The money was intended for the lower-paid employees, and the reason assigned was that these men were not now in receipt of wages sufficient to meet the increased cost of living ; while both the company and the men are bound to a wages award which does not expire until the end of next year.

The Society's objection is to the bonus system in principle.

Armed insurrection and voting for politicians are both out-of-date methods of social warfare, and both are consigned to the junk shop by Syndicalism.

THE MINIMUM WAGE ACT IN SOUTH WALES.

That we have not gotten along very much further toward a settlement of the Welsh coal miners' demands by passing the Minimum Wage Act may be seen from the following schedule of what the men ask and what the owners offer. We quote from the *Manchester Guardian* of April 23.

"The workmen's representatives held the view that the average wages paid should be taken into consideration, whereas the owners maintained that the Act provided that the Joint District Board shall have regard to the daily rate of wages, and that being so they held that only the wages paid to those colliers in receipt of a day rate (and not the average earnings of all the colliers) should be considered in arriving at a minimum rate for colliers. The owners therefore submitted a counter-proposal, proposing a minimum rate—which is the proposed standard rate plus 35 per cent.—for each grade. The following table sets out these rates and those demanded by the men in the classes already considered by the two sides :

	Owners' offer.	Men's demands.
Timbermen	5s. 0¼d.	8s. 0d.
Rippers	4s. 8¾d.	8s. 0d.
Assistant timbermen and rippers	3s. 10d.	6s. 6d.
Hauliers	4s. 10d.	7s. 0d.
Hitchers	3s. 10d. to 4s. 8¾d.	7s. 0d.
Ropemen and trafficmen	4s. 10½d.	7s. 0d.
Roadmen and riders	4s. 0½d.	7s. 0d.
Blocklayers and trammers	4s. 0½d.	7s. 0d.
Ostlers and labourers	3s. 10d.	5s. 0d.
Boys	1s. 9½d.	2s. 6d. to 4s. 6d.

"It will thus be seen that in several cases the men ask for practically 3s. per day more than the owners offer, and the least difference is in the case of the ostlers and labourers, for whom owners offer 1s. 2d. a day less than the men demand."

How absurd it is, anyway, for one class to set out a plan of life for another, and this is practically what the Bill would do.

THE SYNDICALIST CASE.

To the Editor of THE WESTMINSTER GAZETTE.

Sir,—The Crown has thought it worth while to institute a State prosecution, under a statute passed in the worst period of panic which followed the French Revolution, and wisely permitted to fall into abeyance since. No Liberal would care to recall the legislation of that period or the way in which it was used by the Crown to browbeat the friends of freedom.

I submit that this prosecution is not a matter of necessity so much as a matter of executive discretion. The real issue is whether the danger to public order from the action of these three men was so serious as to justify resort to such exceptional procedure. In Ireland we have had of late plenty of loose and foolish talk, which may be far more dangerous in its effects on public feeling. But the Irish Executive, though armed with large powers under recent Acts, have wisely refused to magnify silliness into treason. Many Liberals cannot help regretting that that example was not followed here. Many more, I think, will feel that the prosecution, even if undertaken, should not have been pressed too hard, and that only nominal sentences should have been imposed. The risk is that prosecutions of this nature may inflame opinion far more than the offence.—Yours obediently,

C. E. MALLET.

If any of our readers are sufficiently interested to wish for a daily Syndicalist paper, we would suggest that, pending an English one, the French paper, *La Bataille Syndicaliste,* may be had through the news-stands. We will send it post free for one year on receipt of 14s. Sample free for one red stamp.

If you like the SYNDICALIST why not send in your name as one who will assist in circulating it? Perhaps you might take some off our hands at 1s. 4d, the quire, carriage paid? Get your newsdealer to handle it.

TOM MANN COMMITTED FOR TRIAL.

THE SALFORD SPEECH.

(From THE TIMES, April 1.)

At Salford on Saturday Mr. Hogg, the stipendiary magistrate, committed Mr. Tom Mann to the Manchester Assizes on a charge of inciting persons serving in his Majesty's forces by land to commit traitrous and mutinous practice, contrary to the Incitement to Mutiny Act, 1797. Mr. Gordon Hewart prosecuted on behalf of the Director of Public Prosecutions; and Mr. H. Lindon Riley defended. There was a full bench of magistrates, and the Court was crowded.

Evidence for the Prosecution.

Sergeant Finch, of the Criminal Investigation Department, Scotland Yard, stated that on Sunday, January 14, he attended a meeting convened by the Industrial Syndicalist Education League at the Latchmere Baths, Battersea. The prisoner, who was at the meeting, produced a newspaper which he said contained a clear definition of Syndicalism and could be purchased in the hall. On the third page of the paper was an open letter to British soldiers.

In answer to the Magistrate, Mr. Hewart said that at meetings on March 13 and 14 the prisoner avowed responsibility for the publication of the paper. All the evidence he should call would be directed to responsibility for the original publication. After that evidence was on the depositions two further charges would be framed.

Sergeant Markland, of the Salford Police, said that on March 13 he attended a meeting in the Salford Town Hall convened by the Workers' Union. In the speech he there made the prisoner said: "I have always been one to say to soldiers, Don't shoot your comrade-workers; turn your rifles round and shoot the other people." At that point he said: "I have heard there are two detectives in the room, and I am going to say something which affects me personally; they can take out their notebooks and take down word for word what I say. Last Friday night the police in London apprehended my friend and colleague Guy Bowman over the 'Open Letter to Soldiers' in the paper called the SYNDICALIST. Bowman was the editor and I was the secretary for the paper. After he was apprehended the police searched his rooms and actually stole the copies of the paper that were there. But they did not steal them all. I have brought up about twenty-five copies which I have here and will sell to any person for twopence, but he will have to make personal application at the platform for it."

Mr. Hewart: Did he make any further reference to soldiers?—He said he was pleased to associate himself with the article (the letter), and would always say to soldiers, "Don't shoot."

Continuing his evidence Sergeant Markland said that on the following evening he went to a meeting of the Workers' Union in the Pendleton Town Hall. There, to 600 or 700 people, the prisoner read the first three paragraphs of the "Open Letter to Soldiers," and said he was pleased to take responsibility for the passages. Copies of the paper containing the letter were sold in the room, and the witness bought one.

Cross-examined by Mr. Riley, Markland said he was sure the prisoner was the man who said he would always say to soldiers, "Do not shoot your comrades." No one had ever come to the witness and said, "What an infamous speech that was of Tom Mann's."

Sergeant Joseph Clarke, of the Salford Police corroborated the evidence of the last witness.

Mann's Speech.

Mr. Frederick Milner, shorthand writer, deposed that at the meeting in the Pendleton Town Hall on March 14, he took a shorthand note of the prisoner's speech. At the meeting Mann read from the "Open letter ":—Men, comrades, and brothers,—You are in the Army, so are we. You in the Army of destruction; we in the industrial or army of construction. We work at mine, mill, forge, factory, or dock, &c., producing and transporting all the goods, clothing, stuffs, &c., which make it possible for people to live. You are working-men's sons. When we go on strike to better our lot which is the lot also of your fathers, mothers, brothers, and sisters, you are called upon by your officers to murder us. Don't do it." Mann then referred to the Liverpool strike, saying :—" Were they not called upon to murder in Liverpool?" Continuing, Mann said, " In God's name, where do they come from, these soldiers—from the ranks of the toilers and the homes of the workers. For the most part they are sons squeezed out of a job, not allowed to be able to get a job, not to get food and clothing. They go to the Army and become the servants of the capitalists. It is one thing to be working on the battlefield and another thing to be brought into a strike area among the

very class from which these soldiers are drawn, sometimes their own relatives struggling, as the miners are now, to obtain a tolerable living wage. For these men, these soldiers, to be ordered to fire and to murder, to fire and to kill, for that is how they have been told how to fire, and then to tell us we dare not and shall not on pain of imprisonment utter our voice, utter a sentiment or dare to address them and urge them not to do so—then if we obey we are indeed cowards and mean things. But we are built of different stuff, and by all the gods and devils I will let the Government know that I will not stand it.

" I do not know to what extent there are detectives or plain-clothes policemen in this hall, but at each meeting I have been at for a long time there have been men sent by the police for the express purpose of taking notes. It may be just as our comrade Bowman has been charged with treason, felony, and what not for being identified with the paper he has issued, that if he is punished for that and it is an offence so serious that they will not allow him to come out on bail, I don't see how I shall escape as chairman of the committee. You must not be surprised if I, too, am arrested and find myself in Court. But because of that possibility I am not going to cease from denouncing those tactics."

The case for the prosecution was closed.

Mr. Riley submitted that no case had been proved to justify the Court in sending the prisoner for trial. Before the Bench could put a man in peril of imprisonment on this charge there must be some proof that the incitement had reached some quarters of British soldiers. On the evidence there was only proof that the SYNDICALIST had been published at halls in Battersea, Salford, and Pendleton.

Mr. Hewart said that the prisoner was not charged with having seduced, but with endeavouring to seduce.

Mr. Riley admitted that that was so, but again urged that it was as remote as the mind of man could imagine to suggest that the sale of a few copies of the paper in the way described was an endeavour, maliciously and advisedly, to induce British soldiers to be false to their allegiance

In reply to the Stipendiary, as to whether it was not an act of mutiny for a soldier to refuse to obey the lawful order of his superior officer, Mr. Riley admitted that that was so on active service, when not on active service, he claimed that a soldier was entitled to decide for himself whether a command was lawful.

The Stipendiary.—Do you ask us to say that we should not commit?

Mr. Riley.—Yes, that there is no *prima facie* case made out.

The Bench decided that there was a case for trial at the Assizes.

Statement by the Defendant.

The defendant then made the following statement : "I plead ' Not guilty.' At the same time, as regards the evidence given concerning some of the things I have said, particularly that of identifying myself with the chairmanship of the Industrial Syndicalist Education League, that is perfectly correct, and it was that league that was responsible for the paper called the SYNDICALIST being brought into existence, and as chairman I am quite prepared to share all necessary responsibility. Some of that which has been given as evidence against me is contrary to fact, and at the Assizes I shall give evidence on oath. The statement that I used the words 'Don't shoot your comrades; turn your rifles round and shoot the other people ' is absolutely untrue. Neither have I personally been identified with the writing, the publishing, or issuing of that ' Open letter to soldiers ' beyond that I have already stated in my capacity as chairman, I did not know of the existence of the open letter until several days after the issue of the January number of the SYNDICALIST. I do not say that because I had any reluctance to go to prison or endure any other punishment imposed, but as friend and comrade of men who have already been convicted in connection therewith I fail to understand why further conviction should be called for. I am advised by my counsel that the matter immediately at issue is my personal culpability or otherwise in connection with the ' Open letter to soldiers.' I am quite fearless of the consequences. I unhesitatingly repeat that I agree entirely with the spirit and the object of that letter. I would like to make one remark concerning that extract quoted from the reporter's notebook. I believe it to be absolutely correct and I stand by it in every particular."

Mann was then committed for trial at the Manchester Assizes, and again admitted to bail on the same terms as before—that is, himself in £200 and two sureties of £100 each.

AS TO GUSTAVE HERVÉ.

We would suggest to our Socialist editors who have suddenly warmed up to Gustave Hervé, styling him the arch-syndicalist, whatever that may be, apparently merely because he has recently congratulated the German Social Democrats, that they might have discovered his position in Syndicalism somewhat sooner.

Hervé bears about the same relation to Syndicalism that the Rev. R. J. Campbell does to Socialism.

Hervé is essentially an " anti-militarist," and it was much more because he found a warmer welcome for his views from the Syndicalists in France than from the Socialists that he identified himself with the former.

(To the Editor of the SYNDICALIST.)

Syndicalism is another of the short cuts to Socialism. It is as justifiable as the Trusts—not more so.   JOSEPH BURGESS.
Bradford. March 28, 1912.

BROTHERS BUCK OUT.
By VAL McENTEE.

(From THE DAILY HERALD, April 19.)

I had heard that the brothers Charlie and Ben Buck, as their friends call them, the printers of the famous appeal to soldiers not to shoot their fellow-workers during a strike, were likely to be released from gaol on Thursday, so I journeyed to Walthamstow in the afternoon to interview them. When I knocked at the door of No. 9, Stainsforth Road, it was opened by Mrs. Buck, and when I saw her cheerful smile I knew the brothers had returned.

I handed in my *Daily Herald* card, and was immediately invited to " Come in." " What a pity the *Daily Herald* did not come out a couple of months earlier," said Mrs. Buck, as we went through the hall. " It could have done such splendid service in the cause of freedom of speech and of justice ! "

When I entered their sitting-room I found the brothers already busy on their books, seeking to find out how their business had fared during their absence.

They told me they had no idea when they reprinted the Open Letter to Soldiers, which had previously circulated all through the country, that the result would be imprisonment. The action of the Government they could account for on no other ground than panic. They probably felt that somebody must be punished, to overawe others, and consequently they were selected, along with Bowman, as the victims. They felt strongly that the Recorder's remarks to the jury had prejudiced their case. They attributed the reduction of the sentence from six months' hard labour to one month in the second division to the splendid fight put up by a few men in Parliament, and by the many workers' organisations outside, whom they asked me to thank through the the columns of the *Herald*. From their practical experience of the prison system they regarded it as calculated to degrade and brutalise men.

Handcuffed to Burglars.

" Did you go in ' Black Maria '?" I asked.

" Oh, no," said one of the brothers, " the conveyance was all right, but we were handcuffed together."

This surprised me, and on further inquiry I found that Guy Bowman and Charles Buck were handcuffed together, whilst Mr. Ben Buck was handcuffed to a burglar going for his third term of imprisonment.

" What did you think of your company? " I asked.

" He was probably more sinned against than sinning," said Mr. Ben Buck. " He is a product of our system."

" Did you have a bed to sleep on? "

" Not when we were on hard labour ! We had a plank bed with three blankets, a coverlet, and pillow."

" In the second division you were, of course, not so badly treated? "

" It was rather better," they said. " Books were allowed, but the prison library was limited."

The only book Mr. Charlie Buck could get was a French reader, whilst his brother had to be satisfied with a Christian manual which informed him his bed represented a grave, and the man asleep was " like unto a corpse," and threatened him with dreadful punishments in the world to come.

I discovered also that the two brothers were sent out on the morning of their release an hour and a quarter before the time at which their wives were informed they would be released. As a consequence, the majority of those who went to meet them coming out did not see them. As none of the other prisoners were released before time, they were probably right in thinking that this was done to prevent any demonstration.

A reception in honour of the brothers will be held to-night at the William Morris Hall, Somers Road, Palmerston Road, Walthamstow.

FROM GEO. LANSBURY, M.P.

Sir,—The prosecution of Bowman and the Brothers Buck is the first of its kind since 1804. The Act itself under which the prosecutions are taken was passed in 1797. The Attorney-General in the House of Commons declared that the proceedings were taken for the purpose of deciding, and of letting it be known, that such articles were illegal and a grave offence against the State.

Liberals and Radicals have at all times welcomed to these shores men and women who defied their Governments. Many of us have honoured the late Count Tolstoy, and many of us have honoured and revered the memory of John Bright for the stand he took against militarism in this country, and it is to these I make this appeal.

If it is to be said, and if to remain a law, that those of us who hate the military spirit and say so are liable to be thrown into prison and treated with hard labour, what remains of freedom of expression, freedom of speech, freedom of the Press?

This is no question of Syndicalism, no question of any particular doctrine, except the right of men and women to have freedom of expression—especially freedom to express their views that militarism is a curse, that the sending of armed soldiers against unarmed men and women is a crime, and one which should be prevented.

GEORGE LANSBURY.

"DON'T SHOOT" PROSECUTION.

The following resolution was passed by the Provisional Executive of the British Socialist Party :

" The British Socialist Party vehemently denounces the tyrannous conduct of the Liberal Government in arresting Tom Mann, Guy Bowman, B. E. and C. E. Buck, Thomas Mayfield, J. Morley, and Nelson King, for adjuring their soldier countrymen not to shoot down their fellow-men and women on strike, at the command of the employers, and views with horror the savage sentences already passed upon Bowman and the two Bucks, after the infamous charge made to the Grand Jury by the Recorder, Sir Forrest Fulton. Such Muscovite action is obviously a deliberate attempt on the part of our rulers to put down free speech, a policy which must sooner or later be met by organised and forcible resistance from the people, if even a vestige of our liberties is to be preserved.

" The British Socialist Party calls upon all its speakers and lecturers to condemn these outrages of the Liberal Cabinet, which has allowed direct incitement to civil war by eminent Ulstermen like Sir Edward Carson, Lord Templetown, the Duke of Abercorn, and the Marquis of Londonderry to pass unchallenged. That honest and self-sacrificing champions of the workers should be haled into custody and treated as the worst of criminals in torturing prisons under an obsolete law, because they appeal to the national Army not to allow itself to be used in order to uphold the sweating and swindling methods of unscrupulous monopolists, shows that, as we Socialists have always declared, both political factions are the enemies of the wage-earners."

Many resolutions of protest have reached us : From a public meeting held at Shepherds' Hall, Bristol, on Sunday; from a meeting in South Shields Market Place, under the auspices of the Seamen's Union and Transport Workers' Federation; from a meeting at Hamilton (Lanarkshire; from Dudley Hill and Tong Socialist Club; from the Southend Branch of the Gasworkers' Union; from the Bristol Trades Council; from the Pollokshaws Engineers; from the Stratford Branch A.S.R.S.; from the Leicester Branch of the Tramway and Vehicle Workers; and from the Smethwick, Watford, East Liverpool, Golder's Green, and other branches of the British Socialist Party. We have also received many letters of protest.

"OFF WITH THE ARMOUR."

(DAILY CHRONICLE Correspondent.)
BERLIN, March 30.

Socialists consider that the impending introduction into the Reichstag of the Supplementary Army and Navy Bills renders it necessary for them officially to define their attitude towards the military question in general. The views of the party are proclaimed in a leading article entitled " Off with the Armour," appearing in to-day's " Vorwärts," its central organ.

Germany, says this article, may be likened to a giant who stalks about heavily armoured with a two-handed sword drawn ready to strike a fatal blow on the first occasion. Rulers of the country, it adds, contend that not even this armament suffices for the maintenance of peace, and that it must be strengthened in numerous places.

" We Social'sts, however," it continues, " are not deceived by this hypocritical game, for we know that a strong army and a strong navy are demanded by an Imperialist policy, which competition for world markets compels civilised States to pursue, and we know that pursuance of such a policy is a danger to peace."

Sucking the People's Lifeblood.

Militarism, they declare, has gained such a hold on Germany that no party except their own, not even party of Liberal progress, now dares to set itself against the principle of unceasing increases to the army. Liberals, they state, admit that armaments are indispensable, and discuss only the ways and means for paying for them. In these circumstances, writes the " Vorwärts," it becomes the bounden duty of the Socialist party to oppose the prevailing system of maintaining a standing army, with its permanent tendency to augmentation, with its constant danger to peace, and gradually sucking the lifeblood of the people.

This is all the more necessary (it adds) because the danger is imminent in Germany of an outbreak of offensive war. The principle adopted by the heads of the German army is, it says, that of strategic and tactical offensive, and this principle is idolised by German officers.

A PAT ON OUR BACK.

DEAR SYNDICALIST.—I hereby wish you and your paper every success. If I were to pat you on the back as you ask for in your last issue, I am afraid I should do it too hard. Our war-cry should be " Forward," no matter who stood in the way.

It's time for the workers of all countries to put an end to the auctioneering that has taken place, and to let the leaders (swanks) know that if there is any " selling " to be done, that it must be done by themselves.

I heartily wish you every success, and if there is any help that I can do it's yours for the asking.—I am,

JACK GRIFFITHS.
London, S.W., April 9, 1912.

THE TREASON TRIALS.

MR. BERNARD SHAW ON THE SENTENCES.

(To the Editor of THE DAILY NEWS.)

Sir,—In the report of the Syndicalist trial in the *Times* it is stated simply that the prisoners were found guilty. But in your report a very different conclusion is reported. It is there stated that three questions of fact were put to the jury; and that the answers were in the form of three separate verdicts of guilty. Now, in the absence of a complete verbatim report, it is impossible for me to say exactly what this means. If the judge directed the jury that all they had to do was to ascertain the facts, he misdirected them, and there should be an appeal on this ground. A jury has two distinct duties. One is to ascertain whether prisoner at the Bar actually committed the acts set forth in the indictment. That is clearly an indispensable preliminary to the discharge of the really solemn part of their duty—the part for which alone juries exist. That part is to decide whether the prisoner is an innocent of a guilty man. Thoughtless jurymen are apt to think that there is no difference and judges are tempted to encourage them in this error, because its effect is to take the case out of the hands of the jury and leave it to that of the judge. A few instances will show how profound the difference really is.

It is a crime to break a stranger's windows without his permission : Mrs. Pankhurst is at present in prison for doing it. But whenever there is a fire in London the members of the Fire Brigade commit this unlawful act openly and impudently. They are not indicted for it, not through any sympathy on the part of the Government with window-breaking, but because it is certain that if a fireman were so indicted, the jury would first decide among themselves that he had committed the act, and then find him " not guilty," with, probably, a rider expressing high commendation. If they did, anything else, they should be sent to a lunatic asylum.

It happens that the very case now in question brings out this distinction between the verdict and the mere ascertainment of fact in the most startling way. No crime known to the law is more severely punished than the crime of murder. The act involved in murder is the act of killing a human being. Yet every civilised country has to keep an immense body of men both on land and sea expressly equipped and trained for this very act, and sedulously impressed on every possible occasion with the conviction that such killing is their most sacred duty. We actually go so far as to make a law under which any person can be indicted, and, if found guilty, subjected to ruinous penalties, for asking the members of these forces to refrain from such killing. Under this law any Christian preacher, any publisher of the Bible, the works of Tolstoy, or Carlyle's " Sartor Resartus," or any painter-decorator who writes up the Sixth Commandment on the wall of a church open to soldiers, may be indicted and punished. Yet painter-decorators do these things as openly as firemen break windows, and for the same reason : they know perfectly well that if they were indicted for incitement to mutiny any sane jury would first decide that they had actually committed the act, and then, exactly as in the hypothetical case of the fireman, find them not guilty, and commend their industry and piety.

Now I have no means of knowing whether the jury yesterday, when they had duly ascertained the undoubted and unquestioned fact that the prisoners actually committed the acts alleged in the indictment, proceeded to deal with the entirely separate question of whether the prisoners were guilty or innocent. But it seems to me at least possible that they misunderstood their duties, and imagined not only that they were bound to answer three questions as to facts (which nobody had any right to put to them except as a matter of curiosity appealing to courtesy for information), but that an affirmative reply to these questions committed them in law to a verdict of guilty. If that is so, the Court of Appeal should at once order a new trial, for it is impossible to conceive an error more hideous in its practical consequences, and more utterly subversive of every principle of constitutional law, than this. If it were admitted in theory there would be no sense in having juries at all. If it were carried out in practice there would soon be no law in England except the law of the revolver, which has already too many apologists in high places for the comfort of long-sighted people.   G. BERNARD SHAW.

GUY BOWMAN OUT OF GAOL.

There is one Guy Bowman that Sir Rufus Isaacs has not yet managed to clap into gaol, and he lives at 4, Maude Terrace, Walthamstow, too.

He has been making all sorts of most extremely radical remarks, especially in the early hours of morning, and while there can be no doubt that the burden of his grievance is his disappointment at not seeing a father to greet him on his arrival last week, nevertheless his command of English is not yet sufficiently established for anyone except his mother to fully understand him.

It is certain, however, that if his remarks were correctly interpreted they would afford ample reason for Sir Rufus sending this new Guy to join his father at Wormwood Scrubbs.

The determined way he seizes the means of the food supply indicates that he is imbibing Syndicalism with his mother's milk all right enough.

The Syndicalist

VOL. 1. NO. 5.   LONDON, JUNE, 1912.   MONTHLY, ONE PENNY.

COMRADES,

I have to thank you with all my heart. You have worked wonders, and you have given the public notice that there are at least some guts left in the British working class. No doubt, the efforts of some of you were prompted by personal friendship, but the bulk of you were upholding Syndicalism and one of its concomitants: anti-militarism.

The untiring efforts and devotion of our excellent friends, George Lansbury on the one hand, and Gaylord Wilshire on the other, not only got me out of gaol, but advertised Syndicalism to an extent that we could not have otherwise dreamed of, and the circulation of our paper has now reached 30,000. This shows clearly that the time is now ripe for a weekly paper, and I propose that THE SYNDICALIST should now be turned into a weekly. But to start on this venture we would want an initial capital of £300. It remains for you to say whether you will have the paper and whether you will procure that sum. Let me know what you think, make your suggestions, and I will print your letters in our next issue. I will make our next number a standard one of six pages, so that you might have an idea of what the paper will be like if turned into a weekly.

Scores of manuscripts have been sent by known and unknown comrades. A great many seem to have become Syndicalists now, and want to write and speak on the subject. I am printing some of these manuscripts, but it must be clearly understood that I am not responsible for the views expressed therein.

Tons of ink have been shed in the capitalist Press for the discussion of Syndicalism, but I have not yet come across anything that approaches the real meaning of it. You ought, therefore, to be careful before you draw conclusions.

Several remittances for THE SYNDICALIST Cash-box have reached me, and I will acknowledge them in our next issue. I have not had the time yet to go through the hundreds of letters that were awaiting me. I must, therefore, ask those of you who have not yet heard from me, to excuse me, and I will do my best to write you in the course of next week.

Now, buck up, comrades. This is the time or never. I am as fit as ever, and Tom will be with us in a few weeks.

That which once upon a time was known as "English liberty" is now a dead letter; it is for us to react. They have tried to gag us, but they have piteously failed. They may again clap some of us into goal, but they won't stop us; our propaganda will go on. Let us use our opportunities to remove all stumbling blocks and leave to our children not a fight, but a victory, and the glory of a world redeemed of poverty and iniquity.

GUY BOWMAN.

OUR PRESIDENT IN GAOL.

SENTENCE OF SIX MONTHS REDUCED TO TWO MONTHS.

WE do not propose to bother our readers with any lengthy details about our president's—Tom Mann's—prosecution and imprisonment. The daily Press has done that with full details and comments. Suffice it to say that in about four weeks' time Tom will be with us again, and our agitation will be resumed with renewed vigour and zeal. Said Tom at Coventry just a few days before his trial: "I am an agitator. To the extent to which the term may be correctly applied to me I gladly welcome it; I certainly do not fight shy of it or shirk it. Only superficially respectable people who have conventional opinions as to morality are so silly as to think unkindly of those who do something to call the attention of men and women to vital questions. To be connected with the stirring up of a man to increased mental activity is to be engaged in work with which good men might be glad to be identified.

"I desire to tell you that the course I am pursuing is because long ago I vowed solemnly to myself that I would put forth all the mental and physical energy of which I am capable in fighting down poverty and in uprooting the causes thereof. In doing that I have received many criticisms, but I have no complaint to make. I never reply. There is quite enough for me to do in keeping my energies concentrated upon the most vulnerable points of the enemy with a view to bringing about their speedy overthrow."

Urging the necessity for the workers to take action industrially at once, Mr. Mann said: "I am like unto John the Baptist in attitude. He believed the day of the Lord was at hand. I believe the day of the people is immediately at hand, but I also know that our day of emancipation cannot come of its own accord. It must be ushered in by the workers without the help of the capitalist class. To-day the capitalists are all-powerful, and our object and determination is to transfer power from the capitalists to the working class. We could then immediately solve the unemployed question.

"I discourage you from taking any sectional action, but urge you without delay to solidify your ranks. We are really in for economic freedom. The day of dirty poverty in this country is now to pass away."

(From the Morning Post.)

Syndicalism is corrupting the citizenship of the working man, for it is persuading him that justice is a fraud and that law is a tyranny, that all property belongs to him, and that he has the right to enforce his interests by violence. He is being persuaded into the fallacy that labour creates all wealth, that capital is his natural enemy, and that he is properly in a state of war both against the employer and the State. There is a strong movement afoot in this country at present to turn the British working man into a Nihilist and to use the Trade Union organisation in pursuit of violent ends—ends which, if attained, would be fatal to the whole community, and chiefly to the working man himself. To foil these attempts will require firmness and courage in the Government and the Magistracy, and also in all good subjects. The movement will spread unless it is dealt with seriously and effectively. If it spreads, then its manifestations will compel the use of the military to a much greater extent than at present, and it is of vital importance that the Army should be secured from the insidious advances and plausible doctrines of the able and unscrupulous men who are in charge of the movement. Parliament is neglectful of these things—altogether absorbed in political log-rolling and party measures; but we venture to warn Parliament that it is their authority which is being attacked, and that if they do not look the danger fairly and squarely in the face they may find the power transferred to the hands of the enemy. We had a foretaste of it in the mining strike, when the movement for surrender was so strong that the citadel was for a time in real danger. This danger will come again; "Six months in the second division" will not much

TOM MANN.

retard it. Parliament must have a constructive policy and a clear view of the danger if it is to come unscathed through the ordeal which looms ahead.

(From the New Age.)

Mr. Tom Mann has not been deceived by the technicality of his imprisonment. Not for inciting soldiers to mutiny, but for stirring the workers to strikes and Syndicalism (the same crime in the eyes of the employing classes) has he been prosecuted and condemned. The argument he advanced in his own defence on the stated legal offence was, moreover, perfectly valid, as the members of the profession very well know. By merely becoming a soldier a man does not become either less or more than a citizen; nor is a private soldier immune from private prosecution merely because he acts under military orders. A soldier in a riot is in no more privileged position than any other citizen. It is at his personal peril, whether under orders or not, that he commits an assault on another citizen; and if he has to stand a court-martial for mutiny in the event of refusing to fire against his better judgment, equally he must stand his trial as a civil murderer if he fires and kills. But the Army, like the Church, claims certain privileges over those of the State. The Church, for example, occasionally declines to recognise the legal marriage of a man and his deceased wife's sister. In this case sensible people ignore the Church. The Army, however, by recording the sentence of mutiny for soldiers refusing to perform an illegal act, not only claim privilege, but have again succeeded in enforcing it, even in a civil court. But again we say that had Mr. Mann been somebody else the prosecution would never have been begun, and certainly he would never have been convicted. We can only say that if he should be allowed to remain in prison, either by the law or by the Trade Unionists on whose behalf he went there, somebody will be disgraced. The transport workers should liberate him if the Home Secretary will not.

ENOUGH !

DEDICATED TO TOM MANN.

By ANNA LINCOLN.

Not forever shall the Toilers
  Travel pathways bleak and bare.
To a "Halt !" must come despoilers.
  We the joys of life will share.
We will strike the blow that shatters
  All that keeps us from our own ;
Sweetest thing in life that matters—
  Liberty ! It *shall* be known !

    (Chorus)

Break ! break the chains, my Brothers,
  Though the links be smooth or rough.
Break them ! for yourselves, for others.
  Break them ! We have bled enough.

We have heard our children wailing
  With the pain that hunger brings ;
We have watched our sisters failing,
  All the land with suffering rings.
Shall our children's future children
  Know as little joy as we ?
Must they, too, be born to bondage ?
  Fathers, strike ! and set them free.

    (Chorus)

Write it now, in Fame's gold letters.
  Deed Immortal ! Not mere puff.
Strike the blow that snaps our fetters ;
  Strike it ! We have bled enough.

We have toiled, and starved, and suffered
  On a pittance, mean and bare ;
We have borne what Fate has offered
  With a patience long and rare.
Of the earth's most bounteous giving
  Must the *workers* have no share ?
Shall the ones who *make* the living
  Only life's grim burdens bear ?

    (Chorus)

Workers of the world, unite !
  Blend your voices, sweet or gruff ;
March ! this is Labour's holy fight !
  Hear us ! We have bled enough !

It is shameful ! it is fearful
  That our human flesh and blood
Should be weary, crushed, and tearful.
  Brothers, stop it ! turn the flood ;
Change it, comrades, make life sweeter ;
  Yours the right, and yours the power.
Here is Liberty ! Come, greet her !
  Break your chains this very hour.

    (Chorus)

Comrades, lift the Red Flag higher,
  With these hands, work-worn and tough,
Runs the murmur, like a fire !
  Hear it ! *We have bled enough !*

Strike for Freedom ! strike for Leisure !
  Strike for manhood's inborn right,
For our sisters' rest and pleasure,
  Strike, my Comrades ! Strike with might !
Millions yet unborn will bless us
  For this stand we take to-day.
Courage ! let that thought caress us,
  As we stand amidst the fray !

    (Chorus)

With a calm deliberation
  (And of which is Truth the stuff
Forge your weapons) win the nation
  Justice ! We have bled *enough !*

INDUSTRIAL SYNDICALIST EDUCATION LEAGUE.

A Reception to

GUY BOWMAN

WILL BE HELD AT

The Shoreditch Town Hall

On SATURDAY, JUNE 22nd.

CINDERELLA. WHIST DRIVE. REFRESHMENTS

For particulars, tickets, &c., apply to—

Mrs. TOM MANN, 23, Engadine-street, Southfields, S.W.; or to

DAVE ARMSTRONG, 15, Netherwood-road, West Kensington-park, W.

SYNDICALISM AND SOCIALISM.

By JACK RADCLIFFE.

The rise of Syndicalism gives new hope, renewed life and energy, to those who were losing heart in the long battle for the economic and social emancipation of the world. We have seen the abject failure of the Revolutionary Socialists to gain even an infinitesimal amount of that representation in Parliament which they assured us, and still assure us, is the essential first step towards the end for which they are striving in common with ourselves. We accept the historical basis of Socialism, its economic teachings and general principles, but we cannot, and do not, accept as necessary corollaries the political methods whereby most Socialists seek to carry their principles into effect.

We are told that economic conditions always produce corresponding political effects, that all political movements are but the phenomena of the underlying economic *noumenon.* This is perfectly true. But when we are told, further, that all political movements must necessarily and inevitably be along the conventional parliamentary channels, we differ. And we have good reason to differ when we see clear and unmistakable evidence to the contrary. The most striking fact in the history of the Socialist movement in this country is its signal failure to find expression in Parliament. The only way Socialists have ever succeeded in getting into Parliament has been by sacrificing their Socialist principles. They have had to compromise, to trim and truckle and conciliate. Men who will do these things before election may thoroughly be depended upon to continue the very same practices afterwards, especially if they have their eyes upon permanent and highly-paid office. We have before us such striking examples of gross betrayal of the working classes by men who, at one time, we all believed to be so sound, so honest, and so strong as to be absolutely incorruptible. Small wonder, then, that the workers view with ever-increasing suspicion those who put themselves forward as "working-class" candidates.

Parliament, from the working-class standpoint, is a dangerous delusion and a deadly snare. The sooner the Socialist movement, as a whole, realises this, the better for it. The reason is not far to seek. Parliament is essentially a capitalist instrument. It is designed, simply and solely, to give expression to, to extend, and to safeguard capitalist interests. It could be made to do nothing else, even were there a strong party of uncompromising Socialist members seated there.

The historical conflict of Whig and Tory, Liberal and Conservative, represented the political antagonism of the once hostile economic interests of industrial capitalism and landed aristocracy. The political phenomena displayed were the natural and spontaneous results of the economic causes. To-day, however, we have a virtual merging of those interests, "Aristocracy" rests no longer upon a territorial basis. We find the Upper House filled with titled manufacturers, financiers, merchants, and tradesmen; we even find bearers of ancient names themselves engaged in industry and commerce, and their sons and daughters intermarrying with those of the once socially despised commercial classes.

Industrial capitalism has triumphed economically, and, as a result, we see the development of a plutocracy whose tendency, politically, is more and more towards oligarchic despotism.

The Parliamentary machine is admirably adapted to give expression to this tendency, and it cannot be made to serve any other purpose. Even if we had a respectable minority of thoroughgoing Socialists in the House of Commons they would be quite as impotent as are the 110 Social Democratic members of the German Reichstag. All they could do would be to act as a permanent opposition for the purpose of causing friction, or, if possible, of bringing the machine to a standstill.

(To be continued.)

The Syndicalist

EDITED UNDER THE AUSPICES OF

The Industrial Syndicalist Education League

Offices—
4, MAUDE TERRACE, WALTHAMSTOW, LONDON, E.

MONTHLY - ONE PENNY.

Post Paid Subscription—
Great Britain or Abroad ... 12 months 1s. 6d.

Bundle Rates—
1s. 6d. per quire, Carriage Paid.

The receipt of a Sample Copy is an invitation to Subscribe.

JUNE, 1912.

THE SYNDICALIST MOVEMENT.

Of the thousands of articles and descriptions of Syndicalism which have appeared in the Press during the past month not one has been written by an actual Syndicalist. Not one speech on Syndicalism by a Syndicalist has been reported, though we have had lengthy reports of anti- and non-Syndicalist utterances upon the subject. The movement has loomed suddenly upon the British public because of the Bowman and Mann prosecutions, and the resultant confusion, arising, as it does, from a belief that Syndicalists are primarily Anti-Militarists, has been stupendous, to say the least about it.

Beyond this belief in Anti-Patriotism, the speakers and writers have stated little more upon Syndicalism than the statement that it works to the end of the miners owning the mines, the railwaymen the railways, and so on throughout all the industries.

Messrs. Ramsay MacDonald, Keir Hardie, and E. W. Jowett, amongst others, have made this last statement the text of their objections to Syndicalism, thus making general a statement which no Syndicalist has ever made nor believed.

Syndicalism does not hold with the position of the mines for the miners, though Syndicalists would prefer even that to the present state of affairs—namely, the mines for the mine-owners, the railways for the shareholders, &c., &c. The mines-for-miners policy might not be as good as is possible, but it is infinitely preferable to the present miserable methods, where all is to the non-producers. It may be well to state here and now where the mistake arose. Syndicalism favours the administration of the mines for the miners on the theory that none know as well as the miners themselves the various details connected with the mining industry.

A tailor could advise as little upon mining requirements as the miner upon tailoring ones. Similarly with all industries. Syndicalism claims that it is only in this fashion that the ideal it holds, "the World for the Workers," can be realised.

Some of the daily papers during the late Coal Strike struck the right note when describing it as a Selfish Strike. The Syndicalist unblushingly favours the Selfish Strike and that kind alone. Syndicalism appeals to the working man to become selfish in his industrial capacity and to thus rob his employers of a monopoly of the attribute. The working man, says the Syndicalist, has too long studied the profits of his masters before the stomachs of his children, and calls the halt. He says that the old-fashioned kind of strike, best described as a pitting of his empty pockets against the bank balances of his employers, is worked out. The Syndicalist decides that two or three weeks is the utmost a strike should continue, and that the workers in all the other industries must be prepared to come to the aid of one that is out. When this theory is supported with sufficient strength by the organised workers

the percentage of Trade Union victories will increase gradually from twenty per cent., at which point it has remained for some considerable time, till it reaches the maximum figure.

Some confusion has arisen as to the connection between Socialism and Syndicalism, and the impression has been arrived at in some quarters that both terms are synonymous. This can hardly be said to be the real case, as the argument of the Syndicalists is that the Trade Union, with its open field for all workers, be their political, religious, and ethical opinions what they may, is essentially the principal workers' movement. Syndicalism asks no questions as to a man's personal belief on outside matters, but organises him on the one and only condition of his being a worker. Many Syndicalists are Socialists and many are not. It is true that the ultimate object of Syndicalism may be said to have many things in common with that of the Socialist, but it must be remembered that it is mainly as a present-day movement that Syndicalism considers itself, and it is only through its present efficacy that it claims the attention of the workers, organised and unorganised. Syndicalism appeals to the unorganised as well as the organised by its advocacy of immediate benefits, such as the reduction of working hours, minimum rates of pay, and increases in wages. It is because this new movement shows the best way towards the attainment of these demands that it is receiving the support of the Labour organisations. The impression that the recent Coal Strike was a Syndicalist battle is a mistaken one, though the Syndicalist appreciates it as an experiment in Labour solidarity. Solidarity is a term which Syndicalists are never tired of using, being, as it is in reality, the spirit forcing them forward.

Syndicalists would have conducted the Coal Strike in a different fashion to what took place. They would have given a few hours' notice in place of the six weeks of the miners.

If this had not been sufficient to ensure the success of their demands they would have availed themselves of the aid of the Transport Workers' Federation and of the Railway Servants' Union. The strike would not then have lasted over a month. A week would have seen the men's demands granted, and this with but a tithe of the suffering which has prevailed throughout the country.

Syndicalism has come to stay, and with it has come a broader outlook to the Trade Unionist. It is converting the Unions from an ineffective defensive policy to a successful aggressive one. From a host of petty bickering and struggling Unions it is welding a gigantic hammer of Labour. It will make the poorest organised body of workers as strong and stronger than the strongest of present-day Unions by giving it the backing and support of the massed might of the united workers. This movement was inevitable, apart from the efforts of the Syndicalist agitators. Every industrial country in the world now has its Syndicalist movement under different names. From the American "Industrial Workers of the World" to the South African Industrial Union, from the "Confederations of Labour" in France, Spain, Portugal, and Italy to the latest in Japan, all are advocating the new movement. They will be the force against International Blacklegging just as in each country they prevent internal disputes and until their ideal is gained —the administering of the industries in each country by the workers in the interest of the whole of the working community—there will be no peace.

Syndicalism has come to stay. Not even the Syndicalists could stop it.

AT THE OLD BAILEY.

The sentence of nine months' hard labour inflicted on Guy Bowman, the publisher of the Syndicalist, has resounded painfully in the hearts of all those interested in the doctrines he propagates, and universal indignation is felt at the injustice of this excessive penalty. The six months' hard labour imposed on the printers, the brothers Buck, is still more cruel, especially as one of them "made an appeal for mercy to the judge on the ground that they printed the Syndicalist simply as a matter of busi-

ness, for he and his brother had no sympathy with the ideas expressed in the newspaper."

Even the hostile Press itself has been moved to indignation, and protests loudly against this inadmissible condemnation. The *Pall Mall Gazette* and *Daily Express*, however, must rejoice! Is it not owing to their reiterated denunciation that this pursuit was made? Do they not deserve the title of detectives, for which questionable office they have shown marvellous aptitude?

Yet, if we are to believe the *Daily News*, the Government has acted very injudiciously in according such special attention to the Syndicalist, and endowing it with a notoriety which cannot fail to be profitable to its propaganda and the diffusion of its ideas. The *Daily News* says:

How many or how few of the nation's soldiers have been reached, through the Syndicalist, by the appeal to the Army, which has now, thanks to the Old Bailey trial, been scattered through the length and breadth of the land?

Exactly! Who now in the United Kingdom will ignore the existence of the dear little paper? Thanks to this inimical publicity, it suddenly attains world-wide celebrity. And then the trial! The account of it has been read and re-read, the description of it all, and especially of the enunciation of the famous letter which startled all the judicial apparatus and which rang out as the rhythmic cadence of a poetic strophe :

"*Open Letter to British Soldiers.*"

The words seemed to resound melodiously through the court, pronounced with a different enunciation by Judge, accuser, and advocate; and while some faces became more and more gloomy, others were radiant with a strange, irrepressible emotion.

Oh, glowing memories! Moments never to be forgotten! Unshakable conviction shown in a high resolve!

Such were our impressions of the time spent in the Court of Justice.

History records that the early Christians gazed heavenwards, smiling, while the wild beasts, to whom the Romans threw them, were actually mauling their flesh with bloody jaws. And it was this bloodshed by the martyrs which caused the triumph of Christianity.

In our day Christians are no longer victims, but are persecutors instead. It seems that they forget that every heart-felt cause draws to itself its own apostles and martyrs; that the more cruel and unjust the persecution is the stronger will be the exalted spirit of self-sacrifice which does not hesitate before the gift of life itself. Fierce repression, iniquitous punishments, implacable sentences only serve to favour the triumph of the ideas persecuted, and to render the defamed cause even more beautiful and attractive than before.

The British public has realised this, hence the indignation roused so fiercely against this verdict. The public is right if they realise that neither months nor years of prison, nor even the menace of death, can stifle a living conscience which proclaims universal pity and brotherhood. No earthly condemnation can annihilate the courage and faith of the defenders of true solidarity, the teachers of that spirit of brotherhood which instils mutual love and forbids mutual destruction.

With head erect and gaze fixed on the sublime ideal of peace and universal welfare, they press forward, regardless of blows, insensible to danger, and to the accumulated obstacles of the way; and thus do they draw into their train, not the faint-hearted cowards who would prove a useless encumbrance, but those who are filled with burning conviction, who are athirst for justice, and who suffer acutely in witnessing the cruel social inequalities and iniquities.

To arouse such devotion, to manifest a superb harvest of robust and undaunted enthusiasm, sentences like that pronounced at the Old Bailey on March 22, 1912, are necessary: they are the touchstone of virile resolution, of absolute conviction.

Let us, then, be thankful to these calumniating newspapers who act as purveyors to the British prisons, to these jurymen whose names ought to be immortalised, to Mr. Justice Horridge for his world-famous judgment. They have only helped the Syndicalist to more power: they have only attracted far deeper sympathy to a sacred cause : The Cause of the Workers.

There are many names of prominent Syndicalists, rightly headed by Georges Sorel, mentioned in Sombart's book on "Socialism and Syndicalism," published by Deny, but Hervé's does not appear.

The difference between Syndicalism and Socialism is the difference between walking upstairs and sliding down the banisters. The first is a little more tedious than the other, but it is better exercise, and you can start up from where your are, whereas to slide down you must first mount up, and as mounting up means mounting up a majority vote for Socialism, we are not sure of ever even getting started.

THE LID OF THE DINNER PAIL

By GEORGIA KOTSCH.

Russianised Lawrence has lifted it that the world may look in.

The House Committee on Rules is investigating conditions there, and Socialist Representative Berger presented as an exhibit thirteen " sallow-cheeked, hollow-eyed, poorly-clad children " and six adults.

"I don't believe my children would know the taste of butter," said Samuel Lipson, one of the latter.

"Why did you strike?" he was asked.

"Because I could not make a living for my wife and four children. I am a skilled workman, and my average wages were nine or ten dollars a week. But there was so much slack time in Lawrence that sometimes I got only three and four dollars, and we had to live on that."

He described how John Ramey, a striker, was bayoneted to death by the militia because he exhorted women and children not to return to work unless their demands were granted.

A hat was passed for the benefit of the child workers, and J. H. Cox, a mill-owner, put in a bill. Berger flung it back at him, saying, "It is blood money."

The average wage in Lawrence is six dollars a week. It is figured that a single man could live on that if he never wore a collar, rain-coat, or rubbers, never used a handkerchief or umbrella, never shaved or bathed, never rode on a street car, had a doctor or dentist, bought a book or flower, beer, tobacco, pastry, or condiments of any kind. He must be a human animal. Thirty thousand people in Lawrence have this problem to face.

These people are called "ignorant foreigners," but they are teaching the American workers a lesson in solidarity which they much need to learn. No people on the face of the earth are such self-deceived egotists, such easy marks, as Americans. There is a reason for it, and the day of awakening is at hand. With a fertile continent of seemingly limitless opportunity stretching westward it is no wonder the people did not stop to haggle with the revolutionary forefathers over their valuation of themselves and of the brand of freedom they had achieved, and so while the people were forging their own fortunes the false declarations as to liberty and equality were allowed to stand and fasten themselves on the minds of successive generations. Of late years these, with the spurious patriotism of "My country, right or wrong," have been sedulously instilled into the young through church, school, and Press. Some years ago the workers were insulted by a campaign slogan of "The Full Dinner Pail," and sordidly, shamelessly, followed it to the polls. That was before the pinch of the stomach had reached to the brain, before Socialism had fairly begun its irradiating work in this country. That would be a suicidal slogan for any political party now.

Since the bloody shirt lost its potency, tariff twaddle and gold standard gush have been used to divide the workers and befuddle them until, lo ! under the blessings of both we are face to face with the stark-naked fact of thirty thousand people starving at work. The lid is off.

There are no more fertile lands to be had for the taking. All this country's vast resources are in the control of a handful of capitalists who dictate prices and wages. It seems reasonable that Americans, thus brought up with a sudden jerk, the door of opportunity slammed in their faces, with little of the conservative tradition of older countries to hold them back, may, in spite of past complacency, become the most implacable of rebels.

High tariff has been good for the masters, for one mill paid for itself in profits in two years, and the president of the trust admits he does not know how many automobiles he owns. But tariff or free trade, what of it? The Lawrence strikers were attacked by police under orders of a Republican mayor, soldiers under orders from a Democratic governor and all at the will of Democrat and Republican mill-owners.

This battle for bread was precipitated by the passage of a fifty-four hour per week law, said to have been a compro-

mise between Labour leaders and textile magnates, and, like so many Labour laws, valueless—aye, a positive injury to the workers. It is said the Labour leaders promised to call no strikes in case the Bill was passed, and the mill-owners turned it to advantage by reducing wages and speeding up, saving light and power by the reduction in time and getting the same amount of work done. The Labour leaders did not call the strike. It is an I.W.W. strike and the American Federation of Labour is scabbing against it—rail-road men delivering raw material, craft union electrical workers furnishing light and power, and the stationary firemen working—all helping to drive the strikers back to a lingering death. The I.W.W. is the nearest representative of Syndicalism in America. Among the strikers all craftlines are wiped out. All nationalities are standing together. Haywood says : " The prudence and self-discipline of the strikers have been wonderful. Such a manifestation of solidarity has seldom been displayed in any struggle."

On Saturday, February 24, occurred the blackest disgrace of capitalism in this country. Arrangements were made to care for the children of the strikers by Socialists, and the I.W.W. in New York. Mothers brought them to the train to give them into charge of the committee. The little ones were looking forward to good times, good things to eat, and warm clothes. At the station a "law and order" riot was precipitated by police thugs, who choked and clubbed mothers, knocked down and kicked children about. One pregnant mother was taken to the hospital in a critical condition. Thus does capitalism treat the "sacred" mothers it prates about and the homes it is so afraid Socialism will destroy. Children were kept in cells all day.

Fifteen impartial doctors examined the first delegation of children taken from Lawrence to New York and found every one suffering from malnutrition. Asked by Elizabeth Gurley Flynn if this was from the hard times of the strike, they said, "No; it was *malnutrition extending back to their birth, and even to starvation before their birth.*"

This strike has lifted the lid, exposing a condition which has existed while our Press has been prating about prosperity, and the wool barons have had lecturers in Southern Europe luring dupes to America by showing a picture of working women in Lawrence with aprons full of coin going to the bank.

Mrs. Taft and several handsomely gowned women attended the investigation and "gasped with horror" at its revelations. Their gasps are being printed broadcast by the papers which all these years have had no space for the gasps of hunger and exhaustion of these poor slaves. There will be other gasps due when the class to which these ladies belong realises the meaning of this beginning of solidarity among the workers.

Lawrence is exposed. Other American cities are not—yet. Even in Los Angeles, the city of boost and boom, in the heart of the land of promise, I know of a family of three all working and getting altogether but $15 per week.

Even the capitalist papers are decrying the Lawrence conditions vehemently. The masters themselves are alarmed at being caught with the goods, but are like a man running down hill who cannot stop even though he sees the whirlpools at the bottom. For remedy they only set up their grinning monkey-killer and another shibboleth, " The interests of the people." Many workers will be deceived again, but an ever-increasing number will not, but will base their hope upon solid organisation on the economic field. They are losing interest in the shibboleths of the masters, and are thinking only of getting possession of the industries of the country and running them for their own benefit. It has long been said : " Oh, you can't get the working people to stand together." You English workers are demonstrating that they can and do stand together. The eyes of the world are upon you. The inspiration of your solidarity is telling in America. Nothing so hopeful for working America has ever happened as this germ of solidarity at brave, bleeding Lawrence.

MALATESTA RELEASE COMMITTEE

A Mass Protest Meeting

to Demand the Immediate Release of

MALATESTA

WILL BE HELD IN

TRAFALGAR SQUARE, on Sunday, June 9th, at 4 p.m.

Chairman : **J. F. GREEN,** Secretary International Arbitration and Peace Association.

Speakers : **BEN TILLETT, CUNNINGHAME-GRAHAM, GUY BOWMAN**
Mrs. DESPARD, Mrs. MANN, Mrs. BAKER.

CHARLES E. LEE,	W. PONDER,	J. TOCHATTI,
LESLIE FOYNE,	P. E. TANNER,	W. B. PARKER,
Mrs. AGNES HENRY,	A. B. MACE,	A. RAY,
F. J. PASSEMORE,	GUY A. ALDRED,	R. ROCKER.

AN OPEN LETTER TO THE LABOUR PARTY M.P.'S.

By A WORKING MINER.

Dear Comrades,—I earnestly hope that you will not resent my addressing you as comrades. I will confess that that £400 a year of yours makes me feel small, but, nevertheless, I will venture with your permission to call you comrades.

Having been a staunch supporter of the Labour Party from its inception, I consider I have a right to ask you a few questions regarding your hours of labour, and other details in connection with your Parliamentary duties. There are some statements that have been made by some of you of late which I do not understand, and I hope that you will not put me down as "impertinent" and "cheeky." I have a right to question and criticise your statements and actions because I am one of the class whom you profess to represent. During the debate on the "Mines (Minimum Wage) Bill" I had the pleasure, or perhaps the misfortune to go through your workshop, the House of Commons.

It is a very fine building, and the spring-seated lounges must be very comfortable to sit upon. I would never have dreamt that a capitalist Liberal Government would supply you with such elaborate surroundings and pay you such a nice minimum wage as well.

Comrades, you are lucky. You miners who sit there must feel it strange, no loose roof, no soft coal, no danger of an explosion, no stop pay; you are in clover. Do answer me a few questions, for by so doing you will decide and clear up an argument between myself and a friend.

(1) Do you get paid whether you are there or not?

(2) Is it a weekly salary or a yearly one?

(3) Are there any stoppages?

He says "yes" to the first, and that the salary is yearly and no stoppages.

During my visit there, I saw many of your work-stools vacant and met many of you with your hands in your trousers pockets wandering about the place, or smoking in the refreshment room. Surely you do not get paid for that? If you do, you ought to refuse it, for according to your own statements to us all men that get paid for being idle are parasites, and I am quite certain that you would never allow yourselves to be drawn into any contract that would make parasites of you. Please do not be offended by my asking you these questions, because you all know that all the money that there is in the Treasury Fund was created by and through the sweat of the brow of Labour, and you all believe that all the products of labour ought to be spent as economically as possible.

That is my reason for asking these questions. My friend has taken up an excruciatingly funny attitude of late. He says, "That the £400 a year has been more of a curse than a blessing to our class, that you in your luxurious occupation have forgotten the men who sent you there." He is willing to stake all he holds dear in this life against a wooden spoon that I could not easily find out by your speeches in the House of Commons whether you are members of the Conservative, Liberal, Nationalist, or the Labour Party. "Mr. J. H. Thomas," said he, "in that House during the railway strike, stated that the interests of capital and labour were identical." Lord Claud Hamilton must have lent Mr. Thomas a "bourgeoise book" on

Economics in order to get that statement. They do not represent us; their defence of us could never be so tame if they did. He asks me not to support you any longer. He threw that statement of Stephen Walsh in my face. "I am a citizen first and a trade unionist after, and by the way," he said, "did you hear Mr. Ramsay MacDonald in his speech on the Mines' Bill, when he said, 'that he hoped that there was no member of any Party in the House who would go out and say that the Liberal Government thought that 5s. and 2s. was too much for a day's wage in the mines?'" If MacDonald said that, then I am afraid that what my friend says is true. He must have forgot who sent him there, and was speaking to the gallery and not for his class, for, after the tame appeal which he made, and also the false statement which he made, "that the miners were ready to forego the schedules, if the 5s. and 2s. were inserted in the Bill," every fair-minded man must clearly see that the Liberal Government did see 5s. and 2s. too much.

He also said that the Miners' Labour M.P.'s were as tame as rabbits, and really I am nearly convinced that he spoke the truth, for as I look back over the history of that week I feel ashamed of you.

You knew what the men were out for—you all knew. You ought to have told Mr. Asquith and his Government that you did not object to him passing all kinds of Acts of Parliament, but if they did not contain what the men were asking for, then you would go back to the men and tell them to be firm and to refuse to accept them. You could challenge the whole King's Army and Navy; they could never force us down those black holes through which so many of us have gone down never to return alive. You simply went for palliatives. Why are you so tame in that House? Is there anything in the atmosphere which contaminates you? What is the charm?

I heard a bloated Member of capitalist class making a statement that though the miners were killed and injured they were receiving compensation for it, and, good Heavens! you sat there like so many tame rabbits, when you ought to have forced such a statement down his vile throat.

Why are you gagged? Why not speak inside as you do outside? Can it be possible that what my friend says is true? Oh, ye gods of the Labour Movement, the workers have risen you to your golden pedestal; from there you look down upon us; you are prepared to do anything in order to remain there, betray your own people, sell your very souls, put aside your convictions. "What shall we do to get back if we do get from here by voting the Government out?" Such are some of the questions asked by some of you.

You were a lot of fine fellows outside of that House, and I am going to do my best to get you from there, to reclaim you, to give you back your manhood, to give you back your good names.

The golden tinsel has been too much for you; you are all right at heart. Circumstances have been too strong for you; the limelight of publicity has dazzled you. Fellow workers, be true to your class. Give those that believe and that have an interest in the House of Commons their true place. Ours is the workshop, factory, mines, railways, farms, fields, ships, etc. Let the House of Commons die a natural death, and be men.

Tom Mann's

Penny Pamphlets

No. 1.—PREPARE FOR ACTION.
No. 2.—THE TRANSPORT WORKERS.
No. 3.—FORGING THE WEAPON.
No. 4.—ALL HAIL, SOLIDARITY!
No. 5.—SYMPOSIUM ON SYNDICALISM.
No. 6.—A MANCHESTER MESSAGE TO THE WORKERS OF ENGLAND.
No. 7.—PARLIAMENTARY ACTION versus SYNDICALISM, 2d.
No. 8.—MINERS, WAKE UP!
No. 9.—THE WEAPON SHAPING.
No. 10.—A TWO-FOLD WARNING.
No. 11.—THE RAILWAYMEN.
No. 12.—THE TRANSPORT INDUSTRY.

A dozen will cost you 1s. 3d., post free, and any one of them is worth that. A FACT.

Send to GUY BOWMAN,
4, MAUDE TERRACE, WALTHAMSTOW, LONDON, E.   DO IT NOW!

THE MINERS' SONG.
By JIM CONNELL.

Air—"Deep in Canadian woods we've met."

Deep in the gloom of the great earth's womb
  We force the birth of coal,
The power that moves the nation's wheels
  To the furnace fires we roll.
We dig out wealth at the cost of health
  To guild oppression's shrine;
    'Twill aye be so
    For a wage of woe
Till the miners own the mine.

We furnish forth to the south and north
  The force that drives the mill;
We make the snorting engine dash
  Through forest, fen, and hill;
We rush the lordly ocean craft
  Across the bounding brine;
    'Twill aye be so
    For a wage of woe
Till the miners own the mine.

We move the ranks of the cogs and cranks
  Which grind out food and clothes;
We warm the walls of the festive halls
  When the wintry tempest blows;
We cook the fare and we make the glare
  Where lords and ladies dine;
    'Twill aye be so
    For a wage of woe
Till the miners own the mine.

We take the risk of the awful whisk
  When the rotten cable breaks;
We pierce the deadly after-damp
  When the shattered ceiling shakes;
We search the wreck for mangled mates
  And health and life resign;
    'Twill aye be so
    For a wage of woe
Till the miners own the mine.

But we see a light through the breaking night
  And a smiling dawn we greet.
We'll toil no more in the planet's core
  For a crust and a winding sheet;
We'll drive despair from the bright'ning air,
  And hands and hearts combine;
    And we'll find our health
    In the Commonwealth
When the miners own the mine.

MALATESTA RELEASE FUND.

Subscriptions are received by Guy A. Aldred, 17, Richmond Gardens, Shepherd's Bush, W., and J. F. Tanner, 13, Beadon Road, Hammersmith.

Subscriptions Received.

Acknowledged in *Daily Herald*, May 28	6	10	9
G. Davison	5	0	0
F. T. del Marmol	1	1	0
A Malatesta-ist	1	0	0
Lawrence		2	6
J. C.		2	0
J. B.		5	0
F. C.		1	0
Brighton Comrade		4	0
Amy Haynes		5	0
J. Whitfield		1	0
James Leakey		10	6
Guy Bowman		5	0
	£15	7	9

Where to Buy "The Syndicalist."

The following are the names and addresses of our wholesale and retail newsagents from whom the Syndicalist may be had:—

London.—The National Labour Press, St. Bride's House, Salisbury Square, E.C.

  ,,   London and Suburban Publishing Co., 9, St. Bride's Avenue, E.C.

  ,,   J. Jaques, 191, Old Street, E.C.

  ,,   W. Tarbart, 316, Kentish Town Road, N.W.

  ,,   E. Denton, 427, High Road, Willesden, N.W.

Birmingham.—The National Labour Press, 100, John Bright Street.

Blaina.—Holman, High Street

Bristol.—John Flynn, 19, Horsefair.

Burnley.—J. Tamlyn, 50, Burnley Road

Dundee.—L. Macartney, 203, Overgate

Glasgow.—David G. Lindsay, 139, West Nile Street, and 132, Gairbraid Street, Maryhill.

Leeds.—B. Goldberg, 14, Millwright Street

Manchester.—Sam Brierley, 328, Hyde Road, Ardwick (wholesale).

  ,,   Abel Heywood, 56 and 58, Oldham Street.

  ,,   M. Hyde, 84, Victoria Market, Oldham

  ,,   Brady and Co., 22, London Road

  ,,   J. G. Hewkins, 14A, Cannon Street.

Newcastle-on-Tyne.—J. A. Wilson, 223, Shields Road

Sheffield.—A. M. Barton, 46, Stannington Road.

You can't change human nature. Can't, eh? Did you ever see a raw recruit turned into a veteran? Oh, that is military training. Syndicalism proposes that the raw recruits of labour shall be trained into veterans of labour by training in their Industrial Unions. When the hour strikes for Syndicalism the men to enter the new state of society will already have had their natures changed. It sounds funny, but it is not so funny as it sounds when you get down to the bottom of the Syndicalist philosophy.

THE MALATESTA AND MALECKA CASES.

MALATESTA is an Italian count, who for years has been in the forefront of the struggle for liberty, not only in Italy, but in practically every nation in Europe. In fact, so well known and effective have been his efforts, that he has been banished from Europe, and to-day this country is his only refuge. He has been living here quietly for the past twelve years, unknown to the public, and would be unknown to-day were it not for the police wishing to justify their existence by working up a ridiculous case of libel against him. He was charged with libelling by calling a Turkish spy a certain Belelli, another Italian, who has recently recanted the anarchist faith. Ordinarily a family quarrel between anarchists would never get to court, but in this case the police thought it worth while to arrange that poor Malatesta, dying of consumption, should get his three months hard. Even after the sentence was actually pronounced

MALATESTA.

a police sergeant was allowed to go into the box and deliver a harangue about the dangerous character of Malatesta, and yet when he was pinned down for evidence he had none. But this did not prevent the judge recommending that Malatesta be deported when he has served his sentence.

As the "Manchester Guardian" says:

"It will have astonished some people, a correspondent writes, to learn from the case of Signor Enrico Malatesta that every political refugee in this country is being carefully watched by the police, whether he has done anything wrong or is ever likely to, or not. There are several reasons for this. For one thing the police think that a person who has escaped from the persecutions of his Government is a restless character, and, therefore, likely to cause some trouble even in this country should a critical moment come. This, of course, is sheer prejudice, as everyone can judge who has had the opportunity of coming into private contact with the refugees. But a much stronger reason, and one more characteristic of police methods, is that the police all over the world are acting in the closest co-operation in the pursuit of criminals, and through this co-operation they have evolved a feeling of solidarity and a practice of mutual help which, shameful as it is to have to say it, extends even to political cases which would be no offence in free England. Hence it is that the Russian Government, without incurring much expense in maintaining agents in its own, can find out at any moment from Scotland Yard the whereabouts of this or that refugee and lay hands on him should he leave these shores and proceed to Russia.

"Any political refugee of note, says our correspondent, could tell interesting stories of his experience of the watching methods of the English police. The favourite way is simply to call from time to time at their houses under some fanciful pretext. One day an unknown gentleman will call on a refugee to ascertain on behalf of the Post Office whether a letter of his has not gone astray. Another time a representative of Messrs. Smith and Brown, of Fenchurch-street, will call to ascertain the character of Mr. Harris Myers or Ivan Petroff, who had applied to the said firm for a situation and had given his 'friend' the refugee as reference. The pretexts are so transparent that the pestered foreigner soon gets to know the real character of the callers in jacket-suits and hard felt hats, and begins to send them about their business. But that matters little, as the object of the visit is gained as soon as the detective catches a glimpse of his man. The object is merely to find out whether the refugee is still living at his address, or else to give a fresh man on the job a chance of getting to know his features."

"One of the leading Italian correspondents in London, himself an Italian Imperialist, tells me that there are no two opinions about Signor Malatesta among the Italian community here, whatever their politics may be. Malatesta is universally respected and admired as a great intellectual and idealist who has sacrificed every material interest to his convictions and now earns his livelihood in London 'as a mechanic.' All Italy is interested in the case, and your leading article of Saturday was telephoned (most Continental correspondents send their news by telephone, not by telegraph) to the chief Italian papers."

Let the workers learn international solidarity from the police. We join in the protest against the very thought of deporting Malatesta. Instead of deporting men of such ideals we should really have a Treasury grant enabling others like him to domicile themselves in this country. Spain never recovered from the deportation of the Moors, and if England wishes to descend one step further in her failure to recognise the best and good of mankind, it is quite in line to deport Malatesta. However, we do not fear any such result. Little as the country lives up to its traditional pretence of protection of freedom of conscience we still think we are somewhat better off than Russia.

And this brings us to the Malecka case. Here is a woman, born in this country, and by our laws a British subject. She goes to Poland to teach music. She confessedly had, and has, a belief in Socialism, and she has been on friendly terms with Socialists in Poland. All this is, of course, perfectly legal in this country, and heretofore, presumably legal in any other country. Never before have we known any country take it upon itself to punish its own subjects, let alone a foreigner, on account of merely holding an opinion. And yet this is what Russia proposes to do to Miss Malecka. We pass by as unworthy of credence the evidence offered against her by the professional Russian police perjurers and spies who pretended to connect her with active propaganda. The only evidence against her which holds water is that she is a Socialist, and this she does not attempt to deny.

Although described in the Russian indictment as a British subject, Russia now puts in the claim that, owing to her father having been some forty years ago a Russian subject, although now a Britisher, that, therefore, she is a Russian subject.

Upon the evidence submitted she has been sentenced to Siberia for life, a sentence which, considering her state of health, means her early death.

The question arises, What are we Britishers going to do about it? Are we going to let Miss Malecka be crushed to death between Russian money-bags and British money-bags? Or are we going to use such measures that will make the Russian Bear drop his prey from his bloody hug?

We say advisedly that it is purely a question of money, of property rights, that jeopardises her life. The Russian Capitalist thinks that even having Socialist opinions is a threat on his property rights. And he is right. If enough had the same opinion that Miss Malecka has his rights would be exterminated.

The British Capitalist, on the other hand, fears, if Sir Edward Grey is too insistent upon Miss Malecka's release, that it may cause Russia to throw her friendship to Germany, and thus imperil British interests, capitalist interests, in case of war.

The people who really feel most deeply for Miss Malecka are the workers, and the only way they can effectively make their feelings count is by industrial action. Let the British workers refuse to unload Russian ships, let them refuse to handle any goods either going to Russia or coming from that land of blood, and we would quite soon see Sir Edward Grey change his attitude.

The way to save Miss Malecka is to strike at the money-bag of the nation—not at its heart.

What is said about Miss Malecka applies to Enrico Malatesta, and especially does it apply to Tom Mann. With Solidarity of Labour there would be no such persecutions. The workers would demand, not supplicate. Long live Syndicalism.

CAPITALISTS AND THIEVES.

Les Temps Nouveaux, a Paris journal, published in its number of Feb. 15, 1912, an article by Malatesta which may serve to completely enlighten us upon the principles of the man whom the police have been pleased to show up as a dangerous being. It was at the time of the Houndsditch and Sidney Street tragedies.

These thieves (wrote Malatesta) were Russians, perhaps Russian refugees, and maybe they also went to an Anarchist club on days of public meetings, when they were open to everybody. And naturally the capitalist Press avails itself to declare war upon the Anarchists. If one were to believe the bourgeois papers one would think that anarchy, that dream of justice and love amongst men, is nothing but theft and assassination; and with these lies and calumnies they certainly succeed in turning away from us many people who would be with us if they only knew what we want.

Thus it will not be useless to state once more the position of Anarchists respecting the theory and practice of theft.

One of the fundamental points of Anarchism is the abolition of the monopoly of the land, raw material, and the instruments of production, and thereby the abolition of the exploitation of other people's labour by those who hold the means of production. Any appropriation of other people's labour, everything that serves to enable a man to live without giving to society his quota of production is, from the Anarchist and Socialist point of view, a theft.

The landlords, the capitalists have stolen from the people, by violence or by fraud, the land and all the means of production, and in consequence of this initial theft they are enabled, day by day, to take away from the workers the products of labour. But they were happy thieves, for they became strong; they made laws in order that they might justify their situation, and they have organised a whole system of repression to defend themselves against the claims of the workers as well as against those who would like to replace them by doing as they did themselves. And to-day their theft is called property, commerce, industry, &c., the name of "thief" being reserved, in common language, for those who would like to follow the example of the capitalists, but, because they arrived too late and in adverse circumstances, cannot do it without putting themselves in conflict with the law.

However, the difference of names currently used does not suffice to hide the moral and social character of the two situations. The capitalist is a thief who has succeeded either by his merits or by those of his ancestors; the thief is an aspiring capitalist who is but waiting to succeed to become a capitalist, in fact, and live without working on the product of his theft, that is to say, on other people's labour.

As enemies of the capitalists, we cannot sympathise for the thief who aspires at becoming a capitalist, and being in favour of their expropriation by the people for the profit of all, we cannot, as Anarchists, have anything in common with an operation whose object is to get some wealth to pass from the hands of one owner into those of another. . . .

Thus Anarchist ideas cannot drive people to become thieves any more than to become capitalists. On the contrary, by giving to the discontented an ideal of superior life, and a hope of collective emancipation, they turn away, as far as possible in the present midst, from all these legal or illegal doings which are but an adaptation to the capitalist system and tend towards perpetuating it.

Notwithstanding all this, the social midst being so strong and personal temperaments so different, there might possibly be amongst the Anarchists a few who go in for thieving as there are some who go in for commerce or industry; but in that case both are acting, not because of their Anarchist ideas, but in spite of these.

E. MALATESTA.

CORRESPONDENCE.

SHE LIKES US.

To the Editor of the SYNDICALIST.

SIR,—I wish to thank you for the refreshing draught you have given to my soul, in having created such a paper as the SYNDICALIST.

We (my husband and I) have only just made its acquaintance, but find ourselves immediately at home with its teachings. We have been Socialists for some years now, and have grown weary of waiting for some of its fruit to ripen. But alas! Socialism is a slow growing tree, and we (and many others) have despaired of ever tasting its promised delights.

We have groaned aloud, and wept in secret that nothing was being *done*. That talk, and talk *only*, was the fare of our day.

And lo! We find the SYNDICALIST, and all it stands for!

And our hearts are encouraged by the realisation that the Syndicalists mean to *do* something. At last! at last! Long live the SYNDICALIST!

And all power to the men and women under its flag!

I know you are busy men, who handle life's grim facts from morn till night, but you must find time (and patience) to read my letter, for I am a sick woman. A woman living under the shadow of death. And I want to tell you that though your army is a small one now, it will grow amazingly, and numbers will be lost count of, for there are many, very many, ripe for its plan of action.

Never doubt it! Keep on in great faith, as you are doing, you splendid band of men. And as you are *living* for it, if it be necessary, *die* for it.

I cannot think of a nobler or more-to-be desired death.

If only I might come out and fight amongst you all in this great fight.

But I am helpless. Thanks to the murderous system of life to-day, I am in the ranks of the crushed and broken. The doctors tell us I am dying; not of an incurable disease, but for want of such every-day remedies as bread, and meat, and milk. My husband is nearly blind, and numbers another to the almost countless multitude of victims of the Capitalist system that you are all sworn to destroy.

So you will see we cannot work for you in the open, and we cannot help you with money, eagerly though we wish to. I send you the only help in my power, in the enclosed song. If you care to accept it, you may have and its copyright. If you print it in your columns, and you ask some musical sympathiser to set it to stirring, powerful music, it could be printed and sold for the aid of the SYNDICALIST. May I be happy in the thought that this song of mine is the first *Syndicalist* song? It has been much admired, both by Socialists and Labourites, but—they say it is "too strong," *too* revolutionary.

Can anything *be* too strong to voice the injustice of our day?

Is it "too strong" for the Syndicalists also? If so, then it is hopeless, and I had better cast it to the kindly flames.

My husband and I do not think it is too strong. We both believe it would (when set to music) make any gathering of men and women *feel* these things which its words express.

Can you not print the words on an inexpensive leaflet (like a hand-bill) *immediately*, and sell them, and *get* them sold throughout England for our Tom Mann's "Don't Shoot" fund? Tens of thousands would gladly buy one of the copies at a penny *for* the "Don't Shoot" fund who would have no truck with *Syndicalism*.

I give it to you. It is the only way I can help our Tom Mann. If you want it, use it in any way you think best, with or without my name on it. That is of little moment.

But if it can be used to bring grist to the mill I shall be glad, for I shall feel then that I am helping the cause I have so much at heart. *And* the song (the words of it, I mean) is good propaganda.

I have other Labour songs and poems if you want them. Ano my husband has some "anvil stroke" articles, if you would care to see them.

Our only desire is to help the Cause. And whether you accept my song or reject it, we are with you in aim and sympathy, and will do whatever lies in our power to teach and to preach Syndicalism.

If, for any reason whatever you return my song, give me the satisfaction, please, of knowing *why*.—Faithfully yours,

ANNA LINCOLN.

ASTRONOMICAL SYNDICALISM.

(From the *Daily Standard*.)

BIRTH OF NEW WORLDS.

(From Our New York Correspondent.)

The little group of scientists who are now watching nightly on the summit of Mount Wilson, in California, are being enthralled by a vision of forming worlds and the birth of a new astral system in space, according to reports just received by Professor David P. Todd, of the Amherst College Observatory. A thousand million times greater than our own solar system, a vast celestial system seems to be taking form out of murky nebulæ. A photograph of the mighty event —one of the most remarkable ever made—has been prepared by Dr. Edward A. Fath, the leader of the party, with the aid of the huge 60in. reflector. The picture shows the spiral nebulae apparently in the act of crystallising into new suns.

"The announcement reads as if it were genuine," said Professor Todd on receipt of the news. "I hope that later dispatches fully verify it, for it demonstrates a thing that has long been contended for among astronomers. That is, that we should have telescopes of a much larger size than any now in operation. We have understood for many years that our own solar system was not the only pebble on the solar beach. What is described as having been discovered is just what, according to our theories, may occur at any time, and in any part of the heavens.

"The most remarkable thing is that the process of start formation seems to have been caught at the moment of beginning its change from the nebulous state. Nothing like that has ever occurred before in the history of astronomy. It is only by a long and slow process that the nebulous gases of the heavens become the fixed light points which we know as stars, but is not at all remarkable that a whole system should begin to crystallise out of the gases at one time."

INTERNATIONAL MINERS' CONGRESS.

To the Editor of the SYNDICALIST.

DEAR COMRADE AND FELLOW-WORKER,—As you may know, the International Congress of the Miners will take place in the month of July at Amsterdam. The Conservative trade unions published already their intention to receive the foreign delegates and to make their acquaintance. The revolutionary Syndicalists are no less desirous to meet the foreign delegates. But as we don't know the English delegates, we would be very much obliged to you if you could find out whether some of them are sympathising with the revolutionary movement. If so, would you have the kindness to ask them if they are willing to make the acquaintance of the Dutch comrades and to pronounce a short speech about English labour conditions in a public meeting at Amsterdam? If the English delegates, or one of them, agree, could you ask them to forward their answer directly to the secretary of the Dutch Revolutionary Centre, Comrade H. Kolteck, Secretary of the National Labour Secretariat, 164, Rozengracht, Amsterdam, Holland.—Thanking you beforehand for your kind intervention,

Fraternally yours,

CHRISTIAN CORNELISSEN.

SYNDICALIST MESSAGE FROM OXFORD.

To the Editor of the SYNDICALIST.

SIR,—You have asked me to send the SYNDICALIST a message from Oxford. Such an honour must be obeyed as a command.

Your readers may first like to know the state of opinion in the University. At present Academic Liberalism and Collectivism are predominant. The adherents of the former, though few in number, undoubtedly include some of the minds most characteristic of the best in Oxford culture. The latter has made many converts, especially among the dons. But the last few years have seen the beginning of a great change. On the one hand, neglect and suspicion of party politics has been growing amongst undergraduates—as shown by the large majority Hilaire Belloc secured for his motion at the Union Debating Society last term. On the other hand, and of far more significance, in my opinion, is the defection in the Collectivist ranks—shown by the decline in influence of the Oxford Fabian Society. The undergraduate of to-day is not looking to Collectivism for a remedy. The majority are simply indifferent : some are trying to reconstruct their Socialism, and many of the best minds are seeking for new solutions.

Thus there is a minority ready to welcome the arrival of the SYNDICALIST. I think I can best express that welcome by quoting the words of the article in the last number of the SYNDICALIST called "To the Public." There you say : "We ask that you assert your own right to LEARN what Syndicalism is. We demand the right to teach the British people what Syndicalism is."

Whatever her faults—and they are many—Oxford can claim and does demand that right of LEARNING.

Some of us will welcome Syndicalism simply as a sign of the awakening determination of the wage-earners, as an omen that the popular initiative, which makes a nation great, has not been crushed even by a century of Capitalism. For we are constantly driven to the conclusion that the greatest obstacle to economic reform is not so much the resistance of the propertied classes as the apparent apathy of the English proletariat.

We welcome, too, its criticism of Collectivism, for, as a college friend of mine has written, "If the phrase 'wage slavery' means anything at all, it applies to the wage-system itself and not only to wages paid not by a public body."

Syndicalism is a very young movement in England—the work of a small minority—and its programme is vague. If it has an instrument, and two or three main principles, the principles require elaboration and the instrument perfecting. We in Oxford desire to learn what solution you will apply to the many problems before you. In what manner will you adapt to English conditions and genius a movement which in origin is French? What modifications will you effect in the peculiar position of English Trade Unions, and what view do you hold of their future? Wherein do you differ from the Revolutionary Utopianism of 1833-4 and 1885-9? How will you avoid the blunders that made the schemes of Robert Owen (the first English Socialist) impossible? Under the Syndicalist State what is the function and the nature of the Executive ; and by what means other than the vote (at best, an imperfect instrument) can the will of the people express itself and mould the Democratic State to its desires?

There are answers to these questions ; and the Future is before you!

C. H. C. OSBORNE.

New College, Oxford.

Note by Editor SYNDICALIST.—An endeavour will be made in our next number to take up the points raised in the foregoing.

THE MEXICAN REVOLUTION.

Dear Comrade Guy Bowman,—Jack Wood has written me from Seattle, calling my attention to the SYNDICALIST of February as containing Magon's "The Rifle."

The Mexican Revolution is not receiving from Radicals and Revolutionists a hundredth part of the attention it honestly merits, for I believe it to be the French and Russian revolutions over again, but fought with clearer and more fundamental radical ideas, and far better prospects for success for the masses.

I am sending you five copies of our pamphlet on the subject, and would send more if I knew you could dispose of same to advantage. We are very anxious for a good circulation for this pamphlet, because we think it explains—and that seems the one thing needed. It has been translated into Spanish, is being now rendered into French and German, and, I believe, will be into several other languages.

Magon is a fine writer—as, indeed, is his brother—and the experience of nearly a year's intimate association with them convinces me that they know their country, and the wants and aspirations of the masses in their country as, unfortunately, few revolutionists do.—Fraternally,

WM. C. OWEN.

Office of "Regeneracion," 914, Boston Street, Los Angeles, Cal., U.S.A., March 9.

Organised, man can conquer heaven; unorganised, he is the weakest member in all of the animal kingdom.

THE SYNDICALIST SCARE.

(From the *Star*.)

The very clever speech of the Attorney-General confirms us in the view that the "Syndicalist" prosecutions were a mistake, and that the Government intends as early as possible to repair that administrative blunder. The plain, simple fact is that Toryism thrives on repression, but that Liberalism cannot breathe in an atmosphere of Coercion. The long struggle with Mr. Balfour in Ireland twenty-five years ago was naturally referred to by Mr. Lansbury, who invited the House to "Remember Mitchelstown." Twenty-five years ago Coercion seemed triumphant. But where is that policy now? Coercion is dead in Ireland, and its victims are about to become the first members of the Home Rule Government of Ireland. Sir Rufus Isaacs' speech made it clear that the Cabinet had no responsibility for the "Syndicalist" blunder. The Aldershot arrest was made at the instance of the military authorities, and this isolated enthusiast, who was devoting his spare time to anti-militarist propaganda, promptly converted into a martyr. The next false step was the prosecution of the printers and publisher of the SYNDICALIST, which was followed in a kind of vicious circle by the defiant speech of Mr. Tom Mann, and that in turn by his prosecution. Our view is that this matter does not rest upon the question whether one approves of these views or not. The question is whether these views are to be suppressed by police and prison, or whether they are to be met and refuted by argument in the manner that Liberalism has always approved.

The weakest part of Sir Rufus Isaacs' speech was his treatment of the Orange incitements. We quoted on Saturday the speech of Mr. A. St. G. Hamersley, M.P., and Mr. Wedgwood cited the speech of Mr. William Moore, M.P., who said to the Orangemen :

You need not be a bit afraid of being prosecuted for sedition or rebellion. Let the Government try to lay a finger on any man for asserting principles of freedom, and they would light a fire in Protestant Ulster which would never be put out.

The Attorney-General explained that the Ulstermen had not been prosecuted because they thought these wild utterances were "nothing but bombast," a mere desire to use strong language. But how can he decide that the SYNDICALIST articles are not "bombast," too? To our eye there is a good deal of that commodity about both the Orangemen and the Syndicalists, but of one thing we are certain : that if it is necessary and just to prosecute the one, the other should not escape. The "square deal" is the first necessity of modern Liberal administration.

THE SERVILE STATE.

(From the *Freewoman*.)

It is, indeed, high time for a reversal of this servile notion of government from above. Free government proceeds from the individual outwards, not from the sum-total inwards. It is for this reason that, considering the trend of Syndicalism, we are of opinion that it is likely to make a far more intimate appeal to the nation than Socialism ever has. Its aims are the same : the means of production and exchange to be the property of the community as a whole, but under Syndicalism the control of conditions of work to be in the hands of those who perform it. This latter is a proviso which will raise crafts to the independent status of the professions. It will free them from the blight which follows the laying on of the dead hand of the State, the hand which already hangs over the servers in prisons, workhouses, State schools, post offices, in the Army and the Navy. Syndicalism's method is higher in the plane of evolutionary movement than that of Parliamentary Socialism. State Socialism is impregnated throughout with officialdom and the governmental spirit. It is the régime which would spring up as the retaliation to Capitalism. It is related to Capitalism, and carries the mental stamp of spirits habituated to a slave system. This organisation working from the individual outward, and this Will to snub the officiousness of Parliament is in reality the break out of our long-over-laid racial instinct for free institutions. Free institutions are the genius of the Anglo-Saxon people. What we do not remember often enough is that the English were not only a conquered but a defeated people ; their genius went under, and the Latin mould modelled us, and does so in our institutions to this day. Parliament to-day is not the culmination of the Saxon Village Moot, Town Moot, Hundred Moot, Folk Moot, and Meeting of the Wise Men. It is the offspring of the Magnum Concilium of the Norman, which was the flowering of a slave system, and slave vices inhere in it to this day. A people which acquiesces in it makes a servile state.

THE COAL PHARAOHS.

(From the *Star*.)

He could not quite understand why the Government, having swallowed the principle of the State regulation of wages, should now boggle at the detail of " the 5 and 2," which might be regarded in the light of a living wage only. If " the 5 and 2 " were not inserted in the Bill, he thought the measure would not be acceptable to either section of the men's leaders, and would not end the strike.—Mr. D. A. Thomas.

The Five and Two deadlock continued yesterday. While the country is drifting to destruction the owners have hardened their hearts and refused to grant their worst paid workers a beggarly wage of 25s. per week. The price of peace has been reduced to a song ; and yet our coal Pharaohs will not let the starving people go. It is estimated by Mr. Stanley Jevons that the Five and Two rate would cost the coalowners only £50,000 a year, for the Five and Two rate affects only one in every 200 miners. But the coalowners will not pay £50,000 a year in order to deliver the nation from a strike which is costing it ten millions a week.

Hitherto the coalowners have not felt the force of public anger. If the community can grasp the facts we have set out, their wrath would, perhaps, force the coalowners to realise that they run grave risks by sticking to their stubborn greed. Their profits are vast, although cleverly disguised by financial manipulations. It is idle for them to pretend that their profits would be wiped out if they were to pay one miner in every 200 a bare subsistence wage of 25s. a week. The public know what they pay for coal. They know that the coal trade shows the coal consumer no mercy. It is, therefore, useless to ask the public to believe that the coalowners cannot afford to pay one miner out of 200 a living wage. . . . The poor are bearing the coalowner's agony without squealing. The workers are starving without complaint. There is practically no disorder. Apparently the coalowners are using the self-control of the workers as a cloak for their exactions. They think it is safe to defy the miners, to defy public opinion, and to defy the Government. We tell them plainly that time is up. It is better for them to agree quickly with the Government and the miners, lest a worse thing befall them. The community will be forced to take the control of the mines out of their hands if they refuse to pay their workers a living wage. Their profits are not sacrosanct. Their monopoly is not eternal. They and the royalty owners must be restrained and controlled. It makes us furious when we remember that the royalty owners draw six millions a year from the coal mines without lifting a finger, and yet out of that six millions we cannot get £50,000 to give one miner in 200 a wage of 25s. a week. This is the crime of the strike.

If the coal Pharaohs will not come to an agreement, we hope the Government will reconsider their decision with regard to the Five and Two rate. Let them issue an ultimatum to the owners, and say plainly that the strike must be stopped. If the owners will not agree to pay the Five and Two, let the Government put it in the Bill and pass it without further delay. That course, and that only, will bring the strike quickly to an end.

SYNDICALISM.

G. LOWES DICKINSON, in the *Times*.

Until a few weeks ago the very word "Syndicalism" was unknown to the majority of people in this country. Since it has been discovered it has been exploited as a scarecrow for exaggerating the terrors of the miners' strike. It is, however, true in this particular case that the scarecrow is calculated to scare. Syndicalism really is, what Socialism in general is not, a revolutionary movement. At its base is the axiom of all Socialism—the right of labour to the whole of its product. Ambiguous and controversial as this idea may be, it is the militant idea of our age. It is a spirit seeking incarnation. In many ways, at many points—by co-operation, by profit-sharing, by the single tax, by nationalisation—it seeks to effect an entry of final embodiment in the real world. Syndicalism is one such attempt, and the most desperate. It rejects political action—nay, it rejects the very notion of the State. It defines government in general as coercion, and the government of the modern State in particular as coercion of labour by capital. The State, it declares, means the "Bourgeoisie"—that is, in Socialist jargon, the whole capitalist class. Between it and the worker there can be no transaction. By definition it is the enemy of labour. Labour must work outside and against it.

The serious factor in the present situation is not the unrest of labour ; it is the blind and selfish egotism of property.

Syndicalism, on the other hand, has an idea and an energy behind it. It is Socialistic, but it is against State Socialism. It believes that industries should be controlled by those who work them ; not by a board of directors, but by the labourers themselves. These only know the work. Give them their proper interest in the output, and they are the people with the strongest motive and the greatest capacity to increase it. They will invent, they will save, they will organise ; they will condemn incompetence and foster competence.

CRUSH PARLIAMENT ?

Bernard Shaw, unconsciously, no doubt, made a Near-Syndicalist speech at the Hyndman dinner when he said :

In the future the real development of democracy in this country would only be secured by a study of the science of putting pressure on Parliament from the outside. That was genuine democracy. They had to face a real danger, which was that the capitalists were beginning to perceive that the system of communism was just as useful to them as the individualist system. Capitalists were hoping that in the future they would have Government security for their capital, while the worker would have Government security for his slavery.

We merely suggest that the pressure from without on Parliament will finally be raised from the pushing to the crushing point.

Printed and published by GUY BOWMAN, 4, Maude Terrace, Walthamstow, E.

The Syndicalist

VOL. 1. NO. 6.   LONDON, JULY, 1912.   MONTHLY, ONE PENNY.

COMRADES AND FRIENDS.

Having completed a period of imprisonment, I am very glad to be at liberty again. I do not feel any the worse for the experience, and after a few days' spell for a whiff of ozone, I shall be as fit and as ready for action as ever.

I desire to thank most heartily all those friends who have shown kindness since the time of my arrest. Some wrote to the prison, not realising that the regulations allow a prisoner only one letter a month, so that I was unable to get these till I was discharged. Those I am unable to reply to personally will, I hope, kindly accept my thanks and hearty appreciation in this general acknowledgment.

Now is the time for us to enter upon the campaign for the direct control by the workers themselves of the industries they are engaged in. Simple as this statement may appear, it is really the most far-reaching of any proposal ever seriously entertained by workmen. It carries with it the ending of poverty. It will ensure every child, woman, and man being continuously provided with the requisites of a comfortable existence. It will empty the prisons, the workhouses, and lunatic asylums; for these places, particularly the two first-named, are filled by the poor *in consequence of their poverty.*

When the Trade Unionists fully realise the power and grandeur of this glorious crusade they will enter into it with the necessary vigour and capacity

The struggle for liberty has been a long one and a hard one, and whilst enormous progress has been made, the working-class are still industrially enslaved, and millions are at this hour existing under conditions much below those that obtain in the gaols and pauper-houses.

All intelligent men know that this is so because industry is controlled exclusively in the interest of the capitalist class, and not because the workers cannot produce a sufficiency for all. There is only one cure, and that is, the workers must *themselves regulate and control their labour and the results thereof,* and this can be done and will be done by DIRECT ACTION as soon as the idea is properly grasped by a sufficient number of the workers.

OUR IMMEDIATE DUTY is to carry on a vigorous and extensive educational campaign. The Trade Unionists generally, and the Trades Councils particularly, will yet prove to be the real serviceable agencies by which we shall achieve our emancipation.

Meanwhile we must arrange a series of Syndicalist Conferences in the industrial centres, and one will be held in London as early as possible. This work will be done by the various groups of the Syndicalist Education League, and we ought to have such a group in every industrial district. Our comrade Guy Bowman will gladly give information as to how to get to work to inquirers. Remember, we mean business; we are Direct Actionists; we are not out to quarrel with any, but we are out to achieve something substantial for the workers.

We need a thousand speakers at once, who will, as members of the groups, carry on the campaign in all the unions. A couple of years' solid educational work will secure the volume of opinion necessary for definite action.

This work is too great, too intricate, and altogether too sacred for a plutocratic Parliament to touch. "Who would be free, themselves must strike the blow." That's our case. Instead of allowing the people to be driven out of the country, a process which is now going on, we will, and we can, drive poverty from the land.

TOM MANN.

NATIONALISM AND THE CLASS WAR.

AN ADDRESS THAT WAS TO HAVE BEEN DELIVERED BY SORGUE AT THE ULSTER HALL, BELFAST.

We learn from our friend, Comrade Sorgue, that she was to have addressed a meeting in the Ulster Hall on the 6th of June last. The meeting was organised by the Belfast branch of the I.L.P. But our comrade tells us she was reluctantly compelled to cancel her engagement on account of the situation created in England towards foreigners by the prosecution of Malatesta. To have gone to Belfast at the present time might have created trouble, and as it was stated on all sides that she was to be arrested, she would on no account be a party to putting arms in the hands of those who are carrying on a campaign for the deportation of "dangerous aliens," thereby making a dead letter of the Right of Asylum which up to now has been the glory of this country. We, therefore, are pleased to print below her lecture as she would have delivered it.

COMRADES AND FRIENDS,—

It is with great pleasure that I have come over to old, heroic Ireland; and I am glad to be able to convey to the workers of Belfast the fraternal greetings and hearty good wishes of their Syndicalist comrades of France and of Italy, whom I officially represent.

The subject of my lecture is indeed one of burning actuality, when the probable adoption of Home Rule for Ireland is creating such wild excitement in this province, and especially in this city, and when the class war is waged in Great Britain on ever more gigantic lines. Let me say at once that I have no sympathy with the Unionist agitation, it being most decidedly of a reactionary character.

The Cloak of Religion.

The leaders of Unionism—who are they? They are the men who systematically oppose all social legislation; they are the representatives of political and social conservatism in its most tenacious and violent form. They personify dead and gone ideas—in a word, they are the champions of the past. These supporters of the abominable ancient order of things

SORGUE.

are, nevertheless, very keen on capitalist interests, and one of the reasons why the Belfast captains of industry are so much opposed to Irish self-government is that they fear that Home Rule would be prejudicial to their financial prospects. This is what they admit quite candidly in one of their propaganda pamphlets, which says: "The small farmers of the three southern provinces would be either more or less than human if they did not lessen their own burdens at the expense of the great industries of the province of Ulster, which are almost all in the hands of Protestants"! This quarrel between Protestants and Catholics is an anachronism in the enlightened twentieth century; the cloak of religion is now threadbare, and can no longer hide the real interests which are at the back of it, and which have nothing to do with spiritual concerns.

No, indeed! the Unionist leaders have nothing to recommend them to the sympathy of the workers, and it is high time that Ulster workers should understand how they are duped in backing their exploiters in this present campaign, and thus creating so much ill-feeling between themselves and the other working-men of Ireland. Under no pretext whatever should the proletariat allow itself to be divided into hostile camps.

Notwithstanding all this, and although

I run the chance of incurring your displeasure, I must say that I am strongly in favour of an autonomous and federated Ireland. Why? Because political federalism materialises progressive political evolution; which will lead to a confederated Europe. That is to say, to peace, and then economic federalism will follow as the only logical solution of the social question.

No State Collectivism.

With the French Syndicalists and with the Anarchists, like Elisée Reclus and Prince Kropotkin, I repudiate the idea of State collectivism.

The society of the future must be a community of freedom, where production and division will be organised internationally, according to the principles of federalism and communism combined.

The formidable coal strike has taught us more than one object lesson. Among other things it has clearly put into evidence how economically interdependent all countries are. The repercussion of the stoppage of the British coal supply has been acutely felt from one end of the globe to the other. This black strike has shown us how ultra absurd is the present industrial system, creating competition and antagonism when everything calls for unity and harmony—that unity and harmony which can only find complete and intensive expression in a whole world's economic federalism.

Now there are two hypotheses : one that political federalism will give place to economic federalism; the other that a social convulsion will straight off establish the levelling system, without passing through the intermediate stages. In fact, it is a question of evolution or revolution; and I must say that *revolution* appears to me as the most probable eventuality. A social cataclysm may change the face of the capitalist world at any moment, just in the same way as a seismic cataclysm has so often suddenly transformed the face of the earth. This society, in its pride and strength and wickedness, may be swept away to-morrow by the fierce current of revolt, just as beautiful Messina was washed away by the overwhelming waters of the tidal wave.

Autonomous Unionism.

Let me add this : I believe in the putting into practice of the principles of autonomy in every direction of human activity. I quite agree with the French and Italian Syndicalists in denouncing as anti-progressive and anti-revolutionary the Socialist policy of a centralised and authoritative Unionism. With my comrades of the Continent I am for autonomy; not only at every degree of the scale of Labour organisation, but also for the individual autonomy of each Unionist himself. But autonomy of different units does not imply that voluntary discipline is not absolutely imperative in order to realise effective efficient co-operation between all fighters in the Labour War. What is wanted is not to paralyse, but to encourage initiative.

The Unions, as well as their members, must have the possibility of asserting themselves, of developing in an atmosphere of freedom, so that the power of intelligence should come into play more and more, giving a conscious impetus to the movement. What an irresistible creative force will Labour become when each Union is an aggregate of lucid, comprehensive brains, an aggregate of independent, yet sympathetic wills! The remarkable feature of the present Labour struggle in Great Britain is the intelligent part played by the strikers—who have ceased to be "the men" and have at last become *men.*

To conclude about Home Rule :—Self-government for Ireland is really desirable; it would be the application of a concept on which humanity ought to build its greatest hopes. And for this same reason, I sincerely hope that Home Rule once conferred in Ireland will be a precedent to extend it to Scotland and Wales.

The Curse of Patriotism.

And now, please, do not misunderstand

me! If, as a federalist, I approve of Home Rule, it does not imply in any way that I sympathise with a nationalist ideal as such. Far from it. I say that nationalism, with its corollary of belligerent patriotism, has proved a curse to mankind for all time. The greatest crimes against the race have been committed, and are committed still, for the love of country. Is not patriotism the excuse invoked to justify the criminal expedition of the French in Morocco and the Italians in Tripoli? What fools are these French and Italian "patriots" to give their support to a war brought about—the one by the speculating financiers of Paris, the other by the Roman Catholic shareholders of the Bank of Rome ! In short, what is the mentality of the patriotic, military hero? It is undoubtedly that of the barbarian. Those young soldiers who, from the seat of war in Tripoli, address to their relatives and friends in Italy enthusiastic descriptions of the scenes of carnage—boasting of having done their duty in the slaughtering of Arab men, women, and children—personify active patriotism. When we read their letters which the Italian Press has reproduced as specimens of patriotic literature, we are reminded of the writings of born criminals—whose psychology, as exposed by Lombroso, is absence of human compassion, joy in the suffering of others, and lust of killing.

The frenzied excitement displayed by the soldier on the battlefield—how can these things excite our admiration. Is it not simply the excitement of the beast of prey, maddened by the smell of blood? No ! there is nothing to admire and exalt in the fact that man ceasing to be a man, gives way to the ferocious instincts of wolves and tigers—and the comparison is in favour of the wild beasts, who at least do not attack their kind. What is to be admired instead and put before children as a glorious example is, not this so-called military heroism, but the altruistic self-sacrifice as offered by men of all classes on that tragic night when the pride of Belfast shipbuilders, "the ship that could not sink," *did* sink in the abyss of the ocean. Honour to the memory of the heroes of the "Titanic," honour to those men who loved others better than themselves, honour to those heroes of sublime altruism !

The Menace of War.

It will be still under the flag of patriotism that a European conflagration may break out and rage at any moment. We are seriously menaced with an Anglo-Franco-German conflict. Do you realise what such a conflict would mean? It would mean the mutual extinction of the youth—the future hope of the nations involved. The highly scientific European war which is being actively prepared will be more terrible and disastrous in its effects than words can express, for wonderful killing mechanism will work simultaneously on land and sea, and in the air. The loss of life will be terrific. Try to imagine the military storms which aviation is contriving here, in France, and in Germany. It will make your hair stand on end with horror. What an awful vision !—a hailstorm of shells, of explosive bombs, falling from the heavens on poor mortals, and reducing them to pulp, while whole cities become the prey of flames. That will be Inferno indeed ! What monster could contemplate such a possibility with equanimity? The Kaiser can; the Kaiser, who is determined to conjure up the Red Peril by every means in his power—for the German Emperor considers that a war would change the trend of the workers' thoughts.

After the workers of the three great capitalist nations had come to blows on the capitalists' battlefield, there would be no response (for a long period at least) to Marx's call : "Workers of all countries, unite !" For this reason, the possessing class of all countries is not averse to the idea of war. The French financiers and industrials are wont to say : "Ce qu'il faut c'est une bonne saignée pour calmer la fièvre révolutionnaire du prolétariat !" (what is wanted is a good blood-letting to cool the revolutionary fever of the proletariat). The possessing class, in their monstrous egotism, would prefer to see the most horrifying hecatombs than to see social justice established.

Note the irony of things ! Millerand, the once popular leader of the Socialist International, now Minister of War, is

(Continued on page 2.)

The Syndicalist

EDITED UNDER THE AUSPICES OF

The Industrial Syndicalist Education League

Offices—

4, MAUDE TERRACE, WALTHAMSTOW, LONDON, E.

MONTHLY · ONE PENNY.

Post Paid Subscription—
Great Britain or Abroad ... 12 months 1s. 6d.

Bundle Rates—
1s. 6d. per quire, Carriage Paid.

The receipt of a Sample Copy is an invitation to Subscribe

JULY, 1912.

GEORGE LANSBURY.

At the inaugural meeting of the I.S.E.L., held at the Stratford Town Hall on October 29, 1911, which opened the campaign of propaganda in favour of the Syndicalist movement, circulars were distributed. They contained, condensed into a few lines, the aspirations of the League and an application form for membership.

The first application received was that of our friend George Lansbury, and we cannot forget the smiles of the members of the committee when his name was mentioned. Lansbury ! a Parliamentarian ! How could we accept him !

But the president and the secretary were of a different opinion. They thought, and they explained that what they wanted above all were *men*, and in their opinion George Lansbury *was a man*; that is to say, a man of action and courage; a being possessing a heart and a soul; a being upon whose devotion and abnegation one might rest. The reasons of the president and the secretary prevailed at that meeting, and Lansbury was accepted as a member of the League. Besides, his admission was in no way contrary to the constitution of the League, for the membership clause says :

The membership of the League is open to any person who accepts the above, no matter what views may be held by that person regarding politics ; but no one who does not declare for non-Parliamentary action may share in the responsible work of administration of the League. Therefore, the possession of an ordinary membership card does not imply that the holder is entitled to speak or otherwise act on behalf of the League.

George Lansbury has proved to be the man whom those who answered for him expected him to be. When came the Syndicalist prosecutions, it was thanks to his leadership that the whole rank and file of the Labour movement was able to express its indignation at the injustice that had been committed ; his voice sounded like a clarion, awaking everywhere consciences that had gone to sleep, and at this sonorous appeal men and women of heart came rushing in their thousands. Truly, he found himself seconded, and well seconded, in the task he had imposed upon himself. Encouragement, donations, support came from all parts, but it cannot be denied that he was the soul of the magnificent and unexpected movement which shook the country with a shiver of anger and went to fetch out of their cells earlier than was expected the defenders of a high and true fraternity. It was thanks to his pertinent efforts, to his untiring energy, that the masses rose, and that the Government modified the judges' sentences.

George Lansbury has just been giving us another example of his courage and his frankness by throwing into the Prime Minister's face his disgust at the iniquitous treatment inflicted upon women in British prisons. In vehement and passionate, even harsh, language he has interpreted the sentiments of thousands of persons who are indignant at the conduct of the Liberal Government towards the Suffragettes ; these women whose attachment to their convictions reaches heroism, and who, for those reasons, deserve nothing but respect and admiration.

Lansbury's action has filled with joy all those that are haunted by the spectre of injustice, all those who dream of putting an end to the calamities of which the ruling class is the dispenser, and through his unexpected and "incorrect outburst" he has given us one more proof that he is really the Lansbury whom we had divined, whom we love, and of who n we are proud.

SYNDICALISM AND SOCIALISM.

By JACK RADCLIFFE.

(Continued from last month.)

If the Socialists were to capture Parliament it would be of no use to them, for it could not be made to respond to the needs of the Socialist Commonwealth, which would then be at the point of actual inauguration. But the plutocracy would, if faced by this possibility, resist by force.

The path to Socialism lies inevitably through a Social Revolution, which will destroy the capitalist system root and branch, and with that system must go its most characteristic institution, Parliament. The Co-operative Commonwealth, which will succeed exploitive capitalism, will be the final and most complete expression of the economic interests of a triumphant commune, established for the first time in history since the village communes and the free, federal cities. A Parliament, a Legislature, after the style of that which our Socialists have been yearning all these years to capture, would be impossible.

We see, however, so far from any likelihood of Socialists capturing Parliament, or obtaining any respectable representation there, they find it impossible to win even one seat on the straight Socialist ticket. Nor will they make any better success in forthcoming elections. The fact that many of them still hope, against hope, in this matter, is evidence of their sheer inability to get rid of old prepossessions and to adapt themselves to new methods and new ideas. We wish, indeed, that they will be soundly beaten in every one of the contests they are likely to put up at the next General Election, for the very atmosphere of Parliament is poisonous to honest men. The influences tempting to perfidy are too subtle and too strong. We do not desire to see the roll of dishonour on the part of "labour" representatives any longer than it is at present. Hence we have sought, and have found in Syndicalism and direct action, an alternative policy which promises a more immediate fulfilment of those hopes which we share in common with the misguided Parliamentarian Socialists.

In Syndicalism we see the beginning of a definite policy to express and realise the economic demands of the wage workers. The interests, we all know, of the exploiters, and of the exploited, are antagonistic and irreconcilable. That these interests should *not* express themselves, politically, along identical, or even parallel lines, might have been anticipated. Such is proving to be the case. The Socialist movement itself is destined to be profoundly modified by the Syndicalist idea.

The fundamental mistake which Socialists made in the past, and which it is necessary for them how to correct, is in thinking that the new social order, the Co-operative Commonwealth, must necessarily be imposed from above, downward, through the medium of "elected persons." This is due to their inability to think in terms other than those suggested by their environment. It is, however, now becoming evident that Socialism will arise from below, upward, and Syndicalism is the tangible recognition of this. It is only too often forgotten that authority, government, the State, are artificial conditions imposed upon humanity by the class who own the wealth of the community. Human nature is admittedly a complex and a baffling problem, but we know communism to be the natural state of man ; that whenever the iron hand of class domination and authority is weakened or lifted, mankind instinctively reverts to communism. The communal instinct persists even under the most rigid and tyrannical State despotisms. With the break-up and absorption of the modern plutocratic State, humanity will, of itself, revert to communism. State Socialism, indeed, is a monstrosity, a hybrid, a bastard form of Socialism, a Socialism poisoned by the capitalist environment, and the sooner it is dead and buried the better. State Socialism, with its Government departments, officials, and. mechanical, centralised bureaucracy, would involve a tyranny and a despotism as bad as that of the present plutocratic oligarchy. But it is but a passing phase, a by-product of the transition period. It is dying now, and Syndicalism arises to give it the final quietus.

Our Socialists must understand that an awakened people are quite capable of arranging matters for themselves in their own way; that they do not need "leadership" nor "guidance" by persons who are no more, but, indeed, frequently less, intelligent than those whom they seek to direct. The pedantries of the Socialist doctrinaire will be more and more neglected and ignored as time goes on. We realise that the years of educative propaganda, in which the Socialist doctrinaire has himself rendered good service, are now beginning to bear fruit. The workers are beginning to understand their economic conditions and the causes of these conditions. They realise that class control of the means of life means for them, the producers, political and economic subjection, low wages, miserable conditions of life, poverty, and insecurity of employment, opposed to overflowing wealth, security, comfort, and luxury for the non-productive, dominant few. They realise that, so far from labour being dependent upon capital, the reverse is the case. They know that when labour and natural resources are brought together wealth is the resultant. They know that if either the one or the other of these factors is wanting no wealth can make its appearance. They are realising their power in the monopoly of one of these factors, and they propose to play off this monopoly of theirs against the capitalist monopoly of natural resources. Hence, Syndicalism.

As the Syndicalist idea spreads, we shall witness strikes on a wider and more general scale than heretofore. The first step will be the general withholding of labour power, with the consequent dislocation of industry and stoppage in wealth production. Such a deadlock can only end in one of two ways, either the workers will remain inactive and supine, and be slowly starved into surrender, or they will take the one further step necessary to establish their class interests. They will dispossess those classes which claim to "own" the natural resources. This will precipitate the Social Revolution, which will be peaceful or violent according to the opposition set up by the capitalist classes. It is never the workers who first resort to violence, this is always forced upon them by the classes antagonistic to them. In the general strike that is to be, the workers will organise among themselves what we may call "vigilance committees" to keep the peace as against the irresponsible "hooligan" element which is so useful to the master class when it seeks excuse to coerce the workers. The workers will themselves protect property, realising the folly of destroying what is, after all, their own. The workers in all trades and industries being on strike, ceasing to produce wealth, will understand perfectly that this period of inactivity cannot, and ought not to, continue indefinitely. They will appoint from themselves committees of management for the definite taking over by themselves of the machinery of production, and the natural resources of the country. All workers, in all industries and branches of social activity, will adjust, through their appointed committees, their own inter-relations, quite without regard to the claims and alleged "rights" of the capitalist classes. If these latter do not choose to put themselves into line with the popular movement, they will be at liberty to emigrate.

But before this complete destruction and absorption of the class State is complete the capitalist classes may naturally be expected to make a vigorous resistance. They will depend upon the armed forces, police and military, and upon "volunteers" of both kinds drawn from the non-productive middle-classes. The military and the police are recruited, almost wholly, from the working-class. That these men are beginning to realise their position we have reason to know. That the master-class know what this realisation means is shown by the recent vindictive prosecutions of Syndicalists for appealing to the military. In the last resort the master-class will find this weapon break in their hands if, indeed, it is not even turned against them. The volunteers of the "cheap snob" classes will form the last and most uncertain line of defence for capitalism.

The Society of the future will consist, as has already been pointed out, of free, organised industrial communes, federated nationally and internationally on the basis of production for use, and not for profit. There will be no class distinctions whatever.

This is the real purpose and object of Syndicalism, which is but the means to an end, *not the end itself*. He who has wit to understand, let him understand, for whether he likes the prospect or not he will have to fall into line, or be swept aside, be he Socialist or not, capitalist or wage-worker.

You can only at best vote for Parliament about once every three years, and half the time even then you will find your name is not on the register, especially so if your name happens to be Mary. And when you do vote it's only a little recreation anyway. But you can work for Solidarity every day in the year, Sundays especially included. Working is really more fun than play—that is, working for yourself and comrades.

IS SYNDICALISM UN-ENGLISH ?

By E. J. B. ALLEN.

Many of the opponents of Syndicalism use the argument—if argument it can be called—that Syndicalism is un-English. In various ways they endeavour to prove that Syndicalism may be quite suitable to those hot-headed, impetuous Frenchmen, fiery Spaniards, or passionate Italians, but it will never become a force with the semi-Teutonic Britisher—an excellent argument in its way for those who look at race characteristics in a superficial manner !

Yet only three years ago there was a general strike in Sweden, when even the army raised contributions to the strike funds. Can one imagine a greater contrast than those deliberate, fair-haired giants—the Swedes—and the short, swarthy, active French?

Yet the Syndicalist ideas are the same in both countries. The workers of Norway, Sweden, and Denmark have an International working agreement and exchange of cards with the Unions of the different countries.

Race characteristics weigh much in the minds of those who consider social problems in the light of *mass-psychology* as well as economics. Readily, I'll admit that there appears to be a vast difference between the popularly depicted volatile Frenchman and the stolid, sober-minded Britisher. One may easily mentally contrast a mercurial Parisian comrade with a steady, stodgy Yorkshire "John Willey." But, nevertheless, the Parisian and the Yorkshireman have certain characteristics in common. They have each a stomach, which, when insufficiently or antipathetically filled, causes the same unpleasant thoughts in the heads of each.

Can a person seriously argue that there is less excitement at an English football match than there is at a French political meeting?

True it is, that the French in particular have a revolutionary tradition that has a profound influence upon the national mind, yet also the fact is clear that the Britisher disproved the theory of the Divine Right of Kings by relieving one of his head one hundred and forty-four years before the French removed Louis Capet.

The same economic conditions in various countries produce very similar results. Race characteristics are subordinate to economic ones.

Revolutionary outbursts reach their highest *pitch in mass movements.* The reason is a simple one—the mass movement destroys the sense of individuality. With the absence of that feeling there vanishes also a sense of responsibility. A man in a crowd is a different being to the man by himself. A new mentality is created by mass association, a more intense thought and action.

Tradition counts for much. To the Frenchman the Great Revolution is the epoch in his country's history. Everyone feels it, and thus are more susceptible to revolutionary impulse. On the other hand, the Britisher is seldom reminded of the Revolution against Charles the First, of those Communists the levellers who grew up in that stirring period. Not very often, unfortunately, are they told the tale of the struggles of the early Trade Unionists and the Chartists. Yet, there is hope.

One writer in contrasting the characteristics of the English with those kinsmen of the French—the Irish—used an apt illustration. He said, " All great Irish political movements started out revolutionary, and finished up by becoming constitutional. The Englishmen started out by being constitutional, and finished by becoming revolutionary." Following through the middle-class revolt against the absolute Monarchy, one can see the correctness of that writer's description.

But to return to our muttons. Syndicalism, being the extreme expression of the working-class movement, will only be accepted theoretically by the workers when other means have failed.

The capitalist system itself has, and is still creating the chief psychological factor of a "class-consciousness" amongst the workers, by the concentration in the towns, and the large number of workers employed together in the modern factories, mills, stores, etc. This is of vital importance to the Syndicalists.

The next item is the fact that orthodox, " pure and simple," Trade Unionism was played out before the beginning of this century. The next forward move was the creation of a Parliamentary Labour Party, which has had its day. The workers are worse off than they were before its creation. Profits have gone up, wages either fallen or stationary. Capitalists hold on the necessaries of life as firm as ever because, worst of all mistakes, the workers left off the direct struggle. The Labour Party has, with the brilliant exceptions of George Lansbury and Keir Hardie, proven bankrupt in ideas, courage, and enthusiasm. The recent strikes have remedied things a little. The strike movement has been taken up on a larger scale, with better success than the old sectional methods, and its failures are more due to the stupidity, ignorance, and conservatism of many of the Trade Union officials than anything else.

Meanwhile the more advanced political workers have endeavoured to hide their differences in a united Socialist Party—the B.S.P. Politically, this was the next step after the failure of the Labour Party. Time has yet to prove, when the B.S.P. has its representatives in the House of Commons, whether there is any essential difference or not—whether the species called " politician " is the same always.

But whether there is any great difference or not the workers will continue their efforts of organisation outside amalgamation and federation of their Unions, the replacing of those officials who have shown too strong a preference for conciliation schemes, Insurance Bills, etc., by a more vigorous, aggressive, and frankly revolutionary type. Sooner or later the B.S.P. will demonstrate the obvious fact that a revolution cannot be accomplished by permission of the ruling class. The abolition of the wages system implies the most far-reaching of revolutions that have taken place in society. It means the abolition of profit, rent, and interest, those means by which a parasite class live upon the workers. It carries within itself a revolution at once political, social, economic, and ethical.

The B.S.P., through its theoretical propaganda amongst the workers on the one hand, and the natural evolution of progressive Trade Unionism on the other, brings Socialist ideals and the practical efforts of the Unions into conjunction. The workers must control industry. Co-partnership between the Unions and the capitalists is impossible—the capitalists won't have it peaceably. Co-partnership between the Unions and the State is only with the capitalists sheltered behind politicians and functionaries. It would only be capitalism disguised. The rough and only practical thing remains; viz., the Unions to take control of the industries they operate. Joint ownership by the workers of all industries—this is Syndicalism.

Syndicalism is a natural product, peculiar to no nationality. Its fundamentals are identical, whether advocated by the Confédération Générale du Travail of France, the Freie Vereinigung Deutscher Gewerkschaften of Germany, or the Syndicalists of England. Syndicalism is as much a British product as capitalism was. The Syndicalists are the levellers, or, if you like, the *sans-culottes* of the coming Revolution. They grasp the realities of things. The abolition of the wages system of slavery is their goal. They disdain the whirl of words with which the professional politicians disguise their thoughts and lose themselves in a maze of conventionalities. To paraphrase a familiar advertisement, " Syndicalism is English, you know ; quite English." It is here as well as on the Continent. A Liberal Government has helped to popularise it. Even the British worker can understand the meaning of the phrase—

" The product to the producer, the tools to those who use them."

MILITANT ANTI-MILITARISM.

THE END OF THE PROSECUTIONS.—FRED CROWSLEY'S HEROISM AND DEFIANCE.—THE PROPAGANDA AND MILITANCY WILL CONTINUE AS FIERCELY AS EVER.

Frederick Crowsley has gone to gaol for four months. This is not more than most of us expected who realise the essentially class character of our courts of law, where Justice is not blind and where her scales are used for the weighing of bribes. For this is what it comes to, that the laws exist merely to protect the interests of the wealthy and to prosecute and repress those who espouse the cause of the toiling poor. There is no longer justice in England, and if law be partial—as our law most certainly is—then it cannot be regarded as binding upon those whom it oppresses. Clearly it is not binding upon the capitalist class, the master class. It was framed, and it is interpreted, in their interests. Whatever protection the workers may obtain under it is only incidental.

The sentences passed upon Fred Crowsley,

TOM MANN.

Who was sentenced to six months' imprisonment.

upon Tom Mann, and upon Guy Bowman prove conclusively that the judges are merely the paid retainers of the wealthy, capitalist classes, exactly as are the members of the police force who arrested them, and the soldiery to whom they appealed in the "Open Letter to British Soldiers." This being the plain truth of the matter, which none recognise more clearly than the wealthy classes themselves, however hypocritically they may pretend otherwise, they cannot blame us, who are the champions and defenders of the people's liberties, if at times we act in defiance of their laws. For what may happen hereafter they will have none but themselves to blame.

When Guy Bowman published his translation of Herve's "Leur Patrie" there were some—and, strangely enough, Social Democrats among them—who denied the necessity for an anti-militant movement in England on the ground that there is no militarism here. It is curious how blind to events passing under their very eyes some people can be, and, as we have reason to know in these days, of all men the purblind Socialist is the most hopeless. No effort is being spared to arouse and to cultivate the spirit of militarism among our people. Thus we see the children of the workers as "Boy Scouts" or members of "Boys' Brigades," organised by the hypocritical representatives of the so-called Prince of Peace, in whose name capitalism has perpetrated its most bloody atrocities. We find some of the people—the workers themselves—who are not driven by stress of circumstances as are the majority of the regular army, enlisting in

the Territorials—though, to be sure, the master class does not trust them over much, since it takes away the bolts of their rifles during times of labour trouble! Military pageantry and parade is ever increasing, and the people, not yet clearly perceiving the meaning of it, are dazzled by the meretricious spectacle. Shortly we may see compulsory service, perhaps sooner than the majority of us imagine. For these reasons our work, as Syndicalists, will be in educating the people so that, at the proper time, the master class shall find the weapons they had relied upon for their defence turned against themselves.

The Fourfold Purpose of Militarism.

The purpose of militarism is fourfold. First, to create within the nation a division among its people, the one part armed and ready to shoot down the other (which is carefully deprived of arms) should it seek to free itself from the capitalist class tyranny, which is exploiting and crushing it. Second, to involve the capitalist nations in a general war, or to fling one upon another, should there be any danger of the subject peoples rising in rebellion against their tyrants. Third to create a force for the plunder of weaker nations outside the ring of capitalist "civilisation," so called. Fourth, to derive enormous and ever-increasing profits from the manufacture of armaments during times of peace—profits wrung, as are all profits, from the sweat of the workers who produce those armaments—designed to be used ultimately against the workers themselves.

We have seen the application of the first of these purposes during the past twelve months. In this we had striking examples of "direct action" on the part of the capitalist classes. In Liverpool, Manchester, London, Tonypandy, and other places the military were called out against the workers—always 'against' the workers, be it not forgotten—armed and ordered to fire, if necessary, upon their weaponless fellow-countrymen, did fire, indeed, murdering, in their blindness, several people of their own class. Direct action is always employed by the capitalists against the people whenever they show signs of resisting their extortions. Against foreign nations, weaker than their own, whom they desire to rob for their own enrichment, murdering them brutally, shamelessly, and by wholesale. Such are the "patriots" and such

their deeds. Well might it be said that patriotism is the last refuge of a scoundrel, and of all scoundrels our capitalist patriots are surely the worst.

Direct action can only be effectively met by direct action. But before this can be employed it is necessary that the people shall be educated so that they shall understand what is their true position in relation to the master-class which enriches itself out of the fruits of their labour, which exploits them, plunders them, crushes them down under its extortions, and would not hesitate to slaughter them in the streets of our cities and towns should they dare to resist; should they dare, even, to claim a little larger share of the wealth that their labour creates over and above the miserable pittance—barely enough to keep them alive—which is allowed as their wages. So we get Syndicalism, which is an answer, in kind, to the direct methods employed by the master-class.

How greatly the master class fears this new movement in England was proved by the instant action that was taken against those who sought to open the eyes of the soldiers. It may be well to recall, in brief, what happened. The SYNDICALIST, as is known, published the now famous "Open Letter to British Soldiers." Frederick Crowsley, a fireman employed by the London and North-Western Railway, had some thousands of copies of this letter reprinted at his own cost, and went to Aldershot, where he distributed them to the soldiers. He was arrested, charged under an obsolete Act of 1797, and committed for trial. Thereafter, Tom Mann and Guy Bowman were prosecuted for publishing that letter in the SYNDICALIST, and were sentenced to varying terms of imprisonment, which were afterwards reduced. Finally, Crowsley came up for trial on June 18. His attitude throughout was one of the finest heroism, both when in the hands of the police—those hired bullies of capitalism—before the magistrates (selected, as usual, from the wealthy classes), and before a judge and jury already prejudiced, prepared to find him guilty, and to punish him. Crowsley's speeches in justification of what he did, should be reproduced and circulated among the workers throughout the length and breadth of the land. He said to the magistrates:

A Heroic Defence.

"I am not guilty of any crime. Had I been guilty, my conscience would have told me so.

GUY BOWMAN.

Who was sentenced to nine months' hard labour.

You say I have broken the law, a law made a hundred years ago, in the making of which the middle and working classes had no voice. It was made by a class who live on the labour of another class. Man-made law is not unalterable. Hundreds of laws passed then do not apply now; but I would still tell you, if your law was passed yesterday, that there is a higher law which says, 'Thou shalt not kill.' I have simply made an earnest appeal to the honour of the soldiers not to shoot their brothers who are fighting for the right to live. If that is breaking your law, so much the worse for your unjust law. You say my action was undermining society. If society will not stand the attacks of truth, does not that prove the rottenness of society? And the sooner we have a more just state of society, the better. Your prison missionary called me a traitor for calling attention openly to what he and his class preach, 'Love one another.' You and he are entitled to your opinions on traitors and treachery, and I to mine. You are traitors to your creed, for, although you say with your lips, 'Love one another,' in your hearts you say, 'Shoot, and shoot straight.' Why are you prosecuting me, and not the authors or printers of the pamphlets for preaching the doctrine that Tolstoy preached all his life in Russia undisturbed? If you send me to prison, I shall not be the first or the last to go there unjustly. You will have to send many more before you can hope to suppress the truth, and you will stand condemned for ever before the eyes of all truth- and freedom-loving people. I know and believe every word on the leaflets to be true. Why are you so afraid of the truth? Is it not because of the corruption of the laws and Government? If I have succeeded in dissuading one soldier from being a murderer, my labour will not be in vain. I do not want to go to prison, for I am almost certain to lose my work if I do, but my spirit revolts against asking for mercy from such a ruthless enemy as I have got to fight. You may kill my body, but you cannot kill the truth."

Defiant and Brave.

The hearts of our master-class, we know, are hard as the nether mill-stone. They know neither disinterestedness nor nobility of character when they see them, neither have they ruth, scruple, nor mercy. So Crowsley was committed for trial, and was bailed out of custody by Mr. J. C. Wedgwood, M.P., to whom all honour. Before the judge and jury at his trial, Crowsley said : "My heart bleeds for the way the people are oppressed, and the choice came to me whether to be true or false to the class to which I belong. God forbid I should be false. I hope the day will soon come when the police and soldiers will refuse to be traitors to their class. If I go to prison I shall go with a clear conscience, but if you send me there you will bring a stain on you that will remain on you for ever. For your sakes I hope you won't commit this crime on humanity by sending me to prison. As to the inciting to mutiny, there is no lawful command to kill. It is against the laws of humanity to kill. I think all killing is murder. John Stuart Mill says, 'Act so as to win the approval of Jesus of Nazareth,' and I know He will approve of my action. My conscience tells me I was right in what I did. Of course, I am in your power. You must do as you like." It would seem that even our capitalist-class authorities have some unsuspected sense of shame, some small remainder of unseared conscience, for the judge intimated that if Crowsley would give an undertaking not to repeat the "offence" the Crown (symbol of the capitalist despotism) would not press the charge, and that it might have been passed over without punishment. To his everlasting honour, Crowsley refused the disgraceful terms offered him, and so went to prison.

A brave man, this, and a true. Such men are few in these cowardly days. The action of Crowsley should give us courage to go on with the good fight, confident that whilst we have such men as he with us there is no reason for despair, but for hope in the great fight that now lies before us.

Crowsley must not be allowed to remain in goal. He, of all men concerned in this business, must be released. There must be mass meetings called, and such agitation made as will force the cowardly and brutal enemy to quit their hold

upon this noble, brave, and chivalrous man, That such will be done we have no doubt.

Let's Prepare for the Great Crisis.

Can the capitalist claim and hold for ever the sole right to use force in defence of their gross and infamous usurpations? True it is that the resources of the workers are not such as enable them to meet force with equal force, and herein lies the necessity for us, as Syndicalists, to win over the soldiers, so that when the great crisis comes, as come it must, they shall bring over their weapons—their rifles, their ammunition, their cannon, and shells—to the side of the class to which they belong. The time has gone by for theorising, for discussing, and for passing useless "resolutions," which are but so many empty words. We are upon the eve of the Social Revolution. *The master class is forcing direct action upon us now, and Syndicalism is our conscious reply to it.* Syndicalism, with its advocacy of direct action on the part of the workers and with its anti-militarist teachings, is recognised by the capitalist class, in these prosecutions and in its determination to suppress both free speech and the freedom of the Press, as a far more dangerous enemy than that form of Socialism which repudiates the class war (the most striking phenomenon in modern society), talks about constitutional methods, and allies itself with the capitalist Liberal-Labour Party; more dangerous even than that more "advanced" organisation which calls itself revolutionary, yet can see no other means of social salvation save Parliamentary representation and the peaceful capture of the political machine. The time has gone by for all that. But some of our Socialists, who have shouted so much for the Social Revolution, now that the call has gone forth to prepare for it by *action* and not by words, now that the Revolution is near at hand, demanding action, are showing the white feather, with every disposition to "scuttle."

The development of the idea of the mass strike, in place of the futile sectional strikes as heretofore, brings the Social Revolution clearly within sight. The combined national and international strike is nothing more nor less than the first phase of the Social Revolution. It can lead to nothing else. And this is the result of the teachings of revolutionary Socialism.

The master-class, the land thieves, rackrenters, the capitalist exploiters, dividend extortioners, profit sweaters and usurers, together with all their retainers, toadies, and hangers-on—the idle, useless parasites and drones who live upon the wealth produced by the toiling people—these creatures know well enough what the rapid development of Socialist thought means to them. It means their dispossession, it means the taking away from them of their unearned incomes. They know, well enough, that this can be done only by direct action by the workers themselves, on the industrial field, and not by legislation through an institution that is essentially the instrument of the capitalist class. Thus they are closing their ranks, and, whether we will or no, *they will force direct action upon us.*

The great battle is joining now. The preliminary skirmishes are taking place. Before the final battle, the Armageddon of labour versus capital, there is much to be done. Crowsley has shown us one most necessary work. It is the duty of every true champion of the people's rights, of every genuine revolutionary Socialist, as it is of every Syndicalist, to get hold of the soldiers and the police, to reason with and persuade them, to give them literature, so that, in the final day, the capitalist class shall be vanquished and overcome by the weapons, and the forces they are preparing for the conquest and suppression of the workers.

This, indeed, is the only way to ensure the *peaceful* transition from the present system of capitalist exploitation into the co-operative commonwealth of Socialism. But it needs to be done thoroughly and systematically. Thus we, the Syndicalists, call to all earnest Socialists, reformers, and revolutionists alike, "Come over and help us in this great work of the Social Revolution that shall put an end, once and for all, to the age of barbarism and bring about a better, brighter, and nobler civilisation.

FRED. CROWSLEY.

Who was sentenced to four months' hard labour.

FEUILLETON OF "THE SYNDICALIST."
JULY 1, 1912.

BEFORE THE DELUGE

By BEATRIZ SOUTHER.

CHAPTER ONE.

THE LAST DAY OF CHILDHOOD.

There was nothing in the day itself to suggest that it was to be the most awful of my life—that all in one moment it was to change me from a carefree, romantic little girl of twelve to a saddened woman.

The place was Guerrero, the village in Northern Mexico where I was born. The hour was sunset of a fine October afternoon. I was sitting in the doorway of our tiny, earth-coloured adobe house, with my bare knees humped up in front of me, my elbows on them and my chin between my hands, my black hair tumbling over my shoulders as thick and unruly as a pony's mane. My eyes were fixed upon the distant mountains, then bathed in the liquid, rosy glow of the sunset, but my heart was full of that I had heard my father and the other men say, or rather whisper, in the evenings when they met secretly in our house and the door was tightly shut and the cracks covered with a blanket, that no ray of light might escape to give warning of the gathering assembled there.

They spoke of the great silver companies who half starved the miners such as they, of haciendados (landed proprietors) who treated their peons worse than beasts, and of unjust judges who oppressed the people and tried to wring from them their few centavos. Most of all, they told of Judge Gomez, the wicked magistrate of our own village, who stole the people's money, and had sent more than one innocent man to prison or slavery on the plantations that he might seize the victim's scanty possessions.

Then my father, Mateo Ruiz, who had some smattering of education, would read to them from "La Libertad," a newspaper that came to him from Mexico City, where he was once a shopkeeper. This paper was an organ of the Mexican Liberal Party, a new organisation pledged to work peacefully for the re-establishment of the constitution which the present Government had overthrown, and for the restoration of the ancient rights of the people for which Juarez and other brave men had striven.

My father and his friends thought little of us children as they crouched there whispering; we drank it all in. I doubt if there were a more devoted Liberal in the land that day than I, poor little, bare-legged Inez, who sat in the doorway and dreamed of what she would like to do for Mexico.

Our doorway opened almost on the road, a bare, well-trodden highway with only one house in sight beside our own. There in the dust a group of children were playing, laughing, shouting, and chasing each other about in the manner of healthy young creatures. They were dirty and tattered, bare-footed and bare-headed, but they were brimming with innocent glee. Foremost among them was my seven-year-old brother Jose, our only boy, a handsome child, black-haired,

black-eyed, straight-limbed, and sturdy.

Another sound mingling with their play aroused me from my vision. A rider, unperceived, until almost upon us, had come galloping up the road.

It was Gomez himself, the cruel judge. He was a man of between forty or fifty, high-complexioned, with frowning, dark brows, a great beak of a nose, and an ugly mouth nearly hidden by his bristling, black moustache. Although over-heavy, he possessed tremendous physical strength, and he sat on his great bay horse with perfect ease. Dust grimed his fine, grey coat, and his face was wet from the heat. Plainly, he was much out of temper.

The children drew to one side to let him pass, but they could not resist their desire to jeer at him.

"Hi!" they shouted. "Look at him! Big nose! Thief! . . . ."

Jose, the boldest of them all, was in the foreground. The rider, furious at the children's cries, uttered an oath and wheeled his horse suddenly. Jose sprang backward, but too late—the judge's hands had caught him by the throat. Leaning from the saddle, the man twisted the child's neck with both powerful hands then flung him to the ground almost at my feet.

I heard Jose's one terrible, gurgling cry; I heard my mother's scream as she rushed past me, and then the "thud, thud," of the horse's hoofs bearing Judge Gomez down the road. I saw the terror-stricken faces of the children, and I saw my mother falling unconscious to the earth where, before us, in the trampled dust of the highway that still bore the prints of his tiny, naked feet, lay a huddled shape with open mouth and horrible, staring eyes—all that was left of our pride and darling !

When we somewhat regained our senses after our paroxysm of terror, we children dragged my mother out of the road and placed her close to the side of the house. None of us dared to approach Jose.

Then, while my sister, Marta, and I crouched beside our mother, rubbing her hands and calling to her, the other children ran home to fetch their mother, our nearest neighbour.

This good woman, Senora Josefa, was the only person for whom we could send, since we had no other neighbours and our father was at work in the mines. She came at once and knelt down in the dust beside Jose. Then, with many a sob and passionate exclamation of grief and anger, she lifted his motionless form in her arms and, bearing it into the house, laid it tenderly down and covered it with a blanket.

Our childish instinct had told us truly Jose was past our aid. Not only was he choked, but his neck had been actually broken by the judge's awful hands.

CHAPTER TWO.

MY MOTHER'S FATE.

My mother never recovered from the shock of Jose's death. She grew melancholy and distracted, seemed scarcely to see us, and barely answered us when we spoke to her. Each day she passed hours in the bare and wind-swept cemetery beside her child's grave. One afternoon, while she was mourning there, a sudden storm arose. The wind howled and shrieked, driving before it great sheets of

rain, and Marta and I held our breath with terror of the thunder while we stumbled against the low mounds and pitiful, wooden crosses of the cemetery as we sought our mother.

We found her by our brother's grave. She crouched there lost in grief, drenched to the skin, unconscious of the wind and rain, the raging fury of the skies. We begged of her to come home, and she made no resistance but let us lead her there. She never went out again alive. The exposure in her weakened state had brought on rapid pneumonia, which she had no strength to resist. There was no doctor near. We had no money to have paid one had there been. Within three days after the storm we laid her to rest beside her child.

My father's anger against Judge Gomez, who had brought upon him double loss of wife and son, was, perhaps, the deeper that he dared not express it for fear of the consequences to Marta and me. Redress, except through act of violence, he could not obtain. Minor courts were not. Gomez was the sole representative of the law and—one does not look for justification in a suit where the criminal is also the judge. An appeal to the higher judiciary would have required all the money and influence which we did not possess. Justice—since it has become a commodity to be bought and sold—lies beyond the reach of the poor.

My father's one desire was to obtain the money with which to leave Guerrero. Perhaps some subtle intuition warned him that yet greater trouble was in store for him there—that even his remaining children were not safe.

(To be continued.)

HOW TO WORK.

SYNDICALISM, like all vital and historic movements, is destined to succeed because it is a natural outgrowth of pre-existing conditions. It is not in any sense a mere academic theory. It is the action of the industrial life of our times breaking for itself a new channel through obstructions heaped up by the tyrannies of the past. It is the birth of a new society from the womb of the old; and individual humans can aspire only to be the midwives at this birth.

Avoid Waste Effort.

Those who are called to this inspiring work of giving aid to the ushering in of a reign of industrial justice are naturally persons who have themselves become awakened to the profound significance of the industrial happenings of our time; and their task of bringing their fellow-workers to a similar understanding should be performed with zeal, but also with intelligence and system. On one hand every awakened Syndicalist should be eager to become multiplied many times over, so to speak, through the continuous winning of new converts so thoroughly convinced of the truth and utility of Syndicalism that they in turn will start out indefatigably upon a similar career of self-multiplication. But, on the other hand, every Syndicalist should seek to plant his or her efforts where they will do the most good, rather than waste a greater or less percentage of effectiveness through carelessness in selecting the persons toward the persuading of whom this propaganda should be aimed.

Win the Unions.

The special aim of the Industrial Syndicalist Education League is to carry on this propaganda among those workers who have already manifested sufficient initiative and respect for their class to have become affiliated with their appropriate trade unions. Such already organised workers are more likely to have become convinced, through the experiences of their respective unions, that the time has gone by when really effective results can be obtained from the old-time tactics adopted years ago, before the minds of the workers had even begun to become emancipated from intellectual bondage to conceptions and modes of thought instilled into the minds of the people by the ruling class through its control of all the avenues of education.

Aim Wisely.

Trades union experience, therefore, will have had the effect of making these organised workers much more capable of appreciating the magnificent hopefulness of the direct action promoted by Syndicalism, and, since it is therefore evident that a given amount of time and effort expended among trades unionists will produce many more workers for the spread of Syndicalism than if it were expended among non-unionists, it follows that this policy of firing our broadsides where every shot will count is the policy that promises the speediest realisation of justice for the working class.

Push this Paper.

Therefore, Comrades, be everywhere active among your fellow-unionists—in your workshops, in your homes, in your trades union meetings, and at working class meetings generally. Concentrate on those who show a responsive spirit, and ply them with literature and with spoken appeal until they, too, shall have enrolled themselves in this propagandist action which is pioneering the peoples on their march to the fair land of justice and liberty.

THE INDUSTRIAL SYNDICALIST EDUCATION LEAGUE

President - - TOM MANN.

OBJECT. To carry on among Trade Unionists, and the workers generally, a campaign of education in the principles of **Syndicalism**—which may be described as **revolutionary Trade Unionism**, since its immediate purpose is to conduct a **Scientific class War** against Capitalism—such war having as its objective, or ultimate aim, the **Capture of the Industrial System** and its management by the Workers themselves **for the benefit of the Whole community.**

COMMITTEE:
J. WALTER, ERNEST BARNES (Treasurer), JOHN TURNER, J. BARNES, JOHN LLOYD.
GENERAL SECRETARY:
GUY BOWMAN, 4, Maude Terrace, Walthamstow, London, E.

IF YOU REALISE

Firstly, that in the Labour Movement the need of the hour is to prove to the workers that the many faults of the present industrial system can never be remedied, except by DIRECT ACTION, i.e., by revolutionary industrial action within and upon the industries themselves;

Secondly, that in order to put this DIRECT ACTION into practice, it is necessary to keep up a general observation and study of modern industrial development;

Thirdly, that for the collating of the varied information obtained in various quarters, the workers should have a centre to which such information may be reported and thoroughly discussed;

Fourthly, that the workers should make use of the same centre for publishing and distributing pamphlets and for the carrying on of a literary propaganda;

Fifthly, that comrades having leisure to devote more or less time, in a colporteur or scout capacity, should act as a scout brigade for the sale of literature, at public meetings, in the workshops, and wherever possible;

Sixthly, that there is need that from the same centre of effort there should go forth comrades prepared not only to make public speeches on the subject of Direct Industrial Action, or Syndicalism as it is generally termed, but also to follow up such public efforts by responding to calls from Trade Unions, Trades Councils, Workmen's Clubs, etc.;

THEN WILL IT NOT BE THE RIGHT THING

for you to give practical effect to this realisation by becoming a member of the I.S.E.L., now in process of formation on the following basis of membership?

IF YOU WILL DO THIS

The League will thereafter keep you posted and in line to apply your efforts in effective team-work with other comrades.

MEMBERSHIP.

The membership of the League is open to any person who accepts the foregoing, no matter what views may be held by that person regarding politics; but no one who does not declare for non-parliamentary action may share in the responsible work of administration of the League. Therefore the possession of an ordinary membership card does not imply that the holder is entitled to speak or otherwise act on behalf of the League.

The following categories of persons are specially solicited to become members:—

I.—**Investigating Members.**—Those who are in a position to obtain inside information in regard to particular industries.

II.—**Literary Members.**—Those who have the time and ability to analyse and collate the information sent in by the investigators and observers, and to embody the results of the work in pamphlets and in special articles for the Press.

III.—**Colporteur Members.**—Those who want to see these Syndicalist pamphlets bought up and read by the Working Class, and are therefore willing to go and sell them both in their workshops and at public meetings.

IV.—**Speaking Members.**—Those who have the time and talent for public speaking, and are willing to place before public assemblies and Labour bodies the conclusions reached by the investigators and writers.

V.—**Supporting Members.**—Those who from all walks of life may be willing to assist work by their personal influence or by money contributions, or both.

SUBSCRIPTIONS.

The minimum subscription for members is 1s. per year; but the League is further supported by the voluntary contributions of its friends and sympathisers.

FILL UP THIS APPLICATION FORM, NOW!

APPLICATION FORM FOR MEMBERSHIP.

Fill in, cut out and post to Gen. Sec., who will enrol you.

Please enrol my name as a (1) Investigating / Literary / Colporteur / Speaking / Supporting Member of the I.S.E.L. I enclose £ : : as, a Yearly Part subscription to the League's Propaganda.

Name (in full)...
Occupation...
(and other useful particulars about yourself)
Address (clearly written)................................
(1) Strike out those items which do not apply.

PUSH OUR LITERATURE.

OUR PAMPHLETS—FORGING THE WEAPON.

Thousands of the rank and file in the Trade Unions up and down the country are now in thorough sympathy with the aims, objects, and methods of the I.S.E.L.

We welcome their sympathy, but we want to see it expressed in some useful, tangible form. To achieve this the best thing they can do is to

WORK UP AND PERMEATE,

with Syndicalist ideas, the branches of the Unions to which they belong.

From July, 1910, to June, 1911, we issued a series of pamphlets by Tom Mann, under the title *The Industrial Syndicalist*. These pamphlets are exactly what is wanted for beginners, and a perusal of them by Trade Unionists will do a lot towards putting them on the right lines.

But No. 3 of the series, *Forging the Weapon*, is of special importance to those who want to do something at once. In it Tom Mann deals with the situation at the period of writing; but the most important part of it is the section dealing with

THE WAY TO HELP.

Here it is suggested that those who are in sympathy with our principles should make a start in the branch of the Union to which they belong by moving a resolution expressing the opinion that the time has arrived when steps should be taken to unify the Union movement on the basis of Industrial Syndicalism. This will cause a discussion to take place, and the opener of the discussion should have a quantity of *Forging the Weapon* with him, thus enabling him to continue the educational work of his address. Endeavours should be made to get any such resolution, if carried, sent on to the District Council of the Union, and also to the Executive, thereby creating a discussion throughout the whole of the Union. Our friends should get their delegates to

THE LOCAL TRADES COUNCIL

instructed to move a resolution on the matter. From personal experience we can testify to the splendid facilities for propaganda which a Trades Council offers. As a rule the delegates there are the most active men of their Union branch. There are always plenty of opportunities arising in which our principles can be expounded, both from the point of view of organisation and also our revolutionary purpose. For example, the Cabinet Makers' resolution at the Sheffield T.U. Congress and the Railway Strike offered a timely opening. Then if one is a delegate to the Trades Council let him get a resolution through, that the Council organise joint open-air propaganda during the summer. This will give Syndicalist speakers a chance to explain from this point of view why

WORKERS SHOULD JOIN UNIONS.

Volunteers are wanted to address other societies upon Syndicalism, and to use all Trade Union and Socialist meetings to sell literature, and get in touch with sympathisers. Above all, at this juncture, circulate

"FORGING THE WEAPON."

wherever you can, and write Guy Bowman asking for membership in the Industrial Syndicalist Education League, so that an organised, cohesive, and sustained effort can be made to win the Trade Unions to our principles.

THE SYNDICALIST WEEKLY—£300 WANTED.

Comrades, never was the time more ripe for our paper, the SYNDICALIST, to appear weekly. The growing unrest amongst the rank and file of the workers generally calls for a more energetic propaganda. The manner in which the railwaymen's officials have held their men back during the London Transport Strike, the way in which old officials are holding back the metal-workers in the North, all point to the necessity of a paper for the fighting rank and file of all unions.

We want to concentrate the growing discontent of the workers into a useful channel. We must not allow this mass of enthusiasm and energy to run to waste. It must be drawn into a revolutionary path. *It needs a weekly journal* to persistently follow up an agitation. A month's interval is too long. A strike may be lost for want of a fighting spirit, or prolonged negotiations might damp down the ardour of the rank and file, leaving them a prey to the bosses and their labour lieutenants, the old-style officials. *We want and must have a weekly* to propagate our views. A weekly has more than four times the influence of a monthly. A weekly could easily be made the unofficial organ of all the rebels of the Trade Union world.

If an "appeal to soldiers" in a monthly journal terrifies our rulers, how much more so will a "Don't Shoot" article appearing four times as often? And the anti-militarist propaganda is not going to be slackened but intensified. Not only anti-militarism, but anti-policemanism as well. In our large cities life is becoming unbearable through the increasing officiousness of the police. All the forces that the employing class use against us must be combated.

To give our fellow-workers all over the country an adequate idea of what is taking place we need a weekly paper; to encourage the fighters by letting them know what each district is doing; to strengthen the weaker ones by letting them know what the fighters may do and dare; to emphasise the necessity for a continual warfare against the present system of wage slavery; to link up our forces to a still greater perfection; to rally the members of the working class for the General Strike we need and must have *a weekly* SYNDICALIST.

Below appears a preliminary list of subscriptions, but these emanate merely from personal friends and sympathisers, and £300 is the least that the venture can be made on. Send in some money yourself; get your workmate to; get your society to, and see that it comes to have the SYNDICALIST weekly from next month on.

FOR THE "WEEKLY SYNDICALIST."

	£	s.	d.
J. Vernier	0	2	6
L. Bathsians	0	3	6
H. Philip	0	1	0
Rev. Sadler	0	1	3
John Gordon	0	1	0
J. Sestili	0	0	6
H. MacFall	0	1	0
Henry Bool	2	0	0
Leonard D. Abbott	0	4	0
C. C. Everson	0	6	0
Joseph Lane	1	0	0
Mrs. Dallas-Askew	1	0	0
S. Butterworth	0	10	0
Mrs. C. H. Holiday	0	5	0
London Group Social Studies	1	12	6½
Railway Servants (Glazebrook Branch)	0	2	6
Amalgamated Engineers (Hammersmith Branch)	0	10	0
	£8	6	9

(Continued from page 1)

using all means at his disposal to rouse once more among the people of France the military and Chauvinist (jingo) craze!

In Case of War.

Things would look black indeed if there were not in all countries revolutionary minorities to impress with ardour the doctrine of Internationalism which finds its highest and most logical expression in anti-patriotism—the humanitarian ideal par excellence. The advocates of Syndicalism repudiate the patriotic dogma, and this is the advice they give to the workers: "In case of war, *declare the general strike*; especially you, the transport workers! You have in your hands the power to obviate international massacre!"

If the leaders of the "Social-Democracy" of Germany had not done everything in their power to thwart the admirable scheme put before the International Congress of Transport Workers at Copenhagen by Mr. Havelock Wilson, and had their seamen co-operated in the fight of last summer, a movement of such gigantic proportions would have been in operation that most probably the Kaiser would have thought twice before voicing his anticipations of war: for he would have realised what threatening possibilities for the future are contained in a maritime strike of an international character.

Let me add that we—the Syndicalists—condemn militarism in all its manifestations; therefore, all our efforts tend to prevent the renewal of fratricide on the economic battlefield as well. That is why the capitalist Press denounces us as the most dangerous offenders!

Ah! how shallow are the Christian convictions of the governing class when their terrestrial interests are at stake! What do they care that those they condemn to hard labour are the true disciples of Christ, and are furthering His precepts and those of His spiritual descendants, the Fathers of the Church? Has not Tertullian said: "How can a Christian go to war? How can he bear arms in times of peace, when the Lord has forbidden the use of a sword? Jesus Christ, in disarming St. Peter, disarmed all soldiers." The Christians persecute the anti-militarists just as the pagans persecuted the Christians who denounced lawful assassination. In Catholic Italy the prisons are positively crammed with anti-militarist militants.

The "Don't Shoot" Propaganda.

The *International*, the paper of the Syndicalist Camore di Labore di Parma, which I also represent, stated the other day that, since the horrible Turco-Italian war began, sentences have been passed on the courageous men and women who protested against the Italian atrocities at Tripoli, aggregating to 250 years of imprisonment. Amongst these victims of the Italian Government's abominable persecution is my heroic young friend Maria Rygier, who has been condemned to three years' solitary confinement!

But whatever Governments may do, the "Don't Shoot" propaganda is gaining ground every day; and the hour is fast approaching when the soldier, sent to the strike area to re-establish order, divided between discipline and conscience, will obey the latter, and thus act as a conscious Christian. As an encouraging sign of the times, we note that during the recent riots in Budapest, the soldiers, instead of shooting down the insurgents as they were commanded to do, shot in the air.

Apart from all Christian considerations, the Nationalist idea must be uprooted from the popular mind. Irish Unionists, and you, Irish Nationalists, grasp this fact! A country, a nation, let us say Ireland or England, is far from being a homogeneous whole. A country, a nation, a state, is nothing in the nature of a community of equals, of loving brothers. A nation—even the most liberal and democratic one—is divided into two zones: the zone of the "haves" with their paradise, the zone of the "have nots" with their hell.

A nation is not even the expression of ethnical unity, for capitalism is everywhere a factor of racial differentiation, a factor of racial retrogression for the labouring part of the community. The exploitation of man by man, with all its evils, has had the result (as established by Professor Nicheftoro's investigations) of generating an under-race, which he has called *the race of the poor*, and that race is characterised by the physical and mental deficiencies of its members, who are doomed to premature death.

The Red Flag of the New Order.

Now, do you not see how absurd it is on the part of the victimised section of a nation to allow itself to fall under the spell of the capitalist patriotic suggestion, and to be led to believe that there can possibly be solidarity of interests between the victims and their parasites?

Workers! if you are class conscious, you must realise and assert that you are fellow-citizens, fellow-compatriots of the workers of all nationalities; that you repudiate all frontiers but one, the class frontier; that the only war you will wage shall be the class war; and that your flag is the red flag of social revolution, the flag of the new order of things!

In spite of the wonderful progress of applied science, and in spite of marvellous discoveries, we are not really living in civilised times. In the twentieth century man is exploited by man, just as he was exploited in ancient times. The lot of the present-day wage-earner is as bad as was the lot of the slaves of antiquity, or the serfs of the Middle Ages. It is even worse; because, while the slaves and serfs were at least sure of their daily crust, the labourer of modern times lives from hand to mouth, with the spectre of starvation for himself, wife and children, ever at his side. The industrial worker's lot is "toil, toil, toil in poverty, hunger and dirt"; make money, make money, in order to keep the money market going while your own children are in the gutter and your daughter is on the street—and then; when you are used up, worn-out, and unfit for any work, then starve; starve! die in the workhouse or commit suicide!

Such a society is a society of iniquity and of abomination; nevertheless the capitalists are determined that this society shall not change, shall not evolve. Thus it is fatally a continual tug of war between Labour and Capital. When Labour gains anything it is only by sheer force, and it has always to be on the alert, for Capital is always seeking to take back what it has been compelled to concede. The present attitude of the Shipping Federation singularly illustrates this assertion. The employers have never been more aggressive than they are, now that they are organised nationally, and even internationally, in the hope of breaking the men's Unions and enforcing cheap labour. Industrial conflicts are bound to take colossal proportions in the near future. Very soon every isolated effort, collective or individual, will be a thing of the past: the lesser will be merged in the greater. Sectional organisations and sectional strikes are played out.

Direct Action.

Workers of Belfast! this is my message: Do not allow yourselves to be blindfolded any more, either by the Unionist or the Nationalist leaders. Keep your eyes wide open, so as not to go in the wrong direction. Many reads, as you know, lead to Rome, but there is only one which leads to the abolition of pauperism, and that is the international road. Internationalist effective solidarity must be your watchword; complete success can only be obtained through the *direct action* of the world's industrial workers.

"Direct action!" These words may jar on the ears of many of my hearers who put their trust in political action; but, my friends, let the facts speak for themselves. Parliamentary Socialism, as a revolutionary factor, has proved a failure everywhere!

What is the great electoral victory of the Social Democrats of Germany compared with the victories gained by the strikers' army of Great Britain? The maritime strike of last summer; the coal strike more gigantic still and tremendous in its effects, stopping the machinery of the industrial and social system as with a magic wand, have brought into the limelight of an immense stage the tremendous power of direct action, throwing Parliamentary action into the shade for ever. The epoch-making organisation is not the political organisation of Socialism; *it is your Federation of Transport Workers*, whose advance has been continuous, which is ever ready to give battle and to prove effective solidarity, not only towards its own section, but towards all the fractions of the organised proletariat. This Federation of Transport Workers, which put into operation the Syndicalist methods during the great strike of last summer, will, if it continues to work on the right lines, and assists the railwaymen, be looked upon as the leader, not only of the Labour movement in the British Isles, but as the leader of the whole world's Labour movement.

A Power of Social Transformation.

The epoch-making man is not the social Parliamentary leader: a Ramsay Macdonald may raise himself to power, as John Burns, Millerand, and Briand have done, but he will never raise the proletariat to a higher standard of life. The epoch-making man is the propagandist of Syndicalism, the man who transforms the masses from a flock of sheep, blindly running after their shepherd, to a mass of thinking, acting, willing, combative units, all vibrating in unison to the exalting sentiment of self-help and of active fraternal solidarity combined. The epoch-making men are my active friends—Tom Mann, Guy Bowman, and all the others who are identified with active Syndicalism and anti-Militarism, and who were thrown into gaol because the governing class realises, only too well what a power of social transformation they incarnate.

There is no doubt that through the work accomplished by Tom Mann, Guy Bowman, and his colleagues, Great Britain is at the present moment the country where the greatest revolutionary potentialities exist. Only a few years ago, the British Trade Unionists were in the rear of the Labour movement; now they have sprung to the front with one bound.

And you, Irish, may be proud, because the Irish boycott has become one of the great weapons of the social battle! Boycotting of everything concerning scab labour, blackleg goods, and repression will be the decisive factor in the termination of the class conflict, because inevitably it must take all power away from capitalism.

The Dogged Opposer of the General Strike.

Everybody feels that the wind is blowing towards a general strike in Great Britain; yet a national, a solely British revolution, would be premature, because it would be suppressed by the neighbouring Powers. We think, therefore, that the British proletariat will have to wait before it comes into its own, wait until the other sections of the International are ready to come into line, and this will not be before the colossal German social democracy, the dogged opposer of the general strike, has lost its influence on the workers. Already—sign of the times! —the social democratic workers are divided among themselves; Syndicalism is attracting them more and more, while international determination against the master class is bound to bring about International Syndicalist Unity before long.

Meanwhile, my Irish friends, give *all* your fighting spirit to your own cause. Inspired by the admirable example of the British strikers, whose pluck and solidarity are hailed with unbounded enthusiasm by the proletariat of the universe, prepare to take an active part in the movement. Agitate, agitate, agitate, for better conditions, for shorter hours, for a minimum wage, and live in the exalting hope of a day, which may be near at hand, when the trumpets of revolution shall sound, and the high walls of the capitalist Jerichos shall fall down with a formidable crash.

I conclude: Down with nationalism that divides men, and Hurrah for Internationalism that unites them!

OUR PRISON SYSTEM.

By GUY A. ALDRED.

The optimism that is ever ready to defend authorised iniquity has led us to believe that huge improvements were witnessed in our prison system from the time of Godwin to that of Dickens, and between the age of Dickens and the present time. If this was true, we should shudder to think what it must have been like when Godwin wrote his "Caleb Williams." That work must have been a very poor indictment indeed.

The case of Mr. Ball, the Suffragist, must have come as a surprise to persons who are given to believing that prison life is being reduced surely if slowly to a humane system of detention.

In November, 1910, Mr. Hugh Franklin was sentenced to six weeks' imprisonment in the second division for deliberately and intentionally assaulting Mr. Churchill. A month later Mr. McDougall was convicted of a unpremeditated, and consequently unintentional, assault on Mr. Lloyd George. McDougall was only eighteen, and Lloyd George received no injury whatever. It was thought consequently that McDougall would receive a light sentence. Instead of this he was sent to hard labour for two months. The difference between the two cases was this: Franklin was a relative of a Cabinet Minister, whereas McDougall was only a poor lad.

Mr. William Ball was a friend of McDougall, and, regarding the divergence of sentence as a political and social outrage, he very rightly broke a window as a protest against the sentence. He was sentenced to two months' hard labour as a result. Ball insisted that his offence was a political one, as it unquestionably was. No heed was given to his protest, however, and he accordingly went on the hunger strike.

It was on Christmas Day, 1911, that Mr. Ball was submitted to forcible feeding. For five and a half weeks the treatment was continued, and although Mr. Ball was strong enough physically to remain alive under this disgusting treatment, his mentality weakened, and he was driven insane.

I hope persons who live in Pentonville district will take his case to heart, and I hope the dastardly warders and their superiors who participated in this outrage will be boycotted and publicly hissed. I trust that friends, or at least the acquaintances of the wives of these men, will let them see how disgraceful a thing it is to be the underpaid housekeeper of a craven agent of our prison despotism. The boycott could be applied in the neighbourhood of other prisons as well with advantage.

Mr. Ball complained, and complains, of electricity and noises in his head. Driven mad by hirelings under a system of barbarous torture and secret despotism, he was removed to a lunatic asylum as a pauper lunatic without his wife being consulted in the matter. To some extent this iniquity has been righted; but that such a barbarous procedure was possible serves as some index to the sufferings that must fall to the lot of a friendless prisoner.

Now it is pretended in defence of the prison system that all this is essential to discipline, and discipline is necessary to reform. I submit that this is but the red-tape way of spelling slavery and that, under all circumstances, slavery breeds vice, and not virtue. And discipline, as a trade job, trampling on every human principle for a hireling wage, is productive of so much evil that it adopts secrecy because it fears a public exposure of its corruption; and the only way with despotism is to fight and expose it, never to plead with it.

In the autumn of 1909 that reactionary son of the hypocritical G.O.M., Home Secretary Gladstone, sanctioned the process of forcible feeding, and the first victim was Mrs. Mary Leigh. She was pinioned by having her arms and legs held down, and her head was forced backwards. An indiarubber tube was then inserted through the nose or mouth and pushed down the throat. At the end of the tube was a cup, through which liquid was poured. Perhaps the chaplain was looking on, in case he was required to read the burial service. That would be in accord with his duties. It was consequently established by the testimony of leading medical men that, in the case of sane, conscious, and unwilling patients, this feeding by force does not nourish the victim. It is consequently not only futile, but brutal and dangerous, being an attempt to undermine the strength of a starved stomach.

Under a system where despotism did not pry into the communication of every prisoner, and punish with barbarities the slave who "splits," such hideous torture could not continue a day.

At Newcastle, father than forcibly feed Lady Constance Lytton, the authorities discharged her on medical evidence, stating that she suffered from a weak heart. To her lasting credit let it be recalled how Lady Constance exposed this hypocrisy. Disguising herself as Jane Wharton, a factory girl, she again went to gaol—and was forcibly fed. Only when, after seven days, her identity was discovered did the medical officer unearth her weak heart. Of course Gladstone gladly took responsibility! Such is Liberal hypocrisy!

In all twenty-nine women were submitted to this degrading treatment. Then the authorities succumbed somewhat to the public scandal. Under Churchill, a new set of rules were adopted for prisoners of the second division, which removed the criminal marks and practically admitted the right of the Suffragists to be treated as political prisoners.

I.S.E.L.
(Manchester Group.)

At a meeting held in Manchester, at which Tom Mann and Guy Bowman were present, it was decided to hold a Syndicalist Conference at Manchester in November next.

Invitations will be sent out to all Trade Union branches and Trades Councils in Lancashire and Yorkshire, but any Trade Union in Great Britain and Ireland may send a delegate, who will receive a cordial welcome. It is desired that as many branches as possible throughout the country may be represented.

The conference will take place on a Saturday afternoon and evening—probably on November 30. Bodies desirous of being represented should communicate with the Secretary, I.S.E.L., 50A, Market Street, Manchester.

Tom Mann's
Penny Pamphlets

No. 1.—PREPARE FOR ACTION.
No. 2.—THE TRANSPORT WORKERS.
No. 3.—FORGING THE WEAPON.
No. 4.—ALL HAIL, SOLIDARITY!
No 5.—SYMPOSIUM ON SYNDICALISM.
No. 6.—A MANCHESTER MESSAGE TO THE WORKERS OF ENGLAND.
No. 7.—PARLIAMENTARY ACTION versus SYNDICALISM, 2d.
No. 8.—MINERS, WAKE UP!
No. 9.—THE WEAPON SHAPING.
No. 10.—A TWO-FOLD WARNING.
No. 11.—THE RAILWAYMEN.
No. 12.—THE TRANSPORT INDUSTRY.

A dozen will cost you 1s. 3d., post free, and any one of them is worth that. A FACT.

Send to GUY BOWMAN,
4, MAUDE TERRACE, WALTHAMSTOW, LONDON, E.

DO IT NOW!

List of Lectures
By Tom Mann.

No. 1.—SYNDICALISM: EXPLAINED AND DEFENDED.
No. 2.—HOW TO EMPTY THE PRISONS, WORKHOUSES, AND ASYLUMS.
No. 3.—INDUSTRIAL SOLIDARITY MORE POTENT THAN PARLIAMENT.
No. 4.—CAPITALISM, SOCIALISM, AND SYNDICALISM.
No. 5.—THE DUTIES, FUNCTIONS, AND RESPONSIBILITIES OF TRADES COUNCILS.
No. 6.—THE CURE FOR POVERTY BY "DIRECT ACTION."
No 7.—THE COMING INDUSTRIAL REVOLUTION: HOW TO HASTEN IT.
No. 8.—THE SYNDICALISTS OF FRANCE: WHO THEY ARE AND WHAT THEY ARE DOING.
No. 9.—WHY EMIGRATE? WHAT'S WRONG WITH ENGLAND?
No. 10.—FRANCIS PLACE AND ROBERT OWEN.
No. 11.—JOHN RUSKIN AND WILLIAM MORRIS.
No. 12.—WINSTANLEY THE DIGGER AND LILBURNE THE LEVELLER.
No. 13.—WHY PARLIAMENT CANNOT SAVE THE PEOPLE!
No. 14.—STATE INDUSTRIAL ARBITRATION INCOMPATIBLE WITH ECONOMIC FREEDOM.

Unions, Societies, or Trades Councils wishful to arrange for Lectures, should communicate direct with TOM MANN, 23, Engadine Street, Southfields, London, S.W.

CORRESPONDENCE.

ETTOR—GIOVANNITTI DEFENCE COMMITTEE.

COMRADES,—

This great textile centre, which was only recently the scene of a startling industrial revolt, is again attracting widespread attention. This is due to the continued imprisonment of the two I. W. W. strike leaders, Joseph J. Ettor and Arthuro Giovannitti, and the efforts now being made to secure their freedom. Their case is agitating Europe and the United States. In Italy, it was the cause of an interpellation by Cabrini, a member of the Chamber of Deputies, and is now the subject of correspondence between the Italian and United States Governments. It also agitates the Italian Press, owing to the efforts of Aristiolo Giovannitti, who appeals for justice on behalf of his brother, who is an Italian subject. In France and England, mass meetings are being held on behalf of both imprisoned men, and letters of protest have been sent by them to President and Governor Foss.

In this country a like course is being followed in all large industrial centres. Labour organisations, regardless of affiliations, are joining with the Socialist Party in holding protest conferences and demonstrations and in collecting funds to provide legal defence. Resolutions are being adopted and sent out to Governor Foss and District Attorney Atwill. Some of the conferences, like that of Philadelphia, advocate a general strike of all the workers throughout the country in order to force judicial action favourable to the two men. A similar strike in their behalf is now being agitated in all the textile cities of New England. The feeling displayed is intensely better. Rev. Nicholas Van Der Pyl, of Haverhill, who investigated the situation, declares that the permanent imprisonment of the labour leaders "will be one of the most serious crises we have to meet in the industrial situation."

The reason for this condition of affairs is to be found in the circumstances attending the arrest and imprisonment of the two leaders, Ettor and Giovannitti, who are both held as accessories before the fact to the murder of Annio La Pizza, who was killed during a clash between the police and strikers. It is claimed that advantage was taken of the shooting to arrest the leaders in the hopes of breaking the strike. Neither Ettor nor Giovannitti was actually present at the shooting; both were admittedly two miles away at the time. Nor did they desire the woman's death, as she was a striker in their ranks. Fourteen eye-witnesses for the defence testify that the fatal shot was fired by a policeman named Burbit. In this country, the Ettor—Giovannitti case is declared to be similar to that of the Chicago anarchists. In France it is compared with the case of Durand, the secretary of the local Shovelers' Union.

In brief, the workers hold that Ettor and Giovannitti are innocent.

Lawrence, Mass., U.S.A.,
June 18, 1912.

SYNDICALISM AND THE STATE.

To the Editor of the SYNDICALIST.

DEAR COMRADE—I should like to make a few comments on Odon Por's article in the first number of the SYNDICALIST, as it opens up the whole question of the relation of the industrial syndicate to the community.

I enclose copy of my pamphlet, "The Universal Strike: Why it is needed, and how it is possible," from which you will see I am with you in emphasising the importance of direct industrial action. But whereas you appear to favour syndical possession and control of the means of life, I feel that that should be the function of the organised community, call it the State or what you will.

It will be noted that Odon Por favours leasing of the railroads by the Trade Unions (though probably only a step to complete possession). But is there any difference in principle between Syndical ownership and company ownership? The tendency would be to restrict membership to those already in the Union, and to regard the railroads as means of making money for the railroaders, instead of the common good. Of course, if the State imposes certain conditions to prevent this, well and good; and national ownership through the State, together with Syndical, in place of bureaucratic management, seems a feasible and desirable ideal, but this is far removed from Syndical ownership or possession.

The danger of Syndicalism seems to me to be that unions will enter partnership with employers and exclude outsiders. The Bradford woolcombers, for example, made a compact with the masters and then "closed" the union. The glassmakers actually went on strike to force certain firms to join the combine of masters.

It may be retorted that this is not true Syndicalism. Agreed. But just as the Labour Party are not true Socialists. But something more than sentiment must stop the development when circumstances are favourable to it.

My ideal of society is William Morris's "News from Nowhere," but as a stage (and perhaps a long one) I favour Bellamy's idea of an equal income for all—to be paid to all as citizens, not as producers. As steps thereto, we need public ownership of social utilities and minimum and maximum incomes, the former gradually converging to the latter level. Indeed the maximum is of more importance than the minimum, as without it, the relative share of the worker to the total product may remain the same or even grow less. And excessive inequality means the eternal struggle for riches, which leads to all our social evils. On the other hand, the maximum income once attained, there would be no incentive to exploit others for riches, and other motives would come into prominence.

My Syndicalism is therefore a method—a means of abolishing Capitalism and the capitalist State, but the ideal is Communism, when the functions of the syndicates will be to manage their respective functions in the common interest, subject to the control of the Common Council of the nation.—Yours fraternally, ALF. BARTON.

Sheffield, February 16.

FEDERATION OF TRADES COUNCILS.

To the Editor of the SYNDICALIST.

It can be said with safety that Syndicalism is reviving the labour movement, or rather its work is acting with other factors in causing a general awakening of the labour forces in this country. This is good. May it long be a driving force. Trade Unions are sadly in need of such.

The SYNDICALIST of February publishes an article on the Federation of Trades Councils. Though the idea seems to be anything but new, the time is most opportune for the formation of this federation. Such a federation must lead to good results. Dismemberment of Trades Councils is bad. Co-operation is needed. The linking up of all Trades Councils into one body is a policy all Trade Unionists must strive for, and it remains for Trades Councils which see the wisdom of such a policy to at once take active stps to bring about the desired federation. If Syndicalist propaganda can lead to this it might be truly said that it has done something extremely useful for the future of labour of their country.

The above-mentioned article should receive the attention it deserves.

ARTHUR JONES,
Shop Assistants' Union.

Forest Gate, February 28.

THE I.S.E.L. OVER SEAS.

To the Editor of the SYNDICALIST.

DEAR SIR,—Please find enclosed money order, for which send us the SYNDICALIST. We take several Labour and Socialist publications, and have had two copies of the SYNDICALIST. We consider it the best of all, and it is read through and through by all the members.

Most of us belong to the I.W.W., which is pure Syndicalism, and we send greetings, and hope you can educate the workers so that in their future strike they will not let Labour leaders and politicians rob them of th• fruit of their victories, as in recent strikes.—Yours for the Revolution, PROLETARIAT CLUB.

Los Angeles (Cal.) U.S.A., June 6, 1912.

To the Editor of the SYNDICALIST.

FELLOW WORKER,—Enclosed find money order for $1.00. Put us on the subscription list of the SYNDICALIST AND TRANSPORT WORKER for same. If there is any literature dealing on this question, you might let me know. We have started a Syndicalist League here, and we are making headway. We were up till two weeks ago a part of the I.W.W., the A.F. of L. starting an organisation in opposition to us. The bosses were delighted—expecting a factional fight. We joined the A.F. of L., and fooled them.

I have been a member of the I.W.W. for over five years, and I am beginning to realise the impossible task they have on hand—namely, the building up of an entire new Labour movement, by destroying, instead of capturing the A.F. of L. They say that the A.F. of L. can't be revolutionary. There are a great many of us, members of the I.W.W., who not only deny it, but have arguments so strong that the I.W.W. Press refuses to publish any of them.—Yours for the Cause,

J. W. JOHNSTONE,
Sec. Syndicalist League No. 1.

Nelson (B.C.), Canada, April 15, 1912.

THE MOVEMENT OF THE LIVING WORLD.

To the Editor of the SYNDICALIST.

DEAR SIR,—Having at last procured the SYNDICALIST for June through my friend, Mr. Quelch, I should like to congratulate you and Mr. Mann warmly. I have been convinced of the necessity for Syndicalism for more than six years, but found it impossible to get any expression from that point of view published in England. The very hostility towards it shows how really it reflects the working movement, which is to say the movement in a real sense of the living world.

I enclose £1, and beg you will send on the paper regularly (I hope a weekly edition), and also let me know if you could allow me room, and if so how much, for an article on representation as opposed to oppression, a discussion I want very much to see opened out.—Yours fraternally,

FRIDA DALLAS ASKEW.

June 19, 1912.

To the Editor of the SYNDICALIST.

MY DEAR GUY BOWMAN,—I am very much obliged to you for your kindness in sending me the SYNDICALIST; it is a lively little paper, and will do much good, the first copy especially. The letter to a soldier and the article on the Italian railways ought to be reprinted. They are very good. Personally, I am a Socialist who believes in direct action, and like yourself in a new morality, but we have a long way to go yet, for to my mind, neither Syndicalism nor Socialism, as taught to-day will do; but both combined. Syndicalism alone would lead to the re-enacting of the history of the Guilds; Socialism alone, to State capitalism and officialism.

Education is still very much wanted. The idea that has been at the back of my head for years is an order of propagandists, non-party and non-political, which will pay and work. Such a body, once organised, would control the Labour and Socialist movement in this country the same as the order of the propaganda controlled the old Catholic Church.

I am not rich, so have enclosed a little towards the Maintenance Fund. P.O. for 1s. enclosed.

Kind regards,
F. J. PINNELL.

Dalston, February 24.

ENGLAND!

By ANNA LINCOLN.

England! my soul is filled with anguish
  That I call thy land my own,
For thy helpless victims languish,
  And their song is Sorrow's moan.
On yond high seas thy proud flag floats,
  And splendour gilds thy throne;
But hideous over all there gloats
  King Greed, with heart of stone.

Thy wealth! Where is it, England,
  When thy children cry for bread?
Where thy Beauty, vaunted England,
  To the lives in slumdom bred?
O'er all the earth thy wealth is sung,
  But what of thy greater Ilth?
To all thy land that taint has clung—
  The taint of Moral Filth.

Thy many "Courts of Justice" stand
  All dressed in borrowed dignity.
For everywhere, in every land,
  Should *Justice* for us all be *free!*
Thou *hast* no Justice for thy poor,
  And they have *no* Recompense
For toil that leaves them bent and sore,
  And starves both soul and sense.

If one be rich, that one can *buy*
  Thy Justice—Oh! quite the best.
If one be poor, then law courts fly,
  "He is but a Workhouse guest."
For he who toils not lives at ease
  And multiplies his riches
The Idle Rich own land and trees—
  The Poor, not even ditches

That shameful thing, the "Poor Law"
    game:
  The Hells thy workers people:
Of Want, Despair, and Pain, and Blame:
  Oh! higher than a steeple
Now surges this great sea of Wrong,
  Where, proudly, England's flag unfurls!
Aye! listen to Life's dreadful song
  From victims caught within thy swirls!

This is thy Greatness, my England!
  This misery here bred by thee.
This thy mantle is—*of Glory,*
  And I am ashamèd of thee,
Ashamèd of thee, my England!
  England! the land of my birth.
For suffering groans on every hand,
  And thou hast martyred worth,

Upon an altar raised to Gold.
  To thy undying shame
Shall this black page of life be told,
  And told *in England's name!*
For the Coffers of England's Glory
  Are full and are running o'er
With its victims, bruised and gory,
  And the sad, and the sick, and the poor.

There's a wail that is reaching to Heaven
  That robs us of sleep and of rest:
It's the cry of the hearts that are riven
  And the bodies with burdens hard pressed.
And the Flag of our Nation is flying,
  And Gold is the god of our land:
But when in Time's shade we are lying—
  How with God are we going to stand?

THE CONSCRIPTION AND THE BOY SCOUTS.

(From the *International Socialist,* Sydney.)

The conscription crime and the Boy Scout madness is beginning to shed fruit that is rotten-ripe. On Dec. 9, according to daily Press reports, while some "scouting" was being done, one set of boys met another detachment of scouts and ordered them to "bail up." The scouts "bailed up" all right, and then the rifle of one of the bailing-up party went off, and the bullet made a hole in the hat of a bailed-up scout, whereupon the latter emitted a terrified yell, and sprinted towards the reluctant distance nearly, as suddenly as Jim Page fell down Majuba Hill. The bailing-up detachment fired two volleys after the retreating foe, and then the law came along and in the name of the Labour Party scragged the kids for doing what they had been taught to do under the Labour Party's murder scheme, and flung them into jail, where they stayed until their friends bailed them out.

CUTTINGS.

MR. TOM MANN'S RELEASE.

(From *Manchester Evening News.*)

Though sentenced to six months' imprisonment for inciting soldiers to mutiny, Mr. Tom Mann has been released after suffering little more than imprisonment for six weeks. He seems to have been impressed by the humanity of the prison system, being complimentary rather than critical about it. Now, like a giant refreshed (for that is the sort of feeling which such prison life as he has experienced seems to have upon him), he talks of organising a great campaign in favour of his pet theory: the control of industry by the workers for the workers without any appeal to Parliament or to any class outside the working class. It is not a theory which finds acceptance among practical men. As long as the value of work varies, the value of the return given for it will vary. There are bound to be officers in the industrial army as there are in the regular army, and the men who do work which calls for the exercise of exceptional skill and exceptional knowledge will continue to exercise managerial powers and to draw high salaries, however eloquently Mr. Mann and his friends may argue in favour of equality. There is no such thing as all-round equality. Even in the labour world there are men picked out to be leaders, and some of them are more eminent leaders than others, and some of them get better pay than others.

THE FRAUD OF POLITICAL ENFRANCHISEMENT.

(From the *Open Road.*)

The governing class is faced with a problem which is becoming ever more serious. The people are becoming desperate—and desperate with a considerable degree of forced enlightenment. A large proportion of them have exacted just sufficient leisure to enable them to study social questions. And cheap literature, as well as an ever-increasing facility for communication, has put them into touch with the thoughts of seers, politicians, and charlatans—men who call out their truest and best, those promise them emancipation by the transference of political power, and others who merely make capital out of their misery.

And we are witnessing the hopeless spectacle of the propertyless trying to shake off the yoke that is imposed upon them by the application of the same bad principles which are applied for its imposition. Their representatives imagine, or appear to imagine, that the misery of humanity arises from the fact that other men are on top instead of themselves. If only they were in power, they would have all their subjects on a level with themselves. Wrongdoers would be "reformed" instead of being punished. Thus the evil is perpetuated and aggravated by the very means adopted to minimise or abolish it. Men have groaned under an old tyranny until in their turn they struggled into power, and in the name of their more exalted ideals created the tyranny of the new age. All history proves the absurdity or the delusion that any one set of men can govern their fellows better than any other set. Aristocracies have given way to aristocracies, aristocracies to plutocracies, and plutocracies to democracies, each new form reviving and intensifying the evils supposed to be peculiar to its predecessors. Representative government is only an ingenious device by which those already in power have retained under new forms the allegiance of their old retainers.

But we are on the verge of political bankruptcy, and the rulers know it. The people are beginning to see through the fraud of political enfranchisement, and are looking for other means to realise their aspirations and desires. The rulers are faced with the problem in its acutest form, which, if for nothing else, then for their own preservation, they will have to solve—viz., the persistence of undeserved poverty in the midst of abundant wealth; of unemployment in the midst of unsatisfied desires.

WHERE TO BUY "THE SYNDICALIST."

Printed and published by GUY BOWMAN, 4, Maude Terrace, Walthamstow, E.

The Syndicalist

VOL. 1. NO. 7.   LONDON, AUGUST, 1912.   MONTHLY, ONE PENNY.

THE TRANSPORT STRIKE IN LONDON.

One year ago the Transport Workers arrested the attention of the world by the fight they put up for better conditions; that struggle was remarkable chiefly because all sections of workers in all ports of the country made common cause; for the first time in the history of such fights unity characterised the men.

As a consequence the gains were substantial, including the refusal on the part of the men to continue to take the Shipowners' Federation ticket, the joining of such genuine union as suited the men's interest and the wearing of the union button or badge when and how they pleased, the increase of wages for various grades averaging a shilling a day advance, in a number of instances the reduction of hours, proper make-up of gangs, and for sea-faring men the right to have a union official visit the men on arrival and departure of vessels.

These improvements were not won in a day or a week, nor was solidarity among all sections shown at the start of the struggle; the organisations were imperfect, but the vigorous advocacy of the advantages of common action fired the enthusiasm of the men, and the struggle, began in June, wound up triumphantly for the men in August.

The union membership was increased beyond anything ever before experienced, several departments one hundred per cent. were organised; taking the seagoing men, dockers, stevedores, lightermen, warehousemen, and carters and carmen directly connected with port work, over ninety per cent. are in the unions.

In London many of the agreements between men and employers were arranged through and by the Transport Workers' Federation, and the method pursued has been for the men to show their Federation ticket at the taking-on stand when engaged for work; and the union button, whilst it indicates membership of the union, is of a general character, and is not changed periodically to indicate that the man is a *financial* member. In Liverpool the unions are identified with the Federation, but the Dockers' Union button is changed quarterly and can only be obtained by those who are clear on the books, and this covers identification with the Federated Unions.

The present London strike took place over one man, a member of the Lightermen's Union, but who had been a foreman, and was, it is alleged, being supported by firms to behave in a way detrimental to the men, with the avowed object of breaking up the solidarity brought about by the Transport Workers' Federation. In addition to this was the fact that a number of employers were not paying the rates of wages agreed upon at the settlement last year, and which was a source of continual trouble. So, naturally, when action was taken by refusing to allow the lighterman to break the solidarity that existed and that was the men's only safeguard against demoralisation of their unions and themselves, it was decided to claim the wages and conditions previously agreed to, but not complied with, by the employers.

The fight, beyond all question, ought to have been in all ports, i.e., all connected with the Transport Workers should have exhibited the same solidarity that was the sole reason of their victory last year. No good can be done by any recital of negotiations to bring this about. For myself, I was in Manchester prison at the time and knew nothing about it, being sentenced on the 9th of May, and the strike beginning on 23rd of May. It had been on a month before I heard of it, and J. Havelock Wilson, president of the National Sailors' and Firemen's Union, and who engineered last year's struggle for seafaring men, was in the United States.

The casual nature of dock work, which results in day and half-day engagements, plays into the hands of capitalists to encourage and to keep near the docks swarms of men including the victims of other districts squeezed out and demoralised by a vicious environment. There is no cure for this but perfect industrial organisation. Take away the unions and immediately a social hell is the result, all who know the facts know this is so, and the betterment of recent years is entirely traceable to Trade Union action. UNITY MORE AND MORE PERFECT IS THE ONE HOPE OF FURTHER BETTERMENT.

It was hoped that by this time the various railwaymen's unions would have been lined up as part of the National Transport Workers' Federation, but they have so far been chiefly occupied in endeavours to amalgamate their own forces. Now three of the organisations have emphatically declared by vote of members to amalgamate; and this is good. It is, however, rumoured that some influential members of the A.S.R.S. are not showing any keenness to consummate amalgamation, the only grounds for such an attitude appears to be that the G.R.W.U., having added to their membership about three times the number they had last year, in the nature of things cannot bring much per man with them into the proposed amalgamation, but this is too trifling to be seriously entertained. That which is really vital is that the whole of the railwaymen shall be in organised relationship, and the power thus obtained is enormously greater than the possession of a banking account, although this is desirable also, and is made easily possible by concerted action.

Having sounded many railwaymen on their ideas as to becoming a part of the Transport Workers' Federation, we find that the disposition is entirely favourable, but a sensible caution keeps them at present in the observant position, being wishful to be identified but not willing to be dragged into numerous strikes nor willing to be pitched into industrial struggles without due reason. All this is not only to be approved of, but anything less would be utterly unworkable.

We rely upon strikes, but upon organisation, solidarity, and the power that this gives to negotiate, supplemented, of course, by the added power to strike and the determination to do so when circumstances really demand it.

We must have a Federation that will be properly autonomous for each district and each section, coupled certainly with the principle and practical method of securing solidarity of all sections. How much local autonomy will be truly consistent with general solidarity is not the easiest of things to decide, but the Miners' Federation have had a good deal of experience in this matter, and have not found it insuperable.

The future must be for SOLIDARITY AND DIRECT ACTION. BEWARE OF THE GOVERNMENT. It is this day officially announced that the Government intends to introduce a measure establishing COMPULSORY ARBITRATION. No measure this or any other Government may introduce can ever cause Capitalists to run an industrial establishment on lines under conditions that the Capitalists really disapprove of. The Capitalist will always retain the power to close his *factory*, his *mill*, his *mine*, his *shop*, and the Government propose to make it illegal for the workers to have the right to take concerted action for the control of their Labour.

TOM MANN.

THE TOLL OF THE WORKERS.

By ANNA LINCOLN.

Lay them away all silently,
  The world no longer needs them.
We, too, soon shall be as they,
  And who is there that heeds them?

Only a " worker " gone to his rest,
  Gone to the land that is far the best.
Aye! it is thus that Toil is blessed—
  Despised, and hunted, crushed, oppressed.

Nothing to show for years of labour;
  Nothing to own in pride and joy.
Each one weary, like his neighbour,
  Underfed as man and boy.

Lay him away, there's others waiting
  Eager and glad his place to fill.
God! is it Life or *Death* I'm stating?
  How many more shall Greed yet kill?

He was a miner, born to danger,
  This was a weaver, rich in skill.
Can there be in Life aught stranger—
  That we allow it? Kill! Kill! Kill!

Nobody cares that they have perished
  Forty years before their time.
Where are their children? Loved and cherished?
  Cherish the workers! Madness sublime!

No; crush them and grind them for ever,
  Yes! breed them to bleed them for aye.
Justice? In England? O, never!
  While Capitalism holds sway.

Aye! lay them away in their boxes,
  The tiny sweet babes we have lost.
Not half so much " value " as foxes,
  Or hay that for horses is tossed.

(Mothers, stop that sad, sad sobbing;
  Had they lived, they must have toiled
As their parents toil: nerve throbbing,
  Health and Beauty all despoiled.)

This was a mother, sweet and tender,
  Patient and kind in all her ways:
But she has died of " means too slender."
  Whose is the blame? Ah! whose is the praise?

It's " only a labourer's baby.
  What matters it if it be dead?
Another will follow, soon maybe,
  To clamour for pieces of bread.

Aye! this is the life of the workers—
  To clamour for pieces of bread!
How different from that of the shirkers,
  Whose life is of Roses a bed!

What matter that hearts are breaking?
  That young lives must come to an end?
It's " what are the *Profits* we're making?"
  And " What was its last Dividend?"

Of Gods in Heaven, or Gods on Earth,
  Oh! is there not *one* God to care
That workers' children, at their birth,
  Are doomed to this most dread Despair?

DOCKERS' DISTRESS FUND.

The following sums have been received at this office and forwarded to Mr. George Lansbury:

	£	s.	d.
Albert Davis	2	0	0
Collection taken at I.S.E.L. meeting at Holborn Hall, July 17	1	15	10
Total	**£3**	**15**	**10**

OTHER VIEWS ON THE DOCK STRIKE.

FRANK CRITICISM OF THE LEADERS.

(From the Stratford Express.)

"THE COWARDLY MANIFESTO."

There was a frank criticism of the action of the members of the Strike Committee at the meeting held on Monday night at the corner of Beckton Road. None of the members of the committee were present, but several men who have taken a great interest in the strike addressed the gathering.

The chairman was Mr. Roden, who presided over a very large gathering. He said that time after time the working classes of this country had been sold by their leaders, and it seemed as if the same thing had again taken place. At the outset they said they would never order the men to go back till they had obtained a recognition of the Federation ticket and an undertaking had been given that all men should be reinstated. That was the irreducible minimum, and he must say that he was disgusted when he read the leaders' manifesto in Saturday's papers. That was a fight of the rank and file, and before any manifestos were issued the men should have been consulted. (Applause.) The manifesto was a disgrace to the trade union movement and to the leaders who were responsible for bringing it out. The spirit of the manifesto was that they were out for absolute surrender on the part of the men, but the men were just as determined as Lord Devonport or the Shipping Federation. His opinion was that if they continued the fight to the bitter end they would teach those responsible for the upset of last week that the working classes were not to be played with in that manner. He would tell them candidly that it was no question of being sold; it was a question of being

Absolutely Given Away.

He was absolutely disgusted with the way in which the leaders had treated them during the last week, and he hoped the men would now take the matter in their own hands and fight the battle themselves.

Mr. Allison said that when he read the manifesto he purposely refrained from giving an expression of opinion until he had heard an explanation from the leaders and whether or not they accepted the explanation; he did not. (Hear, hear.) A member of the Strike Committee had since told him that it was only done in order to test the men, but the men who would deliberately do that kind of thing in order to test the men must be idiots. That manifesto had done more harm than they could repair for some time. The issue of the manifesto was not only a blunder, but an act of folly, and had it been designed to drive men apart and cause trouble it could not have been done better. All the way through that fight there had been too much Tower Hill and not enough Custom House.

Mr. Harry Picard said he had already had his say on the matter at Southwark Park, and as a result had gained the black looks of some of their prominent leaders. The previous speaker that evening had suggested that a small committee should be appointed with plenary powers to settle the dispute, but he contended that before any settlement was arrived at they must have a mandate from the men. (Applause.) What was the agreement come to at the beginning of the strike? It was that all men should be reinstated, and that no agreement should be come to until the men had been consulted and twenty-four hours' notice had been given. (Applause.) Had they done that? (Loud cries of "No.") No; they had committed a blunder, and were trying to throw the responsibility on the men. They said it would show the employers that it was not the leaders' fight, but the men's fight, but the employers knew that weeks ago. He wanted to let them know that as early as Thursday night the Strike Committee knew all about issuing that manifesto to the Press on Saturday afternoon. If they went back to work under the manifesto of the Strike Committee they would go back under the flag of surrender, cries of " No surrender."

The chairman said he agreed with what Harry Picard had said. They had been sold by these men, and they should be told that the trade union movement had no further use for them. All the way through he had held that the only members of Parliament who had done anything to assist them were George Lansbury and Jim O'Grady. If Thorne and the others found that they could do no good in Parliament, why did not they come out and state to these men the interest of the men? (Applause.)

CAN SYNDICALISM BE FAR BEHIND?

(From the Freewoman.)

THE STRIKE.

All things work together for Syndicalism, it appears, even the Dockers' Strike, this ghastly business, which should be a warning from now till Repudiation Day against sectional warfare. Sectional warfare is hopeless, and unless the appeal to make it national is successful, labour will not be able even to save its face. A strike is social war, and to waltz airily into warfare brings its own retribution. To cry out against retribution—the natural discipline of consequences—is utterly without reason. It is childish. A man would not get on sporting terms with a tiger and expect the beast to be content with a lick of his hand. Beasts of prey are beasts of prey, and working men who expect them suddenly to be transformed into gentlemen are fools, and can only expect to be well cuffed for witlessness. The London Dockers decided on their own account to declare war, and this without taking any thought as to their supplies, ammunition, or allies. To declare war under such conditions may be right, but it is desperate, and those who do so must be prepared for desperate measures. But they are not! At present the dockers are accepting " charity." They are waiting on the doorstep of the enemy. It is preposterous. There is only one reasonable course for strikers without allies and without means. They have to take up the position of outlaws and utilise the means which exist for dealing with such. First, they could, if possible, put their children in the workhouses, and, if they agree, their womenfolk too. Then they are free to fight. When they are beaten in open fight, they can fall back on the prisons. There is always very good bread in prison. As for organised charity, they would be in a position to tell the organisers to take it to blazes. This is the only common-sense attitude for casual rebels to take up. To speak magniloquently of rebellion in its first stages; then to slide down insensibly on to a lower and a lower key; finally to accept any terms in order to save labour's face—these are methods which hurt rebellion itself, and in the end they prove wholly useless. The only way to fight capitalism successfully is to take measures in proportion to the strength of the enemy. It needs " All Workers " to fight capital. To crush it are needed measures as drastic as those which are used to exterminate the man-eating tiger. The jungle is fired all round, and men with guns stand ready to shoot should the beast spring. Workers will have to adopt measures as drastic if they are to deal with the capitalist man-eater.

Happily, in the present instance, the strikers have been saved by the swelled-headed imbecility of the person who is styled " Lord Devonport." This person, who, happily for them, is blessed with the intelligence of the monkey-like variety, has the itch to make manifest to what limits capital *can* go. As though we were not fully aware! It is surely not the " game " of capitalists to make clear to the wealth-producers how utterly they are divorced from the money-interests. It is the *whole* game of capital, indeed, to persuade the wealth-producers that in some way their interests are allied. It is, therefore, to be expected that " Lord Devonport " will find himself sharply rapped across the knuckles by his fellow-conspirators if he goes any further lengths towards divulging capital's sinister control. In the meantime, allies are coming to the dockers' rescue. Their dogged tenacity has won what their unconsidered rashness failed to secure. It is likely that the local strike will be converted into a national strike of transport workers, and so find its own solution. Mr. Tom Mann, for the first time, has taken a hand in the struggle, and makes an appeal for a national transport strike. It is to be hoped it will be responded to. The dockers in this fight of nine weeks have proved themselves heroes. They deepen belief in the basic goodness of humanity. The moneyholders, the tricksters, the gamblers, the financial things, are merely an evil scum which has risen to the surface. Below, where men work honestly, goodness and spirit still survive. The dockers have proved their bread. Poetry, religion, and honour are here with them. They are grand lads.

We have said that all things are working together for Syndicalism. As a direct result of the strike *impasse*, Mr. Ben Tillett is advising, in the pages of the *Daily Herald*, a single union of all transport workers; but if the principle of the unified union comes, can Syndicalism be far behind? We think not, and when we read of Mr. Vernon Hartshorn advising joint action on the part of all transport workers and miners, we feel that the logic of events has established a logic of method.

The Syndicalist

EDITED UNDER THE AUSPICES OF

The Industrial Syndicalist Education League

Offices—

4, MAUDE TERRACE, WALTHAMSTOW,

LONDON, E.

MONTHLY · ONE PENNY.

Post Paid Subscription—

Great Britain or Abroad ... 12 months 1s. 6d.

Bundle Rates—

1s. 6d. per quire, Carriage Paid.

The receipt of a Sample Copy is an invitation to Subscribe.

AUGUST, 1912.

PARLIAMENT.

Is there any historic instance of a subjugated class using for its own emancipation the organisation that was used to emancipate the preceding class? If not, why should we now expect a new development? Previously to the development of the middle class there was no Parliament known in the sense in which we use the term to-day. Parliament was the organisation used to develop the middle class which afterwards developed into the capitalist class. It was not invented, but grew out of economic conditions. Its growth displaced the Church and Monarchy. These had been the organisations which had developed the then-governing class. Why did not the new middle class adapt the Church and Monarchy to its own requirements? These were already to hand. It did not do so because to re-model is not to follow the line of least resistance. In selecting a new instrument the men of that time were simply following a law we constantly see in operation around us. Soon our parks will be covered with dead leaves. These very leaves last year pushed out their predecessors. While they were on the tree they helped to supply life and energy for the new shoots which in turn replace them. The same holds good in society. We have just seen the Government Post Office opening new premises. It was just because business developed in the old buildings that new ones became necessary. The Government recognised what men of business always recognise, that it is easier to build new premises adapted to new developments than to reconstruct old ones.

What functions were principally necessary to be performed by the organ which the middle class was using for its own development? The chief thing was that it should assist in the production of wealth. Previously production had not been considered of so much importance as fair distribution. This began with giving a tenth part to the Church. If the new institution had only functioned in promoting fair distribution as it did in fostering production, we should not be witnessing the misery that we see at the present day. But the new middle class were not more concerned in the increased production of wealth than they were that it should be entirely for their own benefit. If Parliament ever had the function of distribution it has quite lost it. For how can we tell if an organ is functioning or not? Simply by the ease with which it responds. If the organs of hearing are functioning well, then the organism of which they form part will hear with ease. If the organs of sight are functioning well, the organism will see with ease. But if these organs do not function well, there will be difficulty in seeing and hearing. In the same way if Parliament responds easily to the demand of conditions favourable to the production of wealth for the capitalist class, then it is functioning well in assisting to produce wealth for that class. If it does not respond easily to the demand for conditions favourable to an equal distribution of wealth or the safety and well-being of the people, then it is not functioning to assist distribution or the safety and well-being of the people. That it is not the function of Parliament to distribute wealth is admitted by the present Government. They told the miners that it was not the function of Parliament to give the miners 5s. a day, although they ought to have that, or more.

The Plimsoll line was instituted to safeguard the lives of sailors. Plimsoll spent nearly the whole of his life in agitating to get this. Clearly then the saving of sailors' lives is not the function of Parliament. Removing the Plimsoll line assisted the capitalist class in accumulating wealth. It was done by the stroke of a pen. Clearly, then, it is the function of Parliament to assist the capitalist class in accumulating wealth. No one imagines that a stroke of a pen will replace the Plimsoll line. It will need many years' agitation and several general elections.

No one denies that the feeding of school children will conduce to the health, happiness, and well-being of the people. For over thirty years there has been a vigorous agitation to get them fed, and they are not fed yet. Clearly it is not the function of Parliament to feed children.

Look at the present trouble with the Port of London Authority. This authority was created by Parliament in order that it might assist in creating wealth for the capitalist class. If in order to do that it has to uphold those who are defrauding their workers—that the workers have been defrauded was admitted by the Government's own investigator, Sir Edward Clarke — so much the worse for the workers. If they go on strike they must starve. It is unfortunate that it is so, but if by their starving the Transport Workers' Federation is destroyed, and through that destruction the capitalist class is able to accumulate more wealth, so much the better for the capitalist class. And all the power of the police, the Board of Trade, etc., etc., even to the Army and Navy, if necessary, will be used to support the Port of London Authority. But if it is found that the strike is preventing the capitalist class from accumulating wealth, and it is the Port of London Authority that stands in the way, then that authority will go, and go quickly. Why? Because Parliament does not function easily to protect workers, except they are engaged in producing wealth for the capitalist class, but it does function easily in assisting the capitalist class to procure that wealth.

If the workers want a better distribution they must develop an organ that will function in that way; and just as the middle class did not use the Church or the Monarch, nor the trees their own leaves, nor the Post Office and the business firms their old premises, so neither will the working class use Parliament. This brings us to another point. Why could not the middle class have put men after their own hearts on the throne and into the Bishoprics and Benefices? Because the conditions of the Church were not conducive to produce men fitted to build up this new middle class. Once they were in their Church their chief concern was to perpetuate the organisation of which they formed part. History teems with such instances. One of the most notable is furnished by Thomas à Beckett. When he acquired authority in the Church he used that authority against the very King who had put him there. It seems to be a universal law. How long will a man that is agitating against the capitalist class continue to do so if he himself becomes a capitalist? Or if you sow Shirley poppies with field poppies how long will their descendants remain Shirley poppies? How many men are now "doing time" that would have lived and died honest citizens but for the opportunity to become thieves? How many men would have remained true to their class if there had been no opportunity to sell that class. Nowhere is there a better opportunity of selling that class than in Parliament. When a man has those qualities that make him valuable to his class, and he is put into Parliament, the same qualities make him valuable to the capitalist class; and we soon hear that the Government "Has need of him." Government can afford to pay for its needs, and since its principal need is the procuring of wealth for the capitalist, where is the worker to come in? Or who can blame these men and say he would not have acted similarly under similar circumstances? Perhaps the better way is to lead them not into temptation.

THE DOCK STRIKE.

The Syndicalists are not out to find fault with the leaders of the present Trade Unions. Their work is more serious than that, and, from the point of view of their propaganda, it does not matter a bit about leaders. But both the capitalist and the Socialist Press have been pointing to the failure of Syndicalism on account of the dismal failure of the dock strike. We cannot, therefore, let this pass without a few words of comment.

No Syndicalist has had anything whatever to do with the leading of this dock strike, which is the most preposterous and the most insane trade-union action that has taken place for a long time.

No Syndicalist method was ever resorted to during this strike. Of course not, and why not? Because the strike was led by politicians who are most certainly no lovers of Syndicalism, provided they have other fish to fry, and as the triumph of Direct Action would prove the futility of parliamentarism, in which they are personally interested, they must not be so very anxious to apply it.

None of the speakers at Tower Hill (mostly non-dockers, but almost all of them politicians) ever proposed to make use of Syndicalist tactics. Of course not, and why not? Because militant Syndicalism might lead to prison, whereas cracking jokes about Lord Devonport might lead to Parliament.

They have been imploring Parliament, they have been asking for the interference of bishops, they have been praying to God; but they have never once been making any practical proposal by which the dockers might get what they wanted *through their own direct action.*

The I.S.E.L., which was brought into existence solely to link up those Trade Unionists in all industries already imbued with Syndicalist ideas, has nothing whatever to do with strikes. Its work is chiefly of a permeating character, and as the thorough permeation of any of the industries is probably still a long way off, no present-day strike can be said to have been influenced by it.

But this dismal business may perhaps have taught a lesson or two: first, that no direct action of any kind will ever succeed if left in the hands of politicians; secondly, that if Trade Unionists want their claims to be successful, they must rely upon *themselves* only.

This is now beginning to be felt by most people who have followed our propaganda and watched the development of the dock strike. Thus, in an article in the *Daily Herald*, under the signature of Ben Tillett, who deals with blackleggism, we find the following:

Propaganda Work.

We can only tackle the blackleg problem by understanding the unemployed problem, and the unemployed problem is a wage-system problem. The worker does not share the wealth he creates, or all the workers would be rich in the means of life to-day. The Unions must undertake propaganda work which will teach the toilers to realise and become conscious of the fact, that they must capture for their class the means of life and all the facilities of industry, all the control of Government, ownership, and administration, before the back of the blackleg can be lost sight of for ever. There must be one Union for all trades and occupations, *the abolition of the unemployed by a reduction of labour corresponding to the percentage of the unemployed,* and we shall begin the revolution and the abolition of the parasites, both rich and blackleg. (Italics ours.)

We do not agree with the capturing of the control of government and administration, for that would be of no use whatever to the workers, but we are glad to see that our constant propaganda for the reduction of working hours is beginning to bear fruit. This is the first time, we believe, that our principle has been advocated by a union official.

Good luck, Ben; hope you'll succeed, but you will want more solidarity and less parliamentarism next time.

EXPRESSION OR REPRESENTATION?

By FREDA DALLAS-ASKEW.

In answer to your request for suggestions on the proposal to issue a weekly edition, may I offer these notes?

It is now six years since I welcomed Syndicalism as the next stage in the revolution. Even then the tendency of the orthodox Socialists (or "Marxians," as they called themselves, regardless of Marx's horror of the term) was forcing the question on, beyond the limits of its political form. The opposition to all attempts—by myself or others—to discuss the efficacy of representation—either by word of mouth or by translation from the writings of celebrated sociologists, from Marx onwards—showed infallibly that politics and economics in England were still looked upon as identical, though in reality *direct action* was the far better and more efficacious way of progressing. Yet Anarchism, the individual form of direct action, did not satisfy me. Although my sympathy with individual characters in the movement was great, the feebleness of their discussion of social questions struck me, as well as the lengthiness of their expressions, which seemed to me, who regard theory as a dreary necessity, to amount to incoherence, before getting to the point! They seemed incapable of really examining the merits and demerits of representation in a constitutionally governed country. When they did not merely ignore it, they abused it!

Still, one felt that one must wait with an open mind to see what results might possibly be won by the Labour movement and the women's claim for political liberty.

Then came the elections of 1906, with the double defeat of the S.D.P., the organisation I had sympathised with and supported for the last eight years. Double defeat, I call it, because not only were their candidates rejected, but the advice adopted of voting Conservative placed the association definitely on the shelf. It was precisely that ideology—that theory divorced from practice—condemned by Marx and Engels, which had dissolved this group. Whatever might be the deficiencies of the Liberal-Labour combination, it was at least an advance on such impotence.

Is not the experimental or deductive method the only rule of direct action of Syndicalism? All has to be worked up, re-made, developed. A study precisely on this aspect of the matter by a celebrated Italian sociologist, Professor A. D. Asturaro, of Genoa—a study demonstrating the experimental nature of sociology—was just one of the translations which we had submitted for consideration, and which had been refused!

If direct action implied the minimum of theory, did it not imply the maximum of efficiency, that is to say, of technique? A renewed effort to present the case, but on psychological lines only, was made by the Fabian Society and the *New Age* weekly paper. This gives the psychological and sociological expression of Syndicalism in England—i.e., the problematic and theoretic aspect for discussion—but the practical need must be met by the technique of method, which shows the way to move.

We have to remember that official politics have been criticised and condemned for the last fifty years, not only internally by the Independent Labour Party in the House of Commons, but externally by the Social Democratic Party and the Woman's Social and Political Union. The very form of Parliamentary representation itself is freely criticised; the banking interest is being attacked as impeding commercial development; and current journalism has laid itself open to grave objections. Whether any periodical publication of expression can be kept free from the taint of party politics remains to be seen.

I am sure that the proposal for a weekly issue of the SYNDICALIST arises from the recognition that a monthly issue cannot vie with all the competition and opposition which surrounds such a paper. A monthly issue *must* be inadequate for such a task. If the workers cannot express and discuss their claim it must continue to be obscured and, in fact, misrepresented, as I am trying to show. This is proved by the attitude of the Press towards Syndicalism. Not only the official and bourgeois journals and papers, but also the Socialist ones, have expressed varying degrees of hostility to it, gradually slowing down towards contempt. Even the comments upon the recent prosecutions of Syndicalist editors, writers, or printers have been as much as possible confined to the special trade interest of the Press, the question of the so-called "liberty of the Press." Much was said about the ridiculousness of the subject, and the obscurity of the paper attacked, but on the question of social liberty demanded for human beings in refusing to shoot down their kind, few and little were the comments made. But, after all, what else could be expected? All had committed themselves to the fetish of militarism in one form or another, and, as we all know too well, escape from fetishes or out-of-date abstractions is not an easy or rapid matter.

Thus misrepresented in government and commerce, and deprived of the enjoyment of the sheer necessaries of life, what liberty remains to men and women workers? Yet direct action, which would be their only honest and coherent form of expression, is incessantly denounced and condemned.

"Marxian economics" (mercantile methods thinly disguised) are not enough for live working people, and questions of currency, education, rational defence, catholicism, theosophy, &c., are all but side issues, and indirect matters compared to direct action. Yet the latter rouses such furious opposition that it is impossible to imagine it ending in anything but physical force and bodily attacks. Indeed, this has already been practised by governments, when they attack strikers with armed soldiers, and if physical force is not to be *reciprocated,* then, at least, let Syndicalism and its methods have a fair field and hearty support from all!

CHALLENGE TO SYNDICALISM.

The forthcoming Trade Union Congress is likely to give some indication of the extent to which Syndicalism has obtained a hold in the trade union movement.

The Parliamentary Committee has decided to submit to the Congress the following resolution:

That this Congress reaffirms its continued support of independent, working-class political action in helping the industrial fight for a more equitable share of the wealth produced, and also declares for a larger share of representation, nationally and locally, in view of the continued centralisation of social and industrial questions in the hands of the Government and other authorities.

This motion is a direct challenge to the anti-Parliamentary attitude of the Syndicalists and their claim that the battle must be fought out in the workshops.

THE UGLY WORD "SYNDICALISM."

It is in vain that one searches in English dictionaries for the word Syndicalism. It is a French stranger in our language, with no registered abode as yet. Had it not been an ugly word it would probably never have been brought over, for it has achieved fame by reason of its capacity to frighten. The House of Commons is often dull and is rarely amusing, but if any one who has studied Syndicalist literature is left with nothing but the forbidding pages of *Hansard* for recreation, he will find the debate on Syndicalism, which took place on the 27th of March, 1912, refreshingly delectable in its simple innocence and its charming revelation of the ordinary Englishman's mind under the influence of a bogey.

RAMSAY MACDONALD.

OPEN LETTER TO MOTOR DRIVERS.

A WARNING.

Comrades,—The London Cabdrivers' Trade Union has issued the following leaflet to its members :

Warning to Cabdrivers.

The Executive Council wishes to warn Taxidrivers to be careful about joining the

Motor Reserve Category C,

and draws their attention to the danger of Organised Labour in the

Attestation Form,

which renders them liable to be called up for a

National Danger or Great Emergency.

Issued by Order of the Executive Council.

Read this carefully, you Workers, and reflect ! What is this "National Danger "? What is this "Great Emergency "? Reflect who it is that warns you of these things—it is your Master Class.

Workers, the "National Danger ". is YOURSELVES.

The "Great Emergency " is the world-wide spirit of revolt on YOUR part against the ever-increasing exploitation and des-potism of the Master Class.

Motor Drivers, beware ! All you Workers, beware ! ! The war-schemes of the governing class are *always* directed *against you.*

If you, or the people of any other country show signs of asserting your manhood, of resuming ownership of the country that is rightly yours, demanding that you shall yourselves enjoy the wealth your toil produces, *then there is danger of war.*

If this country is to be invaded by the Germans it will have been arranged be-forehand by your own Master Class. If Germany is to be attacked by England and France, it will have been arranged by the Master Classes of Germany, England, and France together. The object will be " *to bleed the rebellious blood out* " of *the Workers* of all three countries.

Remember, it is always the Master Class that provokes war, *and forces you, the Workers, to wage it.*

The capitalist and financial thieves—our Master Class—*know no country. They have no "patriotism."* Their in-terests are *cosmopolitan and inter-national.* They regard all peoples alike as " raw material " to be used up in the creation of wealth for them, the thieves, to enjoy, or as " food for cannon," when they seek to add wholesale murder to their other crimes.

The Master Class of this and of other countries have a perfect under-standing together. *They are united and class-conscious.* It is time that the Workers of the World had an under-standing and were also united and class-conscious. This is coming about, slowly but surely, and *the Master Class of all nations know it.* THIS IS WHY THERE IS A DANGER OF WAR.

At no time have the Workers of one country any cause of quarrel with those of another. Their interests and their well-being are in fraternal co-operation in the arts of peace, so that there shall be an abundance of all good things for all men in all lands. There is no need for war.

What benefit have the Workers of any country ever gained by war? None ! They have laid down their lives ; they have returned maimed and broken—to starve ; their wives and children have

suffered and pined. And the blood-stained plunder of the war has gone to swell the already teeming riches of the brutal wretches who provoked it.

Whatever happens in war, remember, *it is always you, the Workers, who suffer.* The Master Class never suffers, but always profits.

Therefore, Workers, have nothing to do with the war-service of the Master Class. Refuse to enlist in its army, navy, or police. REFUSE TO BE ENROLLED IN THIS " MOTOR RESERVE." Forbid your children to have anything to do with boys' brigades, boy scouts, and the like.

If the Master Class desires war, let them do their own fighting, and if they will but exterminate each other, so much the better for you, the Workers !

But it is not only this kind of warfare that you will be required to wage in the "Motor Reserve." There is another war that is always with us. THIS IS THE CLASS WAR.

The motto of the Master Class is always " Divide and rule." So long as you, the Workers, are disorganised, all is well for the Master Class. They can plunder you to their hearts' content. So long as you are fighting one another for jobs, they can buy you cheap and sweat bigger profits out of your toil. *But, when you begin to understand the situation, you begin to understand each other.* Then you combine and make common cause against the common enemy. *The better your understanding, the closer your combination.* As you saw the futility of each man fighting for his own hand in the industrial field, so do you begin to see the futility of each trade or industry fighting separately for its own hand.

If an army were to enter the field, one regiment, or one division, at a time, each to encounter in turn the full forces of the enemy, that army would be annihi-lated. *This is what is happening to you now.*

When will you learn that sectional strikes are fatal to you? When will you understand that those " leaders " who still believe in sectional trades-unionism are either senile imbeciles or men de-liberately in the pay of the enemy?—One of the two they must be.

So long as the Master Class can bribe your " leaders " to keep you divided, and so long as you are willing to 'be kept divided, the Master Class has you at its mercy.

How many hard lessons will you need before you have properly learned these facts?

The Master Class does not think you have learned them, or it would not be forming a " Motor Reserve " under " Category C," by which you will be required to carry goods and passengers to help break railway or transport strikes, or to convey police and soldiers to bludgeon and shoot down miners, or others, into submission. *It is this service the Master Class has in mind even more than service against a foreign enemy.*

Therefore, Motor Drivers, refuse to have anything to do with this " Motor Reserve." REFUSE TO ACT AGAINST YOUR COMRADES OF OTHER TRADES, AS YOU HOPE THEY MAY REFUSE TO ACT AGAINST YOU.

Above all, Comrades, cultivate Class Consciousness and Class Solidarity. Reach out the hand of active help to all your fellow-Workers, not only in this country but throughout the world. Thus, and thus only, shall the brutal tyranny of Capitalist Class domination be broken down and Labour come into its own.

CROWSLEY FREE.

HIS PRISON EXPERIENCES.

Our friend Fred Crowsley is now out of gaol, after serving forty-six days—exactly the same number as did Tom Mann. He relates his experiences as follows :

" YOUNG AND BIGOTED."

" Immediately I was sentenced I was shown downstairs, where I expected to see my friends, but the Judge had refused permission on the ground that I was ' young and bigoted, and wanted my friends to know it.' I was therefore bundled into a Black Maria without having seen anybody, and I arrived at Winchester Gaol between six and seven in the evening.

" The next day, no sooner had I had conversation with one of the warders, than I was ' placed on bread and water ' for twenty-four hours, on the ground that I had been insolent. This lost me two days of the remission of my sentence. My insolence consisted in having told the warder that I was not able to use a needle. I did not appeal against the punishment at the time, because I thought the warder might get his own back in other ways. I therefore waited until three days before my release, when I asked to see the Governor. I explained the case to him, but he told me he was unable to alter the decision, which the Home Secretary him-self could not have done ; that it was a sort of a law of the 'Medes and Persians.' But he said that if I would like to write a letter he would willingly grant me that privilege, which under ordinary circum-stances I would not have been entitled to.

" For the first fortnight I was engaged in sewing mailbags and picking horse-hair, after which I had to make nosebags.

" I have not to complain about per-sonal ill-treatment by the warders, as I was treated like any other prisoner, but my personal opinion of warders is that they have no sense of humanity ; for once a prisoner enters gaol he ceases to be looked upon as a human being—as a matter of fact, he is treated and spoken to worse than an animal. He is not sup-posed to possess a soul ; he does not even possess a name, being called by a number. My general opinion of prison is that it is a most abominable place of inhumanity.

BLASPHEMY AND HYPOCRISY.

" The day before leaving I had the visit of the prison chaplain, who, on entering my cell, said : ' You are going out to-morrow, then, Crossley? ' I replied, ' Yes, sir, and I shall not be sorry.' Whereupon he said, ' No ; but there, I suppose you have been well paid for the job? ' I said that what I had done I had done on principle ; but he tossed his head, and said, ' I don't believe you have done it on principle.' Then, after muttering a few more words about ' our duty,' he went away, slamming the door. I did not feel hurt at such cowardly behaviour on the part of this " disciple " of Jesus of Nazareth, for in my estimation he had sunk so low that I thought he was even beneath contempt. I regard the religious service as hideous blasphemy and the height of hypocrisy. Whilst one is sup-posed to listen to a teaching of love and humanity, all one's surroundings are but hate and fear. To look round and see the faces of the poor, crushed souls who fill the prison is a most heartrending sight, and the singing in chapel often brought tears into my eyes when I saw that herd of poor, unfortunate victims of our cruel system of society.

" HELP ONE ANOTHER."

" The railway company at which I was employed as a fireman has up till now treated me with every consideration, and I am now waiting to hear from them whether I will be reinstated ; but I cannot say the same of the secretary of my union, Mr. J. H. Thomas, M.P., and his assistant secretary, Mr. Williams. When I went to see the former at Unity House to ask him whether I was entitled to out-of-work or suspension pay, he prac-tically waved me on one side with a ges-ture of his arm, and walked away, saying, ' I don't know anything about your case.' Afterwards I saw Mr. Williams, whose only consolation for me was ' that I should consider myself lucky if I got off with merely being suspended.' These be your gods, O Israel ! And be it noticed that I never received a farthing from the A.S.R.S., whose motto is : ' Help one another '."

SYNDICALIST METHODS IN OPERATION.

THE CONSCIOUSNESS OF THE RANK AND FILE.

" William," a correspondent, whose letter appears in our correspondence columns, asks us to show " that Syndi-calism will not incur the slaughter of those workers who try to put Syndicalist methods of taking possession of the means of life into operation."

To picture the expropriation of the capitalists by direct action, it is necessary to conceive of the workers being much better organised than they are to-day. Not only much better organised, but ani-mated by a revolutionary spirit. In short, that the spirit of solidarity and resistance has swept over their minds and completely possessed them. Repeated strikes in single industries and a number of indus-tries has developed the requisite technique for attempting a General Strike. The growth of the General Strike idea is quite a natural development of the ordinary strike movement.

At the same time, as the Syndicalists are developing the General Strike idea, so are they also carrying on their anti-militarist propaganda. Our preaching of our anti-patriotic and anti-militarist ideas will have a profound influence upon work-ing-class thought. The use of the mili-tary and the brutality of the police during the recent strikes, and affairs attendant upon them, have opened the eyes of thou-sands of workers as to the real purpose and function of these bodies—viz., to hold the workers in subjection. Thus we shall bring the police and military into contempt with the average worker who is as con-scious of his class interests. This even-tually will have a great effect upon recruiting. This in its turn will simply hasten the day of compulsory military service for all workers. Then, as our French comrades say, " the barracks are the best school for anti-militarism." Slowly but surely we shall create a public opinion amongst the working - class soldiers that it is treachery to their class to allow themselves to be used against strikers. Discipline will be weakened. The soldiers will cease to be machines and will begin to think. They will act in con-cert with their fellow wage slaves.

The perpetual attack upon the capitalist class which the Syndicalist workers will wage will have the effect of hastening the growth of joint-stock concerns. The em-ployers' federation will multiply, the trust system will extend. This means the forc-ing of a still greater number of persons into the ranks of wage-workers. What is more, even where the small employer, the small landowner, still retains hold on his shop, and the other on his land and cattle the growing insecurity of living, the dread of becoming a wage slave, will render them in favour of a social change, though they will probably lack the necessary courage and earnestness to take any active part. They will be perpetually swayed between the thoughts of preserving their existence and their hatred of the forces squeezing them. This mental unrest, due to a sense of insecurity, is already wide-spread in the large centres of population.

The anti-militarist propaganda has a de-velopment of its own. It starts from the negative side of urging soldiers not to fire. But as feeling grows it develops from a passive disobedience to an active one, from negative to positive, from desertion and refusal to fire to insubordination and mutiny and revolt. Equally so will the strike tactics develop. From exhibitions like the Transport Workers' Strike, where one section in one town of the transport industry is allowed the passive measure of a trial of starvation, much will be learnt. The strike of an entire industry, and not merely a section, will be the next move. And in place of weeks of starvation, sabo-tage will be resorted to. It can be made practically impossible for blacklegs to work even if the employers get them. When the employers know that a strike will be conducted in a revolutionary fashion they will think twice before they force one. They will think still longer before they force men to desperation by keeping them out of work for weeks to starve. Strikers, instead of whining to parsons and Press and other channels of " public opinion," will simply see themselves right with the working class and its Press, and will ig-nore " public opinion," as represented by the capitalist Press of all political shades. The capitalist Press exists not to represent public opinion, but to try and mould it to suit the interests of the particular group of financial interests in control of that par-ticular paper. The General Strike move-ment will thus develop in extent. It will develop also in revolutionary impulse. The Syndicalists will endeavour to create a revolutionary working class at the same time as they sap the power from those forces of repression that our masters use against us. During the period of develop-ment also, Socialist and Labour M.P.'s will be elected. Their elections will take place almost irrespective of the Syndicalist movement, which is non-Parliamentary. Such of those of them who are not mere Liberal bourgeois-minded prigs, and who eventually accept " positions under the State," and who take holidays in order to do work " of Imperial importance," will be compelled, by the logic of events like George Lansbury, to openly sympa-thise with and assist the Syndicalist agi-tation. All the forces working together may show the capitalist that it would be best to make terms and arrange for the handing over of the productive forces to the organised revolutionary workers. If they refuse to heed the voice of those few genuine Socialists who will be elected to Parliament, if, by compulsory arbitration and displays of armed force, they continue to intimidate strikers, then, though suc-cessful for a time, this screwing down of the safety valve, whilst the fires of social discontent are still alight in the shape of profit, rent, and interest, then even the easy-going writers of THE SYNDICALIST will be unable to show " William " " how Syndicalism will not involve the slaughter of those who try to put the Syndicalist methods of taking possession of the means of life," and yet also of those who try to prevent them.

NOTES BY T. M.

HOW THE POOR SHIPOWNERS LIVE!

THE TATEM STEAM NAVIGATION COMPANY.

At the annual meeting of the Tatem Steam Navigation Company, limited, held at Cardiff a week ago, Mr. W. J. Tatem, chairman and managing director, submitted the balance-sheet to the end of June covering a period of fifteen months, and said: "There have been certainly many cross-currents which have combined to diminish profits, notably the closing of the Dardanelles owing to the Turkish-Italian war, the prolonged strike in the River Plate, the shipping and railway strikes of last summer, and the colliery stoppage at the spring of this year. This resulted in the dislocation of trade and long detentions, and had the effect also of driving up the cost of bunker coals both at home and abroad."

We can imagine the shareholders beginning to tremble after hearing this statement, lest the figures would show there was no dividend. The following statement, given by the chairman, no doubt eased their minds: "The profits (on voyages completed to date), including £10,792 13s. 3d. brought forward from last account, amount to £261,864 9s. 6d., out of which has been paid in dividends £52,500 (being 15 per cent.), written off cost £11,000, transferred to insurance reserve fund £30,000 transferred to special reserve and contingency fund £155,000, making £248,500, and leaving a balance of £13,364 9s. 6d. to carry forward to next account. . . . *Within two and a half years a net profit has been made which exceeds the amount of the capital of the company.*" The chairman explained in connection with the amount written off for depreciation "that the whole fleet has appreciated in value, the old steamers as well as the new."

It will be admitted that even though an increase of wages took place last year, and "dislocations" were numerous, that to get the original capital returned in two and a half years and still to have that capital with added value does not quite spell ruin, and it is time that attention was given to the Manning Scale—and it must be done. An increase of 20 per cent. is required to put the merchant service seafaring men in tolerable condition. This would be a mere bagatelle in the way of cost. That the trade could stand it the above statement from the *Daily Mail* of July 17, 1912, bears witness.

TOWARDS SOLIDARITY.

A HUGE AMALGAMATION MOVEMENT.

From the Trade Circular of the Operative Bricklayers' Society, July issue, we learn that the proposed amalgamation of societies in the building industry covers the following fourteen societies: Amalgamated Carpenters and Joiners, National Association Operative Plasterers, United Builders' Labourers, United Operative Plumbers, National Association Builders' Labourers, Operative Stone Masons, Manchester Unity Bricklayers, Wood-Cutting and Machinists, Mosaic and Tile Fixers, General Labourers, House and Ship Painters, Smiths and Fitters, Street Masons and Paviors, and Operative Bricklayers. On the proposals being submitted to the branches of the O.B.S., 186 branches voted in favour and 12 against. Good luck, and complete success we wish them!

STILL MORE FOR SOLIDARITY.

It is with great pleasure that we learn that the delegate meeting of the Amalgamated Society of Engineers, just held in Manchester, has decided to broaden the basis of the organisation to Helpers and Assistants in such fashion that all male workers connected with the (Metal) industry will be eligible to join. This means, we understand, that all handy men and labourers of any and every grade connected with any phase of engineering will, when the new rules become operative (January next year), be eligible for the A.S.E.

In another direction good work was done. It is well known that the agreements tying the men up and preventing solidarity have been a source of much irritation, also that the Premium Bonus System is responsible for what is really in many shops an unendurable state of affairs. It is good, therefore, to learn that the following decision has been arrived at:

"The Executive Council shall, within three months of these rules coming into force, take the votes of the members in favour of giving the Engineering Employers' Federation; three months' notice to end the 'Terms of Agreement, 1907'; with the 'Memorandum re Premium Bonus System.' If a majority are in favour of ending them, the three months' notice shall be given by the Executive Council to the Federation at once."

ENVELOPE MAKERS.

I have received from some envelope makers a statement of grievances, with an earnest request that action be taken to help them get improvements. They are good enough to say they have watched with much pleasure how much some of us have done for men workers through organisation, &c., and add that nothing whatever has been done for girls like them.

To prove their earnestness they enclose 2s. 6d. in halfpenny stamps as a start towards action being taken. As the writers of the letter give no address, and add "we do not sign our names, as we know we should be immediately discharged if it were known," I am unable to state the district, or even the town where the young women are engaged. If they will send such bare details as are necessary for definiteness they may rely upon nothing being divulged to cause them any trouble.

THE DISPUTE IN THE FURNITURE TRADES.

MANCHESTER AND ELSEWHERE.

The employees of about 140 firms were on strike in the Manchester district some eleven weeks ago, including French Polishers (male and female), Upholsterers, Cabinet Makers, Carvers, Turners, Machinists, Glass Workers, and all labourers.

They asked for a 48-hour week without any reduction of pay in any case, whilst in nearly all cases an increase was demanded. The strikers were Britishers, Jews, Poles, Lithuanians, &c., and it is very encouraging to know perfect solidarity has characterised all sections, and at the time of writing 110 of the firms in the Manchester district have conceded the terms demanded, and the work is going on now under the altered conditions.

Many of the young women were before the strike getting 17s. a week for a 54 hours' week, some were receiving only 16s. 3d. Now the same young women are receiving a minimum of 20s. for a week of 48 hours.

The men were working various times in the different shops ranging from 54 to 60 hours a week. All these are now on the 48-hour week, and have obtained an increase of 4s. a week on the average, besides the substantial reduction of working hours. We heartily congratulate Brother A. A. Purcell and his colleagues on the excellent fight they have put up, and we expect to hear of corresponding gains in Liverpool and Nottingham.

THE INDUSTRIAL SYNDICALIST EDUCATION LEAGUE

President - - TOM MANN.

OBJECT. To carry on among Trade Unionists, and the workers generally, a campaign of education in the principles of **Syndicalism**—which may be described as **revolutionary Trade Unionism**, since its immediate purpose is to conduct **a Scientific class War** against Capitalism—such war having as its objective, or ultimate aim, the **Capture of the Industrial System** and its management by the Workers themselves **for the benefit of the Whole community.**

COMMITTEE: J. WALTER, ERNEST BARNES (Treasurer), JOHN TURNER, J. BARNES, JOHN LLOYD.

GENERAL SECRETARY: GUY BOWMAN, 4, Maude Terrace, Walthamstow, London, E.

IF YOU REALISE

Firstly, that in the Labour Movement the need of the hour is to prove to the workers that the many faults of the present industrial system can never be remedied, except by **DIRECT ACTION**, *i.e.*, by revolutionary industrial action within and upon the industries themselves;

Secondly, that in order to put this **DIRECT ACTION** into practice, it is necessary to keep up a general observation and study of modern industrial development;

Thirdly, that for the collating of the varied information obtained in various quarters, the workers should have a centre to which such information may be reported and thoroughly discussed;

Fourthly, that the workers should make use of the same centre for publishing and distributing pamphlets and for the carrying on of a literary propaganda;

Fifthly, that comrades having leisure to devote more or less time, in a colporteur or scout capacity, should act as a scout brigade for the sale of literature, at public meetings, in the workshops, and wherever possible;

Sixthly, that there is need that from the same centre of effort there should go forth comrades prepared not only to make public speeches on the subject of Direct Industrial Action, or Syndicalism as it is generally termed, but also to follow up such public efforts by responding to calls from Trade Unions, Trades Councils, Workmen's Clubs, etc.;

THEN WILL IT NOT BE THE RIGHT THING

for you to give practical effect to this realisation by becoming a member of the I.S.E.L., now in process of formation on the following basis of membership?

IF YOU WILL DO THIS

The League will thereafter keep you posted and in line to apply your efforts in effective team-work with other comrades.

MEMBERSHIP.

The membership of the League is open to any person who accepts the foregoing, no matter what views may be held by that person regarding politics; but no one who does not declare for non-parliamentary action may share in the responsible work of administration of the League. Therefore the possession of an ordinary membership card does not imply that the holder is entitled to speak or otherwise act on behalf of the League.

The following categories of persons are specially solicited to become members:—

I.—**Investigating Members.**—Those who are in a position to obtain inside information in regard to particular industries.

II.—**Literary Members.**—Those who have the time and ability to analyse and collate the information sent in by the investigators and observers, and to embody the results of the work in pamphlets and in special articles for the Press.

III.—**Colporteur Members.**—Those who want to see these Syndicalist pamphlets bought up and read by the Working Class, and are therefore willing to go and sell them both in their workshops and at public meetings.

IV.—**Speaking Members.**—Those who have the time and talent for public speaking, and are willing to place before public assemblies and Labour bodies the conclusions reached by the investigators and writers.

V.—**Supporting Members.**—Those who from all walks of life may be willing to assist work by their personal influence or by money contributions, or both.

SUBSCRIPTIONS.

The minimum subscription for members is 1s. per year; but the League is further supported by the voluntary contributions of its friends and sympathisers.

FILL UP THIS APPLICATION FORM, NOW!

APPLICATION FORM FOR MEMBERSHIP. Fill in, cut out and post to Gen. Sec., who will enrol you.

Please enrol my name as a (1) Investigating / Literary / Colporteur / Speaking / Supporting Member of the I.S.E.L. I enclose £ : : as, a Yearly Part subscription to the League's Propaganda.

Name (in full)...

Occupation.. (and other useful particulars about yourself)

Address (clearly written)..

(1) Strike out those items which do not apply.

THE SYNDICALIST WEEKLY.

£300 WANTED.

The issue of a weekly SYNDICALIST has been received with enthusiasm by our known and unknown friends, if we are to judge by the numerous letters of encouragement and approval we have received since last month.

An excellent friend of ours, Comrade Henry Bool, who believes in the necessity of the work to be accomplished, and who has the greatest confidence in the Syndicalist propaganda for the liberation of the working class from its present enslavement, has already sent £50 on the condition that a few comrades who can afford it imitate him at once, thereby showing in an active and liberal fashion their sympathy for the exclusive organ of Direct Action of the Working Class.

On hearing this another friend of ours, Mrs. Dallas-Askew, immediately promised another £50 on the same conditions—that is, if the balance be forthcoming in a comparatively short time.

Since, we have received £55 11s. 6d., the details of which appears hereunder. This, with the £8 0s. 9½d. already acknowledged and Mrs. Askew's £50, makes a total of £113 12s. 3½d. Thus, to reach the £300 we need but another £186 7s. 8½d. Let the £36 7s. 8½d. come in in small sums from our poorer friends, and we are confident that three of those friends of ours who are more favoured by Dame Fortune will turn up with £50 each; for we have a right to count upon the support of those whom our propaganda interests—those who believe in the necessity to alter the false and absurd system upon which present society rests.

And to draw us nearer and nearer to such a result *we need and must have a weekly,* for it is one of the most practical means for spreading our views and our ideas, to make them penetrate little by little, and with untiring energy, into the brains of those that are to bring about the Revolution. A weekly is a weapon at least ten times more powerful than a monthly; for, thanks to it, one remains in contact with its readers, discussion follows without leaving time to the conceptions that accrue from the reading of the paper to evaporate, and this is inevitable with a sheet that appears but every month.

Thus, for the good of all, a Syndicalist weekly is absolutely necessary, but it requires constant support on the part of our friends. It is thanks to their efforts that it must live and prosper; it is through them that it has got to develop. They ought to bring into this task the same devotion they would dedicate to a child of their flesh and blood, provided this weekly would become the child of their brains, the very essence of their sacrifice, to a cause which appears to them to be just and dignified. Let there be no indifference, no egoism. Let everyone contribute according to his or her means to the expansion of our dear SYNDICALIST, and let the results obtained later on be the reward of the generous hearts who suffer to see the sad situation of the working class, and dream of the advent of its emancipation.

Readers and friends, bestir yourselves, and ere long our *Weekly* will no longer be a dream, but a reality.

For the WEEKLY SYNDICALIST.

	£	s.	d.
Acknowledged	8	0	9½
C. H. Grinling	0	2	6
Henry Bool	50	0	0
H. F. Northcote	0	1	0
Myer Greenberg	0	3	0
William Mutter	0	2	0
Workers' Union (Coventry Branch)	1	0	0
Miss Helen Fox	1	0	0
Mrs. F. R. Andrews	0	0	0
Mrs. A. V. Montgomery	1	0	0
E. C. Cornett	0	1	6
E. Bathziany	1	0	0
Mrs. C. Holiday	1	1	0
	£63	12	3½

CUTTINGS.

THE NEW PARLIAMENT.

(From the *Link*, Geo. Lansbury.)

If Parliament can do no better than this—if the Labour Party, with all the goodwill in the world for their fellows outside of Parliament, can do no better than this—then Parliamentary action must be a hopeless kind of business. But I do not think that this is the last word on the subject. The whole working-class conception of Parliament must be altered. We must no longer look upon Parliament as an assembly of rich men who have gained admittance to the best club in the world, but as a body of working-class representatives whose sole object is to change private ownership into public ownership. This is the only way out of industrial unrest and disturbance.

SERFS THAT HAVE BECOME MEN.

(From the *Freewoman*.)

It is futile to question further as to our opinion of the respective methods of insurrection and political reform. If the spirit of the serf is wholly crushed and fireless, it is outside common sense to talk of insurrection. Therefore try Political Reform. You may so fan the fires into life again, and some future age may make them free. But if it is surely alive, if insurrection is already there, then feed it lavishly, in joy and thankfulness.

"MY COUNTRY RIGHT OR WRONG."

(From "The Way of Peace," by Reginald Wright Kauffman. Moffat, Yard, and Company, Publishers, New York City, U.S.A.)

We have too much patriotism in the United States. I mean the common or garden variety. Were you never in a theatre when the orchestra played "Dixie"? There is always a storm of applause from a dozen youths under twenty-one years of age, all born north of the Mason-Dixon Line. And when the tune is "The Star Spangled Banner," at least a hundred persons will rise—persons that don't know the words of this anthem and that won't hesitate to cheat their government by re-using a cancelled two-cent postage stamp. That is the sort of patriotism I mean.

Now is the time for it. The three days of agony—preparation, celebration, and cauterisation—that we call the Fourth of July, when we fire toy pistols and get drunk for the greater glory of our country. In a mad endeavour to forget that independence is an impossible dream and liberty an attainable reality, we call it Independence Day. The honourable member of Congress from the Meat Trust addresses the celebrating citizens. He says: "Our country may she always be in the right; but our country right or wrong." Celebrating citizens cheer.

Yet that sentiment is damnable. If Washington had believed in it he would have fought against the colonies and under King George. Not one of the worth-while men that made this republic would have tolerated the republic had it become oppressive or unjustly aggressive, and that is why these men were able to make it. It takes a finer courage to oppose a popular mistake than to die for the mistake's perpetuation, and, in war or peace, as much to-day as in colonial days, the man that is first to help his country, to be right is the last to applaud her when she is wrong.

Independence is a denial of fact. It shuts the eyes to the infrangible bonds that knit man to man and nation to nation. Liberty, on the contrary, rests on the truth that the welfare of all is the welfare of each. Devotion to the common welfare is real patriotism, and patriotic devotion to anything else is a sham. If our country is doing the best things in the best way, we owe her our devotion; if she begins to do some things in a wrong way, we owe her our criticism. But no man owes any country the price of his own sense of right.

"My country right or wrong!" Why? Because there is anything fine in her wrong? No. Because she is *mine*. There is as much logic in hissing on your dog to kill more of your neighbour's chickens because, although he has already killed some, he likes it, and he is *your* dog. If "My country right or wrong," why not "My employer right or wrong"? Why not *myself* right or wrong—and chiefly wrong—first, last, and all the time?

LABOUR REVOLT.

(From the *Age*, Melbourne.)

A big amalgamation of Australian labourers' unions, which may turn its back on the Labour Party, and refuse to have anything to do with legal arbitration, is a possibility within the next few days. If consolidation is fully effected it will possess a membership of about 25,000. It proposes to exercise unlimited power of absorption, and may swallow smaller bodies, irrespective of craft considerations.

In October last a conference of representatives of labourers' unions from various States of the Commonwealth, arrived at a basis of amalgamation, which was considered in many quarters to be of a startling character. Since then events have progressed to the point of the actual formation of the unified body, and another inter-State conference is to meet to-morrow for the purpose of finalising the details. The Victorian and South Australian delegates, who arrived to-day, were emphatic in expressing determination to carry the amalgamation through on the lines laid down in October. "We shall go through with it," they said, "whether other unions of the Commonwealth are ready or not."

The secretary of the United Labourers' Union of Victoria (D. Culliney) stated that his union was utterly sick of wages boards and arbitration courts. "There is nothing," he remarked, "to be gained by waiting for boards or courts, or for action through political channels. We are satisfied with our own working basis of organisation, as we find we are only able to get as much as we are well enough organised to drag from the employers by force. We are disgusted with craft unions, and dissatisfied with craft federations, as they are maintained for the purpose of going to the Arbitration Court. They only serve to provide a number of officials with the pleasures of office. Our idea is 'one union for Australia.' It is intended to be an organic amalgamation, to contain an unlimited number of bonâ-fide workers."

Are you in favour of the general strike? he was asked.

"When we are strong enough for that," he replied, "we shall be able to get all we want without it."

INSURRECTION AND POLITICAL REFORM.

(From the *Freewoman*.)

The "free labourers" who did the dockers in during the recent strike might shout themselves purple proclaiming they were free, but even they would hesitate to say they were their own masters. "To be our own masters." It needs repeating, as its implications are not all self-evident, for it is something the vast majority of us have never been. It is clear the farm labourer is not his own master. It is equally clear that the mechanical labourer is not. Nor is his overseer, nor the manager, nor the manufacturer. A political agent is not; nor is the member of Parliament, nor the Cabinet Minister, nor yet the Prime Minister. A journalist is not, nor an editor, nor yet a publisher. We are, all of us, puppets on strings. We dance to the tune of those who control money. If, then, we are to be our own masters, we have the task, not merely of ridding ourselves of those who control money, but the task of destroying these characteristics in money which lend themselves to the establishment of mastery over other men. To this double task of destruction the advisers of labour offer two methods of treatment—the one political, the other economic; and up to the present the political method has been viewed with most favour.

The reluctance against dropping the political method is founded on something deeper. It is founded on the reluctance of the individual to shoulder the responsibility of "belling the cat" himself. It is easy enough to be revolutionary by proxy, by elected representative, no less. Welcome as well as brave is the music of the *distant* drum. It is when it draws near that things begin to look uncomfortably like business. No, in this fight which is to make each his own master, restore to each man his freedom of will and freedom of action, the act of taking possession has to be committed by the would-be master. Masters are created in that way, and in that way only: by taking up the mastery. Mastery cannot be conferred; it must be assumed.

THE ETTOR-GIOVANNITTI CASE.

INTERNATIONAL SOLIDARITY NOT TO BE A VAIN WORD.

(From the *Industrial Worker*, Spokane.)

Now, in Lawrence, two men languish in jail—Joseph J. Ettor and Arturo Giovannitti. They are working men, imbued with a spirit of freedom that should permeate every liberty-loving human being. They are now deprived of their rights and are soon to be tried for their lives because they have successfully led the down-trodden wage-slaves of Lawrence against the mill-owners of that locality; because they compelled the fiendish monsters, who sapped the life and strength of the workers and their children, to grant the toilers a greater pittance than had theretofore been allotted them.

The approaching trials of Joseph J. Ettor and Arturo Giovannitti once more brings their personalities and the facts relating to their case into prominent view. Both men possess personalities that can stand close scrutiny and that should, in connection with the injustice done them, win the warm support and interest of the entire working class. Both are capable labour champions whose ability is attested by the persecution now being waged against them. Both are young, intelligent, ardent and brave men of convictions and ideals. Ettor is 27 years old, and a native of Brooklyn, N.Y. Giovannitti is an Italian by birth. He first saw the light 28 years ago.

Disinterested students of events in Lawrence join with outspoken enemies in their praise and admiration. This is especially true of Ettor. Because of his greater prominence in the Lawrence strike, he has been made the subject of many newspaper and magazine articles.

"The One Desideratum."

Henry Emerson Fosdick, writing in the *Outlook* of June 15, also inclines to the opinion that "to put him out of the way" seemed to the authorities of Lawrence "the one desideratum." Fosdick puts the matter thus:

"There is Ettor, a young man of twenty-seven, born in New York City, educated in our public schools, genial, magnetic, a born leader. His unconquered good humour is still in evidence after seventeen weeks in jail. His personality so became the animating centre of the strike that to put him out of the way seemed to the authorities of Lawrence the one desideratum. When, therefore, an Italian, in a minor disturbance, was shot by some unknown person, the homicide was made the occasion for the arrest of Ettor. Although in no way concerned in the killing and although he himself was two miles away, he is held without bail and stands in danger of the electric chair, on the general charge that his language encouraged disturbance. The law that properly considers the one who incites to murder equally guilty with the one who does the deed is being stretched (so his supporters think) to make any strike leader whose speech can be construed as at all incendiary, criminally responsible for homicide that occurs even in personal encounters during the strike. 'You may turn your hose upon the strikers,' he said, after that freezing day in January, when water was played over a crowd of the striking labourers, 'but there is being kindled a flame in the heart of the workers, a flame of proletarian revolt, which no fire hose in the world can ever extinguish.'"

An Infamous Doctrine.

Regeneracion, the Los Angeles, Cal., organ of the Mexican labour movement, has this to say regarding the theory of the prosecution:

"It is admitted that the accused men had no direct connection with the death on which the charge is based, but it is alleged that the things they said resulted in the deed. That is an infamous doctrine, for under it there is not an educator in the world who could not be held for having taught something that induced some one to commit a crime. Let me write the incontestable truth that capitalism often sacrifices life to profits, and under that doctrine, I may be held for the killing of a capitalist by an outraged worker of whom I never heard."

Of Ettor and Giovannitti, *Regeneracion* says:

"Apart from this, Ettor and Giovannitti are fine men, with fine records. They are not of the old money-seeking, notoriety-hunting type of organisers and agitators, with whom we have been cursed so many years. They have stood in the front rank of the battle, they have sunk themselves in the movement of which they are a vital part. These men are types of the new breed this struggle is producing, and we should follow the example they have set for us, making their cause our own."

"To get" Ettor and Giovannitti, then, was obviously the object of the prosecution; Annie La Pizza's death was the opportunity.

Arturo Giovannitti.

Giovannitti arrived on the scene of action some days after Ettor, but once in Lawrence, co-operated with Ettor with such success as to necessitate their joint arrest in order to break the strike. The capitalists do not arrest and imprison nincompoops. Men of ability who jeopardise their interests are their special prey. And so Arturo Giovannitti is honoured by capitalism, however short-sighted the Press may be in its estimate of him.

Giovannitti did great service during the strike as orator, especially among the Italians, who formed a large part of the strikers, and were therefore an important factor. For this particular service Giovannitti is well fitted. He is a powerful speaker, of imposing appearance and incisive speech. His rousing invective and appeals did much to create enthusiasm and produce good results. As a speaker, Giovannitti came to Lawrence well-prepared by experience for his tasks. He had performed a similar service in many other strikes, especially in the Brooklyn Shoeworkers' strike of 1911.

In addition to being a speaker, Giovannitti is also an editor and writer. For over three years he edited *Il Proletario*, an Italian industrial union weekly newspaper of New York City. Under his editorship *Il Proletario* became a power in Italian labour circles. It made him better known and increased his effectiveness.

As a writer, Giovannitti is equally as well at home in English as in Italian. His English contributions to the magazines on the economic causes of the Italian war show him to be an author of considerable virility and force, not to mention his powers as a thinker. As a poetic writer, Giovannitti is just beginning to loom-up. His imprisonment has resulted in the production of some poetry that stamps him a rising genius. Especially is this true of his poem, "The Walker," wherein he describes the psychology of the imprisoned of all degrees. In this poem Giovannitti reaches the climax of his present powers. As a study of the desire for freedom under the most adverse circumstances, this poem is intense and vivid. Few men will read it without pondering what reason there may be, especially for entombing men like Giovannitti. Giovannitti by no means pleads for himself, but sympathises and commiserates with his fellow-prisoners, with a tolerance and a mercy that is broad and all-embracing, dignified and noble.

As he writes his poetry from practical experience, so also does Giovannitti speak and edit. His proletarian speeches and writings are but part of his proletarian struggle for existence. Giovannitti was a miner in Canada, and a book-keeper and teacher of languages in Springfield, Mass., and New York City, before he became writer, editor, and poet. He has known the pangs of unemployment as he has slept, starved and homeless, in winter, on the benches of the New York parks.

Giovannitti is a native of Compobasso, a city of 40,000 inhabitants, in the province of Abruzi, Italy. He has been in this country ten years and is 28 years of age. His education was begun in the university of his native city, where his family are well known and influential. His father and elder-brother are physicians; his younger brother, Aristedes, a lawyer. He will be present at the coming trials in behalf of Arturo; and is doing much to interest the Italian Government in the case. Giovannitti is an Italian subject, never having been naturalised. His case has, on that account, been the subject of diplomatic correspondence between the Italian Government and the United States Government.

Giovannitti is a modest and optimistic man. His chief concern in prison is not so much himself as his friends and comrades on the outside. For their happiness and welfare he is most solicitous. He is confident of acquittal, as he believes the prosecution so palpably unjust as to be rejected by fair-minded men, regardless of class. Such is Arturo Giovannitti.

Thus, our duty is to deliver these two honest Workers from the clutches of the American prison warders. Their companions of misery are already working for their liberation over there, with as much stubbornness and courage as they displayed for Moyer, Haywood, and Pettibone. By adding our protest to theirs, and claiming Ettor and Giovannitti's liberty with untiring energy, we will be showing our *masters* that working-class solidarity is not a vain word, and that they shall have to reckon with international fraternity.

UNLIMITED MAJORITY RULE.

Do you believe in unlimited majority rule? If you do, remember what it means. It means that three men have all rights and two men have no rights. It means that the three men are made all-powerful, as if they were little gods, over the two men. It means that the three men are lifted up into something greater than men, and the two men are degraded into something less than men. It means that the nation is split up into two or more factions, always at bitter war with each other—the majority who own, and the minority who are owned. But all such ideas of subjection and supremacy are brutal, stupid, and unreasonable; they are ideas that have come down to us, with only a slight change of form, from the dark ages when men knelt to popes and emperors. We bid you accept a manlier and worthier belief. Believe in men and women as self-owners, "self-rulers." Desire to have no power yourselves over the lives and property of others; and allow nobody—whether majority or minority—to have power over your lives and your property.

When, then, may men reasonably make use of a majority vote? They may reasonably do so when they all freely agree to accept a majority decision, as in a club or joint stock company; or perhaps when they truly and as a matter of right own some property in common, and can find no other way of settlement; or in the few cases when it is right [as in the prevention of force] to employ force—for you must remember that majority rule, unless accepted by everybody concerned, is force, and nothing but force. Except by disregarding what is morally true and just men cannot employ majority rule to force their own opinions and interests on each other; to take property from each other to compel others to contribute to certain objects of which they do not approve, or to advance any cause or undertaking, however good in itself. Majority rule is not founded—any more than emperor's rule—on reason or justice. There is no reason or justice in making two men subject to three men. The opinions of two men are just as sacred for them as the opinions and interests of three men are for them. Nobody has the moral right to seek his own advantage by force. That is the one unalterable, inviolable condition of a true society. Whether we are many, or whether we are few, we must learn only to use the weapons of reason, discussion and persuasion.—*Free Life*, London.

SPARKS.

I heartily accept the motto "That government is best which governs least," and I should like to see it lived up to more rapidly and systematically. Carried out, it finally amounts to this, which also I believe: "That government is best which governs not at all"; and when men are prepared for it that will be the kind of government which they will have.—H. D. Thoreau.

    *   *   *

Of one thing I am, and always have been, convinced: it is not by the State that men can be regenerated, and the terrible woes of this darkened world effectually lightened.—Wm. E. Gladstone.

    *   *   *

Whoever will be free must make himself free. Freedom is no fairy's gift to fall into any man's lap. What is freedom? To have the will to be responsible for one's self.—Nietzsche.

    *   *   *

One is free in proportion as one is strong; there is no real liberty save that which one takes for one's self.—Stirner.

"WILSHIRE'S MAGAZINE."

CORRESPONDENCE.

"WEEKLY SYNDICALIST."

To the Editor of the SYNDICALIST.

DEAR BOWMAN,—"Make the SYNDICALIST a weekly." Yes! Your American readers would be right glad. Send them all extra subscription blanks. The SYNDICALIST comes like a spring wind, full of life and incentive.

Reminds one of the outcoming of the good old *Clarion*, twenty years ago, when its readers "couldn't sleep of a Thursday" till they had it! Print it weekly; yes, it's needed! The fight that Capitalism is putting up against Industrialism proves that the New Method is more than in the air.

And it's international. Have an "Other Countries" column, and let us know of activities. There'll be plenty here.

Sown in blood, steel, pain, and death, the new industrial wars of San Diego, Aberdeen, Hoqudim, Fresno, Spokane, and British Columbia are monumental for all time. It's hands across the sea in reality.

Affairs in Italy, Australia, and your own transport, dockers, and miners' activities all indicate the growing sense of solidarity and mass action. We've lots of trials in the free-speech fight of San Diego pending, and Ettor and Giovanetti, in jail at Lawrence, Mass., for their work in the late victory there, have got to be saved from the gallows, and a weekly SYNDICALIST will help indeed.

JACK WOOD.

Seattle (U.S.A.), June 25, 1912.

THE WAY WE WRITE.

To the Editor of the SYNDICALIST.

DEAR SIR,—A friend of mine, a young carman, showed me a copy of your paper the other day. He said he could not understand it—the words used were so long and hard and the sentences long. This is the first copy I have seen of the SYNDICALIST, and I must say I quite agree with my friend. No labourer could understand it. It might as well be written in Greek. If you are issuing the paper for the educated classes, college undergraduates, &c., then it will do very well. But I don't see how you are going to get a circulation amongst manual workers if you don't speak to them in the simple Saxon of one or two syllables which they understand. Strangely enough, this seems to be the glaring fault of all the Labour literature I have seen. One would think all the manual workers had been to Ruskin College. The Gospel mission people and jingo propagandists don't make this stupid mistake. It is left for writers in the Labour Press. Take a leaf from the enemy's book, and use simple Saxon such as an agricultural or general labourer can understand.

And, again, why not have in each issue a standing declaration in simple words of what your creed is? Of course, if the paper is only for the "converted," then it does not matter; but it is possible that new readers and people entirely ignorant of your teachings would like to see a simple statement of them in any issue they might chance to buy. This would save them a lot of trouble.

Trusting you will take my criticisms in the same friendly spirit as given and excuse anonymous letter, I remain, yours sincerely,

A FRIEND.

Walthamstow, July 25, 1912.

SYNDICALISM IN AMERICA.

We are requested by Geo. P. S. Bonner to print the following :—

Local 57.

Philadelphia, Pa., June 30, 1912.

Industrial Workers of the World, 728, West Columbia Avenue, Philadelphia, Pa.

Fellow-Workers,—I assume ye all, Industrial Unionist, Anarchist, &c., want to overthrow Capitalism now, as we don't bother voting to elect rulers to make faster the chains which bind us. There is no necessity for political parties. Step at a time to Socialism, S.P. brand, revolutionary party organised by industries, or a simple political party, without immediate demands, such as Socialistic Party of Great Britain, or one without immediate demands (S.L.P.), that claims it is only a shield to usher in and protect an industrial revolutionary union when only 16 per cent. of its own members belong to the "Dupery," better known as the Detroit Faction of the I.W.W. Now, as the "Dupery" claims to have more members in it than the S.L.P., it shows that it is a recruiting ground for the S.L.P.—which is, in fact, a simple political party, too, as it only preaches, and does not put into practice its Industrial Unionism—and if anything shields the S.L.P., and not it them.

I have been a member of the Detroit I.W.W., which has a political clause in its preamble which their recent strikes have shown is not a shield, and now seeing that there is not only no necessity for a political party, but also that there is no necessity for trying to set up a dual union, as the "Bummery"—better known as the Chicago I.W.W. faction—is also doing, thereby causing much confusion, dividing of the workers, and creating a disgust for all unionism.

Now, I request of this Local to have a discussion on this matter, and not to railroad it through.

It remains for you to decide whether you will still help to kindle factional fights, and not unite together to fight your common enemy.

I would suggest those who agree with me vote on the following proposition—viz. :

"This Local 57 I.W.W. hereby severs its connection with the I.W.W., to form (which they claim, but do not represent) a Syndicalist League for the purpose of propaganda, and advises its members to affiliate with the Labour Movement, the American Federation of Labour, and through a militant minority work to get delegates elected to a General Labour Bureau, such as the C.G.T. of France, and there they will exchange views, and go over all differences and eventually the militant minority will have made and direct the A.F. of L. along revolutionary lines."

Hoping you will investigate this, read over again that letter from I.W.W. Local Nelson, B.C., stating it withdrew out of I.W.W.; also W. Z. Foster's letters that were brought to a quick close in both *Solidarity* and the *Industrial Worker* about six months ago, I am, yours for your enlightenment,

GEO. P. S. BONNER, 1427, North Howard Street, Philadelphia, Pa.

P.S.—This will leave a vacancy as a trustee, also, on propaganda committee.

G. P. S. B.

SOCIALISM IN AMERICA.

To the Editor of the SYNDICALIST.

DEAR COMRADE,—There is now before the Socialist Party of the United States a proposition to insert in the organisation's constitution a clause that should have the attention of all believers in the international solidarity of the working-class. The clause in question has already passed the party's national convention, and is now offered to the rank and file for their endorsement. It is known as "Section 6, Article II.," and reads :

"Any member of the party who opposes political action, or advocates crime, sabotage, or violence, as a weapon of the working-class to aid in its emancipation, shall be expelled from the party."

This masterpiece of statecraft is, of course, the work of a few politicians and reformers, who have entered the party, who want success even at the cost of compromise, and who seem really to believe in the possibility of a revolution by diplomacy! What they mean is that they desire the votes of the "socialistic" rather than the votes of the Socialists : that they want to regain the "socialistic" confidence lost by the party's support of the McNamara brothers, since convicted of dynamiting; that they fear the influence of the industrial workers of the world and other Syndicalists, and that they are jealous of the popularity in the party of that courageous member of the I.W.W., Haywood.

Our diplomats (I say "our," for I am a member of the Socialist Party of the United States) are few in number, but they are dangerous, and there is some danger of their converting a majority, and passing "Section 6." If they succeed, they will set back by an entire decade the progress of the proletariat in the United States.

REGINALD WRIGHT KAUFFMAN.

Cloughton, Yorks. July 14, 1912.

SYNDICALIST METHODS IN OPERATION.

To the Editor of the SYNDICALIST.

DEAR SIR,—Possessing an unbiassed mind towards Syndicalism, can you show to me that Syndicalism will not incur the slaughter of those workers who try to put the Syndicalist methods of taking possession of the means of life into operation? Shall look in next number of SYNDICALIST for reply.—I am yours faithfully,

"WILLIAM."

Islington, July, 1912.

SHALL WE AMALGAMATE?

To the Editor of the SYNDICALIST.

DEAR SIR,—Syndicalist workers are constantly discovering that they are compelled to make a revaluation of ideas and methods. Projects which seemed the most feasible and logical have suddenly to be abandoned on account of the fresh light given by some event in the labour world.

Some are slower in making the required change than are their comrades, with the result that a certain amount of confusion becomes inevitable. All this is a good sign and must prevent the stagnation which is so apparent in many of our "progressive" organisations. "Nothing is constant but change" is the eternal truism. But what of the well-intentioned slow person?

Is he to be summarily dismissed as a reactionary and allowed to drift away into antagonism or, what is possibly worse, apathy? Especially when, as sometimes happens, he is *right*.

We are all aware that time will solve the question—may possibly be the only solvent—but where do we stand at the moment? These thoughts have been forced on the writer by reason of recent occurrences in the British Syndicalist movement, if the adjective is permissible. The movement is so young that the uninitiated may wonder at the question having arrived so early in the day. But, as I have hinted, this is but a proof of the "liveness" of the Syndicalist movement in this country.

We have had, as an instance, the question of active anti-militarist propaganda thrust upon us, it is true, by the government prosecutions. At the inception of the movement very few of us cared a scrap about the immediate propagation of anti-militarism. We realised that such an active movement would be bound to come in time, but we were quite content that it should rest on the knees of the future. All our attention was given to the actual economic organisation of the workers, and we felt the task sufficient to occupy our full energies and those of thousands of others.

But this has changed. Many of us are eager for active anti-militarist work whilst the rest are cool upon the matter. Which is right?

There is no necessity to hide this difference of opinion. Discussion on the matter will help many of the members and sympathisers to decide on the question, and the outcome can only be of advantage to the movement.

Anti-militarism is not the only subject on which such a discussion is desirable. There is another which may be said to be of vastly greater importance, bearing as it does on the integral organisation of the future Syndicalist movement in these islands. I refer to the merits of the amalgamation of unions as against their Federation.

The policy of amalgamation is the one that has been advocated in Great Britain since the commencement of our propaganda. In a pamphlet I wrote four years ago on "Industrial Unionism: Its Principles and Meaning," I pointed out the superiority of amalgamation to federation, with the arguments, amongst others, of the unity of purpose, and the saving of finances effected by such a policy of amalgamation. I have had no reason to alter my ideas on the subject, though, conceivably, I may be one of the aforesaid "slow" Syndicalists.

Whilst not an opponent of federation—as one indeed, who has fought for it—when amalgamation was impossible—I could not close my eyes to the numerous cases of black-legging which have occurred between federated unions. This notwithstanding the fact that which I was fully aware: that black-legging was, and is at present, not unknown between various branches of the same trade union. In this last case, however, the cause is the improper working of the union. Between federated unions black-legging is due to the between the unions not being sufficiently strong. I have little need to emphasise this last point. The recent occurrences in the Transport Workers' Federation are too fresh in our memories.

What then, is our present propaganda and the future organisation to be?

All of us realise the danger of a highly centralised union of workers.

Such a thing is a hindrance to the growth of initiative and self-reliance amongst the organised workers. However democratic its executive may

intend to be, there must always be complaints of the provincial members that their local conditions are not sufficiently appreciated. Charges of "bureaucratic methods" must be conceded to be not entirely unjust, and cohesiveness of opinion and feeling is rendered extremely difficult. These are a few of the charges which can be levelled against the amalgamation policy.

Let us now look at the reverse side of the picture.

With 1,500 trade unions in Great Britain solidarity is rendered impossible, however strong the federation may be. The multiplicity of unions breeds jealousy and hatred amongst those organisations catering for the same class of workers. The superabundance of paid officials prevent the breaking down of barriers between the respective unions, causing strife internally where it should express externally and against the master-class. Really concerted action is unknown, as every trade union Syndicalist knows from bitter experience. In a few words, the British unions are too numerous to be affected by federation.

There is the position as it appears to me.

These charges do not apply to the Syndicalist movement of other countries. France, owing to its comparatively few and non-rival unions, can afford to do without amalgamation. Similarly with Germany and most of the Continental countries. America suffers, as does Great Britain from too many unions; hence its cry for "One Big Union." Conditions being different, so must be the method of organisation.

What, then, shall we work for here in Great Britain? Centralisation is bad. The present decentralisation is worse.

I am in no position to dogmatise, but I would suggest that the best line of action would be a compromise between the two extremes. One Big Union, but with the utmost local autonomy consistent with the efficient working of the whole. That should, in my opinion, be the immediate aim.

Let us now hear the counsel for the opposition.

A. B. ELSBURY.

Newcastle-on-Tyne, July, 1912.

DO IT NOW.

To the Editor of the SYNDICALIST.

SIR,—Reading in the *Daily Herald* the above heading from Mr. Tom Mann's advice to Transport men—and that is, as regards *all* sections of Transport workers, the most rational and effective system is to have one big union—I agree. Also advocate that men of all grades would then be under the Transportation Department. But the Tom Mann report in the *Daily Herald* states "seafaring men of all grades, lightermen, dockers, stevedores, quay labourers, wharf and warehouse workers, and carmen." I would like to know if the carmen are considered in with the railway workers, tram and 'bus workers, and also taxi-cab drivers, because I know too well that trams and 'buses blacklegged railway workers when on strike, also taxi-cabs, all vehicle workers.—Yours for solidarity.

GET TOGETHER.

When the factory whistle blows it does not call us to work as Irishmen, Germans, Americans, Russians, Greeks, Poles, Negroes, or Mexicans. It calls us to work as wage-workers, regardless of the country in which we were born or colour of our skin. Why not get together, then; not on national or race lines, but as wage-workers, just as we are compelled to do in the shop when the whistle blows? We have only one enemy—the profit-skinning "boss."

TRADES ORGANISED IN SECTIONS.

I am a married man with eighteen children (six by my first wife, six by second wife, and married a widow with six children). Now they are all in different trades. Now, if they do wrong I hit them one at a time, but if they organised into one body I should stand a poor chance.

CHURCH HYMN.

"Once I was blind, but now I can see The light of the world is Unity."

EX-TRAM CONDUCTOR L.C.C.

Battersea, S.W., July, 1912.

LONDON DISTRICT BOARD OF BAKERS.

A meeting of specially-elected delegates was held at the Mail Coach, Farringdon Street, E.C., on the 19th ult., to consider the organising movement. Fifty-one delegates were present, with Mr. Hutchings in the chair. It was agreed "That an Emergency Committee be elected, to be called together when in the opinion of the board the opportune time has arrived that we should take a ballot of the members on the question of *Down Tools* policy, every man organising movement to be pushed on in the meantime to the utmost"; further, "that the Emergency Committee consist of a delegate from each branch, and also that they be elected on September quarter night." A motion that the platform be altered to the effect that factory hands work one hour per day less than shop hands was withdrawn after brief discussion.

The Syndicalist

VOL. 1. NO. 8.   LONDON, SEPTEMBER, 1912.   MONTHLY, ONE PENNY.

THE UNIONS MUST UNITE.

MUST UNITE TO FIGHT.

MUST FIGHT TO CONTROL INDUSTRY.

During the past two years, since the Sheffield Congress, considerable progress has been made in the matter of Amalgamation of Kindred Unions and the Federation of Industries. In several instances such success has attended the efforts made as to warrant the belief that real business is meant.

The prospect in the Building Industry of uniting in one Amalgamated Union fourteen Societies of all grades, Mechanics and Labourers alike, is very bright and already within an ace of full achievement.

The three Unions of Railwaymen are now one organisation, awaiting only the final touches to consummate affairs.

In the Metal Industry, Engineers, Boiler Makers, Shipwrights, and others are showing a determination to get nearer to each other and to broaden the bases upon which they have hitherto rested.

In the Furnishing Trades complete success has attended the Amalgamation policy of thirteen sectional Unions.

Amongst the slowest to merge are the seven or eight Labourers' Unions, who each took the vote of their members eighteen months ago and thereby obtained the hearty endorsement of the principle of Amalgamation; but owing to "pressure of business" very little progress has been made to carry out and apply the principle. However, we hope this will be attended to without further delay.

In the Transport Industry, Amalgamation is the only policy that can provide the solidarity the situation demands, and ultimately the Railwaymen will become part of the National Transport Workers' Union.

The unification of the Trade Union forces is still the most urgent necessity of the hour, for sectional overlapping and general inefficiency, because of sectionalism, is the main characteristic of the Trade Union Movement.

To ensure success in making towards betterment and the Industrial Revolution, INDUSTRIAL SOLIDARITY is a vital necessity.

And for what do we require Industrial Solidarity? In order that the Working Class shall efficiently conduct the CLASS STRUGGLE which is always going on whether we are conscious of it or not.

The Capitalist Class is the Ruling, Dominant Class in present-day Society; they dominate and control the Working Class because they control industry and, therefore, wealth production. The Working Class have now to challenge them and wrest from them the supremacy they enjoy as a Capitalist Class. If this is not the position, what is? Do we want Unions merely to adjust the wages a trifle now and again; to facilitate the formation of Wages Boards, and to help return workmen to Parliament? This we Syndicalists declare is not the genuine work of the Trade Union Movement.

The ultimate destiny of the Working Class is to become the entire controllers of the Industry of the World, leaving no room for the Capitalist Class. The way to achieve this is by Direct Action in the industries, at which the organised Workers are engaged.

It is not merely the organisation of the Workers that we are after. It is much more than that. It is the ORGANISATION OF WORK ITSELF BY THE ORGANISED WORKERS; and this is the same as saying the Trade Unionists will become the direct controllers of industry, the actual deciding factors as to how industry shall be conducted.

The first and most urgent matter to be dealt with by the Unions is to agree to take drastic action as regards unemployment. It is quite possible for the organised Workers so to regulate working hours as to ensure all being at work who ought to be at work. There is no need whatever for unemployed. The men and women thrown out of work by the Capitalists are so thrown out because the Working Class allow the Capitalist Class to be the deciding factors. The organised Working Class must themselves become the regulators of hours and conditions of work and never allow any of them to be thrown out. Production for use, and not for profit, is the keynote; but it will always be production for profit, accompanied by thousands of unemployed, until the Workers take the responsibility of refusing to work unless all share in the work of production.

And this controlling can best be done—nay, can only be done—through and by the Industrial Organisations.

If the Parliamentarians continue to keep the Unions subservient to Parliamentary tactics and their personal interests, the day is not far off when there will be a line of cleavage so marked as to be very unpleasant for professional politicians. We hope, however, no necessity for this will arise. Let every man exercise his own judgment as to the value of Parliamentary action, but the Unions must be purely industrial in character and out for the Control of Industry, and not for the support of politicians.

If the Trade Union Congress is really alive to the necessities of the hour it will, as a preliminary step to more drastic action, unanimously decide in favour of an EIGHT-HOUR DAY in all industries, to be obtained by industrial action, and not by Parliamentary petitioning. There is no hope in the world to get this by means of Parliament, whilst by DIRECT ACTION it would be perfectly easy if the whole of the organised Forces were prepared to demonstrate their solidarity.

We appeal to Delegates to remember that ever-increasing thousands of fellow-Workers on the Continent and in the United States are heartily endorsing DIRECT ACTION methods. It is the Working-Class method of dislodging the Capitalist exploiters, which most certainly will never be done by Board of Trade officials or Government Departments. Whatever they may be in private life, these officials and departments are always officially and professionally the scouts and watch-dogs of the Ruling Class.

Dare, and again Dare, and always Dare, as part of the Working Class, to fight with, and for, the Working Class, and to get the control of Industry by Industrial Organisation out of the hands of the Capitalist Class.

TOM MANN.

THE FRAUD OF EMIGRATION TO AUSTRALIA.

GOVERNMENT CATERING FOR THE SHIPPING COMPANIES,

REGISTRY OFFICES FLEECING THE IMMIGRANTS.

I am frequently asked as to the chances of work in Australia, as to whether the glowing statements made by emigration agents are to be accepted as correct. I here give a few extracts from the Parliamentary proceedings in Melbourne, the capital of Victoria. These are taken from Hansard, the official report for July 9, 1912, just to hand.

Mr. G. M. Prendergast, M.L.A., is the Leader of the Parliamentary Labour Party of Victoria and of the Opposition in Parliament. In the debate on the Address, in reply to the Governor's speech, Mr. Prendergast criticised the Government re its "bold immigration policy," and at the request of the District Committee of the Amalgamated Engineers of Melbourne he read the following letter to the House, which I feel sure will be of considerable interest to readers here:—   **T. M.**

Amalgamated Society of Engineers,
Melbourne, July 4, 1912.
Mr. G. M. Prendergast, M.L.A.,

Dear Sir,—I am directed by my committee to bring under your notice the serious aspect of the unemployed problem facing the engineering trade, and the ruthless way mechanics are being induced to leave Great Britain for Australia, and undoubtedly under false impressions. In the first place, forty members of our society landed in Melbourne during the week ending June 22, and, together with twenty who were idle (previous arrivals), made a total of sixty out of work, comprising fitters, turners, machinists, blacksmiths. The position is or has already got to be indeed serious, and we consider something should be done to stem the tide of immigration of engineering mechanics to these shores. Mr. Ashby, secretary, &c., to the Chamber of Manufacturers, has had great difficulty in placing the men engaged through Mr. Whitehead, although preference is shown to them, and the unfortunates who pay their full passage money are left to get work themselves, and after getting a job are often discharged to make room for those engaged by Mr. Whitehead, who arrive later. I can prove that dozens have obtained work and have been discharged after a few days or weeks, undoubtedly to make room for the newest comer who, in turn, is treated similarly. One case in particular—a turner engaged by Mr. Whitehead—started work at Newport on June 26 and worked under most unfavourable conditions, and was discharged on July 2, 1912, working altogether about one week. This man has good references, covering twenty years in two shops. The new arrivals complain very bitterly of the way they have been induced to throw up their employment in England, and sell up homes, at a considerable loss, and book for Victoria. They are told by Mr. Whitehead and the Government agents that they need have no fear, as work is plentiful, and that the employers cannot get engineering mechanics, so they come full of hope, only to find that a great surplus of labour exists, and they are brought to the very verge of starvation. Several told me this week that they left as much money as they could with their wives at home, and only brought a couple of pounds with them, as they were certain of getting employment on landing. Now they are without one shilling and have nothing to send home for their wives and families. The position is an absolute disgrace to the State Government. The numbers out of work are so great that when the notice appeared in the paper that the Austral Otis Company had received the contract to build the locomotives for the Victorian Government, the place was fairly besieged with applicants for employment, so much so, that the gates had to be closed against the crowd, and have been kept shut ever since. For every one mechanic engaged by Mr. Whitehead there are about five others arrive, who either pay their full fare or work their passage. We would like to know how many mechanics in the engineering trade have landed up to date, and who were engaged by Mr. Whitehead. We can guarantee and prove that 250 have arrived during the last twelve months, and 100 since Mr. Whitehead left Victoria. Names and addresses, in most cases, can be given. Another grievance is that the shipping companies are engaging men as stewards to work their passage out. Most of these are mechanics. On the Belgic, out of a total of 100 or 120 stewards, fifty remained in Melbourne; of these, seven were engineers and the others were of different trades. The Government seem to be catering chiefly for the shipping companies. I know several fitters and turners who are working, and they state that as soon as they get together enough to pay their fares back home they will go. In conclusion, I must state, and I can bring proof, that Mr. Whitehead is giving preference to married men with families; that the Government dockyard will not require men for some months yet, and that the Austral Otis Company will be some time before they require to increase their staff. So the men were brought out here and were assured of work on arrival, "as far as those responsible are concerned," are to just wait and starve, which only takes about one week.

Trusting you can make use of this, and ventilate this matter fully,

I am, Sir,
Yours faithfully,
A. S. EVERNDEN,
Secy. Dis. Ctee.

Mr. Prendergast added that in Colac, in the West of Victoria, he was informed that:—

A large number of immigrants are wandering about here at present begging for food. One poor fellow arrived at Larpent yesterday by train from Melbourne. He was sent by the Labour Bureau to employment, not being informed as to the wage he was to receive until his arrival at Larpent. This information, which awaited him by letter, informed him that he was to proceed to his employer on the arrival of the train and would be paid the handsome sum of 10s. per week. The young man stated that he had left a good position in England to come to this country with the expectation of becoming a prosperous citizen, but instead had had nothing to eat since the previous day. The poor man at this stage broke down and wept bitterly. He was supplied with eatables by a number of railway employees, for which he was very grateful.

As further evidence Mr. Prendergast gave the following:—

The Mining Conference which was held at Ballarat on March 1, passed a resolution of protest against the immigrants who were being brought into competition with them. They said there was no chance of employment for the immigrants unless the present miners were put out of their jobs. When I stated that 200 immigrants had gone back to England the Age stretched it and made the number 2,000. I would like to read the affidavit which I then referred to. It is as follows:—

Hurd Street,
Portland,
March 8th, 1912

I, George Taylor, of Hurd-street, meat preserver, do solemnly and sincerely declare that on Dec. 20, 1911, I visited the ss. Ayrshire, and I noticed a number of returning immigrants. I interviewed a number of them. They were a fine, sturdy lot of people from all parts of England, including a good number from Scotland. They all complained bitterly of the way they had been deceived. Some had been told they were to get 10s. for eight hours, but instead they had been offered 8d. per acre for ringbarking trees, and said they could do about four to five acres by working long hours in a day. They all seemed glad they were going back, and said if the Government would take them home for the same as they brought them out that they believed thousands would go home. They all said how lucky they were to have the means to return. On Feb. 17 I visited the ss. Suffolk. There I found a large number of returning immigrants. They informed me they were about one hundred, and these, like the Ayrshire's passengers, were even more bitter at the way promises that had been made to them had not been fulfilled. These were all paying their passages, and said that a few others were working their way back in the stokehole in order to get away. These also were a sturdy lot of people from all parts of England, Ireland, and Scotland, and would have made good colonists if sufficient inducement had been offered them to stay. They, too, said how thankful they were that they had the means of returning home again.

(Signed) GEORGE TAYLOR.
Witness—A. W. Leneker, J.P.
8th March, 1912.

In the *Portland Observer* (Victoria) of the 20th Feb. last there appears the following statement:—

We, the undersigned passengers on board the ss. Suffolk, who are returning to England, Ireland, and Scotland, hereby certify that we are leaving Australia because we are greatly dissatisfied with conditions of labour in the country; that the prospects of work held out to us by immigration agents in Great Britain have not been realised. We have done our best to find work, but have been unable to do so. We are glad to see that Mr. O'Keefe cannot deceive the Irishmen, as they gave him a bad reception when he tried to get young men to come out from there.

(Signed) HENRY J. AGNEW.
JOHN W. REED.
CHARLES A. PRATLEY.
W. F. KIRKPATRICK.
ALEX. ANDERSON.
W. WRIGHT.
ETHEL REED.
H. GORMAN.
M. E. REED.
SAMUEL GREGORY.
SARAH HYDE.

The foregoing statement was supplemented by the individual experiences of Mr. Agnew, as follows:—"I am one of about a hundred passengers who are returning home. I have spent about three years in Queensland. I was told before I left home that it was a great country for farmers. Well, I have had as much experience of farming in the Old Country as any man that ever crossed the sea, and my experience of Australia is that they don't want farm hands at all. The best wage I could get from a farmer in Australia was £1 per week, and then the farmer only wanted a man for a few weeks."

Here is a letter from a farmer at Boisdale, addressed to myself (Mr. Prendergast):—

"Dear Sir,—I was glad to read your remarks about immigrants returning home again. It is one of the most disgraceful things our State Government will some day have to account for. Its bold policy of immigration! Dear Sir, I have been told by immigrants that if there was a road so that they could walk back to England they would go right back. But they are ashamed to go back to their friends to be laughed at. There has been here since October last, and to-day they do not know which way to turn to meet their liabilities, and if anything you can do or say that will, in any way, prevent these people coming here, you will be doing good both for them and the people here, especially landseekers. The land in this State is too dear altogether for the people of other countries to make a living off. Before they get into the conditions of working out here their capital is all gone. God help these immigrants when, as large farmer told me last week, he said, will we get some more of these people out here and a bad season comes, then we will starve the — out. I may state they got their harvesting done for 6s. per day this last season. I am writing to you as a farmer who has been in this district close on fifty years, and, I believe, of some standing. In concluding, notwithstanding the *Argus* leader of Wednesday, everything you can do I am sure you will not regret it later on."

To the Editor of THE SYNDICALIST.
Unemployed Agitation League, Melbourne, Victoria, July 11, 1912, Trades' Hall, Carlton.

DEAR COMRADES,—I am instructed by the above to inform your readers of the state of unemployment here at the time of writing. The Trades' Hall Council published the fact that 1,700 unemployed were registered in Union books; also 2,000 to 3,000 men had registered on the Commonwealth unemployment book awaiting for work expected from the Federal Government, which is controlled by a large majority of so-called labour members, who are at the present time kidding the working-class that a higher tariff is what is wanted to find work for all.

They are more concerned in the building of an Australian Navy and Army, also offering men, if they joined, they will receive a trip home, to receive further instruction from the Liberal Government, instructors at Portsmouth and Devonport, in the respectable art of murdering the workers of other lands and for the protection of property and capitalist interests, which are safer in the hands of the Labour Party than any other party. Well, the League have urged upon the Trades and Labour Council to get a mass demonstration of unemployed to shake the Premier (Wily Watt, a Liberal) to get work for the workless—about two months ago we first asked them. Yesterday this peace and loving respectable leaders of craft unionism took a step to have a demonstration. About 1,200 unemployed turned up, and Mr. Watt refused to see them on the grounds that he was very busy, also he had not made any arrangements with the council to meet them. Anyhow, as per usual, they got stones instead of bread—that is what the tame, time-serving blind leaders of the blind received for their tame, weak-kneed attitude. Well this Government, through its Agent in England, and other Agents, are sending to these shores shiploads of helpless men, women, and children, who are decoyed by liars living in clover, and when these persons get here they find plenty of surplus labour of all kinds, ready to sell their labour power for any wages; also the immigrants put up in the various boarding-houses, where the living is dear, and then the immigrant's money goes, and he and his wife sell their clothes. Why the farmers here actually sent to the Government Labour Bureau offering to provide work for keep only. Now then, the workers here are putting advertisements in the two morning papers—the *Argus* and *Age*—also the registry offices (sharks) are having a glorious time of it, fleecing the immigrants and others. I am enclosing cuttings to prove there is an already congested labour market, and that the Agents, and Agents' Generals in the various States in England, know that the immigration policies of the various States are simply to provide plenty of wage-slaves, at cheap wages, for the capitalists; also to prevent the vanguards of the one big union ideas to flourish. Anyhow, I trust you will do your best to place the statements above in your paper, which is read here, and if you make a strong case out the Government here and their Agents in England will be heckled.

What prompts my committee is to show that here capitalism, although not developed in as much degree as in older commercial countries, we find the fruits are just as bitter to the wage-slaves as elsewhere. The workers must unite industrially; and, unfortunately, I notice that here, as well as in England, they look upon Parliament as if it can give them freedom. They at least have now knowledge enough to know the futility of ever expecting justice from such sources. No matter where a worker goes he will learn that he will only be wanted so long as he is willing to work for cheap wages, also that when his muscle is weak he will be thrown out on the industrial scrap-heap, like the worker, when he sucks the goodness out of an orange, he throws the skin away. Never mind, you cannot escape from the claws of capitalists' despotism nor unemployment. You all can make a heaven in England or anywhere when you will. I conclude, yours for social revolution,

F. S. SPILLMAN (Hon. Secretary).

The Syndicalist

EDITED UNDER THE AUSPICES OF

The Industrial Syndicalist Education League

Offices—

4, MAUDE TERRACE, WALTHAMSTOW,
LONDON, E.

MONTHLY - ONE PENNY.

Post Paid Subscription—

Great Britain or Abroad ... 12 months 1s. 6d.

Bundle Rates—

1s. 6d. per quire, Carriage Paid.

The receipt of a Sample Copy is an invitation to Subscribe.

SEPTEMBER, 1912.

THE AMERICAN SOCIALIST PARTY AND SYNDICALISM.

In the *Milwaukee Leader*, a Social Democratic paper, of July 9, is a article from the pen of Mr. Job Harriman entitled " The Socialist Party and the Labour Unions."

Mr. Harriman is a lawyer who always upheld the old-style trades unionism against any criticism by the more advanced thinkers. Some thirteen years ago, when the Socialist Labour Party took up an advanced attitude by declaring that Unions that were not organising for the destruction of the Capitalist system were supporting it, and should be opposed by Unions that were organised to end the wages system, it was Mr. Job Harriman who opposed De Leon, the representative of the S.L.P. in debate.

Times have changed, and it is no longer an advance in Union ideas to endeavour to control Unions by a political party. Experience has proven that the Union movement, once its members realise that Capitalism is their enemy, is best to be autonomous and follow its own path without the interference of middle-class minded politicians.

Mr. Harriman practically asks for the American Socialist Party and the Unions to create a body similar to our Labour Party. He claims that the Party and Unions must be united, that every Socialist wage-worker should be in his Union, and that every Unionist should join the Party. In other words, Mr. Harriman has now advanced to where his opponent De Leon stood thirteen years ago!

Professional politicians are always late —always years behind the times.

De Leon, who was advanced with the policy Mr. Harriman now advocates thirteen years ago, has become simply a mummified Pope.

When the I.W.W., which was originally built out of De Leon's Socialist Trades and Labour Alliance, the Western Federation of Miners, the United Brotherhood of Railroad Employees, the American Labour Union, and various other advanced bodies, refused to march to the tune of the Socialist Labour Party, De Leon formed an Industrial Workers of the World of his own.

The I.W.W. has passed through a trying experience; but if the I.W.W. died to-morrow it would have justified its existence because of the facts relative to Unionism and politics that it has demonstrated.

Formed in 1905, in order to organise the workers on the lines of industries instead of crafts, and with the abolition of Capitalism as its object, the I.W.W. drew all militant Unionists to its ranks. Most of the prominent members of the Socialist Party oppose it. However, politicians dominated its first Convention, and a clause relative to political action was inserted in the preamble. *This proved to be a stumbling block to the I.W.W., as it will to all Unions.* For nearly two years the I.W.W. was hampered by the quarrels of the two rival Socialist Parties striving to control the organisation. When, ultimately, the party that Mr. Harriman represents was turned down things apparently settled. Soon the De Leonite faction became troublesome, and instead of an eternal debate as to which party was the proper " reflex " of the I.W.W., it became a question of politics versus direct action. The direct actionists won in theory and practice.

This is the reason why Mr. Harriman strove so hard, and is delighted with the fact that the Socialist Party endorsed the evolution of craft Unions towards industrial organisation and at the same time passed resolutions condemning sabotage, &c. It was a neat move to try

and capture the Trade Unions affiliated to the American Federation of Labour, and to give a back-handed knock to the members like Haywood and others who belong to the Industrial Workers of the World, which body has been evolved into a Syndicalist organisation as regards theory and policy.

Mr. Harriman wants a state of affairs similar to that in England. He wants to see a working political alliance between the Unions and the Socialist Party, similar to our Unions and the Independent Labour Party, which are united in the composite body, the Parliamentary Labour Party. Mr. Harriman's mental progress has been so great that he now takes up the attitude that De Leon did in his debate with him thirteen years ago.

If the American workers are wise they will leave gentlemen like Lawyer Job Harriman to talk to the wind. The Industrial Workers of the World have at least shown the power of direct action. Politicians did not win the fights at Lawrence, Spokane, Portland, MacKec's Rocks, and all those other victories. If the opposition of the A.F. of L. should make the continued life of the I.W.W. impossible, then there is the remedy by which both Capitalists and politicians can be defeated by rejoining the A.F. of L. Unions and taking up the work with the men inside in order that a militant minority can expound and propagate the Syndicalist ideas and methods. This minority coming forward in each strike and opposing their methods and tactics to those of the politicians and reactionaries.

Direct action, sabotage, the general strike are more effective than the perorations of politicians. To raise the standard of life for the workers, teaching them to demand more, is better work than having Berger as a Congressman, Siedel as a Mayor, only to find these political victories vanish at the next elections.

Syndicalism makes more revolution, it breeds self-reliance, determination, decision; parliamentarianism makes for reform, it breeds compromise, treachery, and impotence.

TIGHTENING THE SCREWS.

Not only does Capitalism seek to nullify the fruits of victory by raising prices when a strike has won an increase of wages, but it endeavours to make every move of the class war the occasion for tightening its grip upon Labour.

This is glaringly illustrated in the cases of Ettor and Giovannitti. In their arrest and trial for being accessory to the murder of Anna La Pizza, a precedent is sought to be established which will make it dangerous for any speaker to point out the evils of the infamous system under which we live.

Regeneracion, of Los Angeles, organ of the Mexican Liberal Party, says : " It is admitted that the accused men had no direct connection with the death on which the charge is based, but it is alleged that the things they said resulted in the deed. That is an infamous doctrine, for under it there is not an educator in the world who could not be held for having taught something that induced someone to commit a crime. Let me write the incontestable truth that Capitalism often sacrifices life to profits, and, under that doctrine, I may be held for the killing of a Capitalist by an outraged worker of whom I never heard."

Says the *Chicago Evening World* (Socialist) : " The situation in this case is very grave, and demands far more serious attention than it has received. As a matter of fact, Ettor and Giovannitti are not on trial. What is on trial, first, is the right of free speech, and, second, the attempt of the American Woollen Trust, sore and angry at its defeat of last winter, to revenge itself upon the men that it holds responsible for its heavy losses. If the prosecution should be able to carry out its purpose, there will be inflicted upon this country an evil greater than riots.

" Once allow the principle to become established that no man may denounce unjust conditions lest some person or interest be injured and once make clear that for the purpose of the revenge of the powerful the courts can be manipulated and justice overridden, and you have performed the greatest and deadliest act of violence that the country has ever known, for you have overturned at once every foundation upon which a republic is supposed to rest.

" No ; it is not Ettor and Giovannitti that are being tried, but the right of the oppressed to protest against oppression. And if we think that right is worth maintaining, we should understand clearly the extent to which it is involved here."

These supposed foundations of the republic do not amount to very much where the rights of the working class are concerned, but until we have sufficient organised strength to speak to the masters in terms of our class, we must maintain such rights as we have by fighting in their terms in their courts. It would be most unfortunate, both for the sake of this

precedent and because of the value of these two fine men to the movement to allow ourselves to be defeated in this case. Of the men Debs says :

" In the unceasing struggle of the workers with their exploiters the truly loyal leaders are always marked for prosecution. Joseph Ettor and Arturo Giovannitti would not now be in jail awaiting trial for murder had they betrayed the slaves of the Lawrence mills. They were staunch and true ; their leadership made the industrial unity and victory, and for this reason only the enraged and defeated mill-owners are now bent on sending them to the electric chair."

Let Labour the wide world make the cause of these men its own, even as they have made our cause their own, even unto the risking of their own lives.

OUR AIM.

By ANNA LINCOLN.

It matters not that we should carve our name
Upon that tablet which the world calls
  " Fame ";
It matters much that we should earn no blame
Of adding to our Nation's awful shame.

What *is* of moment is the love of Truth ;
The balanced working of its wise, wise Ruth.
Then shall old England boast a Noble Youth—
When her twin service is of Love and Truth !

Her service now, to-day, is one of Death.
Death to the highest Life does give with breath.
Death to the buds of promise that each babe does give ;
Death to the souls of men who yet do live.

It matters not at all that we be " great,"
As England writes the word upon her slate ;
But *much* it matters that we *make* a Fate,
And build upon Fair Righteousness a Holy State.

Some of us here, who fight and suffer now,
Will never have the laurel leaves upon our brow ;
But what of that? Do I repine? Dost thou?
We fight and suffer those who follow to endow.

We want a Saner England, Rich—in Beauty ;
Where man, to all his kind, shall do his duty.
Where Worth is honoured for its own fair sake,
And Justice is the Nation's highest stake.

We want a *happy* England, *free* from woe,
Where Health and truest Gladsomeness shall flow,
And to an honoured heritage ALL children grow ;
And we will die, if need be, that these shall be so.

TO THE DAY.

By NORMAN YOUNG.

Cast down those blood-stained banners, old and rent,
  Which hang in mock'ry on the grey church walls !
Grim sign of all the men and millions spent
  To force free foemen to be Britain's thralls.

Thy priests and popes did bless them in Thy name,
  O Christ ! who cam'st with tidings of Goodwill
And Peace on Earth. Thy servants without shame
  Sent men for Mammon forth their blood to spill.

Symbols of reeking slaughter there they hang !
  Of greed for land and trade, of lust for gold.
They echo down the centuries the clang
  And crash of battles from their every fold.

*   *   *   *   *

Our rank and file at last are " reasoning why ";
No longer will they aid in piracy ;
No longer will they blindly " do or die,"
  Or shoot down toilers struggling to be free.

One flag, one nation, will the future give :
One people and one broad humanity,
When workers of all lands are free to live
  And labour for one great community.

THE ETTOR - GIOVANNITTI CASE.

The following resolutions of protest and sympathy were passed unanimously by the Glasgow Trades Council, the Glasgow Branch of the B.S.P., the Glasgow Administrative Council of the I.L.P., and by a mass meeting on Glasgow Green, held under the auspices of the Transport Workers Union.

These bodies were addressed by W. A. Nelson Collier, an American revolutionist, whose appeals on behalf of the imprisoned comrades met with generous response. A brief account of the strike, and of the incidents which led to the arrest of the leaders, was given by the visiting comrade.

When the workers in the Textile industry at Lawrence, Mass., gained their contention for a 54-hour week, the mill owners retaliated by a corresponding reduction of wages. This brought on the strike. Some 27,000 workers went out—men of all nationalities—speaking about forty different languages. They were organised and led to victory by the prominent Labour leaders, Joseph Ettor and Arturo Giovannitti, and after these were thrown into prison, by Wm. D. Haywood.

The strike was conducted in a peaceful manner by these men, but during some trouble which arose a young girl—one of the strike sympathisers—was shot by a policeman. Thereupon Ettor and Giovannitti—both of whom, it is admitted, were two miles away at the time of the tragedy—were jerked up and put in prison as accessory to the murder. The charge, of course, is preposterous, and is merely a subterfuge on the part of the profit-mongers to get these disturbers of their system out of their way.

It is estimated that the victory of the strikers has resulted in an increase of from 5,000,000 to 15,000,000 dollars in wages for the workers of New England, as well as many other benefits. The cause of Labour cannot afford to lose two such leaders—so " dangerous " to the Capitalist class and schemes.

The Trades Council — representing 60,000 workers in Glasgow and the West of Scotland—expressed their heartiest sympathy with their fellow-workers in duress, and pledged them any further support within their power. Mr. James A. Allan, chairman of the Council for the I.L.P., expressed gratitude that the case had been brought before that body for action, and the Executive Committee of the B.S.P. has taken up the matter of forming an Ettor-Giovannitti Defence Committee in Glasgow. The demonstration of several thousands on the Green was addressed by Madame Sorgue, the famous organiser and agitator, from Brussels, who took occasion to make a plea for the imprisoned men.

Resolutions:

Whereas : Our comrades, Joseph J. Ettor and Arturo Giovannitti, having proven their devotion to the cause of Labour by their activities in directing the strike of the textile workers at Lawrence, Massachusetts, U.S.A., and bringing the same to a successful termination, thereby furthering the interests of the workers, materially and otherwise, throughout New England and the world ;

Whereas : The capitalists of New England have therefore singled out these two prominent leaders and benefactors of the working class for punishment because of their said activities, and have caused them to be thrown into prison, where they are now held, on charges absurd and false ;

Whereas : We believe the false charges preferred against these our comrades to have been brought for the sole purpose of crippling the Labour Movement in its universal struggle for freedom from injustice and oppression ; and

Whereas : The workers of all nations are rallying to the support of their comrades in distress ; and we feel that it behoves the working men of Scotland to take some action to save these innocent men from death ;

Be it therefore resolved, by the Glasgow Trades Council,

That we protest against the continued confinement of our fellow-workers, Ettor and Giovannitti, by the authorities of the State of Massachusetts, U.S.A., and demand their release ;

That we extend our sympathy to our comrades behind the bars in " Free America," and pledge them our support in their trials.

Be it further resolved,

That representatives be appointed by this Council to serve on a defence committee now being formed in Glasgow ; and

That a copy of these resolutions be forwarded

by the Secretary to the Hon. Whitelaw Reid, U.S. Embassy, London, West ; to the Governor of the State of Massachusetts ; and to the Ettor-Giovannitti Defence League, Lawrence, Mass.

We fear that these protests will be thrown, unread, into the waste basket. With the knowledge we possess of the American capitalist class, we believe that they intend, in spite of all protests, to take the lives of Ettor and Giovannitti, if harsher means are not resorted to. And we consider it an imperative duty for the workers of Europe to do their utmost, in order to force the American capitalists to set these two labour leaders free.

In thus taking the initiative towards international action by bringing the matter before the international central organisations, we could advance many good reasons for so doing.

Not counting the fact that labour's cause is one and common throughout the whole world, thus making an injury to one an injury to all, we have this splendid cause for interceding, that about one-third of the Swedish working-class lives in America and there suffers under the oppression of capitalism. We also have a debt of gratitude to pay to the American workers who, during the general strike of 1909, so liberally came to our assistance.

But even if these special causes did not exist, we need not make any apologies for the step we are taking.

THE YOUNG SOCIALIST PARTY OF SWEDEN.

After due deliberation the General Executive Board of the Young Socialist Party of Sweden has come to the conclusion that International solidarity demands that measures be taken which are more effective than a mere written protest.

We wish, therefore, to request the INTERNATIONAL TRADE UNION SECRETARIATE :

1. To take steps towards establishing a world-wide boycott of all American goods, and

2. To request the organisations of transportation workers in all the countries of the world to refuse, from a certain date, to have anything to do with vessels and goods arriving from or departing for America, until Ettor and Giovannitti shall have been liberated.

We, furthermore, address a request to the INTERNATIONAL SECRETARIATE and to the INTERNATIONAL SOCIALIST BUREAU to cause the matter to receive the greatest possible publicity, in order that the world's workers may arouse themselves to an understanding of the necessity of immediate action, if the lives of Ettor and Giovannitti are to be saved.

We are convinced that in the face of such a world-boycott of American goods and a world-blockade of American vessels, the American capitalist class will stop and consider ; the tremendous loss we could inflict upon them in this manner surely would be of greater effect than written protests.

Finally, we request and admonish all SWEDISH WORKERS from this day until the liberation of Ettor and Giovannitti, to completely boycott all American goods of all kinds, such as bacon, meat, fish, flour and canned goods ; shoes, hats, collars ; bicycles, gramophones, knives, arms, &c., &c., &c., of whatever kind they may be. We also request all Swedish sailors, longshoremen, and transportation workers to absolutely refuse to handle vessels going to or coming from America.

We also wish to suggest to all brother organisations in other countries to start a similar agitation and to continue same until Ettor and Giovannitti are free.

Should we neglect to do our utmost, and thus allow the murderous designs of the American capitalist class to be carried, then the blood of our brothers is upon our conscience.

Let us, therefore, over the whole world unite our forces to liberate Ettor and Giovannitti.

Long live International Solidarity !
Young Socialist Party of Sweden,
  General Executive Board,
    Per C. R. NILSSON, Sec.
Sv. Ungsocialistiska Partis, Centralkomite, Olandsgatan, 48, Stockholm.

MR. BATTLORI'S DEATH.

THE FRIEND OF FERRER.

At the age of only 51, Mariano Battlori, a personal friend of Ferrer, has just died at Walthamstow.

As manager of Ferrer's publishing business at Barcelona, he found himself exposed to the persecutions that followed the insurrectionary movement of July, 1909, and became one of its innocent and unfortunate victims.

Battlori had formed with Ferrer, during their schooldays, one of those solid friendships that resist time and all sorts of trials.

When Ferrer was charged with complicity in Morral's attempt on the life of the King and Queen of Spain, and thrown in prison, some of the friends of Morral found in a letter, addressed to them by the latter, sentences which completely proved Ferrer's innocence; but not daring to trust the post-office with such a precious document, they sought in Ferrer's surroundings for a trustworthy person who might carry it to Madrid and put it in the hands of the solicitor; the choice fell upon Mariano Battlori.

As manager of the Modern School, he had had at that time already to endure the vexations and threats of the police, and for a whole year had been trembling for the life of his friend.

When, after his acquittal, Ferrer understood the uselessness of his efforts to re-open his school, and decided to start a

THE EXILES IN TERUEL.

Mrs. Maria Ferrer (wife of Ferrer's brother) and her little daughter Alba; in the middle Mariano Battlori; at the back Jose Ferrer (with beard).

publishing business, it was upon Battlori he conferred the post of manager and his power of attorney.

Then came the tragic events of July, 1909. Battlori was arrested in the shop, at the Calle Cortès, and to reach the prison he had to walk through the streets of Barcelona, handcuffed with Señor Casasola, the former headmaster of the Modern School. Without any preparation, without anything on him except a few bob, without even being allowed to go home to inform his family, he was taken to the station surrounded by the civil guard, and exiled to Alcaniz, in the province of Tarragona. There he found himself with José, Ferrer's brother, José's wife, and their little girl, the veteran Anselmo Lorenzo, the teacher Casasola, and other employees of Ferrer. It will be easily understood what anguishes Mariano must have gone through after he had left Barcelona without being able to address a word or two of farewell to his wife, who was thus left alone with a little girl of five and her ailing mother.

From Alcaniz the exiles were transferred to Ternel, another Spanish province, which is still under the yoke of the narrowest fanaticism and where life became thus unbearable. In fact, they were living in a house which was watched day and night by the police and the civil guard, who had erected, at a few yards' distance, a wooden shelter, so that their watch should not belie itself for a single moment. Their house door was bolted at 7 p.m., and no one was allowed to enter or leave that kind of fortress after that time. During the day they were not allowed to go out without being accompanied by

one or more policemen. The same escort followed the postman and the purveyors. Thus unable to do any work and to earn any money, they saw the spectre of famine threatening them, and especially so because their correspondence was opened and the registered letters containing money had disappeared. It was but in November, more than a month after the execution of Ferrer, that these tortures came to an end.

Back in Barcelona, Battlori had to seek employment for his living, for Ferrer's publishing house had been moral suffering, undermined his health every day a little more.

It was then that our friend Guy Bowman, informed of this sad situation, offered him a berth in his newly-opened publishing business, and that was how, submitting himself to a new exile, he came to England and settled down at Walthamstow with his wife and his little girl.

The friends who are in the habit of visiting the little cottage at Maude Terrace will no doubt remember the kind and modest comrade whom an imperfect knowledge of our tongue rendered very coy, and whose face bore the indelible imprint of the torments he had previously undergone. In the midst of the sympathy with which he was surrounded, he looked at one time as if he were going to recover, but the illusion did not last long. Undermined by disease and grief, his organism had lost all resistance, and death met scarcely any obstacles to accomplish its work.

Mariano Battlori leaves to all those who have known him the memory of a loyal, disinterested, and devoted friend.

Open Letter to the Delegates to the Trade Union Congress at Newport.

London, September 1st, 1912.

FELLOW WORKERS,

You are again meeting to consider ways and means for improving the condition of the Working Class.

The splendid achievement of the Transport Workers a year ago; the magnificent display of the Railwaymen; and the solidarity of the miners this year, should have given you some proof of what can be accomplished by Organisation, Direct Action, and Solidarity.

True, the two last mentioned were robbed of the just fruits of their victory by the ineptitude of their politicians.

The Sheffield Congress marked the beginning of a new epoch in the British labour world. It is for you to see to it that no backward move is made.

Remember, the railwaymen and the miners would have won, but they allowed themselves to be seduced by the siren song of their politicians, their reformists, those who cry Peace! Peace! when there can be no peace. All those labour politicians did was to rob the men of their victory, leaving them still to fight by direct methods for better conditions and enforcement of the minimum wage awards.

Your Parliamentary Committee has the following resolution to submit to you :—

That this Congress reaffirms its continued support of independent working-class political action in helping the industrial fight for a more equitable share of the wealth produced, and also declares for a larger share of representation, nationally and locally, in view of the continued centralisation of social and industrial questions in the hands of the Government and other authorities.

Is there any *independent working class political action*?

How many Labour M.P.'s hold their seats by arrangements with, or permission of the Liberal Party? What of the double-barrelled constituencies, such as Leicester, Blackburn, Derby, Dundee, &c.?

Where was the *independence* of Crooks and Duncan, who voted for increased Naval expenditure, though the Labour Party is professedly against the big Navy policy?

Where is the *independence* of Ramsay MacDonald, who accepts a Commission of "Imperial importance" under the Liberal Government that shoots workers at Liverpool and Llanelly, and imprisons their champions like Guy Bowman, Tom Mann, Fred Crowsley, and the others?

Where is the *independence* of Henderson, who draws a fine salary for being on the Insurance Commission to administer an Act whose purpose is to destroy Trades Unionism as a fighting force.

Why have the Labour Party so "*independently*" striven to keep in power a Liberal Government composed of men who have put every sailor's life at stake by altering the Plimsoll line?—a Government that has established Labour Exchanges in order to find blacklegs more easily for the employers. But has not that Government found jobs for parasites, including many "independent" labour politicians?

Where was the "independence" of the Labour Party when Grayson made his protest on behalf of the unemployed? Where was it when O'Grady championed the dockers?

Enough!

There never was, and there never will be, "independence" in parliamentary politics. Even with a separate Labour Party, compromise reigns supreme; there are conferences, committees, bargainings, and what not, with the political parties of our employers.

Comrades, how much longer will you allow yourselves to be deceived by smooth-tongued politicians with their eyes on £400 a year, and Government jobs like those that have already been given to them?

Nationalisation and municipalisation is no real guarantee of better working conditions now, still less is it bound to be a necessary step to our salvation. The financiers still get their interest, even though they loan their money to the State and municipality. The State and municipality merely guarantee to see that wage workers are exploited in order to pay that interest.

Whilst the workers rely upon someone else to effect their emancipation they will remain slaves.

The more honest the man who goes in for "practical" parliamentary politics, the worse things become. To remain honest to himself, he would remain impotent; to get something done, he must conciliate the majority; he must go with the stream.

Where there was once a burning zeal for the abolition of the wages system of slavery, there is a propaganda for the minority report.

Where men were once enthusiastic fighters breathing inspiration amongst the masses, they now avoid strikes and conflicts for fear of losing the goodwill of non-working class voters who must be propitiated.

One of the Labour Party politicians once said: "The people without a vision perish!" but our politicians have become blinded to everything except immediate electoral advantages both personally and as a party.

Comrades, the **Parliament Politics of the Labour Party are not and never will be independent.**

Leave parliamentarianism to the purely political organisations. Concentrate upon organisation and use only those weapons which the workers as a class can use.

Unity alone will win, and unity can only be achieved by the direct struggle in the workshops, mills, mines, and railways.

Not as Liberals, not as Tories, not as Socialists, but in our common category as wage slaves, let us unite and fight. This way lies victory. Struggle and hardship may face us, but solidarity will win.

Through Parliament lies disaster, splits, secessions, betrayals, treacheries of those who take office under a Government that shoots strikers and imprisons their champions, damps down the workers' ardour, weakens their enthusiasm, divides their forces.

Comrades, let us stand firm for Direct Action, Solidarity, and Emancipation.

DOWN with parliamentary politics that divide the workers, and **UP** with Direct Action that unites them.

---

closed; but for more than two years his efforts remained unfruitful. His exile, his relations with Ferrer had closed to him the doors of all the employers, and he saw with terror his scanty savings go. A bronchitis which he had caught during Ferrer's first trial became more acute, and physical suffering adding itself to

HINDU PROFESSOR MAKES PLEA FOR SOLIDARITY OF LABOUR.

HAR DAYAL OF STANFORD UNIVERSITY POINTS OUT NEEDS OF WORKERS' MOVEMENT.

A striking speech is reported in the San Francisco *Bulletin*, as delivered by Har Dayal, professor of Hindu philosophy at Stanford University, on "The Future of the Labour Movement." According to Professor Har Dayal, central labour colleges, manned by men and not by money, where the sons of labour can be educated to lead the onward march of the workers, is one of the most urgent needs of to-day. Har Dayal is an Oxford man, and has spent six years travelling in England and the Continent, studying international labour conditions. He is an advocate of the universal labour movement, which he defines as the fight of the poor against the rich, raging in all the civilised countries of the earth, and even now stirring the great sleeping nations of the East.

The speaker took note of the present situation, and enumerated the obstacles which beset the path of the worker. Sounding the prophetic note, he declared that there are six things wanted before the fight for industrial freedom can be won.

Solidarity Necessary.

"There are six things wanted before labour can achieve complete success," he said. "The first thing is solidarity. Labour must think in terms of the whole world, not in terms of the city, the State or the nation. Should one nation acquire freedom, the rich of another nation will crush it. In the eighteenth century the labour movement failed because it was isolated. For moral and practical reasons the labour movement must be universal.

"In the second place, labour must have a complete ideal. We want not only economic emancipation, but moral and intellectual emancipation as well. You cannot have an ignorant proletariat and have it free. Therefore, the processes of emancipation must cut at the roots of every form of slavery. An intellectual slave will not think in terms of economic freedom. If you leave one thorn growing, it will grow up and choke the good seed. We know that no man will lay down his life for a partial ideal.

Rich Cannot Lead Labour.

"We need good workers. The rich and respectable cannot lead us. If the rich man cannot enter the Kingdom of Heaven, neither can he enter the kingdom of Labour. If a person is ashamed of Labour, we are ashamed of him. The spirit of brotherhood cannot thrive on economic inequality. Grime and shabbiness are the crowns of thorns to-day, which will be turned into crowns of gold to-morrow.

"We will have two kinds of leaders—First, the ascetics who have renounced riches and respectability for the love of the working-man, men like Kropotkin, the St. Franciscs and St. Bernards of Labour. These will be difficult to find, for such renunciations are scarce and such intellects are few. Secondly, we must have the sons of toil themselves, who must take up their own cross and lead their brothers on.

"Then we will need co-operation between the Labour movement and the woman's movement. The workers and the women are two enslaved classes and must fight their battles together.

"We have great need of a constructive educational system. We want central labour colleges where our young men can be taught, not by money, but by men. We do not want endowments, because endowments, with their incomes, are another form of exploitation. An endowment cannot teach the truth, and our colleges should stand for the truth.

Brotherhood Essential.

"Lastly, we will need a feeling of actual brotherhood. The Poor must love the poor. The shame of labour is that the poor must accept charity from the rich. We are not so poor but we can care for our own poor. We don't want their stolen goods, but if a burglar comes to our house let us open the window and invite him in to partake of what we have. We must realise the solidarity of labour before we can achieve our great emancipation. This lack of solidarity is the reason that economic equality has been so rare a thing. This is why economic equality has been but like short lucid intervals in the insanity of history, and why economic history has been like a nightmare to every right-thinking person. So we must stand together.

"If we fail in this titanic struggle of the twentieth century, no one can imagine how dark will be the future of human labourers. The feudalism of money will be more cruel and heartless than the feudalism which the French Revolution ended. It will be a feudalism without heart, hope, or love."

In recounting the dangers ahead in the labour movement, the speaker warned his

(Continued on page Six.)

NOTES BY T. M.

One Union for Transport Workers.

At Southampton a considerable number of men have fallen out of the Dockers' Union, alleging as the cause that "they came out for ten days to help the London men, and were then ordered back, and many of their places were filled, so that they are left in the cold." This appears to be true, and no wonder it causes dry-rot. The only cure is ONE UNION for Transport Workers.

Liverpool Transport Workers.

The demonstration in Shiel Park, Liverpool, on Sunday, August 11, in celebration of Red Sunday of 1911, was an immense success. All sections took part in the procession, and marched to the rendezvous. Fully 40,000 were present, and at every platform the resolution calling for AMALGAMATION of all Transport Unions was carried unanimously.

Repudiating Syndicalism.

It is odd that a Liverpool Union has sent in to the Trades Congress Parliamentary Committee for the agenda a resolution *repudiating* Syndicalism. Officialism, we understand you, and have our eyes on you all-right.

Cooks and Stewards.

The Cooks and Stewards and Butchers and Bakers' Union held an agreeable function in Liverpool to which I was invited. Pleasant things were said by Bro. Joe Cotter, who presided, Bro. Quilliam, of the Carters' Union, and Bro. Robinson and others. They were unanimous for ONE BIG UNION.

Miners' Daughters as Blacklegs.

At a meeting at Hednesford for industrial organisation, evidence of the advance in Union affairs was shown by the cheerful spirit of the tailoresses who had just been through a strike, but which finished not too satisfactorily. Still, the girls, members of the Workers' Union, proved that they understood and fully appreciated the necessity for organisation. Less pleasing was it to find that the miners in the district were dropping out of the Union because of their serious dissatisfaction with the termination of the miners' strike, and that these men had deliberately encouraged their daughters to blackleg on the tailoresses on strike. No educational or propagandist meetings are held amongst the miners of the district. Once a quarter the "stall" men have a meeting to deal with their own affairs. This is not the kind of conduct to build up a militant and powerful industrial organisation.

More Organising Required.

The Swadlincote pipe-yard men have scored a good success through the Workers' Union, some of the men getting 5s. a week increase. I urge that increased attention be given to more organising before attempts are made with other firms. There are 800 members in the W.U. Branch, but there are 2,800 employed in the pipe-yards of the district.

Engineers at 30 Bob a Week.

Why don't the engineers at the Great Northern plant at Doncaster wake up and demand and get something better than 30s. a week? Such a paltry wage for men that build the engines of the G.N.R. doing a mile a minute is a positive disgrace. They seem to be asleep, with a double dose of an opiate which forbids them to wake. There are labourers at 19s. 6d. a week for full time, and not 10 per cent. of them organised. They are waiting for political action to come to their rescue, forcibly feeble crowd that they are, a drag weight upon the workers' movement, hinderers to progress, too feeble to do other than work and sleep and eat and work, always for the company. Fortunately others there are alive, alert, willing, ready, determined, and courageous. These are the salt of the working class, and by these the great change will be made.

CIRCULATION NOTES.

By SAM BRIERLEY.
Northern Circulation Manager.

During the month of August I have visited (along with Brother Tom Mann) Liverpool, Doncaster, Featherstone, Wakefield, Sheffield, Preston and Todmorden. The crowd was so dense at Liverpool that effective sales on a large scale were out of the question. However, 600 of the August issue were disposed of. I have made agents at all the places we have visited, a list of which will be found in this issue. At every meeting resolutions have been carried in favour of our methods of propaganda. We have also promises of assistance for our Manchester Conference in November. This should be called "The Northern Conference." I am expecting that Yorkshire this time will do its duty. I am glad to be able to report that 2,000 copies of the August issue, sent to me on August 10th, will all be disposed of. We must, however, have them in hand earlier in the month. Delays cause worry and expense to the wholesalers in answering inquiries. This damages our reputation. I must impress this on the editors: Circulations cannot be got up if we delay publication. I have been elected by the Manchester Branch of the Newsagents' Union on the E.C. of the National (U.K.F.) Union. I beg to intimate to all Union agents that THE SYNDICALIST should be obtained from the wholesale houses at 12 copies for 6d. Anyone requiring Gustave Hervé's book, "My Country Right or Wrong," wholesale or retail, please apply to S. Brierley, 328, Hyde Road, Ardwick, Manchester.

The Industrial Syndicalist Education League.

President:
TOM MANN.

OBJECT. To carry on among Trade Unionists, and the workers generally, a campaign of education in the principles of Syndicalism—which may be described as **revolutionary Trade Unionism,** since its immediate purpose is to conduct a **Scientific class War** against Capitalism—such war having as its objective, or ultimate aim, the **Capture of the Industrial System** and its management by the Workers themselves for the benefit of the Whole community.

Gen. Sec.:
GUY BOWMAN,
4, Maude Terrace,
Walthamstow,
London, E.

If You Realise

Firstly, that in the Labour Movement the need of the hour is to prove to the workers that the many faults of the present industrial system can never be remedied, except by DIRECT ACTION, *i.e.*, by revolutionary industrial action within and upon the industries themselves;

Secondly, that in order to put this DIRECT ACTION into practice, it is necessary to keep up a general observation and study of modern industrial development;

Thirdly, that for the collating of the varied information obtained in various quarters, the workers should have a centre to which such information may be reported and thoroughly discussed;

Fourthly, that the workers should make use of the same centre for publishing and distributing pamphlets and for the carrying on of a literary propaganda;

Fifthly, that comrades having leisure to devote more or less time, in a colporteur or scout capacity, should act as a scout brigade for the sale of literature, at public meetings, in the workshops, and wherever possible;

Sixthly, that there is need that from the same centre of effort there should go forth comrades prepared not only to make public speeches on the subject of Direct Industrial Action, or Syndicalism as it is generally termed, but also to follow up such public efforts by responding to calls from Trade Unions, Trades Councils, Workmen's Clubs. etc.;

Then, will it not be The Right Thing

for you to give practical effect to this realisation by becoming a member of the I.S.E.L., now in process of formation on the following basis of membership!

If you will Do This

The League will thereafter keep you posted and in line to apply your efforts in effective team-work with other comrades.

The Organisation.

The organisation of the I.S.E.L. is in strict accordance with its practical and fighting principles, and is perfectly simple.

The members are made up of five categories, each under the direction of an adviser selected on account of his special qualifications.

There is no executive, as such. There are a President, a Secretary, an Assistant-Secretary, and a Treasurer; these, with the five advisers, form the Committee.

There are no "branches," as such, of the League. The function of the Central Committee is to assist and to advise members in their work, not to exercise an autocratic control. It is in order to give and to gain the full benefit of the individual's services for the general purposes of the League as a whole that members join directly with the centre in London.

But members group themselves in their own localities as may prove most convenient to themselves, for the purposes of local work, consultation, and study. Each of these groups appoint a Secretary for the purpose of linking up the groups with each other and with the central office.

Membership

The membership of the League is open to any person who accepts the foregoing, no matter what views may be held by that person regarding politics; but no one who does not declare for non-parliamentary action may share in the responsible work of administration of the League. Therefore the possession of an ordinary membership card does not imply that the holder is entitled to speak or otherwise act on behalf of the League.

The following categories of persons are specially solicited to become members:—

I.—**Investigating Members.**—Those who are in a position to obtain inside information in regard to particular industries.

II.—**Literary Members.**—Those who have the time and ability to analyse and collate the information sent in by the investigators and observers, and to embody the results of the work in pamphlets and in special articles for the Press.

III.—**Colporteur Members.**—Those who want to see these Syndicalist pamphlets bought up and read by the Working Class, and are therefore willing to go and sell them both in their workshops and at public meetings.

IV.—**Speaking Members.**—Those who have the time and talent for public speaking, and are willing to place before public assemblies and Labour bodies the conclusions reached by the investigators and writers.

V.—**Supporting Members.**—Those who from all walks of life may be willing to assist work by their personal influence or by money contributions, or both.

Subscriptions

The minimum subscription for members is 1s. per year; but the League is further supported by the voluntary contributions of its friends and sympathisers.

The question of subscription is always an important one. But the I.S.E.L. sets more value upon personal service than upon monetary subscription. The minimum subscription for membership is one shilling a year, but no one is asked to pay even this shilling. What is wanted is active work. There is no room for idlers. Each member must do something, and the categories of membership are so arranged that each individual may do the best in his power, according to his abilities, his opportunities, and his circumstances, and he is helped and encouraged along the lines he is best fitted for.

Anyone who does not see his or her way to become useful to the League's propaganda work in any of the five capacities mentioned above, need not apply, for the I.S.E.L. is not out for useless talk. With the I.S.E.L. and its members, it is the Movement, first, last, and all the time.

C. J. SMITH,
8, St. James Street,
WALTHAMSTOW.

High-Class Pianos from £12 12s. Cash.

OUR CELEBRATED PIANOS
— DEFY COMPETITION. —
Cash, or from 10s. monthly.

All Pianos Fully Warranted for 15 Years.

COMING INDUSTRIAL SYNDICALIST CONFERENCES.

The two proposed conferences to be held in London and in Manchester have now been definitely decided upon. The former will take place on Saturday, November 9, and Sunday, November 10, at the Holborn Hall. The latter will be held on Saturday, November 30.

A circular letter of invitation is now being sent out to all Branches of Trade Unions and Trades Councils within the metropolitan area, and in Lancashire and Yorkshire; none are invited except those who belong to a Trade Organisation of the genuine order on the workers' side.

The London circular letter is signed by the following: Tom Mann, President, I.S.E.L.; Ted Leggatt, London Carman; Charles Benson, Postmen's Federation; Dave Armstrong, Engineers; John Turner, Shop Assistants; H. E. Stringfellow, Engineers; F. J. Passmore, A.S.R.S.; Arthur Jones, Shop Assistants; J. McCann, A.S.R.S.; and Guy Bowman, Gen. Sec. I.S.E.L. The Manchester letter is signed by A. A. Purcell, Furnishing Trades; Harry Green, Engineers; Sam Brierley, A.S.R.S.; William Muller, Operative Bleachers; and K. Brierley, A.S.R.S.

In order to admit of adequate time for the issue of credential cards and other details, it is desirable that Societies sending delegates should acquaint us with their decision not later than the end of September.

It is therefore necessary that your branch should appoint its delegates as soon as possible. SEE TO IT THAT THIS BE DONE AT ONCE!

NOTE.—It is to be clearly understood that the Industrial Syndicalist Educaion League is not a rival organisation to the existing Trade Unions; on the contrary, we seek to perfect the existing Unions by (a) helping to enrol all Non-Unionists into the organisations representing the industry in which the workers are employed; (b) by bringing these organisations into right relationship with all similar Unions to secure

INDUSTRIAL SOLIDARITY.

THE LEAGUE'S ACTIVITIES.

APPOINTMENT OF AN ASSISTANT SECRETARY AND AN ORGANISER FOR LONDON.

At a meeting of the League held in London on Thursday night, August 28, two important appointments were made, that of an assistant secretary and that of an organiser for London

Hitherto the honorary assistant secretaryship had been held by our very good friend John Lloyd, who became one of the pioneers of the Syndicalist movement in England after the return of Tom Mann from Australia. But the post was purely honorary, and John could but give his services as a speaker, as a writer, and at committee meetings. In reality, the scribbling was done and the accounts of the League were kept by poor old Battlori, whose death we report in another column.

This sad occurrence and the ever-growing activities of the League have compelled us to appoint an assistant secretary, who will have to devote the whole of his time to our work, and we do not think that our choice could have fallen better than on E. J. B. Allen, who joined the Social Democratic Federation about 1897 at Oxford. Became literature secretary and performed other work of a like character. In 1901, came to London and transferred to Chelsea and Fulham branch S.D.F., took an active part in Socialist movement. Was an "impossiblist," and had supported the movement for a more revolutionary policy, particularly in connection with the Trade Union. When, in 1904, the circular letter was issued, calling the conference at Chicago for the formation of I.W.W., Allen entered into correspondence with Trautmann and circulated literature inside the Socialist Parties and Trade Unions upon Industrial Unionism; entered into an active campaign, and soon joined forces with members of the I.L.P. and formed the London Advocates of Industrial Unionism; was sent as their delegate to the Birmingham Conference that united the local bodies of Advocates into a national organisation; was pressed at that time to take up editorship of the *Industrial Unionist*; was elected member of National Executive Committee.

When attempts were made by I.L.P. members to control the Industrial Union movement and use it as a recruiting ground for S.L.P. he led the opposition. When the split occurred about parliamentarianism and Allen and others were expelled, he organised the Industrialist League as a non-parliamentary body. With six others started the *Industrialist*, and edited it for the first year. During this period entered into communication with Tom Mann and exchanged quantities of pamphlet "Revolutionary Unionism" for Mann's "Way to Win." Reprinted Mann's pamphlet in *Industrialist*. Fell unemployed and went north as organiser of Industrialist League. Payments stopped. Allen found work in Huddersfield and took up the agitation amongst the Trade Unions and Socialist Parties. Was delegate to Huddersfield Trades Council from the local branch of Gasworkers Union. Was elected to the Executive at the first election of officers after joining Council. Was sent as Trades Council representative to various conferences, &c. Had to leave the Huddersfield district for Lancashire, and took an active part in the workers' movement there. Principally known for his advocacy of the General Strike.

Allen is also an effective speaker, who will undoubtedly render us great services in the metropolis. But London offers such a vast field for our activities that it is almost impossible to do effective work without putting a man permanently on the road. This the League has decided to do by appointing a London organiser, and they have, we think, been fortunate in selecting for that task our comrade F. J. Passmore, who has been a non-commissioned officer in the Royal Engineers and a signalman on the London Electric Railways.

Francis John Passmore joined the railway service in 1907, and his union, the A.S.R.S., in the same year. From the first he took an active part in trade union affairs, and has occupied the positions of organiser, assistant secretary, vice-chairman, and chairman to his branch. In 1909 he was elected as chairman of the London Underground Railways employees' deputation, and, in spite of the company's refusal to grant any increase of wages, succeeded in obtaining substantial increases of wages and improved conditions by his intelligence and forensic powers.

He played an important part during the national railway strike, and was victimised by the railway company in October of that year. Fearless and bold, he fights with his coat on, and fights all the time; possessed of tremendous will power and perfectly class conscious, he has dedicated his life to the uplifting of his class, and should accomplish great things for Labour

CUTTINGS.

THOSE FORTY INVERTEBRATES.

(From the *Manchester Evening News*, Frank Rose.)

The Last Shot.

Lord Murray's parting shot at the Labour Party has struck nearer the core of the sham than he may think. Though few men on his side of politics have taken a more accurate measure of their strength, it is improbable that he could imagine them to be as feeble as they have proved in this Midlothian business. For he placates them by offering to influence the official Liberal candidate to retire in favour of Mr. Brown, who is also a Liberal, but is willing to run as a Labour man, and sit, if returned, with the forty invertebrates already there and vote as religiously at the command of his successor in the Whip's office as the most pliable. He could hardly have thought they would bite at such a bait—but they did. He retires from politics with more laurels than he expected, or, perhaps, deserves. No useful purpose is to be served by keeping up a farce like this; its one element of humour has worn so thin by constant repetition. Piece by piece the constitution of the Labour Party has been cast away, its first principles contradicted by acts which bear little or no connection with either their spirit or letter. The blatant platform boasts of independence are never backed by practice, and rarely justified by such sincerity as the workers have a right to demand. No quarrel remains between Liberals and Labourists on matters of principle; there is nothing but a squalid controversy about seats, and that looks like being definitely settled in favour of the predominant partner.

Mr. MacDonald's Job.

It is significant that Lord Murray's retirement synchronises with the acceptance by Mr. J. R. MacDonald of a temporary Government appointment—and that with the full approval of his colleagues. The apology offered for this flagrant violation of the Labour party's constitution is that his great abilities—which no reasonable man disputes—will enable him to do useful work in the interests of Indian education. But might not similar reasons be as convincingly assigned to men who have done similar things, and have been stigmatised as traitors and renegades for doing them. The late Mr. Broadhurst might—indeed, did—say in effect that he took office as Under Secretary to the Board of Trade entirely because he saw enlarged opportunities for helping Labour in an official capacity. Mr. Burns might reasonably plead that his own assumption of office had no other purpose than that of promoting the cause of the poor. A dozen loud-mouthed Labourists who have taken Government jobs under recent legislation have just the same right to excuse acts of virtual apostasy and desertion by the same lame apologia. We have arrived at this pass, that avowed Liberal politicians may be accepted for representative positions in the Labour movement with no higher diploma than a declaration of willingness to wear yellow favours in their buttonholes. It would be pretentious and untrue to suggest that Mr. MacDonald is not the possessor of great intellectual and personal gifts, and stupidly wrong to suggest that he will not use the best he has for a perfectly upright public purpose. But it does not spell independence.

The Point for Decision.

What impresses me most at this juncture is the virtual amalgamation of the Labour and Liberal parties. The Master of Elibank's efforts have done most towards achieving this end. It is the third boat of this design which has drifted with the same tide in the same direction, because its crew were too weak to pull against it. If Labour must work with Liberalism in the House, there is no excuse for fighting in the constituencies. What difference can it make to the rank and file of the Labour movement whether their representatives are Liberals who call themselves Liberals, or Liberals who call themselves Labour men? If there is any room for choice it is in the direction of the former. If Labour as an independent political force has become impossible, we are forced to contemplate the existing alternative, and that lies between Liberalism and Liberalism's traditional opponent. If "keep the Liberal out!" is the climax of political wisdom, let us ask ourselves who we must let in if not the Labour man? If the choice lies between an official Liberal and an independent advocate of Labour interests, we know how to work to induce other men to choose as well as to determine our own course. But it no longer lies there. The alternative is to strengthen the other political element in the country. The alternative is more desperately hopeless than men can calculate without contemplation.

THE SYNDICALISTS IN AMERICA.

(From the *Daily Chronicle*.)

A short while ago William D. Haywood, the orator of the American "Industrial Workers of the World," went down to Pittsburg to address a monster protest meeting on behalf of Joseph Ettor and Arturo Giovannitti. Ettor and Giovannitti are to be tried in Massachusetts for inciting to violence and murder during the recent textile workers' strike at Lawrence, Massachusetts. The trial is to take place in September.

Before it comes on—probably at about the end of August—a weekly paper, with a specific object, will have been started by the "Industrial Workers of the World." It will borrow the name of a French syndicalist organ, and be called *Direct Action*. I have had long talks with the editor-elect of this journal (Mr. S. A. Stodel) and other officials of the I.W.W. The starting of this paper is significant, because it is designed to forward a particular strike campaign in one of the biggest industries in America; it is claimed that this strike will involve workers in all branches of this industry, and in allied industries, and that it will be the greatest and most far-reaching labour contest that has yet taken place in America.

Nothing less than Revolution.

I am not in a position to confirm this prophecy, but I can vouch for the great influence of the American syndicalists, both through their own separate organisation and within the ranks of the Socialist party and the trade unionists. For the I.W.W. are the syndicalists of America. They aim at nothing less than revolution. They explicitly declare war upon society as it is now organised. Their avowed enemies are all wage-payers, but primarily the great trusts. They differ from the Socialist party in believing that little can be effected through politics and legislation, and they fundamentally differ from the American Federation of Labour in that they object to all agreements with employers, and distrust ameliorative measures such as increased wages or reduced hours. They object to the political method because the working classes, they believe, can never be effectively represented in Congress or through the Presidency. They distrust the trade union method because it divides workers into grades, and enables the capitalist to play off one grade against another, and skilled workers against the unskilled; and because it endorses the wage system which they wish to abolish altogether.

In a preamble similar to that of the English Industrialist League they set forth that "the trade unions aid the employing class to mislead the workers into the belief that the working class have interests in common with the employer." They take their stand upon the theory that "the working class and the employing class have nothing in common. There can be no peace so long as hunger and want are found among millions of working people and the few who make up the employing class have all the good things of life."

Their ultimate objects are to take possession of the land and the machinery of production, to abolish the wage system, and give the worker the full product of his work; their immediate object is to gain any and every temporary advantage. Their weapon is the strike, applied as strategy may dictate. Their constructive mission is to organise labour so that production may be carried on when capitalism is overthrown.

THE PEST OF OFFICIALISM.

From the *Manchester Evening News*, Frank Rose.)

The strange impossibility of unifying the forces of organised labour for any industrial purpose is accounted for by the character of the elements, personal and politic, which dominate every revival of militant industrial activity. Industrial movements are always matters of huge public importance, and those who engineer them necessarily become prominent and important in some measure. The vast field which is opened up for the increase and exaltation of leaders and officials is alluring not only to men of capacity and probity, but perhaps more so to adventurous and ambitious charlatans. The more sectional unions, the more official positions, the more sectional animosities, the greater security for official profit and public prominence. In order to give some colour to professions of solicitude for "solidarity," federations are formed and financed just sufficiently to endow more official seats. Ostensibly these federations are centres of fraternal harmony and purpose; actually they are the focussing points of personal hatred and conflicting official ambition. It would take an immensity of effort and research to accurately state the precise sum which would cover the cost of trade union officialism, but we do know that nearly 25 per cent. of the total expenditure of the 1,500 or more existing associations goes in maintenance, and there is good reason to suppose the largest part of this money is absorbed in salaries, fees, and other official emoluments. A rough estimate of £750,000 per annum as the aggregate cost of trade union officialism will be well within the mark.

LABOUR MARKET AT BROKEN HILL.

Complaint by Immigrants.

(From the *Age*, Melbourne.)

Complaint is made by two men who have arrived in Melbourne from Broken Hill that they were cruelly misled as to the position there with regard to employment. They state that they landed in Australia in February. They were first in Sydney, and in seeking for employment went to the Sydney office of a Broken Hill mining company and were told there was plenty of work at the mine. On their explaining that they were not miners, but would take labouring work, they were given a letter to the mine manager, advised to go to Broken Hill, and informed that if they stayed on six months their fares would be refunded. They spent £5 15s. each in going to Broken Hill, only to be told by the manager that he did not know what to do with them. They pointed out that they had been induced to go to Broken Hill by the Sydney office, and had been assured of work. They were then told to see the under-manager, but he also said he had no work for them. After considerable argument they were given two days' trucking coal, and then finished up. Finding that there were hundreds of men out of work in Broken Hill they came back to Adelaide, and have arrived in Melbourne after spending practically the whole of their money.—July 10, 1912.

SYNDICALISM & TRADE UNIONISM.

By M. J. DAVIS.

There is no essential difference in principle between Syndicalism and Trade Unionism so far as organisation is concerned. They are both out to organise Labour. The one is the up-to-date weapon to get complete solidarity of the workers, and the other has become almost obsolete because of the wrongful use of what could have been a most valuable medium to emancipate Labour eventually.

Trade Unionism in itself is not an antiquated weapon by which the workers could be organised properly, though it is many years old. The same tool should be differently fashioned to what it has been up to the present time, and should be more skilfully used in the interests of the workers, so that every worker will be impelled to become class conscious and must see the real advantage of being thoroughly organised.

Syndicalism seeks to establish a better state of things for the wealth producers on the quick basis, and by methods which may be peaceful or otherwise—though not necessarily by violent means—but in any event the organising of the toilers must be made complete, and the organisation throughout the country must be perfected before any real benefit can accrue to the workers. Therefore there can be no antagonism whatever between those who support the aims of Syndicalism and those who favour the idea of Trade Unionism—what it should and might be.

Trade Unionism since its inception has not been of real benefit to the workers, but unionism is not at fault for that lamentable state of affairs—that is to say, the principle is all right if carried out on proper lines, but the ship of Unionism has been drifting all the time instead of going ahead. This, obviously, must not continue any longer, otherwise it will meet the fate it deserves—and that is destruction.

There are great possibilities in Trade Unionism if the policy is a forward one, and that is what it ought to be, for no great movement can possibly remain still. It must be progress or stagnation, and the latter means retrogression every time, and then its collapse.

The potentialities of the Trade Union movement at its beginning should have been more than partly realised long before this if the workers only understood what a power for good—in the direction of giving them full control of their own labour—Unionism could be, and to them, as the producing class, to be able to dictate their own terms and conditions of employment of the workers as a class, and not for sections of employees only. Not until the workers are in a position to demand the best terms for every member of the working-class will Trade Unionism have carried out its mission.

The leaders, or officials, or mouth-pieces of the various Unions have not made, all these years, the best use of the material at their disposal. It is true only a percentage of the workers have been all along, and are, organised to-day, but if the ideal of what Trade Unionism was meant to achieve had always been kept in front of those leading the movement, and by those participating in Trade Unionism—and, after all, a great deal, if not everything, depends on the rank and file of the Trade Unionists taking an intelligent interest in their own concern—then real substantial and solid results would have been gained, not only for a great minority of the workers, but for the large majority of the toiling masses, because during these long years the vast majority of the workers would have seen that the movement is out entirely for the workers, and they would naturally have joined the ranks of the Trade Unionist Army.

I do not run down Trade Unionism even as the great principles are at present carried out. I am merely offering criticism of the conducting and controlling of the whole movement, and of the way opportunities have been lost which should have been taken advantage of. I give credit to Trade Union combination in the preventing of greater evils being imposed upon certain sections of the workers by the capitalist employers than would otherwise obtain, but apart from the fact that the workers are no better off after nearly sixty years of Trade Unionism—they are worse off to-day in spite of Trade Unionism—though the average Trade Unionist is not so bad off as he would be if the Unions were no more. But the movement by this time should show something better after being in existence for so many years, than merely striving to hold on to the little bit gained, and fighting again for that which is filched or pilfered from them by the bossing class. It is a case of losing a penny, getting it back again, and the game is going on in this paltry manner when the best efforts of the men should be devoted to something much more ambitious.

Trade Unionism can be of real value to the workers, but what happens to-day is a farce, and the workers, even in the Unions, will never get "no forrader" in regard to receiving a fairer share of the wealth they produce if they wait till Doomsday, unless the movement is handled differently and the rank and file among Trade Unionists force the pace in their own interests, and see that they get a fairer share of the wealth that is created by their labour, and thus get the workers as a whole to become organised with some definite object in view, and that is—a higher rate of wages, the right to work, and the working day to be so curtailed as to include every man and woman wanting employment, and the very best possible conditions under which to work, for every member of the toiling class.

It rests with each individual Trade Unionist—and the fact that he or she is a member of a Trade Union proves that they believe that they must help themselves as it were to get any improvement in wages, hours of work, etc.—to understand what they are out for, and to make Trade Unionism worthy of the name, in the interest, not only of themselves, but of the class they belong to, and to induce their fellow workers, who at present are not members of a Union, to join the only army that is worth enlisting in and that is the Trade Union movement, so that the position of every worker will be greatly improved when the forces become too strong for the master class to resist just demands of the workers as a class. This is long overdue. The entire rank and file of the Trade Unionists should be the advancing army of workers to demand a much fairer share of the wealth created by Labour, and they should become imbued with the idea that right and justice, in so far as wealth distribution is concerned, will not be a reality until the full produce of Labour is received by those who created the whole of it—namely, the workers.

To get the best out of Trade Unionism there must be more Unity and less Unions. The basis of organisation ought to be amalgamation of all Federations of Labour, and one Union for one Industry. Solidarity of Labour must be the aim of every Trade Unionist. There is much leeway to make up before Trade Unionism can be justified, not only in regard to organisation, but in respect of the results so far achieved by the policy of which so much was expected.

Syndicalism is Trade Unionism on a revolutionary basis. The Syndicalist is an advanced Trade Unionist who recognises that there must of necessity be antagonism between Capital and Labour. The ordinary Trade Unionist dimly realises the fact that the capitalist is out to exploit and to still further rob the wealth-producers, and the worker has to defend, and it takes him all his time, the little bit that he receives in the form of wages, otherwise the grasping employer would even take away a big proportion from the miserable pittance of the workers who, at the best, only receive a third of the pay they are entitled to; and they are robbed again, in a more or less extent, when the wages have to be expended.

Syndicalism is out to capture the Industrial system. This will, of course, abolish wage slavery entirely, and for ever. By means of Syndicalism the creators of the wealth will enjoy the full fruits of their toil. The workers will get the lot, because they produce all the wealth.

There is plenty of good work to do for Trade Unionism, and Syndicalism rightly has, as its immediate purpose, the conduct of a class war on scientific lines against Capitalism. Every Trade Unionist can, and ought to, take a share in this glorious work which means the ultimate emancipation of the workers. It depends on the toilers when they wish to have redemption.

CORRESPONDENCE.

THE I.S.E.L. OVER-SEAS.
To the Editor of the SYNDICALIST.

DEAR COMRADE,—You must have noticed that the *Agitator* has taken up the cause of Syndicalism and has begun to spread its teaching among the American barbarians; and let me say it is a "doctrine" for barbarians only. The "cultured" won't touch it. They fear it. They fight it. They see in it a real enemy—an enemy they cannot cajole with fine speech and moral precepts.

The way to kill a new idea is to accept it and then divert it from its course in any or many of the numerous ways known to the tricksters.

Isn't Social Democracy a safe and sane movement to-day in every country in the world? Can't "respectable" men and women join it without fear of losing their social standing? Haven't the "respectables" been "converted," and don't they occupy the seats of power in the party? And what tyrant fears it any more? And, by the same token, what knowing slave has any more faith in it?

How can the respectables accept Syndicalism with its barbarous doctrines of strikes and sabotage? And, accepting, how could they control? Impossible. Syndicalism seems safe from the middle class, for it is distinctly a class movement.

Unionism is the only distinctly working-class movement that has ever existed, and Syndicalism is simply Unionism up to date. Syndicalism is the application of the scientific method whereby experience displaces tradition in the economic relations of the working class.

Syndicalist Leagues are springing up in every part of the country, and a National League is now in process of formation. Our aim, like yours, is the spreading of education. We will work in the old Unions, and in no case will we organise dual Unions, which could only have the effect of further dividing the workers, and thereby destroy the main object of Syndicalism. For Syndicalism is the cement that will solidify the wage-slaves. It is becoming a world movement, in spite of Labour politicians and Capitalist masters.

Its powerful opposition proves its worth. It is headed for the goal of Freedom. It is irresistible.

These are my words of fellowship to you, comrades and fellow-fighters.
JAY FOX.
Home (Lakebay P.O.), Wash., U.S.A.,
August, 1912.

A SYNDICALIST ESPERANTIST LEAGUE.
To the Editor of the SYNDICALIST.

DEAR MR. EDITOR,—Before I get to the theme of my letter, allow me to praise the SYNDICALIST, and to hope that it will live long and that the management will very soon be in a position to publish it weekly.

My reason for writing to you, and for taking up space, which I am sure at present you can ill afford, is this: As the Syndicalist movement is essentially an International movement, I claim that English Syndicalists are ignoring a very valuable—nay, absolutely essential—instrument of industrial solidarity. We are pursuing a course of propaganda that will make us as much sectional as the trade union movement which we are trying to convert, because eventually we shall find ourselves separated from our foreign comrades by the old barrier—that of language. I take it that the international solidarity cannot be realised without occasional meetings, not of leaders particularly, but of genuine representatives of the rank and file of the movement in all lands. Unless these representatives are linguists (and I think I am safe in saying that they will not be), they will only receive a very vague and nebulous idea of what has been said and done through an interpreter. The only people who will be able to take part in the discussions, too, with any effect will be the delegates of the country in which the conference takes place.

Therefore, in my opinion, it is absolutely essential that the Syndicalist movement, in its early stages, should acknowledge the world language—Esperanto—and declare it to be its official auxiliary language.

Esperanto is easy enough to learn, and is a pleasant study. It is not a language to be left to "his lordship the clerk," as our horny-handed comrades so sardonically name us "scribes." I know several manual labourers here in Sheffield who have taken to it enthusiastically, and have become adepts. Its rules are not numerous, there being sixteen only, and no irregularities. It can be learnt, without previous knowledge of English grammar, for sixpence, from Miss Helen Fryer's "Esperanto Teacher." Miss Fryer is a Socialist, and is always glad to give hints to students.

In conclusion, Mr. Editor, may I ask you to give your opinion, and to grant a corner in your paper periodically for Esperanto? I will be responsible for its being filled if you can see your way to give it. England rarely takes the initiative, and here is a chance for us to seize a very useful weapon, without which, I am convinced, Syndicalism will be sorely hampered.

I shall be glad to hear from anyone who either knows Esperanto or who would like to do so, with a view to forming a Syndicalist Esperantist League. Esperantistaj kamaradoj, kompreneble, skribos en "la kara lingvo."—Yours fraternally,
PERCY E. WELLS.
Sheffield, August, 1912.

A NEW USE FOR AN OLD WEAPON.
To the Editor of the SYNDICALIST.

DEAR SIR,—As a worker and an observant trade unionist, I have been greatly disappointed at the comparatively small results achieved compared with the great solidarity shown, dating from August last year. Now, since that date we have greatly increased in numbers, and I suppose the number of trade unionists cannot now be far short of 2,000,000.

The present London strike, I consider, would have been a success if matters had been left to the rank and file; but when we get a "manifesto" from the likes of Father Hopkins, and an "order" to the Scottish dockers from Kessack not to strike until he tells them, and another from Cathery to the sailors and firemen, and ditto from Sexton and his clique, and a nice wet blanket from Chedlow, it's a poor look-out for solidarity!

Papal edicts are nothing as to tone compared with the "orders" issued by some of the leaders in the trade union movement. Even the good old *Transport Worker* had some of this about it, as last December its placard contained this nice little sentence: "Official order: buttons up January 1." A word to the wise is, or should be, enough.

But to turn to the real purpose of this letter. Take the coal strike as an example of what might have been done with this weapon. Had the different E.C.'s been prepared, branch meetings might have been called and resolutions passed that until such time as the colliers had their demands granted the trade unionists of this country would not pay any more rent. I think the result would have been a bit different to what it was. I fancy the 5s. and 2s. would have been inserted with alacrity.

Further, if this idea were adopted, the position would then be reversed—that is, they, the landlord class, would be asking us for something, and we, like their brethren, the capitalists, would be in a position to refuse; and, further, the authorities could do absolutely nothing. We would be the masters of the situation for once, and that would be a nice change. I think this would be better than *all* the workers coming out on strike, as all the workers who could work could go on doing it, with the one exception, the others to help them by not paying any rent. With this weapon we can go straight to the point—no conciliation, conference, arbitration, inquiry, "seeing into it," &c., &c. We simply stop supplies. I hope that our good comrade Tom Mann and his able fellow-workers will give this subject their earnest consideration, as I think it is a much-neglected and very valuable weapon.—Yours fraternally,
NO PAY.
Liverpool, August 12.

(Continued from page 3.)

hearers against the quacks, cowards, and cranks whose purpose is to divert the stream to their own private advantage or hobby. Among those he mentioned parliamentarism and parliamentary Socialism, which, he said, has ended in a blind alley in Germany and Belgium, where it is strongest. He said the fallacy of this method is that it gives to labour the weapons furnished by capitalism and expects them to free themselves therewith.

Terrorism he spoke of as a greater danger, and characterised it as a mixture of heroism and folly.

Terrorism a Waste.

Said he: "Terrorism is a waste of force, and gives the other party a chance for needless persecution. It provides martyrs, but the labour movement, which eschews terrorism, will have its own martyrs in plenty. Ferrer was a real martyr, but he was killed not for killing, but for his greater love. Preach and suffer, but don't retaliate now. A man who lives and acts in the interests of freedom is himself living social dynamite."

In regard to the danger of Trade Unionism, he said that if the unions can be persuaded to acquire capital they will be of help to capitalism, but if not they will be of value to labour.

Patriotism he described as another danger, because it was devised to divide the labourers into their various countries, and thus into a false division of society. He said the true division of society is that which holds on shipboard. He turned to history to show that whenever a social revolution has been imminent the powers have picked a quarrel with their neighbours and roused the citizens to a false spirit of patriotism, which made them go forth and fight their brothers, and in this way forget their own struggle.

DO REVOLUTIONARY SOCIALISTS DESIRE A REVOLUTION?

From THE LINK, Norman Young.

It is amusing, as well as tragic, to see that in many quarters, especially in doctrinaire political circles, Syndicalist ideas are opposed before any attempt has been made to understand them. The would-be scientific Socialist approaches the question in a very unscientific and partial attitude of mind. Like Women's Suffrage, Syndicalism has met with a lot of thoughtless opposition from quarters where one would at least have expected reasoned argument.

Are we, too, Ulsterians? Do we also, like Bonar Law and Carson, mouth revolution with tongue in cheek? When we talk of a change of system is it mere street-corner clap-trap? Do we mean it? If we do mean it, is it possible, then, to have a change of system merely by political means? Must it not be, if it be anything at all, an economic revolution, engineered, not by bourgeois Socialists, not even so much by our Tom Manns and Ben Tilletts, but by the rank and file of industry, organised, alert, acting purposively, intelligently and constructively, *through the Unions*, the latter organised as fighting units ready to control and run their own industries for the community? Are we afraid of the general strike?

Morris has said:
"Yea, the voiceless wrath of the wretched, and their unlearned discontent,
We must give it voice and wisdom till the waiting tide be spent."

I should like to ask the middle-class intellectuals, the superior Fabians, whether they have not been giving voice rather to their own pet ideas and theories than to any "voiceless, wrath of the wretched"; whether they have not made themselves drunk on statistics, and deluded themselves that nationalisation, which can, and probably will, leave a parasite, interest-receiving class, is revolutionary?

If only that Syndicalism points to a healthy reaction from bureaucracy and middle-class conceptions of Socialism, with its servile collectivist State, where our Sidney Webbs will analyse, docket, and inspect an inferior working class, where the present departmental head and Civil Service demi-god is the future administrator of centralised industry—if Syndicalism had done only this, it would have deserved well of Socialists who are not Revisionists. But if one regards Syndicalism, not as antagonistic, but as contributory to Socialist thought, it has done much more. It has emphasised a method which will give the "consummation devoutly to be wished" by Socialist and Syndicalist—the expropriation of the capitalist class. It lays stress, too, on the fact that a few middle-class revolutionary (?) leaders are of little value compared with an organised, revolutionary working class; that it is the producer, organised and educated towards the control of his own industry, who has the power to lock out the owning class by means of the general strike.

Anything which dethrones tin-gods, anything which does away with false hero-worship, anything which helps the mob (so-called) to work out their own salvation, by their own self-reliance, is good; it means, in the ultimate, an intelligent democracy. At present we have set down God, Jesus Christ, and the King from divinity only to raise in their stead—well, fill in your own special Deity from Lloyd George, the Socialist, down to——

When one comes to sabotage (disowned by Sorel, the French exponent) there is a difficulty. The working class in England, at any rate, will have to free themselves from the thraldom of capitalist religion and morality before they will attempt the "irritation strike," the destruction of property, &c. They must learn that loyalty to a cause, to a principle, to their own class, is sublime; but loyalty to a master, an owner, is damnable and detestable. But the time is coming when the workers will form their own religious perception, their own art and literature, based on their own lives, aims, and aspirations. The need is for an independent view-point in education, industry, and politics. Immorality lies not in sabotage, but in remaining a class of wage-slaves while any weapon remains untried. "Slacking," open to reproach in itself, loses that reproach when it becomes purposive, collective, a weapon of emancipation. There is no indignity then.

Meanwhile, the schools to which the future workers go teach a bourgeois patriotism, a grotesque religion. The Boy Scouts, recruited from working-class children, while doing the work of the Syndicalist in training boys in alertness, self-reliance, fitness, &c., also have as their tenets "Obedience and respectfulness to employers," "Reverence for God, King, and Country."

Now, you Syndicalists and Socialists, is it not possible to start before the future worker enters the labour market?

Printed and published by GUY BOWMAN, 4, Maude Terrace, Walthamstow, E.

The Syndicalist

VOL. 1. NO. 9.   LONDON, OCTOBER, 1912.   MONTHLY, ONE PENNY.

SYNDICALISM IN SWEDEN AND DENMARK.

RAPID GROWTH OF THE MOVEMENT.

YOUNG SOCIALISTS of SWEDEN DECLARE for DIRECT ACTION

By TOM MANN.

I have had a strenuous three weeks in Scandinavia, interminable travelling and addressing meetings, at a different town every night, with only one night free in the lot; but it has been full to overflowing with vital forces, a real vigorous propagandist campaign for Syndicalism, under the auspices of the Swedish Workers' Central Organisation, the Syndicalist body. The first ten days it rained more or less nearly every day, but we adhered to the programme in every particular. I was accompanied all the time by Comrade John Sandgren as interpreter. He is a fine, intellectual man of thirty-eight years, a Swede who has had ten years rough-and-tumble experience in the United States—engine-driving, government surveying in Alaska, etc. He is also the author of several Syndicalist books that have already commanded a wide circulation in Sweden.

It was decided to commence the campaign amongst the Stone-cutters (Quarrymen) in the Isle of Malmön, in the Province of Bohnslan, these men being an exceptionally sturdy lot with characteristics worthy of imitation. They have secured the eight-hour day as Quarrymen; they work under relatively pleasant conditions; and the wages are relatively high. I have been amongst the Iron Ore Miners, the Cutlers of Eskilstuna, the Transport Workers of various ports, including Stockholm, Gefle, and Copenhagen, the chief engineering and match-making centres, and am writing this at Lund, a University city.

To-morrow the Swedish Syndicalists commence their Conference at Obrero. I was to have attended, but that would have cut short some of the propagandist meetings, so I shall not do so.

It will surprise many in England to know that there is a definitely organised Syndicalist body in Sweden running a fortnightly paper named the *Syndikalisten*, straight out fully avowed in favour of Industrial Solidarity and Direct Action.

Fifteen years ago I had an organising run through Scandinavia on behalf of the International Transport Workers' Federation, and it has been of very special interest to me to observe developments since then. The great Lock-out of 1909 led of necessity to the General Strike of that year in Sweden. I remember keenly watching every item of news in connection with this fight whilst in Australia, and as the workers of other nations allowed the Swedes to fight the battle single-handed, whilst the Capitalists had the International backing of their class, it was small wonder that the workers did not win much. At the finish the men returned to work, but the Employers' Associations rubbed in the ointment and compelled the men to work with non-unionists whenever called upon to do so.

How far there is truth in the statements made by some that the leadership of the Strike was seriously at fault, I am unable to say, but that the men showed great resentment and dissatisfaction at the close is a certainty; and whilst the Land's Organisation (the National Trades Organisation) had a membership of 164,000 at the time of the Lock-out, and the Railwaymen and Typographical men not in the Land's Organisation, brought the total membership up to 180,000, six months after there were only half that number in the Unions.

Meantime Syndicalism was being seriously discussed, and those favourable thereto finding all the officials of the Unions strongly opposed to any broadening of the basis, or to any difference of tactics, decided to launch out on a Direct Action basis, and in the spring of 1910 the Central Organisation was formed. This is a Trade Union organisation pledged to Syndicalist principles and methods. The Head Office is in Malmö; the growth is rapid; the future, I believe, is with them. I knew of the Swedish movement prior to reaching here, but I did not know to what extent the Danish Syndicalist movement, was an organised reality, and on reaching Copenhagen I was much surprised to find quite a vigorous and well-developed organisation with a weekly paper called *Solidaritet*.

The population of Copenhagen with suburbs is 500,000, and of the adult male population fifty per cent. are in the Unions; but great dissatisfaction exists with the quiet, stodgy, fat officials of the older type. Still, the Syndicalists held to the view that the existing organisations ought to be revolutionised, and that the right way to do it was for them to remain members of the existing Unions, and to form also a Syndicalist organisation to enrol any existing *Trade Unionist* in, but *no one else*. So that an Engineer carries two cards, the old Union card and the Engineers' Section of the Syndicalist Union, and pays cheerfully into both. This gives them a splendid chance; they are only two years old, but have made much headway, and in the Machine-Workers' Section already they have twenty-five per cent. of the old Union members as members of the Syndicalist body. This is a most interesting development; and one that deserves serious consideration by us in England, where, like the Danes, we have refused to sever our connection with the old Unions. I, personally, am strongly opposed to any such policy of severance for Britain. There are many reasons why we should not, and as far as my knowledge goes, not one satisfactory reason why we should; but the Danes have struck on a most effective method of forming a Syndicalist section for each trade, but a man must show his Union card of *the existing Union* as a qualification for joining the Syndicalist Union.

Nearly all the Syndicalists are young men between the ages of twenty-two and thirty-five. Naturally, having life in front of them, they desire to fix conditions as nicely as possible, but are prepared for any action that may be necessary to assert and apply Syndicalist principles. It is of great importance that we in England should duly note the behaviour of the old officials, particularly the parliamentary members. Let their actions be duly noted and recorded when they afford opportunities for the discussion of Syndicalist methods, and, equally so, when they do anything to balk such discussion. We have seen and heard what some of them will do at the Trade Union Congress, where they have gratuitously done their best to disparage Syndicalism, when there was not one Syndicalist present who raised a question, moved a resolution, or supported an amendment; and, as far as I knew, not one Syndicalist present at the Conference, although there were several believing in Industrial Solidarity coupled with parliamentary action. We do not complain of anything that transpired, but it would be silly of us not to give consideration to the same. We shall not only remain in the existing Unions, but shall definitely and systematically work to convert them to Syndicalism, and if balked in one direction, we shall be ready immediately to try another.

There are three men directly and officially connected with the Swedish Syndicalist movement. These are comrades Lindström, Sjöström, and Andersson. They are battling splendidly and doing magnificent work, but no man has been more helpful to the movement in Sweden than Comrade Albert Jensen, who, as Editor of the young Socialist journal called *Brand*, has rendered the greatest service to the Syndicalist propaganda. Recently Jensen retired from the editorship of *Brand*, and it is thought likely that

(Continued on page Four.)

GUSTAVE HERVE IN ENGLAND.

Gustave Hervé is to address an English audience upon Anti-Militarism. Many well-known Continental Socialists have come to address the English workers on various themes at various times. Our hospitality has been proffered to a Jaurés as well as to a Molkenburg. But of all the many prominent personalities of the Continental Socialist movement none have the same claim to our attention as Hervé. He is no great orator as rhetorical oratory is understood in France. He is simple, direct, and forcible in his delivery. He has no long years of the limelight as a Parliamentary leader; he has refused to stand as a candidate. Yet he has an international reputation few men possess. His speeches to his fellow - members of the Socialist Party, his addresses to juries that have convicted him, his chief work ("Leur Patrie"), "My Country, Right or Wrong," has been translated into many languages. This quiet, unassuming man has become a world power. His thoughts have leapt all frontiers. He has caused more discussions in the Socialist parties and Labour bodies of the world than any other man has done; for he has an international reputation as an anti-Nationalist. Whilst many Socialists have endeavoured to frame their policy to avoid shocking non-Socialist opinion, Hervé has attacked the most sacred fetish of the governing class—their Fatherland. He realised that whilst the workers of any country thought it their duty to fight for that country, their rulers were safe. Even among Socialists there are so many who are patriots, who have not yet realised that whilst they are willing to allow themselves to be shot for a country of which they possess no particle, it is only necessary for the Capitalists to bring about a war in order to throw back the whole Socialist movement in all its phases. However, Hervé is coming. He can speak for himself.

Even his enemies must admit the courage of a man who *will* keep on with his propaganda, in spite of the eleven years of imprisonment to which he has been sentenced. In prison or out of it he steadily pursues his path. From 1900, when he was tried for an article in the *Travailleur Socialiste (Socialist Worker)* and was dismissed from his professorship by the Minister of Education, down till to-day he has had one continuous struggle. It was then that he "planted the flag on the dung-heap."

In 1905 he was sentenced to four years' imprisonment for his share in an anti-militarist placard addressed to young conscripts, which was posted all over Paris. They were urged not to fire on strikers. "All war is criminal; to the order of mobilisation respond by an immediate strike and insurrection," ran one paragraph. After serving about six months he was released with other political prisoners on a general amnesty. Then his fighting journal, *La Guerre Sociale*, was started. In this paper his views were published. His keen attacks upon the Army and the expansionist policy of the Government have brought him further punishment. There have been four prosecutions and sentences for him since its foundation. Ever ready to champion the oppressed, whether the murdered Moroccans or bullied conscripts, or the victims of the police of Paris, he sacrifices all in their defence. In a recent interview Hervé told us himself that he is the same Hervé as before his imprisonment. The same Anti-Militarist, the same Sans-Patrie who during the strike of the postal workers and railway servants could tantalise the Government by publishing cartoons of the acts of "sabotage" that were committed. The sketches of the cloaked conspirators in their long robes and huge sombreros, who with giant shears strode through France snip-snipping the telegraph wires; the same insurrectionist of old; the same supporter of the Syndicalists of the Confederation Generale du Travail as formerly. Whatever his changed attitude towards the Socialist Party may be, he has not altered his views on Anti-Militarism. It is in his rôle of Anti-Militarist that he is coming amongst us.

THOSE £300 FOR THE "SYNDICALIST WEEKLY."

COMRADES,—

What is the matter with you, comrades? I have received very few contributions towards the SYNDICALIST WEEKLY since the appearance of our last issue, and I fancy you imagine that because there is a likelihood of two or three friends of ours sending another £50 each, you may now rest on your oars.

If that is so, you ought to undeceive yourselves immediately, my boys, for those friends of ours are waiting to see what *you* are going to do before they send in their lump sums. They want to know whether the SYNDICALIST WEEKLY is really wanted by the Workers, and the only way to show them that it really is so is to send in your contributions, however small their amount. Cannot you see that a weekly is absolutely necessary to keep up with the magnificent development of our propaganda? We have now an Assistant Secretary and an Organiser for London, two men who are devoting their whole time to our work. Surely you want to know *week by week* what they are doing and how we are progressing everywhere.

Not only must the members know what they are doing, but we must find some larger scope for their activities. Seeing that this is so, comrades, it is necessary for us to have a weekly paper in order that they may relate the facts concerned with the Trade Union movement. To go and address a Trade Union branch every night in the week is good, but it is not sufficient. We must have a much larger field than this affords. The facts relative to working-class life and the Trade Union movement must be spread over a large area, and at much more frequent intervals. We must convert thousands, not a few, in order that their activities may bring results.

When I was in prison I suffered agonies of mind for fear the SYNDICALIST would go under during my incarceration. Judge of my joyful surprise, when released, to find that not only was the SYNDICALIST still in existence, but had been enlarged, and its circulation had risen from 3,000 copies to 20,000. In my enthusiasm I wrote to you in the June issue and said that I would bring out the July number on six pages, so as to give you an idea of what the paper would be like if turned into a weekly. I not only did this for the July issue, but I kept up the paper to the same size for the three succeeding issues, including this one. But you have not responded as you ought to have done. Cannot you see that a monthly paper cannot be got out as a *fighting* organ, because it cannot keep pace with events? In fact, the most interesting events, that we ought to deal with from our point of view, very often have become stale before our next issue can appear, and have therefore lost all interest to our readers.

Do you think that I am a millionaire, who runs this paper as a hobby? If so, please undeceive yourselves at once, and kindly note that I am only a journalist who has got to earn his own living, like all of us.

Don't let there be any misunderstanding; if you will not keep this paper going financially, I cease publication of the paper as it is. In every new movement there are a number of men who are attracted to it because it is new. They have been in everything, and will be in everything that may crop up. They are of little use; they lack energy and determination. Their one strong point is talking. Actual work in raising funds, engaging in propaganda, pushing the sale of literature is too hard. They want to shine, but do not like the necessary labour to be put in before that can be done. We do not want these novelty-mongers. We want workers—propagandists, literature sellers, and others who will help in the work of the League and help to make this paper a weekly. I hope sincerely that this will clear your minds about the situation, and that everyone of those of you who want immediately to see this movement reach its utmost efficiency will send in their contributions towards the SYNDICALIST WEEKLY.

Buck up, brothers, and send in your mites at once.

GUY BOWMAN.

The Syndicalist

EDITED UNDER THE AUSPICES OF

The Industrial Syndicalist Education League

Offices—

4, MAUDE TERRACE, WALTHAMSTOW,
LONDON, E.

MONTHLY - ONE PENNY.

Post Paid Subscription—

Great Britain or Abroad ... 12 months 1s. 6d.

Bundle Rates—

1s. 6d. per quire, Carriage Paid.

*The receipt of a Sample Copy is an
invitation to Subscribe.*

OCTOBER, 1912.

THE POLICY OF THE SYNDICALIST WEEKLY.

In our weekly journal, which we hope, with the co-operation of the militant members of the working class, to make an effective organ of combat, we shall express clear thoughts in a frank (brutally so at times) and clear manner. We are workers writing for workers in a language which they can understand. If—as some of our correspondents have claimed—our style of expression favours that of the student from Ruskin College, we are not to blame. It has been so because those writers have been the only ones that have assisted us in the work of producing the paper. The thing most remote from our minds is to make the SYNDICALIST merely an academic journal. Our ambition is to deal with live issues in a live manner. We candidly admit that we may lack polish and culture as understood by those of the leisured class. In event of a strike we want to give the progress of the fight. If some rebellious workers have practised sabotage upon a job we want news of it, and we will retail the information in a manner which other workers, reading that account, cannot fail to understand why it was done, and also how it was done.

Many of our ideas will be repugnant to those who have not felt the oppression of the Capitalist class. But those who have been unemployed, tramping the country in a state of semi-starvation in a vain endeavour to find a purchaser for their body and brains, will appreciate the view-point of those who have also had to do it. Those whose spirit rises in revolt at being compelled to work fifty to sixty or more hours per week for a miserable wage will nod their heads in sympathy with our denunciation of that system. Their minds will enlarge in sympathy with us as we urge the wage slaves to revolt. That increasing number who realise that only by Direct Action can the workers obtain any immediate improvement of their condition and their final emancipation from wage slavery will find in us their allies.

Every day the employing class make some fresh move to fix their hold upon the workers more secure. Every day their Government considers some fresh methods of damming the growing stream of revolt. With care they foster the spirit of militarism amongst the youth of the nation. Every day the industrial machine slaughters the workers at their task in the mines, on the railways, on the buildings, and on the seas. We want a weekly organ to take up the fight in a more adequate manner than we can in a monthly issue. We must be placed in the position to assail the enemy more often. To reply to each fresh blow by a quick and vigorous return. A weekly and then a daily to give Labour daily news of Labour's wars. We ask for the co-operation and support of our readers to make the SYNDICALIST a weekly by the end of the year.

Fellow-workers, this is your paper, the paper for rebels and for making rebels. Give us your support, in articles dealing with your experience in the shop and the methods by which you combat your employers. Support us by aiding in the effective distribution of the paper. Give us what financial assistance you can in order to get a weekly SYNDICALIST, journal of Direct Action, Sabotage, and militant Anti-Militarism.

THE TRADE UNION CONGRESS AND SYNDICALISM.

Most of our readers, like ourselves, have regarded the attitude of the Trade Union Congress towards Syndicalism with the utmost unconcern. It was gratifying, of course, to record the quickening of public interest at the sound of the word "Syndicalism" and to hear the hesitating judgment passed upon it by various delegates, and then, most gratifying of all, to get back to our own constructive propaganda, lighting that small flame of discontent soon to be fanned into a fire of revolt. The flame and zest of the battle is so quickly lost in the tedious exchange of commonplaces and the fruitless discussions that occur at every Congress. That element of unctuous respectability that clings around our teetotal, P.S.A., Labour M.P.'s and J.P.'s is not one that makes for either vigorous thought or action. The real conferences are those held in every mine, mill, and shed where small and earnest groups of men, intent upon their emancipation, gather to discuss the next steps to be taken in their warfare with the employers. Not by the sleek-faced, cleanly-clad respectables who have left shop life behind them, but by the men in their rough clothes and toil-stained hands is the movement carried on. These constitute the real "conferences"—the shop committee discussing the coming strike. Here is the heart of the Union movement; the discussion on the job of ways and means to strike for better conditions.

The most interesting result of the Trade Union Congress, as far as we are concerned, is that Syndicalism and Direct Action have been disapproved of in a half-hearted fashion by the would-be leaders of the Labour movement. And this is as it should be, since Syndicalists want no leaders. We prefer to win or lose off our own bat, and not run the risk of losing off somebody else's, which is an admirable and, in the long run, victorious fighting tactic.

MILITARISM AND THE POLITICIANS.

Our friends the politicians are fonder of the sound of their own voices raised in declamations than they are of the sounds of revolt. Those who roared loudest at the Congress will be found cooing like doves at the next opening of Parliament. But there is one thing that might have been discussed and rediscussed and thrashed out from beginning to end, even if it had taken up the greater part of its time, and that is militarism. Than militarism there is no greater menace to the success of the working-class movement to-day. It shows itself through the different Boys' Brigades, the National Service League, the Boy Scout movement, and in the manifestations of journalistic "public opinion" that broke out at the recent drowning of several members of that organisation. For the rank and file of their armed forces the Capitalist class have to depend upon the workers. Armies are only used against the working class—against its soldier sons in time of war, against the worker in revolt in times of peace. The Congress should have said to the master class that the workers of Great Britain are prepared to strike in a body at the first signs of war. Also that in the event of the making of any laws for the enforcing of Conscription they will burst out into open revolt. Now, as in the past, we say "Don't Shoot." But if the workers have weapons forced into their hands, let them use them in self-defence; those rifles not to be used against their mothers' sons of the proletariat, but against their exploiters; as an instrument of emancipation, and not a tool for subjection.

PROGRESS IN THE B.S.P.

In a paper published by the Birmingham branches of the B.S.P., entitled the *Torch*, we find much of interest. For instance, in No. 1 there is an admirable article in praise of Direct Action. In the same issue and the succeeding one the necessity for the combination of the Unions and for the sympathetic strike in place of sectional methods are ably demonstrated. True, there are those who desire to "fight with both weapons "—" Industrial Unionism plus Social Demo-cratic political action," as one writer puts it. We differ, but the appearance of these sentiments in a political paper is a sign of advance. We know that just as the reaction against the treachery or incompetence of the politicians of the Labour Party led to the B.S.P., so will there be a revolt against the politicians who will be manufactured by the B.S.P. Syndicalism will grow here as elsewhere. The numerically small S.L.P. led to the development of many workers into Syndicalists. The B.S.P. is only the S.L.P. of a larger growth. Ere long our recruits from them will be just so much larger in proportion as the B.S.P. is to the S.L.P. The period of incubation may be longer, but the results are assured. In the meantime such propaganda is preparing even a larger number of the rank and file of the working class to receive and digest our principles.

BILL HAYWOOD.

Our friend Bill Haywood has been arrested in connection with the Ettor-Giovannetti conspiracy charge. The *Daily Herald* has published the information on this matter from time to time. Not knowing how events will turn out at the time of going to press, we wish him the best of luck, and hope that this second attempt on the part of the American capitalists to "get" him and his colleagues will fail. We know, too, that soon the organised forces of the American working-class will be too strong for such methods to be resorted to again.

GEORGE LANSBURY.

In our correspondence columns will be found a letter from our friend George Lansbury. He protests that Henderson is not paid for serving on the Insurance Commission. We mistakenly thought that *all* the Commissioners were paid. The point at issue is not the receiving of payment, but of serving the Government in this capacity, MacDonald is not paid for being on the Commission on India. But to what paid Government appointments do these unpaid ones pave the way? Our friend Lansbury thinks that all politicians are as honest as himself. We do not wish to flatter him, but he is one man in a thousand amongst politicians. The bourgeois politician goes to Parliament because he has some axe or other to grind. The Labour men go there to grind Labour's axe. But the atmosphere of the House has no effect upon the bourgeoise; it is no different to that which they have always been used to. The wage-worker who goes there leaps from the Hell of working-class life to the Heaven of bourgeois ease. But Comrade Lansbury is a working-man. As he writes, when he served on a Commission his meals were similar to those which he had at home. We do claim that the movement outside Parliament is purer. Syndicalism is purer, and must be so, because it teaches the workers to rely upon themselves and not delegate either their power or responsibility to someone else. In Comrade Lansbury's opinion, "the time has arrived when all of us should *believe* that each one is doing his or her best." That, Comrade Lansbury, is an impossibility. For we have had too many examples, and in all countries, of what Parliamentary life may make of our best and most revolutionary friends. As the Arab proverb runs: "If a man deceive thee once, shame on him; if he deceive thee twice, shame on thee!"

A WAR FOR PEACE.

By NORMAN YOUNG.

While millions toil and live a sordid life,
  While men are but machines to grind out gain,
While slavery is forced on child and wife,
  And "hands" are born, tho' minds and souls are slain,
    O God of battles, let there still be strife !

'Tis but hypocrisy to prate of peace
  And gentle brotherhood 'twixt bond and free ;
For who could wish industrial wars to cease
  While landless, hopeless, wage-slaves still must be?
    While such exist, O let there still be strife !

They read not our great destiny aright
  Who deem we ask for bread—a little ease—
A little rest from toil ere it is night—
  A trifling comfort—why, the beasts have these !
    Our end is freedom, 'tis for all we fight ;
    Till that is gained, O God, let there be strife !

IS SABOTAGE UN-ENGLISH ?

By E. J. B. ALLEN.

Just as eagerly as our misinformed opponents tell us that Syndicalism is un-English, so with a greater emphasis do they condemn Sabotage as being quite alien to the guileless Britisher's mind.

Let us examine the origin of the word and see if the practice that it denotes is such a foreign affair, after all. The word itself is French. It became part of the revolutionary vocabulary in quite an interesting way. A man was working at his machine in a shop in Paris ; his employer had subjected him to an unusual amount of annoyance, and in his rage the workman stooped down, pulled one of his sabots (wooden shoes) from his feet and threw at the machine, rendering it useless. Hence a new word was coined.

Like our English "lock-out," which has become international, to denote that action on the part of employers, so has the word "sabotage" become internationally used to denote injury done to an employer's machinery or material by his workpeople.

But if the word "sabotage" is French the practice is undoubtedly English. It is as old as the Labour movement. The British workers were the first Trade Unionists ; they were also the first to have practised "sabotage." Not only did they engage in it practically, but they formulated a theory and philosophy. Our most common workshop phrase—"Bad pay, bad work "—is a whole philosophy in miniature.

In 1816 the textile workers created a sabotage of their own when they had their Luddite movement. All through the valleys of the West Riding of Yorkshire, Lancashire, and the North machines were smashed, engines broken by those bands of men who went "plug-drawing." In the Huddersfield area they had a specially heavy hammer made for this work, and in their meetings at the houses of friendly publicans before they set out for their night's work they sang the praises of this giant hammer, "Great Enoch," as they had named it. During the years from 1850 to 1870 Trade Unionists used violence to intimidate blacklegs and recalcitrant employers. In those days they called it "rattening." If, for example, a grinder in Sheffield refused to pay his dues to the union, he would go to work one morning and find his tools and belt, which connected his grinding wheel, with the power gone ; there would be a note from "Mary Ann" telling him to pay up. When he had done so, next day another note signed "Mary Ann" would tell him where to find them. If he was obdurate then he never had them. These were mild methods. Emery was put in axles instead of oil. Sweating employers had their boilers blown up, were shot, and had explosions occur at their homes. The Royal Commission of 1867 that inquired into the Sheffield outrages also held inquiries into the acts committed by the Brickmakers' Union in Manchester. Bottles were filled with naphtha, gunpowder, and slugs, and hurled into the bedroom windows of blacklegs and sweaters, stables full of valuable horses were fired, capitalists were shot, and policemen met the same fate. Members of the Warpers' Union dashed vitriol in the face of a blackleg. So much for the innocent Britisher of those times. Other times, other manners.

In 1889 the dockers of Glasgow went on strike for increased pay. The employers engaged large numbers of farm labourers to displace them. The blacklegs were sufficiently numerous to break the strike. The dockers had to go back on the old terms. Just before they started work the general secretary of the union called them together, and said : "You go to return to work to-day at the old rate. The employers have said repeatedly that they have been delighted with the services of the farm hands who have taken our places for some weeks. We have seen them ; we have seen that they don't know even how to walk on a vessel, that they leave behind about half the stuff they are supposed to carry ; in short, that between two of them they hardly do the work of one of us. Now, then, the employers have sung the praises of these men, let us match them and practise 'ca'-canny.' Work like they worked. Only it has happened sometimes that they fell into the water, it is useless for you to fall also."

The men followed this advice for some days. The employers sent for the secretary and asked him to get the men to work how they had formerly, and they should have the rise.

This example of the spirit of the men of that time has become classical. Emile Pouget quotes it in his book, "Le Sabotage," for the instruction of the French workers.

One can safely say that there is as much sabotage practised habitually in England as there is in any other country. True, it is not talked upon, written about, or rendered so much a fine art as it is, perhaps, in France. The "militants" of the South Wales Miners' Federation give an instance in their pamphlet "The Miners' Next Step " : "At a certain colliery, some years ago, the management desired to introduce the use of screens for checking small coal. The men who were paid through and through for coal-getting—e.g., for large and small coal in gross—objected, as they saw in this the thin end of the wedge of a move to reduce their earnings. The management persisted, and the men, instead of coming out on strike, reduced their output by half. Instead of sending four trams of coal from a stall, two only were filled. The management thus saw its output cut in half, whilst running expenses remained the same. A few days' experience of a profitable industry turned into a losing one ended in the men winning hands down." At the time of the Railway Strike last year the shunters in a town near Manchester did well. They very carefully shunted the goods trains so that the trucks for the same stations were scattered in a dozen sidings. When the strike was settled it took weeks to get the traffic to rights. There was an organised disorder. Sometimes the destination cards had managed to get on the wrong trucks, which was extremely inconvenient at such a large junction.

When a certain very large hotel was in the course of erection near Piccadilly Circus a strange affair happened. The firm was "rushing" it; the men were being bullied ; so, when some of them had to fix up a fine carved ceiling, they somehow put long nails in just where the water-pipes and electric light wiring ran. When these things came to be used, of course it meant the ceiling had to come down, and the plumbers and electricians had to work over again. This was one way of finding "more work." I recollect with amusement the trick of some irreligious workers whom I knew. They were engaged in the job of decorating a rather fashionable church. The contractor had undertaken to get it all finished off for the Sunday. Apparently it was so ; but when the devout dames and damsels sat down in their pews in their best and latest toilettes for each others edification or envy, they found that their silks and satins possessed an extraordinary desire to stop on whichever part of the pew they rested. So tenacious was the hold of the seats that rising became a difficulty ! Those wicked painters had put too much oil in the varnish when thinning it ! How often have men who were whitewashing ceilings got tired of the too long inspection by the boss, and by the proper flick of the brush whilst industriously working managed to leave on his hat and coat unmistakable traces of where he has been ?

So, after all, sabotage is English. Just as we have made Syndicalism a household word, so shall we also make the word "sabotage" equally as well known. Who knows ? Perhaps before so many years have gone even the teachers in the Council schools during the lessons in grammar will ask the children for the declension of the verb sabot, and we shall hear their shrill, treble voices repeating aloud : "I sabot ; thou saboteth ; he sabots ; we sabot ; you sabot ; they sabot." And, begorra, they will !

Open Letter to the Miners' and Railwaymen's Delegates

WILLIAM WALKER,
FORMERLY a Carpenter and Joiner and Trade Union official;
NOW an Insurance Commissioner in the pay of the Government at £500 a year.

DAVID SHACKLETON,
FORMERLY in the pay of the Textile Workers to look after **their** interests;
NOW an Insurance Commissioner for the Government at a salary of £1,000 a year.

JOHN BURNS.
FORMERLY in the pay of the Amalgamated Society of Engineers at a salary of £100 a year;
NOW in the service of a capitalist Government at a salary of £5,000 a year.

RICHARD BELL,
FORMERLY General Sec. A.S.R.S.;
NOW working for the Government blackleg agencies called "Labour Exchanges" at a salary of from £500 to £1,000 a year.

To the Miners.

London, October 1st, 1912.

FELLOW-WORKERS,

You are again assembling to deliberate upon measures to benefit yourselves as workers. At this particular period it well behoves you to consider carefully all those proposals that are submitted to you. There are able men in the ranks of the miners who are alive to the situation, and are active with the propaganda of Direct Action and the General Strike.

Whatever advantages the miners possess above those conceded to the bulk of the wage-workers of these isles, those advantages, those privileges, are due solely to the potency of Direct Action.

You know that for thirty years Liberal and Tory Governments alike accepted the *principle* of an eight-hours' day, but refused to put it into operation. It became *a fact* when the miners of Great Britain threatened the employers and the Government with a demonstration of Direct Activity.

Last year you gave a splendid example of Solidarity. A million men were united as one. No longer did the men of Durham and Northumberland refuse to make common cause with the men in Wales. From Wales to Lanark, from Northumberland to Lancashire, the miners stood united. For the first time in history the whole of the miners presented one solid phalanx to their foe.

Comrades, in this Solidarity and Direct Action alone lies your hope.

It was by allowing those treacherous invertebrates, the Labour politicians, to split your forces into District Boards that broke the back of your first real national movement.

The politicians gulled you into accepting a *principle* when you demanded a fact.

For the future there must be no more Conciliation Boards. No more "impartial" arbitrators, who probably hold shares in mining companies. War to the knife upon the employers! Their elimination is the only thing to give you peace. Fight the direct fight. Have no more "Jack-of-both-sides" politicians interposed between the fighting forces.

As our well-known American comrade of the Western Federation of Miners and the Industrial Workers of the World, William D. Haywood, said :

"No contracts, no agreements, no compacts; these are unholy alliances, and must be damned as treason when entered into with the capitalist class."

Beware of politics and politicians.

Look at the men whose photos appear on this page. It was the political State that debauched their manhood.

Ignorant friends or cunning foes ask you to accept the State as your sole employer. To what end? The aggrandisement of still more Labour politicians? The State is your employer's machine. When the State takes a Labour leader into its service it is only because of services rendered or to be rendered. You—whom the State has shot at Mold, at Featherstone, at Llanelly—are asked to make this machine your one master from whose tyranny and black list there is no escape or appeal. The State would not alter its functions because it had extended its control. It would still be there to repress you, even if your erstwhile comrades entered its service.

To take a Government position is only another way for a Labour leader to accept your master's bribes.

The nationalisation of the mines would mean the control of the mines by the State. But the State is the instrument of the financiers; these would therefore become your anonymous exploiters.

D. A. Thomas, you know; Lord Merthyr, you know; Hanns, you know; but who is the State? The State is the mask that hides the vulpine features of the cosmopolitan financiers. *They* owe allegiance to no country, though they own all countries. For them the hills of Wales are but heaps of earth to be bored to pay a dividend. The miners are but their slaves to that end. So long as you remain wage-workers you will be robbed, be you employed by private companies or by the exploiting State.

To the Railwaymen.

London, October 1st, 1912.

FELLOW-WORKERS,

Once again you are meeting to discuss and devise ways and means of bettering the position of the men you represent. Remember that the Capitalists will be watching you, and that if you pass pious resolutions that mean nothing and will accomplish nothing, they will chuckle with glee.

The only method by which Railwaymen (like all other workers) have benefited, or can benefit, is that of **Direct Action.** By the THREAT of direct action, in 1907, you gained a few paltry benefits under the con-swindleation scheme; by the USE of Direct Action in August, 1911, you brought the Railway Companies to their knees, but **the ineptitude of your politicians** deprived you of the just fruits of your victory.

Hitherto you have held the mistaken belief that if you could obtain solidarity in the Railway Unions your task would be accomplished. Do you still hold that belief since the Railway Companies stood shoulder to shoulder with the other Masters and the P.L.A. during the London Transport Strike?

Dockers, Lightermen, Seamen, and Firemen, Bus and Tram-men, Cab Drivers, Railwaymen, etc., all are part and parcel of the transport industry; why then hold yourselves aloof from those who suffer from the identical wrongs that you suffer from?

You have the opportunity of correcting your mistakes; grasp it ere it be too late, and carry the resolution on your agenda for affiliation to the Transport Workers Federation. Better still; declare in favour of **One Transport Union,** and instruct your representatives to set about its formation and see they carry out your instructions.

Beware of cunning amendments, such as the "Nationalisation of Railways" and "Political Action." The employees of the State Railways of Germany, France, Belgium, Australia, etc., are just as badly off as you; they are even worse off than you. Besides, an exchange of private Capitalists for State Capitalists will not bring you either freedom or better conditions.

Leave political action to those people who like to have babies christened in the crypt of the House of Commons.

You carried troops and police for the Capitalists who used them against YOUR interests last August. Do you imagine that you are going to defeat Capital whilst you foolishly persist in defeating yourselves and your fellow-workers?

Where is your resolution on the agenda *re* the transportation of troops and police during industrial disputes?

The A.S.R.S. officials refused to support your anti-militarist champion, Fred Crowsley; have you tendered any advice to the thousands of reserve soldiers in your ranks? In the event of their being called upon to act as strikebreakers (as they were in France recently), are they to obey military orders or refrain from obeying? Are they to fight *for* you or *against* you; or don't you care?

You have an item on your agenda requesting you to accept a deputation from Ruskin College, though you have expressed your dissatisfaction on various occasions with that institution and its methods. Have you heard it whispered that Professor Lees Smith, Liberal M.P. for Northampton, corresponded with one of your officials, asking him if it was possible to get your students transferred from the Central Labour College to Ruskin College? You ought to ascertain who caused this item to be placed on your agenda, and why?

Are you in favour of sweated labour being employed at your Headquarters? If you are not, express your disapproval of the persons responsible for covering your Society with ridicule, and support your victimised members who have been grossly insulted by those who ought to be your servants, but who actually boss you.

Your programmes to the Companies usually contain a demand for the abolishment of intermediate grades, because you believe in the "one man one job" policy. If you are consistent, you will vote for the Ormskirk resolution, and see that people who already have their bread well buttered do not have the opportunity of drawing two men's salaries; besides, if you pay a man to devote his whole time to your interests in one particular direction, and then allow him to devote a portion of that time to some other object, though *he* is gaining, *you* are losing, whether he be occupied as an M.P., J.P., or on the Industrial Council.

Finally, see that *you* call the tune, for the men you represent are paying the piper; abolish your delusions of officials and leaders, and institute representatives who will truly carry out the desires of the men they represent.

MINERS AND RAILWAYMEN!—Refuse to be caught in the subtle snare of Mines and Railway Nationalisation. It isn't State control you need; it's your own you want. Fight both your employers and the State, and win **the Mines for the Miners, the Railways for the Railwaymen, and THE WORLD FOR THE WORKERS!**

OUR STUDENTS' COLUMN.

We receive many more articles than we can publish. Many are from comrades new in the movement. We do not want articles on theory. We want articles containing information, on strikes in different districts of the unions, of the changes in industry, of the employers' organisations and methods. Our space is limited, but we will print one or more each month for our students. They will note how their articles have been altered and adapted. We wish to give every encouragement to those converts who desire to assist us if they will bear the above points in mind.

AN EIGHT HOURS DAY.

By SYNDICUS.

A most glaring instance of the futility of depending upon Parliament to grant anything that is likely to benefit the workers is to be found in the attitude of Parliament on the Eight Hours question. For twenty-five years the Trade Union Congress has passed resolutions asking Parliament for an eight hours day. We are no nearer the general shortening of hours than when they started. The original demand was for an eight hours day and a five days week. Now the demand is toned down to a forty-eight hours week, which means more than eight hours a day when there is a half-day holiday. The forty hours week was urgent twenty-five years ago, so surely now the time is ripe for it without adding an additional eight hours per week. The Trade Union Congress has grown in influence because it represents a larger number of Trade Unionists. The Trade Union leaders must be like jellyfish to repeat a demand for an eight hours day for a quarter of a century. They should be demanding more from Parliament now, seeing that their hopes are centred on the Labour Party. The advent of the Parliamentary Labour Party has done more harm than good to the Trade Unions. During the six years which they have been in Parliament they should at least have got a forty-eight hours week established by law. But the Trade Union Congress has gone back on its original demand. No satisfaction can be got from Parliament on this one question alone, in spite of a body of Labour M.P.'s in the House, who are supposed to look after the interests of the workers. Parliament treats with contempt the Unions represented at the Trade Union Congress and the Parliamentary Committee of the Congress also. Let the workers treat Parliament with the same contempt. The workers are finding but that it is no good sending any more Labour members. This is proved by recent electoral events. The working class should do the same with all Parliamentarians and not vote at all. They have been doing this voting business for many years and are no better off. Direct Action will prove a godsend to the workers in regard to the reduction of hours. Direct Action does not mean a general "down tools" policy in a demand of this character. The workers themselves, individually and collectively, should refuse to work more than eight hours per day. Now is the time to give Parliament the go-by. The Unions should declare for an immediate eight hours day, and their members refuse to work longer. They would thus get a forty hours week at an early date, instead of waiting another twenty-five years.

FORMATION OF A TRANSPORT WORKERS' UNION BY THE RANK AND FILE.

A highly successful meeting was held at the Fairbairn Hall, Barking Road, Plaistow, on September 18, when twenty-one Transport Unions were represented by sixty delegates.

The chairman, Mr. McCann, stated "that the meeting had been called in continuance of a series of meetings that had been held during the last few weeks for the purpose of getting some definite steps taken towards the amalgamation of all Unions existing at present, connected with the Transport Workers."

Sam Roden, hon. secretary of the committee, reported on the previous work of the Provisional Committee," and said, "That one Union ought to have been formed years ago, not only for the 'Transport Workers,' but for all Workers. At the present time the Workers were worse off than they ever were before. It was no use crying over spilt milk; what they had to do was to crush sectionalism and organise the Workers solidly, so that they could fight the employers and win the whole result of their labour, thus allowing the Workers to control the means of their own life. Those who had started the movement intended to keep it going until successful, and the best thing to do with the officials of Unions who opposed the formation of a Transport Union was to clear them out. The masters sunk their differences when fighting, and the Workers must do the same," (Applause.)

Many delegates voiced their distrust with politicians and Union officials—the officials of the railwaymen especially—and expressed their belief that the Workers should treat themselves and nobody else. A resolution, inviting Tom Mann to address a Mass Meeting of Transport Workers in the "Canning Town Hall," in the near future, and to give a send-off to the movement, was carried unanimously. The meeting decided to elect a committee to deal with all detail work, and the following men were elected on that work:

Dockers' Union—T. H. Yardley.
Electrical Trades' Union—J. Hazelden.
Amalgamated Stevedores—C. Brown.
Gas Workers' Union—E. Halkett.
London Carmen's Trade Union—W. Cant.
National Operative Labourers' Union—C. Aviss.
Amalgamated Society of Railway Servants—F. J. Passmore.
Bricklayers—C. Showl.
Carpenters and Joiners—C. Blackwell.

The committee will carry out an active indoor and outdoor propaganda immediately, and meetings will be held at Fairbairn Hall on every Wednesday at 8 p.m. All branches of Transport Unions are requested to send representatives to these important meetings. For any other information, write to the hon. sec., S. Roden, 7, Holland Road, West Ham.

T RADE UNIONS, Trades' Councils, or Labour Societies desiring to know more about Syndicalism can have Speakers attend their Meetings. Travelling expenses only are asked for. Write Gen. Sec., I.S.E.L.—

GUY BOWMAN,
4, Maude Terrace, Walthamstow, E.

THE TWELFTH CONGRESS OF THE GENERAL CONFEDERATION OF LABOUR OF FRANCE.

AUTONOMY AND INDEPENDENCE OF THE SYNDICALIST MOVEMENT REAFFIRMED BY OVERWHELMING MAJORITY.

(From "Bulletin International du Movement Syndicaliste," Paris.)

On Monday, Sept. 16, at Havre, the Eighteenth Workers' Congress, the Twelfth Congress of the C.G.T. was opened. 1,093 unions were represented, 39 federations sent delegates, and 92 trades councils were represented. Before speaking of the work of the Congress, here are some figures relative to the development of the C.G.T., that we have extracted from the reports presented to the Congress. The number of unions that were affiliated in 1902 was 1,403, but now there are 2,837. The membership cards and due stamps issued during 1910-1912, taking into account the dues unpaid because of strikes and lockouts, and also the refusal of certain federations to pay on their full number of members, permit us to say that the real membership of the C.G.T. is a minimum of 600,000 members. In 1904 it had about 200,000 direct dues-paying members and about 300,000 members of the federations; to-day the number of dues-paying members exceeds 400,000. The C.G.T. has doubled its effective membership in the course of the last eight years, and this in spite of Governmental repression. The number of trade journals published by the different industrial federations is thirty-eight. Regarding federal activity, we simply cite the figures relating to strikes. The number of strikes, offensive or defensive, engaged in by the union organisation from the period June, 1910, to January, 1911, was 634. Of these:

Victories	117
Partial successes	247
Reverses	270

For the year 1911 there were 1,443 strikes:

Victories	267
Partial successes	563
Reverses	613

During the period January, 1912, to April, 1912, there were 263 strikes:

Victories	51
Partial successes	80
Reverses	114

Without entering into a general description of the resolutions and discussions of the Congress, we simply realise how they have disillusioned all those who were waiting to see the reformist and State-Socialist conceptions capture the French unions, by the infiltration of the ideas prevailing in other lands, notably in Central Europe. It is, above all, the German Social-Democratic Press which has spread, these last few years, the stories, more or less invented, in this connection. A great debate, the importance of which will escape no one, took place, as at the Congresses of Bourges and Amiens. The theses of revolutionary Syndicalism and that of the Reformists came into conflict with each other again. It was Renard, the secretary of the Textile Federation, who, profiting by the report on the Confederal action, explained the conception of the majority of the members of his Federation regarding the policy on which they wished to see the workers' actions based. Renard glorified the centralisation that has been realised more and more in foreign countries, and he combated the action of the Trades Councils, as being a counter-weight to centralisation (realising federalism, decentralisation, Syndicalism) as was expressed in the manifesto published by the Building Trades Federation. Whilst he pronounced against the opposition of the C.G.T. to the Socialist Party, and defended the old ideas of "the two arms" of the proletariat, of which one is called Syndicalist action, and the other Parliamentary action.

The response of the revolutionaries was formal and crushing. Bousquet, of the Waiters, Cooks, and Foodstuffs Workers, explained how the tendencies of the Reformists are the very negation of the class struggle, though upheld theoretically in Parliament, and repeated to Comrade Renard the insults addressed to the militants of the C.G.T. by the craft people and Socialist journals of the North.

"In the Socialist Party, as in all parties, the workers have to mix with employers. It is not a proletarian party."

Dumas, of the Clothing Trades, remarked that the introduction of politics in the unions engendered hatred between the members.

Yvetot recalled the oppression and the authority of the State, that we must combat in our quality of revolutionists.

Dumoulin, the assistant treasurer of the C.G.T., responded in a thorough fashion to the thesis of Renard. He first pointed out that the example of abroad had nothing to do with the debate. "The foreign comrades respect our autonomy; we respect theirs." He explained that Socialist neutrality in the unions is impossible, and gave as an example the strike of the railwaymen. "Do not the comrades who take up the old attitude of Briand see that they are lending themselves to an attack upon the independence of the unions?" Dumoulin recalled, in following, the rôle played by the Socialist Party in the strike of Naval Reservists, and how they withdrew from the struggle when the C.G.T. intervened at the request of the sailors. He cited the present condition of the miners, who could not congratulate themselves upon the political interference which they suffered; the nefarious propaganda of the Socialist M.P., Compere-Morel, during the agricultural workers strike in the South. The C.G.T. and the Socialist Party met one another in certain cases. That suffices. We do not give to these meetings any other importance. We shall maintain in its integrity, always erect, always fighting, the Syndicalism of the C.G.T.

Having consideration of the number of speakers booked to address the Congress, the Congress decided to hear again, on the third day of the Congress, three speakers of the three tendencies that had come to light.

For the Revolutionary Syndicalists there were Broutchoux, Merrheim, Griffuelhes. For the Reformist tendency, Cluet, Gaston Levy, Fiansetti. For the Social Democrats, Renard, Enghels, Vandeputte. The discussion finished, the secretary, Jouhaux, proposed a resolution recounting the characteristics of Syndicalist action, and fixing the position of Syndicalism. "Syndicalism, the offensive movement of the working-class, by the voice of their representatives, meeting at the only authorised Congress, affirms itself again as a force to conserve its autonomy and independence, which has made its strength in the past, and which is the gauge of its progress and development. The Congress declares that, as before, it is resolved to exclude all problems foreign to its proletarian action, susceptible of weakening its unity, so dearly conquered, and of lessening the power of the ideal, followed by the proletariat grouped in the Unions, Trades Councils, and Trades Federations, of which the C.G.T. is the natural representative." Then Jouhaux recalled the declaration of the Confédération at the Amiens Congress, 1906, which is as follows:

"The Confederal Congress of Amiens confirms Article 2 of the Constitution of the C.G.T., as follows: 'The C.G.T. groups, outside all political schools, all the workers conscious of the struggle to be carried on for the disappearance of a wage class and an employing class.'" The resolution formulated thus its theoretical affirmation: "In the daily work of revendication, Syndicalism follows the co-ordination of the workers' efforts, the increasing of better conditions by the realisation of immediate ameliorations, such as the shortening of the hours of labour, and increase of wages, &c. But this task is but one side of the work of Syndicalism; it also prepares for the integral emancipation which cannot be realised except by the expropriation of the capitalists; it recognises as the means of action the General Strike, and it considers that the Unions—to-day organisations of resistance, will be in the future organisations for production and distribution, basis of the social reorganisation. As a consequence, in this that concerns individuals, the Congress affirms, the entire liberty for the Unionist to participate outside of his union in such forms of struggle as correspond to his philosophical or political conceptions, and not to introduce into the unions the opinions he professes outside.

"In that which concerns organisations, the Congress declares that, in order to obtain the maximum of effect, economic action must be exercised directly against the master class. The confederal organisations have not, as Trade Union bodies, to concern themselves with parties and sects, which outside and by the side may pursue in all liberty the social transformation."

Here are the results of the voting on this resolution that strengthens the resolution of Amiens, and affirms distinctly the autonomy and independence of the Syndicalist movement:

Number voting, 1,103.

For	1,057
Against	35
Abstentions	11
	1,103

TO BIRMINGHAM READERS.

A PRELIMINARY MEETING will be held to consider the advisability of forming a

SYNDICALIST GROUP in BIRMINGHAM.

All sympathisers should apply for tickets in the first instance to H. B. WILLIAMS, GOALTON ROAD, BOURNBROOK, BIRMINGHAM.

THE LEAGUE'S ACTIVITIES.

COVENTRY GROUP.

The League has been making favourable headway in Coventry. Mainly owing to the recent visits by our Comrades Tom Mann and Guy Bowman, an active group of Trade Unionists has been formed. It is hoped that in a short time the whole of the Trade Union Branches in the city will have members who are actively engaged upon Syndicalist education propaganda inside their respective organisations. A leaflet is being drawn up which will be circulated throughout the city. Tom Mann addressed a largely-attended meeting held in the Market Square, organised by the Amalgamated Society of Engineers. His speech was listened to attentively, and the listeners were obviously impressed with the doctrines of Syndicalism; and at the same gathering a resolution demanding the release of Ettor and Giovannetti was carried unanimously. The No. 1 Branch of the Workers' Union have passed a resolution declaring that its functions as a Trade Union are industrial and not political, and that its object is the capture of the industries by economic action, to be controlled by the Trade Unions in the interests and general welfare of the community.

The chairman of the group is Comrade H. Summers, and the secretary of the group is H. E. Burdett Ludlam, 62, Sackville Street, Hillfields, Coventry.

LONDON ORGANISER'S REPORT.

Since my appointment I have been engaged on the following duties: Distribution of bills announcing conference at Holborn Hall amongst Trade Union branches; tracing secretaries of Trade Union branches and Trades Councils (removed); collecting reports and addresses of Trade Union branches for circularisation re Holborn Conference; visited newsagents who sell our paper, and found the papers and posters well displayed; canvassed other newsagents who do not sell our paper and succeeded in obtaining some more. I have attended, up to date, ten branches of the railwaymen's union, A.S.R.S., have sold literature at each, and have found very little opposition to my address on Syndicalism. Several branches are attending the Holborn Conference, representing the railwaymen employed on the following railways: Great Eastern, Great Northern, Great Central, South Eastern and Chatham, and Brighton, London Electric, City and South London. I have been able to persuade two comrades of the railway service to become distributing members for the railwaymen in their local branches. The prospects for the future of Syndicalism, as far as London is concerned, are undoubtedly rosy, and although progress must of necessity be slow at first, there are promises of a good harvest in due course. I am booked for several Trade Union meetings, and am assisting in the movement for the formation of one Transport Workers' Union. I shall be pleased if any member of the League who knows of any scope for my services to be utilised—for the benefit of the League—will kindly notify our General Secretary, Guy Bowman.—F. J. PASSMORE.

CIRCULATION NOTES.

By SAM BRIERLEY.

Orders must be obeyed, so I made no bones about it, but went into the lion's den—I mean the Trade Union Congress, Newport, Mon. For eight days I was happy. I arrived in Newport very early, and almost immediately met Jim Sexton. Jim was looking very glum. He purchased a copy of the SYNDICALIST and went off to his hotel smiling. On Saturday I went to the miners' meeting, and sold fourteen copies. I also saw Mrs. Watts Morgan. On Saturday night I got contents sheets placed outside all the shops in the main streets.

"Have you got a *Clarion*?" said one delegate. "No, but we have the SYNDICALIST," then with a gentle, swear, the would-be customer departed. On Sunday we went to church, and to the P.S.A. in the afternoon. Mr. Harvey, M.P., delivered an address on the "Log Cabin to White House" subject. He carefully and graphically explained to the delegates how we could all rise to be M.P.'s, like him, if only we were good, obedient, thrifty, teetotalers, and looked to Jesus, also like him. Outside the place some of the delegates got a severe shock when they found the SYNDICALIST on sale.

On Monday morning I attended the Congress early, and was met by one, Sunday by name—I thought he was all the blessed week by his officious manner towards me—who tried to prevent me from selling the SYNDICALIST. However, Ablett, Wills, and Hedges were on the spot, and told him that I must be allowed the same privilege as the others. After that all went merrily, and soon between 450 and 500 were sold.

I must thank Will Thorne, M.P., for the ready permission which he gave me to sell our paper at their meeting. The I.L.P. also did the same. We have to thank the B.S.P. also for the same courtesy. Mme. Alexander Kollantz, whilst not agreeing with us, ordered a copy to be sent to her monthly. This lady will be in England again in March, 1913, and by that time I hope she will be on our platform.

Tom Mann having been away in Sweden during the month of September, I have not been able to get the same sales as when I was with him at meetings.

I expect to be at Swansea early in October for the Miners' Congress.

The Manchester Conference arrangements are well in hand. Seven hundred and fifty invitations have been sent out, and the credentials are being returned already.

The Coliseum, Ardwick, is engaged for a mass meeting on Sunday, Dec. 1. Tom Mann and Guy Bowman and others will speak. Reserved seats can now be booked, 6d. each at 328, Hyde Road, Ardwick, Manchester.

NOTICE TO SYMPATHISERS.

In order to make the work of the I.S.E.L. effective, we must be able to reach every Trade Union Branch, therefore send all Trade Union Reports and Branch Lists to the General Secretary—

GUY BOWMAN,
4, Maude Terrace, Walthamstow, E.

(Continued from Page 1.)

the Syndicalist Conference meeting now in Obrero will decide to make their fortnightly journal *Syndikalisten* into a weekly one, and request Jensen to act as Editor. Meantime *Brand* is edited by one of the best-known men in Sweden, Hinke Bergegren. One of the organisers for the Syndicalists is John Andersson, of Gothenburg, who was formerly a Transport Worker, but was refused work after the General Strike of 1909. John is now one of the most effective advocates of Solidarity and Direct Action.

At every port I visited, I was pleased to find that a very strong feeling existed favourable to some general action being taken to shorten the imprisonment of the three young men who are now serving life sentences in Swedish prisons for participation in the explosions on board the blackleg ship at Malmö, where the Shipping Federation had taken a shipload of English blacklegs to break the strike of the Swedish Dockers.

To think that it should be England that should have supplied these blacklegs! England, who with her many faults, had to her credit this one thing, that she was really the home of working-class Industrial Organisation, the pioneer and pace-setter in this regard. To think that Capitalism should be so triumphant as to have completely demoralised so many englishmen (I cannot make myself use a capital "E") as to have deprived them of all hope, of all semblance of manhood, of all self-respect, and able to control them for a few paltry pounds and command their active help as deliberate and systematic strike-breakers against Swedes and Hollanders, who had first been encouraged to organise by our example: that such a condition could be reached is the greatest possible humiliation to Englishmen.

I cannot and will not pretend that I was, or am, sorry that the explosion took place. It is not to be forgotten that the very next day all the crawling, wretched, Capitalist victims—blacklegs—in the various Swedish ports, demanded to be taken away at once, and the Shipping Federation had to take them. Three men are in prison for life in connection with this; three of the brightest young men that were in Sweden. To them in the prisons, I send by telepathy, and by any other possible means, my Love and Comradeship, which shall show itself in sturdy work to overturn the wretched Capitalist system responsible for their being where they are. I am sure thousands of others will join in this, and will work unceasingly for INDUSTRIAL SOLIDARITY and DIRECT ACTION.

TOM MANN.

Sweden, Sept. 21, 1912.

Syndicalism and the Intellectuals.

The way to kill a new idea is to accept it and then divert it from its course in any or many of the numerous ways known to the tricksters.

Isn't Social Democracy a safe and sane movement to-day in every country in the world? Can't "respectable" men and women join it without fear of losing their social standing? Haven't the "respectables" been "converted," and don't they occupy the seats of power in the party? And what tyrant fears it any more? And, by the same token, what knowing slave has any more faith in it?

How can the respectables accept Syndicalism with its barbarous doctrines of strikes and sabotage? And, accepting, how could they control? Impossible. Syndicalism seems safe from the middle class, for it is distinctly a class movement.

Unionism is the only distinctly working-class movement that has ever existed, and Syndicalism is simply Unionism up to date. Syndicalism is the application of the scientific method whereby experience displaces tradition in the economic relations of the working class.—J. Fox, Ed. the *Agitator*, Home, U.S.A.

Syndicalism & Undergrads.

This is all quite true, but subject to certain limitations. Some of the Syndicalist papers recently referred to the Syndicalists as "gadflies." The name is good. It describes our mission in life exactly. We intend to sting the sleepy Socialist and Labour kine into a greater sprightliness than they have displayed of late years.

This is all quite true, but subject to certain limitations. Some men .intellectuals who think it gives them an additional kudos if they cultivate a reputation for being "advanced." When the prosecutions over the "Don't shoot" letter took place, it was marvellous the number of people who became—in their imagination—apostles of Syndicalism. We do not deny the right of anyone to criticise Syndicalism, to classify it: if possible amongst all the other "isms," to examine it both as a theory and as a movement. But when some of our good friends, like Gaylord Wilshire, for instance, attempt to organise a Syndicalist movement in the Universities, it is time to protest against this obvious absurdity. In what capacity can undergraduates partake in the struggle between the workers and their masters? The undergraduates at Oxford during the Coal Strike did talk of forming a volunteer corps of blacklegs. Their hearts bled for their country deprived of coal by the wicked miners. *They* would go to the mines. But somehow it did not happen; the coal-owners were, perhaps, too much afraid of the damage which they would do.

Why are these men at the Universities? Some to graduate in some science—well and good; some to become priests—living hypocrites and State-paid deluders of the workers; some in order that later on they may take up commissions in the Army and Navy, in order to slaughter the workers of this or other countries; many to commence their careers as barristers, solicitors, or professional politicians. The debating societies are of great use to the latter. *None* of the undergraduates are there to learn anything about the real facts of the workers' existence and the means for them to win their emancipation from wage-slavery.

Training for Fuzzy-Wigs.

All are at the Universities in order to learn how best to keep the workers in subjection. Many of the fuzzy-wigs who occupy the judicial benches of France to-day were once Anarchists. When studying at the Sorbonne in Paris they were shadowed by the police, and treated as political suspects. But now, when they have grown older, and have found themselves in those positions for which they were sent to the University to study, they are most law-abiding. France swarms with judges, magistrates, and lawyers who were at one time revolutionary. They are now the most reactionary of all classes. It is they that pass the most severe sentences upon those militant Syndicalists who may come before them. There are but few high officials of the Republic who were not at one time called "comrade."

Government Whitewashers.

It may be urged that these young men are sometimes full of enthusiasm for the Socialist movement. They may even profess to be philosophic Anarchists. Yet at one time Briand—the Prime Minister of France—was once an Anarchist. He is now the best bulwark that the French capitalists possess. What about Mr. C. F. G. Masterman, noted for his interest in social matters; has not Mr. Bottomley aptly described him as being in the Whitewashing Department of the Government? They all duly "arrive" at the military, naval, legal, or political positions, and in these capacities proceed to *do their official duty* of maintaining the law and order of the governing class.

No Moses Wanted.

We have no need for priests or politicians. Syndicalism is a workshop affair. We do not look to some stray member of the capitalist class to come down to us as a modern Moses to lead us to the Promised Land. He could not if he would. We don't want such presents thrust upon us. We can do better without them. We want the navvy, not the lawyer; the mechanic, not the priest; fighters, not word-spinners. Syndicalism is action, not philosophy.

Social Democracy.

As to Gaylord Wilshire, he is a good friend of the SYNDICALIST; he is better still, a personal friend of ours. We feel sure that he has no Social Democratic obstinacy, and that before long he will see that we are right. We, therefore, feel confident that in the future he will no more bother about undergraduates than he will about discussing Syndicalism with a Social Democrat, for Social Democracy is the apotheosis of the weak, the exaltation of the defeated, the enthronement of the inefficient, and the survival of the unfittest!

Their Views and Ours.

"Syndicalism" .... J. H. HARLEY, M.A.
"Syndicalism and Labour" .... Sir ARTHUR CLAY, Bart.
"Syndicalism" .... J. RAMSAY MACDONALD, M.P.
"What Syndicalism Means" .... SIDNEY and BEATRICE WEBB.
"Syndicalism and the General Strike" ARTHUR D. LEWIS (Fisher Unwin, 6s.).

It is striking testimony to the public interest in Syndicalism to find so many formidable looking books on the subject. Some of them—those by our friend MacDonald and the Webbs, for instance—betray their contents by displaying the names of the authors. We suspect, however, that the identity of the writer of Ramsay's effusion could not long remain hidden even if his name were not on the cover. Also it is not difficult to detect the manner of the arch-Fabians Sidney and Beatrice Webb. Anyhow, let us dispose of the publications in the order printed above. First, there is a cheap sixpenny edition by Harley. Now, Mr. Harley is a University man. If we mistake not, he writes in the *Contemporary Review*. This seems to damn him from the outset. However, let us be lenient and deal with the book on its merits or demerits. We say the book is cheap. So it is. It is a very neat little volume, handy to put in the pocket to while away a long railway journey—only the journey must be very, very long. To tell the truth, we are not greatly impressed with Mr. Harley. His style, for one thing, is not our style; his ways are University ways, and not our ways. Now, Ramsay's style is very good—quite the Syndicalist style. He takes all sorts of liberties with the flexible English tongue. In fact, he moulds it to his own liking. . . . But, there, we are on Ramsay's track again! And we promised to deal with these books in their proper order.

To return to our muttons—and Harley. Harley is a clever man, and a very nice and entertaining man, too. We believe he writes very nice books—children's books and fairy tales. If he doesn't is it our misfortune, and not our fault. He is frankly interested in his subject—perhaps that's why he wrote a book on it. We wish we could be as interested in his book as he is in his subject. But, there, we are not University men, and we have no appreciation of the University style; when we are older and wiser we shall certainly read Mr. Harley's book again. But now for the worthy Clay (Baronet).

Sir Arthur Clay, the Genial Baronet.

Comrade Clay—organising secretary of the Federation of Capitalists' Trades Unions about to be formed—is nothing if not genial. He has the cheery, octogenarian style of the *Times* and the *Morning Post*. Indeed, he displays a fatherly interest in the cause of the working class. We must certainly get comrade Clay (Baronet) to subscribe to the new SYNDICALIST weekly. He certainly sympathises with Syndicalists. He would have us all confined in a nice comfortable home for pauper imbeciles if he could—which is very nice of him, very nice indeed. Not to be too enthusiastic in our praises, we are certainly interested in the Baronet's book. If he would just tell us what Syndicalists propose to do, instead of what he thinks Syndicalism means, we should know whether to agree with him or not. As it is, we can only admire his kind intentions, and—throw away the book.

Loud cheers! At last we come to our old friend Ramsay. We turn over the pages carefully, with bated breath, to see what the great man has to say about us. As we said before, Ramsay writes in our style, which—though we say it ourselves—is a very good style. He breaks away from the fossilised and dead forms of the English language, and writes in a clear and (almost) convincing language. To cut a long tale short, he is a little contemptuous of us Syndicalists. He does not say so in so many words—in fact, words could not express his contempt. But we suspect he secretly regards us as a lot of young men in a hurry.

Ramsay MacDonald Doing the Half-Nelson on Us.

So we are, so we are, dear readers. And the most painful sight to us is to see the slowness of the working-man. Horse-whipping isn't in it. Of course Ramsay, as the tin god of the Parliamentary Labour Party, has a right to do this. In fact, that's what he's there for! However, after ploughing through pretty well the whole of the book, we came across one passage that nearly knocked us down—did the half-Nelson on us, so to speak .(not to be careful about the correct use of wrestling terms). We found it buried right at the end, intended probably as a reward for a good boy, and after we recovered from the shock we promptly dug it up, and now wear it as a charm to conceal the effect of a small Guinness. And here it is :

The old revolutionist I respect. He understood his business. He prepared for the work of barricades and street fighting. He knew that a revolution had to be carried through by activity, not passivity. The childish dream of a revolution by paralysing society never entered his head. Revolution must always be more or less paralysing, but he knew that the less paralysing the better.

There! What do you think of that? Not to regard the little thrust at us, how blind we have been all these years not to notice what a bloody revolutionist Ramsay is! We shall never forgive ourselves for this, never!

Out-Syndicating the Syndicalists.

As a pleasant relief to the earnest, not to say prophetic, style of the one and the only Ramsay comes the learned treatise of the Webbs. We are afraid we must take it seriously. Nobody, so far as we remember, has ever treated the Webbs in jest and escaped from the wrath to come. Indeed, this treatise is so learned that we have much more to learn before we can understand it. It out-Syndicates the Syndicalists. Up to now we thought we knew something about Syndicalism, but we were mistaken.

Out of the wilderness where the Fabians live on locusts and wild honey come the foretellers of our doom! In terrible voices, like those of the twin jemini of the Romans, they predict the failure of Syndicalism. And they tell us more about Syndicalism than we know ourselves. We are again suspected of being young men in a hurry. So much for the Webbs.

A Sheep in Wolf's Clothing.

Like a sheep in wolf's clothing comes our friend Arthur Lewis with a formidable volume on Syndicalism. He, at any rate, has taken the pains to find out who and what we are, and we almost believe he is a Syndicalist himself. Only a Syndicalist could not find time to write such a big book. At any rate, friend Lewis lets us down lightly, and is half inclined to pat us on the back. He certainly has no love for Hyndman and the Old Guard. There is only one fault about this book—which is a very good book indeed—and that is, it is too dear. Possibly, however, its price will recommend it to some nice, comfortable, middle-class people, who will read it, and then write letters to the publisher, in virtuous horror at his audacity in issuing such a book. And then, perhaps, Fisher Unwin will let us have his reply to publish in the SYNDICALIST!

But in order that the Workers may have a book explaining what Syndicalism really is, we will get our friend Tom Mann to write one for us in time to come out as a Christmas-box.

A French View.

These last few months the great revolutionary strikes in England, France, and the United States have led a large number of persons to write on revolutionary Syndicalism. We continue to receive newspaper articles in which they combat or defend Syndicalism, its tactics of Direct Action, General Strike, Sabotage, &c. But we are astonished to see how few of these men who study the movement have gone to its sources, to the strikes, the workers' struggles, or even the working-class publications. The authors of the various countries generally attribute the birth of the revolutionary movement and its theories of Direct Action to the influence of French Syndicalism, as if it were sufficient for them to declare that "it is a foreign product" that has no vitality in our country. Instead, however, of studying the French movement from its official organ *La Voix du Peuple*, for example, or from the pamphlets of the Syndicalists, or from the militants, the authors of the articles on Syndicalism address themselves to French and Italian writers, &c., who are living quite outside of the movement, and whom nobody in the French unions even trouble themselves about. Thus, for some weeks we could read in an English daily a series of articles by the English Socialist M.P., Ramsay MacDonald, where the origin of the French Syndicalist movement was found in the theories of M. Georges Sorel, and among those of his master, the professor at the Sorbonne, Bergson. In the July number of the *International Socialist Review*, of Chicago, we find an article on "Sabotage and Revolutionary Unionism." We are sent back again to the school of the neo-Marxians, again with M. Sorel. And so they follow. We should be foolish to waste our time in insisting upon the nonsense contained in these and similar articles. Let us point out one fact, that the revolutionary Syndicalist movement in France, as in England, as in the United States and elsewhere, is everywhere *a real movement of the masses*. It is the militant revolutionaries that have created the movement in France by the experience of many years of struggle, and quite apart from all "new schools"—old Marxian, neo-Marxian, or Bergsonian. The same in England and the United States; it is the great strikes of recent months that have drawn—as we said —attention on this movement, and that which has preceded these strikes. It is not a new school of philosophy whatever, but the arduous task of organisation and the practical experience of the masses in the service of capitalism: and in the daily struggle against that capitalism.—Christian Cornélissen, in *Bulletin International*, Paris.

ABOUT GADFLIES—AND OTHER THINGS.

By JACK RADCLIFFE.

The most fossilised and hide-bound of our Socialist papers recently referred to the Syndicalists as "gadflies." The name is good. It describes our mission in life exactly. We intend to sting the sleepy Socialist and Labour kine into a greater sprightliness than they have displayed of late years. We are tired of their slow, plodding pace, and their chewing of the cud of ancient platitudes. Yes; we are gadflies!

Our grandfatherly organ (dreary old hurdy-gurdy) also prophesied for us a brief existence. Well, a short life and a merry one, if it must be so! The wish was, doubtless, father to the thought. But we will see all about that. At any rate, we will keep the cattle moving so long as we last, which is likely to be much longer than grandad thinks.

Syndicalism was "turned down" by the Trades Union Congress, as we expected it would be. But it was something to have got the idea brought forward. It will take several more turns of the "economic screw" on the part of the master-class before the rank and file of the Trades Unions make up their minds to the necessity of "sacking" their fossilised leaders and officials, and taking matters more directly into their own hands.

The truth is that the leaders and the officials do not want a final settlement of Labour's demands. This is the last thing they would welcome. It would mean an end to comfortable "jobs" and to the emoluments direct, and *indirect*, that office brings. A final settlement would mean Socialism, no less. And Socialism is the last thing many of those who call themselves Socialists desire to see. Socialism of late years, unfortunately, has become a road to place and power for those unscrupulous enough to prostitute it to this end. So have we seen, and no doubt will see again in more than one or two of those setting out on a Parliamentary career, professing Socialism.

Beware of the Parliamentary Socialist. He is fooling thee! Distrust him! The desire for the magic letters "M.P".after one's name has more in it than appears in an election address. It pays well to betray the workers to their enemies. But no one can betray the workers until he is in a position to do it. Can you see that? When a person becomes a Trade Union official or, better still, a "Socialist"-Labour M.P., he is pre-eminently in that position. Can you see *that*?

The Trades Union Congress also went back on the secular education resolution. This was evidence of the untiring activity of that arch-enemy of the workers, Clericalism. Clericalism and Militarism! These are the twin pillars of class tyranny and oppression. God and the Country! Religion and Patriotism! So long as these superstitions bind the limbs of Labour, Labour can never be free.

It is easy to trace the activity of that remarkable international Jesuit *lay* organisation known as the "Militia of Christ" in this matter. Over in America the Militia of Christ is a force to be reckoned with in the Labour movement. Here, in England, we hear little of it; nothing at all of its name. But we know this, that a Catholic serves his Church before all things, and a man who allows his mind to be enslaved by ecclesiasticism will never be able to emancipate his body from the thraldom of secular tyranny. You, Catholic Labour men, Catholic Socialists! what of the Militia of Christ?

Those Socialists who say that Socialism has nothing to do with religion, as such, are either singularly ingenuous or particularly astute in the service of interests other than those of Socialism. It would be curious to know, if it were possible, why Catholics (or Anglicans, or Nonconformist Christians, for that matter) interest themselves in Socialism. In the mind of a Christian, of course, the welfare of the soul is an infinitely more important matter than the welfare of the body. But Socialism has no interest save the improvement of purely material conditions. Hence, what do these good Christian "souls" want with Socialism? God is their master, and His heaven is their reward. Let them look to that.

We know that the attitude of Clericalism, Catholic or other, is one of uncompromising hostility to Socialism. Individuals among the clerics, or their "lay" dupes, may be ingenuous enough to imagine, or astute enough to pretend otherwise. But the history of the past teaches us, beyond all cavil or doubt, that "God" is always on the side of the rich and the powerful, even as He is always on the side of the "big battalions."

Clericalism and Militarism are now, as ever, inseparable allies, indispensable to one another. The spiritual and the temporal, the right and left arms of Tyranny, they are raised to-day against Freedom, as bitterly hostile, as cruel and unscrupulous, as murderous and remorseless as ever they have been all through the bloodstained history of Humanity's centuries-long struggle towards emancipation.

Clericalism and Militarism! There they are striking down those who would loosen Labour's chains, riveting those chains on again ever and anon. And what are you doing about it, poor, old, doddering grandfather? You, with your political-Parliamentary platitudes at a time when Parliamentarism is utterly played out; when the Social Revolution (which you were wont to proclaim so grandly) is in sight? You, with your Clerical councillors (Militia of Christ) and your crazy Citizen Army scheme! Gadflies? Yes, old gentleman, in *justice* to you, let us tell you our intentions towards you: By the "God" that you protest is no business of yours, we will sting you to death if we cannot rejuvenate you!

The Trades Union Congress has also betrayed Trades Unionism to the most cunning and deeply-laid Capitalist conspiracy of modern times. The object and purpose of the National Insurance Act was plain enough for anyone to see, save the purblind fossils who are the "representatives" of organised labour. They are prepared to hand over the future of Trades Unionism to the tender mercies of the Sassoons, the Rothschilds, and "High Finance," acting on behalf of class-conscious Capitalism. These enemies of the workers have made little disguise of their intentions in this respect. They have been, in some respects, cynically frank. But the old-style Trade Unionism has always believed in the identity of interest between capital and labour. No doubt it has been made worth the while of certain among the old-style Trades Unionists to pretend to believe it.

Old-style Trades Unionism is played out. Nothing could have made this fact more evident than the Trades Union Congress has done. Well, if the workers will not learn in any other way, it must be left for the Sassoons, the Rothschilds, and class-conscious Capitalism to teach them. The lessons are going to be rubbed in hard. It will remain for Syndicalists to point out the moral of these lessons. We shall have plenty of occasions.

With all this it is evident that the deadliest enemies of the workers are not their avowed foes, the capitalists, but those who pretend, and in many cases doubtless believe, that they are the only true friends of the workers. The rank and file of the working class must learn that *they are their own best friends*, and that if they would achieve their emancipation *they must do it themselves*. Meantime Syndicalists will get busy educating the workers, and especially the Socialists, as to what Syndicalism really means.

What it *does not mean* is being stated with vicious mendacity by many of those who really know better, who are writing books to falsify Syndicalism, who declare that "Syndicalism means the ownership and control of any industry, not by society, but by those engaged in that industry, *who, workmen and owners alike, have a bond of union against the rest of society.*" This lie is from the senile organ at first referred to. Some of our professedly Socialist sheets could give the most unscrupulous of the Capitalist papers points and beat them at cold, calculated, carefully-thought-out falsehood.

Sassoon, Rothschild, and company. These, it seems, are to be our schoolmasters. It is regrettable that they should have to do the work of *forcing* the workers, by cumulative tyranny and repression (we shall see plenty of this by and by), and by intensified. exploitation to resort to the only method that can be of any use—that is, Direct Action on the *industrial field*, whilst the majority of our Socialists are gibbering and mouthing their worn-out political platitudes, instead of taking hold of the only efficient weapon lying ready to their hands—Syndicalism.

WHO IS SORGUE?

This question may arise quite naturally when one thinks of the South Wales Miners' and Transport Workers' strikes of a year ago. That year which will mark an epoch in the British workers' calendar.

However, in spite of the splendid impression that Mme. Sorgue (or "Sorgue," as she prefers) created everywhere, the voice of querulous reproach was heard. Sorgue was on the strike committee in Glasgow. Whilst there she gave a lecture in one of the large theatres upon "The Conscious Minority." The magnificent success of this exposition of revolutionary thought, with its support of Syndicalism, exasperated the politicians. *Forward*, the political Labour paper, printed a series of insinuations. In a more or

Sorgue addressing Strikers at Tower Hill, London.

less mysterious and enigmatic manner it suggested that it would be well if they were told where her money came from, who she really was, etc. All sorts of conclusions could be drawn from their article.

Mme. Sorgue is the daughter of the celebrated French scientist Durand du Gros, to honour whom his fellow-countrymen are to raise a statue of him in his native town of Rodez. Foremost upon the committee are M. Bergson, known by reason of his philosophic works everywhere, and M. Ribot, the distinguished scientist. Her mother was an aristocrat, Lady of Honour to the Grand Duchess Constantine; her grandfather was at one period Director of Customs at Odessa—the General Kripkoff. Her uncle, Estomme, was Senior Admiral of the Baltic Fleet. Nearly all her mother's relatives were officers in the Czar's Guard or Pages of Honour to him.

At eighteen Sorgue rebelled openly against parental control, and in spite of her father's opposition gave her hand to the man she loved. At nineteen she entered life as an independent wage-earner, as an actress, and for a time was associated with Sarah Bernhardt. After a while, tired of the trivialities of the stage, she took to journalism as a profession. The first-hand study of the workers' lives which this led her to, definitely moulded her to revolutionary thought. The necessity for deep-seated and perhaps violent changes was apparent to her. The revolutionary basis pervaded her writings. The editor of the *Journal des Débats*, to which she contributed, raised objections. But what he despised she championed. Sorgue was on the staff of *La Petite République* for four years, under the direction of Millerand. She became one of the most popular writers and orators in the French Socialist movement. Her ideas outgrew those of the Millerand, Jaurès, Gérault-Richard combination. She saw that their ideas inevitably led to Government, even as Millerand accepted Government office as Minister of Way.

Now she is known everywhere as the ardent propagandist of Direct Action, Syndicalism, the General Strike, and all those things that are abomination to the respectables. In her revolutionary career she has taken part in over fifty strikes. Twice she has been imprisoned, once in Portugal and once in Italy. Condemned in Portugal for her revolutionary propaganda, when she was released and expelled, the Government had her escorted by gunboats down the river Tagus from Lisbon.

In Italy she was tried for regicide, but was acquitted. During her trial the prosecutor exclaimed that behind her in the cage he beheld the pale face of Bresci, the remover of King Humbert. Whilst acquitted on that charge she was imprisoned with solitary confinement for her advocacy of Anti-Militarism and the General Strike.

About six years ago she was with the "land-grabbers" of Triangle Camp, West Ham, when the unemployed attempted to go "back-to-the-land," by seizing unoccupied land.

Was amongst the peasants in their strike in the Italian province of Parmesan, and was also amongst the miners in the Pas-de-Calais in their struggle.

Amongst other accomplishments of hers was that of being the first woman admitted to the table of the judiciary Press at Antwerp.

When Ferrer was seized, her indignation forced her to the front of the agitation for release.

She came to England with her credentials as correspondent to our valued comrade *La Bataille Syndicaliste* of Paris. The editor of *L'Internationale* of Lugano recommends her, whilst she has credentials from the Labour Council of Parma and of the national organisation affiliated to the committee there. They warmly commend her to the English workers. The Federal Committee of the National Federation of Ports, Docks, Transports, etc., of France give her their recommendation to England. The Arsenal Workers of Toulon thank her for the powerful work she accomplished for them, whilst the Union of Workers Syndicate, St. Quentin and District, gave her a mandate as their representative. So this is the woman—the living symbol of international revolutionary activity—that the politicians suspect. She is a devoted friend of the C. G. T., the Syndicalists of France.

Her settled income is derived from interest on the money realised by the sale of the large Domaine d'Arsac in the South of France. This was bequeathed to her by her father. Five years ago she sold it, because owing to a boycott against her it was almost impossible to sell the produce of her estate. The landed proprietors of the district were her sworn enemies, for she had given her farm workers an eight hours' day, whilst theirs slaved from fourteen to fifteen hours. They had no mercy for her, who would not treat her serfs the same as they.

ANSWERS TO INQUIRERS.

T. B. SMITH.—In answer to your query as to what forms of organisation are suggested for mental activities: In the primary matter of education we claim that teaching is the business of the teachers. That these men and women of the "intellectual proletariat" who have studied in order to qualify as teachers are the ones best capable of seeing to matters of education. To-day, the professional duties of the teachers absorb much of their spare time and consideration. In their paper, *The Schoolmaster*, they state that it is their particular function to look after the teaching profession. Syndicalism has developed amongst the teachers, and it is quite likely that before long there will be a journal issued on Syndicalist lines to specially circulate amongst the members of the profession. Just as a manual worker who is a Syndicalist looks to his Union to take control of the industry in which he works, making regulations and conditions for the better development of that industry, so will the teachers, through their professional organisation, discuss the best methods of obtaining superior results in the matters of education. Education will be entrusted to those who have made that their particular consideration, and they will have practically free scope to adopt which methods they think best, free from the vexatious interference of politicians whose chief preoccupation in educational affairs is not educational efficiency, but thrusting the dogmas of their particular sect into the minds of the children. As regards art, apart from the more elementary training in drawing and colours, it is a purely individual affair. The artist with his brush, or the sculptor with his chisel, each endeavour to express the ideal which they hold. Approval or disapproval of the multitude has no weight with these. They express themselves, that is all. One thing is certain, that as the increased leisure which all will have, will give a chance of development to the artistic faculties which the many may possess. There will be a possibility of a real and beneficial co-operation of the arts and crafts—a co-operation which production for profit makes almost impossible.

Printed and published by GUY BOWMAN, 4, Maude Terrace, Walthamstow, E.

The Syndicalist

VOL. 1. NO. 10.　　　LONDON, NOVEMBER, 1912.　　　MONTHLY, ONE PENNY.

THE MANIFESTO OF THE B.S.P.

The British Socialist Party must be in a bad way by the time they find it necessary to issue such a document as that appearing in the *Daily Herald* of October 31. One might have thought that the uniting of the forces of the old S.D.F. and the Clarionettes would have secured such a standing as to be altogether beyond the necessity for crying out against the comparatively insignificant efforts of us poor Syndicalists. They have their old-established papers, the national and local machinery of organisation, hundreds of trained propagandists, and a historical continuity of nearly thirty years. Surely such a combination of propagandist forces could well afford to ignore the doings of a "mere handful" like ourselves. Yet something or other has happened, or is happening, causing the B.S.P., or, to be more correct, some members of the Executive of the B.S.P., to exhibit much perturbation. I honestly assure them, in the name of our "handful," that we Syndicalists are completely indifferent as to their numbers. We certainly are not laying special siege to their forces and would disdain to ask any one of them to forswear their faith in the "all-saving power of Parliamentary action."

We are, however, concerned about the Trade Unionists, even though we may be the "hopeless failure" in influencing the British Trade Unionists that the B.S.P. manifesto says we are. Still, we frankly say we are wishful to influence them, and, according to our opportunities, we intend to continue to influence them; but it is quite open for the B.S.P. to do the same, and we don't at all complain of any efforts they make in this direction or any success they claim or achieve.

Indeed, we think there is ample room for the B.S.P. to do good work, and honestly wish them success in the doing of it. However large their membership may be, the number of non-members is many hundreds of times larger; so there is a very big field for work. It is true we Syndicalists are at work, and shall continue to work with the utmost zeal and goodwill. The fact is, whatever some members of the Executive of the B.S.P. may think, a growing percentage of the rank and file not only are not afraid of the terms DIRECT ACTION and SABOTAGE, but are recognising the absolute necessity of the first, and are not all averse to a well-directed use of the second. It is really so, let who will get exasperated. It is really so, let happen what may to the B.S.P. or any other organisation.

Those who know the real attitude of Syndicalists towards parliament, know full well that our ignoring of parliamentary methods is not as the manifesto states, "because the present Labour Party in the House of Commons has failed to voice the real needs of the people." Our objection is a much more serious one, it is that parliament is part of the decaying capitalist régime, and institution wholly unsuited to afford the workers opportunities of getting control of the industries and the wealth produced by the workers in these industries. We look upon parliament as utterly unsuited to the enabling of the workers to apply their own power in the controlling and ultimate owning of all wealth-producing agencies. All that many members of the B.S.P. claim for it is that it is an excellent platform for propaganda purposes, but frankly admit its uselessness for the purposes of revolution and reconstruction of society. We declare it to be not of the smallest value that there should be a few Socialist speeches made in such a place. Such speeches would give the workers no power nor would they send

fear to the hearts of the capitalists. Naturally the capitalists will fear nothing until they find they are losing the power to control the Working-Class. Our Syndicalist method is the encouragement of the Working-Class to control itself. There is absolutely no agency in existence or projected at all suitable to this great work except the industrial organisations of the workers. These unions at present have many faults, many officials are utterly and stupidly reactionary; even so, the unions have all the essentials for enabling the workers to actually function as controllers of wealth production, and, what is equally important—of wealth distribution. Industrial solidarity is the one and only all-powerful agency through which and by which work will be controlled, all unemployment solved, and capitalist exploitation stopped for ever.

TOM MANN.

SONG OF THE SYNDICALIST.

By JAS. W. K. LEIPER.

Our Fathers fought with pikes and swords,
With other weapons we
Assail the might of Labour's lords,
And struggle to be free!
Our banded might's our folded hands,
As our strike-signal ran;
And Lords of Labour and of lands
Curse deep the striking man.

We're beaten oft—but yet again,
Like giants from the earth,
We rise in mass, with might and main,
To wring our right of birth.
And each for all and all for each
Our cry shall ever run,
Till we the Socialist Commune reach
And Labour's fight is won.

Then join us, brothers of the mine,
The factory or the plough,
The dock, the wharf, the railway line,
Join up, the time is now!
The system rocks when Labour stands,
As we stand *still* to-day,
And the vision of our idle hands
Gives tyrants all dismay!

TOWARD THE LIGHT.

By NORMAN YOUNG

O men of Britain, still in bondage vile—
Still slaves, tho' centuries have onward
　　roll'd
Since Israel made bricks by Egypt's Nile
And hewed and drew to swell another's
　　gold.

No buttresses of property will give—
By blowing on rams' horns a feeble
　　blast
By asking meekly for the Right to Live
From those whose will it is to hold ye
　　fast

Ye are as chained as Roman chattel slave
Or Saxon serf when Curfew Bell was
　　toll'd
And still the fallen crumbs ye humbly
　　crave
And stand alarmed at being somewhat
　　bold!

Ah! Would ye struggle upward to the
　　light,
No longer beg, but organise—and fight!

AL ĈIUJ ESPERANTISTAJ GEKAMARADOJ.

KARAJ GEKAMARADOJ,

La redaktoro, bonvole permesis ke mi uzu iomete da sia valora spaco por Esperanto, ĉiumonate. Pro tiu ĉi mi estas certa ke ĉiu esperantista Sindikalisto kore dankos lin.

Mi intencas, do, en sekvontaj numeroj doni iun novajon, pri la frenda flanko de la movado, kiun mi povas obteni. Tiel, mi tre ĝojos se la gekamaradoj sendos al mi ian legajon, kiu, en ilia opinio, estas interesanta.

Mi ne ricevis multajn respondojn al mia letero en la Septembra numero. Cu mi estas la nura Sindikalista Esperantisto en Anglujo? Se ne, tuj skribu al mi.

Via, por la socia revolucio,
　　PERCY E. WELLS.
52, Mushroom Lane,
　　Sheffield.

War Against War

GREAT ANTI-MILITARIST DEMONSTRATION

GUSTAVE HERVÉ'S ELOQUENT APPEAL FOR PEACE.

At the Shoreditch Town Hall, on Monday, October 21, a magnificent meeting was held under the presidency of Mr. Tom Mann. Mr. Josiah Wedgewood and Mr. George Lansbury denounced war. The meeting was extremely enthusiastic, and the pronouncements of the various speakers against militarism were cheered to the echo. Our friend Gustave Hervé was in fine form, and this is in substance what he said:

M. GUSTAVE HERVÉ.

LADIES AND GENTLEMEN,—
COMRADES AND FRIENDS,—

I have come here on a request of my friends on the platform, who, like myself, have suffered imprisonment for expressing ideas that are common to most of us.

I have come here to propose to you an Entente Cordiale, but not one like that which was hatched a few years ago by our Governments, which they brought about amongst themselves without even consulting us.

It was made by the financiers and industry owners of the two countries against Germany, without even considering whether Germany had a right to a place under the sun, or whether she had a right to expand.

But our financiers wanted an ally on the Continent. Previously the two countries had been at daggers drawn with each other. We were "natural enemies." This state of affairs had lasted many years, and at last culminated in the Fashoda affair, when we nearly went to war with each other.

Then M. Delcasse, our Minister for Foreign Affairs, or rather the financiers who controlled him, found a solution, which would satisfy both and be a guarantee of peace between them for the future.

He said we have come to conflict over the occupation of Egypt; very good, now

let us see if there is not a way out of our trouble. You English do not like the Germans, who are your trade rivals; let us unite as against them; we will allow you a clear field in Egypt, whilst we must be left free to open up Morocco to our civilisation. They agreed to this division of spoils; hence the Entente Cordiale between "Perfidious Albion" and "La Belle France." The politicians talk of localising the war, of confining the outbreak to the Balkans, but I see three places where the flames of the conflagration might burst through.

First of all, there is Russia. The Czar is surrounded by Pan-Slavists, who constitute a veritable Camarilla around him. They want war; their profession is war; both glory and material gain may result from one.

Even if the governing clique do not desire war; there is the dangerous possibility of the naïve peasants entering upon a Holy Crusade to assist their brother Slavs, who are of the same religious faith, against the infidel Mohammedan Turks.

Then there is Austria. The Grand Duke, who really rules, is also surrounded by a group of military, clerical, and financial advisers who for years have desired to possess Salonika, as a window from which to look over the blue waters of the Mediterranean, even as Russia wants Constantinople as a warm-water port and to promote her interests in Persia en route for India.

Then in Asia Minor there are important works to be undertaken, the Bagdad Railway to be built and ports to be made. This, again, will bring the English and German financial interests into conflict.

Thus, if war breaks out, there will be England with France, and the ally of

(*Continued on page 6.*)

JOTTINGS.

JOTTINGS.

TRANSPORT WORKERS' AMALGAMATION COMMITTEE.

Sam Roden, secretary of the above Committee, writes saying that in order to raise funds they have printed a number of books of tickets to sell to sympathisers. The money is wanted to be used for circularising the whole of the branches of the Transport Unions. Write for them to Sam Roden, 7, Holland Road, West Ham, E.

THE ONLY MOVEMENT DISPLAYING ANY ENTHUSIASM.

But where is there a movement with any life in it? Where is there a movement with any real message, or any genuine faith in itself?

Take what is said to be the most advanced and revolutionary movement, and really, about the only one that is displaying any enthusiasm: Syndicalism. Well, there is only a handful of men who are possessed with the divine power of the agitator, who understand anything about the philosophy, and roots of Syndicalism. The rest are attracted and enthused because there is evidence of a real fight, but they have only yet a vague idea of what Syndicalism is. However, they are showing some signs of life.—*Daily Herald.*

ENGINEERING AND SHIPBUILDING AMALGAMATION COMMITTEE.

A meeting of this Committee will be held on Saturday, November 16. All interested in this work should write for fuller particulars to the hon. secretary, W. F. Watson, 26, Priory Road, Acton Green, W.

NOTICE TO SYMPATHISERS.

In order to make the work of the I.S.E.L. effective, we must be able to reach every Trade Union Branch; therefore send all Trade Union Reports and Branch Lists to the General Secretary.

SYNDICALIST LECTURES.

Trade Unions, Trades' Councils, or Labour Societies desiring to know more about Syndicalism can have speakers attend their meetings. Travelling expenses only are asked for. Write General Secretary, I.S.E.L.

GENERAL PROPAGANDA FUND.

Comrade Joseph Lane sends 5s. to open a General Propaganda Fund, because if the people won't come to you, you must go to them, and you must have cash to do so. I hope many will imitate him.

LEAFLET PROPAGANDA FUND.

Comrade Joseph Lane sends another 5s. to start the above fund, and wants to see hundreds of thousands of small leaflets issued on all questions from time to time for free distribution at all meetings. Now, roll up in your thousands with the cash, pounds, shillings, or pence from everyone according to his ability, that we may live to see the time when everyone shall receive according to his needs. The first leaflet of this kind will appear during this month.

THE "WEEKLY SYNDICALIST" FUND.

Wanted, one thousand subscribers to pay down 6s. 6d. each by January 1, 1913, as their year's subscription for a copy by post each week.

This would make a fund to start the paper of £325.

Wanted, one thousand sympathisers to pay down all they can afford by January 1, 1913, to start and keep going the paper for the first twelve months.

Wanted, one thousand Syndicalists to guarantee amounts of 1s. to 10s. per month for the first twelve months to give the paper a fair chance.

Wanted, one thousand earnest, sincere men who, for the love of the cause, will sell and distribute the paper week by week.

Contributions towards the above fund received during this month will be acknowledged in our next issue.

I have got a lot to talk to you about, but I am too busy to do so now, I will next time. Good luck!

GUY BOWMAN.

The Syndicalist

EDITED UNDER THE AUSPICES OF

The Industrial Syndicalist Education League

Offices—

4, MAUDE TERRACE, WALTHAMSTOW,
LONDON, E.

MONTHLY – ONE PENNY.

Post Paid Subscription—

Great Britain or Abroad ... 12 months 1s. 6d.

Bundle Rates—

1s. 6d. per quire, Carriage Paid.

The receipt of a Sample Copy is an invitation to Subscribe.

NOVEMBER, 1912.

GUSTAVE HERVE.

Some men are doomed to be misunderstood, even by their friends. This is the case with Gustave Hervé.

All the Parliamentary Socialists, particularly those of the reformist section, are triumphantly shouting that Hervé has been converted to parliamentary action, and they applaud him accordingly, whilst the Anarchists are denouncing him for the same reason.

"Extremes meet," says the proverb, but they usually meet when they are both wrong, and this is the case respecting Hervé, for Hervé is not what either of them claim him to be.

Hervé is a Blanquist, and August Blanqui believed in parliamentary action, but also in Insurrection. He believed in an economic organisation, but that organisation was to have an autonomous existence.

Hervé does not believe in building up a revolutionary Union movement, to be used merely as a voting machine. He does not believe that the co-operative societies should be merely milch cows for the politicians. He does not believe that the Social Revolution will be inaugurated by the vote. He is as firmly convinced as ever he was that the Revolution will come through the fight in the streets. Whilst his new policy of dual organisation resembles very much that of the S.L.P. and that of some members of the B.S.P., he differs from them in his belief that the Revolution will come by Insurrection.

As far as we are concerned, we must confess that we are totally unable to follow him in his imitation of Blanqui, who lived many years ago, and who spent forty years in prison. To the men of '48, the gaining of the franchise appeared to be a great stride towards equality, especially as their idea of a new Society was based upon Society itself; but as our ideas of the Society of the future are based upon Industry, no franchise of any size is of interest to us.

We are not concerned with running an anti-parliamentary propaganda; it would not be worth the candle. We are quite willing to let men vote for Socialist and Labour candidates if they so wish; that is their concern, not ours. In fact, we do not object any more to that than if a man declares himself to be a teetotaler or takes us to have a small Guinness with him. But when the self-same politicians would have us believe that all our activity must be subordinated to their parade of the ballot box, we object.

When in his speech Hervé talks of an ever-increasing Socialist Party in parliament, *under the control of its members outside*, he must have forgotten that he came from France, Where was the Party's control over Millerand, Viviani, Briand?

Oh, yes; they, like a crowd of lesser lights, can all *be under the control of the Party*, till they have been elected and have become politically celebrated; *then* starts the procession out of the Party. The first thing is to rebel against party discipline, and become "Independent" Socialists; then the next step is to go into the "Radical Party," and run the whole gamut to governmental opportunism, and perhaps, if lucky, to government position.

No, Comrade Hervé, we have seen the Labour Party of Australia introduce conscription and break strikes; we have seen your fellow-countrymen enter parliament and then betray us; we have seen the Italian Socialist M.P.'s land themselves in the Radical reform camp; and we have seen our Labour Party at the beck and call of a Liberal Government that we detest as much as you do yours; we decline to trot in double harness with politicians and be driven by adventurers.

There are men like Hervé whose honesty of purpose no one can question, and whose disinterestedness is obvious to all. There are men like George Lans-

bury, who, as Hervé, is but one amongst thousands in the parliamentary scramble, but there are others. And the others outweigh, in power and influence these honest champions.

Syndicalism seeks to unite the workers in their unions and unite the unions, so that they shall be able to control the productive forces which they operate; then, by Direct Action in all its forms, they will be able to destroy the power of the exploiting class, and live in equity and peace.

Direct Action breeds self-reliance, initiative, and sacrifice, all of which are necessary for the accomplishment of a great task. Parliamentarism is the school for making troops of sheep-like voters, who all depend upon someone else to do something for them. It is a continuous delegation of power and responsibility to others. Syndicalism, with its policy of Direct Action, teaches the workers to shoulder their own burdens and accomplish their own emancipation.

As to Gustave Hervé himself, he remains our friend as in the past. Whatever his change of tactics in his endeavour to bring about the Social Revolution, we are as convinced of his honesty of purpose as we are of George Lansbury's. If there were a few more men of the stamp of these, the work ahead would proceed a hundred times quicker than it does at present, when there are so many who prefer to tear one another to pieces, in many cases out of personal jealousy.

OUR COMING CONFERENCES.

During this month we are holding two conferences—one in London, one in Manchester. Both will be followed by large public meetings at which the aims and methods of the Syndicalists will be expounded.

At the conferences themselves a series of resolutions will be submitted which, if carried and acted upon, will create a militant working-class organisation—a body that will be far superior to any one yet existing in this country as a fighting force. Ample provision will also be made for a definite revolutionary propaganda. The various functions of the different Union organisations will be outlined, and a strenuous attempt made to realign the workers' forces so that they shall be effective in the class struggle. These conferences, undoubtedly, will mark the beginning of a new epoch in the Labour Movement of this country.

All the progressive workers are acting in co-operation with us. The most energetic of the men on the various Amalgamation Committees are our friends, and ours is an effective team-work. Likewise, the advanced members of the Trades Councils see eye to eye with us in the matter of forming a National Federation of Trades Councils.

The Unions are destined to become the most powerful factors for economic and social betterment in the workers' lives. Our conferences will endeavour to give the Union movement that power that results from intelligent and purposeful organisation. Waste of effort will be eliminated by a real co-ordination of the different sections with their different functions.

Methods of combat will be considered, forms of organisation remodelled, and a wave of educational enthusiasm sent over the whole working-class movement. In our common capacity of wage-workers we shall confer and act.

Not the least important step will be the proposal for the establishment of an International Syndicalist body, similar to that which the political Socialists already possess in the shape of the International Socialist Bureau. Unemployment and militarism will be considered and steps taken to check both of these evils. Hurrah for the pioneers!

A SONG OF SOCIALISM.

By ANNA LINCOLN.

Brave hearts uniting,
Dark Ignorance fighting,
Its Selfishness blighting,
So move we along.

Holy things adoring,
Selfless Love outpouring,
Upward ever soaring,
This—this is our song :

That all true men are Brothers ;
All women, Sisters, Mothers.
O, make it known to others
That Love is Life—is all.

Love's service freely given,
A Message is from Heaven.
Then let your Doubts be riven,
And rally as we call !

Our Song is life, not self-renewing,
Love's Roses we are strewing,
And Wisdom we are wooing ;
O ! hear our joyous Song !

Come ! help to make Life brighter
By making burdens lighter ;
Yea ! come and be A Fighter
In this our Righteous Throng !

Open Letter to the Members of the British Socialist Party.

COMRADES AND FELLOW-WORKERS,

Most of us who are members of the Industrial Syndicalist Education League were, and many are now, members of one or other of the bodies that fused together to constitute the B.S.P.

For many years most of us had given our energy, time, and money to the advocacy of Socialism. Whilst members of the former organisations, chiefly the S.D.F., no one impeached our honesty or doubted our sincerity. Even our opponents in the Party recognised our honesty of purpose. *They* all knew that we were fighting Capitalism to the best of our knowledge and ability. This being so, how comes it that *Justice* of September 28th can so mendaciously pretend otherwise ? In that paper appeared the following :—

MORE SYNDICALISM.

On Monday the Executive of the Sailors' and Firemen's Union again entertained Sir Walter Runciman as their guest at their annual dinner. Mr. J. Havelock Wilson presided, and Sir Walter Runciman said that the sailors and firemen had been well organised, but the men were not going to get all their own way. They now knew that it was good to have a Shipping Federation, but also a strong and sound Seamen's Union. He believed that the majority of shipowners recognised that. To make a seafaring life more attractive he thought they should pay better wages to the men. Prosperity had come, and he did not think that next year many owners would refuse the men a share in that prosperity. That is all quite in keeping with the theories of Syndicalism ; no "class" war ; no antagonism between the exploiting capitalist and the exploited workman, but a combination and agreement between the two—between the monopolist and the retainers, to prey upon society ; to force up rates and freights and prices, and then for the monopolist to share a little of the extra swag with his slaves. That is the ideal of Syndicalism —ownership by Syndicates—as against that of Socialism, or ownership by society.

This is a remarkable example of the deliberate lying by which "the organ of the Social Democracy " seeks to discredit Syndicalism. It is unfortunate that our worst enemies should be those "of our own household." It is unfortunate—for them. On this point, the distortion of Syndicalism, note the touching example of mutual agreement which exists between those loving friends Philip Snowden, M.P., and Harry Quelch, would-be M.P., H. M. Hyndman, the rejected of Burnley, and Ramsay MacDonald, the elected of Leicester.

Thus does "adversity breed strange bedfellows."

The paragraph is unsigned ; but it would not be difficult to guess, fairly accurately, who indited or inspired it. It looks very like the work of an individual who, in the editorial pages of *Justice* several years ago, declared that that very live organisation, the Industrial Workers of the World, was duly dead and buried ; though, strange to say, when W. D. Haywood, one of the chief organisers of the I.W.W., the said defunct organisation, came to England, it was the S.D.P. that fêted him.

However, the paragraph provides striking evidence of the serious moral degeneration into which certain leading exponents of the B.S.P. have fallen. The object of it is clear enough. It is to create, if possible, a prejudice in the minds of the members of the B.S.P. against Syndicalism, to arouse a hostility which shall prevent them inquiring into the matter fairly for themselves. This kind of thing is on all fours with the contemptible policy of some of the lower Capitalist papers in misrepresenting Socialism. That *Justice* could sink to that level would have been unthinkable in the fighting days of the old S.D.F. Yet it is so. That paragraph proves the fact beyond dispute.

We readily acknowledge the great services to Socialism that were so freely, so readily, and so unselfishly given by the "Old Guard " of Social Democracy. They did a great work, and a brave work, in their time.

We freely admit our indebtedness to their workings and speeches for much of our earlier education in Socialism.

It is well known that in most cases, after a certain age, a person's mind refuses to respond to, or be receptive of, new ideas. This is due to the gradual decay of the brain as old age advances. Thus we did not expect to be understood, or appreciated, by those who are unable to think in terms other than those of twenty or thirty years ago. We were prepared to accept their attitude towards us, and to charitably excuse it on these grounds. But when we find a moral as well as mental degeneration expressing itself in venomous falsehood we are compelled to protest vigorously.

It is not necessary for us to reply at any great length to the falsehood of that paragraph. It is sufficient just to print it as it was published, to leave to our readers who understand our position to draw their own conclusions.

It provides striking proof of the evil effects of *Parliamentarism* in the B.S.P. It also indicates the bitter disappointment of the S.D.F. (S.D.P. now B.S.P.) place-seekers at their repeated failure to get into Parliament. We realise, now, that had the S.D.F. been successful in getting its candidates into Parliament, they, the S.D.F. (or B.S.P. as it now is), would have gone the way of the I.L.P., not to mention the even more horrible example of the non-Socialist Labour Party.

We Syndicalists have quite as much objection to any union entertaining Sir Walter Runciman, or any other representative of the capitalist class, to dinners as our friends of the B.S.P. have. That the Sailors' and Firemen's Union should have entertained Sir Walter Runciman, under the presidency of Havelock Wilson, assisted by the ineffable MacGhee, and listened patiently to and approvingly (so far as we know from the paragraph) to the sentiments expressed, only confirms what has been said over and over again by Syndicalists as regards old-style Trades Unionism, and the essential treachery of non-class-conscious Labour misleaders.

As the idea of Syndicalism spreads among the younger, up-to-date members of the B.S.P. they will realise more and more the necessity for getting rid of the "Old Guard." If they don't, the "Old Guard" will destroy the B.S.P. Grayson, Leonard Hall, and the younger element are more advanced in this matter.

With the final remark that we as Syndicalists are not opposed to the B.S.P., as it affords an outlet to many middle-class people who feel constrained to do something for the workers.

We appeal to you, comrades of the B.S.P., to make a clean sweep of the mentally and, as it also appears, morally degenerate "Old Guard" leaders. These, unfortunately, have served their turn and outlived their usefulness. They should be definitely retired before they succeed in destroying completely that respect with which we would wish to regard them in their old age.

Do not let the "Old Guard" stand in the way of those who are now becoming the "Advance Guard." Step in line with that younger, more militant section who support Industrial Solidarity and Direct Action, and remember that no Revolution was ever made or ever will be made by Parliament alone. The final issue has always been fought outside. Now, as in the past, force will have to be the deciding factor.

NATIONAL FEDERATION
OF
INDUSTRIAL UNIONS.

When the Trade Unionists allowed the Government to impose the Insurance Act upon them, they accepted a measure that was specially designed to rob them of all militancy. The General Federation of Trade Unions that should be pre-eminently a fighting force has become to all intents and purposes a gigantic Insurance Society. The sumptuous offices in Adelphi Terrace, overlooking the Thames Embankment, are filled with insurance clerks—the Federation has become like a Prudential.

As the General Federation of Trade Unions promises to become less and less of a factor in economic warfare, it rests with the militant workers to decide how best to re-align their forces, so as to give them unity and power.

The need for greater unity has been felt, and the desire for a more militant policy has been expressed, and a number of energetic workers in various industries have constituted themselves the provisional committee for Amalgamating Existing Unions.

We, as Syndicalists, welcome these efforts at a closer union and more fighting policy. We urge all our members and sympathisers to partake in this work.

Out of the original provisional committee have been formed various other committees.

These committees exist at present for the building industry, the printing industry, the metal industry. There has also been formed a Transport Workers' Committee for amalgamating all unions connected with transport. This body was formed independently of the original provisional committee, but will most probably affiliate to it. A committee is also at work amongst the clothing workers.

If the men who are on these committees would look ahead, they could easily foresee a most necessary and useful function being performed by these bodies, that function being the reorganisation of the unions on revolutionary lines.

The existing machinery of the General Federation of Trade Unions has become simply an adjunct of the Insurance Commission. Now, seeing that many unions in themselves are approved societies, there is nothing to prevent the members of these unions amalgamating with others in a fighting body. Thus, supposing that seven of the unions connected with transport are now individually approved societies, that is no obstacle to those unions amalgamating into one fighting organisation. Thus, these various amalgamation committees can fix their object primarily in the amalgamation of the Trade Unions in their industries; secondly, to secure a federation of the national amalgamated industrial unions once that amalgamation has taken place. If the various industries are tackled as they should be, and amalgamation committees formed in each for the purpose of uniting the various Trade Unions within an industry, there should within a reasonable time be formed a Federation of Industrial Unions. This Federation to be composed of a number of delegates from each national industrial union, and could be the real fighting force of the combined workers.

This form of organisation would guarantee complete solidarity inside of any one industry, and would prepare the way for united national action of all industries.

When these amalgamations take place great care must be used not to destroy the craft unit. Whilst machinery has made great strides, and tends toward the elimination of craft destruction, many problems of a craft technical nature still remain, and are likely to do so. Thus, for example, painters, as painters, have certain professional matters entirely their own. They have to devise new and fresh schemes of colour decoration; to value the distempers, paints, enamels, etc., that are being invented, to discuss and consider how best to increase technical efficiency of the painters. Because these industrial unions will not be formed for the fun of the thing, but to have a better fighting organisation on the one hand, and to be so organised *that the workers in those industries can take control of and operate them through their unions.* The workers when they obtain control of industry, will want the highest technical efficiency from all. Thus the painters, as painters, in professional technical matters, have a craft interest. But their craft interest ceases. When it is a question of fighting the employers, it is not so much as painters as it is in their capacity common to *all* workers of being wage-slaves. Fighting ceases to be a question of craft; it becomes the greater economic question of class.

Thus each craft is entitled to craft autonomy in purely craft matters, but all *fighting* must be the business of the Amalgamated Building Workers' Industrial Union. *All* crafts in the building industry have to fight the same employer. Fights are industrial and class. Education and training is technical and craft. A painter has technical craft interests with all other painters in the country as painters. He has also immediate economic interests with all other workers in the building industry. Thus he should hold a card in the painters' section of the local Building Workers' Industrial Union. This will give him a connection with all the other organised members of his craft for professional, technical, mental advancement. He is linked with other workers in the same industry as wage-workers for fighting purposes. The National Industrial Union should be federated with all national industrial unions for class solidarity. The various national unions could constitute a real fighting body: The National Federation of Industrial Unions.

UNITY IS STRENGTH!

STRENGTH UNITED IS STRONGER!

Trade Unions Amalgamating—Trades Councils Federating.

WHY NOT CONFEDERATE?

AMALGAMATION COMMITTEES ACTIVE.

The agitation for amalgamating the various trade unions in an industry into one union is making splendid progress. Through the instrumentality of

THE BUILDING TRADES' CONSOLIDATION COMMITTEE.

the following societies have been balloted on amalgamation with the following results:—

	For Amalgamation.	Against Amalgamation.
Amalgamated Carpenters and Joiners	18,690	10,593
Operative Bricklayers' Society	4,371	763
United Operative Plumbers	1,606	291
Operative Stonemasons	1,209	61
National Association of Plasterers	1,738	310
Builders' Labourers (National)	756	2
United Builders' Labourers	2,369	40
Bricklayers (Manchester Unity)	427	61
Street Masons and Paviors	152	104
Painters and Decorators (London and Provincial Federation)	223	1
	31,541	12,156
Votes for Amalgamation	31,541	
Votes against Amalgamation	12,156	
Majority in favour	19,385	

As a result of the above gratifying figures, a conference of all the unions concerned is to be held soon, when a definite scheme of amalgamation and working rules will be drawn up, which will be submitted to the members for their approval or otherwise. Societies can still obtain ballot papers for taking a vote on amalgamation, and should apply at once to C. W. Bowerman, Secretary of the Parliamentary Committee of the Trade Union Congress. The committee urge societies to take a ballot at once to get a real united building workers' union. For further particulars write the honorary secretary, G. Hicks, 16, Joubert Street, Battersea, S.W.

ENGINEERING AND SHIPBUILDING AMALGAMATION COMMITTEE.

A very successful conference of trade unionists in the Engineering and Shipbuilding industry, convened by the Provisional Committee for Amalgamating Existing Trade Unions, was held on Saturday, September 25th, at Workmen's Hall, Stratford. W. Scott (A.S.C. & J.) presided, and J. A. Stubbings (Saddle and Harness Makers) gave a short but lucid address on the need for amalgamation. A very interesting discussion followed, the audience showing great enthusiasm on the matter of solidarity. W. F. Watson (A.S.E.) then moved the following resolution, which was adopted unanimously:

, That the trade unionists here assembled, recognising that the time has arrived for a closer unity amongst the unions, hereby pledge themselves to work in the branches and workshops advocating the amalgamation of trade unions on the principle of one industry, one union, one card. To further this object, we here and now agree to form an Engineering and Shipbuilding Amalgamation Committee.

W. F. Watson (A.S.E.) was elected hon. secretary, with D. Armstrong as assistant secretary. An executive committee, comprising one man for each union, was also elected, with instructions to call another conference and outline a plan of campaign. All active trade unionists in Engineering and Shipbuilding industry should help us link up the trade union movement. For speakers and information write W. F. Watson, 26, Priory Road, Acton Green, W.

PRINTING TRADES' AMALGAMATION COMMITTEE.

The Printing Trades' Amalgamation Committee have been successful in getting a national conference called on this subject. The future of the movement is in the hands of one or two provincial unions, who do not seem anxious to proceed further. But the provisional committee is building up an organisation of associates throughout the United Kingdom, and establishing committees in the various towns, to move the unions and urge the executives forward. All printers, of all unions, who are in favour of amalgamation should send their name and address in full, stating their union, to the hon. secretary, Chas. F. Woodward, 76, Tylecroft Road, Norbury, S.W.

MINERS' UNOFFICIAL REFORM COMMITTEE.

The organisation of linked groups of the rank and file within the existing organisations, and otherwise to cover the whole of the Coal, Ore, Slate, Stone, Clay, Salt Mining or Quarrying Industry of Great Britain, having for objects the watching and pressing of the interests of the rank and file by genuine combined action, and not through officials or intermediatory Boards.

Fellow-Workers,

We, the undersigned, believe that the time has arrived when the whole of the Workers in any industry should be in one organisation, with a view to the carrying on of that industry in the interests of all the community, instead of, as to-day, in the interests of a few shareholders.

Since the publication of "The Miners' Next Step" by a group of Working Miners in South Wales, a movement has arisen through the whole of the Coalfield, and we wish to see the Workers of the Durham Coalfield step into line with their fellows. We realise the magnitude of our task, and we believe that this object cannot be attained by a mere change of leaders, but by each individual member taking his part in the work. We are not, therefore, concerned with electing official representatives upon any Executive Committee, but of putting before the rank and file our ideal by aid of Local Groups and Conference, the first of which was held at the Workmen's Club Hall, Chopwell, on Saturday, October 12, at 3 p.m. Chairman: Tom Barron, St. Hilda Lodge, South Shields. Secretary, Will Lawther, 25, Trent Street, Chopwell, Co. Durham.

TRANSPORT WORKERS' AMALGAMATION COMMITTEE.

This committee has made much progress. Outdoor meetings have been held in Canning Town, East Greenwich, Custom House, and other districts where the message of the Transport Workers' Union has been delivered to large and enthusiastic audiences of transport workers. The hon. secretary of the committee, Sam Roden, has been in correspondence with the various London branches of transport trade unions. Arrangements have been made to hold a demonstration in the Public Hall, Canning Town, with Tom Mann as chief speaker, on October 24th. All the general secretaries of the transport Unions have been invited to attend. The committee are now ready to assist in the establishing of local and provincial committees. All transport workers who desire to see amalgamation brought about should communicate with the hon. secretary, Sam Roden, , Holland Road, West Ham, E.

TRADES COUNCILS MOVING.

Following upon the publication of an article in the February issue of THE SYNDICALIST, considerable discussion and correspondence has ensued. Various Trades Councils have discussed this matter of forming a National Federation of Trades Councils. In many instances they hardly seem to wish to take the initiative in this matter. Here are some expression of opinion:

WALTHAMSTOW TRADES AND LABOUR COUNCIL,

68, Springfield Road, Walthamstow.

October 11th, 1912.

Dear Sir,—The above Council have for some time considered that the Trades Councils are weak and ineffective owing to the fact that no organisation exists among them. Further, we consider the time ripe for a move toward the establishment of a National Federation of Trades Councils, thereby linking up the whole of the Trades Councils of the country. This would add strength to the Trade Union movement by bringing the whole of the progressive Trade Unionists into close touch with each other.

The above resolution was passed at the last meeting of the Council, and I was instructed to forward same to the Editor of THE SYNDICALIST with a request for publication.—I remain, yours fraternally,

A. G. TUFTON.

RUNCORN AND DISTRICT TRADES AND LABOUR COUNCIL,

27, Ellesmere Street.

August 13th, 1912.

Dear Sir,—The above Council have had for several months before them the question of "A National Federation of Trades Councils," which was inspired by your article in the February number of THE SYNDICALIST, and have at last passed a resolution approving the formation of such a Federation. Please send me any information that may be useful.—Yours fraternally,

J. BANCROFT.

To Mr. Guy Bowman.

In addition to the letters printed above there are a large number of other Trades Councils that are in sympathy with this idea, though they have not yet sent us any official communication to confirm the verbal reports. In London alone there are *Wimbledon, Woolwich, West Ham,* and *Willesden. Wrexham* is in sympathy with us. There must be many more Trades Councils, both in London and the provinces, whose members are in favour of a national federation being formed. The best way in which this can be accomplished is for the various councils throughout the United Kingdom to pass a resolution definitely stating their agreement with the proposals. These resolutions, when carried, should be sent on to THE SYNDICALIST for publication. We shall be only too pleased to assist this work of unification by tabulating the resolutions forwarded to us, informing the various Councils as to the number desiring to form such a national federation. We offer our services in this work and hope that the Councils will avail themselves of our good offices for this measure. If there is anything like the good response that there should be, we shall be willing to bring about a *Conference of Delegates of Trades Councils,* in order that the *National Federation of Trades Councils shall speedily* become an accomplished fact, and by this means the whole of the trade union movement strengthened, its agitation increased, and the welfare of the working class promoted. Send your letters to

Guy Bowman,

4, Maude Terrace,

Walthamstow,

London, E.

NATIONAL FEDERATION
OF
TRADES COUNCILS.

In our article in the first column of this page, dealing with the General Federation of Trade Unions, we show how a craftsman (a painter) can be linked up with all the painters, as painters, for technical and craft matters, and how he is invited as a wage-worker with all other workers in the building industry, and through the National Federation of Industrial Unions with all other organised workers nationally and internationally. On the other hand, all local industrial unions should form a local industrial or trades council, affiliating to them where they exist, or forming them where they do not. By uniting the movement in this way it would be a simple matter for the organised workers in a given locality to have a central trades hall. Here could be rooms for the meetings of the different sections of the unions, committee rooms, and so forth. With a large room where delegates from every trade could meet and constitute the Trades Council, wherein matters of interest to all workers could be discussed.

The Trades Councils, seeing that they group all the workers in a given locality on the basis of their class interests, should be the real centres of union agitation and propaganda. Instead of being the adjunct of the Independent Labour Party, or any other politicians, revolutionary workers should endeavour to make them the place to which to focus working-class thought and action. Seeing that they deal with the general interest of the workers as workers, they should be the starting-points for preaching the class struggle, fomenting that struggle, raising it to its utmost revolutionary height as expressed in the Social General Strike for the Expropriation of the Capitalist Class. There is this important duty for them to undertake now; they have the still more important function to fulfil in future society—that is, they are to take the place of the municipal councils of to-day and form the industrial councils of the future. In outlining this function the workers can see a definite organic growth towards the organisation of a Labour Commonwealth. The Trades Councils will perform the local administrative work in a working-class society. Through these bodies will the needs of the inhabitants of a given locality be stated, and satisfied. Through the Trades Councils the tactics adopted by the capitalists in the district covered by each of these councils can be thoroughly discussed by the members who assemble in them, but there must also be carried on a systematic and intelligent campaign for the constant reinforcement of the workers in both their trade struggles and their individual struggles with local capitalists.

Towards this assumption by the Trades Councils of their proper functions, an important start has been made. There are at present four federations of existing Trades Councils—the North-Eastern Federation, the Yorkshire Federation, the Lancashire and Cheshire Federation, and the South-Western Federation. The fact that in the London territory there is no such Federation—although there are no less than a score of scattered Trades Councils—is sufficient proof that the systematic co-ordinating of the Trades Councils for effective action has been sadly neglected. Those areas where there are a number of Trades Councils who have not yet combined into District Federations should do so. These District Federations should be made something better than a happy hunting ground for politicians. Not only should the Trades Councils combine within a given district, but they should line up nationally, and form a National Federation of Trades Councils. Elsewhere on this page will be found communications from various Trades Councils, expressing their views upon the matter. Let us set about the formation of a National Federation of Trades Councils immediately.

Then progressive trade unionists have a splendid work before them in order to make the union movement that power for improving the workers' conditions that it should be. There are the amalgamation committees to be joined, their work to be aided in the different branches of the various unions. Members are to be educated to understand the necessity for amalgamating the various trade unions within an industry into one body. Then to see to the formation of a National Federation of Industrial Unions.

Then, to complete the work of unification and to obtain the greatest solidarity possible, and still more important, to be building up properly our structure of a future Labour Commonwealth which is to take the place of present-day capitalist society, there are the Trades Councils to be formed where they do not exist, District Federations to link them up within their various areas, and a National Federation to be formed in order to have a cohesive body of the Trades Councils. Thus national campaigns and agitations could be more effective; news of the different localities exchanged; the whole tone of the working-class movment raised; and its members invigorated by these bodies, which must have a joint committee formed of delegates from the National Federation of Industrial Unions and from the National Federation of Trades Councils, thus constituting the General Confederation of Labour, whose work should be the creation, strengthening, and unification of Labour's forces, the education, propaganda, and action to win Labour's Emancipation.

OUR STUDENTS' COLUMN.

We receive many more articles than we can publish. Many are from comrades new in the movement. We do not want articles on theory. We want articles containing information, on strikes in different districts of the unions, of the changes of industry, of the employers' organisations and methods. Our space is limited, but we will print one or more each month for our students. They will note how their articles have been altered and adapted. We wish to give every encouragement to those converts who desire to assist us if they will bear the above points in mind.

SOME FUNDAMENTAL POINTS.

By BURDETT LUDLAM.

The object I have in view in writing this article is to place before the readers of the SYNDICALIST the fundamental basis of Syndicalism. All movements have a fundamental basis from which to work. Objects or ideals do not fall from the heavens, but are formulated by people who generally have in view a means of action by which they can eventually arrive at a desired state in which they are socially and economically raised. Now, Syndicalism finds its basis in the direct desires of the working class; that it is the natural outgrowth of working-class antagonism towards the owners of the means whereby the workers obtain their bread and butter. Without the wage-earners there cannot possibly be any Syndicalist movement. If our doctrine of revolutionary Trade Unionism were not the outcome of the tendencies of the working-class movement then it would not be genuine, because it would have been originated by people of another class in society who have nothing more and nothing less than a class object in view of attainment. But it is, of course, not the case. A capitalist cannot be a Syndicalist. A Syndicalist must be a wage-receiver.

The Socialist political, so-called working-class, party is not a movement exclusively for workers of the fields, factories, and mines. A capitalist can be a Social-Democrat and have nothing to fear, whatsoever, in his or her lifetime. In fact, the Social-Democratic parties all the world over "stink" with the middle class. These "working-class" parties are now in the control of capitalists of the sentimental character, and therefore these parties are not proletarian parties, but are the debating societies of the sagacious politicians. One can easily account, then, why it is that Social-Democracy has failed to be of any benefit to the workers, in so far as emancipation is concerned. All movements that are political and that arrange themselves under working-class banners are bound to fail, because they have, and will come into contact with, particular circumstances that force the leaders into compromise with the capitalist parties, in order to obtain a few pettifogging reforms in order to give appearance that the party is making progress. And all these reforms are of no material benefit to the working men and women whatsoever.

The Syndicalist, therefore, is a wage-earner who has learnt the lesson of political cajolery. He therefore ceases to rely on political action, and he declares that he is non-Parliamentary; that he is an industrialist in the revolutionary meaning of the word. It is now obvious that no capitalist, whether he be big or small, can be a Syndicalist. It does not matter who he be, if he does not earn a living at the bench, in the factory, or in the field, or in the mine, he cannot even claim to be a Syndicalist. There are, I know, a number of men and women in England as the present moment who are posing as Revolutionary Syndicalists, and are actually advocating its doctrines in speech and by pen! They are not Syndicalists! I certainly do not want to deliberately throw ice at them, because I will readily admit that they are no doubt in earnest. But it is essential that it should be pointed out here that the other words for Industrial Syndicalism are Revolutionary Trade Unionism. Now, it is quite clear that a middle-class person cannot obtain membership in a Trade Union, and, therefore, I hope that the reader will now quite understand that the Syndicalist movement is absolutely proletarian. It behoves the organised workers, then, to steer their own course, and not allow middle-class bigots to trade upon the cause of emancipation. We have, then, arrived at this contention, that Revolutionary Trade Unionism (Syndicalism) is not for University students, it is not for middle-class exploiters, and it is not for capitalist philanthropists. These kind of people have found their footing inside the so-called workers' political parties, but they cannot, and will not, find their way into the workers' industrial movement.

Syndicalism, as stated above, is the outcome of the economic antagonism in society, and therefore it is only by working-class direct action that the industrial co-operative commonwealth can be realised. But I must say in all fairness that no doubt there are a number of middle-class men and women who are sincere in the interest of the workers' movement, but we must declare that it would be certainly doing more harm than good if we were to allow these well-intentioned people to take in hands the reins of our economic coach.

There is a glaring fact staring us in the face, and that is the complete failure of the Social-Democratic movement. It is in point of illustration that I will here relate why Social-Democracy has so ignominiously degenerated in influence. We know that when it first started on its career it gained a deal of ground in the political world, simply because it was then not absolutely handled by middle-class adventurers. But no sooner did the middle class obtain a footing in the party than it began to lose its political force and significance, and now the workers' political ship is a wreck upon merciless waves.

The Syndicalist movement is not destined to failure in the way that Social-Democracy has, because those of the working class who have a spark of intelligence have now realised that it is treachery to allow capitalists to take part in their affairs. We have learnt the mistakes of the past, and we are now building up the great invulnerable working-class unionism that is going to carry out to the full extent the social revolution. Now that Syndicalism is an established doctrine we must emphatically refuse the help or advice of middle-class muddlers in the great and ennobling work or duty that we have before us. On the appreciation of this course of action the workers, not only of the United Kingdom, but of the whole of the capitalised world, will gain their economic freedom from wage-slavery. We will steer directly through the iniquities of the present epoch in history. The ship of Liberty is already awaiting us in the harbour of Justice, and now the crew is being formed that is to do the world's greatest work.

Education is now the only thing that is required. There are sufficient self-contained men in these islands who will strongly march under the banner of revolution. I do not believe that the transformation will be the outcome of

ethical reasoning with the exploiters. The exploiters have not got any ethics at all, and I am sure that they will not listen to the ethics of the revolutionary. Ethical predominance is not going to accomplish anything. What is going to do something is physical predominance. Our propaganda is inspiring! The Trade Unionists are awaking! Self-contained individuality is required—and also grim determination to conquer. The new ideology has set in the minds of the workers. Woe to those middle-class hypocrites who may try to retard the march of progress!

The basis of Syndicalism lies in the fact that while there are wage-earners; while there is an exploiting class and an exploited class in society, an uncompromising scientific class war must be carried on against the exploiters of labour. It declares for unceasing industrial war against wagedom in negation to "ballot-box striking," political amour, and compromise with the hirelings of the economic dominant class.

THE FINAL AIM OF INDUSTRIAL SYNDICALISM.

By H. L. E. HOWARTH.

That the capitalist Press should misrepresent the propaganda of the Syndicalists and the basic principles upon which their activity, aims, and aspirations are founded, comes as no surprise to the intelligent workers who realise the mission which the capitalist class are out to 'conduct. Fortunately, the Syndicalists have a mouthpiece to voice their opinions—otherwise the capitalist Press might have the field entirely to themselves. To allow them to have things all their own way without being criticised would greatly please the well-paid hirelings of the master class, as it would enable them to continue undisturbed their partially successful campaign of keeping the workers in ignorance of their class interests. The Syndicalists, however, have no intention of leaving the capitalists a clear field of action, and their misrepresentation will be ceaselessly exposed in the SYNDICALIST and other papers which will be published until the final aim of Syndicalism is attained. Probably no misconceptions are so varied and so universally widespread as the misconceptions regarding the final aim of the Syndicalist movement. In order to fully comprehend the significance of this final aim, it will be necessary to examine briefly the basic principles of Syndicalism and the circumstances which have given rise to the movement. Ever since the institution of modern machinery and the consequent development of the capitalist system of production a struggle—fierce and unceasing—has been going on between the employers and the employed, the palliation of their conditions of toil being the object of the employed and the maintenance of their status of luxury and laziness the object of the employers. This struggle is essentially part and parcel of the social system now in operation consequent upon the possession of the means of life by the few and the dispossession of the many. Syndicalism, therefore, recognising this all-important fact, bases its activity on the CLASS STRUGGLE. The working class and the employing class have nothing in common. So long as the class struggle exists, the interests of the workers and the interests of the capitalists can never be identical. Herein, therefore, lies the explanation of the attitude of the capitalist class towards the Syndicalist or any revolutionary movement which kindles the spirit of revolt in the workers. Such is the nature of our present social system that the only method open to the workers of preserving their existence is by continuous struggle on the economic field with the capitalists and open revolt with the sordid conditions of life which the capitalist system compels them to put up with. It is the historical mission of the workers to do away with capitalism, and it is through Syndicalism that they will achieve this object. With the abolition of the capitalist system, the class struggle will for ever cease. The ultimate aim of Syndicalism is therefore to ABOLISH THE CLASS STRUGGLE AND INSTITUTE THE INDUSTRIAL COMMONWEALTH.

Syndicalists are often accused of creating a class struggle. Far from creating one, the Syndicalists have no desire to see one. Such a struggle already exists, and it is this struggle that causes the misery and suffering which the workers endure. If there was no capitalist system—and this is exactly what the Syndicalists desire; but while this class struggle continues the workers must wage war on the capitalists with all the power they possess. This they can do effectively along the lines of industrial Syndicalism. The workers must consolidate their forces, and when there is a strike for higher wages or better conditions of labour, they must stand together conscious of their interests and be prepared to consider "an injury to one an injury to all." The strike, the boycott, and sabotage are all useful weapons in the struggle which the workers wage—and the struggle must go on until the toilers come together on the economic field to take and hold the means of production. When that is accomplished, the class struggle ceases. The workers will then enjoy the full product of their labour. The work of the Syndicalists is therefore apparent. We must educate and organise the working class in so efficient a manner that they will be able to effect the transformation of capitalist society into the Socialist method of production. The task that lies before us is one that requires courage, endurance, and sacrifice, and it is without hesitation that we announce our belief that these qualities will be forthcoming. The only danger is that the workers are too much inclined to rely on leaders and not on their own efforts. The betrayals of the past, however, should convince them of the truth of this assertion. Karl Marx said: "The emancipation of the workers must be the work of the workers themselves." Priests, politicians, and philanthropists will shed crocodile tears over the sufferings of the workers, but they will not and can never be of any use to the workers as far as their emancipation is concerned. While the workers are content to put their faith in politicians—be they Liberals, Tories, or Labour bleeders—they will remain in poverty and degradation. The capitalist class are not afraid of pious expressions or even revolutionary phrases. What they are afraid of is REVOLUTIONARY ACTION. They will do anything for the workers except get off their backs. Yes, they will pour out pity by the volume, they will organise charities, present the workers with free libraries, and do many other things of a similar nature, but there is one thing they will not do, and that is CEASE TO LIVE ON THE UNPAID LABOUR OF THE WORKING CLASS. It is therefore behoves the workers to organise along the lines of industry for the great task which is before them. All other classes in society have emancipated themselves; it now remains for the workers to work out their salvation and to banish poverty, tyranny, and oppression for ever.

SYNDICALISM inspires the workers with new hope, for it teaches them to rely upon their own efforts. Never was there a greater or more inspiring movement throughout the history of

the world. It is the movement of all movements, for through it will come the dawn of FREEDOM, SOCIAL EQUALITY, and HAPPINESS.

THE LEAGUE'S ACTIVITIES.

LONDON ORGANISER'S REPORT.

During the last month I visited a good number of A.S.R.S. branches. Though I encountered a certain amount of opposition at most of the meetings, I received a still greater measure of support. The branches visited were Kensington, Joint West London Extension Railway; Neasden, G.C. & M.R.; West Brompton, Met. District; King's Cross, G.N.R.; Acton and Ealing, District Railway; Stratford, G.E.R.; Bow, L.N.W.R.; Chalk Farm, L.N.W.R.; New Cross, S.E.C.R.; Farringdon Street, G.N.R.; and also the London Society of Tailors and Tailoresses.

As a member of the Transport Workers' Amalgamation Committee, I attended several of their Executive Committee meetings officially, and was also present at the meeting that was addressed by Tom Mann, under their auspices.

I attended the meetings of the Provisional Committee for Amalgamating Existing Trade Unions, and was elected to their Executive Committee, which I have to address shortly on Syndicalism.

As part of my work as organiser, I was present at the formation of some of our local groups in the London area. At Wimbledon Comrade F. Baker was elected secretary. Their next meeting will be held next Monday, November 11, at the Labour Hall, Broadway, Wimbledon.

Hammersmith met on Tuesday, October 22, when D. Armstrong was elected secretary. They decided to meet weekly at the Grove Studios, 2, Adie Road, The Grove, Hammersmith, on Tuesdays.

The Islington comrades formed a group on Thursday, October 17. P. Rodda was elected secretary. At present they meet at the Prince Brunswick, Barnsbury Road. They decided to hold the group meetings fortnightly.—F. J. PASSMORE.

OTHER MEETINGS ADDRESSED IN LONDON.

GUY BOWMAN went to several societies to lecture on Syndicalism during the last month. On October 5 he attended the Brixton branch of the Amalgamated Society of House and Ship Painters and Decorators. They had a most interesting discussion, and the following resolution was carried:

"That the time has now arrived when organised painters should take part in the consolidation movement of the building industry as a basis for emancipation, and that Parliamentary action being played out, the workers will have to resort to more direct methods of fighting the employers."

This resolution was adopted at a subsequent meeting on the motion of Dick Moore, and ordered to be sent to the Executive Committee of the Society.

On October 11 he spoke at the St. George's-in-the-East Town Hall, on the occasion of the anniversary of the murder of Ferrer and the opening of the Ferrer Sunday School in that district, and was able to expound our international and anti-militarist conceptions.

On Sunday, October 27, he visited the St. George's and Wapping B.S.P., at their request. This was a very disappointing affair, as they seemed imbued with the old S.D.F. spirit, of getting a speaker there, not for the purpose of considering his ideas, but to have the pleasure of repeating ad infinitum their Parliamentary platitudes.

A pleasing contrast to the last affair was his visit to the Union Scientific and Literary Society at Lewisham. Here he received a cordial and courteous reception, even from his keenest opponents. It was an enjoyable evening, spent amongst real intelligent people, who could offer opposition in a civil manner.

E. J. B. ALLEN spoke to the Stoke Newington branch of the National Union of Clerks. It was a poorly attended meeting, but a vigorous discussion ensued.

On October 9 he attended the Stoke Newington B.S.P., and received a splendid reception. The questions were intelligent, and much sympathy was expressed for Syndicalist teaching. As a matter of fact, this is practically a Syndicalist group.

On the 29th he was at the Working Men's College, Crowndale Road, Camden Town, to take part in a debate. His opponent was Mr. Ewer, B.A. The debate showed that B.A.'s, as well as other folks, fail to grasp the immense change that the abolition of the wages-system implies. An interesting discussion took place amongst the members of the class, and Syndicalism received a very fair support from such an audience.

FORMATION OF NEW GROUPS.

LONDON DISTRICT.

LIST OF GROUP SECRETARIES.

BRIXTON.—A. S. Albery, 16, St. George's Road, Southwark, S.E. This group is intended—not only for members living in this particular district, but also for comrades who are not in a neighbour in which a group exists yet. Write to the secretary for particulars of meeting nights.

CITY.—A. S. Bewlay, 95, Guildford Street, W.C. This group is linking up the members in the centre of London.

HAMMERSMITH.—D. Armstrong, 15, Netherwood Road, West Kensington Park, W. A strong group has been formed here, and has already made a start towards getting an active agitation going. We are going to issue a leaflet to the Trade Unions in the district, giving a brief explanation of Syndicalism, and asking them to allow one of our members to address them. We meet every Tuesday, at the Grove Studios, 2, Adie Road, The Grove, Hammersmith.

ISLINGTON.—P. Rodda, 130, Barnsbury Road, Islington, N. This group was started on Thursday, October 17. We have decided to meet fortnightly for the present, at the Prince Brunswick, Barnsbury Road, on Thursdays.

WIMBLEDON.—F. L. Baker, High Street, Colliers Wood, Merton, S.W. We are determined to make this group an active one. Several well-known trade unionists belong to us. Our meeting-place is at the Labour Hall, Broadway, Wimbledon.

PROVINCIAL GROUPS.

BIRMINGHAM.—E. R. Robinson, 31, Ashmere Road, Cotteridge. The Birmingham comrades are busy. We intend to educate ourselves as well as the workers generally, and to this end we are going to have some classes. There is a large field for a revolutionary propaganda in this city, and we intend to work it.

COVENTRY.—Burdett Ludlam, 62, Sackville Street, Hillfields. We have commenced our life as a group by arranging for comrades to attend different Trade Union branches in the
(Continued on next column.)

SYNDICALISM IN AMERICA.

VIEWS OF AN AMERICAN SYNDICALIST,

W. Armstead Nelson Collier, an American revolutionary and student of philosophy, is in London for the winter—having come to Europe for the purpose of acquainting himself with the movement in England and on the Continent, and of studying the fundamental principles and ideas underlying the revolutionary activities in their various phases. With this end in view he has taken lodgings at 228, The Grove, Hammersmith, in the William Morris neighbourhood—and is mingling with the numerous groups of workers and agitators about London.

A Southerner by birth, and reared in the Conservative traditions of the old slave-holding class, Mr. Nelson Collier became a convert to the ideas of the Social Revolution while studying along advanced lines at American Universities, and endeavouring to get into philanthropic work in the slums of New York and Philadelphia.

The horrible conditions prevailing amongst the underpaid workers of these wealthy and prosperous communities opened a new world of thought to the observant student—and in the case of this product of the "aristocracy of America" brought about a revulsion of feeling that forced him to realise that nothing but a complete transformation of society could save the race from decay and ruin.

Having had considerable experience in political organisation work, he perceived the futility of the ballot as a means of effecting the necessary renovation of social conditions, and became from the first a firm believer in the methods of direct action and the General Strike as the most effective weapon to bring about the Social Revolution. Hence he may be classed as a Revolutionary Syndicalist. His views may differ in some respects from those we hold—but Syndicalism is no hard-and-fast creed that allows no room for individual interpretation. At an interview with Guy Bowman and Assistant-Secretary Allen he explained his views.

In reply to the question "How is the I.W.W. going in America? Is it getting stronger? Are its prospects bright?" Comrade Collier was of the opinion that the recent strikes had shown the power of the I.W.W., and the value of its methods of propaganda and organisation. That it was a growing force, with its prospects brightening.

Do you think that Syndicalist ideas are growing in America? "Oh, undoubtedly. The I.W.W. might be termed the American form of Syndicalism. It is practically a Syndicalist organisation now in its theory and tactics. The workers of the world have no time nor patience for parliamentary methods—they are too indirect and too uncertain of results. Direct industrial action is the most powerful revolutionary weapon the workers possess—and they are beginning to realise it. Still, whilst the leaders of the I.W.W. realise this and act accordingly, they remain on fairly good terms—on ' speaking terms ' at least with the Socialist Party. They generally co-operate in Free Speech fights."

(Continued from previous column.)
town. Our message is well received by the workers here, and we confidently look forward to being one of the strongholds of Syndicalism in the near future. If work will make a movement grow, Coventry is safe.

MANCHESTER.—The Secretary, 50A, Market Street. The arrangements for the coming conference are well in hand. Some thousands of invitations have been sent out, and the responses are numerous.

Would it not be better for the I.W.W. to disband as an organisation, and its members rejoin the unions in the A.F. of L. in order to permeate them with Syndicalist ideas? "No; there is no organisation capable of taking the place of the I.W.W. For the I.W.W. to disband now would be to simply hand over the working-class to the tender mercies of the Civic Federation fakers and other Capitalists who run most of the unions in the A.F. of L. The I.W.W. is here to stay. Whilst this one big union is there, with its power to run strikes like those of McKees Rocks and Lawrence, it can be used as an example to the men in the A.F. of L. The rebels have a better chance inside the old unions with the I.W.W. outside. Besides, whilst the I.W.W. is strong and effective as a fighting revolutionary organisation, the great mass of members or units composing it are, excepting the leaders, not deeply enough imbued with the revolutionary idea to stand and fight alone without the support that comes from association. They are not strong enough in knowledge or in numbers to make individual permeators. They would be swallowed up in the mass. I have been surprised at the difference here. Your Syndicalist advocates seem well versed in knowledge of union matters, of economics, and revolutionary thought. They are capable of holding their own in any section meeting of a union."

Do you think that the A.F. of L. may be revolutionised? "I don't think so. The A.F. of L. unions may, but I would rather take an active part in the I.W.W. than try to convert the A.F. of L. bunch."

Well, Comrade Collier, what is your opinion regarding the formation of Syndicalist Education Leagues like ours? We have received quite a number of letters from members of the I.W.W., and those who have rejoined the A.F. of L., saying that they are starting educational leagues. "Oh, I think the idea is a good one, for not only would it strengthen the I.W.W. itself, but it would spread the idea in the A.F. of L. unions. The members of the Syndicalist Education Leagues, who are members of the old unions, would not attack the I.W.W. or allow attacks to pass unchallenged. It would be a good move."

Have the strikes in England had any influence upon the American workers? "Yes; it was new life to them, when they heard of the magnificent Transport strike of last year. That railroad strike was great. We almost expected to hear of the revolution next. When the English workers move it is a sign of a general international advance."

So, Comrade Collier, you are of the opinion that Syndicalist ideas are spreading over the other side of the herring-pond? "Yes; Syndicalism is a growing power. Direct action is the most effective weapon—especially where so many workers are voteless. The wage slaves are beginning to realise their condition and their power; and the most revolutionary and intelligent among them will never be satisfied with those reforms of the present system that may be effected by recourse to the Capitalist method of counting votes by the ballot. The I.W.W. in America stands boldly for the abolition of the wage system and restitution to the workers of the entire product of their toil. The Syndicalist movement is a tremendous step in the right direction."

Here, after giving us some further views of his upon matters generally, our comrade parted company with us.

The Railwaymen and the A.G.M.

CONCILIATION AND DIRECT ACTION.

By A MIDLAND GUARD.

Of all the resolutions down for discussion in the agenda of the Railwaymen's "Annual General Meeting," held at Dublin in October, the only one that mattered, the only one that could have materially benefited railwaymen, was the one moved by Clay Cross Branch, asking the delegates to repudiate the Conciliation Scheme. If the delegates had really grasped the true position, it is within the realms of possibility that the scheme would have been repudiated, the railwaymen, freed from the chains that bind them, and they would by this time have been reaping the benefits they have so long been promised, but which have never yet materialised. Mr. J. H. Thomas, M.P. (assistant secretary), speaking on the resolution to repudiate Conciliation, pleaded for the retention of the scheme, and said " the resolution was one of the most dangerous proposals," and that " it was not one which reflected the opinion of the rank and file." Possibly the delegates forgot, or were not aware, that their executive committee, who are supposed to represent and reflect the opinion of the members—a fact that even Mr. Thomas cannot dispute—carried a resolution unanimously at their September sitting,

In Mr. Thomas's Presence,

" regretting the *impossibility* of obtaining the observation of contracts entered into between organised labour and the capitalist class, and urging upon their members to consolidate their forces by the abolition of sectionalism and by complete organisation in order to be in the position of *enforcing* any contract made." As a matter of fact, their executive committee condemned the scheme and advocated the use of "*DIRECT ACTION* " as their only salvation. The men were asked to give a fair trial to the scheme (which has already been on trial for the past four years), and it was even admitted that " over thirty railway companies had *not yet put the scheme into operation*." Then the general secretary, who hobnobs with the capitalists on the " Industrial Council," castigated Brother Leahy (who was dismissed, with five others, from the railway service for daring to ask his company to adopt the scheme and put it into practice) because he stated that the scheme was a farce and ought to be abolished. Then the same official (who was *at one time* a railwayman) said " that the progress made during the last eighteen months was greater than it was in the past twenty years." (Really the grammar is shocking, but it is not ours.)

12,000 Men Sacked.

Progress, forsooth ! Is a reduction of over 12,000 of the permanent staff progress ? Does he term the action of the Midland and other companies (who have increased a few of the men's wages two or three shillings per week and reduced a large number of their employees' wages by two or three shillings) progress ? Then a little later he proceeded to inform the delegates that the companies' receipts had increased by £5,000,000, and that if they were to grant an all-round increase of a couple of shillings per week they would still have £2,000,000 left as a surplus. Why on earth didn't he tell the delegates that the few miserable increases that have been granted by the companies were not worth the having, and that if they wanted any portion of the £5,000,000 they would have to fight for it ? No one can wonder that, after all, the delegates foolishly believed that Conciliation was worth having, and that they defeated the motion to repudiate the scheme.

Inconsistency All Round.

A little while afterwards, just to show their inconsistency, the delegates (with the acquiescence of the officials) declared " they would not allow *any agreements* to stand in the way of the defence of their victimised members."

Yet, again, they decided to support the Clay Cross Branch's resolution, " to abolish the capitalist class and take over the possession of the industries themselves." Isn't it absurd to think of conciliating with people whom you want to wipe out of existence ? Truly, there is plenty of scope and necessity for an educational activity in the ranks of the A.S.R.S. And so the " Annual General Meeting " has ended, and for all the benefits that are likely to accrue from it, it might just as well have never been held at all. When will the Railwaymen awake to the fact that they can obtain anything if they will only make up their minds to get it ?

Syndicalism and the Electrical Workers.

SUPPLY STATION HANDS HOLD THE KEY.

Syndicalism is the outcome of the failure of sectional Trade Unionism and the futility of Parliamentary Representation. Syndicalism stands for class solidarity on the principle, " An injury to one is an injury to all."

The workers must organise themselves nationally and internationally, the same as the capitalists. For example, the Shipping Combines are organised internationally so as to be able to break the back of any sectional strike that may take place amongst the seamen. The same applies to practically every industry.

The power of the workers lies in their organisation and the withholding of their labour power. Syndicalism is Revolutionary Unionism. The workers must organise within their industries with one common goal in front of them, that is to control and work those industries in the interests of the community.

Emancipation From Below.

This emancipation comes from within the workers themselves, not from the top of society downwards, but from the bottom upwards, as all revolutionary movements have done in the past.

Having briefly explained Syndicalism, let us see its relation to the Electrical workers. It requires very little observation to see that the great motive-power in modern production is the applied force of electrical energy. Take a survey of any of our staple industries and, with hardly any exception, we see the great use of that energy. We see by the closing of a switch the large masses of machinery stirred into action. Deep down in the mines it is used for working the pumps, drawing the trams, and lighting the levels. See how the transit systems have been revolutionised by the same force.

The electric tramways, railways, lifts, and signals. On the large buildings in course of erection we see the electrical hoist.

We see it used as an illuminant in the factories, halls, and the streets. Yet we find that, like all other great discoveries, it has been turned to the advantage of the employing class.

Instead of it shortening the working day, as it should do, we still find the majority of workers spending long hours in the workshops and factories.

We find amongst electrical workers, owing to our cut-throat, competitive system, an ever-increasing difficulty to find work. We find supply stations working long shifts, and the men bossed by incompetent officials and unable to obtain any redress because they have not yet realised the great power of " Solidarity " !

When you have realised the necessity for organisation you must get inside your Union, not for the purpose of building up big funds for sick benefits, or for the upkeep of officials, but for the purpose of building up within it a complete organisation on class and not sectional lines.

Every Worker, Skilled or Unskilled.

Your organisation must embrace all the workers in the electrical industry, wiremen, mates, switch-board hands, lamp makers, armature-winders, and even the often despised but indispensable to the capitalists, the meter readers. In short, every worker, skilled or so-called unskilled.

There is no doubt that the supply-station hands would hold the key to any action taken by the workers against the employing class.

Suppose, for instance, that the time had arrived for forcing a strike for a shorter working day—without a reduction in the week's wages—amongst the installation workers. This would greatly reduce the percentage of unemployed, the greatest weapon that the masters have to use against us. A general stoppage would be called ; this would not only include the wiremen, electrical fitters, and mates, but also the shop hands, the armature-winders, switchboard assemblers, etc. If the employers tried to prolong the strike, and so defeat the workers, then the supply-station hands would come out as a natural result of their organisation and solidarity.

Note the importance of such a step. We have already shown that a large number of factories and workshops rely for their motive power upon electricity supplied in bulk from the central supply stations. Thus we should then have the employers in other industries affected, and then they, in their turn, would bring pressure to bear upon the electrical firms involved. This shows what would be the power of the workers if they were organised.

RED RUBBER.

WORKERS' APATHY LEADS TO MASTERS' FORTUNES.

By RUBBERITE.

I.

If there is one trade that requires organising as much as any other it is surely the Rubber Trade. This trade employs thousands of workers of both sexes, the majority of whom receive small wages utterly inadequate for a decent existence. These wages are quite out of proportion to the skill required.

It would be as well to give a treatise on how rubber is " made." It is a juice tapped from trees bearing that name. It is chiefly grown in Para, the Congo, and India. After tapping, it is placed in cauldrons and heated until its elasticity causes it to gather into balls or batches. It is then shipped to the various manufacturers for treatment. The first piece came from India, hence it was called " India-Rubber." In the old days experimental researches were carried on in order to find a means of adapting so resilient an article to some commercial and industrial use. Rubber mats were the first general commercial articles which were made.

Luxury for the Wealthy.

But owing to the " para " not being " vulcanised," and consequently soft, and the price being so high, only the wealthier classes could purchase these luxuries. Further experiments were made with a view to finding some process for hardening the rubber. To James Lyne Hancock belongs the honour of the discovery of the secret of hardening rubber. His process of " vulcanisation " consists of sulphur being mixed with the rubber and subjected to steam at high pressure. This discovery proved to be the foundation of many fortunes. The manufacture developed. Coloured rubbers were made with pigment leads, until every shade in the printer's colour-book was mastered. The industry kept progressing, from small works to large factories, and now huge mills employing thousands of workpeople are the rule rather than the exception. In its earliest days workpeople with even the scantiest knowledge were at a premium ; wages of from £3 to £4 per week were the rule. But not so now. Why ? Because the employers have been very much alive, and have organised an Employers' Federation. The workers have been sleeping and letting things slide until now they find themselves in a quagmire of low wages, excessive hours, and hustling piece-work.

Fines for the Workers.

A damnable system of " fines," speeding up, girls ousting youths, youths ousting men, and young boys being put where they can. All this to the detriment of the workpeople, whilst bringing higher profits to the employers.

The uses of rubber are variant in character ; it has become an important item in the industrial system. It can be manufactured to withstand all attacks of steam, oils, acids, and climatic conditions, and its powers are not yet exhausted.

Steamships could not leave the ports until refitted anew with valves, piston rings, and packings. Railway trains would be held up if there were no " buffers " handy. Billiard enthusiasts would miss their game pretty much if there were no rubber strip to make the " cush." The Road-Hogs would have to revert again to horse and gig if there were no rubber motor tyres. So many are the different uses to which it is put that it would be difficult to find a trade or sport in which it is not used in some form or other.

Employers Not Philanthropists.

Readers of the SYNDICALIST who are rubber workers must be reminded that if better conditions are to prevail they must organise in a union. The employers are not in business for fun, or for philanthropic purposes, but for profits. Say, they want their 100 per cent., and, like Oliver Twist, want more. They care not how they are got. Sweat the workers, bully them, piece-work them, pay them on count, weight, length, or anything and everything to gain another farthing profit. What care they if girls become languid or exhausted, there are plenty more outside the gates seeking work at any price that is offered. When trade is brisk, scour the towns for Labour, run the mills at breakneck speed night and day. Irregardless of religious beliefs they run the mills on Sundays as well as night and day through the week. They put pressure on the foremen to get out, throw out, or fling out the work, or they themselves may be flung out. When trade is slack again, they throw out the reserve army of labour with as much compassion as would be shown to a dog with rabies, until they are again required.

(To be continued.)

The Transport Workers Demand One Union.

TOM MANN ON JEHOVAH AND SABOTAGE.

Under the auspices of the Transport Workers' Amalgamation Committee, a highly successful meeting of Transport Workers was held in the Public Hall, Canning Town, on Thursday, October 24. Quite 2,000 persons were present.

Sam Roden (Hon. Sec. of the Amalgamation Committee) presided, and in his opening remarks stated that the object of the committee was the formation of One Transport Union, not by forming any new Union, but by amalgamating the existing ones. He then read the following resolution :

Seeing that industrial organisation is absolutely necessary to the workers to achieve economic betterment, and seeing that a lengthy experience has fully demonstrated the lamentable inefficiency of sectional unionism, this meeting of transport workers declares in favour of one organisation for the whole of the transport workers, and to guard against centralised official bureaucracy, urges the immediate necessity for the amalgamation of the existing Unions in the transport industry, with adequate provision for local and sectional autonomy consistent with general efficiency.

The resolution was moved by J. F. Passmore, of the A.S.R.S., and seconded by W. Blackwell, a well-known and enthusiastic worker in the locality. W. F. Watson, Secretary of the " Provisional Committee for the Amalgamation of existing Trade Unions," supported, emphasising the necessity of one union and one policy, instead of fifty-eight Transport Unions to fight one Masters' Transport organisation. Ted Leggatt, of the Carmen's Union, also supported, and then our Comrade

Tom Mann.

He said he looked upon that meeting as one that was likely to be referred to in the future ; it would become historical. He congratulated the committee upon their splendid work. The movement was destined to transfer from the dominant class that power that is absolutely necessary to rescue the workers from the poverty that so many of them were in. Organisation alone was not sufficient ; there was nothing on this earth so essential to the welfare of the working class as the spirit of solidarity. The Transport Strike of 1911 was a success because the spirit of solidarity was present, but this year the London Transport Workers had been defeated because of its absence. He was compelled to come to the conclusion that the Federation was hopeless ; he was not for complete amalgamation. Unions that were poor were prepared to take common action, but as soon as they managed to increase their funds, the spirit of solidarity began to disappear, the desire to conserve their little exchequer began to manifest itself, and when some other union was involved in a fight, then they were reluctant to make common cause. They had £10,000 ; they didn't want to lose it, but they expressed their sympathy, their wishes for success, and considered what action they should take, hoping that something would turn up before long to save their face. They must have one organisation, with one common fund. When that object was obtained, he did not want a centralised bureaucracy ; he was against that just as much as he was against sectionalism. The Transport Union officials had all been invited to attend that meeting and support the formation of one union, but they were not present. He was not out to slate them ; he could do more effective work without that. He had heard officials say " My Union." How could it be *their* union ? It belonged to the men who composed it. Just as soon as the men were determined to amalgamate, the officials would be compelled to sympathise or else get out of it altogether. He was connected with the Transport Strike of 1911 at Liverpool, and about ten weeks ago they celebrated the event, and about 40,000 Transport Workers carried a resolution for the formation of One Transport Union.

The Building Trades' Unions had made their officials sympathetic, and were on the point of amalgamating.

Referring to Parliamentary action, he said that for twenty-five years the workers had been petitioning, pleading, and begging of Parliament to do something for them, but nothing had been done ; were the workers prepared to continue doing this ?

Direct Action and Sabotage.

Direct action must be used. In the time of the Israelites a man named Moses came along and said to them. " Come, friends, are you willing to revolt against your terrible conditions ? " " Revolt," said they, " what do you mean ? " " Why," said Moses, " the strike. Use Direct Action," and he went from one to another of the twelve tribes and obtained their consent, and then they all said to Pharaoh, " Let us go." But the capitalists hardened their hearts and would not let them go : then Jehovah applied " sabotage," the plagues of lice, darkness, &c., and finally killed their eldest sons to punish them for their wickedness. He mentioned " sabotage " because he knew the finnicky minds of the men, their weak-kneedness, and he declared that the Israelites never treated so terribly as the workers, the slaves of to-day, were by their Pharaohs—the capitalists—and so he advocated that the men should punish them, that they should sabot.

At the conclusion of his address the resolution was submitted to the meeting, and was first carried amidst cheers without a single opponent. But on Tom Mann asking a second time for opposition, a solitary individual raised his hand as being an opponent of working-class unity.

Syndicalism and the School Teacher.

A SELF-DISCIPLINED PROFESSION.

By NORMAN YOUNG.

I don't mean to say for a moment that the English school teacher would endorse an anti-militarist campaign or an advocacy of sabotage. (The latter he would oppose violently on moral (!) grounds, for he regards capitalist morality as the only morality.) His attitude to the manual workers, from which class he is as a rule but a generation removed, is not at all friendly. He teaches their children, but does not recognise that he, too, is of the proletariat, and that his conditions of work, his social status, and the regard in which he is held by the Whitehall Mandarins and local Council snobocracy, are dependent on the fact that he is, indeed, a very wage slave, with no control of his own destiny.

How to be Brought to Their Proper Position.

At present he has not achieved reality. In times of strike he is on the side of the masters.

He doesn't want to be reminded that his father was a navvy, or his grandfather a weaver. He wants to leave that all behind. He would agree heartily with Sir Forrest Fulton. Yet it is the growth of bureaucratic methods on the part of officialdom which is going to make a man of the English teacher, and bring him to his proper position—that of fighting in one solid battalion with his brothers of the working class against the common enemy.

The basis of Syndicalism lies in the teaching that the workers themselves shall control the method of working of their own industries ; that no one has a right to have a voice in the internal economy of the mines, unless he is connected with the mining industry. This means the abolition of wage-slavery, in that the mark of a wage-slave is just the fact that he has no say in the method and condition of production, no say in the distribution of the commodity when produced. It is this which the teachers are grasping sub-consciously. They are beginning to demand the right of supreme control in those things which ought to be their sole concern.

Promotion Should Lie With Teachers.

The annual report of the work of the London Teachers' Association (numbering over 17,000 members) was given as a supplement to the *London Teacher*. It bristles with contributions to Syndicalist teaching. The workers ought to know. What is necessary for the dockers, miners, weavers, etc. One of the burning questions for London teachers has been that of " compulsory promotions." The official point of view is, " Given a school, how to keep the class-rooms full ? " The officials attempt to do this by rushing the children through the curriculum at breakneck speed, in defiance of all theories of education, in defiance of all warning from teachers. It is the application of " speeding up," as it is known in industry, to education. The result is disastrous. This is the pronouncement of the London Teachers' Association : " It cannot be too strongly insisted that the promotion of elementary school children must be vested entirely in the teachers, whose judgment and knowledge should be supreme."

Then comes this startling piece of Syndicalist teaching : " One of the most hopeful signs of the growth of the professional spirit among teachers is the desire, which is steadily increasing, that in all professional matters the profession should be self-disciplined. It is of the utmost importance that the standards of professional conduct should be settled by teachers themselves, and that breaches of professional etiquette should be dealt with inside the profession."

Freedom of Teaching Methods.

Following this is a statement which asserts the necessity for safeguarding the freedom of the teacher in questions of the adoption of teaching methods which *he* (or *she*) considers most reliable.

Finally, there is this pronouncement regarding Central Schools : " There has been a disposition on the part of the Administration to interfere unduly with the organisation of these schools, and the Central Schools Sub-Committee had to intervene on several occasions *to secure full liberty for the teachers to conduct the schools in the way which they deemed best.*" The italics are mine.

All the foregoing points to a gratifying desire on the part of the school teacher to make himself supreme in matters of " craft." As the SYNDICALIST pointed out last month, it is surely just that for which he has been trained. Some day he may revolt against teaching capitalist untruths about Empire, etc., to working-class children ; some day he may be in and of a militant working-class movement towards Freedom. Who knows !

WAR AGAINST WAR.

(Continued from page 1.)

France (Russia) on one side, and opposed to them will be Germany, Austria, and Italy. The whole of Europe involved in a devastating war!

Then there is the curse of Patriotism; for if this catastrophe produces itself they will say: "It's the other chap, not me!" The blame of being aggressor will be thrown from one to the other.

This is the crime that is about to be perpetrated against Humanity, against Civilisation! I have come here to denounce that crime.

So there! For the private interests of a few financiers in London and Berlin millions would be condemned to the most horrible misery and death. And all this in the name of their country—a beautiful country indeed. What is their country? Two groups of human beings, one living upon the other, which in France I am fond of illustrating with the following parable:

There is a richly-loaded table, at which sits the great landowners like your Duke of Bedford and Duke of Westminster; the great captains of industry, like Macara of the Cotton Ring, and Mond of the Chemical World, Paget of the Railways, Thomas of the Mines, and Runciman of the Shipping. To them: all the well-being and comfort that the progress of science allows; to them all the intellectual enjoyments also; to them a human life.

With them are the politicians whom they pet and flatter in order that they shall do their bidding. But far from that table of luxury I can perceive millions of slaves: slaves of Industry, slaves of the Factories; the slaves of Militarism, the soldiers and sailors; the slaves of the State, the Civil Servants; the slaves of their households, the domestic servants; these provide those seated at the table with flesh for factories, flesh for cannon, flesh for pleasure.

Put the two together, this small minority enjoying all, and the vast majority possessing nothing, and in the name of such countries they ask us to accept all the horrors of an European war, in which the oppressed portion, the workers of Germany, Austria, and Russia, will be murdering each other. If we are to make war, we prefer to wage it against our real enemies, the capitalist class.

For us Democrats, Syndicalists, and Socialists of the world, all the exploited are our brothers, whatever the nation of exploited they may belong to. If we are to fight, let it be against the European capitalist class who lives upon the oppression of the Proletariat.

Wars may have been justified in the past, but to-day we have nothing more to gain from any war whatsoever. And, therefore, the only war we might gain anything from is the class war—Civil War.

The only war which ought to interest you English workers is not a fratricidal war against the unexploited like yourselves, but the war against your capitalist class at home; the war which will make you masters of the Mines, the Railways, the Land, and all the means of production and exchange exploited to-day as private concerns by private persons, but which to-morrow will be the collective property of the General Confederation of Labour the producers.

To-morrow, instead of serving to provide a stupid luxury to a million men, of whom many are parasites, you will serve to provide all children with the material and intellectual bread to which they all have a right. All adults will do work that does not go beyond human strength, and they will do it under hygienic conditions. And those who have performed their social task will find security and comfort in their old age.

When we are victors in that struggle—that day we shall have a country. But such a country—to which the Proletariat is aspiring—is not to be erected against other Countries; we shall want it linked up with all other countries by a federal link, such as the one which is uniting the states of the United States of America.

By working this way in our different countries, we are working for the advent of the United States of Europe.

Oh, I know it would have been Utopian in times gone by, to draw all the men in Europe into the same Confederation, but to-day science, steam, electricity have, like the stroke of a magic wand, made the world smaller.

It is easier to communicate from one end of Europe to the other to-day than it was a hundred years ago to communicate from one end of England to the other.

The capitalist régime has, through the Internationale of Capital, which knows no frontiers, created in Europe and the Far-East a civilisation which is uniform, or almost so.

Capitalism has prepared the bed of the Internationale of the Peoples. And don't let us be told about the frontier of races. The only frontier there is is the one that separates you and me at the present moment, the frontier of language, but even that is disappearing, because of our new International language, Esperanto.

What about America? America is a country that contains more Irishmen and Scotchmen than there are in Ireland and Scotland. America is a country which contains more Danes than there are Danes in Denmark. America is a country which contains more Germans than there are Germans in Prussia. America is a country which contains more Belgians than there are Belgians in Belgium. America is a country which contains more Italians than there are Italians in the northern provinces of Italy.

Well, if all these people can live in peace in America, why can't we live in peace in Europe?

Our dream of Social Justice and Fraternity, we ask no more than to realise it by peace, and all our preference goes towards peaceful methods. We reckon in every country to bring about the Social Republic by means of the two organisations—Political and Economic.

By political organisation we mean the organisation of the workers in a united, disciplined party, which will be able to bring about in every country daily papers as large in circulation, and as powerful in influence, as those of the capitalists.

A Party which will be able to send to the law-making factory a group of representatives of the people more and more numerous and ever more ardent; whom the Party will endeavour to maintain under its discipline, whom the Party will stop from sliding into the Parliamentary quagmire.

When it is known that in France the ballot paper has founded the lay school, that colossal achievement; when one sees that in Germany the Social Democracy has succeeded in giving itself one hundred dailies, groups a million subscribers, and four and a half million electors—one has no right to completely reject as a means of transformation the instrument of Universal Suffrage.

Your Suffragettes, whose combative energy we admire so much in France, are right in wanting to obtain it, and we shall rejoice in them getting it, so sure are we that women electors will be our most ardent allies in the legislative struggle against militarism, alcoholism, and prostitution.

I only wish, you comrades of England, at the time when your women are claiming the vote for themselves, that you should see to it that the suffrage for men should not remain a caricature. I wish you workers of Free England, who often laugh at the autocracy of the Kaiser, would conquer for yourselves a suffrage like the German suffrage, which at least does not exclude two million from voting.

Quite as much as we reckon on political organisation, so do we rely upon the Trade Union and Co-operative organisations, which in the society of to-morrow will be the organisations of production and distribution, when we have socialised the means of production and exchange.

We partly depend upon Trade Union action because of the spirit of self-sacrifice and solidarity which strikes develop in the heart of the Proletariat.

We wish through this twofold action to be able to evolve in peace and quietness from the present capitalist system into the Socialist régime of our dreams.

Only to prevent us accomplishing that our present masters must not come with a European war and compel us to have recourse to violence. Before having recourse to this violence, the supreme violence of the Social Revolution, we are ready to attempt anything, and this is how we will address our masters whom we feel are sliding towards the abyss of war: "We are not bad boys; the only thing we are asking you for the time being is peace. We summon you gently; we are going to summon you in all your Parliaments at the same time to inscribe in your legislative books 'Compulsory Arbitration,' and don't come and tell us that you will not submit to Arbitration Courts certain cases in which national honour and vital interests of the country are at stake.

"For us, the only national honour we know is to avoid war which would be a shame for the nation; the only vital interest for the country we know of is to avoid a war—a catastrophe for business, and thereby making a terrible misery and ruin for all poor people.

"You will, therefore, be good enough to inscribe International Arbitration in your Statute Book—and after that you will be able to talk amongst yourselves of the limitation of armaments. It is putting the cart before the horse to talk about the limitation of armaments whilst you have not inscribed International Arbitration on the Statute Books.

"If you refuse to accept our ultimatum, which is the ultimature of human reason and humanity, then woe to thee.

"Woe to thee who will have unfolded violence. WE consider ourselves in a state of legitimate defence against you, and in all countries simultaneously we shall answer your order for mobilisation by the General Strike and Insurrection. I pray certain of our friends who admit as legitimate our principle of revolt against war not to raise the objection to us: 'Yes; all that's very fine, but how do we know that in all lands the people will follow; that the most advanced people will not be victims, seeing that it is in their country that the movement for Instruction will have developed, whereas in other countries they will march deceived by those who govern them."

I should say, on the contrary, to those who speak of the possible dupery of the more advanced nations, that it is for us to pioneer the War against War; it is for us, whatever national catastrophe may happen, to stab War in the back. We are dishonoured if we do not attempt that supreme protest of revolt.

And you are asking yourselves the question: "What will the German Social-Democrats do?" "Will they do their duty against war?"

I believe they will. I am firmly convinced that if the Kaiser gave an order for mobilisation it would be the last in his life. I am certain that in a country where there are four and a half million Socialist electors, disciplined and regimented, all knowing the use of arms, the Kaiser would thereby sign the fall of his Empire and the advent of the German Republic.

That which confirms my hope, in spite of the timidity of the official German Social Democracy, is the necessity under which it found itself at Stuttgart, by the pressure of its own Socialist troops, to accept the Stuttgart resolution, which ends with this significant sentence: "If war broke out in spite of all our efforts to prevent it, it is the duty of all proletarians to profit by the disturbance brought about by the fall of the capitalist régime."

What increases my hopes are the monster demonstrations which took place all over Germany two years ago over Morocco, and that open-air demonstration where 200,000 Berliners showed their fists to threatening war, and acclaimed Peace and the Workers' International.

Within a week the International Socialist Bureau is meeting at Brussels. I wish you, together with me, to ask it to organise in all the capitals of Europe a tour of the most noted Socialist M.P.'s of all Parliaments who would join with representatives of all the National Trade Union Centres. This delegation of all prominent men in the Socialist and Trade Union movement would receive an enthusiastic welcome at the stations by the peoples of London, Paris, Vienna, Berlin, Rome—I daren't say of St. Petersburg. And in vast open-air meetings, which no Government—not even that of the Kaiser—would dare to stop, these gigantic meetings on behalf of Peace would show to all Governments our unshakable determination that Peace has to be respected, and it would be the beginning of a great agitation.

Comrades of England, my future fellow-citizens of the United States of Europe, we reckon in France that you will do your duty. We reckon first upon the two Socialist organisations of this country, the British Socialist Party and the Independent Labour Party, for the unification of which we fervently wish on the other side of the Channel, and we know that we can count upon them; and it was a great joy for us, at the International Socialist Congress at Copenhagen, to see Keir Hardie put his name by the side of Vaillant's at the bottom of the resolution asking for the General Strike in case of war.

We trust that the Labour Party and the Trade Unions, convinced by that and stimulated by the handful of English Syndicalists who have already accomplished so much, will at the decisive hour feel that solidarity which is to unite the workers from one end of the world to the other.

We also rely upon the élite of that Radical bourgeoisie, those Nonconformist Christians who at the time of the Boer War had the courage to resist the wave of Jingoism that spread over the country; all those men whose money-bags have not yet killed in them all humanitarian instincts. In a few words, we count on all English citizens who desire the title of civilised men.

All of you, I ask to join the new crusade, with the cry of:

DOWN WITH JINGOISM: WAR AGAINST WAR!

LONG LIVE THE UNITED STATES OF EUROPE!

LONG LIVE THE INTERNATIONALE!

— THE —

Ferrer School

now meets at

107, Charlotte Street, W.

On SUNDAY AFTERNOON,
at 2.30 p.m.

SYNDICALIST LITERATURE.

We are repeatedly being asked for a book on Syndicalism. If inquirers will read through the pamphlets and books of which we print a list underneath, they will obtain a fair idea of what Syndicalism means. Meanwhile, we are bringing out a series of comprehensive books at one shilling, under the general title of "The Syndicalist Library." The first of the series will be by Tom-Mann, as advertised below.

TOM MANN'S PAMPHLETS.

No. 1. PREPARE FOR ACTION. — 1D.
Explains the need for linking up the unions, and adopting a fighting policy.
The pamphlet that made the strike year of 1911. Only a few of these left. Order early.

No. 2. THE TRANSPORT WORKERS. — 1D.
Calls for united action amongst Transport Workers. Brought the National Transport Workers' Federation into being, which Federation is to pave the way for ONE union for the Transport industry.

No. 3. FORGING THE WEAPON. — 1D.
Explains the steps to be taken by sympathisers in order to build up a fighting union movement. The pamphlet to be pushed. The best for workers. Most useful to propagandists.

No. 4. ALL HAIL SOLIDARITY. — 1D.
Shows the growth of solidarity amongst the workers of various industries. Deals with the Cambrian Combine Strike, and contains messages from W. D. Haywood, I.W.W., and Eugene V. Debs, of the American Socialist Party.

No. 5. SYMPOSIUM ON SYNDICALISM. — 1D.
Contains both an account of the practical work to be performed by Syndicalists and a brief statement of our object and methods. A splendid educator. There are not many of these left.

No. 6. A MANCHESTER MESSAGE TO THE WORKERS OF ENGLAND. — 6D.
A verbatim report of the whole of the proceedings of the first national conference held on Syndicalism. Records the formation of the Industrial Syndicalist Education League. This will become a historic document, useful alike to workers and students. Only about a dozen left.

No. 7. PARLIAMENTARY ACTION versus SYNDICALISM. — 2D.
Being a report of a debate between TOM MANN and FRANK ROSE, both well-known members of the A.S.E., and both prominent in the Labour World. The conflict between Unionism and Direct Action, and the policy of the "pure and simple" politicians as a means to emancipation. 60 pages for 2d.

No. 8. MINERS WAKE UP. — 6D.
Contains essays by members of the South Wales Miners' Federation, who are at work in the pits. This pamphlet with Number 5 was quoted by the Coal-owners to Mr. Asquith in order to kill the Miners' Minimum Wage Bill, and to show the "dangerous" trend of advanced opinion amongst the Miners and workers generally. Only about two dozen left.

No. 9. THE WEAPON SHAPING. — 6D.
A compact work, showing the growth of Syndicalism; full of suggestions; indicates the interest in Syndicalism aroused amongst the Trades Councils. Should be read by all members of the Trades Councils, for it contains an account of the Derby Trades Council's action, and an address by the Secretary of the Walthamstow Trades Council to its members.

No. 10. A TWO-FOLD WARNING. — 1D.
This contains a splendid account of the International Cotton Manufacturers' Federation. A lucid statement of the growth of this important industry, and of the tactics used by the Federated employers. Contains a powerful plea for solidarity amongst the Textile workers, and shows the necessity for the workers being educated as to the development of machinery that the masters are bringing in. Explains that the only hope lies in their controlling the industry. Shows up the Cotton Ring.

No. 11. THE RAILWAYMEN. — 1D.
A splendid essay upon the growth and development of the Railway Service. Railwaymen will find it packed full of useful information. Explains how they must organise, and what means to use to combat the power of the Companies. Conciliation Boards exposed.

No. 12. THE TRANSPORT INDUSTRY. — 1D.
This details the inner history of the Shipping Federation, against which arose the National Transport Workers' Federation. Shows the cunning and unscrupulous methods of the men who pull the strings in the Shipping World. None of these left. We shall probably reprint. Order immediately if required.

MASS MEETING

To Demand the Release of

ETTOR, GIOVANNITTI, HAYWOOD, and CARUSO,

Now on Trial at SALEM, U.S.A.,

Will be held in the

ST. ANDREW'S HALL,

Newman Street, Oxford Street, W.,

On **Wednesday, November 13th,**

At 7.30 p.m.

Look out for further Announcements.

OTHER BOOKS.

MY COUNTRY: RIGHT OR WRONG.
By Gustave Hervé.
Translated by Guy Bowman;
Library Edition, 3s. 6d.
The Yorkshire Daily Observer says:—"It is a fiery, sustained, and often eloquent plea for a union among the workers of all countries against capitalism, and incidentally against war, which, Mr. Hervé has no difficulty in showing, never by any chance benefits the industrial population of the conquering or of the conquered country, and is of service only to financiers."

MY COUNTRY: RIGHT OR WRONG.
By Gustave Hervé.
Cheap Popular Edition, — 1/-

THE MINERS' NEXT STEP. — 6D.
A stirring appeal for the reorganisation of the Miners' Federation on fighting lines—the bible of the militant miners. Has been circulated all over the United Kingdom.

INDEPENDENCE, or CO-PARTNERSHIP IN EDUCATION, by A. H. M. Robertson. — 1D.
A pamphlet containing the private and strictly confidential draft memorial on University Education, lately issued to the Parliamentary Committee of the Trades Union Congress by the Workers' Educational Association, with comment thereon, partly reprinted from the "Railway Review."

THE SYNDICALIST RAILWAYMAN. — 1D.
Copies of Numbers 1, 2, 3, and 4 can still be obtained. Contains matter of general interest to Syndicalists, and will serve the purpose of any student, as well as that of any member of the Syndicalist.

THE SYNDICALIST. — 1D.
A limited number of the January and February issues that were seized by the police can be had. Collectors can have copies of these to complete their collections at 5/- each, to go towards the "Weekly Syndicalist" fund.
Any of the succeeding issues can be obtained for.
GUY BOWMAN, Publisher, 4, Maude Terrace, Walthamstow.

C. J. SMITH,
8, St. James Street,
WALTHAMSTOW

High-Class Pianos from £12 12s. Cash.

OUR CELEBRATED PIANOS — DEFY COMPETITION. — Cash, or from 10s. monthly.

All Pianos Fully Warranted for 15 Years.

Printed and Published by GUY BOWMAN, 4, Maude Terrace, Walthamstow, E.

The Syndicalist

VOL. 1. NO. 11.   LONDON, DECEMBER, 1912.   MONTHLY, ONE PENNY.

GEORGE LANSBURY.

The political contest at Bow commanded attention beyond the ordinary. George Lansbury had exhibited a degree of independence and courage in parliament that secured for him the disapprobation of all the machine politicians. Lansbury was a Socialist and a Labour man, agreeing thoroughly in the methods of advocacy of the Labour Party, but with exceptionally deep sympathies for the sufferings of the impoverished, and a large-heartedness that dominated his life compelling him to make effort upon effort in attacking what he believed were the chief sources of economic servitude and working-class degradation.

Lansbury is not a man to sit quiet for fear of hurting the feelings of some government official or parliamentary Front Bencher, so let who cared to approve or otherwise, whenever he saw a chance to ventilate a workers' grievance or to take to task a member of the government for indifference or neglect, Lansbury would be up and "at him."

To the writer of this article it is a matter of unusual interest to observe the development of George Lansbury. I have known him well over twenty years, and soon after Lansbury entered the House of Commons as a member I happened to be there, speaking with Keir Hardie on industrial affairs. George happened to pass us; he pulled up, and joined briefly in the subject of conversation, but soon stretched out his hand to me to say goodbye, and added : "Tom; you have gone back forty years." By this he meant that my declaring that the right method for the workers to fight was by industrial action, and that parliament was a negligible quantity. I was on the wrong tack, and, as George left me, the tone of his voice implied : "I say it more in sorrow than in anger."

As everyone knows, industrial affairs began to move, and in the following year, 1911, when I was in Liverpool, and the city was absolutely held up, and solidarity was manifested on an hitherto unknown scale, and the substantial demands were receiving respectful consideration, George Lansbury went down to Liverpool to observe affairs ; he was evidently impressed. The power to get at grips with economic evils in parliament had not shown itself, but the possible chance to get grip seemed farther and farther off, and here in front of him he saw ordinary workmen actually functioning as the direct controllers of the conditions, that should obtain in the vast and wealthy industry they were identified with. George declared he had not believed it possible, but he saw it and knew it to be so. From that time his attitude was changed, and his faith in industrial solidarity grew ; but George was, and, I suppose, still is, a State-ist ; he views the State as Society ; he does not take the Syndicalist view that the organised State, with its government and officials and armed forces, was brought into existence by the opponents of the Workers, and functions only in the interests of the enemies of the Workers.

If George Lansbury gives himself free rein to calmly contemplate the all-sufficiency of industrial solidarity and resorting to DIRECT ACTION methods for grappling with economic servitude he will probably be unable to remain where he is at present, expressing disgust with, and contempt for, parliament, and yet wishful to get there.

We are neither sorry nor glad at the result of the Bow election. In our opinion it does not matter a straw what the political complexion of members of parliament may be. The only thing that is really vital is that the percentage of the working class, who have the right conceptions of solidarity and its use to enable the Workers to function as the actual controllers of industry, shall continue to increase. They are increasing rapidly now, and nothing that parliament or government can do can seriously retard their growth. The economic emancipation of the working class will be a certainty in the near future, and we hope George Lansbury will soon find full scope in the all-important industrial arena for his warm heart and honest mind, and abundant physical energy.

TOM MANN.

AMALGAMATION COMMITTEES' FEDERATION.

ONE INDUSTRY! ONE UNION!! ONE CARD!!!

FIRST OUTCOME OF OUR LONDON CONFERENCE.

JACK WILLS AS SECRETARY.

In accordance with resolution No. 3, carried at the Conference convened by the I.S.E.L., and held in the Holborn Hall on November 9 and 10, a Conference of the Amalgamation Committees was convened by the I.S.E.L., and was held at the Trafalgar, St. Martin's Lane, W.C., on Sunday, November 24.

The following Amalgamation Committees were represented : Building Trades Consolidation Committee, by Messrs. J. V. Wills, F. Traquair, and B. Garnsey ; Engineering and Shipbuilding Committee, by D. Armstrong, J. P. Lloyd, and W. Bax ; Transport Workers' Amalgamation Committee, S. Roden, F. Halkett, F. J. Passmore ; Provisional Committee for Amalgamating Existing Trades Unions, W. Scott, P. Edmonds, and R. A. Bender.

Guy Bowman, who presided for the first part of the evening, read letters from W. Lawther and W. H. Mainwaring, secretaries of the Miners' Unofficial Committees of Durham and South Wales, wishing the Conference every success, and stating that before long they would join the Federation.

The Printing Trades' Amalgamation Committee were not represented, a letter being read from the Secretary objecting to the manner in which the Conference was called, and stating that they could not see their way to attend.

A resolution was moved by J. P. Lloyd and W. Scott : "That the Conference recommend the Provisional Committee to convene a conference of the committees for the purpose of forming the Federation."

An amendment was moved by J. V. Wills and D. Armstrong : "That this Conference decides to form a Federation of the Amalgamation Committees." J. V. Wills, in moving the amendment, said that the Conference was the logical outcome of the Holborn Hall Conference, and he wanted to get to business and so did the majority of those who came for amalgamation, and he did not care who initiated the Federation so long as it was formed.

The day was past for silly talk, they were not children playing with marbles, but men out for business. To get the Federation formed was the most important business, irrespective of who convened the Conference for that purpose.

On the amendment being put to the vote, it was carried with only one dissentient.

On its being put as a substantiated resolution, the amendment was carried with one abstention.

Guy Bowman said he was very pleased that the decision had been arrived at, and now that the Federation was formed, they would conduct their own business as

JACK WILLS,
Secretary, Amalgamation Committees' Federation.

Trade Unionists, and he would vacate the chair.

D. Armstrong was then elected to the chair. W. Scott was elected treasurer, and J. V. Wills was appointed secretary.

A vote of thanks to the I.S.E.L. was carried for their services in convening the Conference.

The Federation decided to issue a general manifesto for circulation amongst all Trade Unionists on the subject of amalgamation.

Our comrade J. V. Wills was appointed secretary of the Federation. He is well known in the Trade Union movement. He has been a delegate from his Society to the Trade Union Congress, where, on behalf of the Operative Bricklayers' Society, he moved a resolution in favour of the Trade Unions amalgamating by Industries. For thirteen years he has been an active member of his Union, and for ten years he served his branch as their delegate upon the Bermondsey and Rotherhithe Trades Council. He has been keenly interested in the amalgamation of the Unions, and was one of the earliest associates of the Building Trades Consolidation Committee. J. V. Wills was a delegate from that body to the Operative Bricklayers' Society's official Consolidation Committee. who have been largely responsible for bringing about the recent vote in the Building Trades Unions in favour of amalgamation into ONE Industrial Union. For about nine years he was a member of the S.D.F., S.D.P., and now B.S.P. For three years he occupied the position of secretary of the Bermondsey branch, which position he resigned on account of his opinions on Industrial Unionism, which came into conflict with the official attitude of the Party. He ultimately resigned the B.S.P. on account of their Anti-Syndicalist attitude. He has been on the Bermondsey Borough Council for three years, and is now an Alderman.

During the great industrial upheaval of 1911 he played a very prominent part. During that period and during the Dock Strike of 1912 he was actively engaged as a propagandist. Bermondsey being one of the largest of the waterside districts in London, he had ample scope for his abilities. He has a thorough practical knowledge of the working-class movement, the knowledge that can only be obtained by those who have actually been in, and are part of, the movement. He is thoroughly convinced of the necessity of industrial organisation, sees that through that alone is the emancipation of the workers to be achieved. He is extremely active in the Labour movement, and has won the confidence of his fellows by his integrity and energy.

The position could not be occupied by a more fitting man.

May he have a long and useful career in his new post.

JOTTINGS.

In our August number, in which we appealed for an initial sum of £300 to start on a WEEKLY SYNDICALIST, I mentioned Mrs. Dallas-Askew's offer of £50 subject to the condition that the balance be forthcoming in a comparatively short time.

At the same time Mrs. Askew asked me to publish an article of hers entitled "Expression or Representation." I agreed to print the article at the time, but when I saw it in print I found it contained a diatribe of Hyndman and a praise of Quelch. This I considered was absolutely out of order, and would serve no purpose whatsoever. I therefore struck out the passage referred to, and printed her article as it appeared in our August issue. This Mrs. Askew did not like, and accordingly wrote saying she withdrew her offer of £50.

As I wish my readers to know how we stand at present with regard to the fund for the WEEKLY SYNDICALIST, I wrote to Mrs. Askew and here is her answer :

La Pineta, Monti Trinita, Ticino, Switzerland,
Nov. 22.

Dear Mr. Editor,—In reply to your letter regarding the withdrawal of my offer, I can only repeat what I wrote to you in September. My offer was entirely subjected to two conditions : First, the opportunity to discuss the question of *representation as opposed to expression*; secondly, six other subscribers to be found to give the same sum. When the first of these conditions was broken by alteration without my consent of my article, I wrote almost immediately to withdraw the offer. This was not published. I can only repeat regretfully the withdrawal made then.

You objected to the examples I gave as illustrations of the method or theory, but surely application is an essential stage. No analysis is complete without illustration. The case of monopoly to which I referred was so marked as to be impossible to ignore, unless for political reasons. With these we agreed Syndicalism has nothing to do. Moreover, every word in the article you accepted was most carefully weighed, and reference was made to any but well-known and authenticated facts, and as regards conclusions I accepted full responsibility in signing my name. Amongst the many changes made without my consent the most damaging to the sense was the insertion of the word *misrepresentation*, an expression I carefully refrained from using, from the point of view of the æsthetic, which is that of expression considered under the scientific or general form, all representation is misrepresentation. False or spurious expression, apologies for the labour or effort involved in the real.

I have already subscribed to your paper so far as I think justified, and hope to be able to continue to do so. I am convinced that the Syndicalist method of Direct Action must reveal direct expression as the only real form in time.

Yours cordially,
F. DALLAS-ASKEW.

Now, Mrs. Askew is a personal friend of ours, and she has been very kind to me personally. I do not want to quarrel with her, and I want to remain her friend ; but may I point out to her and all concerned that the policy of THE SYNDICALIST cannot be influenced by anyone merely because of their offer to support the paper financially. But in any case, and under no circumstances, are we going to imitate the pernicious policy of the Socialist Parties—namely, to tear one another to pieces, which has proved so disastrous for the last quarter of a century. We desire to carry on our propaganda without taking any notice of what other people may do or say, and our friend Tom Mann would certainly refuse to have any longer anything to do with a paper that devotes its space to attacking other people.

Mrs. Askew will be welcome to write as many articles as she likes on any subject that is of interest to us, and we should be glad to publish them ; but if they contain personal attacks, or too much praise of other people, I shall do as I did before—use my blue pencil.

The following are the contributions received for the WEEKLY SYNDICALIST :

	£	s.	d.
Previously acknowledged	63	12	3½
Norman Young	0	1	6
Ewald Draugs	0	4	0
Lucy Parsons	0	2	10½
Geo. Jackson	0	5	0
F. Sadler	0	5	0
John and Anna Lincoln	0	2	0
W. H. Paine	0	1	0
B. Saunders	0	1	0
R. Poulter	0	2	0
Fred Pinnell	0	2	6
Peter Carton	0	2	0
Gaylord Wilshire	1	1	0
Holborn Hall Conference (collection)	1	3	7
Lily Gair Wilkinson	1	0	0
Total	£68	8	9

In response to our friend Joseph Lane's suggestion in our last issue, we have received two annual subscriptions, paid in advance, for receipt of a copy by post each week as soon as THE SYNDICALIST appears as a weekly :

Shadwell	6	6
Joseph Lane	6	6

This is a long way off the £325 which this particular method is intended to raise. How many more subscriptions will come in before we get our next issue out ?

*   *   *

I cannot make out why the money has not been forthcoming. Don't you want a WEEKLY SYNDICALIST ? Our circulation is now larger than any Socialist paper in Britain except the *Clarion*. Look at the enormous influence we could wield if only it were a weekly. Rally up, comrades, and let us have a WEEKLY SYNDICALIST soon. We want it absolutely if the working class is to make any headway.

GUY BOWMAN.

The Syndicalist

EDITED UNDER THE AUSPICES OF

The Industrial Syndicalist Education League

Offices—

4, MAUDE TERRACE, WALTHAMSTOW,
LONDON, E.

MONTHLY - ONE PENNY.

Post Paid Subscription—

Great Britain or Abroad ... 12 months 1s. 6d.

Bundle Rates—

1s. 6d. per quire, Carriage Paid.

The receipt of a Sample Copy is an invitation to Subscribe.

DECEMBER, 1912.

WHERE WE STAND.

Since the government prosecutions over the Open Letter in the SYNDICALIST Syndicalism has been to the fore. A great number of people have called themselves Syndicalists without even troubling as to whether the ideas they advocated were really Syndicalist or not. Every person who is at all connected with the union movement, and even many who are not, have invented a Syndicalism of their own. Weird and wonderful are some of the suggestions which are put forward as Syndicalist proposals. The first thing that is trotted out is the commissariat idea. That is easily accounted for. The people who put this forward have caught a glimmering of the power that Syndicalist methods of organisation would produce. They can imagine an almost universal stoppage, or at least the stoppage of a whole industry; then they think of the food supply: the commissariat to beat the capitalists by starvation. Futile method, productive of nothing except the killing of all militant spirit; excellent means of providing the government with rations for others than the strikers. There is no Syndicalism in a suggestion of this kind. There may be better organisation, there may be the supply, but there is no revolutionary driving power in this method. The capitalists' government could obtain control of the food supply in this country by expropriation. The workers must do the same. Equally absurd is the suggestion of competing the capitalists out of existence by money. For the organised workers of this country to build up co-operative enterprises may do a little good, but also a great deal of harm. The Co-operative movement of to-day affords a striking example of the power of a little wealth to kill revolutionary instincts. The co-operative movement was started, in the first place, as a means to bring in a new social system. Now, to a large extent, they are bulwarks of capitalism. How many workmen with the accumulation of the "divi" have managed to get a sum of money invested? The share capital grows, the interest accumulates, and the revolutionary spirit diminishes in an inverse ratio to the growth of the account in the share book. Social revolutionists become social reformers. The sole element that can form the basis of a proletarian movement—direct and forcible expropriation of the owners of land and capital—disappears. Modifications of the capitalist system are accepted, school clinics, municipal housing schemes —when they can be obtained—Poor Law reform, and the extension of State Bureaucracy; but profit, rent, and interest are left untouched; or, if touched at all, only in such a way as to make the continuation of the system possible by making it tolerable. The average teetotal, thrifty, divi-saving co-operator pictures a garden city, with a benevolent Cadbury, or other employer of a like kind, paying "good" wages, letting "good" houses at "fair" rents, as the God of this little Paradise, which, by some strange illusion, has become their conception of an "emancipated" working class. There are scores of "good" employers who dream of this and who endeavour to accomplish it. They tell us that they are not greedy, that they will have a co-partnership, that they only want 5 per cent. on capital invested, and then they will share the other profit with us. They are so good that they voluntarily reduce their exploitation to only 5 per cent. Bah! The practical, business-like, hardheaded co-operator is usually the first to be "codded" by a scheme of this kind, which simply means the perpetuation of the wages system of wage-slavery.

A few taxi-drivers, by clubbing together, may manage to purchase their own vehicles, but that does not alter the fact that the companies own most, and that they could practically run the others off the streets if they so wished. A small increase of the price of petrol and a few shillings less per day in fares will seriously affect the owner of a single vehicle, but not to the same extent the companies. Try how they will, the workers will never be able to defeat capital with capital. Some section of the capitalists may be beaten by these means, but not all. Co-operation and co-partnership are not Syndicalism; nor do they necessarily support the Syndicalist worker. They can easily be used as an instrument against the success of Syndicalism. The growth of co-operatives and co-partnerships does not affect the transfer of the ownership of capital from the capitalist to the workers. We are equally as much misjudged by those people who seem to think that Syndicalism simply means a share in the management of an industry by the organised workers. A variety of people propagate this idea. The *New Age* has a theory of co-partnership between the Unions and the State which is suggested as a solution of the problem. But it is no solution. This "Guild Socialism," as its supporters have christened this bastard of State Socialism and Syndicalism, ignores the fact that the political State itself is one of the chief means of exploitation. It exploits both as an employer and as a government. Why should the Unions have a partnership with the State? What is the State? Merely a political machine for a ruling class to dominate an exploited class and to provide the means of violence to maintain that exploitation. "Ah! but we mean a democratic State," say the Guild Socialists. But what is a democratic State? It is one where the permanent officials, the bureaucrats, can safely say, "The State—that's me." And who are these people who are to be the predominant partners in this unlimited liability company of the State and the Unions? Why, whom do you think? Could they possibly be other than Civil servants, bureaucrats, who, after making their living by sucking the ideas from the brains of the workers, have the cool impudence to suggest a permanent lodgment on our backs? Whilst personally as polite to these people as they are to us, we know where their interests lie and how they must live on us. We are not deceived. Syndicalism means the organisation of the workers for the expropriation of the capitalists by the organised workers, and the ownership and control of industry by, and through, their Unions.

PETER KROPOTKIN.

On December 9 Peter Kropotkin celebrated his 70th birthday. All those who know of his devoted and unselfish work for the Social Revolution will join with us in paying our tribute of love and admiration which we have for him. Unfortunately, the mass of the workers have never yet been brought into contact with his splendid work. If Kropotkin had done nothing more than give the world his Fields, Factories, and Workshops, his Mutual Aid, and that magnificent revolutionary study, "The Conquest of Bread," he would have accomplished sufficient to have carved for himself a niche in the hearts of all those who wish Well-Being, Freedom, and Happiness for All.

He has devoted his whole life, regardless of comfort and security, to the work of emancipation. Everyone should read his "Memoirs of a Revolutionist" to gain some insight into the sweet and wholesome character of this man, who threw aside title, rank, honour, and wealth in order to devote himself to the self-imposed task of helping to rid the world of economic slavery and its twin evil—political government.

The best homage all can pay to him is to study his works, imitate his unselfishness, and propagate his ideas. He will live long as one of the greatest of Emancipators of the Human Race.

RED RUBBER.

MASTERS' QUEER ARITHMETIC

By RUBBERITE.

(Continued from last month.)

II.

The work requires a fair amount of skill, some of the finished articles requiring micrometer measurements, as most rubber workers know. Many works of note have night and day gangs. One firm works their hands from twelve and a half to thirteen hours per night, with only half an hour break for a bite and a sup; it cannot be called a meal. When they enter the mill at night they are kept there till next morning.

What the position of the workers would be like if there were no trade unions in existence at all would be too awful to contemplate. If we were living in the eighteenth century, when anyone attempting to form a union would be banished for seven years, one could understand the workers being afraid to join their unions. We know that this happened to the well-known Dorchester labourers in the year 1829, but our forefathers fought and won legal recognition for the unions, after much suffering and imprisonment. There is nothing to keep the workers out of the unions now but their own apathy and indifference. They should avail themselves of every opportunity that comes their way to secure some amelioration. If rubber workers think that the employers are going to higher wages, shorten hours, and give better working conditions of their own free will, they are under an illusion. Piecework is made a fine art, and with its twin evil, "fines," so arranged that Shylock is outdone. God knows that the workers have to work hard to get anything of a wage as it is, without having "fines" for faults which may not be caused by the operatives.

One firm has an arithmetic of its own. They pay for joining up inner-tubes the rate of 5½d. *per hundred*, yet if there are any "rejects" the girls are stopped 3½d. *per dozen*. There are eight items on the fines list, and the least fine is 3d. per dozen.

Girls Clamouring for Sweated Work.

With the girls working at a breakneck speed, their fingers working like springs manipulating the rubber tubes, to get bread and make the employers' profits, is it any wonder there are "rejects"? They clamour for work like mad wolves for food, to "get their day in." Then there is the bad effects of the naphtha fumes which pervade the shops, making the air sickly.

To save expense, a vitriolic liquid, "Camphene," is used, which makes the girls' hands all swelled, chapped, and bleeding, as though they had been slashed with knives. The workers pay one penny per week hospital money, and thus are entitled to the doctor's skill to get their hands well again, only to go back to work to go through the same process again. It costs the girls no small sum out of their wages each week in buying preparations for their hands. Girls are also called upon to do "Cold Cure" work; every rubber worker knows the harmful effects that this has on one's system. Its bad effects can be retarded by quantities of milk, but the employers—like their rubber—can stretch the law if need be, and openly ignore it. Let cyclists when they are awheel reflect for a moment as to how their tyres and inner tubes are made. They are the product of the sweat and tears of the operatives.

Day Shift v. Night Shift.

The men are sweated just as much as the women. The night shift is pitted against the day shift, to see which gang can turn out most in a given time, which is set out by clerks who, if they had to run a business on their own would make small headway with a whelk stall. Under the guise of looking after the men, they have the business taught them. Managers are changed, new methods tried, fresh substitutes in the rubber in order to cheapen it and make more profit.

When men are inside the works they lose all individuality; they become so many cogs in the wheel, to be worked at the sweet will of their employers ten, twelve, and fourteen hours per day or night, Sundays included, when orders have to be got out, and when not wanted outside they have to go.

NOTICE TO SYMPATHISERS.

In order to make the work of the I.S.E.L. effective, we must be able to reach every Trade Union Branch; therefore send all Trade Union Reports and Branch Lists to the General Secretary.

SYNDICALIST LECTURES.

Trade Unions, Trades' Councils, or Labour Societies desiring to know more about Syndicalism can have speakers attend their meetings. Travelling expenses only are asked for. Write General Secretary, I.S.E.L.

A MESSAGE TO THE WORKERS.

FROM A MONMOUTHSHIRE MINER.

Change, change; all things are in a state of incessant change. Animate and inanimate Nature, things, man, and institutions—all, all obey the laws of Nature and go through the cycle of change. Spring, Summer, Autumn, Winter—such is the cycle of seasons. The elements contained in the atmosphere are converted by Nature into vegetable, reconverted into animal matter, die, decay, and return to the atmosphere, and their former state. One state succeeds another in an unbroken chain, and human institutions are no exception to the rule. Institutions are but the embodiments of ideas, and ideas change with succeeding generations. We have had thrust upon us, whether we like it or not, in the most remarkable and sensational manner, during that magnificent upheaval known as the national coal strike, the idea of Syndicalism. What does it mean? We have responsible and respectable Labour leaders and Socialists repudiating any connection whatever with this audacious upstart. But, despite this, it is your duty, fellow-worker, and mine, as well-wishers of, and workers for, the common weal, to discuss this idea, and try to comprehend its meaning.

Nature, whether wisely or unwisely, has brought into existence a world; it has evolved a race of supposedly rational beings; let us live up to this supposition and think—think, and act. We have a world. We are a human race, and nature has decreed that, in order to live and propagate we must work. It is ours to make the best of things, and not to be content with the worst. We have had monarchical government, both absolute and limited. Can it be claimed that either has been a success from the workers' point of view? Republicanism, which was hailed as a boon, has been tried in the balance and found wanting. When we look around us and examine the different forms of government in vogue, there is only one conclusion we can arrive at, and that is that politics is the synonym of cunning, and the acts of politicians and parties are knavish tricks designed to deceive the people. We have what is called a science of political economy. What does it deal with? It treats of the consumption, production, distribution, and exchange of wealth. What is wealth? Wealth is all those goods and services which satisfies human wants, and requires an effort to obtain. No good can come of calling a spade an implement of agriculture; it leads to confusion. And we had may as well call this science, if science it is, the science of industrial economy.

The argument, obsolete though it is, still used by non-Socialists against Socialism, that it means dividing up, is just as absurd as the argument, or more properly speaking the statement, for it is no argument, used by Socialists against Syndicalism, that it means that those people working in a particular industry should own and control the tools and natural resources necessary to that industry and exploit the workers in all other industries. The statement is made in good faith, perhaps; but nothing is adduced to prove that it is at all likely to turn out that way. There was one economist, unorthodox of course, who asserted, and proved to my humble mind at least that commodities exchange with commodities in equal ratio—that is, in proportion to the amount of socially necessary labour embodied in them, or in other words, in proportion to the amount of labour socially necessary to produce them. That profits are made by exploiting the workers, by paying the workers wages varying in amounts less than what they really earn. If it takes a tailor one working day of eight hours to make a coat, and a bootmaker an equal time to make a pair of boots, the cost of the raw material in both cases being the same, the coat will exchange for the pair of boots—no more, no less. But if one man employs a number of tailors, and another man employs a number of bootmakers, and each employer pays his employees for seven hours' labour while exacting ten from them, the manner of profit-making indulged in by our employers is obvious. What is the underlying principle of our trade unions? Is it not to band ourselves together, so as to be better able to demand higher wages and better conditions of labour? Or, if you prefer it, to compel our employers to accept less profits?

Industrial economy, then, if you accept the term, treats of the consumption, production, distribution, and exchange of wealth. Let people consume that which they consider is best for them. We will deal here with production, distribution, and exchange, as they fundamentally affect society. Who produces the wealth of nations? Why, the workers! No one denies it. Who performs the real function of exchanging this wealth? The workers again. We produce and exchange wealth under the protection of the Police, Army, and Navy, a worthy university professor tells me. Quite so, and is it not reasonable to argue that industrious folk and none other should control these protective forces, and not be cowed by them into submission and acceptance of living conditions which are simply hellish. The past twelve months has seen a grand revolt of workers, and the attempt also to cow them by means of these very forces. The tide must turn! Who should have the authority to say how many hours per day and how many days per year men should be compelled to toil in the darkness and danger of the mine, in order to win for society the precious nuggets of coal? Who has mere right to control the hours and conditions of labour, in field, factory, and workshop than the people who have to toil in those places? The whole fabric of society rests on the bent backs of the workers, and they hardly dare look up for fear of being shot down. But there are men among them who have dared, and who are looking up. Men who have asked themselves, why is this so? And, after long searching, they have found the answer. It is this: That while the workers produce and exchange wealth, a comparatively small number of shirkers distribute this wealth, taking unto themselves the major portion, doling out to the workers the minor portion, to enable them to exist, and have for the sole object in life —what? Why, work. How do these noble shirkers manage it? By legalised thievery and pious fraud. They control the Legislature, the Police, the Army, and the Navy. They have a firm hold on the helm of the ship of State, and we suffer them to guide and to govern us. We are the nation. They are the State. When we aspire to take hold of the helm, they give us the Osborne Judgment; when we grumble, payment of Members; when we demand reform in thundering tones, they give us a Royal Commission of Inquiry. What a farce is politics. Let us have no more fooling. We have works committees, executive committees, agents, secretaries, and presidents. We have national conferences and congresses, also international. Let us bestir ourselves and utilise the means at our disposal to regain possession of the land and the instruments of industry, to be used with our labour for the good of the community. In Trade Unionism we have the machinery necessary for self-government. Fellow workers, I appeal to you, organise; organise with a definite object in view, and be assured that as we perfect our Trade Organisations, and conversely, as we assert ourselves, the old ideas of State and politics must wither and decay. The old State will pass away and with its passing the new one will have arisen when men shall brothers be, and overbearing superiority and cringing servility with all their attendant evils will have disappeared for ever. Syndicalism means :—

The World for the Workers,
Perdition to Shirkers,
Peace! Happiness! and Plenty.

SOME FALLACIES STATED AND ANSWERED.

THE GENERAL STRIKE AND THE COMMISSARIAT.

A GREAT ILLUSION.

There are some good friends of ours who imagine that the most important items in the economic warfare between the workers and the Capitalists is for the former to accumulate huge funds and from these funds to purchase large quantities of foodstuffs in order that, when a general strike takes place, the workers may have a food supply of their own, and thus, "irony of ironies," starve the ruling class into submission.

But we Syndicalists must insist that it is not by huge treasuries or large stores that the ruling class can be defeated and expropriated, for this tactic merely resolves itself into the absurd position of the workers trying to fight Capital with capital. So long as the workers rely merely upon money, they are face to face with the obvious fact that the Capitalists possess most.

Our comrade Tom Mann has, in our October issue, given us some idea of the enormous growth of Syndicalism in Sweden. This growth really dates from the end of the Swedish general strike of 1909. The general strike was a defeat. Why? Because it was peaceful, because the workers relied upon their commissariat. With the utmost stupidity the strike leaders suggested the formation of a "strikers' police" in order to maintain "the peace, order, and tranquillity" of the cities.

Preserving the Peace.

There was no violence, no sabotage, no Direct Action. With but one or two exceptions everything was left to the test of the commissariat trial of strength.

When the bourgeois found that blacklegs could go to work with impunity, when they knew that all the various plants were in good order, when they saw the strikers appoint men from their own ranks "to preserve the peace," they realised that it was only a peaceful "withdrawal of labour," and that they could act in safety. Calls were issued for men to join "The Public Security Brigade," like our special constables and civilian police. All those salaried officials, whose interests were identical with the capitalists, expressed their willingness to engage in the most urgent and necessary of tasks, and under the guidance of managers, sub-managers, and foremen, the men of the middle class forsook their ease and indolence and obtained some useful exercise by acting as strike-breakers.

To quote an example given in the *Times* of Aug. 10, 1909, the editorial staff of the *Stockholm Dagblad* carried out the production of their paper and presented a copy to the pickets outside the office. The Swedish general strike of 1909 was lost because they relied upon their money-bags.

With the Politicians.

Even less effective was the general strike in Belgium about 1904. This was a collapse. Organised in order to demand universal suffrage, the Socialist politicians saw that it was kept a peaceful affair. They withdrew their defiant utterances, and the strike was allowed to collapse. They are now engaged upon another attempt to provoke a general strike. Arrangements have been made through the co-operative societies to supply food only to those with tickets, and so forth. We can safely predict beforehand that, whilst they *may* obtain some minor political concessions, which will not injure the employers as employers, if the strike is conducted merely on passive lines, another defeat is ahead of them.

In Great Britain these last few years there has been a splendid growth in the solidarity of the workers. The transport strike of 1911 was a splendid and successful manifestation of unity. The miners' strike of 1911-1912 was a fine example of combination. But, successful as this strike was as a strike, its good results were thrown away by the stupidity of the men's leaders, mostly politicians, who allowed a national movement to be broken into districts, and thus betrayed the men. Arising out of its unfortunate settlement were a number of critics and advisers who condemned the methods used and advocated some other moves for use in the next national miners' strike. Some of the suggestions for their line of action were, like the curate's egg, excellent in parts.

Flirting with Direct Action.

Some members of the B.S.P., who, whilst being wedded to Parliamentarism, nevertheless like to be daring enough to flirt with Direct Action, pronounced their oracles upon this matter. They have *their* own particular brand of Syndicalism, which amounts to this: We will flirt with Syndicalism, we will toy with her, we will enjoy to the utmost our illicit relations with her; but if she dares to insist upon our full-hearted devotion we will leave her and return like respectable married Britishers to our legal wife at home in the

FIGHTING GOLD WITH GOLD.

NO REMEDY.

Homœopathic sends us a scheme for getting rid of the capitalist class by fighting them with gold. On the ground of like for like and same for same, he suggests that the two million odd Trade Unionists should pay in to a fund £1 per year for two years. This would bring in £4,000,000, which are to be withdrawn from circulation until two years were over, and then the Unions are to start rival banks to those existing, and thus compete the capitalists out of existence. We are afraid that we are dense. We say that gold could be demonetised; that the workers could not all pay in that pound per year apart from other payments as suggested; that to compete the whole of the capitalists out by rival concerns overlooks the State-sanctioned monopolies that different concerns possess; that the withdrawal of so much gold coin would rush up prices to the extent of hitting those workers who were saving the £1 per year; that if this £4,000,000 were accumulated, where are they going to be invested to get the three per cent. that would maintain several Labour Banks and their staffs? And how is interest to be paid except by exploiting the workers? And the fact of exploitation is the same thing whether the employer owns all his own capital, borrows from a capitalist bank, from a co-operative bank, a Labour bank, or a £4,000,000 war chest.

Westminster Talking Shop, and leave her to face the rest of life without us. They want all the excitement of Direct Action without any of its unpleasantness.

Then they told the miners that before they had another general strike they had to attend to the commissariat. Contracts ought to be made with the Co-operative Wholesale Society and other co-operative societies to deliver certain quantities of food in return for tickets issued by the strike committees. This idea has been seized upon with avidity. Our politicians who flirt with Direct Action have developed it to the extent of declaring that the combined unions should accumulate huge stores of foodstuffs in order that a national general strike of all industries should be called, and that the strikers could hold out long enough to compel the capitalists to submit through starvation. Now that which is good sense in a limited area may easily become nonsense when enlarged. As an example, a person may absorb a small quantity of strychnine into his system with other chemicals and it will have beneficial results as a nerve tonic, but a large dose of strychnine is of use only for making corpses.

Confiscation, the Prerogative of Governments.

Let us suppose that all the miners' unions proceeded to entrust their funds to the Co-operative Bank and Co-operative Wholesale Society on the understanding that they could claim food to the value of the money invested; that they allowed a period to elapse, and that they gave in their notices of strike in the usual long-winded way. They maintain this peaceful constitutional attitude and commence their holiday. First of all they would have to wait for the supplies at the pit-heads, wharves, and railway sidings to be exhausted before any great uneasiness was caused. Let us suppose that the railway service was curtailed and that voluntarily the railwaymen had made common cause with the miners, that the textile workers and metal workers were at a standstill. Well? The Government would get the Royal Engineers to run some sort of railway service, such as they did during the Irish railway strike. The country would be placed under martial law. What foodstuffs came to the ports would be commandeered, the non-striking populace placed on siege rations, and if this was insufficient for their needs, particularly for the Army, then those accumulated stores of the strikers would be requisitioned in "His Majesty's name" by the military and distributed by them and the police in different localities. The National Reserve, the special constables, the civilian police, and a large proportion of the non-working-class male population would assist.

To the argument that for the Government to take these stores would be illegal, as if that being so would prevent it, is to betray an abysmal ignorance on the part of those who use it. Confiscation is the prerogative of Governments. The Government would speedily legalise such action.

The Absurdity of Passivism.

The Taff Vale decision was really an illegal one.

The legality of the act is nothing; the thing is, Would the Government have the power to accomplish it? If things were as they are at present, if the workers merely ceased work, the answer is undoubtedly they would.

For Syndicalists to preach passivism is absurd. The expropriation of the capitalists is not going to be accomplished by the starvation of the workers. For us the general strike is not a national movement for working-class starvation but the commencement of the capitalists' expropriation. The "commissariat" idea may be a good one for sectional strikes, but we are not enamoured of it.

(Continued on page 6.)

THE CONTINUOUS STRIKE OF JUST VERSUS UNJUST.

By REV. G. T. SADLER.

To the Editor of the SYNDICALIST.

Dear Sir,—I always look forward to your paper, and wish it were a weekly. I like its bringing of men together, and I like its anti-war spirit. But why advocate the class-war between workers and capitalists? Is that a true division? What of shopkeepers? They are both capitalists and workers. What of the thousands of working-men with savings in the Post Office or elsewhere? They are capitalists and workers. What of a managing-director of a company? Is his work necessary? Sectional strikes are proved useless (or almost so). What have the railway men, the miners, the dockers gained—net gain, remember—after deducting what they lost in fighting their strikes? Not much. The General Strike you want. It is a myth, according to Sorel; a myth, like the hope of the Second Coming on the clouds. It may inspire for a time, but it comes not. You really need something bigger than a general strike of "workers" against capitalists—vague and inconsistent as that is. You want a continuous strike of *those who are just against those who are unjust*. (1) The land has been stolen by force of arms and parliament from the people by the great landlords. It is justice to have it back. Let the owners only own it therefore for "lives in being." To vote for that is justice without harshness. *Unite all who want such justice.* That is the true, deep, strong Syndicalism. (2) Working-men must begin now, with the middle classes, to work out justice to the childhood of the nation. It is unjust to a child to bring it into the world if you have not a fair chance to provide for it healthily, and in thousands of cases there is no such fair chance, and men know it. "They ought to be able to provide." Perhaps; but let them have the means ere they ask God or Nature for so many children. Justice is our basis of reform. It means self-control and effort; but God defends the right! Here are two examples. I add a third and a fourth and fifth with which you will agree. (3) Workers should share profits they have helped to make, and even losses share to a small extent. (4) It is not justice to go to parliament and vote like sheep to keep any party in office. Let all seats face one way, and every member be a man first of all! (5) It is not justice for financiers to send working-men, called soldiers, to fight and die that they, the few rich, may get concessions at the ends of the earth. Let men refuse to be soldiers, therefore. (6) Justice to women, economic and political emancipation. There is no other basis, but justice, for a permanent social order. Unite *all* who feel this and will work on such lines.

Yours faithfully,
GILBERT T. SADLER.

Mr. Sadler has proven himself a good friend of ours by his support. Whether or not that support has been given under a misapprehension is hard to say. We hope not. However, his letter raises many points. His first question, "Why advocate the class war between workers and capitalists?" is quickly answered. Our sense of *justice* compels us to urge a conflict of those who produce wealth against those who do not produce, but appropriate. From the viewpoint of economic *justice*, profits appear in reality as value created by the workers for which the capitalists give no equivalent when they take it. It is simply legalised theft. We make war on these thieves. There must be an antagonism between those who work for wages and create profits and those who do no work, but are able to appropriate the proceeds of those who do. Our sense of *justice* says that this is a true division. Shopkeepers are not wage workers. They are not dependent upon an employer. They are small capitalists. Where they are merely middlemen they are simply a parasitic class upon the community. With an effective organisation of production and distribution they would disappear. The co-operative movement has demonstrated that they are unnecessary. With regard to the working-men with savings, we admit that they exist, but that the interest received upon their savings is insufficient to keep them without working. Technically speaking, they are capitalists. In so far as receiving interest proves that, directly or indirectly, labour is robbed for their benefit. They have to work for employers, and as such they have to come under the same competition, the same conditions of labour, &c., as those who are penniless. They have better sense of security, that is all. They do not cease to be wage slaves. Some managing directors perform a useful task, but workers can be trained for those positions, and when the work of managing directors is changed from that of seeing how much "unpaid value" can be extracted from the employees to that of seeing to the increased technical efficiency of the staff and their comfort, workers in the various departments would best qualify for the post. "The general strike is a myth, like the second coming on the clouds." Yes, Mr. Sadler, the second coming on the clouds is undoubtedly a myth, but not so the general strike. The whole course of union development of the last three years has been towards it. When other industries are organised to the same extent that the miners are at present and animated by a revolutionary impulse, the "myth" will soon be a reality.

"*We want a continuous strike of those who are just against those who are unjust.*" We are agreed, Mr. Sadler; but what is *justice*? Does it not vary according to the economic, social, and political status of the individual that contemplates this ideal *justice*? The capitalist thinks that it is *just* to extort "profit" from those he employs. The landlord thinks that it is *just* to buy and sell land and extort a tax from the non-landowners who are compelled to live upon it. The financier thinks that it is *just* to hire working-men as uniformed murderers to gain him concessions at the end of the earth. The average working man, at present, thinks that it is *just* to sell his manhood for a wage and follow an officer to the ends of the earth, and to do that officer's bidding, though his whole moral sense may revolt. The average M.P., and unfortunately most other men, too, think that it is *just* that women should economically and politically

"THE RAILWAYS TO THE RAILWAYMEN."

THE ONLY SOLUTION.

Oh, what visions of heated debates does the above sentence bring to one? The letters of protest from Socialists and even our own supporters! How we are accused of wanting to set up another form of class ownership! We reiterate the railways to the railwaymen, for the simple reason that the railway workers are the ones best capable of actually and efficiently running the railways. They do so to-day on behalf of the shareholders; they will do so in the future on behalf of themselves and the rest of a working-class commonwealth.

When our Socialist critics predict all sorts of anti-social, predatory actions by the workers of the different industries, because of their directly controlling their own activities, they are fashioning an argument against themselves. What is to prevent the State-controlled workers in a State-Socialist community from wanting different conditions? And how would they obtain them? By the strike? Our Socialist friends say that they want ownership by Society. But what constitutes Society? It is not a homogenous whole by any manner of means. It is composed of diverse and conflicting classes. When things are owned by "Society," like the Post Office, Dockyards and Arsenals, and Labour Exchanges, it simply means that the dominant capitalist class has control. Our political friends overlook the class-struggle which has to be fought to a finish, culminating in the expropriation of the capitalists.

State Ownership No Change.

We object to State control because it simply strengthens the hands of the ruling class by giving them a centralised and universal control. State ownership is the perpetuation of class exploitation. The wages system is not abolished. The State, and likewise the municipalities, guarantee the financiers their interest arising from the robbery of the workers.

The railwaymen could not act as brigands by refusing to carry goods except to their own disadvantage. They could not live by running trains, they could not feed upon the window straps, or yet sleep in safety and comfort on the permanent way. Their refusal to transport food, clothing, raw material, or manufactured goods would simply mean the denial of the use of these things to the railwaymen as much as it would to any other section of the community.

Self-Consciousness.

The success of Syndicalism depends entirely upon solidarity, mutual aid, joint action. Syndicalism teaches the greatest development of co-operation amongst all workers.

Whilst its tactics of Direct Action develop to the full the powers of the individual's initiative, its whole line of action is towards ever-extended mass movements of self conscious individuals, and not the blind rush of a flock of sheep. Our methods develop the virtues of initiative, courage, and the social instinct of cohesion.

By some unknown mental process our Parliamentary opponents picture a Social Revolution which is to leave everything as it is. The wages system is to be retained, profits are to be made from unpaid labour, money is to be kept.

Our conception of the Social Revolution, effected by the direct and forcible expropriation of the capitalists, abolishes at once and for all the wages system, production for profit, and the need for money. It means the communist reorganisation of society, the abolition of all political government, all society being workers, and these regulating and controlling their own conditions of existence through their economic organisations that have been shaped to that end.

SHOULD TRADE UNIONS BUY RIFLES?

WE SAY "NO!"

We are asked the question, "Seeing that the aim of the Syndicalists is to bring about the forcible expropriation of the capitalists, do you advocate that the Unions should buy rifles?"

We do not. It would be an impossibility for this to be done in an effective manner. The regulations concerning the sale of firearms are so stringent that no large quantity could be purchased without the Government being well aware of what was going on and taking action accordingly.

Of course, in a country where the carrying of arms is common, such as it still is in the Western States of America, it would be a wise thing for every unionist to be armed for self-defence against the brutality of the detectives, both of the regular police and private firms, and the military. The members of the Western Federation of Miners are at present holding up an entire city by reason of being armed. They are on strike, and frankly state that the importation of blacklegs under the protection of an armed force will be met with an armed resistance.

Learn to Shoot Straight.

Here in England it will take some generations before the average man is habituated to the use of arms. The advice in the advertisement in our columns, "Learn to shoot straight," will have to be followed much more than it generally is. To attempt the accumulation of arms is a queer business. The "physical force" section of the Home Rule Party found that out some twenty to thirty years ago. They had an armoury of theirs seized in London as well as some in Ireland. To endeavour to copy their methods is to resort to the old-style conspiracies, which have ever been the breeding-places of traitors and are the means by which the "agents provocateurs" accomplish their dirty business. We have no secrets for the slimy crew of detectives to nose out. We proclaim our objects from the housetops.

Get Them for Nothing.

Besides, why buy rifles when you can get them for nothing?

When the coal strike commenced the Territorials in South Wales had to bring in their rifles.

But we think that the advent of conscription is not far off. This will mean compulsory military training for all—an expert knowledge of the use of firearms. Then perhaps these considerations may be of use.

Meanwhile the strike weapon has to be developed and perfected. Revolutionary principles have to be spread. Our anti-militarist propaganda has to be extended. There is the great hope that our anti-militarist propaganda will teach the workers to understand why the weapons are placed in their hands by conscription. Then the weapons and magazines that have been established to uphold the reign of capitalism may be used for another purpose. We sap the power of the armed forces by the education of the workers both before and after they are compelled to join the services.

Scott's Temperance Commercial Hotel,

9, Halliwell Street, Corporation Street
(Near Victoria Station),

MANCHESTER.

Bed and Breakfast from 2/6.   Boots extra.

J. SCOTT, Proprietor

and in a *just* sense loss-sharing, we disagree. We have already given it out that our sense of *justice* says that profits are theft—unpaid value, created by the workers. The workers would have to create profits before they could "share" them. It is a device used for speeding up, for setting one worker against another, in order that a larger surplus may be created for the employers. The capitalist says create me 25 per cent. more profit than usual, and you shall have 10 per cent. divided amongst you. In plain English, he says, create me 15 per cent. more than formerly, and speed yourselves up to do it. We share most of the losses now. We get thrown out into the ranks of the unemployed or have wages reduced.

When our good friend Mr. Sadler can define *justice* other than in the way we have done we will consider our advocacy of it as "a basis for a permanent social order."

The one point on which we are in wholehearted agreement is where he says: "It is unjust to bring a child into the world if you have not a fair chance to provide for it healthily." Mr. Sadler is to be congratulated upon having the moral courage to make this statement. It is so vastly different to the average gentleman of the cloth. The landlords, the financiers, the military chiefs want the workers to breed large families to provide flesh for exploitation, flesh for their brothels, and flesh for the cannon. If the workers are wise they won't supply it. The wage worker with a large family is compelled to be the most abject slave of all.

LONDON AND MANCHESTER DECLARE FOR SYNDICALISM.

From Solidarity to the General Strike.

150,000 WORKERS REPRESENTED AT THE TWO I.S.E.L. CONFERENCES.

Two Conferences have been held under the auspices of the Industrial Syndicalist Education League. They far surpassed the hopes of the promoters.

Syndicalism was accepted as the only working policy for the wage-slaves.

At London resolutions calling for the amalgamation of Trade Unions according to industry, for the federation of the Industrial Unions, the federation of Trades Councils, and the Confederation of the two bodies when formed, were adopted almost unanimously.

The method of a complete organisation of a General Confederation of Labour was endorsed. The calling of an International Syndicalist Conference was agreed to.

At Manchester the whole of the London resolutions were endorsed. The methods to be used in the struggle of the workers against exploiters were considered.

In spite of the fear that means that were too drastic were proposed, and that the delegates would not support them, the Manchester Conference carried them all.

Direct Action was agreed to. Sabotage, Boycott, and Anti-militarism were taken as weapons for the workers' arsenal. With log cat convction the Conference agreed to call upon all workers to prepare for the expropriation of capitalists by means of the General Strike.

Syndicalism and its methods have the whole-hearted support of the militant workers. Contrary to foolish statements, it does not depend upon either Tom Mann or Guy Bowman. The rank and file are determined to work for it.

The I.S.E.L. has opened the flood-gates of Revolution; neither capitalists nor their State can hold back the deluge.

LONDON CONFERENCE, November 9th & 10th, 1912.

On Saturday, November 9, at the Holborn Hall, 98 delegates, representing 58 Societies, and over 50,000 Trade Unionists of London, met under the presidency of Guy Bowman. From the commencement, at 1.30 p.m., until its close, at 6 p.m., the Conference maintained its order and earnestly discussed and considered the proposals submitted.

The chairman called the delegates to order prompt to time and opened the proceedings by delivering the following address:—

Chairman's Address.

COMRADES AND FELLOW WORKERS,—I presume that by now you have all received agendas, and are thus fully aware of the nature of the proposals which we have to lay before you.

For a long time now the need of a better organisation of the workers has been felt. With the immense growth of machinery, craft divisions have tended to disappear, huge numbers of workers, whose crafts widely differ, are now assembled in the premises of one employer; and it is essential that if we are even to maintain our present standard of existence, we must so organise that there will remain but one Union in any one plant. As our friends of the Provisional Committee for the Amalgamation of Existing Trade Unions" so well put it:—

One Industry, One Union, One Card,

and I would also add: *One Policy,* and that a *FIGHTING ONE.*

And let us call our French comrades who have only about 50 Unions all told.

It is essential, whilst we are amalgamating that we should have in view, and, bear in mind, the end for which that amalgamation is advocated.

Our support of industrial organisation is not for the fun of the thing; it is given for the specific purpose of uniting in such a way as to enable the workers to take control of the industry in which they work.

Some of our friends, already connected with the different Amalgamation Committees, will presently tell us what they have already accomplished, how they have accomplished it, and what steps they intend to take in the future.

When we have been able to get our National Industrial Unions formed, we must have an efficient co-operation between them all.

To avoid the possibility of a centralised bureaucracy, with its paralysing influence, I think that a National Federation of Industrial Unions would be best.

This would give the necessary cohesion, minus too much centralised authority; it would be the recognition of the right of each industrial Union to autonomy in purely industrial matters.

With regard to the TRADES COUNCILS, the real function of these bodies have been but little understood.

It is essential that all assembled here should comprehend how and why it is that the Trades Councils should be the educational bodies that we wish them to become.

In a Trades Council, representatives of all the different trades in a given area meet. The fine points of a purely technical consideration, which are often discussed in the Trade Union branch room, do not appear here; or if they do so they are dealt with in a broader spirit; they are considered in the light of how they affect the whole of the workers concerned.

The Trades Councils emphasise the Class character of the Trade Union movement, as apart from craft interests. These should be federated by districts so as to cover a number of closely lying towns; and in the case of London, which is not merely a city, but almost a province, all the Councils should be united.

Now let us get our National Federation of Industrial Unions and our National Committee of Trades Councils, each having particular work of their own to do.

Join the National Committees of both together, and you will have a Confederation of Labour, in all manners and for all purposes.

We can then deal effectively with National and International questions. We shall thus have a general committee of propaganda and action, a veritable permanent strike committee, whose time will be devoted to the study and consideration of ways and means and of securing unity of action on all matters pertaining thereto, and to best accomplish our emancipation.

This is the work in front of us.

This is the task to be accomplished.

Comrades, if you do this, November 9 and 10 of the Year 1912 will be marked as Red-Letter days in British working-class history, when the workers set out definitely to wrest from the master class control of the means whereby they live.

Opening Remarks.

The Chairman then called the delegates' attention to the fact that the agendas had not been sent to the branches for discussion, and therefore it was not possible for the delegates to pledge their societies. They could only give a personal expression of opinion and take a report back to their branches and explain the arguments used for or against the different resolutions.

A letter was then read from Mr. Haigh, the delegate of the Hornsey and Wood Green A.S.R.S. as follows:—

Guy Bowman, Gen. Sec. I.S.E.L.

Dear Sir,

At the Conference on the 9th inst. I request permission to move the following amendments to:—

Resolution No. 1 : Insert after Solidarity "Both on the Political and Industrial Field."

Resolution No. 2 : Delete "Political School or."

Resolution No. 5 : Insert after the word union "for Political and Industrial purposes."

Yours, &c.,
H. HAIGH.

The Chairman then read the reply sent to Comrade Haigh:

Dear Comrade,

In reply to yours received this morning, and requesting permission to move amendments to Resolutions 1, 2, and 5, may I point out to you that the Conference is convened to discuss *INDUSTRIAL SOLIDARITY* and the *importance and necessity for DIRECT ACTION?* Therefore any amendments raising the question of parliamentary politics will be ruled out of order.

May I also point out that this is a non-political organisation? The only and logical way for anybody who disagrees with the resolutions to express their objections is to speak against and vote against them.

Yours for Industrial Freedom,
GUY BOWMAN.

Greetings from the French C.G.T.

ALFRED ROSMER then addressed the Conference as the fraternal delegate of the Confederation Générale du Travail. On rising he received an enthusiastic welcome. He delivered his speech as follows:—

DEAR COMRADES,—In the name of my fellow-workers of *La Bataille Syndicaliste* I bring you the fraternal greetings of the French Syndicalists.

We Frenchmen are very interested, and much pleased by the progress of Syndicalism in England—progress which is attested by the great strikes of last year and of the beginning of this year, by the great curiosity excited by this new theory in all the classes of society. Many people write and more people speak on the subject of Syndicalism. Well, there is much nonsense written and spoken—in France too—but it does not matter.

What matters is, that you, by your acts, show what Syndicalism is; because Syndicalism is not a subject for academic discussion: it is, before all, a peculiar form of action. It has its own ways, its own aim. Its practical ways are to be found in Direct Action—i.e., action of the workers themselves against their employers, culminating in the general strike. Its aim is the establishment of a society where there will be no more of either employers or wage-earners, but only equal men.

It resolutely refuses to identify itself with any political party, because political parties are not constituted according to the class struggle, and because the Socialist party, which sometimes asserts it is pursuing the same purpose as Syndicalism, puts its trust in the State, whilst Syndicalism is against the State and opposed to such measures like nationalisation of mines, railways, &c.

And, after all, is not England the native land of Syndicalism? Is not England the land of Robert Owen, of the "Grand National Consolidated Trades' Union," which advocated the general strike as early as in the thirties of the last century?

So Syndicalism is only a renaissance, and we hope that this time it will not disappear before having realised its object.

Long live the I.S.E.L.!

Long live the international of the workers! The Chairman then read Resolution No. 1, as follows:

Solidarity.

"Whereas the only way by which the workers can emancipate themselves is by the most complete solidarity:

"The Conference calls upon all workers to join the Unions of their respective trades;

"Urges upon those already organised the vital necessity of causing all the Trade Unions, in any one industry, to amalgamate, and

"Recommends Trade Unionists to organise Amalgamation Committees for all industries."

Tom Mann then moved it.

He said that before directing his remarks specifically to the resolution he would speak on the general situation. They all knew what had taken place during recent years in the industrial movement. The situation was most unsatisfactory. The Trade Union machinery was lamentably deficient. There was no proper systematic method of one set of forces picking up with another, to achieve the best results. The officials knew and declared, some in private and some in public, that it was lamentably deficient, and they desired some day to reach a better situation. Some with a lifetime of experience, were conscious of these deficiencies, but were so surrounded by their positions as officials, that it was impossible for them to lift themselves out of the rut. He had never yet struck a capable man in the Trade Union movement who could link the Unionists into one machine, and thereby achieve our emancipation. Some had felt this, and, regardless of fear, had for many years endeavoured to get the Unions out of their rut. It behoved such to take initial action, and express their conviction of a satisfactory method whereby such a re-arrangement should take place, that would allow of common action of any body of workers in a given locality at a given time. He ventured to say that the Parliamentary Committee of the Trade Union Congress, the General Federation, most Trade Unions, the respective Amalgamation Committees, and the Trades Councils—all put together, did not present a unified movement whereby we could get definitely to work to the desired end. It showed a policy of drift, with much overlapping and stultification. One could not go to an industrial firm without bothering about which was the proper Union to be in; instead of having one card he had to have two or three. We want one common ground of action, one policy. If inspired by fraternity, we must have such machinery as will advance this and not retard it. In London there were various organisations whose methods of control hindered unity. They developed coldness and suspicion. There were some who encouraged sectionalism. He was out for amalgamating all the Unions in one industry. This meant the removal of some of the executive officers, but other offices would be found for them, though not executive offices. He wanted amalgamation of the whole of the bodies of Unionists. The first step was for those in favour of the resolution to form active Amalgamation Committees in their branches. He hoped the resolution would be carried.

Amalgamation Committees' Reports.

The Chairman then called upon W. F. Watson of the Provisional Committee for the Amalgamation of Existing Trade Unions, to give his report.

W. F. WATSON, who also seconded the resolution, gave a history of the two years existence of the Provisional Committee, and explained how the Printing Trades' Amalgamation Committee had sprung out of it. He said that the Engineering and Shipbuilding Committee had been formed by calling a conference of organised men at the Workmen's Hall, Stratford, and that they were holding another conference on Saturday, November 16, to strengthen the movement. They first set up in all branches of the unions in an industry propaganda committees. They sent speakers to the branches to show the necessity for amalgamation. They proposed to issue pamphlets to the rank and file. They endeavoured to bring pressure on the branches, and the branches in their turn on the executive.

SAM RODEN (Transport Workers' Amalgamation Committee), stated that 90 per cent. of the workers in that industry would never again enter upon a sectional strike. They wanted to amalgamate all unions connected with transport. The Federation would not solve the difficulty—this was shown by the recent strike. They must get into the amalgamation all the unions—those not in the Transport Workers' Federation, as well as those that are in. They had been able to form committees at Greenwich and various other districts, and the work was progressing well.

C. J. WOODWARD (Printing Trades' Amalgamation Committee) next addressed the Conference. He said at the last annual meeting of the London Society of Compositors, a resolution was accepted to ask the Parliamentary Committee of the Trade Union Congress to take a ballot of the Printing Trades for amalgamation. A conference was held, and they were told that it was impractical to amalgamate only the London societies, as some were national Unions. It proved the necessity for one Union. The Printing Trades' Federation were going to call another meeting on amalgamation. The Amalgamation were not satisfied with merely getting the workers called together, but were working inside the unions and branches, giving lectures, distributing literature, &c., in order to convert the two-thirds majority necessary for bringing about amalgamation according to Trade Union law.

The CHAIRMAN here explained that, unfortunately, George Hicks (secretary of the Building Trades' Consolidation Committee) was away organising in South Wales, and no report of this committee could be given, though Comrade Hicks was heartily in sympathy with the work of the Conference.

V. VOLINSKY (Independent Cabinet Makers' Association) supported. He said that the resolution did not show how the workers could get non-unionists to join the unions. It was the duty of unionists to refuse to work with non-unionists. Many men were kept out of the unions because they were unskilled. He did not believe in that.

H. GREENBAUM (Jewish Branch of the London Society of Tailors and Tailoresses) wanted to know how it was possible to amalgamate and have local autonomy?

H. HAIGH (A.S.R.S.) said that he was the delegate who wanted to move the amendments on politics. The I.S.E.L. had drawn up the resolutions in such a manner that the delegates as Trade Unionists must support them.

R. L. WIGZELL (A.S.R.S.) said that he considered that his Comrade Haigh had proved the case for the principles laid down in the resolution. As he (Wigzell) understood the resolution, it does not matter whether the delegates were Liberals or Tories. They were there concerned with industrial questions, how long they should work, how much they would get for the work. He gave a vivid account of the recent Transport Strike, and of the harm done by the railwaymen remaining at work, and asked if the members of the A.S.R.S. were taking steps to prevent it from happening again.

S. NETTLE (Furnishing Trades Association) said that if we were to amalgamate upon the present craft jealousy of Trade Unions the workers would not get much further, but if we are to amalgamate for a "down tools" policy on the lines of Direct Action, he believed that they would gain and get more members made, which could not be done the way the Trade Unions are managed now.

C. MILLER (Amalgamated House and Ship Painters) said that he was glad to have heard Haigh's letter read and the answer thereto. It cleared the air. The delegates were there for *industrial matters.* We are out for amalgamation, but the point we seem to miss is how are going to fight officialism. The Executive of his Union had refused the members the right to ballot on this matter.

J. HITCHINGS (Furnishing Trade) said, in supporting, that he was going to teach his fellow members that officialism was wrong. The delegates ought to enter their branches and individually advocate their position as Syndicalists, although he was not a member of the Syndicalist League he was a Syndicalist in spirit.

H. ROSE (London Society Tailors and Tailoresses) said that they had to fight against sectionalism not only in their own Society, but in every one represented there. If they had asked permission of their officials to attend there, they would have been refused. The London Society of Tailors was convening a Conference to combine the whole of the clothing trade in London.

P. TANNER (A.S.E.), in supporting the resolution, pointed out the danger of autocracy and bureaucracy, and said that he did not consider that there would be any more danger from 15 executives than there was from 1,500. The danger of autocracy in the National Council could be obviated by the members, seeing that they had the right men. Another point that was missed was, what were they going to amalgamate for? If they were going to get a crowd of men together they must know what they were out for. With regard to executives who would not take ballots on amalgamation, he suggested stopping their finance, then they would soon toe the line.

J. BROWN (Woolwich Trades Council) remarked that he had heard a lot about officialism. He contended that when the working class was sufficiently educated to amalgamate, those educated forces would be represented as they wished. He had implicit faith in the educated workers, in Human Solidarity, when they were conscious of where they were going. Their organisations had been built up through adversity and would have to go through adversity to emancipation.

HYMAN GREEN (Amalgamated Society of Tailors and Tailoresses) wanted to know if the London Society of Tailors went on strike, would it be compulsory for every Union to strike?

C. CORBETT (A.S.R.S.) said that sectionalism was absurd. On the Midland Railway drivers' strikes had failed and guards' strikes had failed. In 1911 in three days the railways were at a standstill, and if the men had not been let down, they would now have been reaping the benefits. Out of that strike, in which the A.S.R.S., the Associated Locomotive Engineers and Firemen, the General Railway Workers' Union, the Signalmen and Pointsmens' Society were engaged, the executive committees, through that, after the fight, thought that the Unions should join in one. A conference was arranged, and, as a result, the A.S.R.S., the G.R.W.U., and the U.P. and S.S. would in a few months be one. There was only one Society that refused to amalgamate, that was the A.S.L.E. and F., and he wanted their delegate to go back to his branch and help them to benefit by the discussion. At the Triennial Conference of the A.S.L.E. and F. only three votes were cast for amalgamation.

W. CLARKE (A.S.L.E. and F.) said that he thought that the Conference was called to form one Union, and not to start washing dirty linen. He wanted to tell the A.S.R.—(here the Chairman intervened and ruled the delegate's remarks out of order).

A. HITCHAM (A.S.R.S.) supported the resolution, saying that it was the damnable system of education of the country that kept the workers back. We had to go beyond the questions of hours and wages. The workers should say that they were dissatisfied and be prepared to take a little risk and get hold of the economic system by which they lived. He did not want craft autonomous groups, and hoped they would be left out of any scheme of amalgamation.

Tom Mann replied to the questions of Volinsky and Greenbaum, saying that no machinery can make wise men of dunderheads. This machinery that we are suggesting will develop the working-class organisation instead of retarding it. The Resolution was then voted upon.

For the Resolution 68
Against the Resolution ... 2
Abstentions, 2.

Propaganda.

"This Conference urges all organised bodies of workers to affiliate to the Trades Council of their district, or to take immediate steps to form Trades Councils where none are existent.

"Whereas the Trades Councils ought to be the real centres of Trade Unionist propaganda, and be used for building up the Trade Union movement as a movement of wage-workers, outside and independent of the control of any political school or religious sect.

TOM MANN, in moving, said that here again was a resolution that contained nothing political or anti-political. Whatever phase of politics men hold it is not a wise course to commit those who organise industrially to any one particular method of politics. Any organiser would find that those who wished to organise had half a dozen political faiths, and if he started a meeting with a political address it would be found impossible to do organising work. Similarly with the Trades Councils. All Unionists ought to be identified with the Trades Councils to enable them to do effective organising and propaganda work and become the machines for bettering their positions. The Trades Councils were pre-eminently the bodies for organising work; they ought to direct the organising of the working class until there were none left to organise. It was the duty of the Trade Unions to affiliate to the Trades Councils. Where none existed it was the duty of the workers to institute them. There should be no religious or political ties; nothing should be done that would interrupt the work of industrial organisation.

A. G. TUFTON (Walthamstow Trades Council) seconded, saying that it was essential that the Councils of outlying districts should be supported. The Trades Councils had made themselves ridiculous when they had devoted their time to political action, they could not find the power to enforce their wishes. He knew of Trades Councils where their members were divided on politics, the sections were imbued with the party spirit, and so their work came to a stop. But as soon as they dropped politics they were more in request by the Trade Unionists, who came to support them and to receive support. With regard to forming Trades Councils in many districts, the workers would soon form them if they only realised their importance from an organising standpoint. In Walthamstow two or three Trade Unions, on calling a meeting, were only able to gather an audience of about 300, but when the Trades Council called a meeting they could always rely on having an audience of 1,000.

H. JACKMAN (Labour Protection League) said he was in favour of the resolution except it said "outside of all political schools." If the resolution was carried it would be taken for granted that the delegates were in favour of ignoring political action altogether. If it had not been for political action the chaps working for the Woolwich Corporation would never have got 30s. per week. It could not be got by industrial organisation. He wished to delete the words complained of, and if he could not, he must vote against it.

Mr. PELL (Shop Assistants) supported the resolution because he had been a delegate to Trades Councils for some time, and found that they were dead assemblies. If the Trades Councils set the policy you would have a live, strong one, and not the Engineers taking one policy and the Shop Assistants another. This Conference is called because of economic pressure. We have tried every other method and found that they have failed. If there was any utility in the Trades Councils, it was because there they should discuss their grievances, and a policy could be given forth to the general body of Labour from that centre.

A. E. SMYTHE (Labour Protection League) wanted to explain the position of the L.P.L. We are bound to have a certain number of State employees in our Union, and we may have to bring a certain amount of influence on candidates in our locality for the local governing body or for parliament. WE have to take political action when we want an increase of wages, send deputations to the War Office, or demonstrations to Trafalgar Square. If this resolution rules out these things that may be termed political, we shall have to vote against the resolution. We have positively gained by these methods.

J. F. D. DIXON (London Society of Compositors) agreed that the Trades Councils should assist the organised workers in their respective trades and to organise the unorganised. Where he disagreed a little was over the question of politics. They had found it useless to deputise. The Compositors got Unionists to see that members of our Society run as candidates for various bodies to see that contracts are carried out under the Fair Wages Clause. He agreed with the main principle of serving industrial Unionism, but we must still get these contracts. It was a matter of importance to-day.

A. HITCHAM (A.S.R.S.) said that he did not see anything in the resolution for discussion. Of course, one could believe in Syndicalist methods and yet believe in taking political action.

D. ARMSTRONG (A.S.E.) was in favour of the resolution because of his experience with Trades Councils. He had been on one that had become affiliated with the I.L.P., and had developed into a Labour Representation Committee. They had dropped industrial action and advocated politics. Now they were turning round again because they saw industrial action coming to the front. If they were not out for emancipation they were out for a new form of slavery. There was a danger in advocating two things. We were out purely for industrial action. He declared that politics were the last refuge of a scoundrel.

S. NETTLE (Furnishing Trade) said that we were brought together here simply for discussing industrial questions. He had found all along the line that political action had not been much good to the workers. No delegate ought to be present if it was to play the game of politics. A man is sent to parliament and the government pay him £400 a year, and then what does he trouble about the workers? He had gained his emancipation. So long as the workers put up with them, and guarantee them their salaries, so long would the politicians be creeping up and talking and exploiting the Labour class, and the Trade Union movement. He contended that if they were out for industrialism, they were out for a thing that was honest, but with politics they would be supporting a machine that was inaugurated by the capitalist class.

SAM RODEN (Transport Workers' Amalgamation Committee) said that he maintained strongly that if they were going to organise the workers in one body on scientific lines, the delegates would have, to adopt the tactics laid down in the resolution. He had done organising work in different parts of the country, and knew what appealed to the workers. Look at Belfast. Belfast is a town that everybody could understand. His native town was the same. When the strike was on in North Staffordshire, men came from Ireland and Wales to blackleg. They had different religions and different politics. At Belfast, in the same shipyards, on the same ships, working side by side, are Home Rulers and Orangemen, Roman Catholics and Protestants, all being starved and sweated, all being wage-slaves. Tell them that they are wage-slaves, and for that reason adopt the Syndicalist policy and act independent of any political or religious school.

Tom Mann replied, pointing out that the Labour Protection League, in deputising the War Office and the Admiralty were only doing what all other workman did to their employers. There was no need to go in a round-about way through politicians or parliament to do that.

The resolution was carried by 56 for and 4 against.

The Conference then adjourned at six o'clock.

Second Day.

The proceedings commenced soon after 9.30 a.m. by Tom Mann moving Resolution No. 3, as follows :—

Amalgamation.

"Whereas it is necessary that the Amalgamation Committees should consult one another for common action, co-ordination, and propaganda, this Conference urges upon all Amalgamation Committees already formed, and to be formed, the necessity to federate, thereby forming the nucleus of a National Federation of all industries."

He claimed that it was necessary for the committees to meet and consult one another. Some delegates held the opinion that it was necessary to amalgamate them; they were impressed with the idea of one big Union. There were some who wanted to federate the National Industrial Unions. We don't appreciate the carrying of amalgamation further than that, . otherwise it would be unworkable and impractical. We definitely advocate the federation, and not the amalgamation, of the national organisations that were at present represented by the Amalgamation Committees. We don't think that one big Union containing all industries is the right policy. We want a general body formed by the federation of the National Industrial Unions.

P. Rodda (A.S.R.S.) asked a question about the formation of special sub-committees from the Amalgamation Committees.

The Chairman replied that was a question for the Committees to decide, and the Conference could not interfere with the business of the Amalgamation Committees.

C. J. Woodward (Printing Trades Amalgamation Committee) seconded, and said he was in favour of one committee for each industry. The Printing Trades Amalgamation Committee are agitating amongst the Unions catering for the printing trades, the Engineering and Shipbuilding, Building Trades, and the Transport Committees did the same. The four committees representing the four industries should keep in touch with each other. They had little finance, and had great difficulties, quite apart from the question of amalgamating such industries as those of the mining and textile industries. It was unfortunate that they had different names, some being called amalgamation committees, some consolidation committees, and some reformed committees. It would be better for all to be called amalgamation committees. Much good could be done by meeting together and discussing schemes, arranging business, and so on. He wanted to see all the Amalgamation Committees federated, and the Syndicalists supporting the committees as far as possible by putting all the news on amalgamation in their paper, the Syndicalist, and all suggestions and matter that would assist the committees in their work.

Sam Roden (Secretary Transport Workers' Amalgamation Committee) said what he wanted to emphasise was the necessity in the future of deciding the matter of the different Amalgamation Committees acting as a federated body. We have the "Transport Workers' and Amalgamation Committee," and we have formed local committees in other places. When we first went to form local committees the first question asked was:—"Are we going to be controlled by the committee in Canning Town?" Now if we had decided to do so we should not have had half the work done, for it would have taken away local autonomy and individual initiative. The principles day everybody had been complaining about officialism, and what we had to avoid in the future was the autocracy and bureaucracy of officials. If only the men in different unions would show a little more individuality, then as far as those unions were concerned officialism would be dead, and the officials would become the servants of the men.

C. Miller (Amalgamated House and Ship Painters) said we have already arrived at the stage where Amalgamation Committees are formed; we are now concerned with the question of shall we federate or amalgamate these committee? The people in one industry are not able to suggest how the people in another industry shall carry on their business, and so he supported federation and the resolution.

R. L. Wigzell (A.S.R.S.) said he did not wish to pledge himself at that stage. He wanted to put one or two questions to Comrade Watson when he spoke. He wanted to be clear on the point as Comrade Roden had said, the Amalgamation of all Trade Unions in one industry; then the resolution said we were to have a federation of all Industrial Unions. He wanted to know if this policy was accepted by the Conference would it get the support of the Provisional Committee for Amalgamation of Existing Trade Unions? If we support the policy laid down by Tom Mann, are we to have the support of the Provisional Committee, or are they going on in their own sweet way? If so, will their action and methods be best, or is it possible for the two to work together? He hoped the position would be made clear.

W. F. Watson (A.S.E.) said that he wished to move an amendment that the word "federation" be deleted and the "amalgamation" be inserted. We have arrived at a point where we must give reflection to it, and be careful over it, and see that we all go together. The objection to amalgamation is that it will mean too much centralisation, too much bureaucracy. He was not so much afraid of that centralisation, because the members would recognise their individual responsibility and prevent bureaucracy. Federation was a very loose form of voluntary organisation. There must be a combined fund to fight with. He had moved an amendment, but it did not mean to say that if the amendment was defeated that he was against the resolution. If the Conference was

not in favour of amalgamation, then he would vote for federation.

H. Haigh (A.S.R.S.) seconded the amendment, saying that he could clearly see on the basis of federation certain actions which might be done that he was willing to agree with, but there may be certain actions that he would disagree with, as they might be a danger to the community at large. Amalgamation would make the unions think upon the effects of their conduct upon workers of all industries.

B. Rose (L.S.T. and T.) said that he would heartily support the resolution of Tom Mann, for the simple reason that he could see the policy of amalgamation of the industrial unions, "instead of freeing yourselves bit by bit, bit by bit enslave yourselves." Whether we succeeded or failed under federation, we have one thing to learn—that is, so long as we have executive power, the domination of one over another—that this somebody in a certain body shall say how we shall live, how we shall do, what we shall want, we shall still remain slaves. We have to lift ourselves up a little, or else the weight will come from the top and crush us down. He wanted to show some of the contradictions of the mover and seconder of the amendment. The mover said that he was quite in agreement with the logical outcome—free association. You have not got, and therefore must use, force. The seconder had tried practical means to do the same thing. He had pointed out a certain conditions of a particular industry that he belonged to, and he had been given a free entrance into their branch rooms in order to discuss together means to improve their conditions. When they rejected the offer, he could not force the men to go there. You cannot compel men to strike against their will, because then they are not free men.

J. V. Wills (Chairman of the Building Trades' Consolidation Committee), who had entered the hall a little time previously, asked to speak. He wished to explain why the Consolidation Committee had not kent delegates. They only met once a month, and, unfortunately, their meeting was being held that morning, and thus they had not been able to discuss the matter. As far as he could speak as an individual, he hoped that the resolution would have the full approbation of the committee he was connected with. In his opinion the resolution was a very important one. In his opinion, if the committees were amalgamated it would be a blunder. The most essential thing for them to do was to point out the changed conditions of employment. The craft which had formed such a great power in the early days of the Trade Union movement had gradually been taken from the workers' hands, the tools had passed from their hands to the machines of the employers. Could a clerk go into the building trades branch and put forward the technicalities that are necessary to convince men of the necessity of amalgamating the unions? Fancy him (Wills) going into a printing trades branch and talking on the question of industrial unionism. He could talk on general terms, but they were not good enough for this purpose. We have to educate our members and get them to recognise what really does matter before we can form our Industrial Amalgamation Committees, and develop this new plan. We have a bureaucracy that is more dangerous than even the capitalist class. That bureaucracy will only be settled by the increasing development of the democracy. In the building industry we are going to take more notice of our officials. We are going to take more notice of whom we elect as officials of our unions than we do of whom we elect to borough councils or to parliament. We recognise that it is important for us to have men who are good revolutionaries at the head of our movement, with their heart and soul—regardless of ridicule or anything else—for the cause; leading the workers on to that revolutionary goal we all hope and desire to reach.

W. F. Watson (A.S.E.), as mover of the amendment, replied that when the democracy was sufficiently educated they would not submit to any sort of bureaucracy or autocracy. He did not advocate any executive body but an administrative body under the control of the rank and file. The workers should be the rulers of our working-class movement.

Tom Mann closed the discussion.

The amendment was voted upon and was lost.

Voting against... 47
Voting for 4

The resolution was then submitted and 66 voted for, 0 against.

Tom Mann then moved Resolution No. 4.

Federation.

"Whereas it is urgent that the Trades Council should take up their proper functions as educational and propagandist bodies for the working class ;

"Whereas it is desirable that they should prepare themselves for the functions they will have to fulfil in future society as the centre of social and economic life ;

"Whereas they should make themselves effective for collating and disseminating information in other localities ;

"This Conference urges upon all Trade Unionists the necessity of bringing about a National Federation of Trades' Councils."

He said that it was hardly likely that there would be much difference of opinion. The Conference had just decided upon the federation of the Amalgamation Committees, now they were asked to proceed a step further and vote in favour of the federation of the Trades Councils. We believe that they will become vastly more important than they are to-day, and that they will be largely substituted for our present Borough Councils. Therefore, we are asking all who are here, those who believe in the Trades Councils becoming the chief centres for organisation, more important than all the other Councils, to support their belief. By degrees the working class will function so effectively through these Trades Councils that it will be an utter impossibility for the functioning of those sore the London County Council and so on. All that believe that the Trades Councils should be federated will vote accordingly. We ask that the Trades Councils should be made effective for the collating and disseminating of information over a large area. It is regrettable that we should have to be urging such a request upon our Trades Councils at this time.

R. L. Wigzell (A.S.R.S.), in seconding, said he did not agree with Tom Mann that it was regrettable that we should have to advocate this cause at this stage. He (Tom Mann) seemed to infer that it was because a large number of workers had never been in agreement with this. He (Wigzell) thought that why they had never supported such a resolution before was because they had been afraid of the consequences. He did not regret that it had not been done before, because if it had been done in a half-hearted manner a mess would have been made of it. We want to see that in the future we get an industrial position put clearly for the industrial workers. We could then bring before the Trades Councils facts and figures which we could not

to-day. Then on the question of getting rid of "dud" officials, the branches could discuss the pros and cons of the question, and then the Trades Council could take action, first locally, then nationally.

J. Staines (Associated Locomotive Engineers and Firemen) supported, saying that all ought to try and look at the tremendous force in the Trade Union world, and represented at the Conference that morning. With the power of the rank and file behind the Trades Councils, they could properly function for the benefit of the rank and file. He was a member of the revolutionary minority in the A.S.L.E. and F., who called the A.S.R.S. brothers. Look at the way their organisers went to work—the inducements that were held to men to join. The organiser points out the benefits of his particular union; the chap says, "Do I get all these benefits? Oh, not a bad investment. I will join." You had then introduced a Trade Unionist whose function was to bleed the Trade Union and pull the organisation down. The Trades Councils should be used as the means of educating the workers and organising them. They should be made to fulfil that which they had not yet achieved. It was desirable that they should be forwarded by every means in their power.

J. Brown (Woolwich Trades Council) expressed his opinion that before the working class and the Trades Councils would be able to study the question of economics, they would have to understand what economics are. He refused to accept middle-class economics because the middle-class did not understand working-class economics. The working-class had been insulted for years by middle-class politicians trotting out their propositions that bewildered the workers. When the working class understood that living in the workhouses was better than working for the capitalists, capitalism would disappear.

W. F. Watson (A.S.E.) supported, because he believed that the Trades Councils would eventually fulfil the functions of the Urban District Councils and Borough Councils. When the Industrial Unions showed that they were sufficiently organised to get control of the industrial side of society, the Trades Councils would get hold of the administrative side.

P. Rodda (A.S.R.S.) said he was glad to see in their resolution the recognition for educational propaganda. He took it that the Trades Councils themselves were in need of education first, just as much as the Union leaders of to-day. The education of the proletariat, as well as of the leaders was the biggest problem that the Syndicalists had to face.

H. Greenbaum (L.S.T. and T.) supported and said that Comrade Brown had referred to middle-class politicians. He had conceived the idea long since that it was not the middle-class politicians who were a barrier to human progress, but it was all politicians.

V. Volinsky (Independent Cabinet Makers) opposed on the grounds that it would take too long to revolutionise the Trades Councils. He believed it would be better to form District Councils, because it would take too much time to bring the Trades Councils along with the new ideas.

Tom Mann then replied, and the resolution was carried, with 1 against.

Resolution No. 5 was then moved by Tom Mann :

Confederation.

"Whereas to obtain the most complete solidarity, the maximum results in propaganda, agitation, and our daily warfare,

"This Conference urges the formation of a joint committee of

(a) The National Federation of Trades Councils.

(b) The National Federation of Industrial Unions ;

thereby forming a general confederation of Labour.

"The duty of such confederal committee to be the systematic work of general propaganda ; the organising of national campaigns for the reduction of working hours ; the raising of the workers' standard of living ; a general education in working-class economics ; a propaganda of Direct Action in all its forms ; and the preparing of the workers for their final emancipation from wage slavery."

He claimed that this resolution was to simply link up the two bodies—the federated Trades Councils and the federated Industrial Unions. We now called for the completion of the scheme by confederating the two federations. This had been resorted to elsewhere with good effect, and we know of no better form whereby we can crown the scheme.

J. F. D. Dixon (L.S.C.) seconded, and did so on the ground that we wanted a genuine co-operation of forces to bring about a reduction of working hours.

S. Nettle (Furnishing Trades) supported, saying it seemed to him that a great deal had been said about economics, but it did not require a great deal of intelligence for them to know that those who produced everything got nothing, and those who produced nothing got everything ; so the whole talk about economics was a lot of fizzle. We have to look at the leaders, and we allow them to live and "represent" us, and exploit our unions. If the rank and file of the Trade Unions were cognisant of the fact that they belong to the exploited class and the others to the exploiting class, there would be no need for leadership in any shape or form.

The resolution was carried by 64 for, 1 against ; and 1 abstention.

The Chairman then announced that a series of lectures would be organised by the I.S.E.L. on the subjects of amalgamation, federation, &c.

Tom Mann then moved resolution No. 6 :

Internationalism.

"Whereas cases of international importance are getting every day more numerous, the work of the Trade Unionists of all countries should be co-ordinated, and an international policy decided upon ;

"Whereas war is the greatest calamity that could befall the international working-class movement, it is most urgent that common action should be decided upon by the workers of all countries ;

"This Conference calls upon the I.S.E.L. to convene an International Syndicalist Congress to be held in London as soon as possible."

He said that the Industrial Syndicalist League, of course, was the convener of this particular Conference. Nothing was more necessary than a Conference convened on straight-out Syndicalist lines. It was necessary to have an International Congress if we were to have the voice of Labour expressed.

H. Haigh (A.S.R.S.), as one of the workers who had taken an active part in the movement, thought it was desirable. He had, as a soldier, seen all the horrors of war, and he wanted an understanding amongst the workers of all nations to prevent it.

J. Staines (A.S.L.E. and F.) supported

because it was necessary for the workers of all countries to be united for all purposes.

N. Roberts (Teachers' Union) said that the teachers were not yet sufficiently educated to send delegates to this Conference. He realised the great necessity of convening an International Conference of Syndicalists.

The resolution was carried unanimously.

J. Staines (A.S.L.E. and F.) suggested that all the good points and items with regard to amalgamation should be sent to one common centre, and that they should be published in the Syndicalist.

D. Armstrong and W. F. Watson then moved the following resolution, which was carried unanimously :

"That this meeting of delegates from the English Trade Unions, representing over 50,000 organised workers, assembled in Conference at the Holborn Town Hall for the purpose of furthering National and International Solidarity of Labour, send greetings to Brothers J. J. ETTOR, A. GIOVANITTI, WILL HAYWOOD, and J. CARUSO, now facing a police-manufactured charge of murder in Salem, U.S.A.

"We recognise that their real crime, in the eyes of the masters, is that they have achieved, to a great extent, that which this Conference and all who are true to Labour aspire to, Industrial Solidarity.

"Further, we vehemently protest against this last attempted crime and outrage against Labour, and call upon all workers to demand their immediate release.

"Further, that a copy of this resolution be sent to the American Ambassador in London, and to the Daily Herald."

R. L. Wigzell (A.S.R.S.) suggested a collection towards establishing the Syndicalist as a weekly. This was agreed to, and was taken up. The amount of £1. 3s. 7d. was subscribed.

There had been four detectives present on Saturday ; on Sunday there was only one. When the delegates were photographed by Comrade Renault, late of the French Railway Workers, one delegate humorously suggested that a copy be presented to the gentleman from Scotland Yard, who, at the same time, was requested very urgently to stand on the seat that the delegates might admire him and recognise him on other occasions. Seeing that the request was unanimous, he obligingly did so.

Tom Mann wound up the proceedings by thanking the delegates for the splendid harmony that had prevailed during the Conference. He expressed his belief in the fruitfulness of the work accomplished.

The Conference terminated at 1.30 p.m.

MANCHESTER CONFERENCE,
November 30th, 1912.

Following on the London Conference, one of a similar character was held on Saturday, November 30, at the Coal Exchange, Manchester. There were 137 representatives from 76 branches of 42 Trade Unions, 10 Trades Councils, and 3 Amalgamated Committees present.

A. Rosmer, of La Bataille Syndicaliste, and L. Jouhoux, Secretary of the C.G.T., of France, were also present as fraternal delegates.

The Conference was presided over by A. A. Purcell, of the Furnishing Trades' Association. In his opening remarks he pointed out that the gathering was a more representative one than that which was held there two years ago. He said that the spirit of Solidarity that had been expressed in the recent strikes was quite comforting and showed the possibilities of the future. If the workers wished to materially improve their conditions, they must move upon lines that favoured a reduction of working hours and increased pay, at all times keeping their object in view, the overthrow of the wages system. Furthermore, he said that although it had often been said that the emancipation of the workers must be wrought by the workers themselves, he again wished to emphasise it.

Tom Mann was then called upon to move Resolution No. 1.

Solidarity Re-affirmed.

"Whereas it is essential for the workers to practise Industrial Solidarity on a much larger scale than hitherto, if they are to improve their present position and ultimately emancipate themselves from wage slavery ;

"Whereas such Solidarity must be expressed and maintained through, and by the agency of, much better-developed organisations than exist at present, both nationally and internationally ;

"Whereas Direct Action offers the only method whereby the unity of the workers, as a class, can be obtained ;

"This Conference hereby endorses the findings of the London Conference, held on the 9th and 10th instant, which carried the following resolutions :

"(a) The Amalgamation of all Trade Unions within an industry into one Industrial Union.

"(b) The Trades Councils to become the centres of Trade Union propaganda, independent of any political school or religious sect.

"(c) The formation of a National Federation of all Industrial Unions.

"(d) The formation of a National Federation of Trades Councils.

"(e) A Joint Committee of the National Federation of Industrial Unions and the National Federation of Trades Councils, thereby forming a General Confederation of Labour.

"(f) The holding of an International Syndicalist Conference in London."

Tom Mann pointed out that the London Conference findings were embodied in the first resolution ; it dealt with the formation of organisation—whereas the resolutions that were about to be submitted for the consideration of the delegates that afternoon, dealt with the object of industrial organisation. He had come to the conclusion that the Trade Unions, as at present organised, were faulty ; the various Unions were stultifying the efforts of one another. He deprecated the stupidity and strife between craft Unions ; he pointed out that the workers were to organise as a class and not as crafts, independent of craft or sect. He said that if they looked back over the last two years, they would realise how little had been achieved, and yet, comparatively, how much had been expended by the spirit of Class Solidarity that had been displayed. They were there to state the steps which they were to travel, and the form of organisation which they wanted to travel with. He said that our Trades Councils were weak and useless in value, but his idea was that they should educate, organise, and direct the fighting force of their locality.

After the resolution had been duly seconded and spoken to, it was agreed to transfer Paragraph 3 to Resolution No. 2, and take the remaining portion of the resolution in two sections, the first down to (a), which was carried unanimously. The remainder of the first resolution was then taken as a separate resolution, to which an amendment was moved to delete the words "independent of any political school or religious sect." A very interesting and enthusiastic discussion took place upon the amendment, which was finally defeated by 78 votes to 17. The resolution was then carried with only 7 against. Resolution No. 2.

Direct Action.

"Whereas the General Confederation of Labour, as previously outlined, can only become an effective fighting machine and ultimately the structure of an Industrial Commonwealth, by the direct activity of the members composing it ;

"Whereas Direct Action means the pressure of the workers' power upon the employers without the aid of the intermediaries of any description ; this Conference declares for Direct Action," was moved by Blundell, of the Dockers' Union, and seconded by Armstrong, of the A.S.E. Blundell said that if we only tried Direct Action we could not make matters worse than they were to-day. Armstrong said that somebody had said that political action was a reflection ; seeing that was so, he did not think we could spend our time usefully in chasing shadows.

Owen (A.S.E.) said our failure in political action was because we had not had an industrial organisation behind us.

Hay (Workers' Union) said that he was out for politics, but not Labour politics, but politics of a revolutionary kind, but until capitalism gave up politics he did not think it was advisable for the workers to do so, and they must realise that politics beat the Railwaymen and the Miners. (Laughter.)

Chandler (R.C.A.) said that when the last speaker stated that politics had beaten the Railwaymen and the Miners, he was quite correct. If their Secretary had kept away from the House of Commons, the last Railway Strike, which was already won, would have wound up alright. (Applause.)

The Conference then adjourned for tea. On resuming, Comrade Jouhoux, of the C.G.T., of France, gave a short but very stirring address, which A. Rosmer translated. It was received by the delegates with much enthusiasm.

Resolution No. 3 :

Regulation of Working Hours.

"Whereas mental and physical relaxation are necessary for the workers' normal development ;

"Whereas it is absolutely necessary that the workers should obtain leisure to educate themselves in their class interests, thereby preparing themselves for the management of industry ;

"This Conference urges the necessity upon Trade Unionists to bring pressure to bear upon their organisations with a view to the progressive reduction of working hours."

This resolution was moved by A. A. Purcell, who vacated the chair for the time being, Mr. Donaghue, Secretary of the Building Trades' Federation, acting as chairman.

Purcell said that too much importance had been attached, in the past, to the question of raising wages, and not enough importance to the reduction of hours. In his opinion, this was the most important part of their programme. If they were able to progressively reduce the hours of Labour, he contended that wages would automatically rise. Any introduction of any labour-saving machine should be the signal to move for a further reduction of hours.

Orrel (Toolmakers' Society) seconded, and said that if they could reduce the hours to eight in his industry, it would very quickly absorb the larger portion of the unemployed members of his Society, and so lessen the competition for jobs. It was then suggested that the following words should be added to the resolution, "so as to bring about a complete absorption of Labour."

The resolution was carried unanimously.

Resolution No. 4.

Methods of Direct Action.

"Whereas the State is always prepared to use its armed forces in the interest of the capitalists to coerce the workers into submission whenever they attempt to better their conditions ;

"Whereas the capitalists have even gone so far as to raise armed forces of their own ;

"Whereas the workers, who have no country, have no interest in any war, except the class war ;

"This Conference declares the necessity for the workers to devise means of Direct Action against the State as well as against the capitalists—such as the Strike, the Irritation Strike, the Pearl Strike, Sabotage, the Boycott, and Anti-Militarism ;"

—was moved by Tom Mann and seconded by Chandler (R.C.A.). Tom Mann explained the Irritation Strike, the Pearl Strike, and Sabotage, which explanation was followed by a very keen and energetic discussion.

The resolution was carried with applause with only one dissentient.

A discussion was raised at this juncture as to how the resolution was to be put into operation, and the Chairman called upon J. V. Wills (O.B.S.) and Secretary of the Amalgamated Committees Federation, who has had a considerable experience on this subject, to give his views upon the matter. Wills said that if the work of the Amalgamated Committees was to be carried forward successfully, it could only be done by the members of the various Unions that covered a given industrial organisation, forming themselves into Amalgamation Committees ; first, with a view to the carrying on of general propaganda, and, secondly, taking united and unanimous action inside their Unions in favour of amalgamation. This could only be done successfully by organisation, therefore the object of the Federation, of which he was secretary, was to stimulate and assist the formation of Amalgamation Committees in every industry and every industrial centre. The Conference decided to elect a committee of sixteen delegates to form a Amalgamation Committee in the Manchester district, and to form a similar one in the Liverpool district.

Resolution No. 5.

The Revolutionary General Strike.

"Whereas the General Confederation of Labour is to become the basis of a new social system on the morrow of the General Strike ;

"This Conference calls upon all wage-workers to prepare for the expropriation of the capitalist class, thus making the means of production and distribution the common property of all ; this expropriation to be effected by means of the Revolutionary General Strike."

This resolution was moved by Cotton (S.S.U.) and duly seconded, and carried unanimously. The Conference then terminated.

THE RAILWAYMEN AND "THE AGREEMENT."

PRESIDENT PRAISES DIRECT ACTION.

By A MIDLAND GUARD.

Mr. A. Bellamy, the President of the A.S.R.S., addressed a public meeting at the Bury Textile Hall recently on the general position of the Railwaymen.

Referring to the 1911 Railway Strike, he said: That although as a result of that strike they had not got all that they desired, yet their condition generally was far better than it was before August, 1911. Before the strike the representatives of the Government said they were not going to allow a strike of Railwaymen. Two days afterwards they found they could not carry out their threat. That was the first defeat the Government sustained, and it was not a snap division.

Now, as a Railwayman, I heartily agree with the President's sentiments, and thank him for this unsolicited testimonial to Direct Action and Syndicalism, but is it not rather immoral and just a little wicked on the part of a Trade Union official to teach the workers that they alone possess the power to rectify their grievances! Have not the Syndicalists been preaching the same thing over and over again? But they were wicked fellows in August, 1911, and they are still called wicked chaps to-day for advocating the policy which Mr. Bellamy spoke so highly of, and which he claimed had gained better conditions for the men concerned. And is it not funny that our General and Assistant-Secretaries always say that Syndicalism is opposed to the interests of Railwaymen?

When our brothers in Liverpool and Manchester desired to assist the Transport Workers last year they were told that they must not strike without the sanction of the executive, and if they did they would not receive the support of the Society. But the men, luckily for themselves, ignored the official advice; they took their fate in their own hands; they used Direct Action and won a glorious victory. Unfortunately, the politicians, Mr. Bellamy's friends, helped to deprive them of that victory by assisting the State to befool them with their Royal Commission. Where is your logic, Mr. Bellamy?

Mr. Bellamy seems to think that Railwaymen ought now to be highly satisfied with their condition; but I have not yet heard of any of the thousand and one grievances, such as victimisation, &c., having been redressed. Mr. Williams, of course, says there is no victimisation except on the Midland.

Have I had a bad dream, or has my brain become disarranged? I was under the impression that several victimisations had taken place on the Great Eastern, South-Eastern, London and North-Western, Central London, and many other Railways. But I must be wrong, and perforce must see a doctor, for I have it on the General Secretary's own authority that the Midland is now the only Railway that persecutes the men. What a paradise the Railway would must now be!

Little Tin Gods with Feet of Clay.

But the A.S.R.S. has now issued a warning to the Midland Railway. I suppose victimisation is going to cease here also, for Railway Companies generally tremble when warnings are issued. I am told, however, that they tremble much more when the trains stop. Direct Action is a very effective medicine, for the Railway Companies got was so, at all events. Why not try a second and a third? That is the only method by which grievances can be remedied. Little tin gods with feet of clay cannot rectify grievances, as Mr. Bellamy has so capably demonstrated. If the men want a £3 a week minimum; a six hour day, a five day week, and a ten month year, they can get it, but they can only get it themselves. They must do as the medical and other professions do—make agreements between themselves re the amount of remuneration that is commensurate with their services. Then, like the medical and other professions, their employers will ask them how much they want for their labour, instead of the Railwaymen asking how much the Companies are prepared to give for their labour, as they do to-day.

Not Worth More Than £3 per Week.

Talking about £3 a week reminds me that the South Wales miners have decided that that shall be the maximum salary of their officials. Are Railway Union officials worth any more than Miners' Union officials? If they don't like it, well, let them go on strike; then we will give them the sack the same as we do our casual clerks. Now, brothers, don't forget this when the next alteration of rules comes along. I have met several of my chums on the Midland and other Railways recently. They tell me that they have embraced Syndicalism, and I really was surprised when I heard that seventeen delegates were present at the I.S.E.L. Conference on November 9 and 10, representing eleven A.S.R.S. Branches in London. That is glorious news, and if Syndicalism continues to make such splendid progress amongst the Railwaymen, then there is a chance even yet of obtaining something worth living for.

METAL, ENGINEERING, AND SHIPBUILDING AMALGAMATION COMMITTEE.

A Conference convened by the above committee was held at the White Swan, Tudor Street, London, E.C., on Saturday, November 16. Mr. A. Wardle, of the United Kingdom Pattern Makers, occupied the chair. The secretary, Mr. F. Watson, read out a batch of correspondence from various branches of Unions connected with the aforementioned industry that was distinctly encouraging; requests for literature, speakers, and further information on Amalgamation were plentiful. One letter from an active comrade announced that the Combined Smiths, the Operative Smiths, and the Associated Smiths had formed into one Union. (Cheers.) The Secretary gave a very lucid address on the necessity of Amalgamation, when it was moved that "That Amalgamation Committees be established in all Unions of the industry." The resolution was carried unanimously. The Conference decided to send the assistant-secretary, Mr. D. Armstrong, and two delegates to the I.S.E.L. for November 24th, to form a Federation of the Amalgamation Committees. It was also decided to be represented at the I.S.E.L. Conference, at Manchester, on November 30, and Mr. Armstrong was elected as the delegate. A plan of campaign was discussed, and several smart ideas were adopted. A collection to defray expenses realised 16s. 6d., and concluded the business.

GROUP REPORTS.

ISLINGTON.

We are at present holding our group meetings at the Prince of Brunswick, Barnsbury Road, N. We meet there fortnightly on Wednesdays, at 8 p.m. Our next meeting will be on December 11th. We are expecting to commence our outdoor meetings shortly, and will no doubt have some reports of these in the next issue of the Syndicalist. I have visited several branches of Trade Unions in the district to lecture, and expect to shortly increase our membership as a result. Two other members of the group have been doing the same. We expect to have two prominent members of the local Trades Council join us directly. Sales of literature are good. Our distributing members are attending all the meetings they can to dispose of it. Any one in the district wishing to join should communicate with the secretary, P. Rodda, 130, Barnsbury Road, N.

WIMBLEDON.

The members have not turned up to the group meetings like they should have done. Syndicalism is the only subject talked of here. On Sunday, the 17th, Comrade E. J. B. Allen lectured before the Wimbledon Socialist Society on Syndicalism. On Monday, Gaylord Wilshire lectured on the same subject, in the Compton Hall, to a large audience. The Rev. Sadler took the chair, and he stated that he had been a reader of the Syndicalist from its first issue. He dealt at some length with the "Don't Shoot" prosecution. Comrade Broadbridge is working inside the O.B.S. and takes one and a half quires of the Syndicalist each month. I am convinced that the most effective work is to be done inside the Trade Union movement. Sec., F. L. Baker, 1 High Street, Colliers Wood, Merton, S.W.

COVENTRY.

The Trade Unions here are well entrenched, and are increasing their membership every week. An Amalgamation Committee has been formed for the Engineering Industry, and a good number of its members are Syndicalists, who are working energetically for the consolidation of the various sectional unions into one great fighting force. The local Trades and Labour Council will consider at their next meeting the need for a National Federation of Trades Councils, and a resolution urging the vital necessity of such will be moved by the local I.S.E.L. secretary. We find no difficulty in disposing of the Syndicalist; in fact, the Trade Unionists who are members of the most important committees are quite keen on seeing that they obtain a copy of each month's issue. The Amalgamation Committee have decided to sell the "Tom Mann" pamphlets at their meetings. There is a great deal of patriotic militarism manifested in the city from time to time, and the local group will in the future combat this nonsense by holding both indoor and outdoor meetings. The outdoor gatherings will be held in Market Square on Sunday evenings at 7 p.m. A number of Trade Unionists who are Socialists of the genuine type are being asked to take part in these meetings. The main object is to find a sale for "My Country Right or Wrong" among the general public. The local Trade Union branch secretaries are being asked to give the I.S.E.L. dates on which a lecturer will be able to address the branch on the aims and methods of Syndicalism. Information of the work of the I.S.E.L. in Coventry can be obtained by dropping a postcard to the secretary, H. E. Burdett Ludlam, 62, Sackville Street, Hillfields.

MANCHESTER CENTRE.

This group has been very active during the last few weeks. The Manchester Conference is to be held on Saturday, November 30, and arrangements have also been made for a monster demonstration on Sunday, December 1, in the Coliseum, Ardwick, Manchester. Our secretary visited the London Conference at Holborn Hall and secured a few of the delegates for the Manchester Conference. There is great consternation amongst the parliamentarians here because we refuse to come away from the Industrial field. Many of the members of this group are working heard inside their Trade Union branches, with the result that many of the younger Trade Unionists are devoting their activities entirely to the propagation of Industrial Solidarity and Direct Action. Our group is already too large and will have to split up. Mr. J. J. Smith, 13, Fairburn Street, Horwich, Lancs, is making preparations for the formation of a group at Horwich, and he will be glad to hear from Syndicalists in the neighbourhood with a view to getting to work at once amongst the Trade Union branches in the district. Sec., Manchester Group, 50A, Market Street, Manchester.

HAMMERSMITH.

Our group meetings have been well attended. We have had good discussions with the members and non-members, with the object of encouraging young Trade Unionists to advocate the amalgamation of the various Trade Unions within an industry and to point the need for Direct Action. I have received many letters from these comrades asking for fuller information. This is a good spirit, and gives us hope. Our literature sales are increasing. As the weather has not been favourable for outdoor meetings we have concentrated on the Trade Union branches in this district. I can safely say that our eight speaking members will be busy from November onwards. Comrade Barr is to address the Southall branch of the A.C.E. on November 30. We are looking forward to receiving the new Weekly Syndicalist. Our women members complain that they have not enough work to do half the month now. All the Trade Union branches in West London should write to us for a speaker to come to them and explain Syndicalism. Our weekly meetings are held at Morris Studio, Adie Road, The Grove, Hammersmith, on Tuesdays. Sec., D. Armstrong, 52, The Grove, Hammersmith.

"WEEKLY SYNDICALIST" COLLECTING SHEETS.

We are issuing collecting sheets for our sympathisers to use in their endeavour to raise funds for the Weekly Syndicalist. Comrades requiring these sheets should write to me for them.

AN ACKNOWLEDGMENT.

The splendid photograph of Gustave Hervé which appeared in our last issue was lent to us by the *Christian Commonwealth*. We wish to thank the editor for his courtesy, and hereby express our regret that we inadvertently missed our acknowledgment then. The *Christian Commonwealth* gave a good report of our Holborn Hall Conference.

THE GENERAL STRIKE AND THE COMMISSARIAT

(Continued from Page 3).

It is not by accumulating money or stores that the employers can be fought. That is a relic of eighty years ago. Direct Action, sabotage, militant anti-militarism, and insurrectional activity are the only things that will win the ultimate fight.

The A.S.R.S. possessed large funds which the Taff Vale Railway Company dipped into pretty deeply.

The London Society of Compositors had to make a present to Hammond's of £600 arising out of their strike there in 1906. Most likely the textile workers at Oldham will find some money for the Ram Spinning Company, against whom they have struck. This commissariat, huge treasury business is a flat negation of militant methods.

Legality of the Final Issue.

Militant activity, not reformist-passivity, is the key to success. Force alone is the legality of the final issues of the struggle.

A peaceful national general strike may be a good thing for politicians, but not for workers who seek their emancipation.

A squad of soldiers with loaded rifles would have a better claim to ownership of the Co-operative Stores than a strike committee possessing half a dozen receipts from the Co-operative Wholesale Society.

As we said at the beginning, this suggestion has its good parts. We earnestly advise all workers to join the Co-operative Societies, as well as join their Unions. Through the co-operatives the workers may control some of the productive works of the country, and be able to insist upon their Union membership and conditions in their works. They can control their local societies and insist upon Union membership and conditions for those engaged in the distribution of co-operative produce. They can demonstrate that the private trader, the middleman, is an obnoxious parasite upon society.

The Only Method.

In working-class districts in the East-End of London thousands of street traders who sell in the market streets at the week-end went to the docks to get their 11s. a day for scabbing upon the people, who were their customers and found them a living. The co-operative movement offers the workers a way of "getting their own back" on these week-end tradesmen, and they should take advantage of it.

But everything in its place and in its due proportion. Co-operation does not abolish the wages system, and cannot. Don't let us imagine that a co-op. coal mine is going to save the miners, the cotton mill at Rochdale the cotton operatives, or the mills at Batley the woollen weavers.

Don't let us magnify a detail of guerilla warfare into the strategy and tactics for the overthrow of the present system.

Direct Action, sabotage, general strike, insurrection leading to expropriation are the only methods that Syndicalists can use to emancipate the workers.

GOLDEN PRIVET.

Finest Stock in the World.

100,000 to choose from.

15in. to 18in. 3s.; 18in. to 2ft., 4s.; 2ft. to 2ft. 6in., 5s.; 2ft. 6in. to 3ft., 6s.; 3ft., 9s. per doz. Specimens from 2s. each.

All other Shrubs equally cheap.

Carriage paid on order of 10s.

F. BAKER & SONS,

The Nurseries,

LOWER TOOTING and MERTON.

1 minute from Merton Tram Terminus.

C. J. SMITH,

8, St. James Street,

WALTHAMSTOW.

High-Class Pianos from £12 12s. Cash.

OUR CELEBRATED PIANOS — DEFY COMPETITION. — Cash, or from 10s. monthly.

All Pianos Fully Warranted for 15 Years.

SYNDICALIST LITERATURE.

We are repeatedly being asked for a book on Syndicalism. If inquirers will read through the pamphlets and books of which we print a list underneath, they will obtain a fair idea of what Syndicalism means. Meanwhile, we are bringing out a series of comprehensive books at one shilling, under the general title of "The Syndicalist Library." The first of the series will be by Tom Mann, as advertised below.

TOM MANN'S PAMPHLETS.

No. 1. PREPARE FOR ACTION. 1D.

Explains the need for linking up the unions, and adopting a fighting policy. The pamphlet that made the strike year of 1911. Only a few of these left. Order early.

No. 2. THE TRANSPORT WORKERS. 1D.

Calls for united action amongst Transport Workers. Brought the National Transport Workers' Federation into being, which Federation is to pave the way for ONE union for the Transport industry.

No. 3. FORGING THE WEAPON. 1D.

Explains the steps to be taken by sympathisers in order to build up a fighting union movement. The pamphlet to be pushed. The best for workers. Most useful to propagandists.

No. 4. ALL HAIL SOLIDARITY. 1D.

Shows the growth of solidarity amongst the workers of various industries. Deals with the Cambrian Combine Strike, and contains messages from W. D. Haywood, I.W.W., and Eugene V. Debs, of the American Socialist Party.

No. 5. SYMPOSIUM ON SYNDICALISM. 1D.

Contains both an account of the practical work to be performed by Syndicalists and a brief statement of our object and methods. A splendid educator. There are not many of these left.

No. 6. A MANCHESTER MESSAGE TO THE WORKERS OF ENGLAND. 6D.

A verbatim report of the whole of the proceedings of the first national conference held on Syndicalism. Records the formation of the Industrial Syndicalist Education League. This will become a historic document, useful alike to workers and students. Only about a dozen left.

No. 7. PARLIAMENTARY ACTION versus SYNDICALISM. 2D.

Being a report of a debate between TOM MANN and FRANK ROSE, both well-known members of the A.S.E., and both prominent in the Labour World. The conflict between Unionism and Direct Action, and the policy of the "pure and simple" politicians as a means to emancipation. 60 pages for 2d.

No. 8. MINERS WAKE UP. 6D.

Contains essays by members of the South Wales Miners' Federation, who are at work in the pits. This pamphlet with Number 5 was quoted by the Coal-owners to Mr. Asquith in order to kill the Miners' Minimum Wage Bill, and to show the "dangerous" trend of advanced opinion amongst the Miners and workers generally. Only about two dozen left.

No. 9. THE WEAPON SHAPING. 6D.

A compact work, showing the growth of Syndicalism; full of suggestions; indicates the interest in Syndicalism aroused amongst the Trades Councils. Should be read by all members of the Trades Councils, for it contains an account of the Derby Trades Council's action, and an address by the Secretary of the Walthamstow Trades Council to its members.

No. 10. A TWO-FOLD WARNING.

This contains a splendid account of the International Cotton Manufacturers' Federation. A lucid statement of the growth of this important industry, and of the tactics used by the Federated employers. Contains a powerful plea for solidarity amongst the Textile workers, and shows the necessity for the workers being educated as to the development of machinery that the masters are bringing in. Explains that the only hope lies in their controlling the industry. Shows up the Cotton Ring.

No. 11. THE RAILWAYMEN. 1D.

A splendid essay upon the growth and development of the Railway Service. Railwaymen will find it packed full of useful information. Explains how they must organise, and what means to use to combat the power of the Companies. Conciliation Boards exposed.

No. 12. THE TRANSPORT INDUSTRY 1D.

This details the inner history of the Shipping Federation, against which arose the National Transport Workers Federation. Shows the cunning and unscrupulous methods of the men who pull the strings in the Shipping World. None of these left. We shall probably reprint. Order immediately if required.

— THE —

Ferrer School

now meets at

Manette Street, W.

(Charing Cross Road),

On SUNDAY AFTERNOON, at 3.30 p.m.

OTHER BOOKS.

MY COUNTRY: RIGHT OR WRONG. By Gustave Hervé.

Translated by Guy Bowman. Library Edition, 3s. 6d.

The Yorkshire Daily Observer says:—"It is a fiery, sustained, and often eloquent plea for a union among the workers of all countries against capitalism, and incidentally against war, which, Mr. Hervé has no difficulty in showing, never by any chance benefits the industrial population of the conquering or of the conquered country, and is of service only to financiers."

MY COUNTRY: RIGHT OR WRONG. By Gustave Hervé. 1/-

Cheap Popular Edition.

THE MINERS' NEXT STEP. 6D.

A stirring appeal for the reorganisation of the Miners' Federation on fighting lines—the bible of the militant miners. Has been circulated all over the United Kingdom.

INDEPENDENCE, or CO-PARTNERSHIP IN EDUCATION, by A. H. M. Robertson. 1D.

A pamphlet containing the private and strictly confidential draft memorial on University Education, lately issued to the Parliamentary Committee of the Trades Union Congress by the Workers' Educational Association, with comment thereon, partly reprinted from the "Railway Review."

THE SYNDICALIST RAILWAYMAN. 1D.

Copies of Numbers 1, 2, 3, and 4 can still be obtained. Contains matter of general interest to Syndicalists, and will serve the purpose of any student, as well as that of any number of the Syndicalist.

THE SYNDICALIST.

A limited number of the January and February issues that were seized by the police can be had. Collectors can have copies of these to complete their collections at 5/- each, to go towards the "Weekly Syndicalist" fund. Any of the succeeding issues can be obtained for 1D.

GUY BOWMAN, Publisher, 4, Maude Terrace, Walthamstow.

TRANSPORT WORKERS' AMALGAMATION COMMITTEE.

At the Conference held in the Holborn Town Hall, organisation slips were distributed amongst the delegates, for them to fill in the names of those engaged in the transport industry, in their respective districts, who would assist in the initial work of forming district sub-committees. Will our friends kindly forward all names and particulars as early as possible, so that we can get to work!

*   *   *

During the last few days the following branches have been visited by the secretary: Dairy Employees (Earl of Essex); Dockers (East Ham); Gas Workers (Deptford); Carmen (Old Friends, Greenwich); General Labourers (Grocers' Arms, Greenwich). These have been specially summoned to discuss "Amalgamation," and at all the meetings absolute unanimity has prevailed. This week the big branch of the Gas Workers and General Labourers, Barking Road, Canning Town, is visited on Tuesday; the West Ham A.S.R.S. on Friday; and on Thursday delegates from all Transport Workers' Unions in the Greenwich district meet at the Conduit House Club.

*   *   *

If any of our comrades can, will they kindly obtain from branches of unions engaged in the transport industry the privilege of a deputation from our committee paying them a visit to discuss amalgamation. It is in the branches the work is done, and during the winter outdoor meetings turn out failures as often as not.

*   *   *

On December 27, Tom Mann speaks at the Stratford Town Hall. The meeting will be succeeded by a musical entertainment. Tickets, 6d. and 3d. each. These tickets must be sold. The hall must be packed.

*   *   *

Will those who have our books of penny tickets for sale kindly return all counterfoils and cash by the first post on December 18! This committee is putting in plenty of work and could do a lot more if it had the money to do it with. We hope all the tickets will be sold.

*   *   *

The secretary and F. J. Passmore visit the Manchester Conference as delegates from this committee. All transport workers visiting the Conference should get into communication with these with a view to propaganda, formation of local sub-committees, and general organisation.

*   *   *

As far as the London Dock district is concerned, the Amalgamation question is now the sole topic of conversation in Trade Union circles. Everyone is advocating it now—the more reason why we should redouble our efforts. We are not going to be awakened by any "half-way," "one thing at a time" proposal, if such a thing is suggested. We want and intend to have "one union for all transport workers."

*   *   *

This committee is now employing Sam. Roden as organiser, and he is devoting his whole time to the work. The rank and file are securing guarantees of weekly sums to provide a wages fund. The treasurer is E. Halkett, 33, Richmond Street, Plaistow.

*   *   *

One last word, and this the most important. Will every transport worker from railwayman to bread-rounds man, taxi-driver to coal-trimmer, who reads this, kindly write at once? To get into touch with all transport workers; any one, anywhere, is the wish of SAM RODEN.

Sec., Transport Workers' Amalg. Com., 7, Holland Road, West Ham, E.

Printed and Published by GUY BOWMAN, 4, Maude Terrace, Walthamstow, E.

1913

The Syndicalist
and Amalgamation News

Edited under the auspices of the Industrial Syndicalist Education League. ::

President
TOM MANN

Secretary
GUY BOWMAN

VOL. II. NO. 1.   LONDON, JANUARY, 1913.   MONTHLY. ONE PENNY.

PROPAGANDIST EFFORTS FOR 1913.

Those who attended the meeting at Anderton's Hotel on New Year's Night, 1912, when George Lansbury presided, will realise how far we have travelled in twelve months. Syndicalism has been advanced out of all proportion to any other phase of the revolutionary propaganda during the past year. The absurd action on the part of the government in prosecuting those who spread the "Don't Shoot" leaflet gave a stimulus to our propagandist efforts for which we have good reason to be grateful. We cannot expect the fates to be equally propitious during 1913, and we must, therefore, undertake with greater definitness and vigour—if that is possible—to conduct a systematic propagandist campaign amongst the Trade Union branch members. Nothing tells so powerfully as this educational work in the Trade Unions. There are three million of trade unionists in the United Kingdom. Of these, one-third may be counted as of serious importance—i.e., the other two-thirds are relatively passive. It is the active third that counts. It is of more importance to the revolutionary movement that the active one million of trade unionists shall be influenced aright than six times that number of others. Had there been more Syndicalist propaganda done in the Miners' Lodges in 1911 they would have shown more of the right kind of Direct Action tactics in the struggle of 1912. There are several big fights to come on during the next two years, and the nature of these struggles will be decided by the proportion of workers who understand the meaning of SOLIDARITY and DIRECT ACTION. The I.S.E.L. need not strive to obtain an enormous membership, but it must be equal to reaching the rank and file of the trade unionists, and every advocate must himself or herself be a trade unionist.

The efforts at amalgamating the sectional Unions in each industry have borne good fruit, and the prospect is good for the achievement of far greater things on these lines during the present year.

The Conferences held at London and Manchester each emphasised the increasing importance of Trades Councils, and Direct Actionists will render good service by giving special attention to these bodies. Energetic, tactful work here will repay the effort effectually.

For myself, I feel strongly the necessity for centring my energies more than I have done the last few years, so I give this intimation that from now on I intend to make Manchester my centre, and shall confine my efforts within a radius of some eighty miles or so of that industrial centre. My Lancashire address will be 18, Beech Range, Levenshulme, Manchester.

TOM MANN.

FORWARD, SYNDICALISM !

A CALL TO ARMS.

By GEORGE SIMPSON.

"None are so blind as those who will not see." This is an adage which political Socialists have been extremely fond of using towards those liberal and tory workmen who refused to listen to Socialist teachings, or who, having listened, could not see "the wood for trees."

Since the advent, within the last few years, of Syndicalist ideas into Great Britain, the Socialist politicians have placed themselves in the very same category that they placed liberals and tories.

Two writers in the organ which to all intents and purposes is the official organ of the B.S.P., or at least the S.D.P. majority in that body, have stated that there is no Syndicalism in this country. If they really believe what they say, it seems foolish that these writers should continually go out of their way to attack and misrepresent both Syndicalists and Syndicalism.

As a matter of fact, there is no truth in the statement, for while there has not yet been any really serious attempt to organise Syndicalists, the SYNDICALIST has a larger circulation than any Socialist paper in Great Britain, with the single exception of the *Clarion*.

A few weeks ago, as stated in the November issue of the SYNDICALIST, the organ above referred to made a particularly lying attack on Syndicalism, to which I strongly protested. In reply to my protest, a well-known member of the Birmingham B.S.P. stated that there was "more Syndicalism in the B.S.P. than Social-Democracy," and this particular comrade has, I venture to believe, far more knowledge of the B.S.P. rank and file than either the editor or the other scribe of the sheet in question.

The fact is that the leaders of the B.S.P. are seriously alarmed because of the number of resignations from that organisation, and because of the lack of energy and enthusiasm in the party. It must be very annoying to find that the rank and file refuse to have their ideas and principles moulded on the same identical pattern as their "leaders'," and undoubtedly it was due to my spirited defence of Syndicalism in *Justice* that the conservative element of the B.S.P. executive issued the manifesto against Syndicalism to which Messrs. Leonard Hall, Russell Smart, and Conrad Noel took such exception.

Indeed, Syndicalism is so strong in the B.S.P. that at the October Executive Council meeting it was suggested that the party would have to seriously consider the advisability of expelling all known Syndicalists.

There is not a single political Socialist party in this country to-day which is not as dead as the proverbial kippered herring, in so far as effectiveness is concerned.

Of course, the politicians, eager to seize upon any excuse, try to make out that this "recrudescence of anarchy" is due to the failure of the Labour party when it is nothing of the kind.

Syndicalism is the expression of the revolt of the proletariat against, and is the natural outcome of, existing economic conditions—the exploitation of the wageworkers by the capitalist class.

This economic revolution can never be brought about by politicians, and by means of such a machine as the house of parliament, which is the instrument by means of which the capitalist class enslaves us. It can, however, and will, be

GEORGE SIMPSON,
Ex-Treasurer B.S.P.,
Now Northern Organiser I.S.E.L.

effected by the wage workers themselves, through their own united action on the industrial field.

Syndicalism offers the only real method of abolishing unemployment. I will here state a case, and I wonder how parliament would deal with it.

In the September issue of the *International Socialist Review* there was an article by Robert Johnstone Wheeler on "Automatic Machinery in the Glass Bottle Industry, and its Effect on the Employment of Skilled Craftsmen":

In 1903 an automatic machine was made for making glass bottles. In 1905 it was admitted by experts to be a success, and a company was formed to take advantage of the invention which has revolutionised the American glass bottle industry.

In the year 1909, 49 automatic machines, having a producing capacity per machine of 111.5 gross per day of 24 hours, or a yearly production of 1,700,824 gross, based upon a year of 300 working days, were at work in the industry. It would require 440 shops, or 1,320 skilled blowers to produce 1,700,824 gross. The Census Bulletin says that there was only 493,341 gross more produced in 1909 than in 1904. Therefore, since the machines were working, a large number of skilled men must have been idle. And it is so.

In 1909 there were 8,501 journeymen and 1,840 apprentices under the jurisdiction of the Union, and about 900 non-Union blowers.

In the month of December of that year the Union had 2,395 idle.

According to Mr. Wheeler, this automatic machine for making glass bottles is the first machine to take over the entire work of production in a great industry and to eliminate the skilled workman. In fact, *not only are the whole of the SKILLED men being displaced, but also most of the* UNSKILLED.

In seven years two-fifths of the American glass bottle workers have been thrown upon the scrap-heap through the introduction of machinery, and this is happening all over the world.

When the workers are organised on Syndicalist lines, they will, in order to meet such a situation, merely reduce the hours of labour of the men engaged in that particular industry, which will at once absorb those men who otherwise would be thrown out of employment, and in addition will enable the workers to enjoy a shorter working day, with the minimum expenditure of energy and the maximum amount of comfort.

At the beginning of this article I stated that the SYNDICALIST had a circulation which exceeded that of any Socialist paper in this country, with the exception of the *Clarion*. That being so, there is every reason to believe that large numbers of Syndicalists are waiting to be organised in order to spread the gospel of Syndicalism throughout Great Britain.

At present, the Industrial Syndicalist Education League exists for that purpose, but the question of effectively organising the Syndicalists in order that they might co-ordinate their propaganda has not been seriously attempted so far; if it has, it has not yet taken a very definite shape, for the I.S.E.L. consists at present of a small number of loosely organised groups and a large number of individuals scattered all over the country.

The time is now ripe for the formation of a strong Syndicalist organisation on national lines, whose function shall be the spread of Syndicalism throughout the length and breadth of the land. This could be done by means of autonomous local groups of Syndicalists federated into a national body, without, if possible, an Executive Committee, for executives are always caucuses.

We could hold meetings at factory and workshop doors and at street corners, but our greatest work should be the distribution of Syndicalist literature.

Our aims would be to:

1. To induce non-Trade Unionists to join Trade Unions.
2. To induce Trade Unionists to spread Syndicalist ideas inside their Trade Unions.
3. To obtain members for the Syndicalist League in order to effectively organise our propaganda.

I earnestly appeal to all Syndicalists to seriously consider this question of an organised National Syndicalist Movement, and to communicate their ideas WITHOUT DELAY to the Editor of the SYNDICALIST.

Do it now! Hurrah for the Industrial Revolution!

WEEKLY SYNDICALIST FOR 1913.

COMRADES,—Again I want to say something about that £300 for the WEEKLY SYNDICALIST. Never was the time more propitious for the launching of our paper as a weekly. A monthly journal cannot aspire as becoming anything other than an "academic" sheet because it cannot possibly keep pace with current events.

Strikes may have taken place and be over between the appearance of two numbers, such as the North-Eastern strike was; lock-outs may have defeated the workers; wars may have been engaged in; adverse legislation may have been rushed through. All this may have taken place without the SYNDICALIST having had an opportunity of offering the worker any plan of action.

A monthly paper cannot have the influence we Syndicalists wish it to exercise. A WEEKLY SYNDICALIST is exactly the kind of paper which is wanted as a "Fighting Organ" because:

It would wield more than four times the influence that a monthly could ever hope to have; it would be in the position to show the workers the best immediate line of action to follow.

For example, we could have taken up the North-Eastern strike and endeavoured to have got a national strike of railwaymen. The men are seething with discontent all over the country owing to the many victimisations and the deceitful awards of the conciliation boards. With the railwaymen out, would the seamen have been held back? I think not; and so we could have had a repetition of 1911 with all its educational value and propaganda. As Direct Actionists our agitation thrives best when strikes are on. It is our duty as well as policy to play the part of agitators. Action is the sovereign educator. Nothing succeeds like success, and we thrive best in the midst of the fight.

The power of the SYNDICALIST has grown. We have already made a profound impression upon the British Labour movement. Do not let the paucity of funds stand in the way of success. Everything is in favour of a WEEKLY SYNDICALIST. The Labour Party has ceased to hold the attention of militant workers. The B.S.P. is torn asunder owing to the attitude of its executive to Syndicalism. There is a vast mass of unorganised Syndicalists waiting for a policy on which to concentrate. A WEEKLY SYNDICALIST would bring these hesitating ones definitely to our side and in our ranks.

Besides, a WEEKLY SYNDICALIST is a sound financial venture. Newsagents will handle a weekly and push it where they do not trouble about a monthly. Men will take a weekly regularly because their interest is maintained. They will order a weekly and see that they get it, where a monthly is too long in between issues for them to trouble over.

A large circulation of the SYNDICALIST such as a weekly would give means more Syndicalism, more members, more finance, more propagandist value, more influence on the general body of workers, and the quicker accomplishment of our object.

A WEEKLY SYNDICALIST would soon become the recognised mouthpiece of all militant workers. The rank and file would find in us their champion, always ready to take up their grievance against the employers or their officials.

As a step towards obtaining the necessary £300 as initial capital, we have drawn up collecting sheets, which all our friends can have by applying to me.

£300 is a large sum to raise from the workers, but it is not so large that they can raise it if they wish. It is up to you if you want a WEEKLY SYNDICALIST to get busy and send the cash along. The I.S.E.L. was asked to convene an International Syndicalist Congress. A WEEKLY SYNDICALIST would greatly facilitate that matter. We have accomplished much with our small resources. Help the SYNDICALIST to accomplish more. January, 1912, found the SYNDICALIST a power which the government had to attack. Let January, 1913, place the SYNDICALIST in a stronger position to attack the government. We have earned the hatred of the Press, the employers, and the state. Give us more power by making us a weekly that we can fight them all even more effectively than we have done.

The workers are turning to Direct Action as their only method. Set up the WEEKLY SYNDICALIST as *the* journal of Direct Action, Sabotage, and Anti-Militarism.

GUY BOWMAN.

The Syndicalist.

EDITED UNDER THE AUSPICES OF

The Industrial Syndicalist Education League

Offices—
4, MAUDE TERRACE, WALTHAMSTOW,
LONDON, E

MONTHLY - ONE PENNY.

Post Paid Subscription—
Great Britain or Abroad ... 12 months 1s. 6d.

Bundle Rates—
1s. 6d. per quire, Carriage Paid.

The receipt of a Sample Copy is an invitation to Subscribe.

JANUARY, 1913.

THE LEGACY OF 1912 TO 1913.

With this number we commence a new volume. One year's life has seen many changes. Twelve months ago Syndicalism was a word hardly used by the English-speaking races, but by the government's aid it has now become an accepted part of the English language, like many another word of "alien" origin. Since January, 1912, not only has there been a widely-spread propaganda of Syndicalism, but some of the results of that propaganda have also commenced to appear.

The first result of importance was the acceptance of a Direct Action policy by the militant workers, be they Miners or Railwaymen; the potency of their own direct activity has taught them to rely on nothing else but their own efforts.

Conciliation boards and agreements must go. No more compromise with those who live upon our labour, for compromise in the class struggle is treason. The only peace is that assured by victory; the only truce that which allows for a re-formation of the workers' forces.

With the increased revolutionary spirit there goes the understanding for a better organised force. The SYNDICALIST and the Syndicalists have given an immense boom to the various Amalgamation Committees. We have placed them in the position whereby they can best accomplish their task of securing the unity of Labour's forces.

The past year has witnessed above all the damning exposure of the parliamentary Labour Party, and the obsequious Trade Union officials who compose it have sunk into insignificance. The workers are now recognising that parliament is no longer the place for their Union officials, and that their place is outside in the fight.

Whilst many workers had ceased to have any faith whatsoever in the Labour Party, other parties have fared as poorly. The B.S.P. is dying of inanition; the stupidity of the "Old Guard" of the S.D.F. is responsible for this. "Revolutionary" politics have fared as badly as those of the "practical" Labour Party.

The Syndicalists, the advocates of Direct Action, are the only ones who can boast of an increased power and influence.

The two large conferences, the one in London and the other in Manchester, held under the auspices of the Industrial Syndicalist Education League, gave clear proof of the growth of Syndicalist ideas amongst militant workers.

Much has been accomplished; but still more remains to be done. In order that our efforts should not be lost, we must increase the pressure upon the Trade Unions.

The work of the Amalgamation Committees must be pushed forward, and the large number of men and women with Syndicalist principles must be brought into definite organisation as one another, as suggested by George Simpson in another column; the I.S.E.L. must have its groups extended throughout the whole of the country. Every reader of the SYNDICALIST who agrees with the policy we advocate should become a member of the League. The I.S.E.L. is not an organisation in opposition to the Trade Unions or the Amalgamation Committees; it is but an educational propagandist body. Every meeting held under its auspices strengthens the Trade Union movement. The first thing the Syndicalists call for is for every worker to join the Union of his respective trade. Every

meeting held under the auspices of the Industrial Syndicalist Education League is a fillip to the amalgamation movement, for we ask the workers to join their Unions, and then to take active steps with a view to the amalgamation of all the Trade Unions within any one industry.

Then we have a mission to fulfil beyond the joining of a Union, or the amalgamation of the Unions so joined, and that is to outline the functions and purposes for which the Union movement should exist.

There are plenty of men who will support the Unions; there are an increasing number who will join and support the Amalgamation Committees, and there is an ever-increasing number who understand the message of the SYNDICALIST. It is to this ever-increasing number that we appeal, asking them to join us and take up a share of the work of the I.S.E.L.

We have been afforded ample proof that the workers realise the necessity for a greater unity. It is for us Syndicalists to see that this greater unity, which is being evolved, is not wasted in vain effort afterwards.

We want members inside every Trade Union branch, District Council, and Trades Council fighting all the time for Amalgamation and Direct Action. We want more groups, because by the general propaganda at the street corner and elsewhere we not only reach the non-Unionists, but also large numbers of Trade Unionists who for some reason or other never attend their branch meetings.

The Unions and Amalgamation Committees have got to perfect the worker's organisations technically; the Industrial Syndicalist Education League has got to carry on that revolutionary propaganda which is to inspire the rank and file with the idea that the perfected machinery will have to be used for a definite object; and that object is the overthrowing of the power of the employers entirely, by the organised workers taking possession of the tools with which they work, and the wealth they produce.

We have to thank the Socialist Labour Party, the Advocates of Industrial Unionism, the Industrialist League, and all those who preceded us in the various policies and methods of preaching Industrial Solidarity. We ask all those who have realised the necessity for industrial organisation, both for the present as a fighting force and in the future as the structure of an Industrial Commonwealth, to join hands with us in our work of utilising the material at hand by educating the rank and file of the Trade Unions to an understanding of our message.

A new Union movement cannot be built up outside of the existing one in this country. Even if this could be done, it would be unwise to attempt it whilst the old one is there. Besides, the Unions can be made to be what the rank and file will choose to make of them.

We call upon all those who believe in Industrial Organisation, Direct Action, and the expropriation of the capitalist class to join the I.S.E.L., thereby giving the New Year a hearty send-off for increased activity in every direction.

ANOTHER UNCONSTITUTIONAL STRIKE.

The North-Eastern Railwaymen have again demonstrated their power of Solidarity and the efficacy of Direct Action.

The strike for the reinstatement of Driver Knox was a challenge to their own Union officials, to the company, and to the state.

Like all successful strikes of the last few years, it was led by the actual participants—so they won; whereas official strikes, like the miners', have ended disastrously. There is no doubt that the withholding of the official advising assisted the strikers. The capitalist Press, particularly the tory papers, apart from their lying articles about a strike for "the right to get drunk," saw the full significance of this dramatic fight. They claimed, and claimed rightly, that the success of the strike was a blow at the prestige of the state.

The magistrates who sentenced Knox in the first instance have protested, since Chester Jones' reversal of their sentence, that their verdict was given in accordance with the evidence given them. Then why did Chester Jones find that the man was not "drunk in law"? Can anyone imagine that the government sent him there for any other purpose?

The men on the North-Eastern have demonstrated that Direct Action and Solidarity can beat the company and the company's protector—the state. This strike has been the finest example of the power of Syndicalist tactics and methods.

If the organised on one railway line can compel the capitulation of the employers and the state over the reinstatement of one man, what is to prevent the organised Working Class from using the same methods to compel the unconditional surrender of the capitalist class and the state? And as the North-Eastern men won, so would the Working Class win.

Go, thou, and do likewise.

RED RUBBER.

By RUBBERITE.

(Continued from last month.)

III.

We have heard much of red rubber and slavery in the Congo, but if the lusty-throated philanthropists would look more after the rubber slaves at home, under their own eyes, it would be better.

When a black becomes infirm they have a quicker and more humane system of finishing his earthly life, they club his head. Then there is a chorus of denunciation from the prelates. Investigations are started, columns of sentimental slosh fill our patriotic papers. They "kid" the workers what vile tyrants these taskmasters must be. Under "civilised conditions" when a man shows grey hairs it is a sign that his wages have to be reduced, thus further lowering his low supply of the necessaries of life. It does not matter that his labour, in co-operation with others, has been instrumental in making a small works into a gigantic limited company concern. The workers are "hands," profit-making machines, pale, languid girls, overworked, underpaid men and boys. Dividends have been rising whilst wages have remained stationary, in reality falling, owing to the increased cost of the necessaries of life.

Unfortunately the employers are not likely to grant anything. Still more unfortunately, the workers have acquiesced in everything the employers have done to them. It remains for the workers to rub their eyes and ask, whether men sifting that poisonous stuff red antimony, carrying rolls of rubber, "pressmen" working the day or night through, with no meal time, "trolling" tyres about, rushing at their work as if it was the last day, shall continue to work for their 4½d. and 5d. per hour? Whether girls shall be sacrificed on the altar of dividends for their 10 or 12 shillings per week? The employers consider it a crime for a girl to be seen with a red face, they think they are being robbed of dividends

It is estimated that there are over thirty thousand persons engaged in the rubber trade. The total value of rubber sold for consumption is 8½ millions sterling. It is obvious to all what magnitude the rubber industry attains.

If by some subtle influence the whole of the workers were to stop working until they had secured a minimum wage, it would be almost as effective as the coal strike.

It is reported that an independent investigator once stood outside some rubber works when the horde of slaves came out. He was astonished! He said, "I never saw a man or woman with colour on their faces, nor decent clothing on their backs."

No wonder! They do not get sufficient wages to buy enough ordinary food for seven days a week. And music, drama, amusements are out of the question, a "twopenny lean-over" is their highest extravagance. Not that they would refuse high-class art, but their wages are too low.

The workers will have to take a leaf out of the employers' book. They are organised so perfectly that no matter to what part of England, Scotland, or Wales one may go, the wages are about the same. When labour begins to organise we hear a lot about capital leaving the country, but they may be reminded that during the last few years English firms have established works already in Japan, Ceylon, and China. There are English managers to teach the Orientals the mystic art of rubber manufacture. Labour is cheaper in these places where the workers live on rice and curry—they only receive rice and curry wages, no more, sometimes less.

If anyone doubts this, let them read the speech of Mr. Frederick Anderson, chairman of the Gulakalumpong Rubber Estates Co., Ltd., when moving the first annual report of that company at its shareholders' meeting, held in the Cannon Street Hotel, London, in April, 1911. Speaking on "The Labour Force" he said: "Wages have advanced fully 50 per cent. more than two years ago in the East as in the West. Experience had shown that when high wages are paid, the tendency is for manual labour not to make the most out of prosperous times, but to take things more easily and work less. They—the coolies—can live quite comfortably on about 12 cents (about 3½d.) per day.

There you have it. In a few years time this will prove a bugbear to the English rubber - worker. Organised Capital can only be met with organised Labour. Spasmodic outbursts on the part of a few workmen are useless. Far be it from me to censure them for smarting under their grievances and rebelling, thus losing a day's or, perhaps, a week's wages, even when some of them are married and have wives and little children dependent on them. We are proud to know that some, at any rate, will not submit to the conditions imposed upon them. The slave that will not rise against his master, but who turns his cheek to the smiter, that slave is hopeless.

THE WORKING-CLASS AND POLITICAL ACTION.

By W. F. HAY.

I.

In all the discussions which take place as to how and by what means the working class should seek to ameliorate its present condition, and finally to accomplish its emancipation, the terms "parliamentary" and "political action" are constantly being used. It is, therefore, essential to clearly understand what these terms connote, and also to see how far it is permissible to use the two terms to convey the same idea. There is also a tendency to scribe the term "political action" to the taking part by the organised workers in elections for Councils and boards of local administration. In my opinion, this is a misnomer, which arises directly from a misconception as to what constitutes political action. The following analysis and resultant deductions may assist us in coming to definite conclusions on this important point.

What Is Parliament?

Parliament is, as its name denotes, a talking place, a deliberative assembly, where persons representing diverse interests may meet in a civilised fashion, and by a process of debate and voting come to some compromise which, while it serves the interest of none entirely, yet serves the interest of all by cancelling differences. Called into being first of all to cancel out differences existing between landowners, it afforded the battle ground on which the rising capitalist class fought and beat the landlords, utilising the working class as pawns in this game of political chess; afterwards compromising with the landowners in the hour of victory. Cromwell's order to "take away that bauble" marked the period which terminated the reign of the landlord singly and ushered in the joint reign of land and capital. The struggle for supremacy between these two for power is written large in the constitutional history of the past 200 years. It consists, in the main, in the struggle on the one hand to expand and on the other to contract economic rent. This internecine struggle, however, did not prevent both landlord and capitalist seeing clearly that, whichever had the best of the struggle between the two, it was to their common interest to keep the working class in subjection and also in such ignorance as was compatible with the working class becoming continuously more efficient as wealth producers. Parliament thus became increasingly necessary for both land and capital. It became the Forum on which could be argued and fought the antagonistic interests of the two sections of the governing class—land and capital. As each side found themselves in difficulties in their struggle with each other, they enlisted armies of mercenaries, i.e., they extended the franchise—the Tories in the rural districts where they were strong, because the ownership of land gave them power to control the lives of the rural voter; and the Liberals in the urban districts, where their ownership of capital gave them control over the urban voter. There was a double sophistry employed against the workers in these manœuvres. The first, that their interests, either as rural or urban workers, were identical with their employers. The second, that they were "citizens" because they had the use of a vote. The plain truth being that just as the state was invented to protect private property, so parliament was invented to equate the differences between individual owners. Equal value and equal rights to vote are logical when understood in connection with a community of large and small property owners, because the ownership of property gives the basis of citizenship. To the man who owns no property, the vote is not a badge of citizenship, but a sign that he is one of the voting cattle, just as he is one of the working cattle for the same reason.

Pills from Parliament.

This can be easily seen if we take the result of a parliamentary general election. Among the members returned will be men closely identified with finance—banking, loan-mongering, Stock Exchange, &c.

—with land, manufacturing capital, and distributive capital—merchants, shopkeepers, &c. Included amongst the tagrag and bobtail will be found a few Labour members who are supposed to represent "Labour." In parenthesis, it may be noted that they simply represent the labour leaders' itch to become more respectable and influential. The net result of this hotch-potch of interests represented is that parliament becomes a mortar in which all these interests are braised by the pestle of public opinion and political trickery. The resulting compound is made into pills, or "Bills," and presented to the electorate. Each section gets a little of what it wants—and a good deal that it does not! Those who contribute most to the amalgam—i.e., land and big capital—get most, and those who contribute least get the usual results of taking pills! Such an institution can never afford the pathway along which a subject class shall travel to freedom. It can only obscure the issues,—blunt the instincts of the working class, and throw a veil over the class struggle by making the worker lose his class identity as a worker, in the simulacrum of citizenship. Society, the nation, the community, the people, are all phrases which serve as a snare for the workers, phrases which are used to beguile the workers by the pimps, panders, and prostitutes who play the game of politics in parliament.

Politics—"the Art of Government."

So long as the "art" is practised, it presupposes the existence of two classes politically — the governors and the governed. Useful to the first-named, since it serves to delimit property rights and to codify laws which serve as "taboos." Nine-tenths of the laws already in existence are negative in their nature, and consist in permutations of "Thou shalt not" do anything contrary to the interests of land and capital. These laws obviate the necessity for a continuous discussion of what constitutes an invasion of property rights. A series of principles are propounded and embodied in these laws, against which, if any law offend, the machinery of the law automatically takes action. No discussion takes place upon the principle of the law: that has long enough ago been settled and decided. All that is discussed is the FACT of the offence against the law. "He who breaks pays," and the machinery for making the individual pay, either in purse or person, once set in motion, works on with all the force of law and order behind it. That is, the full force of ALL the interests affected —i.e., property interests concentrate to protect the interests of all.

This is clearly brought out, if we consider that legislation which usually comes under the term of SOCIAL REFORM. If we go right back to the first Factory Act, and carefully consider all the facts, it will be clearly shown that the power of the individual employer to exploit was limited in the interests of ALL the employers, in precisely the same way as a close time for wild birds, fish, or seals is enacted, not, of course, in the interests of the birds, fish, or seals, but simply in order that they shall not be exterminated, and thus a profitable industry be ruined. Incidentally, the birds, &c., have a little more comfortable time of it during the breeding season; but this is usually made up for by the rigour of the hunt when it has ended! And even those persons who are so enchanted with the sixty years of social reform legislation we have experienced would themselves deem it absurd to expect the ox to be grateful for the oilcake which fattened him for the market! Let any of this legislation be examined—Factory Acts, Education Acts, aye, even the beneficent (?) Insurance Act and Old-Age Pensions—and it will be seen that either it is prompted by the same considerations which force a horse-owner to feed and shelter his horse comfortably, or that a cheaper—to the governing class—method of dealing with some particular "poverty problem" has been evolved.

(To be continued.)

SYNDICALISM IN MANY LANDS.

DIRECT ACTION, SABOTAGE, & ANTI-MILITARISM ADOPTED BY TEUTONS AS WELL AS LATINS

AMERICA.

SYNDICALISM IN THE UNITED STATES.

Within the past few months there has been organised in the United States a national Syndicalist propaganda organisation known as "The Syndicalist League of North America." Perhaps a few words regarding its purposes and reasons for being may interest English rebels.

The I.W.W., which until the advent of the S.L. of N.A. alone embodied the revolutionary Union movement in the U.S., claims jurisdiction over the whole working class. It is based on the theory that the old Trade Unions are incapable of evolution and must be supplanted by an entirely new and revolutionary labour movement.

The members of the S.L. of N.A., or Syndicalists—as distinguished from the Industrial Unionists of the I.W.W.—are dissenters from this theory and programme. They hold that an attempt will have to be made to revolutionise the old Unions. Their contention is based on the fact that the bulk of the old Unions are not only not dying out, as they should according to the I.W.W. programme, but are exhibiting unmistakable signs of progress; while the I.W.W., in spite of seven years of intense propaganda, is unable to secure a foothold in the industries in which the Trade Unions have any strength. The Syndicalists reason that if the mountain won't come to Mahomet, Mahomet will have to go to the mountain. Consequently they are proceeding to carry the message of Revolutionary Unionism to the Trade Unions.

The reason why the workers in the Trade Unions have not forsaken them and joined the I.W.W. are numerous and various. Perhaps one of the most important is that the old Unions, bad as they are, offer a great measure of protection to their members, as their comparatively high standard of living proves. Consequently they are loth to leave them on the speculation of finding something better in the I.W.W. Instinctively they cling to them, and they try to purge them of their abuses. Another factor is the extreme radicalism of the I.W.W. Its melange of anti-patriotism, anti-militarism, anti-parliamentarism, anti-religion, contempt for law, and labour contracts, &c., presented en masse to the conservative Trade Unionists by an organisation in competition with their own—and consequently viewed with more or less suspicion—arouses their prejudices rather than wins their support. The I.W.W. has experienced this time and again. Another important factor is the unpopularity among Trade Unionists of the " One Big Union " form of Unionism advocated by the I.W.W. The trade Unionists, schooled in the tenets and practices of craft unionism, and jealously watching over the interests of their crafts don't relish the prospect of submerging themselves in big industrial Unions in which their crafts will have no autonomy. Their tendency is to gradually bring their Unions into closer relationship just in the measure they learn this is necessary, and that they can protect the interests of their crafts in so doing.

It is noteworthy that in the textile industry, the only one in which the I.W.W. has, as yet, gained any considerable strength, practically all the above-mentioned obstacles to the success of the I.W.W. were absent. The textile workers were a gang of wretched slaves working on a common level of starvation. The few remnants of the Trade Unions among them offered them no protection and had no prestige. They were practically all foreigners, and; naturally, not repelled by the I.W.W.'s " anti-Isms." They had no " craft interests " to protect. They were " rotten ripe " for the I.W.W. type of Unionism. In passing, it may be noted that several other industries, notably the Steel Industry, present similar conditions.

But whatever the reason, the inescapable fact exists, as pointed out above, that the vast bulk of the Trade Unions are not disintegrating as the I.W.W. would have them, but are going the contrary route of evolution. And the future holds but little hope for their demise, as they are rapidly passing into the hands of the Socialists—at the recent A. F. of L. Convention the Socialists controlled one-third of the vote. If their strength increases as much in the New Year as it did in the past one, they will be in the majority at the Convention of the A. F. of L. a year hence. The Socialists, once in control, can be depended on to so modify the Unions as to, at least, prolong their life indefinitely.

In consideration of these facts, it seems the Syndicalists extremely poor tactics
(Continued on next column.)

FRANCE.

FRENCH SYNDICALIST'S PROTEST AGAINST WAR.

On Monday, December 16, the General Strike as a protest against war took place. There was a magnificent demonstration against war. In Paris and the district of the Seine there were over 110,000 strikers, whilst in the provinces there was also a splendid response. In the Ardennes there were 30,000 men out, who were mostly metal workers. On the eastern frontier there were 50,000 strikers all told. Throughout the whole of France it was estimated, from news received by *La Bataille Syndicaliste*, that some 600,000 men were on strike in order to demonstrate their hatred against war. In Paris the police invaded the offices of the committees to impair, if possible, the work of the committees. At Lyon the mayor and prefect of police attempted to prevent the demonstration taking place, but more than 50,000 workers paraded the streets. On the evening of the 16th there were thirty-five arrests, and the magistrate distributed sentences amongst these strikers varying from five months to two years of imprisonment.

All in all, it was a grand movement, full of promise for the future. The General Strike against War is the precursor of the General Strike for Expropriation.

We can safely venture to say that the European Governments fear more the action of the workers when they follow the line of action of the French Syndicalists than they do of a dozen Social Democratic Congresses at Basle.

Our comrades of the C.G.T. of France are to be congratulated upon the success of their efforts.

to act on the theory that the Trade Unions are all going to die out; and to continue the present policy of abstention from activity in them. The extent of this abstention policy may be judged from the fact that though the Socialists at the recent A.F. of L. Convention controlled one-third of the votes, the rebel-Direct Actionists had no representation whatever. There was no one to even sound the note of revolutionary Unionism by proposing a resolution to endorse sabotage or the general strike. Similar conditions exist in practically all of the individual Unions.

The irony of the situation is that much of the radical sentiment in the A.F. of L., which the Socialists are busily organising without the least competition, was created by the Industrial Unionists. The Socialists are exploiting the work of the Industrial Unionists.

The Syndicalists propose that the Direct Actionists become active in the Trade Unions and make their influence felt. To this end they are endeavouring to organise the militant minority throughout the Trade Union movement—which movement numbers all told about 2,500,000. Their plan of organisation is very similar to that of the I.S.E.L. Branch propaganda leagues have been formed in numerous cities and national Trade Unions.

The Trade Union militants are readily accepting the propaganda, and no doubt the S.L. of N.A. will soon be an important factor in the Labour movement. The I.W.W. has also been considerably influenced by its propaganda, and through its ranks there is a growing demand that a sane attitude toward the Trade Unions be adopted.

The S.L. of N.A. is not an anti-I.W.W. organisation; nor is it pro-A.F. of L. The Syndicalists don't recognise any of the general organisations claiming jurisdiction over the whole working class (there are four of these—the A.F. of L., I.W.W., Knights of Labour, and the S.L.P.-I.W.W.) as having a monopoly on the Labour movement. They take the position that each of them—as well as the numerous independent craft Unions—may well be a part of the Labour movement. They consider the interests of the working class to be paramount to those of any of the ambitious, general organisations. Consequently, they intend to enter whole-heartedly into all the struggles of the workers regardless of what organisation may be conducting them. They will urge the adoption of those tactics (regarding affiliation, &c.) in the various industries as will, in their opinion, best further the interests of the workers in these industries. They will endeavour to keep strictly clear of the " organisation patriotism " that is working so much harm in the American Labour movement at present.

WM. Z. FOSTER, Sec. S.L. of N.A.

"WEEKLY SYNDICALIST"
Collection Sheets may be had from the General Secretary of the I.S.E.L., 4, Maude Terrace, Walthamstow, E.

ITALY.

THE ITALIAN SYNDICALIST CONGRESS.

On Saturday, Sunday, and Monday, November 23, 24, and 25, there was held at Modena a Congress of representatives of 100,000 Italian workers, who met to affirm their faith in Revolutionary Syndicalism and Direct Action. It is important, above all, to see what composed the forces of this important advance guard.

Grouped by branches of industry, there were about

```
300  Unions of agricultural workers with 30,000
      members.
100  Unions of transport, communication, and public
      service with 30,000 members.
150  Unions of building and furnishing trades with
      20,000 members.
 25  Unions of metal workers with 7,000 members.
 30  Unions of foodstuff workers with 3,000 members.
 30  Unions of garment workers with 2,000 members.
 10  Unions of miners and quarrymen with 5,000
      members.
 10  Unions of diverse industries with 3,000
      members.
```

These figures are naturally only approximate, but they give a sufficiently exact idea of the situation.

The work of the Committee of Direct Action that has guided the revolutionary Syndicalist movement here was approved unanimously after a lively debate. A resolution was carried unanimously in favour of an amnesty for all the political and military prisoners, of whom there are more than 2,000 in prison.

Comrade Corridoni, who on the Wednesday previous came out of prison at Bologna, presented a report (which had been printed beforehand) on " The Forms of Struggle and of Solidarity." His conclusions were as follows : " That there should be instituted in each Trades Council a fund solely for propaganda and resistance, in which should be placed the financial efforts of all categories, and which must be raised and maintained by federal and confederal contributions. " The Congress affirms that it is solely by the class struggle being carried on most vigorously directly by the Unions that the proletariat can conquer its emancipation from the slavery of the wages system where they are held by capital.

" We recognise as transitory weapons of combat for the Unions the partial strike, the boycott, sabotage, by the aid of which we tear away from the capitalists day by day their profits, and thus compelling them to have recourse to the most extreme means of defence.

" We declare that the General Strike of the workers of all branches of production is the sole effective means for realising the definite expropriation of the capitalists." The Congress voted this resolution by an enormous majority.

The following day (November 24) marked the definite separation of the revolutionary Italian Syndicalists and the Confederation of Labour, and the founding of a new autonomous organisation, by which it is hoped some day to realise the unity of the working class.

The discussions had been most lively and lasted about ten hours. Comrade Bitelli, on the one hand, sustained valiantly the necessity for remaining affiliated to the Confederation, in spite of the attitude of that body. But, on the other hand, Amilcare d'Ambris, Tocchi, Corridoni, and Masotti have demonstrated superabundantly the practical impossibility of effecting unity in the bosom of the Confederation.

The motion presented by the last-mentioned has triumphed by 42,114 against 28,152 given to the motion of Bitelli, with 3,000 abstentions.

In consequence of this motion a new organisation has been created called the Italian Syndicalist Union.

We must note of the 28,152 votes received by the motion of Bitelli, 25,000 have been given by the Railwaymen. This shows that, apart from this category of workers, almost totally the revolutionary Italian proletariat feels the necessity of separating themselves from the Confederation in the interest of the future of Syndicalism.

The journal *L'Internazionale* has been designated as the official organ of the Union, the rules of which have been approved of as a whole, as they were presented by the committee. A proposition of Corridoni that the organisations in the South should be under the immediate direction of the Central Committee was carried.

Parma has been chosen as the headquarters of the Union and its Executive Council. The next Congress will be held at Parma at the end of 1913.

GERMANY.

AN INTERNATIONAL CONGRESS.

The journal *Die Einigkeit*, the organ of the revolutionary Unions of Germany, dealt at some length with the decision of the Syndicalist Conference held in London, November 9 and 10, of convoking an International Syndicalist Congress with the end of taking common action against war.

" We Syndicalists of Germany," says *Die Einigkeit*, " desire nothing more ardently than to see the realisation of this idea most quickly. We also for some years, and again at our tenth congress, expressed our views on the necessity of holding an International Syndicalist Congress. It is now even more necessary than ever that the Syndicalists of France, Sweden, Holland, America, and Spain should occupy themselves with the calling of a congress in common."

Christian Cornélissen, the editor of the *Bulletin International du Mouvement Syndicaliste*, in commenting on this writes :

" We can well see the difficulties that rise, notably in France, where the revolutionary Syndicalists dominate the workers' movement. Meanwhile, it is difficult for the French C.G.T., because of the position it occupies in the international organisation of the Unions, to take upon itself the task of becoming the centre for convoking an international Syndicalist congress. We estimate that the same difficulties do not exist for the National Federation of Trades and the Trades Councils, which are autonomous, and are mostly revolutionary enough in their action to believe it useful to help other nations and not abstain from the congress."

On December 9th, the editor of *Der Pionier*, appeared in the police court, because of an article published in that paper, on May 29th. It was a reply to a study by Kautsky on " The First of May and Militarism," which appeared in the *Neue Zeit*. This reply examined, purely from the theoretical point of view, the value of the means of struggle of the working-class—solidarity, strikes, and general strikes, and proved Kautsky to be in complete contradiction, on this point, with the doctrines of his master, Karl Marx.

" It is only in this fashion," concluded the *Pionier*, " that the proletariat can realise in the state those reforms which, instead of consolidating present society, lead to Socialism. The expropriation of the capitalists by the refusal to continue as wage-workers must be the Alpha and Omega of all proletarian tactics in class struggle. Naturally, the Social Democracy cannot admit such a tactic. The Social Democracy, trail at their feet the weight of the central committees, and cannot advance. Only the Syndicalist workers' movement can obtain realities."

The public prosecutor contended that the article " placed in peril the safety of the state," and said that it contained a " provocation to break the law," and asked for a punishment of six months' imprisonment.

The counsel for the defence, Dr. Halpert, gave, in the course of his remarks, a splendid exposition of the basis of Syndicalism. After opening by asking for an acquittal on the plea that the article was an academic discussion on the difference between Syndicalism and Social Democracy, he gave a very lucid statement of the difference between Social Democracy and Syndicalism, their end and means. The *Pionier*, in commenting on the sentence, considers that it will have good results. It will make the mass of the workers reflect, and will help them to see which are the real means by which they can attack the capitalist system.

Scott's Temperance Commercial Hotel,

9, Halliwell Street, Corporation Street
(Near Victoria Station),

MANCHESTER.

Bed and Breakfast from 2/6. Boots extra.

J. SCOTT, Proprietor

DENMARK.

SYNDICALISM IN DENMARK.

The revolutionary opposition, that in the Danish Unions proposes to reorganise the Unions on the basis of the old movement, have constituted at Copenhagen a dozen propaganda clubs with a total membership of 600. At Kjøge, Aarhus, and Kastrup have been founded and the groups together count up to 1,000 members. Outside of Copenhagen the groups are not limited to a single trade or industry, but constitute one large discussion group to which are affiliated workers of many industries. This revolutionary minority has published, as an organ, the Syndicalist journal *Solidarites*. They have issued a manifesto to the Danish workers exposing the weakness of the old Union organisations, showing the old Unions to be incapable of guiding with success the struggle against capitalism. The leaders of these organisations exercise everywhere a reactionary influence ; by all means they reinforce themselves to stifle opposition—for their own interest. The workers are tied to the employers by collective contracts—true contracts of slaves. But opposition has raised itself in order to preserve the Labour movement from complete ruin, and this opposition has made an appeal to the Danish workers for them to affiliate with it, and to help the revolutionary Syndicalists to win in their efforts to transform the workers' organisations into real organisations of combat.

SCANDINAVIA.

SYNDICALISM IN NORWAY.

Norway is, perhaps, by its recent industrial development, the country where Syndicalist propaganda promises to have most success. During December lecturing tours have been arranged for Albert Jensen, of Stockholm, and a Swedish comrade, John Anderson. Martin Tranmoel has also had an extensive lecturing tour. In spite of the opposition of the leaders of the party, he has been elected editor of the Social-Democratic paper, *Ni Tid*, at Trondhjem. The annual Conference of the Young Socialists was held during the last fortnight of December. The question of Syndicalism between others was discussed on this occasion. In the official organ of the party, *Klassenkampen*, the editor writes that the resolution of Trondhjem will serve as a base for the discussion on this subject. He even recommends this resolution, in which is recounted the revolutionary Syndicalist formula, as being a real programme, expressing the principles of the workers towards Union organisation. To conclude, the journal declares frankly in favour of revolutionary Socialism, and against the moderate leaders. A new paper has been started there called *Direkte Aktion*, which is the third in the Scandinavian countries, which altogether have a circulation of about 15,000 copies.

THE SWEDISH SYNDICALIST CONGRESS.

The revolutionary Syndicalists of Sweden held their Congress at Orebro. At the opening of the Congress there were present 22 delegates representing 29 local Unions. The Central Organisation of Swedish Workers actually is composed of 68 local Unions, and in 1911 the number of its members had risen by 700. Amongst the questions down for discussion on the agenda was the question of strikes that had taken place under the direction of the old Central Organisation of Unions of reformist tendencies. The Congress decided to participate in the strikes called by the old Unions, if suitable, in order to profit by the propagation of revolutionary Syndicalist ideas. When on the question of strike funds, the Congress declared that this was not the principal element in a strike ; under this reservation meanwhile they recommended all local Unions to create a fighting fund. The Congress decided to issue a manifesto to the Swedish workers in favour of the reduction of the hours of labour—a manifesto that has been published by *Syndicalisten*, the organ of the Central Organisation. At the conclusion of the Congress strongly disapproved of the workers belonging at the same time to the Central Organisation, and to the old body the Landsorganisation—except in the case where they are forced, in their branch of industry, by the Union belonging to the Landsorganisation

BUILDING TRADES SERIOUSLY AT WORK.

We have been fortunate enough to secure a copy of the proposed scheme for the amalgamation of the Trade Unions in the Building Industry. We print it below for the information of Building Trades' workers who may not have seen the original, and also because the scheme will serve the purpose of a model for other workers interested in amalgamation.

PART I.

Proposed Scheme for Amalgamation of Trade Unions in the Building Industry for Trade Purposes only.

NAME.

That the Union be called "The Building Workers' Union."

OBJECT.

1. To unite all workmen in the building industry into one Union embracing the whole of the wage workers engaged therein.

2. To maintain a fighting organisation, working to improve the material conditions of the workers engaged in the building industry; to take joint action with other similar Unions in the furtherance of the interests of the workers nationally and internationally, believing that the interests of all wage workers are identical.

3. The systematic organisation of propaganda among the workers upon the necessity of becoming organised on the industrial field, upon the basis of class instead of craft. Organise by industry as workers, instead of by sections as craftsmen.

COMPOSITION.

The Union shall at its inauguration be composed of the existing building Trade Unions who may decide to join the new organisation.

Any existing building Trade Union not availing itself of the opportunity of joining with the new organisation at its inauguration shall be eligible to join at a later date if it so desires.

Any person employed in the building industry in the United Kingdom shall be eligible for membership.

CONTRIBUTIONS AND BENEFITS.

The contribution payable by each member of the new Union and the benefits to which each member shall be entitled shall be uniform.

The contribution shall be 2¼d. per member per week (2d. for benefit, ¼d. for management).

The benefits to be given shall be as follow:—

In the case of a strike or lock-out .... 15s. per week.

In the case of victimisation .... 4s. 6d. per day for a period not exceeding one month.

Trade privileges .... 2s. 6d. per day for a period not exceeding one month.

No benefits shall be paid during the first six months from the starting of the fund.

No reserve for any existing Union for the above-mentioned benefits shall be interfered with in any way, each Union to be responsible for each benefits during the aforesaid period.

At the commencement of the amalgamation each society affiliating shall be called upon to pay a total of 1s. per member in advance, this sum to be counted as part of the first quarter's contribution.

LEGAL ASSISTANCE.

Provision shall be made in the rules empowering the Executive to grant legal assistance to members in civil action and compensation cases connected with the Union.

CRAFT BENEFIT.

It is recommended that a tool insurance fund be provided for in the rules, and that it shall be optional to members to contribute or not thereto.

PROVISION FOR EXISTING OFFICIALS.

Provision shall be made by the new organisation for the employment of the employés of the Trade Unions forming the new organisation for a period of three years, at not less than the pay received and the conditions enjoyed at the date of inauguration. In the event of any officer or member of the staff of any of the Unions not accepting the position assigned to him he shall be suitably compensated.

ANNUAL CONFERENCE.

There shall be an annual movable Conference, which shall be composed of representatives of each section of each district in the Union, to be nominated by branches in each district, and elected by ballot throughout each district.

EXECUTIVE COUNCIL.

The Executive Council of the new organisation shall be composed of one representative (at least) from each craft forming the Union (craft to be understood to mean each section of the building industry), but provisions shall be made for proportional representation, provided that no section has more than three representatives on the Executive Council at any time.

Each section forming the new organisation shall nominate and elect its own representative on the Executive Council. The election shall be by ballot throughout the organisation. Only members in the section affected to vote on their election.

The Executive Council shall consider and decide upon all matters relating to the funds of the Union, and carry out the policy of the organisation as decided by the Annual Conference.

OFFICIALS' POSITION.

In order that the policy of the Union shall not be dominated by officials of the organisation, no paid general officer shall vote on any Council, Conference, or Committee in the Union.

INFORMATION BUREAU.

In order to carry on a general organised propaganda there shall be a central information bureau established.

BRANCHES.

Branches of the new organisation shall be composed of all workers in the building industry. There shall be a branch or branches of the Union in each district, to which all workers of the building industry shall be eligible for admission.

SECTIONAL BUSINESS.

In each branch facilities shall be provided for dealing with sectional business by members of the section affected.

BRANCH COMMITTEES.

Each branch shall appoint a Committee, which shall be representative of each section in the Union for general business.

DISTRICT ORGANISATION.

The Union shall be divided into districts to be hereafter decided, which shall comprise all branches in the district.

There shall be a District Committee elected, which shall be formed of representatives of each section from branches in the district, to be elected by ballot throughout the district.

PART II.

Proposed Scheme for Amalgamation of Trade Unions in the Building Industry for Trade and Friendly Benefits.

SICKNESS BENEFIT.

The Amalgamated Union shall be an Approved Society. We propose that additional scales of Sickness Benefit shall be added.

UNEMPLOYMENT BENEFIT.

We propose to administer Part II. of the National Insurance Act with a minimum additional benefit of three shillings.

DISABLEMENT BENEFIT.

Provision to be made for payment of Disablement Benefit to members if entirely incapacitated from following their employment.

FUNERAL BENEFIT.

Funeral Benefit shall be paid to members.

SUPERANNUATION BENEFIT.

Provision shall be made to continue payment of the Superannuation Benefit to those members in receipt of same at the time of the amalgamation.

The adoption of Part II. is to be optional.

NO MORE SHUFFLING

Now that the movement for amalgamation has spread so far, many officials are determined to fight it, but the militant rank and file are not likely to put up with any more shuffling. We have come across a very interesting document that

---

Amalgamation Committees' Federation.

Manifesto to the Trade Unionists of the United Kingdom.

FELLOW-WORKERS,

The lessons the recent industrial disputes have furnished prove that if we are to be more successful in our fight against the united forces of capitalism we must in future enter the industrial conflict in a more up-to-date and better-equipped form of industrial organisation than we have done in the past, with our craft Unions.

The development of modern industry, with the introduction of labour-saving machinery, specialisation, speeding up, and its new method of production, is displacing the skilled artisan, thereby forcing thousands of workers into the ranks of the unemployed.

The changes have diminished the power of our Trade Unions, and we find ourselves unable to either resist the encroachments of the employers upon our position or to improve our conditions.

The competition between the workers has not only increased, but our time, money, and energy are wasted by demarcation disputes which often break out into open rupture by the Unions fighting each other.

As wage-workers (manual or intellectual) who are compelled to sell our labour power to live, we have a common interest; and instead of quarrelling amongst ourselves as to who shall do a particular piece of work, we must unite as a class to secure the wealth we produce.

WHAT IS NEEDED.

The great need of to-day is for a better form of industrial organisation, coupled with a fighting policy.

We must organise on the basis of class instead of craft.

Our 1,700 Trade Unions must be amalgamated into Industrial Unions, so as to have but one Union for one industry.

Our Industrial Unions should be constructed so as to admit to membership all workers, male or female, skilled or unskilled, engaged in any one industry; and the work of organisation should be extended by uniting all industrial Unions into one federated body.

THE OBJECT IN VIEW.

Our object for organising in this way is two-fold.

First: To take common action, nationally and internationally, to shorten the hours of labour, raise wages, and improve our conditions.

Second: To construct an organisation that will be capable of administering and regulating production in the interests of the whole community, and thus secure to the workers the full proceeds of their labour.

HOW IT MUST BE DONE.

To achieve the above object it has been found necessary to establish "Amalgamation Committees" for each industry. These committees are composed of enthusiastic Trade Unionists drawn from all Unions in the same industry desirous of securing the above object. Such committees have already been formed for the Printing Industry, the Metal Industry, the Building Industry, the Transport Industry, and the Mining Industry.

But in order that the work of these committees might be co-ordinated, a uniform plan of campaign entered upon, and the growth of such committees assisted and stimulated in every industry, and in every industrial centre, it has also been found necessary to federate these committees; hence this federation.

HOW IT WILL BE DONE.

Thus, *The Amalgamation Committees Federation* has been formed to improve our industrial organisations and make them a force for the uplifting of our class.

We are out to amalgamate the Trade Unions, not to destroy them.

Through the medium of speakers and leaflets we shall conduct a vigorous campaign in favour of these proposals.

By establishing committees on the lines above suggested, we shall provide the necessary driving force to bring about the great change we desire, and the question of amalgamation will become a real live one.

What we want is to give practical expression to the prevailing spirit of Industrial Solidarity.

FELLOW-UNIONISTS.

With your moral and financial assistance, we can carry this movement to success.

If you agree with us, see that this manifesto is read and acted upon at your next branch meeting.

Remember, the Unions belong to us, and are what we make them.

The workers must work out their salvation *themselves.*

Organisation on the lines above described will supply us with a weapon that will constantly challenge the consolidated forces of capitalism, until the worker is elevated to his rightful position in society—the owner and controller of the forces of production.

J. V. WILLS,

10, Layard Road,

Rotherhithe, S.E.

---

has been circulated in the United Operative Plumbers' Association, and we are glad to reproduce it here, as showing the progress that is being made, and we hope the desired effect has been obtained.

November, 1912.

FELLOW MEMBERS,

We wish to call your attention to the reactionary attitude of our E.C. to the vital question of Amalgamation. Delegates appointed by our E.C. attended a Conference at Essex Hall, which was the result of the policy that was adopted at the two previous Trade Union Congresses. At this Conference an outline was given of a scheme whereby the Delegates were to go back to their various T.U.'s to draw up something to place before the next Conference. A second Conference was held at Manchester, when a paper from one of the Societies was adopted, to be placed before the various T.U.'s for their approval. A third Conference was held at Essex Hall, when it was decided to send this Paper as a Voting Paper to all individual members of the Building Trades throughout the United Kingdom.

Our Delegates were in favour of the finding of these three Conferences; our E.C. recommended all Members to vote accordingly (*see August Quarterly Returns, 1912*). This having been done, the E.C. neglected to send Voting Papers on to the Parliamentary Committee, until the Secretary, Mr. Bowerman, wrote demanding same, he knowing that the Members of our Association had voted, which proved that our Members were in favour by 5½ to 1 majority. This result was made known at the last Conference, on October 21, 1912, at which we were not represented. *Our E.C. sent letter stating they would not be represented at any future Conferences, complaining of vagueness and indefinite policy. What justification is there to complain of vagueness? The Voting Paper set out clearly and definitely the lines and policy upon which Amalgamation should proceed. To attempt to justify the lame excuse of vagueness is a confession on behalf of our Officials of their bankruptcy of ideas. Whose point of view does their action represent?* Certainly not the majority of our Members, as our voting has proved. It is our duty to bring pressure to bear on our E.C. to see that we are represented at the Conference, on December 3rd, which is to draw up the Constitution before submitting to the Members of the different Trade Unions, therefore, hope you will pass Resolution to that effect and send on to E.C. as early as possible.

The time has passed when we should, by mean excuses, attempt to preserve a glorified policy of isolation. We must keep pace with the growing feelings of industrial solidity; the masters are closing up their ranks, we must do the same. The selfish spirit of sectionalism must go, we must unite into one common brotherhood, for the betterment of our lot, and for the welfare of those who come after.

W. J. SMALE, *President.*

With regard to the manifesto that has been issued to the branches of the General Union of Carpenters and Joiners, George Hicks has received the following postcard:

G.U.C.J., Pendleton Lodge, November 19, 1912.

DEAR SIR,—

I am directed to say that the above Lodge are not in sympathy with any scheme of Amalgamation that has not the sanction of their E.C.

—Yours, &c.,

F. R. JONES, Sec.

METAL, ENG., AND SHIP-BUILDING AMALGAMATION COMMITTEE.

The report of the above appears on page 5

TRANSPORT WORKERS' AMALGAMATION COMMITTEE.

A meeting of all sections of transport workers was held at the Stratford Town Hall on December 27. Ex-Councillor C. Dear (N.U.C.) presided. He pointed out the necessity for the closing up of the workers' ranks for the purpose of fighting the capitalists' organisation and winning their emancipation.

The resolution that was submitted to the meeting read as follows:

Seeing that industrial organisation is absolutely necessary to the workers in order to achieve economic betterment, and seeing that a lengthy experience has fully demonstrated the lamentable inefficiency of sectional unionism, this meeting of transport workers declares in favour of one organisation for the whole of the transport workers, and to guard against centralised official bureaucracy, urges the immediate necessity for the amalgamation of the existing unions in the transport industry, with adequate provision for local and sectional autonomy consistent with general efficiency.

S. WILLIAMS (Corresponding Secretary West Ham Branch A.S.R.S.), in moving the resolution, expressed his pleasure at being able to identify himself with the movement, and was especially pleased that the railwaymen of that district had decided to give it their heartiest support.

F. TANNER (Dockers' Union), in seconding, declared that the transport workers realised that it was useless for them to think of fighting unless the whole of the transport workers were combined. The object of the committee was not for a paltry increase of wages, but to gain the complete emancipation of the workers and the expropriation of the capitalists.

J. V. WILLS (Secretary Amalgamation Committees' Federation) supported, and showed the necessity for the workers to form a superior organisation than exists at present. He said that the workers must weld themselves into one big organisation, one union for each industry, and all linked up together into one gigantic body as a National Federation. They must also prepare for action, and they must fight not only the capitalists, but the State as well. It was their duty to shape the weapon with which they were going to fight, and that weapon would apply Direct Action. (Cheers.)

TOM MANN then supported. After dealing with the follies of sectional unions, he illustrated how the absence of solidarity always defeated the workers when engaged in industrial disputes, whereas if they were properly organised and strikes were conducted on a large scale they could obtain any demand they cared to make within reason. It was of no use petitioning Parliament for Parliament was a machine that had been fashioned by the capitalists for the purpose of serving their interests, and therefore could not possibly function effectively for the workers. The State had robbed the workers; he hated that State. He was a rebel, and would always be a rebel. He advocated the use of Direct Action, and demonstrated by very effective illustrations how the workers could, by the use of Direct Action, obtain control of their own shops, factories, mines, mills, &c. He put the resolution to the vote, with the chairman's permission, and this was carried without a single dissentient.

PRINTING TRADES AMALGAMATION COMMITTEE.

The above committee have issued a three-fold leaflet in which they state that the case for amalgamation of the Printing Trades is fundamentally the same as the case for amalgamation in all other industries. It deals generally with the need for amalgamation. Here are some extracts from it.

Combine and Conquer.

Our employers say that competition is good, yet they are continually combining their businesses and organising themselves into masters' associations to fight the workers. Take less notice of what they *say*. Take more notice of what they *do*. Our masters are organising by industry. So must we.

Demarcation.

The demarcation question has, perhaps, caused more friction between Unions than any other matter. In the grading of the crafts within the industry, the dividing line between the work of one and the other is, in many cases, difficult to determine, and experience has shown that the conflicting Unions are less likely to consolidate themselves than to take part in a general amalgamation.

What Is a "Fair" House?

At election times we tell candidates to have their printing done at a "fair" house. Yet the number of all-round fair houses is shamefully small. The moral effect of *one Union* and *one card* for the whole industry would be a wonderful power towards winning over the non-Union departments.

There are many other interesting items in this manifesto, and all workers engaged in the printing trades who are interested in amalgamation should send a card, with their name and address, and name of Union, to Chas. J. Woodward, 76, Tylecroft Road, Norbury, London, S.W.

FRENCH AND ENGLISH SYNDICALISM.

We are not greatly concerned with the antics of politicians—as a rule, they can well be ignored. Syndicalism represents a growing danger to them in all countries, and it does this without attacking them. We stand in the same relation to politicians as a well-known philosopher did to religion. He said, "I do not attack religion; I explain it." We do not attack the politicians; we explain them and show the workers how to move about them.

One result of this is the "entente cordiale" of the politicians of the various countries, for the purpose of stemming the popular tide in favour of DIRECT ACTION. An example of their methods is to be found in the work of Jean Longuet. This "comrade" is sub-editor of L'Humanité. In this Parisian paper he dare not attack Syndicalism. When he wishes to vent his spleen upon a movement that will not be controlled by politicians he goes to the provincial journals and even those across the Channel—in England. Thus in the Daily Citizen of November 15, Longuet had an article on the "impossible isolation" of French Revolutionary Syndicalism. Of course, our "Labour Party" was glad to receive such an article. It came to them like manna from Heaven. You see, if Syndicalism could be discredited, even if it be French Syndicalism that is being condemned in England, then, perhaps, the steady march of the workers away from politics to DIRECT ACTION may be stayed. Thus, first of all, Longuet attacks the French Syndicalists for their method of representation—viz., one delegate from each branch, whether large or small. Longuet was very careful not to tell his readers that even if proportional representation was adopted, the General Confederation would still be in the hands of the Revolutionaries. Besides, there is something to be said in favour of one branch one delegate, irrespective of membership. We remember representation being discussed at the Congress of the Federation of Waiters, Foodstuffs, Workers, etc., when Bergia pointed out that the strength of the Union movement depended on the number of the workers who were outside the Union. He gave us an example—a small branch of bakers, who only numbered just over twenty, but who had in their ranks every journeyman baker in that town. They had improved their conditions to a large extent. Then Bergia took Paris, and showed that Paris had thousands of bakers in the Union, but there were also thousands outside. From the point of view of Union efficiency, the Union branch, of a score represented a higher development than the Union branch with its thousands. This is a fact that it is well for the critics to bear in mind.

The C.G.T. was condemned because they would not be brought in at the fag-end of the Socialist Party on the anti-war demonstrations. But why should they? The Socialist Party of France has not been any better towards the Syndicalists, on the whole, than the Labour Party has to us. Longuet, Compere-Morel, Basley, and a few others have done their best to kill a fighting movement, and the Militant Syndicalists know this; hence their refusal to allow a political party to control their affairs even for a little time.

The joke in the article in the Daily Citizen lies in the statement of Longuet that the action of the C.G.T. was condemned by powerful critics. Whom do you think he quotes? First of all, Gustave Hervé, who is not a Syndicalist—a member of the C.G.T. never was—and who is never likely to be. His influence upon the workers of France has diminished in just the same proportion as he has backslided from the policy of DIRECT ACTION to parliamentarism. We know the work that he has accomplished, but that does not bind us, as Syndicalists, to let him have weight with us, seeing that he is a non-Syndicalist. That would be as stupid as the English Syndicalists to allow, say, Sidney Webb, to tell us what to do. Then Longuet quotes Pouget against the Syndicalists. Yes; but Pouget, like all other journalists, has to write to suit the paper that he writes for. So Pouget, ex-editor of the Anarchist paper Père Peinard is but a faint echo of Hervé in this matter—the article referred to appeared in Hervé's paper La Guerre Sociale. So the powerful critics have been reduced to one, and that one is a man who has never been in the Syndicalist movement as such. So the criticisms are neither so profound nor important as Longuet would imply.

Georges Yvetot states the case well when he declared that he hoped the Socialist Party's demonstration would be a success everywhere, and declared that the C.G.T. would act on parallel lines. When Longuet attempts to imply that Yvetot apologises for the action of the C.G.T. he knows that he is implying something false.

The French Syndicalists, who have had years of experience with political parties, whose General Confederation of Labour has been built up by those who refuse to allow their economic organisations to be sundered to please the whims and wiles of politicians, are determined to maintain intact their principles as defined in the first article of the Confédération Générale du Travail, where it states that the Confederation has for its end :

1. The grouping of the wage-workers for the defence of their interests—moral and material, economic and professional.

2. It groups; outside of all political schools, all the workers conscious of the struggle to be carried on for the abolition of the wage-class and master-class.

Anarchists, Socialists, parliamentarians, and anti-parliamentarians can meet together on this common ground. But the moment the C.G.T. becomes the tool of any political faction its integrity will be vanquished, its utility destroyed, and ultimately its organisation disbanded.

Longuet can continue to play into the hands of the MacDonalds and Snowdens, by telling their adherents of the wickedness of the French Syndicalists, who refused to march to the tune played by politicians; but we shall continue our work and endeavour to get the British workers to consider their Unions as organisations of combat too useful, too powerful, too revolutionary to become the catspaws of parliamentarians under any circumstances whatever, even those the most specious.

SYNDICALIST ACTIVITIES.

Lack of space has prevented us from inserting the following reports, which have been in type for some time; but we now produce them so as to keep our readers informed of some of our activities.

Farringdon Street A.S.R.S.—On October 25th our comrade F. J. Passmore delivered an address on Syndicalism to the members. He has attended this branch before, and the interest aroused was so great that he was invited to attend again in order that the men on the other shift might have an opportunity of hearing this new gospel of the workers. The men present listened attentively to his appeal for the amalgamation of the Transport Unions and for a real fighting policy. We decided to send delegates to the Conference called by the I.S.E.L. on November 9th and 10th at the Holborn Hall.

West Central Electric A.S.R.S.—We were favoured by our member F. J. Passmore giving the members of this branch an address on Syndicalism. He was in good form. The growth of the Trade Union movement was outlined, and the changed conditions of employment were ably shown. The necessity for railwaymen to move with the times and keep alert was clearly made out. Though we see our brother Passmore fairly regularly, we are always glad for him to open a discussion, such as he did on November 15th.

Brighton Revolutionary Industrialists.—On November 3rd a meeting was held in the Branch Hotel Assembly Rooms, when Guy Bowman gave us a lecture on Syndicalism. The meeting had been arranged by comrade Kerry and his friends. Many of the Trades Councillors were present. The address was a great success. The amalgamation of the Unions was dealt with effectively, and the establishment of a General Confederation of Labour for forming a National Federation of Industrial Unions and a National Federation of Trades Councils, with a Confederal Committee to unite them, was sketched in a very convincing manner. When the lecturer proceeded to explain the revolutionary purpose of the Confederation he was greeted with applause. Sabotage was explained and was shown not to be the foolish criminal acts that it was generally pictured to be, but a means for intelligent people to use. There is every likelihood of a group of the I.S.E.L. being established in Brighton at an early date.

Ilford Branch B.S.P.—This branch was visited by Guy Bowman on November 5th. His lecture on Syndicalism was greatly appreciated by the members of this branch. We were glad to hear the aims of the Syndicalists expounded by an authority. Syndicalism, as thus presented, was vastly different to the syndicate of workmen and capitalists, such as had been pictured by Justice. The movement was shown to be one of the workers for their emancipation from capitalism, and not at all a combination of workmen and capitalists against the rest of society. Most of our members were in hearty agreement with the speaker.

Grays Branch B.S.P.—On Thursday, November 14th, E. J. B. Allen attended the meeting of this branch. The lecture had been arranged through Mr. Jope, who used to be our secretary and who is a member of the National Union of Clerks. There was only a small attendance. The relation of Syndicalism and Socialism was explained. Whilst the members were in agreement with the idea of uniting the various unions, they were not prepared to go the whole hog and accept Syndicalism. Whilst some of our Trade Union members were prepared to accept Sabotage as a weapon against the employers, the secretary of the local Socialist Sunday School opposed it on moral grounds. Comrade Allen repeated Bernard Shaw's phrase, "You may as well sing hymns to a tiger as expect to convert the capitalists by moralising." Those who agreed with Syndicalism, as well as those who did not, were glad to have had the matter explained to them.

Hammersmith Branch B.S.P.—This branch received a visit from Guy Bowman on Sunday, November 17. Great interest was aroused. Dr. Davison was present, and asked how the medical profession could practise Sabotage! This drew the reply from the lecturer that the medical profession had no need to sabot at all. Their Solidarity had proven itself sufficient. But whilst this was the case with a highly educated and trained profession, it did not hold good with the majority of trades that the ordinary workers belong to. The average worker could be easily replaced; therefore a different policy became necessary, and Sabotage was as much an instrument to prevent Trade Unionists being defeated by the un-class conscious majority as it is against the employers.

Wimbledon Socialist Society.—E. J. B. Allen visited this society on Sunday, November 17th. He showed the development of the Syndicalism movement in England. The history of the Trade Unions was traced from the early formation down to the 'eighties. The influence of the S.D.F. and the I.L.P. was shown. The disastrous effect of the Engineers' Strike of 1897 was discussed, and also the result of the Taff Vale decision. The subsequent development of Industrial Unionist ideas and their evolution into Syndicalism was briefly sketched. The status of married women who were not in the position to be organised as Unionists roused a very widespread and interesting discussion. It would

have delighted the hearts of the readers of the Freewoman to have been present and heard the ladies there express their views as to women's position in the future.

West Brompton A.S.R.S.—By special request of the members of this branch, F. J. Passmore, who was recently elected as outside secretary of the Traffic Conciliation Board, London Electric Railway, came and spoke on Syndicalism. After listening carefully to our brother's remarks, we decided to send delegates to the I.S.E.L. Conference at the Holborn Hall. We can see quite clearly that Syndicalism is really Unionism up to date, and though our forefathers did not see beyond the capitalist system, so we must take up their weapons, perfect them, and use them for winning our emancipation.

Knightsbridge Shop Assistants.—At a largely-attended meeting of this branch of the N.A.U.S.A.W. and Co., held in the Sydney Hall, on Wednesday, November 20th, Guy Bowman addressed us on Syndicalism. He gave a good explanation of the Syndicalist conception of society organised on the basis of Industry as opposed to the State Socialists' conception of Society organised on political lines. He illustrated his meaning by describing the fourteen or fifteen large industries as being the pillars upon which society would rest. The Unions of these industries would constitute the pillars. The political Socialist looked to one big pillar—the State. The industries would be self-contained and self-disciplined. The Trades Councils would be like a lot of little local parliaments; they would be improvements on and would supersede the Town, Borough, and Urban District Councils of to-day. Mr. Bowman showed us the means by which the handful of Syndicalist railwaymen of France compelled Rothschild to reinstate the 3,000 men who had been discharged owing to the strike of last year. By means of Sabotage and the Pearly strike, they brought sufficient pressure to bear upon the capitalists generally, that they in their turn brought pressure to bear on the government, and the government on Rothschild, to reinstate the men. By altering the destination labels, by obstruction, by cutting the telegraph wires, capitalist business was interrupted. Not only have the men been given back their shops, but the three journals, L'Humanité, La Bataille Syndicaliste, and La Guerre Sociale, which had been taken off the bookstalls of the stations, were replaced. It was extremely interesting, and many members were enthusiastically in favour of it. A good discussion followed. A large number of SYNDICALISTS were purchased by the members present.

OTHER MEETINGS.

The Letchworth Debating Society arranged to have Guy Bowman to give an address on Syndicalism. The hall was packed. The audience were well satisfied that they had had Syndicalism thoroughly explained to them. This by no means meant that they were in agreement with it. As a matter of fact it was altogether too barbarous a movement for the majority of people who were there. The chairman, a banker, was naturally against it. He remarked that they had had both drama and opera bouffe. By a curious method of expression it was Sabotage that he referred to as opera bouffe. This was evidently not what he intended to imply. Members of the audience 'arose' and testified to the efficacy and prevalence of Sabotage in this country, and that Sabotage, at any rate, was not a French importation. The respectables were disgusted at the methods of the Syndicalists and their object. On the other hand, many there were in favour of the principles advocated by the speaker. A group of the I.S.E.L. is in the course of formation at Letchworth.

Lewisham.—On Sunday, Dec. 8, at the Catford Clarion Club, a large and enthusiastic audience assembled to hear an address by Guy Bowman on Syndicalism. Local enthusiasm had recently run high on the subject of Syndicalism. Previous lectures had centred around the questions of parliamentary action, and Syndicalism; Direct Action, and Sabotage. The fact of so many speakers and propagandists of working-class organisations being present was due to the interest aroused in the latest outcome of working-class activities. Comrade Richardson was chairman, and after opening with a few remarks upon the parliamentary movement, gave a hearty welcome to the speaker, and then called upon Comrade Bowman to address the meeting. On rising to speak Bowman was greeted with great applause. He opened by drawing a comparison between Social Democracy and Syndicalism. He illustrated the difference by saying that Social Democracy constructed its future system upon a single pillar—society as a whole—with parliament as the centre for carrying out through its elected representatives the function of organising and carrying on production and distribution. This, he contended, would lead the workers into a worse form of tyranny than at present, as at the head of each department of industry we should have a politician comfortably fixed in a job of which he knew no more about than the average chairman of a trust does about the industry from which he draws his profits; whereas the Syndicalists based the construction of their future system upon several pillars, a pillar for each industry, to be connected with all other industries, but each of which would have full autonomy to work out its own conditions of labour and everything connected with that industry. This was the only means by which the workers in that industry would have a guarantee of Freedom, and they certainly were the only people capable of functioning in that way. Comrade Bowman explained in a masterly manner the means which Syndicalists advocated the workers should use in order to get possession of the instruments of production. Direct Action was defined as meaning the action of the workers against the employers without the interference of politicians or parliament. When dealing with numerous forms of Direct Action he raised great applause and laughter amongst the audience, particularly in his humorous description of the incidents of the great French railway strike. He has not forgotten that humour can be used for serious educational work, as was fully proved by the manner in which they grasped the necessity for the working class changing their method of attack. The much-abused and misrepresented weapon of Sabotage was very capably dealt with, and did much to remove the prejudice towards this method employed during the recent unrest. Bowman's outspoken and spirited utterances in his closing remarks on anti-militarism and the General Strike, showing that Syndicalists were internationalists in the true sense of the word, called forth general applause. To speak to the workers, "Insurrection rather than war," met with a welcome that indicated that the jingo internationalism of Social Democracy had little influence in his audience.

The discussion brought forth very little opposition, and the speaker's replies left the parliamentarians with some hard facts to think over. The Direct Action propaganda has been firmly planted in the Lewisham district.

We are all looking forward with great interest to the next visit of Comrade Guy Bowman.

F. V. BEACHAM.

METAL, ENG., AND SHIP-BUILDING AMALGAMATION COMMITTEE.

FORGING AHEAD.

Another successful meeting of the above committee was held at the headquarters of the Printers' Warehousemen and Cutters, 220, Blackfriars Road, on Friday, December 13. Great enthusiasm was manifested by those present. It was agreed to meet on the first Saturday in the month at 7.30 p.m., the secretary to find suitable meeting place. It was agreed to invite T.U. branches to become affiliated at $\frac{1}{2}$d. per member per quarter.

The committee recognises that there are thousands of Trade Unionists who are willing to assist, but cannot become delegates. It was therefore decided to ask them to become individual members at 1d. per month. It is now up to the "aristocrats of labour" who see the necessity of amalgamation to come along and help. Committees are formed or are being formed in all engineering centres. So all workers are asked to write to the secretary, who will immediately send his name and address to his local secretary. We are willing to send lecturers to any branch or Trades Council for bare exes, and comrades this is where our work lies. The outlook in this industry is distinctly hopeful, but the help of all is essential.—W. F. Watson, A.S.E., Hon. Sec., 26, Priory Road, Acton Green, London, W.

ESPERANTO.

LA LASTA KANONO.

La lasta kanono! Oh! kiam ĝi iros,
Al la laborej' de la fero-fandist'

Kaj kiam, oh homo, kun ĝojo ni diros.
"De nun ne ekzistos plu un' militist'"?

La lasta soldato, oh! kiam li ĉesos
Ekzerci sin por la kruela meti'?
Kaj ĵetas surteren l'armilojn kaj jesos
La bonon de senmilitista soci'?

El "Internacia Socia Revns."

BONGUSTAJ PECETOJ.

Rego Alfonso pri la mortigo de Canalejas.

"Mi ĵuris defendi la nacion hispanan, kaj dum unu guto de sango elfluos el miaj vejnoj, mi tenos mian ĵuron (El la Madrida ĵurnalo "A.B.C.") Kiel heroa estas la mortiginto de Ferrer!

Gustave Hervé en Parolado je la Shoreditch Town Hall "Kapitalismo pretigas la liton de la Internaciismo de la Gentoj. Kaj ne permesu ke ni estu diritaj pri la landlimoj de la Rasoj. La nura landlimo kiu ekzistas, estav tui, kiu apartigas Vin kaj min je la nuna momento, la landlimo de lingvo, sed eo tiu malaperas pro nia nova Internacia Lingvo, Esperanto.

Tradukita el la Novembra "Syndicalist."

PRI LA BALKANUJA MILITO.

"Kie estas la Simpatio de Socialistoj, je kiu flanko? Eble je neniu flanko, car jen la situacio: Banditoponlos, Friponidov, kaj Rabisovic atakas kune maljunan, sub ciuspecaj kulpoj svenantan krimulon, por traserci liajn posojn kaj depreni al li cion kio estas prenebla. Sed niaj simpatioj certe ne povas esti kun la atakantoj.

El "Internacia Socia Revus."

SINDIKATISMO.

"Ĉu ni estas reakciuloj au revolucianoj, kreduloj au ne kreduloj, socialistoj au anarkiistoj, patriotoj au kontraupatriotoj, la mastraro, trouante nin cintage neniel nin diferencigas. Tiu egaleco en la profesia malfeliĉo, tiu mastra lekspuatado senopinia, jen kio naskas la Sindikatismon, kiu ebligos, ke ĉiu suferantoj malgravigu kiel eble plej multe tiujn suferojn, tagon post tago, atendante la tutplenan reformon."

S'ro Niel en "L'Humanité."

Will all comrades who are curious about the above jargon address themselves to P. E. Wells, 52, Mushroom Lane, Sheffield.

WORKERS, AWAKE!

Workers! Awake!
The time has gone for dreaming;
Nation to nation, send the word along.
Comrades, awake! Let Life be real, not seeming
One vast army gather to this Battle Song.

To Arms! To Arms! my comrades,
In Truth's strong coat of mail;
For Justice we are fighting,
We shall not, cannot, fail!

Workers! Arise!
Shake off that dull repining;
Too long have we Oppression's wrong endured.
Come out with us, to where the sun is shining;
Fight! until the Workers of Justice are assured.

To Arms! To Arms! my comrades,
In Truth's strong coat of mail;
For Justice we are fighting,
We shall not, *must* not, fail!

Workers! March on!
The field is Ours *for taking*.
Who is there amongst us with his pulse unstirred?
Forward into battle! soul and body staking,
Only one word shouting—"Justice!" is the word!

To Arms! To Arms! my comrades,
In Truth's strong coat of mail;
For Justice we are fighting,
We shall; we SHALL prevail!

ANNA LINCOLN.

RAILWAYMEN'S GRAND OBJECT-LESSON OF THE USE OF DIRECT ACTION.

By A MIDLAND GUARD.

Driver Knox and his heroic comrades of the North-Eastern Railway have received shoals of congratulations from all parts of the United Kingdom for their gallant stand for principle. I, too, desire to offer my heartiest congratulations to them. I glory in the fact that they have proved beyond all doubt that DIRECT ACTION is *the* only weapon in the workers' armoury that will achieve their ends.

Knox's comrades determined to vindicate his reputation. As they also happened to possess the knowledge how to obtain it (which apparently their Union officials did not), they proclaimed their intentions of doing so by the method of DIRECT ACTION, and on December 7 the men took action.

The Lord Mayor of Newcastle followed suit—he also took action; so did the state, for it immediately dispatched Mr. Chester Jones to Newcastle to ascertain if their magistrates who had convicted Knox were drunk—no, we mean responsible for their actions or not.

Now, why did the Home Secretary send Mr. Chester Jones to Newcastle? My explanation is that a vast number of resolutions in favour of a National Railway Strike had been enthusiastically carried in all parts of the country. It was quite evident to the state that if Knox's question was not settled in his favour, and quickly at that, there would be another strike of the railwaymen on a scale of immense magnitude. The capitalists have not yet recovered from the shock to their dignity which we, the railwaymen, gave them in 1911, when, in spite of the armed forces and the whole of the capitalists' might and power, the men lowered the capitalists' prestige, humiliated them, made them grovel in the dust, all in the short period of two days—two days of Direct Action.

The Transport Workers were also threatening trouble, so were the Seamen, and the Miners might have found it opportune to have joined common cause. It was a case of " of two evils choose the lesser." It was a bitter pill to swallow, but the only thing the capitalists dread is ACTION. So they climbed down on the question of Knox.

On December 14, just a week after the application of Direct Action, the state decided that their own magistrates were incapable of administering the law; that Driver Knox was not " drunk in law," for which offence of the capitalists they graciously and condescendingly presented Knox with an absolutely free pardon. Who said the law was an ASS?

The *Railway Review* admitted the " deep consequences " of the dispute; secondly, they admitted that " so-called trials, whether in the court of first instance or on appeal," were a mockery and a sham. Then it ran on as follows : " The revolt on the North-Eastern was wholly unauthorised and the method adopted by the men one which the Executive Committee could not sanction or condone." With the next phrase they absolutely take the biscuit. Here it is : " As a matter of fact, the men owe the whole of their success to the prompt and immediate action of the Executive Committee." But in a short while we come to this sentence : " *The Executive sat down and thought out the situation.*" There you are, isn't that what they always do? And by this action of sitting down to think, which appears to have a very stimulating effect on the brains of the officials, they secured for the men the retrial of Knox, and enabled them " to return to work with honour." Surely, if the Executive were able to do all this, after the strike had taken place, because " they sat down and thought," it could have been done just as easily by them before the strike. Then why on earth didn't they do it? It would have removed the necessity for the men to strike at all. But perhaps the genius of their committee had not discovered that justice can be obtained and strikes won simply by the process of sitting down and thinking. The Executive must be possessed of the most sublime cheek imaginable to try and tell the Workers " that they sat down and thought." Oh, it's too bad ! What the officials really did do was to show their incompetency and their inability to defend the Workers' interests. Really, I cannot see, for the life of me, why the men keep such a pack of useless individuals at all for. Why on earth don't they pension them off? It would be much cheaper, anyhow.

Now, regarding the settlement. The men have plenty of time to retrieve their mistake; the fines are not paid yet—let us hope they never will be. When the French Railways, in the great Railway Strike of 1910, succeeded (with the assistance of the Labour aristocrats) in beating the men, they refused to reinstate 3,300 of the strikers. The men who were reinstated played " Old Harry " as a consequence. They caused the goods to be delivered at their wrong destinations, engines accidentally dropped into the turntable pits, signals were reversed, etc.—amongst many other things—with the result that the French Railway organisation became disorganised. Chaos reigned, and eventually the companies capitulated, and the whole of the 3,300 men were reinstated. The North-Eastern men might try an even easier method of bringing the company to their senses. Let them work strictly according to rules and regulations and the North-Eastern will not run half of their ordinary service. I will guarantee that the company will not persist in the fines being paid if this be done. As the Syndicalist teachings are gripped by the Workers, they will be able to discover many other methods for themselves, but the North-Eastern dispute has justified the existence of the " Syndicalist League," the North-Eastern men have justified its teachings, and the thanks of the whole of the Workers are due to them for the splendid manner in which they fought for principle and for their use of DIRECT ACTION !

GROUP REPORTS.

BIRMINGHAM.

The members of this Group visited the Saltley branch of the Workers' Union on Saturday, December 7, and also the National Union of Clerks at Smethwick Town Hall on Friday, the 13th. Comrade Harvey opened the discussion of Syndicalism on both occasions. Will local Trade Unionists who realise that Trade Unionism should be something more than an insurance against sickness and unemployment demand a hearing for us at their local branches?

Remember this is a workers' movement, and it is up to each worker to do his best for the emancipation of his class.

The Group meets at the Coffee House, 15, Special Street, Saturdays, January 11 and 25. Secretary, E. Robinson, 31, Ashmore Road, Cotteridge, Birmingham.

LIVERPOOL.

Though London and Manchester have moved first, Liverpool has fallen into line at the first opportunity. At a monster demonstration held in St. Martin's Hall, the resolution in favour of Syndicalism was carried unanimously.

The chair was taken by Will Jones, of the A.S.R.S. Spirited speeches were made by the proposer and seconder of the resolution, and by Joe Cotter, of the Ships' Stewards' Union, and Fred Bowers, of the Operative Masons. At three o'clock in the same hall the Sailors' and Firemen's Union met, and all the speeches in favour of the complete programme of the Syndicalists were cheered lustily. As an outcome of Guy Bowman's visit of the previous week, and of Tom Mann's on this occasion, a Group of the I.S.E.L. has been formed, and Liverpool is now in the fight. Already our women members have been in gaol as Suffragettes for the vote, and now, seeing the uselessness of it, have come into our movement, which is going to work without parliament. Secretary, Will Jones, 15, Hodges Mount, Toxteth Park, Liverpool.

OUR "BRITISH" PATRIOTS.

On going through an old Post Office Directory of a few years ago, I looked up the names of the residents of Berkeley Square, Grosvenor Square, and Park Lane. These are where the élite of the " British " nation live. *Berkeley Square* had such good old Anglo-Saxon names as : Belleville, Ludwig Mond, Hartmann Steinkoff, Cloete. *Grosvenor Square* possessed these : Neumann, Eckhardstein, Cazalet, Joel Stiebel, Van Raalte, Strauss. That rendezvous of patriots, *Park Lane*, revelled in the British names of Pantlin, Solano, Pikoff, Seligman, Soudes, Thuman, Eckstein, Beit, Sassoon, Volkein, Isaacs, Goetz, Rautenberg, Lazarus, Lowenstein, Argenti, Lopes, Sanbach.

When will the workers cease to be fooled by a " patriotism " that is exploited by these people in every country they control? Let us be as international as the financiers are, or we will never check their power.

SYNDICALIST LECTURES.

Trade Unions, Trades' Councils, or Labour Societies desiring to know more about Syndicalism can have speakers attend their meetings. Travelling expenses only are asked for. Write General Secretary, I.S.E.L.

SYNDICALISM AND THE CLERKS.

" What message has Syndicalism for the city clerk?" is a question that we are asked to answer. And one broker's clerk who asks this question, further inquires, " Will the *necessary* workers of the world hand over their produce to a ' syndicate ' of gamblers' assistants?" We do not despair of propaganda amongst the clerks, whether brokers' clerks or others. All clerks who are in industrial establishments should be linked up with the industrial workers connected with that concern. If, for example, clerks on the railways were in the Railway Clerks Association, and this Union, in its turn, was amalgamated in a national body with the A.S.R.S., the General Railway Workers' Union, the United Pointsmen's and Signalmen's Society, and also the Associated Society of Locomotive Engineers and Firemen, there would be less of the unmanly conduct that has characterised the railway clerks during the strikes, particularly the last one on the North-Eastern Railway. Ships clerks are part of the Transport Industry. Clerks in Metal and Engineering firms should be organised as part of the Engineering and Shipbuilding Industry. In short, all clerks connected with productive and distributive industries should be lined up with their fellow-workers there.

Now comes the other part of the question : what is to be done with the brokers' clerk? First of all, there is the National Union of Clerks to be joined. This will ensure protection, and possibly improvement in conditions as well. Not only so, but the principle of Solidarity with other workers will be developed. The National Union of Clerks is by no means a reactionary Union. Many of its members are ardent Socialists and Syndicalists. The rôle which the clerks will fulfil in a working-class society is fairly easily suggested. Those connected with industries would be with their fellow-workers in those particular industries. Those who are engaged in purely parasitical occupations would be dispersed amongst those that are necessary.

This is no dogmatic assertion. The Syndicalist workers of France, a few years ago, opened an inquiry amongst the Unions, with regard to the work that their members would do after the General Strike.

Their official organ, *La Voix du Peuple*, printed some of the replies. Almost without exception, those workers engaged in parasitic occupations, and even some that were not parasitic, but only concerned with luxuries, gave the answer to the effect that their members should be absorbed into those Unions where the members were engaged in socially necessary occupations, and whose ranks required augmenting.

We Syndicalists have high hopes of the clerks who become Syndicalists. They have an immense field for propaganda. Their better education fits them for activity as writers and speakers. Their knowledge of commercial affairs permits the clerks to foresee and explain many of the acts of commercial jobbery for which the manual workers have to pay. They are in intimate touch with the private affairs of the various companies and know of their agreements, combinations, and manipulations. They can tell the workers how many firms that are supposed to be rivals really are working in agreement ; how one firm agrees to perform the other's work during a strike ; how many of the companies are in the employers' federations ; what steps are being taken to checkmate the men in the event of a strike, and so forth. We have a place for all workers in our ranks—the clerk, the teacher, the journalist is just as necessary as any other worker.

Our Industrial Syndicalist Education League is a purely propagandist body into whose ranks there is a welcome for all. There are but few workers who are not capable of being Unionised. Once in a Union there is always a sphere for propaganda, and moral and material assistance to other workers. Not only is there Syndicalism for the clerks, but we want the clerks for Syndicalism.

The Syndicalist

and Amalgamation News

Edited under the :: auspices of the :: :: Industrial Syndicalist Education League. ::

President
TOM MANN

Secretary
GUY BOWMAN

VOL. II. NO. 2.   LONDON, FEBRUARY, 1913.   MONTHLY, ONE PENNY.

ARBITRATION IN NEW ZEALAND.

The country that has resorted to legalised methods of Industrial Arbitration longer than any other, and which at one period was referred to as "a country without strikes," has just passed through one of the most bitterly-conducted strikes of recent years, and it should be a subject of value to those who adhere to the new idea that State Arbitration is a desirable, or even a possible, method of grappling with economic questions.

New Zealand has been quoted so often as setting an example to other countries as to "how to deal effectively with industrial disputes," that many in this country have been led to believe that the New Zealanders have really hit upon some valuable method which it is desirable should be imitated here as speedily as possible.

The papers just to hand from New Zealand—Capitalist and Socialist alike—give considerable space to the recent happenings at the celebrated gold mine at Waihi, in the North Island, a few hours ride from Auckland.

The miners have had years of experience of the Conciliation and Arbitration Act, and, as a consequence, they unanimously decided to cancel their relationship to the Arbitration Act, and to rely upon Trade Union methods to adjust conditions. They were members of the New Zealand Labour Federation, a militant Trade Union Federation run on I.W.W. lines. Some of the Engine Drivers and Winders at the Waihi Mine, however, favoured Arbitration methods, and registered under the Act. The Miners had suffered so seriously under the Act (I write as one having direct knowledge gained at first hand on the spot) that they refused to be in working alliance with any Union that resorted to state methods of Compulsory Arbitration, and refused to work; they struck, and, following upon this, there was drafted a number of armed police, and organised "scabs," were brought to the district as strike-breakers on modern American lines. It has resulted in scores of men being gaoled, and the trained "Thugs" of the Capitalists, a la "Pinkerton's sloggers," have been paid by the mine-owners to watch opportunities to help the police in bludgeoning the strikers.

The most glaring instance occurred two months ago when, an understanding having been arrived at between the Union and the Commissioner, that for the time pickets should be withdrawn, the next day in the absence of pickets a raid was made by the "scabs" armed with bars of iron and several having revolvers, who entered the Union Hall, where only a few men and their wives were present, and set about the men, one named Evans being batoned to death. The final results of the Court case have not yet reached this country, but New Zealand's silly pretence of being a country without strikes is for ever exploded, and Compulsory State Arbitration has most ignominiously failed to achieve what was claimed for it.

All these methods are simply variants of the constantly changing tactics of the plutocracy to keep their grip as the Ruling Class; Insurance Acts and maternity benefits are of precisely the same order. It will be interesting to our readers to learn the opinions of the more advanced of the Labour papers of Australia as here appended, culled from the *Maoriland Worker* of December 13, 1912:

"No one who has studied the question can see in compulsory industrial arbitration the solution of the industrial problem. The relationship between employer and employee, based on a system of exploitation, can never be ethically adjusted by any court in the land.—*Westralian Worker.*"

TOM MANN.

THE MENACE TO THE WORKERS

CAPITALISTS' PRIVATE ARMY OF ARMED STRIKE BREAKERS
THE CIVILIAN FORCE.

On Trafalgar Day, 1911 (whatever that day may be), was founded the Volunteer Police Force, which unassuming title was, on the motion of the Right Hon. the Earl of Lonsdale, on December 12, 1911, changed to the Civilian Force. This body being brought into existence in 1911, naturally causes one to think of strikebreakers, and a person so thinking would not be far wrong.

In pamphlet No. 2 the anxious inquirer finds the following gem as a kind of introduction:

The Civilian Force.

The Civilian Force endeavours as far as possible to assist the community at large by preventing the disturbance or breakdown of any Service of Public Utility.

"Members of the Civilian Force are in no way 'strike breakers,' as they do not take the part of any particular employer or Trade Union, but voluntarily assist in carrying on Transport and other services of vital importance to the distribution of necessaries of life to the Community at large.

Without taking any partisan attitude as to the merits of any Trade Dispute, the Civilian Force offers its protection to men who desire to work from being compelled by force or threats unwillingly to abandon their employment with a view to prevent any breach of the peace or the disruption of the Food Supply of the Community.

And on the next page we are informed:

Arrangements have been made whereby Members of the Civilian Force will be sworn in as Special Constables before going on duty in any public place. On private property Members of the Civilian Force, without being sworn in as Special Constables, may lawfully act on behalf of the Proprietor as his friends or servants for the purpose of protecting his property from forcible trespass.

Read these two items through again, friends, and ask yourselves the question: "How can persons who volunteer to carry on Transport, if the Transport Workers should be on strike, be other than scabs and blacklegs?"

This is precisely the purpose for which this precious Civilian Force was organised.

Notice the profusion of capitals in the words, and see how property interests dictated the drawing-up of these statements. The words Members and Civilian Force have capitals; so have Special Constable, so has Proprietor; but mark how servants commences with a small " s."

In the Rules and Regulations of the Civilian Force we find amongst its objects are:

1. To assist as a Civilian Force in the maintenance of "Law and Order" and the preservation of the peace.
2. To provide a Reserve Force available for the maintenance of Internal Order during the absence of the Regular Force in time of war.
3. To oppose all those who advocate the use of force or violence in attacks upon the British Constitution, the destruction of national institutions, the confiscation of property, the coercion of free labour, interference with personal liberty, or revolutionary projects of any kind.
4. To render help to railways, ships, docks, tramways, electric power, light, sanitary or other public services in time of emergency, &c.

Obviously, this Civilian Force is making a bold bid to oust Mr. Collinson and the Free Labour Association of Blacklegs.

In the section under the heading of "Composition of the Force," we find Clause 3 states:

"That the Force consist of Service Members, Honorary Members, Special Patrons, and Grand Council."

Clause 4 states: Service Members are to be divided into the following classes:

(a) "Special Service members" being those who are willing to serve throughout the kingdom and hold themselves ready to start at short notice in Flying Columns.

(b) "Trade Service members" being those who are willing to serve in any prescribed trade for the protection of their own business or employment, or with the consent of their employers for the protection of other concerns of a similar kind.

(c) "Service members" are those who join the Force for active service in case of need within a prescribed area.

The operations of the above categories of members are under the control of the Grand Council. Section 8 of the Rules says:

The Grand Council shall consist of British subjects elected (irrespective of sectarian or party consideration) purely out of regard for their patriotism, reputation, influence, knowledge, experience, and ability to direct and assist the Force in attaining its objects.

This Grand Council of all the virtues has such eminent friends of the workers as follows:

His Grace the Duke of Abercorn, K.G.P.C., president.
The Earl of Lonsdale.
The Earl of Meath, P.C., K.P.
Sir Gilbert Parker, M.P.
Sir Albert de Rutzen.

Three lieutenant-colonels, some major-generals, majors, captains, and other military small fry, with that excellent gentleman, Sir Joseph Lyons, celebrated of tea-shop fame; R. Burbidge, of Harrod's, and other folk of that ilk.

In order to still further strengthen the forces of democracy in its deliberations, Section 9 of the Rules states:

The Grand Council may from time to time co-opt additional members from amongst the following categories, or persons recommended by them.

(a) Lords-Lieutenants, High Sheriffs, Chairmen of Quarter Sessions or of County Councils, Recorders, Stipendiary or other Magistrates.

(c) Chambers of Commerce, Railway, Dock, Shipping, or Transport Companies and other industrial undertakings.

(d) Banks, Insurance Companies, &c.

All these gentlemen, of course, would never think of breaking strikes. Oh, no! To even think such a thing is to show that you are unpatriotic.

The whole plan of this organisation is a military one. Provision is made for proper Army arrangements. Thus Rule 24 reads:

Service Members may be formed into Companies consisting of 120 men. Each such Company shall be commanded by a Captain, who shall be appointed by Headquarters.

Composition of a Company of the Civilian Force:
1. One Captain.
2. Two Lieutenants.
3. Two Sub-Lieutenants.
4. One Medical Officer.
5. One Company Sergeant-Major.
6. Ten Section Sergeants.
7. One Signalling Sergeant.
  One Commissariat Sergeant.
8. One Hospital Sergeant.
9. One hundred and twenty men.

Again, the men are only worth a small "m." Provision is made for a supply of motor-cars, cycles, and lorries for use of the force.

The Signalling Instructor is supposed

(a) To supervise the necessary instruction in signalling, telegraphy, telephony, and other methods of communication throughout his District.

(b) To ascertain the names of those Members of the Force and others within the District who are willing to allow the Force to use their telephone instruments in time of emergency.

(c) To supervise preparations for the repair of instruments or wires by Members of the Force in time of emergency, &c.

We commend the last section to the notice of the telephone workers amongst our readers.

The gem of the whole concern is This. The Equipment of the Civilian Force consists of Helmet, Armlet, Whistle, Numeral and WEAPON OF DEFENCE.

Fellow-workers, what are you going to do about this? Note that this government of "Lloyd George Social Reform" is supporting this body, members of the Privy Council, and on the Grand Council of the Civilian Force. Liberal working-men, what have you to say to that? What will you, who listened to Lloyd George at Limehouse, think of the Liberal government that has members on the Grand Council of a Force whose avowed object is to carry on Transport if there should be a strike?

The Army has been used against the workers at Mold, at Belfast, at Featherstone, Llanelly, and at Liverpool.

The Navy has been used against the strikers at Hull, at Grimsby, at Belfast, and at Liverpool.

Remember how the Royal Engineers ran passenger-trains during the Irish Railway Strike; how the troops promenaded the stations and overran the yards during our Railway Strike of 1911.

Call to mind how the R.I.C. in Belfast had to do the work of blacklegs.

How the police in the London Transport Strike drove round the scabs and thus helped in scabbing. Not content with giving us bullets from the Army when we strike, and machine-guns for us in Trafalgar Square when we are unemployed; bullets from the Navy, bâtons and bullets from the Police—for now two thousand Metropolitan Police are armed with the latest pattern Webley-Scott quick-firing pistols that fire nine shots in five seconds—and now on top of that we have this Civilian Police to act as blacklegs, who are armed with A WEAPON OF DEFENCE.

This calls for new tactics, when, with the ordinary strike men gather in huge masses to listen to politicians at Tower Hill or elsewhere, they are in the finest position for the authorities to slaughter them. Think of how the Police bludgeoned the strikers and their friends and wives at Liverpool on Bloody Sunday. Organisation is essential, but it is not the last word in the fight. We as workers cannot, except under conscription, hope to bring an adequate force against these armed brigands; therefore more and more in the future we must refrain from offering ourselves as a mass to be slaughtered.

Their Army, their Navy, their Police, their Civilian Force, their Free Labour Associations are useless to them whilst the Army of Labour remains in the workshops. Therefore, fight the bosses whilst you work for them, sabot their material, exhaust their profits, sabot their plant whilst they are exploiting you, and when none can offer you personal violence or take your place.

To the organised violence of the master-class we offer an individual warfare of sabotage.

The employers have formed their associations to fight us. We must take up the gage of battle in our own way.

Sabotage, anti-militarism, and insurrection is our reply to their coercion.

During the Transport Strike at Liverpool the offices of the Shipping Federation were burnt down. The offices of the Civilian Force are in Kingsway.

WHAT CAN THE TELEPHONE WORKERS DO?

Quite recently I was travelling from the North to London, and in the railway carriage I got into conversation with a fellow-traveller. He had attracted my attention in the first place because of his fine presence. He was well built, of keen and business-like features.

After having been seated a time I heard him humming the "Internationale." This still more aroused my interest, and I said "Boots," which brought the prompt reply "Spurs." Of course now all reserve disappeared, and we were soon engaged in an animated conversation upon Labour matters. He detailed at some length the grievances of the telephone employees.

Now he told me that Mr. Joynson-Hicks, M.P., had taken up the question of the telephone employees, and had asked the Postmaster-General several questions in the House of Commons relating to the treatment of the old staff of the National Telephone Company. The result of the questions had been that one case of extreme hardship had been modified, and that was about all. There had been commissions which had sat a long time, but apparently on a pot egg, for nothing had resulted. He added, as a conclusion, that the only thing to do was to get some telephone employees into parliament.

I asked him if he was satisfied with the Labour Party, and whether telephone employee M.P.'s were likely to do more than the other Labour men. He replied that he was not at all satisfied with the Labour Party, but he did not see what else could be done. The government was simply fooling most of the workers by the long-drawn-out delays.

To this I retorted that, seeing that the government refused to move in spite of the questions in the House, and that the Labour Party was no use in the matter, why on earth did he want more men to go to parliament? Why didn't the telephone employees strike to get their grievances remedied?

This was no good, he said, because the operators have been looked after a bit, and they would not strike. The service would continue, for a long time at least, even if the linesmen and others struck. There was no hope only through getting a telephone employee M.P.

This led me to talk to him in my usual paternal style. I told him that he was "up the pole" to talk of getting anything from another brand-new telephone worker M.P., any more than from the Labour Party, or Liberal Party, or any other bunch of politicians. To hear a practical workman speak in such an apathetic manner made my blood boil. I lost my temper, and asked him how the devil it was that the telephone workers couldn't strike even if the operators remained in. What on earth are the linesmen employed for? Is it not to repair broken wires, lay fresh lines, and make up new connections? Isn't this all necessary so that the operator can utilise the "juice"? And if linesmen make connections, can't you make *dis*-connections? My dear boy, can't the gentlemen of the climbing-irons and pliers sabot? What do I mean? Why, this. If you had to joint a line in order to get the proper connection, can't you make a disconnection, and thus render the operators inoperative? When you are perched at the top of a pole one day, for the profit of Samuel and Co., the edification of sundry small boys, and the consternation of all the old women of both sexes in the neighbourhood, couldn't some stout cord be substituted for a foot of wire by the insulators? Or couldn't you make a connection of a dozen lines and joint them up to the wire that runs to earth? Why, man alive, you can make the operators strike by preventing them from operating. When the government sabots your wages, why not sabot their service?

And I left him looking surprised.

GUY BOWMAN.

The Syndicalist

and Amalgamation News.

EDITED UNDER THE AUSPICES OF

The Industrial Syndicalist Education League

Offices—

4, MAUDE TERRACE, WALTHAMSTOW,
LONDON, E.

MONTHLY - ONE PENNY.

Post Paid Subscription—

Great Britain or Abroad ... 12 months 1s. 6d.

Bundle Rates—

1s. 6d. per quire, Carriage Paid.

U.K.F. TERMS TO NEWSAGENTS.

The receipt of a Sample Copy is an invitation to Subscribe.

FEBRUARY, 1913.

SYNDICALISM TO THE WORKERS.

The Syndicalist movement is growing everywhere, and in countries where well-organised unions already exist Syndicalist propagandist bodies are on foot. Thus, just as we in England are adopting a national constitution, electing officials, &c., the Syndicalist League of North America is doing the same thing. The *Agitator*, which for two years has been ably edited and published by Jay Fox, at Home, Lake Bay, Washington, has now been transferred of place of publication has also changed its name. It is now the *Syndicalist*; and is issued twice monthly by W. Z. Foster, 1,000, South Paulina Street, Chicago, Ill., U.S.A.

Jay Fox, W. Z. Foster, and W. C. Owen are amongst the contributors to the first number of the new series. The following article shows well the policy of our American comrades, with which we are in hearty agreement.

The Syndicalist League is not a party, nor is it a labour union. It is composed of associated groups of workers drawn together for the purpose of educating themselves and their fellow-workers. It is not a body of theorists. It has no new-fangled ideas to propagate. It merely points out the failures of the past, and shows how they may be avoided in the future.

One of the strong points about Syndicalism is that it does not take the workers away from their work. It does not ask them to join any new party or union. It does not take them into new fields of effort, where they are unacquainted. It does not divide their energies and attentions. It does not, on the one hand, tell them their unions are the only thing, and, on the other, that they must vote for this or that party if they want to be free. It does not confuse them with a dualistic philosophy. It is monistic. It is modern.

It says to the workers: "You have been in the unions long enough to know that they are a mighty force in your favour. You have done much so far for yourselves through unionism, but the limit is not yet reached; it is far, far off. Only you have to change your tactics. You must profit by your past experience. If you will follow up, closely, the causes of past failures you will not only improve your conditions under capitalism, but you can even destroy the wage system and institute co-operative production and consumption.

"All this you can do by the simple act of studying your own case; and thusly you can do yourselves, with your own hands, what the politicians glibly promise they will do for you, but cannot. For it is the plainest lesson of history that no man can talk himself or his fellows into freedom, that this precious gift of mankind can only be achieved by those who with their own strong arms strike the blow that shatters the chains of slavery."

A strike is lost. Does that prove that strikes are failures? Nothing of the kind. It simply shows that under certain conditions they fail. The failure shows the weak point, and Syndicalism urges the workers to the task of strengthening that weak spot, and thus by a systematic up-building make the now weak organisation of labour an invulnerable bulwark against defeat.

Does this life of working eternally for a boss pall on you? Would you like a change? Syndicalism points the way. You don't have to leave your union nor join this or that party. Just stay where you are, where you have been schooled, where you have the field to yourself, where you know how to work. Only don't waste all your brain energy on the boss. He thinks while you work. That's how he has enslaved you. You begin to think about your own welfare and your liberty is at hand.

Syndicalism teaches one thing that, above all else, is of vital worth. It is

this: That talk is good, but it takes action, Direct Action, to build a Brooklyn bridge or to spin a top, it shows us—and we should have seen it long ago—that, while the loafers do all the talking, we, the toilers, do all the work, and that if they stopped talking for a thousand years the world would not be affected in the least, except for good. But if we stopped working for a week, those who survived would never forget the catastrophe.

By our silent labour the world is fed and clothed and housed. In our hands lie the destinies of the world.

Here, then, is the key to our emancipation, right in our own hands. Strike, and the world is ours.

THE TRADE UNION BILL.

The Labour representatives have met, and, as expected of them, have again decided to support the Liberal government. This was only to be expected when one considers the conduct of the Labour M.P.'s, and those would-be M.P.'s who dominate the councils of the Labour Party throughout the country.

At the risk of being misunderstood, we must frankly declare that the Osborne judgment gave us no qualms at all. A man joins a Trade Union for economic betterment, and not for parliamentary purposes. If the unions consider that parliamentary action is their prime concern, then, in all fairness, intending members should be told when they are asked to join the union that they will have to support a bunch of political opportunists like MacDonald, Snowden, Crooks, and other honourable gentlemen who believe that there is nothing incongruous in "representing" Labour and accepting government office at one and the same time.

We are not much concerned about parliamentary politics. We say that they have no place in the unions; that the workers are as likely to have as many political and philosophic divisions as any other class in society. Facts prove this. Therefore we seek to unite the workers as a class on the basis of their economic interests, and only engage in such activity as will, and can, be taken by the workers as a class. This class unity can only be obtained by the workers taking action in those places where their identity of interests as a class are most easily seen; that is, in the workshops, mines, and railways.

It may sound a plausible argument that the Trade Unions should have the right to spend their money how they please, but nine-tenths of the men and women who join unions do not do so for parliamentary purposes. This is well proven by the fact that so few Labour candidates are elected, and none where they have been opposed by Liberal candidates. People join political parties for parliamentary politics.

If the government practically prohibits parliamentary politics being engaged in by the unions, it only means an added strength to the out-and-out Socialist parties on the one hand, and on the other the unions will flourish more strongly than ever as organisations of combat.

We Syndicalists shall never forget that it is the Labour politicians who have either killed strike agitations or rendered them abortive, like they did the railwaymen and the miners.

Let us leave parliamentary politics to the politicians, but as workers let us unite in our unions for Direct Action.

RANK SYNDICALISM.

The Trades Councils must own what they need in order to carry on the work of the district and satisfy the needs of the district.

The Trades Council, and not Parliament, because—

It is the miner who knows most about mining. It is the railwayman who knows most about railways.

Not the M.P., who knows nothing of the industries.

The M.P. at the head of an industry is a talker explaining what he does not know to an audience that cannot understand it. Permanent officials teach him. His audience studies Blue-books.

Delegates are not delegates, and representatives do not represent.

If the worker cannot manage his own affairs, no one else can; you cannot give power to a man who cannot undertake responsibilities and who is unable to act by himself.

The M.P. says: "I am powerless, because there is no public opinion, no rioting, no agitation, to drive me on."

He asks to be kicked.

It does not matter to you whether you kick a Conservative or a Socialist.

Both alike say: "We can do nothing unless you kick us."

Why not kick them with riots and strikes, and not bother to elect your man, since without kicks they are all powerless men?

What does it matter to you whom you kick?
—*Daily Herald.*

SHEER SYNDICALISM.

What does it matter to you whether you kick a Conservative or a Socialist?

Send 600 men to Westminster, and they are out of touch with Lancashire and Cornwall, with Wales and Portsmouth.

They become "leaders."

Deal with affairs locally, and you do more for yourself.

A few men can do their own work.

Many men have to appoint a few to do their work for them.

It is better, therefore, that localities should look after themselves and not get Westminster to look after them.

—*Daily Herald.*

RED RUBBER.

NO MORE PETITIONS.

By RUBBERITE.

(Continued from last month.)

IV.

Whatever the masters do is right. They have a weekly trade organ wherein all the latest labour (wage) saving devices are in a conspicuous position. When the workers try to better their position they are morally wrong. The Midland rubber workers are aware that they do not want more work but more wages and less work. They know that there is more work for them now than there was ten years ago; they know, also, that wages have not risen in proportion to the increased work.

No matter what political or theological opinions they hold they should have at least sufficient solidarity to join a union to keep in check the employers' rapacity. Here is something which every man, woman, and girl can do towards laying the foundation of a decent standard of the necessaries of life. It is not right that men should have to work for £1 per week whilst the shareholders can take 10, 15, 25, and even 100 per cent. dividend at the end of the year. It is not right that men and girls should be carried out fainting owing to the nature of their work. It is no use thinking that rubber-workers can get any permanent benefit until they are organised. The old game of circularising the employers with the "bobbin system" is done for. New times call for new methods.

Joining Unions the Only Real Protest.

The only form of protest that is of any use is to join a union. The skilled men as well as the lower-paid workers should be in one union. The lowest paid workers should have the first care of the organisation, because, however highly skilled the better-paid men are they could not do without the "Bottom Dogs" to labour for them. If the "Bottom Dogs," one and all, refused to work it would inevitably mean the skilled men having to come out as well. Besides, the labourers want good food, good clothes, good homes, and leisure necessary for a decent life the same as skilled men do. So it is the duty of those better paid men to come to the help of that much larger number of their lower-paid mates. A few shillings per week increase would be a boon to them; it would also have as much force with those who are better off. Low wage workers are a constant menace to those who are receiving more; this fact should never be lost sight of. Women should organise, the girls, and the boys, the workers of every section. Rubber workers know that all the sections are necessary in the process of rubber manufacture, therefore, all prejudices should be cast on one side and all the workers organise in one union. The only qualification should be that the person is engaged in some capacity in the rubber industry. The Midland rubber workers should organise with those all over England, Scotland, and Wales.

Organised Workers are Better Paid.

Where other trades are organised they have been able to obtain better wages and better conditions of labour. In the rubber industry there are employed a few mechanics, engineers, and carpenters; they work the number of hours fixed by their union; they are paid time and a quarter, time and a half for overtime, and double time for Sunday work. What an object-lesson to the unorganised rubber workers! If these trades can be paid these rates for overtime, so can all the other sections.

The rubber finishers are just as necessary as the engineers. The secret of the difference lies in the fact that the engineers and carpenters are organised. The rubber workers should join a union; all snobbery and sectional antagonisms should be sunk; all should work with one object in view, the raising of the conditions of the rubber workers. See that the officials stand the strictest test. No parleying with the enemy; any union official found so doing should be instantly dismissed. We must do the same as the employers do. They select a manager to increase profits. How he does it does not greatly concern them. They do not hamper him at every turn; they allow him free scope, but if he fails to make headway they dismiss him. So should we select our officials, and give them power to direct us in order to get better wages; and if they failed to get them, then they should be dismissed.

THE WORKING-CLASS AND POLITICAL ACTION.

By W. F. HAY.

II.

Politics can thus be seen to be nothing more than the POLICY of the propertied class. When dealing with each other they are compelled to fight by economic competition. Yet, in order to retain and make the best use of their property—i.e., to exploit the working class to the extreme limit—they must be conscious of their interest as a class and take measures to safeguard them. Seen from this angle, politics lose their chaotic, kaleidoscopic character. Old-Age Pensions, Education Acts, Tariff Reform, Boer and other wars become explicable. The whole policy of the governing class presents itself as one harmonious whole. It is, so to order affairs, that it can extract the greatest amount of values out of its working class, and secure the widest range of markets in which to realise them. But what interest has the working class in that policy?

The Politics of Labour

consist, as does its opponents', in its policy. Labour, therefore, must evolve its own laws passed in its own Forums, the lodge rooms of the Trade Union. These laws must obviously be based on certain principles for which Trade Unionism unitedly stands. Such, as an instance, on minimum rates of wages being paid, old customs and privileges being maintained, victimisation or black-listing being negatived, &c. On these principles codified into laws, Trade Unionism must take its stand. Its laws, edicts, and punishments must run with the same automacy and certainty as that which is called, somewhat humorously, "the King's justice." Nay, on occasion, and more and more as the years go by, it will be brought into direct conflict with that "justice," driven to actively antagonise it, forced to joint in a death grapple with it, to see WHOSE law is valid and can make good—the workers' or the governing classes'.

Solidarity is the great weapon which the workers are slowly forging. If a collier is victimised, underpaid, or deprived of some privilege in any part of the country, then it becomes the interest of all to defend him. What is imposed on one man in Scotland this week will be imposed on the whole of South Wales shortly. Therefore, prompt and decisive measures are the only ones we can use. We deal with an opponent who understands to the full the use of delay. First must be punished the offending employer; then all others who come to his assistance, they are "accessories after the fact." Cumulative action, entailing the linking up of all workers into one big union for each industry is a necessary condition for the future. Only so can they win, only so can they make THEIR law effective.

Let our energies then be directed toward the perfecting of our own, instead of a futile attempt to capture the employers' parliament. The final stages of every big struggle between in parliament. Before any big interest will submit to defeat it will, by placing its case before its peers and by showing that concessions forced from it will be followed by concessions forced from all, endeavour to get joint action taken by the whole of the properties' interests, to save it from defeat. The particular question at issue will there be judged from the point of view of the propertied class as a whole, AND ONLY THOSE WHO REPRESENT PROPERTY INTERESTS WILL HAVE ANY INFLUENCE ON THE DISCUSSION. That this is bound to be so can be readily seen by the discussion on the Minimum Wage Bill. In this discussion the representatives of interests other than coalowning let it be clearly seen that, although smarting under the ruthless extortion of the coalowners, they were prepared to face a prolongation of the strike rather than include definite figures in the Bill. On this point all propertied interests were unanimous, because they knew that a statutory minimum, once fixed for the coal-mining industry, would be rapidly extended to cover all others.

The workers' representatives had no influence in that discussion, because they were attempting to function outside their proper sphere. The very argument which would have been unanswerable before a special Trade Union Congress called to invite the fullest possible support of all trade unionists for the miners was an insuperable objection before parliament.

Therefore, the workers must build up their own institution, their own state, their own code of laws, their own parliament, not in harmony with, but in antagonism to, those institutions of the propertied class, which they must defeat

before they can accomplish their emancipation.

The House of Commons functions as a conciliation board in excelsis. Like all conciliation boards, it seeks to hide the class struggle, and, by mouthing pretty phrases, to fill the workers' bellies with the east wind. Behind parliament lurks the organised force created by the governing class to maintain its power. Behind the workers' congresses and conferences must be ranked a greater power than property can oppose to it. This can only be evolved by an ever-perfecting industrial organisation. Every big strike is a political event of the first importance, and is so understood by the government. Let us then understand at last that "political action" does not consist in sending leaders to parliament to be conciliated, but in the strategy of the strike. In the clear understanding that our enemies' difficulty is our opportunity, and that only when the workers are more strongly organised, and therefore more powerful than the propertied class, ON THE INDUSTRIAL PLANE, can the workers win through to Socialism.

Local Administration

presents itself under different aspects. Here we see capitalist and wage slave both concerned with mutual interests. One desires as much as the other perfect sanitation, proper lighting, paving, building inspection, &c.; although even here the class struggle creeps in and colours the administration of whichever class can dominate the Council. Yet the conditions are set, and admit of only slight variation in favour of one side or the other. But, slight as the variation is, it is important that it should be in the hands of, and on the side of, the workers. Questions of working-class child education, provision of meals and clothing, and of the graces and easements of modern civilised community life are of vital importance to the workers. But a vote to assist in determining these conditions no more constitutes a man a "citizen," in the political sense, than does a vote in his friendly society branch. He is simply taking part in a species of communal housekeeping, and is concerned to see that he gets full value for the rates he pays. If he wishes to extend his powers for local administration, to enhance and amplify them, all such proposals have to meet the approval of the joint property interests represented in parliament; and only those proposals which subscribe the general advantage of those interests stand any chance of becoming law. Whoever has watched the passage of a Bill through parliament empowering a local authority to extend its sphere of usefulness must have been struck by the distinction vividly shown between a ratepayer and a citizen when some local property-owner opposes as a "citizen" a proposal which would be to his advantage as a ratepayer! The workers, who above all need to clear the scales of illusion from their eyes, need to clearly distinguish this important distinction.

Which Road?

Recent events have made it imperative that the working class should make up its mind as to its future line of action. To those who are still obsessed with the idea that the working class can win through to real advantages, gained through sending representatives to parliament, I ask for proof of their contention. If the foregoing analysis is correct, then the working class can neither wrest advantages from nor can it destroy or disrupt the activities of parliament by sending Labour or Socialist members to that ancient and dishonourable institution. The only power the workers can wield is a power drawn from and organised upon the industrial plane, growing to power with the growing consciousness of the workers, drawing its volition from their conscious energy, as they more and more, by the logic of experience, approach the consummation of their historic mission. THE POLITICAL ACTION OF THE WORKING CLASS CONSISTS IN THOSE CONSCIOUS ACTS BY WHICH IT SEEKS TO ACHIEVE ITS OWN EMANCIPATION. Such acts must be continuously under its own control, exercised through its own institutions, and cannot, by their very nature, be performed by "representatives" sent to the council chambers of our enemies. Our only point of contact is when we send a herald with a summons to the Post Office we no longer need to do anything so mediæval! That action, like parliament itself, belongs to a dead or dying method of production. It is for the workers themselves, their own harbingers of the future, to create now, in order to wage their fight, those institutions which will form the framework of the new order, the society of the future—Socialism!

A WORLD-WIDE INVITATION

FIRST INTERNATIONAL SYNDICALIST CONGRESS,
To be Held in LONDON, in MAY, 1913.

THE OLD INTERNATIONAL.

The old International Workingmen's Association was formed in 1864 in London. From then till 1869 it was a Federalist and Revolutionary body. At the Congress held at The Hague in 1872 Marx and Engels captured the Congress and ruled in a thorough high-handed, autocratic manner. Engels in particular was the fanatical centralist who wished to utterly destroy the federal form of organisation.

The General Council of the International was not supposed to interfere with the internal affairs of the national sections affiliated to the International; it was only to act as a central bureau for the correspondence of the different national organisations.

But Engels, who was a member of the General Council, and was correspondent for Spain, on July 25, 1872, wrote to the Federal Council in Spain an abominable letter, in which he demanded "a list of all members of the Alliance," and concluded: "Failing to receive a categorical and satisfactory answer by return of post, the General Council will feel compelled to denounce you publicly."

Bakounine, who was the champion of the Federalist element, was expelled, and the meeting-place of the General Council was changed from London to New York, where the Marxian authoritarians reigned supreme, and were able to " suspend " the Federalists.

The sixth Congress of the International was held at Geneva. The Federalists continued to hold Congresses down till 1881, when they dissolved. On the other hand, the authoritarians, under the guidance of Marx and Engels, evolved from a revolutionary body to a reformist one. They became Social Democrats and foreswore all revolutionary methods.

The revolutionary International was killed.

When the Federalists were expelled, the politicians spared no pains to weaken their influence. They even did the dirty work of police informers.

Thus, in Madrid, Paul Lafargue, the son-in-law of Marx, went so far as to denounce the Federalist members of the International to the police as being revolutionaries. However, just as the authoritarians developed into Social Democratic politicians, so the Federalists kept alive the revolutionary traditions, and in Spain they originated Syndicalism by declaring for the expropriation of the landowners and capitalists and the control of industry by free Federations of the workers.

Ultimately the International Socialist Congress was established, which, at Zurich, in 1893, had the following resolutions submitted by the politicians:

"The struggle against domination and exploitation by the governing class should be political and have for its aim the conquest of political power."

Whereas the old International had declared:

"That the emancipation of the workers must be the work of the workers themselves"; and, "The economic emancipation of the working class is the principal aim, to which all political action should be subordinated."

The International Socialist and " Trade Union " Congress, in 1896, in London, passed resolutions which excluded every organisation that did not declare for parliamentary action. The Trade Unions, unless they were dominated by politicians, had no standing there. Direct Actionists, bona fide delegates from Unions, were excluded, whilst politicians like Jaurès, Deville, and Millerand (now Minister for War), who represented nobody but themselves, were admitted.

The old International had tried to implant their ideas from above. But though the Federalist International disappeared in 1881, its ideas went on developing regionally, and Bakounine's ideas are now more alive than ever.

Syndicalism has evolved in all countries—amongst the Slavs and Teutons, as well as the Latins; even the heterogeneous inhabitants of America have evolved their Syndicalism. It is alive in all countries, and raises itself as the opponent of the centralist, authoritarian State Socialists by putting the free associations of the workers against the hierarchy of State officials, as being the controllers of the workers' destinies.

Seeing that this is so, the time was never more opportune for the institution of a new International—revolutionary, proletarian, and composed of economic organisations of the workers seeking to bring about international and simultaneous action for the economic emancipation of the working class.

Long live the new red International ! Long live the combined Unions of all countries !

INTERNATIONAL SYNDICALIST CONGRESS.

To the Members of Labour Unions and Syndicalist Propagandist Bodies everywhere:

Comrades and Fellow-workers, Greetings.

At present there exists no organisation for bringing together the revolutionary Unionists of the world; this militates against effective Solidarity and hinders our progress to Emancipation.

There is the International Socialist Congress, with its permanent Bureau at Brussels, but we cannot be rendered impotent by having our International relations conducted through a body that exacts a pledge of parliamentarism and is composed of glib-tongued politicians who promise to do things for us, but cannot even if they wanted to. We must meet as Syndicalists and Direct Actionists to prepare and develop our own movement for economic emancipation free from the tutelage of all politicians.

There is the International Conference of Trade Union Centres which is held about every three years and which merely consists of the president and secretary from each country; thus there is no direct representation of the rank and file, and the officials are mostly conservative. We want a Congress where the militants of all countries can rub shoulders with each other, discuss tactics and methods, and by thus removing misunderstandings contribute to the growth of International Solidarity.

The International Bureau of Trade Union Centres at Berlin refuses to allow the vital questions of the General Strike for Expropriation, Anti-militarism, and Sabotage to go on the agendas for the Conferences; but it would not count for much if they did, for the whole of the permanent officials are politicians; most of the delegates are conservative if not absolute reactionaries; and the whole business is controlled by Social Democrats.

At the present time, Unions sending resolutions dealing with Anti-militarism and other matters considered " political " are referred to the Congress of politicians—the International Socialist Congress.

We Syndicalists want a Congress of the rank and file, not of officials. We want to confer on means of action, not merely on pious resolutions. We want common action against war, no parliamentary palaver. We want International Solidarity expressed in Direct Action.

At a Congress of Trade Unionists held under the auspices of the *Industrial Syndicalist Education League*, held in the Holborn Hall, London, November 9 and 10, 1912, a resolution was passed instructing the I.S.E.L. to make arrangements for the holding of an *International Syndicalist Congress in London.*

The Syndicalists of America are asking for it.

The Syndicalists of France desire to see it.

The Syndicalists of Germany wish it.

The Syndicalists of all countries need it.

The Syndicalists of England are preparing it.

The date has been provisionally fixed for May next during Whitsuntide.

Fellow-Workers,

No International Syndicalist Congress has ever been held; therefore no time should be lost in forging the chain which is to link up the workers of the five continents. An International Syndicalist Congress has been desired for many years by Revolutionists of all countries; now is your chance to realise that dream. Let the first International Syndicalist Congress bring together the Militant Workers of all countries.

Select your delegates at once, send in your resolutions for tabulation, and communicate your decisions to me immediately.

On behalf of the I.S.E.L.,

Guy Bowman, General Secretary, 4, Maude Terrace, Walthamstow, London.

CONGRÈS SYNDICALISTE INTERNATIONAL.

Aux membres des Syndicats ouvriers et aux Organisations de Propagande Syndicaliste, en tous lieux.

Camarades et Compagnons de Travail, Salut.

Il n'existe pas actuellement d'organisation qui réunisse dans un même lien les Syndicalistes Révolutionnaires du monde entier; cette situation empêche notre solidarité d'être effective et entrave le progrès de notre Emancipation.

Il existe bien un Congrès Socialiste International, avec son Bureau permanent à Bruxelles, mais nous ne pouvons inutiliser nos forces en permettant à une organisation qui s'appuie sur le parlementarisme et qui est composée de politiciens à langue dorée qui nous promettent des avantages qu'ils sont même incapables d'obtenir, de diriger nos relations Internationales.

Nous devons donc, comme Syndicalistes et partisans de l'Action Directe, nous entendre afin de préparer et de développer notre mouvement d'Emancipation économique, en dehors de la tutelle de n'importe quels politiciens.

Nous avons la Conférence Internationale des Centres Syndicaux qui a lieu environ tous les trois ans et qui est composée d'un président et d'un secrétaire de chaque pays; il n'y a donc pas de représentation directe de la masse et les fonctionnaires sont pour la plupart conservateurs.

Nous voulons avoir un Congrès où les militants de toutes les nations puissent se réunir, se connaître, discuter ensemble les méthodes et les tactiques à observer, et aussi, en détruisant certains malentendus, contribuer au développement de la Solidarité Internationale.

Le Bureau International des Centres Syndicaux à Berlin refuse de porter sur les ordres du jour de la Conférence des questions d'ordre aussi vital que celles de la Grève Générale pour l'Expropriation, de l'Antimilitarisme et du Sabotage. Mais nous ne nous étonnons pas qu'il en soit ainsi, car tous les fonctionnaires permanents sont politiciens; la majorité des délégués sont conservateurs, lorsqu'ils ne sont pas de véritables réactionnaires et l'organisation est dirigée par les Sociaux-Démocrates.

Actuellement les Syndicats qui adressent des resolutions traitant de l'Antimilitarisme et autres sujets considérés comme " politiques " sont renvoyés à la décision du Congrès des politiciens—Le Congrès Socialiste International.

Nous, Syndicalistes, nous désirons avoir un Congrès pour les militants et non pour les leaders.

Nous désirons conférer sur les moyens d'action et non discuter sur des pointes d'aiguilles.

Nous voulons une action commune contre la guerre, non des discours inutiles.

Un Congrès de Trade Unions tenu sous les auspices de la Ligue d'Education Syndicaliste Industrielle (I.S.E.L.) qui eut lieu à Londres les 9 et 10 Novembre, 1912, au Holborn Hall, un ordre du jour fut voté, enjoignant à la Ligue de préparer un Congrès Syndicaliste International qui devra avoir lieu à Londres.

Les Syndicalistes d'Amérique le demandent.

Les Syndicalistes de France le désirent.

Les Syndicalistes d'Allemagne le réclament.

Les Syndicalistes de tous les pays en ont besoin.

Les Syndicalistes d'Angleterre le préparent.

La date a été provisoirement fixée au mois de Mai prochain, à la Pentecôte.

Camarades,—Aucun Congrès Syndicaliste International n'a jamais eu lieu jusqu'à présent, donc il n'y a pas de temps à perdre pour forger la chaine qui doit unir les travailleurs des cinq continents. Un Congrès Syndicaliste International est attendu depuis plusieurs années par les révolutionnaires du monde entier. Voici le moment de réaliser ce rève. Que le premier Congrès Syndicaliste International rassemble les travailleurs de tous les pays.

Choisissez vos délégués immédiatement, envoyez vos résolutions pour la préparation des ordres du jour et communiquez-moi aussitôt vos décisions.

Au nom de la I.S.E.L.,

GUY BOWMAN, Secrétaire,

4, Maude Terrace, Walthamstow, London.

INTERNATIONALER SYNDIKALISTISCHER KONGRESS.

An die Mitglieder der Gewerkshaften und der Syndikalistischen Propaganda Gruppen.

Kameraden und Arbeitsgenossen !

Bis heute existiert noch keinerlei Organisation, die die revolutionären Gewerkschafter der verschiedenen Länder in nähere Beziehungen zu bringen im Stande wäre.

Dieser Zustand verhindert jede tatkräftige Solidarität und die progressive Entwicklung unserer Emanzipationsbestrebungen.

Es bestehen zwar die Internationalen Sozialisten-Kongresse mit ihrem permanenten Büreau in Brüssel, aber wir würden uns freiwillig zur Unfruchtbarkeit verurteilen, wenn wir die Vermittelung unserer Internationalen Beziehungen einer Körperschaft der direkten Aktion, die sich dem parlamentarismus verpfändst hat, einer Körperschaft von zungenfertigen Politikern, die sogar mit dem besten Willen nichts für uns tuen Können. Wir müssen uns begegnen als Syndikalisten und Anhänger der direkten Aktion, damit wir unsere eigene Bewegung vorbereiten und entwickeln Können, frei von der Vormundschaft der Politiker.

Es existieren auch die Internationalen Zusammenkünfte der gewerkschaftlichen Landeszentralen, die alle drei Jahre stattfinden und lediglich aus den Gewerkschaftsbeamten der verschiedenen Länder zusammengesetzt sind; folglich keine direkte Vertretung der militanten Elemente genannt werden können. Die meisten Gewerkschaftsbeamten sind konservativ gesinnt; was wir erstreben, ist ein Kongress der aktiven und tatkräftigen Kameraden aller Länder, der uns die Möglichkeit geben soll, alle taktische Fragen zu behandeln, etwaige Missverständnisse aus dem Wege zu räumen und die Entwicklung der Internationalen Solidarität zu fördern. Das Internationale Büreau der Gewerkschaftlichen Landeszentralen in Berlin weigerte sich sogar elementare Lebensfragen, wie den Generalstreik als Mittel zur Expropriation, den Antimilitarismus und die Sabotage auf die Tagesordnung der Internationalen Konferenzen zu stellen. Aber wenn das Büreau eine Diskusion der betreffenden Fragen sogar nicht abgelehnt hätte, so wäre das von kleiner Bedeutung gewesen, denn alle permanenten Gewerkschaftsbeamten sind Politiker, die Mehrheit der Delegierten ist Konservativ gesinnt, wenn anders sie nicht absolute Reaktionäre sind, und alle Geschäfte der Konferenzen stehen unter der Kontrolle von Sozialdemokraten. Gewerkschaften, die in ihren Versammlungen Resolutionen über den Antimilitarismus zur Abstimmung bringen werden heute damit an die politischen Kongress verwiesen.

Wir Syndikalisten wollen einen Kongress der aktiven und militanten Elemente, nicht einen solchen von Beamten.

Wir wollen uns beraten über die Mittel der Aktion und nicht über statistische Abhandlungen debattieren.

Wir wollen, die gemeinschaftliche Aktion gegen den Krieg, nicht Petitionen an die parlamentarier.

Wir wollen, dass die Internationale Solidarität ihren Ausdruck in der direkten Aktion finden möge.

Anf einen Kongress von Trade Unionisten, der von der " Industrial Syndicalist Education League " einberufen wurde und am 9 und 10 November, 1912, in Holborn Hall, in London, tagte, wurde die I.S.E.L. beanfragt, die nötigen Vorbereitungen für die Abhaltung eines Internationalen Syndikalistischen Kongresses in London zu treffen. Als Dátum wurde vorläufig die Pfingstwoche im Monat Mai bestimmt.

Die Syndikalisten in Amerika fordern einen Kongress.

Die Syndikalisten in Frankreich wünschen ihn.

Die Syndikalisten von Deutschland verlangen danach.

Die Syndikalisten aller Länder benötigen ihn.

Die Syndikalisten von England bereiten ihn vor.

Arbeitsgenossen !

Ein Internationaler Syndikalistischer Kongress hat bis jetzt noch nicht stattgefunden und es sollte daher keine Zeit verloren werden, um das Band zu schmieden, dass die Arbeiter der fünf Erdteile verbinden soll. Ein Internationaler Syndikalistischer Kongress ist schon seit manchen Jahren der Wunsch der Revolutionäre aller Länder; jetzt ist die Zeit gekommen, wo dieser Traum verwirklicht werden soll. Möge der erste Internationale Syndikalistischer Kongress die aktiven Arbeiter aller Länder zusammenführen.

Wählt sofort Eure Delegierte, schickt Eure Resolutionen für die Tagesordnung und übermittelt uns in Bälde Eure Beschlüsse.

Im Auftrage der I.S.E.L.,

GUY BOWMAN, Sekretär.

4, Maude Terrace, Walthamstow, London.

INTERNACIA SINDIKATISTA KONGRESO.

Al la Anoj de Laboraj Unuiĝoj kaj Sindikatistaj propandistaj grupoj

Ciu Kamaradoj kaj Samlaboristoj:— Salutojn !

Nune ekzistas nenia organizaĵo por kunvenigi la revoluciemajn unuigistojn de la mondo. Tiu ĉi batalas kontraŭ efektiva propagando kaj malhelpas nian progreson ĝis la Liberigado.

Estas la Internacia Socialista Kongreso, kun ĝia konstanta oficejo je Brussels, sed ni ne povas esti farita senpotenca ĉar niaj internaciaj rilatoj estas kondukitaj per grupo kiu postulas garantiajon de Parlamentismo; kiu estas konstruita de glatlangaj politikistoj, kiuj promesas ke ili faros iojn pro ni, kaj kiuj ne povas, eĉ se ili volus. Ni devas renkonti, kiel sindikatistoj kaj kredantoj je Rekta Agado, por pretigi kaj vastigi nian propran movadon por ekonomia Liberigado, libera de la protekto de ĉiuj politikistoj.

Estas la Internacia Konferenco de Metiounuigaj centroj, kiu okazas ĉirkaŭ trijare, kaj kiu nure konsistas de la Prezidanto kaj Sekretario el ĉiu lando; tial, ne estas rekta reprezentado de la anoj. La oficialoj estas plejparte konservativoj. Ni bezonas kongreson kie la militemuloj de ĉiuj landoj povas froti la ŝultrojn unu kun la alia, diskuti la taktikojn kaj metodojn, kaj, tiel forigante nekompreneblaĵojn, aldoni al Internacia Solidareco La Internacia Oficejo de Metiounuigaj Centroj je Berlin rifuzis permesi ke la necesegaj demandoj de la Generala Striko por Senproprigado, Antimilitarismo, kaj " Sabotajo " estu metita sur la memorlibro por la Konferencoj. Ĝi ne estus tre valora se ili estus permesita ĝin. La tuto de la konstantaj oficialoj estas politikistoj, plejmulte de la Delegitoj estas konservativoj, se ne absolutaj reakciuloj, kaj la tuta afero estas sub la kontrolo de la Socialdemokratoj. Nune, Unuigoj, kiuj sendas rezoluciojn pri antimilitarismo estas turnataj al la kongreso de la politikistoj.

Ni Sindikatistoj bezonas kongreson de la anoj, ne de oficialoj.

Ni deziras konsideri metodojn de agado, ne statistikojn.

Ni bezonas komunan agadon kontraŭ la milito, ne petskribojn al parlamentanoj.

Ni bezonas Internacian Solidarecon, esprimita en Rekta Agado.

Ĉe Kongreso de Metiounuigistoj, kiu okazis sub la auspicioj de la " Industrial Syndicalist Education League," en la Holborn Hall, Londono, la 9an kaj 10an de Novembro, 1912a, rezolucio estis akceptita, postulante ke la I.S.E.L. arangu por havi Internacian Sindikistan Kongreson en Londono. La dato esti fiksita, provizore, por la proksima Majo, dum la Pentekosta Festo.

La Sindikatistoj de Usono demandas ĝin

La Sindikatistoj de Francujo deziras vidi ĝin

La Sindikatistoj de Germanujo volas ĝin

La Sindikatistoj de ĉiuj landoj bezonas ĝin

La Sindikatistoj de Anglujo pretigas pro ĝin.

Samlaboristoj,

Nenia Internacia Sindikatista Kongreson ankoraŭ okazis; tial, la tempo ne devus esti perdita por forĝi la ĉenon, kiu kunigos la laboristojn de kvin kontinentoj. Internacia Sindikatista Kongreso estas dezirita, dum multe da jaroj, de revoluciemuloj de ĉiuj landoj; jen estas la ŝanco por efektivigi tiun songon. Permesu ke la unua Sindikatista Kongreso kunigu la militemajn laboristojn de ĉiuj landoj.

Elektu viajn delegotojn, sendu viajn rezoluciojn, por ke ili estu arangotaj, kaj komuniku, tuj, viajn decidojn al mi.

Pro la I.S.E.L.,

GUY BOWMAN, Sekretario,

4, Maude Terrace, Walthamstow, Londono, Anglujo.

The 'Amalgamation News' Page.

Notice.

All information respecting amalgamation news and Trade Union activity, intended for publication on this page, must be sent to J. V. Wills, Secretary Amalgamation Committees' Federation, 10, Layard Road Rotherhithe, London, S.E.

AMALGAMATORS, PUSH THIS PAPER.

Fellow Trade Unionists,—One of the difficulties that has retarded progress in the Industrial Movement in the past has been the lack of opportunity to disseminate the news and doings of the advanced guard.

Whilst most organisations have their trade journals, these are chiefly confined to matters concerning the Trade Unions who issue them; and, while serving a useful purpose, they do not and cannot represent the pulse and tendency of the whole movement.

With the increasing demand amongst the rank and file for a more militant policy, and with the broadening conception of the possibilities of industrial action, comes the need for a journal that will report the activities, and publish the views of those bodies making for progress.

In order to meet this need, the Editor of the Syndicalist has generously decided to put as much space aside each month in the Syndicalist as is necessary for reports of Trade Union activity.

Here is an opportunity which all those who wish to see the Trade Union movement develop towards industrial solidarity, and freed from the present domination of the political caucus, cannot fail to use.

So send along your reports, comrades. Let your fellow Unionists know what you are doing in your Branch, at your E. C., at your Trades' Councils, and in your Trade Journals. By so doing, you will make it possible for us to tabulate and co-ordinate such information from the Trade Union world, which otherwise might never come to light, and by so doing reflect the feelings of the rank and file.

J. V. WILLS.

THE FURNISHING TRADES' SPIRITED MOVE.

The following has been issued by the National Amalgamated Furnishing Trades' Association:—

To all Workers in the Woodworking and Furniture Industry.

We all seem agreed that the day of Sectional and Local Trade Unionism is at an end.

The swift and scientific development of industry and the wide field covered by Employers' Organisations is the force which is compelling this.

What, then, is our next move?

The reply is apparent to anyone who has given a moment's thought to the present industrial conditions. It is that we require without delay—

One huge Organisation for the whole of the Workers in the Woodworking Industry, totally regardless of craft, skilled or unskilled.

Observe.—We have several Unions in the Furniture Industry, made up mainly as follows:—

Union.	Membership.
National Amalgamated Furnishing Trades Association	10,000
Amalgamated Union of Cabinet Workers	3,000
Amalgamated Woodcutting Machinists	4,000
Scottish	1,000
Amalgamated Union of Upholsterers	2,000
London French Polishers Society	1,000
Various Societies of similar Workers to above	1,000
Total	22,000

With the exception of the first-named, the whole are distinctly Craft Unions, yet there is barely a day passes without two, or the whole of them, being involved in some shop dispute, or a matter affecting a whole shop district.

This will be more so in the future.

Forward—is the next move.

How? By every Member attending his Branch every Meeting Night and advocating the proposals for Industrial Unity he so frequently applauds at public meetings.

When? Now! and at once.

Why? In order that we may all fight together for reduced hours, higher wages, the absorption of our unemployed, and the overthrow of all intolerable conditions.

An injury to one Branch of Industry, an injury to all.

One big Union for each Industry.

One great Federation of all Industries.

Down with Sectionalism and up with Unity.

Will you help?

A Call to Arms.

Fellow Members,—In the *Furniture Record* for the week ending January 3, 1913, appears an article which is very clearly not intended to be of material value to the members of our Association. Yet it is clear that if the words of the writer of the article mean anything, it is most assuredly that of a call to arms to the Furniture employers. Viewed in that light, the declaration is one that commands our immediate attention. The article is luridly drawn, so that employers will be roped into the Wholesalers' Association. Of this we need not complain; on the contrary, I regard it as a healthy encouragement to us to at once set to work to prepare for action. Of this more later.

The writer, who signs himself "Nemo," says that:

(1) It is notorious that the Unions, as a rule, respect a settlement just so long as it gives immediate advantages, and when they have anything to gain by repudiating it they do not hesitate to do so. Some leaders advise their men to see that clauses that favour their interests are strictly observed, and to ignore the rest.

(2) That in most settlements the old workmen are usually ignored.

(3) That the Union prevents workmen leaving districts where wages are low and obtaining work where it is better paid, and this is probably due to the local officials who attempt to encourage a system of artificial dearth of workmen.

(4) That the employers should not permit the Unions to attack individuals (employers) or districts quite irrespective of the merits of the case.

(5) The employers realise that there must be a rise in wages.

(6) The Unions are busily surveying the country, quietly organising the men in the new centres, planting an agitator, or two in seemingly peaceful spots, and generally doing their very best to increase their membership in preparation for the time when the Spring trade has opened and they can show their strength by demands that, as a rule, are far from reasonable.

He also adds the year will undoubtedly bring its fresh crop of strikes and lock-outs. Further, he says, let us prepare ourselves for them.

"Nemo" says a lot more, but the above will suffice.

He undoubtedly bespeaks what is deep down in the hearts of many employers, and my purpose in drawing attention to the letter is to encourage immediate preparation on our part.

The employers smell the proverbial rat. "Nemo" unconsciously pays a flattering tribute to the noble stand of our members last year. He snivels for loyalty among the employers, He mixes full-blooded truths with brilliant lies. In short, he fears *us*. Good it is for us that it should be thus. And for the reason that it ought and must spur us on to the highest degree.

Preparing for Action.

Let us get to work upon the job. We must get ready, and thereby get strong.

Let the members—every one—see that there is something for them to do. I feel sure there are plenty of willing workers, who only require the word to be passed round in order to get them moving.

We Require Them All.

Let us forget the things which do not much matter and magnify the things which affect us in every town and district.

Judging by what I have seen of my colleagues and the Executive during the last few days, they are at one in the conviction that a strenuous and vigorous campaign must be kept going, and in that sense we are all in hearty accord.

We have a good field. The Spring will soon be here.

Let us sow well in the earliest moments.

Let us hold what we have got. Let what we get stimulate a hungering desire for more *and more*.

Here is *our* chance. And it is our bounden duty to seize it with all the force, vigour, energy, and enthusiasm at our command.

Sincerely yours,

A. A. PURCELL
(Organiser).

"WEEKLY SYNDICALIST" Collection Sheets may be had from the General Secretary of the I.S.E.L., 4, Maude Terrace, Walthamstow, E.

METAL, ENGINEERING, AND SHIP-BUILDING COMMITTEE.

Fine enthusiasm is manifesting itself in this Committee, and I expect great things in the near future. We had our monthly meeting on January 11, and, in spite of the fact that the heavens had opened the floodgates, we had a representative attendance, delegates coming from Walthamstow, Manor Park, Greenwich, Cricklewood, &c.

The Secretary reported that the Greenwich Ironfounders had sent along 10s., and several branches had become affiliated. The Islington Labour Party had been visited; also, a number of T.U. Branches, and requests for lectures were coming in fast. It was decided to meet on the second Saturday in the month at the Apple Tree and Mitre, Cursitor Street, Chancery Lane, at 7.30 p.m. (Engineers take note.) The financial statement was not altogether rosy; it is therefore essential that you should get your branches affiliated, and as many individual members as possible to subscribe.

We don't want huge funds, but we *do* want enough to keep us going.

The following manifesto was unanimously adopted, and the secretary instructed to send a copy to all Branches in the Industry.

Don't forget the next monthly meeting on February 8, at 7.30 p.m.

MANIFESTO.

In the Engineering Industry there are 205 Unions. We Want ONE.

FELLOW WORKERS,—

It must be clear to you that the time is over-ripe for the re-organisation of the Unions in the Metal, Engineering and Shipbuilding Industry. With the development of the Industry, the introduction of high speed machinery (displacing the skilled workers, thereby lowering wages), the adoption of pernicious bonus and other systems, the clocking in and out, and the general speeding up in the workshop, the position of the worker to-day is infinitely worse than it was twenty years ago.

The Engineers' rate, for instance, in 1874 for London was 38s. per week; to-day it is a struggle to get £2. This is a 2s. per week increase in 38 years, and the cost of living continually going up. Surely it is time we woke to a better conception of the value of our labour.

The employers, scientifically organised, not satisfied with their successes, are persistently at work endeavouring to undermine and destroy what little power there is left in the Unions by means of conciliation and arbitration boards, agreements and insidious legislation.

It is quite obvious, then, that if we are even to maintain our present conditions, let alone improve them, different methods of fighting the employers must be devised.

Sectionalism the Cause.

At the end of 1911 there were 414,083 workers organised in the Metal, Engineering, and Shipbuilding Industry with 205 Unions. This is the cause of our failing to make progress. To use a hackneyed phrase, "too many unions and not enough unionists." Just consider for a moment what sectionalism means: Petty jealousies between officials invariably reflected in the ranks; continual squabbles over demarcation, &c.; terrible overlapping and consequent waste of energy.

We are convinced that only by a complete

Amalgamation of All Existing Unions

on the lines of One Industry, One Union, One Card, embracing all workers, whether skilled, semi-skilled, or unskilled, male and female, organised on a class instead of a craft basis, can we ever hope to eliminate this internal strife. Only by recognising that our interests are indentical, that an injury to one is an injury to all, can we ever hope to improve our conditions in the workshop.

The above Committee, formed for the purpose of propagating this principle, invites your branch, if situated in London, to appoint two or more delegates to attend the monthly meetings on the second Saturday in each month, at the "Apple Tree and Mitre," Cursitor Street, Chancery Lane, W.C., 7.30 p.m.; if in the Provinces to link up with local committees where established, or assist in forming one.

The Committee further invites those who may be willing to assist, but unable to become delegates, to become individual members at 1d. per month.

Finances are urgently needed, and all are asked to help. Lecturers will be sent to any branch upon application to the Secretary.

On behalf of the Committee,

W. F. WATSON, Hon. Sec.

FOR THE "WEEKLY SYNDICALIST."

The following contributions have been received:

Previously acknowledged	68	8	9
J. Barnett	0	0	6
Mrs. Montgomery	0	1	6
H. G. Salmon	0	0	6
Jas. W. K. Leipner	0	0	6
Collecting sheet No. 1 (per Barnett Rose), B. Rose 5s., A. Honing 1s., F. Breuning 2s. 6d.; F. Rall 2s., Letnnig 1s., Barth 6d., Kafman 6d., Derchansky 1s., J. Salomon 1s., Manuel 6d., A. Theeger 6d., M. Bernstein 1s., L. Cohen 1s., Leo XIII. 1s., S. Lemel 6d.	0	19	0
Geo. H. Hill	0	1	6
C. C. Everson	1	1	0
Joseph Dalby	5	0	0
J. I. Leacock	0	0	7
	75	13	10

SOUTH WALES.

TRADES UNION REFORM LEAGUE.

A Conference was held at Cardiff on Boxing Day of Comrades from various parts of South Wales, who were called together for the purpose of forming a Propagandist Body in order to educate the Workers in the principles of Industrial Unionism. It is intended to hold a further Conference at Swansea during Easter, when all individuals, Lodges, and Branches of Trade Unions will be invited to be represented, and a Manifesto will also be issued giving our views upon Industrial matters.

The following Resolutions were adopted:

1. That we stand for the Principle of one Union for the whole Workers in a given industry.

2. That any proposal that tends to remove the basis of power from the officials to the Rank and File must be supported.

3. That an education policy be carried on so as to enable the Workers to control and administer the industry in which they are engaged.

Dealing particularly with the Miners' Federation, the following Resolutions were adopted:

Rank and File Control.

Legislative power to be vested in the hands of Members by means of monthly Conferences.

Legislation by Principle.

The grouping and classification of grievances and disputes so that they fall under distinct and separate heads, and thus save a great deal of time which is now frittered away in discussing petty details.

Unofficial Council.

While the official element makes up the Council it is useless to expect Rank and File control or an adequate expression of their opinions; therefore no official holding a permanent position under the organisation shall be eligible for a seat on the Administrative Council.

Departmentalising of Organisations.

That the Organisation be divided into three grades :—1. Piece-workers; 2. Day-wage Workers; 3. Mechanical Workers. Each grade to be represented on all Committees from Local Lodges right up to Administrative Council.

Unification of Conditions.

To be obtained by making a demand for one Minimum Wage to cover all Workers irrespective of craft or grade.

General.

That steps be taken to form Joint Committee with other Organisations in other industries of South Wales for the purpose of defending the interest of the Workers and demand a common Minimum Wage.

That we keep in view the question of amalgamating with bodies similar to our own so as to make our propaganda the more effective.

The following was adopted as the object of the Trade Union Reform League:

This Organisation is established to propagate the following principles among Trade Unionists:

No Democratic Organisation of Industry is possible unless the workmen working in an Industry directly control it.

Therefore the workmen should directly control their own Trade Organisations, so that they may learn to control their own Industries through those Organisations.

Therefore, control of the Industry must be gradually removed from the Masters' Office to the Trade Union Lodge. This of necessity implies that side by side with a Democratic Centralisation of the Workmen's Organisations, full opportunities for the development of individual initiative will be created.

Therefore, since knowledge and power grow hand in hand, and when the Workers know how to control, they will, by the same process, generate the power to control.

Therefore, since the problem of Democratic control of Industry needs to be solved on both its sides, we stand for centralised control of Industry through the Workmen's Organisations, and at the same time seek to evolve amongst the workmen the necessary individuality and initiative, which will enable them to control both.

For further information, write to—

MAINWARING,
Llwyncelyn Clydach Vale,
South Wales.

TAILORS UNITING.

On January 8, a conference of delegates representing 9,000 tailors was held at 41, Cowcross Street, E.C., at the offices of the London Trades Council.

An attempt was made to get the Societies amalgamated. This failed, but it was decided to form a federation.

The newly-formed federation includes the following Societies:

The London Tailors' Union.
The Gentlemen's Tailors' Union.
The Trousers' Makers.
The London Society of Tailors and Tailoresses.

The Secretary of the Federation is Mr. Shipe, and the offices are at 41, Cowcross Street, E.C.

MANCHESTER TRADES COUNCIL MOVING FOR AMALGAMATION.

At the January monthly meeting of the Manchester Trades Council the following resolution was carried:

This Council views with great satisfaction the endeavours being made to Amalgamate existing Trade Unions by Industries, believing it to be a most practical scheme towards our industrial emancipation. To this end we call upon the Council to at once elect an active Amalgamation Committee in order to bring about the above desired object.

An amendment to delete the words "by industries" was lost by 230 delegates voting against and only 10 for.

NOTICE TO SYMPATHISERS.

In order to make the work of the I.S.E.L. effective, we must be able to reach every Trade Union Branch; therefore send us Trade Union Reports and Branch Lists to the General Secretary.

THE LEAGUE'S ACTIVITIES.

On Feb. 1 the first Annual General Meeting of the League will take place, at which the League will be definitely organised as a democratic body, when all officials, honorary as well as the paid assistant secretary, will relinquish office.

Up to now the League has been more or less an amorphous organisation owing to the method of its inception. There were but few comrades who started it, and the need for a definite constitution, rules, and so forth was not felt. We were all personal friends, and we just selected a committee of five and appointed a general secretary and h president without giving definite duties to either, and let them get on with the work of spreading Syndicalist propaganda.

Now, owing to the establishment of provincial groups and the increase of membership in every direction, it is desirable that the whole body of members should have a voice in saying what shall be done and how it shall be done.

The members must organise themselves on the lines which they think are best suited for the work that there is to be accomplished.

I print herewith a Preamble, Object, and Rules for the organisation. These are the embodiment of the ideas of a number of comrades with whom I consulted.

However, they are merely printed as a basis for discussion, subject to amendment and alteration by our members in whatever manner they may think fit. Members and groups are asked to consider them, and send in their suggested alterations as soon as possible, or bring to the A. G. M.

The final decision must, of course, rest with the whole membership as sanctioned by a referendum.

PREAMBLE.

History is the record of class struggles. Dominant to-day is the capitalist class, which can maintain its supremacy only so long as the working-class consents to produce wealth and sacrifice its ownership and control.

Being destitute of property, the Workers, in order to live, are compelled to sell their working power to the capitalists, who only employ them when a surplus can be made from their services—that is, the Workers are paid less in wages than the value of the wealth they produce.

For many years politicians of all creeds have regarded the Trade Unions merely as a means whereby they may reach parliament and obtain state offices. The path of politics is a delusion, because economic power precedes all other, and the Social Revolution can only be brought about by Direct Action on the Industrial Field. Syndicalism insists that through the Direct Activity of their own Members the Unions must first seek to improve their economic conditions; then prepare themselves for the work of expropriating the owning class and manage the Industrial system themselves after they have taken possession of it.

The Workers in the past sought to protect their interests by the formation of craft Unions, but with the development of machinery craft divisions and distinctions have been altered and modified, and in many cases have disappeared. These developments necessitate a corresponding change in the methods of the Unions, so that it will be no longer possible, as hitherto, for some sections of the Workers to help in the defeat of another section by remaining in work when that section is on strike. This change can be wrought by organising according to industry (and with other industries) in order that a united body of Workers can face the employers.

Syndicalism declares that to obtain and retain the unity of the Workers as a class Solidarity and Direct Action are the means to be adopted. Direct Action means those efforts taken by the Workers themselves against the employers and their state, through their own Organisations, without the aid of intermediaries of any description.

In order to spread the above principles, it is necessary to unite in a Propagandist body, which is neither a party nor a Trade Union, but which will be composed of associated groups of Trade Unionists drawn together for the purpose of educating themselves and their Fellow-workers. Such a body should not be composed of theorists, for it must not take the Workers away from the work they have to perform in their own Unions; on the contrary, it asks them to study their own case, thus doing for themselves that which the politicians glibly promise they will do for them but cannot.

Name.

Industrial Syndicalist Education League.

Object.

To carry on among Trade Unionists and Workers generally, a campaign of education in the principles of SYNDICALISM—which may be described as Revolutionary Unionism, since its immediate purpose is to conduct a scientific CLASS WAR against capitalism, such war having for its object the CAPTURE OF THE INDUSTRIAL SYSTEM and its management by the Workers themselves for the benefit of the whole community.

Composition.

The League shall be composed of Groups and Trade Union bodies and Individual members.

Membership.

The membership is open to any person who accepts the Preamble, Object, and Constitution, no matter what views may be held by that person regarding politics; but NO PERSON WHO DOES NOT DECLARE FOR NON-PARLIAMENTARY ACTION, and is not a bona-fide Trade Unionist, may share in the responsible work of administration of the League.

No one who will not become active in one or more of the following categories is expected to join.

1.—INVESTIGATING MEMBERS.—Those who are in a position to obtain inside information in regard to particular industries.

2.—LITERARY MEMBERS.—Those who have the time and ability to analyse and collate the information sent in by the investigators and observers, and to embody the results of the work in special articles for the Press and in pamphlets.

3.—DISTRIBUTING MEMBERS.—Those who want to see Syndicalist literature bought and read by the Working Class, and are therefore willing to go and sell it both in their workshops and at public meetings.

4.—SPEAKING MEMBERS.—Those who have the time and talent for public speaking, and are willing to place before public assemblies and Labour Bodies the conclusions reached by the investigators and writers.

5.—SUPPORTING MEMBERS.—Those who from all walks of life may be willing to assist work by their personal influence or money contributions—or both.

Entrance Fee.

Every intending member must fill in an application form, and send same to the General Secretary with a minimum sum of 1s. as an entrance fee; this sum to cover four weeks' subscriptions, copy of rules, membership card, &c.

Groups.

Any six members of the League residing in a locality may form a Group, whose duty it shall be:

1. To form Amalgamation Committees for each Industry.
2. To visit Trade Union Branches and other Working Class Societies.
3.—To hold indoor and outdoor meetings in order to reach non-Unionists and get them to join the Unions, and to reach those Trade Unionists who for some reason or other do not attend their Branch Meetings.
4.—To endeavour to get Syndicalists elected upon all Trade Union bodies other than political office.
5.—To hold public meetings in halls where Unionists of all Trades may be brought together.
6.—To sell and distribute Syndicalist Literature wherever possible.

Individual Members.

Any persons who do not reside in a locality where a Group exists, or who do not wish to take part in the collective work of a Group, may remain individual members, and subscribe directly to headquarters.

Subscriptions.

All members of Groups shall subscribe One Penny per week to the headquarters to be paid to the Group Secretary, who shall forward the same to the head office at least once per month.

Subscriptions for local purposes to be fixed by the Groups themselves.

Affiliated Trade Unions, Trade Councils, and other Working Class Organisations to pay 2d. per member per year.

Individual members shall pay a minimum subscription of 3d. per week, to be sent direct to the General Secretary.

Any member whose subscriptions are thirteen weeks in arrears shall be struck off the books.

Officials.

A Provisional Executive Committee shall be elected consisting of twelve members, and a President, a General Secretary, an Assistant Secretary, and a Treasurer, all elected annually by the Annual General Meeting. (For the first year the P.E.C. shall be elected by the first G.M., February 1, 1913.)

No member of the E.C. shall hold office for more than two years in succession. One year shall elapse before a member is again eligible for election. Retiring members shall be available for consultation.

Six members shall be elected from the London area and six from the provinces. The London members shall meet fortnightly, thus forming a permanent sub-committee. There shall be a meeting of the whole of the E.C. at least once every three months, at which meeting all matters relative to the internal affairs of the Organisation, and its general business shall be considered. The members of the E.C. shall receive an agenda of each meeting of the E.C. at least two clear days before the holding of each meeting, and all amendments and suggestions sent by provincial members unable to attend shall be considered.

The duties of the E.C. shall be to supervise the general work of the Organisation, initiate and maintain Propaganda, circulate literature, hold Local, National, and International Conferences on Syndicalism and Syndicalist proposals, and activities that are calculated to spread Syndicalist principles.

The E.C. shall send all League notices, manifestoes, resolutions, etc., that are for publication to the official organ of the League.

The General Secretary shall record the transactions of all E.C. meetings, shall draw up agendas for same and send to all E.C. members at least two clear days before E.C. meeting, shall send reports of E.C. meetings to provincial members of E.C. and to all Secretaries of Groups.

Organisers may be appointed by the E.C. if the financial position warrants it. The duty of the Organisers shall be to spread the Propaganda of Syndicalism, circulate the official organ of the League and such other Syndicalist literature that may have been approved by the E.C., to obtain members and organise Groups of the League.

All Organisers and all other officials shall at all times be under the control of the E.C.

Group Officials.

Each Group shall appoint a Secretary whose duty it shall be: to receive contributions from members;

To receive all correspondence from headquarters or elsewhere, and lay same before the members of the Group;

To send a report of the Group's activities to the official organ of the Federation at least once a month;

To carry out the instructions of the Group.

Each Group shall appoint a Literature Secretary, whose duty it shall be:

To receive and distribute copies of the official organ and other Syndicalist literature for sale amongst members of the Group and the general public;

To attend Trade Union and other working-class meetings, private and public, and push the sale of Syndicalist literature;

To supervise the work of the distributing members of his Group.

Temporary Rules for Matters Not Provided for at Present.

The E.C. shall have power to make rules on any matter not provided for in this Constitution. Such rules, however, shall be subject to revision at the Annual General Meeting.

Referendum.

Any three Groups may demand a referendum of the whole Organisation on any matter concerning the conduct of the E.C. or any official of the Federation, which referendum shall be taken by the General Secretary, and the result of any such referendum shall have the same effect as a resolution carried by the Annual General Meeting.

Annual General Meeting

The A.G.M. shall be the supreme governing body of the Federation and shall consist of delegates from each Group and Trade Union Body in the proportion of two for any number of members up to twenty, and one for every additional ten or fraction thereof, provided they are in good standing financially. No Group, etc., shall, however, send more than six delegates.

The A.G.M. to be held every year on the first Saturday in February.

All matter for the agenda of the A.G.M. to be in the hands of the General Secretary at least three weeks before the holding of the A.G.M.

BIRMINGHAM.

Slowly, surely, and quietly Syndicalism is taking root in Birmingham, which is preferable to an upstart growth. Some of our members have been addressing Trade Union branches. All Trade Unionists who believe that our present situation cannot be remedied except by Direct Action and Solidarity of Labour on class lines are invited to join the League. The Group meets at 15, Special Street, on Saturdays, February 15, and March 1, at 7 p.m.—E. Robinson, secretary, 31, Ashmore Road, Cotteridge.

A RESIGNATION.

E. J. B. Allen, who was appointed assistant secretary of the I.S.E.L. last August, has tendered his resignation, and his services with the League terminate on February 1.

Whilst the above is an official announcement, I would like to add a few words.

No doubt it will be with regret that the members will hear of this decision; but it is unavoidable, as he is going to New Zealand where it is to be hoped he will find room to render the same services to the revolutionary movement as he has done here.

Allen was one of the pioneers of Industrial Unionism in this country, and when Tom Mann and I had launched the Syndicalist propaganda in this country, he was asked to co-operate and he wrote for us in No. 5 of the *Industrial Syndicalist* an article entitled "Working Class Socialism," extracts of which have been quoted by such diverse persons as Graham Wallace, at a meeting where A. J. Balfour presided and other well-known public men were present; by Mrs.

E. J. B. ALLEN.

Sidney Webb, in the King's Hall lecture on "Syndicalism and the General Strike," when F. E. Smith presided.

Both the *Syndicalist Railwayman* and the SYNDICALIST received his voluntary contributions.

His appointment to the only paid office in the I.S.E.L., the assistant secretaryship, was approved of unanimously.

From the moment of his appointment to official position our relations have been most cordial. Allen liked his work, and I enjoyed my share of it.

In the morning I would enter the office and read through the correspondence, and if there were any knotty points to be settled we discussed them, and when we were agreed the answers were sent off.

When, as Editor of the SYNDICALIST, I considered it desirable that certain articles should appear on definite matters, we held a "pow-wow," and after agreeing upon the scheme Allen would write it up.

The bulk of the matter appearing in the SYNDICALIST since October last has been either his original matter or has been rewritten or passed by him. His wide knowledge of the Labour movement in this country in its various phases has been of immense service. He was equally at home writing an article upon the American Socialist Party and its leaders' attitude towards Syndicalism, as he was in giving a brief history of the early Trade Union movement in this country, and thereby proving conclusively that Sabotage was not un-English. He would ridicule the fables of a Longuet regarding French Syndicalism or sit down and patiently write answers to a whole host of fallacies that have threatened to crop up in the Syndicalist movement.

A fair knowledge of French enabled him to make translations from that admirable *Bulletin International du Mouvement Syndicaliste* and *La Bataille Syndicaliste*, and other revolutionary journals, which enabled us to give the readers of the SYNDICALIST a good selection of International news. Some fifty revolutionary journals would pass through his hands in a week, and he would carefully mark and call my attention to those items of news, whether in French, German, Danish, Italian, Norwegian, Spanish, or other papers.

No one regrets more than I do the fact that he is going. His place will be difficult to fill.

I am sure our members and readers will join me in wishing him "Good luck and a safe voyage." They will also be glad to know that he has practically finished a book on "Syndicalism at Work," which deals with the development of the movement in this country, and will be of great interest because it will not only give a history of the development of Industrial Unionism and the later development of Syndicalism, but will contain an exposition of the resolutions that were adopted at the London and Manchester Conference, which will in itself be a statement of Syndicalist principles and methods.

SYNDICALIST ACTIVITIES.

Finsbury Park A.S.R.S.—Our comrade, F. J. Passmore, attended this branch on December 30. Though the attendance was small, the enthusiasm aroused by his remarks was great. A very animated discussion took place, and provided a splendid opportunity for our comrade, who proved the case for Syndicalism and convinced his audience of the necessity thereof.

Hornsey and Wood Green A.S.R.S.—A very interesting and capable exposition of Syndicalism was delivered to our members on January 2 by our brother, F. J. Passmore. He was listened to with the greatest attention, as he demonstrated how the railwaymen could hold their own by the application of Syndicalist principles. His illustrations of sabotage were splendid, and the shunters of the G.N.R. agreed that it would be far better to obey the company's rules and only shunt a couple of trains per shift of duty, whilst at the same time avoiding accidents and loss of life, than to court disaster by disobeying the company's rules, which we do for their benefit, and not our own. After a number of questions had been satisfactorily replied to by our brother, a hearty vote of thanks was accorded him. As our secretary had been anxious to debate against Syndicalism, a resolution was moved instructing him to arrange for a debate with the general secretary of the I.S.E.L. Several members purchased a copy of "The Railwayman," a splendid little work written by our brother, C. Watkins, of the Midland Railway.

Harlesden and Willesden B.S.P.—This branch received a visit from Comrade F. J. Passmore on January 5. An attentive audience listened to his address on Syndicalism, which occupied an hour. This was followed by a whole batch of questions, which our comrade answered very satisfactorily. Several members took part in the discussion that followed, and the general opinion expressed was that our comrade had caused us to regret the inactivity of our own party and the necessity for a real live revolutionary body on the industrial field. One of our comrades illustrated the benefits which he and 400 of his fellow-workers had obtained by the use of Direct Action. They had compelled their employer to withdraw his refusal to their demands, and scored a splendid victory over him. The same comrade maintained that the same results could never have been obtained by political action. We wound up at 11.10 p.m. by tendering a hearty vote of thanks to the lecturer for his splendid address.

Kentish Town Branch B.S.P.—An unexpected visitor attended here on January 7 in Comrade F. J. Passmore. A battle royal was carried on for an hour and a half on the merits of Syndicalism by our comrade and some of the branch members. We finally fixed up a debate on the subject between him and Comrade P. Petroff, for Thursday, the 23rd inst., at 8 p.m.

West Central Electric A.S.R.S.—Owing to the desire of our members to hear more about the subject and principles of Syndicalism, our brother, F. J. Passmore, was asked to book us up for January 10 and 17, if possible. We were fortunate in being able to get his services for both dates, and at each meeting a good attendance listened to his stirring address. We all enjoyed his illustrations of Syndicalist principles, and we felt convinced that if railwaymen would only learn to use them they would soon find the way out of their present difficulties. How foolish it is to go on strike, thus placing ourselves in the power of the companies, who can starve us into subjection, when, by a little intelligent use of sabotage, &c., on the job, we could obtain our ends. Brother Passmore must be doing splendid service to the railwaymen, whom he is so frequently amongst, and we can quite understand why he is hated and feared by the reactionary members of our Society. Long may he live to carry on the good work and assist us in obtaining our emancipation!

Wood Green Branch B.S.P.—Mr. J. F. Passmore, London Organiser of the I.S.E.L., attended a meeting at the headquarters of the above branch on Sunday evening, December 15. Although it was a very wet night, over a dozen comrades put in an appearance, and listened attentively to Mr. F. J. Passmore's address. At the conclusion of same, several questions were dealt with by the speaker, dealing with the attitude of the I.S.E.L. on political matters, &c., which were suitably replied to. A short debate afterwards concluded an interesting and instructive evening.

Several of the thoughtful ones are wondering how and why Syndicalism is diametrically opposed to Socialism, as they were recently informed that this is the case by one of our own comrades.

North Camberwell Branch B.S.P.—
To the Editor of the SYNDICALIST.

DEAR GUY,—I am instructed by the above branch to ask you to give publicity in the next issue of your paper to the following resolution against the manifesto on political action and strikes issued by the E.C. of the B.S.P.

The North Camberwell B.S.P. having considered the manifesto issued by the E.C. on political action and strikes, deeply deplores the attack on Syndicalism and the Syndicalist movement contained therein. Seeing that the Syndicalist movement is decidedly revolutionary in character, we contend that it is no part of the business of Socialists to make attacks of this kind. Further, we are of opinion that the forces arrayed against the working-class movement are such that it should be our duty to extend the hand of fellowship to all engaged in the fight to wrest the means of life from the domination of the capitalist class.

I hope you will find space for this in the next number of the SYNDICALIST.

With best regards.—Yours fraternally,
SIDNEY ELLAM, Hon. Sec.

Carpenters, No. 6 Branch, Birmingham.—Comrade Harvey addressed them. The Secretary of the Birmingham Branch I.S.E.L. wrote the President thanking the branch for allowing us the opportunity of expounding our principles. There was a good meeting.

Toolmakers, Birmingham.—A new comrade addressed his branch of the Toolmakers. Whilst speaking he had two contents bills pinned up by the side of him. He spoke for an hour and a quarter. When question time came things began to hum, for he had attacked the state and officialdom. Some big official there tried to save his face by saying that we were all working to the same goal. He was challenged by our comrade to debate some future time. He then climbed down.

T. B. SMITH: Thanks for your suggestions, but we are afraid they will not serve. Our mission is to get the workers to take action, not to philosophise. As you will see elsewhere, we have drawn up a preamble. Many thanks for your good wishes and for your help.

RAILWAYMEN'S SYNDICALIST OFFICIALS.

By A MIDLAND GUARD.

It is astonishing, but nevertheless true, that there are always some people who are opposed to any movement on the part of the rank and file of the workers which tends to emancipate them from the vile conditions of wage slavery.

So I am not at all surprised to see that a few of my brothers of the railway world are opposing Syndicalism; it may be because they themselves would not benefit by Syndicalism, or it may be due to other causes.

Anyhow, I am not troubled much about the cause, for I have always studied the interest and welfare of the many, not the few; and I want the bulk of railwaymen to have a clear conception of their position. I intend, therefore, to dispose of a few of our opponents' fallacies.

Transport Workers to Amalgamate.

A few weeks ago a committee which is endeavouring to amalgamate all Transport Workers' Unions into one big Union held a meeting at the Stratford Town Hall. Tom Mann was the principal speaker, and the remainder of the speakers were all rank and file Trade Unionists.

Two of them were delegated from West Ham branch A.S.R.S., which branch also sends delegates to the aforesaid committee. One of them spoke with enthusiasm of the fact that this movement was strongly supported by the railwaymen of that locality and others.

But a small financial loss was incurred by the promoters of the meeting; this must happen of necessity in all such meetings held by the rank and file, who have no rich coffers to play with; and the scribe of West Ham branch saw a golden opportunity to have a smack at his beloved friends the Syndicalists, who, by the way, had no connection with the meeting whatsoever.

So, with the aid of his vivid imagination, he reported in the *Railway Review* that the financial loss was caused by the unpopularity of Syndicalism in West Ham, and, imbued with a desire to do even better, he stated " that the article in the *Daily Herald* on the investment of the A.S.R.S. funds " was another Syndicalist attempt to belittle the work of the A.S.R.S.

I once knew a cheerful idiot who used to tell everybody he met that " white was black," but, being in a similar predicament to that of the West Ham scribe—namely, 'without any proof of his statement—people told him he was " balmy." He thoroughly deserved it, too.

Our cheerful scribe then winds up by announcing a big railwaymen's rally to take place in the near future, at which Mr. J. H. Thomas, M.P., will act as principal speaker. The meeting is to consider a new scheme of organisation for East Anglia, and I presume Mr. Thomas will appear on the stage of Stratford Town Hall, dressed in shining armour, as the Railwaymen's " St. George," determined to slay the fiery dragon of Syndicalism, which he asserts is out to devour railwaymen.

I remember this once fire-eating Socialist saying that, if Syndicalism meant " the railways for the railwaymen," he was opposed to it. Just so; that means he is in favour of the capitalists retaining control and subjecting their employees to all sorts of indignities and insults, and tyrannising over them as they do now. So he certainly cannot advocate that the companies should be compelled to disgorge their ill-gotten gains, and hand them over to their rightful owners, the railwaymen.

Workers to Boss Themselves.

I am sorry to have to disagree with such an intellectual genius as friend Thomas, but I certainly think it would be better for railwaymen, that they would be happier and freer if they bossed themselves instead of being bossed by other people. But then, you see, if they did so, all the bosses would have to go to work, and it is not so easy to work as it is to boss other people, who do the work; yes, I can quite understand why some people oppose Syndicalism; I hope my fellow-workers will now.

It is somewhat strange that this amiable and docile member of the Labour wing of the capitalist government should advocate amalgamation and solidarity one moment, and repudiate it the next. It was he who took a leading part in the fusion of the railway unions, which will ere long be an accomplished fact; but it is he, again, who is against the formation of one transport workers' union. He is opposed to sectionalism, and advocates our motto, " Workers of the world unite "; but that does not include the transport workers.

The biggest joke of all, though, is that in assisting to unify the railwaymen's forces he has been applying the principles of Syndicalism.

INTERNATIONAL NOTES.

NEW ZEALAND.

" God's Own Country " has recently been experiencing events quite similar to those that have happened in the Western States of America, or at Llanelly and Liverpool in England—namely, workers have been maltreated and killed by the authorities.

The miners at Waihi have been on strike for about six months. The New Zealand Federation of Labour, which is the militant workers' organisation there, placed a levy of 10 per cent. upon the total earnings of its members, to support the men at Waihi. This enabled the men to stand out, and if the strike had run along ordinary lines, there is not the slightest doubt that the men would have won.

To the shame of the New Zealand working class, there were a sufficient number of men who were prepared to blackleg. White men (who were white in nothing but the colour of their skins), half-bred Maoris, toughs and corner-boys, and professional bullies were encouraged by the government to register themselves a (scab) union, under that reformers' acme of wisdom, the Arbitration and Conciliation Act.

The scabs got to work, and then the police were flooded into the town. These things, not men, insulted strikers, their wives and children, and backed up the scabs whenever they were getting the worst of it in a scrimmage.

One day the scabs were given a holiday, and with the help and connivance of the police they stormed the Union Miners' Hall, smashing the property and stealing the correspondence, &c. Some of the Union members were in the hall at the time and attempted to defend it. Revolver shots were exchanged. A Union man, George Frederick Evans, the Union storekeeper, was bludgeoned by the police, and whilst on the ground was kicked by the scabs. He died as the result of a blow on his head from the policeman's bâton.

Women and children, as well as men, have been ridden down by the police. Men have been given twenty-four hours to clear out of the town on the penalty of having their houses burnt or blown up if they don't. Where this did not frighten the men, threats were made against the lives and honour of the men's wives and daughters as well—all this with the police and government in acquiescence. Nothing was done to maintain " Law and Order," of which the capitalists prate so much when the " disorder " threatens their interests.

New Zealand was horrorstruck at the police-sanctioned rioting.

The militants are already proposing a march of the organised workers on Waihi to recapture the Miners' Hall from the scabs and their protectors the police.

New Zealand has become quite up-to-date. It has now its equivalent of our Featherstone, Llanelly, Liverpool, and America's Homestead and Cœur d'Alene.

All Unionists will revere the memory of George Frederick Evans. His name will be inscribed on the list of Labour's martyrs with hundreds of others of capital's victims.

May the New Zealand Federation of Labour prosper until it wipes out every remnant of capitalism and militarism throughout the Dominion.

BELGIUM.

The Belgian Socialist teachers, delegated by various local and regional organisations, have been meeting for some days in great numbers at the Maison du Peuple, Brussels.

During the first day of the Congress a national centre for Socialists in the teaching profession was created.

The new organisation groups all the members of the teaching profession, in public or private schools, from the teachers at the Froebel institutes to the professors at the universities. They have affiliated to the Belgian Labour Party and to the Union Committee, which is the General Confederation of Labour for Belgium. Their object is the reorganisation of the methods of education and the defence of the moral and material interests of the members of the profession.

The central body inserted in the rules that it is obligatory for all members to subscribe to one of the large dailies of the party. They have equally decided that the new Union shall possess a periodical.

A committee of inquiry has been nominated who are to give before February 1 next a report on the ways and means of doing this. The methods to be adopted will be considered at a Congress at Easter. To conclude, the assembly proceeded to the election of its executive committee, composed of seven members. Before separating the Congress voted unanimously an address of great sympathy to their comrades, the French Syndicalist teachers, victims of the French bourgeois Republic.

THE SYNDICALIST MOVEMENT IN RUSSIA.

St. Petersburg is almost the only city in Russia where a certain number of Unions have resisted the government reaction and conserved their characteristics of organisations of combat.

At present there exists in the capital fifteen organisations in the following industries: Printing, textile, wood-working, the gold and silver workers, baking and confectionery, hides and skins (tannery), motor-car construction, building, metal industry, granite and marble, clothing industry, commerce, and the chemical workers.

The metal workers, the printers, the clerks, the tailors, and the bakers each publish a trade paper.

For some months the Metal Workers' Union was dissolved by the police, but the workers reorganised their Union under another name last July, which had about 21,000 members; but this new organisation was attacked by the authorities, who dissolved it.

At Moscow the situation is even blacker. Nominally they have there thirteen Union organisations, but certain of them have again been dissolved, and have found themselves placed in the impossible position of undertaking any action. The Textile Workers' Union, that at one time counted many thousands of members, at present numbers seventy. More lamentable, again, is the situation in the provinces. There exists there a certain number of isolated Unions, but, being under police oppression, they are not able to give any sign of life.

ALL MAKES BOUGHT, SOLD, HIRED, REPAIRED ETC.

THE TYPEWRITER PEOPLE

(LARKIN & LEWIS)

PADS FOR YOST MACHINES AT 6/6

1000 FACSIMILE CIRCULARS FROM 7/6

ASK FOR AVENUE 535

MINCING LANE HOUSE ARCADE

53 to 69 EAST CHEAP LONDON E.C.

INDUSTRIAL SYNDICALIST :: EDUCATION LEAGUE. ::

The ANNUAL GENERAL MEETING of the League

will be held

On SATURDAY, FEBRUARY 1st, 1913,

At the Communist Club, 107, Charlotte St., London, W.

AGENDA:
1. Secretary's Report.
2. London Organiser's Report.
3. Balance-Sheet ending December 31st, 1912.
4. Proposed New Constitution of the League.
5. Election of Officers.

Proceedings will commence at 6 p.m.

Provincial Groups are especially invited to send delegates; the hour of 6 p.m. has been purposely fixed in order to allow them to reach London with half-day trip tickets.

Suggestions re the new Constitution, methods of finance, and nominations for election of officers must be sent in at least a week before the date fixed for the meeting.

GUY BOWMAN, *Secretary*.

4, Maude Terrace, Walthamstow, London, E.

SYNDICALIST LITERATURE.

We are repeatedly being asked for a book on Syndicalism. If inquirers will read through the pamphlets and books of which we print a list underneath, they will obtain a fair idea of what Syndicalism means. Meanwhile, we are bringing out a series of comprehensive books at one shilling, under the general title of " The Syndicalist Library." The first of the series will be by Tom Mann, as advertised below.

TOM MANN'S PAMPHLETS.

No. 1. PREPARE FOR ACTION. 1D.

Explains the need for linking up the unions, and adopting a fighting policy. The pamphlet that made the strike year of 1911. Only a few of these left. Order early.

No. 2. THE TRANSPORT WORKERS. 1D.

Calls for united action amongst Transport Workers. Brought the National Transport Workers' Federation into being, which Federation is to pave the way for ONE union for the Transport industry.

No. 3. FORGING THE WEAPON.

Explains the steps to be taken by sympathisers in order to build up a fighting union movement. The pamphlet to be pushed. The best for workers. Most useful to propagandists.

No. 4. ALL HAIL SOLIDARITY. 1D.

Shows the growth of solidarity amongst the workers of various industries. Deals with the Cambrian Combine Strike, and contains messages from W. D. Haywood, I.W.W., and Eugene V. Debs, of the American Socialist Party.

No. 5. SYMPOSIUM ON SYNDICALISM. 1D.

Contains both an account of the practical work to be performed by Syndicalists and a brief statement of our object and methods. A splendid educator. There are not many of these left.

No. 6. A MANCHESTER MESSAGE TO THE WORKERS OF ENGLAND. 6D.

A verbatim report of the whole of the proceedings of the first national conference held on Syndicalism. Records the formation of the Industrial Syndicalist Education League. This will become a historic document, useful alike to workers and students. Only about a dozen left.

No. 7. PARLIAMENTARY ACTION versus SYNDICALISM. 2D.

Being a report of a debate between TOM MANN and FRANK ROSE, both well-known members of the A.S.E., and both prominent in the Labour World. The conflict between Unionism and Direct Action, and the policy of the " pure and simple " politicians as a means to emancipation. 60 pages for 2d.

No. 8. MINERS WAKE UP. 6D.

Contains essays by members of the South Wales Miners' Federation, who are at work in the pits. This pamphlet with Number 5 was quoted by the Coal-owners to Mr. Asquith in order to kill the Miners' Minimum Wage Bill, and to show the " dangerous " trend of advanced opinion amongst the Miners and workers generally. Only about two dozen left.

No. 9. THE WEAPON SHAPING. 6D.

A compact work, showing the growth of Syndicalism; full of suggestions; indicates the interest in Syndicalism aroused amongst the Trades Councils. Should be read by all members of the Trades Councils, for it contains an account of the Derby Trades Council's action, and an address by the Secretary of the Walthamstow Trades Council to its members.

No. 10. A TWO-FOLD WARNING. 1D.

This contains a splendid account of the International Cotton Manufacturers' Federation. A lucid statement of the growth of this important industry, and of the tactics used by the Federated employers. Contains a powerful plea for solidarity amongst the Textile workers, and shows the necessity for the workers being educated as to the development of machinery that the masters are bringing in. Explains that the only hope lies in their controlling the industry. Shows up the Cotton Ring.

No. 11. THE RAILWAYMEN. 1D.

A splendid essay upon the growth and development of the Railway Service. Railwaymen will find it packed full of useful information. Explains how they must organise, and what means to use to combat the power of the Companies. Conciliation Boards exposed.

No. 12. THE TRANSPORT INDUSTRY. 1D.

This details the inner history of the Shipping Federation, against which arose the National Transport Workers' Federation. Shows the cunning and unscrupulous methods of the men who pull the strings in the Shipping World. None of these left. We shall probably reprint. Order immediately if required.

—THE—
Ferrer School

now meets at

107, Charlotte St., W.

On SUNDAY AFTERNOON, at 3.30.

OTHER BOOKS.

FROM SINGLE TAX TO SYNDICALISM,

by Tom Mann.

Library Edition, 2/6

Cheap Edition, 1/-

(See advt. on page 5.)

MY COUNTRY: RIGHT OR WRONG.
By Gustave Hervé.

Translated by Guy Bowman. Library Edition, 3s. 6d.

The Yorkshire Daily Observer says:—" It is a fiery, sustained, and often eloquent plea for a union among the workers of all countries against capitalism, and incidentally against war, which, Mr. Hervé has no difficulty in showing, never by any chance benefits the industrial population of the conquering or of the conquered country, and is of service only to financiers."

MY COUNTRY: RIGHT OR WRONG.
By Gustave Hervé.

Cheap Popular Edition, 1/-

THE MINERS' NEXT STEP. 6D.

A stirring appeal for the reorganisation of the Miners' Federation on fighting lines—the bible of the militant miners. Has been circulated all over the United Kingdom.

INDEPENDENCE, or CO-PARTNERSHIP IN EDUCATION,
by A. H. M. Robertson. 1D.

A pamphlet containing the private and strictly confidential draft memorial on University Education, lately issued to the Parliamentary Committee of the Trades Union Congress by the Workers' Educational Association, with comment thereon, partly reprinted from the " Railway Review."

THE SYNDICALIST RAILWAYMAN. 1D.

Copies of Numbers 1, 2, 3, and 4 can still be obtained. Contains matter of general interest to Syndicalists, and will serve the purpose of any student, as well as that of any number of the SYNDICALIST.

THE SYNDICALIST.

A limited number of the January and February issues that were seized by the police can be had. Collectors can have copies of these to complete their collections at 5/- each, to go towards the " *Weekly Syndicalist* " fund.

Any of the succeeding issues can be obtained for 1D.

GUY BOWMAN, Publisher, 4, Maude Terrace, Walthamstow.

Printed and Published by GUY BOWMAN, 4, Maude Terrace, Walthamstow, E.

The Syndicalist

and Amalgamation News

Edited under the :: :: auspices of the :: :: Industrial Syndicalist Education League. ::

President
TOM MANN

Secretary
GUY BOWMAN

VOL. II. NOS. 3 & 4.　　　LONDON, MARCH-APRIL, 1913.　　　MONTHLY, ONE PENNY.

SYNDICALISM AND THE STATE.

It is distinctly encouraging to find so many evidences that the workers are recognising the necessity for industrial organisation and Direct Action. The amalgamation of the three sectional societies of railwaymen and the spirit of Solidarity shown by them over the case of Guard Richardson is magnificent evidence of the right kind of development; but it is necessary to point out that we have to travel much further than this before we arrive at a right conception of Syndicalism.

Syndicalism is not perfected "stateism." It is opposed to stateism. It is not a case of developing a force by industrial organisation to be applied through the machinery of the organised state. It is the voluntary organisation of the workers outside of and independent of the state, for the direct control of all industry.

The state is the enemy, and the "stateists" (i.e., those who seek to bring about changes by means of the state machinery) are opponents of voluntary organisation, voluntary control, and voluntary ownership. The state, and with it parliament and all the governmental departments, are opposed to direct control and ownership by the people engaged in the industries. The state caters directly for the ruling class. The ruling class is not the Working Class. The Working Class cannot become the ruling class by state action, nor can its members throw off the yoke of bondage imposed on them by the present ruling class by any means short of refusing absolutely to act as wealth producers for a ruling class or for any body or institution other than themselves.

William Morris always advocated the vital necessity for the workers themselves to control entirely the work they do. The only possibility for the people to become artists again, as our fathers in the Middle Ages certainly were, will be when all responsibility for the entire output of wealth is claimed and discharged by the workers who will form the community. However large or small that community may be, the men and women therein must not be regimented, ordered, and bossed by superiors of any kind. The real life of the people will show itself in the work of the people, and with the abolition of economic servitude all shoddy production—all trade trickery—all forms of adulteration will cease, as no one will be a gainer by resorting to such methods.

The workers to-day must learn to hold the ruling class in contempt and to treat the agency through which they keep alive the glamour, viz., parliament, in the manner it deserves. They must realise that it belongs to their enemies, and see in it an institution that can never be used effectively by the workers. They must view it as belonging to the capitalist régime, tottering, doddering, decaying with capitalist decay. The live men of the country already know it to be more and more a pretentious "Joss House," revered only by the capitalist class itself, and those of the Working Class whose minds are incapable of activity, save within those channels provided by the master class. The despising of that master class and the whole of the judicial and legislative trappings upon which it depends for its continued domination is a necessary condition of a healthy, mental virility.

TOM MANN.

The International Syndicalist Congress.

A POSTPONEMENT.

CHANGE OF DATE FROM WHITSUNTIDE TO AUTUMN.

Our world-wide invitation to the working class to hold an International Syndicalist Congress has been hailed with delight by workers of all countries, and we have already received numerous applications.

The appeal has received cordial comment in the Syndicalist and Socialist presses of the different countries. All are agreed that the holding of a Congress is necessary, and that it would produce splendid results; most are agreed that London is the best centre for the holding of such a Congress; and all are agreed that Whitsuntide—the date provisionally put forward by ourselves—is too premature. It would not leave time for circularising the Unions and making other necessary arrangements. The general feeling is that some time in autumn, say September or October, would be suitable. We agree entirely with them in this matter.

Here are some of the comments of the Continental papers:

Die Einigkeit, the organ of the German Syndicalists, declares that the date fixed (Whitsuntide) is too early, and concludes, "Our Executive Committee will not fail to submit very shortly to the organisations affiliated to the Free Union of German Workers such proposals as will lead to the thorough discussion of the whole matter. As far as lies in its power our Executive Committee will do everything possible to ensure a fine Congress."

Syndikalisten, the organ of the Swedish Central Workers' Organisation, comments to the same effect. The Viennese *Wohlstund für alle* also approves warmly the step we have taken.

L'Internazionale, the organ of the Syndical Union of Italy, points out that the revolutionary committee has already expressed itself in favour of an International Congress.

Now we come to France. It is in this country alone that our appeal has aroused other than favourable criticism—in France, where the Syndicalist Movement is strongest, but also, let us not forget, where the revolutionaries in the C.G.T. and in most of the national federations find their aggressive action paralysed. In its issue of February 20, *La Vie Ouvrière,* the bi-monthly Syndicalist Review, criticises the holding of an International Syndicalist Congress as a means of creating an International link between the organisations which advocate Direct Action. Comrade Monatte states that the French movement could not share the idea of "this *second* International secretariat in opposition to that at Berlin"; further, that "this second secretariat would be as powerless as the existing organisation under Socialist tutelage." He regrets the "initiative of our English Comrades"! He approves of our action up to this point, "aiming at following up within the English Trade Union organisations their propaganda in favour of Syndicalism and industrial federation." "These old organisations," says he, "are being wonderfully rejuvenated within these last few years, and there it is that the English revolutionaries must take their propaganda in favour of a real Working Class International Congress."

We are indeed grateful that Comrade Monatte bestows his paternal blessing on our work in England. We have felt signs and portents of that same rejuvenation of which he speaks. For all that, it is vitally necessary to the future International action of the working-class that their organisations, which are at present placed under the tutelage of parliamentary Socialists through the International Socialist Bureau in Germany, shall be freed from the befogging direction of political bosses.

HOLBORN HALL, LONDON.
In which the First International Syndicalist Congress will be held, September 27th to October 2nd, 1913.

It is impossible for us not to desire—indeed, it is for that we live, and hope, and strive—to take away from them little by little the powers they exercise. The questions which workers all over the world ought to be discussing are industrial questions. Let politics and the politicians take care of themselves. We repeat that there is no machinery at present for the discussion of such questions as sabotage, anti-militarism, and the general strike, at International Congresses. These topics are severely barred. It is our intense desire to create, as the most urgent need of the day, a real working-class Congress, at which the rank and file will voice their own needs.

It is all very well to rejuvenate the Trade Unions. They want it, Christ knows! But our foreign comrades know as well as we do that there is no common agreement on questions of principles and tactics. Nothing but good can be the outcome of a Congress at which revolutionaries from all countries can meet, express their views, and order their strategy in the future. Experience is the only teacher. For International Working Class action we must have International experience.

An article above the signature of A. Luguet in *L'Humanité* of March 4 also expresses a fear that "such a step (i.e., the holding of a Congress) would lead to a division in the ranks of the proletariat of France."

We consider that the proletariat of all countries could not very well be further torn asunder than under the tutelage of political leaders. The root of the whole matter is just this : How are the revolutionary minorities in all countries to find International expression? In a Parliamentary Socialist International Congress? If not there, where then but in an Industrial Syndicalist Congress? As for the fear that this would destroy any unity, even if this unity existed, the revolutionary organisations would know how to maintain it, at the same time maintaining the right to discuss working-class problems at their own International Congress. We know how our French comrades will act when the time draws nearer.

Spain is distinctly sunny and fiery. Spain is all right. Spain is more than ready for the step we have taken. The following is an extract from the Spanish *Tierra y Libertad,* expressing their assent to the idea :

"Spanish and American Workers !

"You who know that you live under a tyrannical oligarchy ! You who work for a wage which is a mere pretence at justifying the exploitation which the capitalists practise ! You who are anxious to free yourselves by your own efforts without placing faith in leaders who generally turn out to be bad shepherds ! You who feel yourselves compelled to sacrifice even liberty and life itself for the emancipation of the workers; you who look upon all half-measures as a traitorous abandonment of the ideal of emancipation—to the Syndicalist Congress of London !

"Trade Unionists, Trade Union Federations, diverse trades, old and new societies now held in bondage by political federations, exercise your primitive right of autonomy; obey that impulse towards freedom which has never been allowed to die—to the Syndicalist Congress of London !

"You Agricultural Unionists who will constitute the next Congress at Cordova ! —to the Syndicalist Congress of London !

"You seventy thousand railwaymen, who instead of travelling at high speed towards working-class emancipation, are merely travelling by ' goods ' train, owing to being held back by less revolutionary Unions, the Syndicalist Congress of London switches you on to the main line to the participation in universal freedom."

Let it be understood that the calling of the Congress is not an individual affair. It is not even an affair of the I.S.E.L. Let it be remembered that both at London and Manchester last November delegates representing over 150,000 workers met and agreed on the necessity for such a Congress. We are carrying out the wishes of the militant workers of this country, who at these conferences agreed to Direct Action as their policy, and took Sabotage, the Boycott, and Anti-militarism as their weapons.

Some of our Dutch comrades have already taken the initiative of putting some questions to the Syndicats. We hope plenty of answers will be received, and that they will let us know as soon as possible what those answers are.

It is then agreed that :

1. An International Syndicalist Congress is necessary.

2. **Autumn, preferably September, is the best time for holding such a Congress.**

3. **We should proceed at once with the necessary arrangements, so as to make the Congress an epoch-making event in the history of the world's working-class.**

PAST, PRESENT, AND FUTURE.

Last year the March number of the SYNDICALIST did not appear owing to the "Don't Shoot" prosecutions. Our very good friend Wilshire nobly stepped into the breach and piloted the March-April number through. Those were stormy times.

This year we have had not so much a stormy March as an agitated one. The League has been reorganised, and, as will be seen elsewhere in our columns, put on a sound working basis. This took time and trouble. On the top of this there was the arranging of the Syndicalist Library (the first book of which is to appear immediately), now under the editorship of Norman Young. A double dose of influenza made the appearance of the SYNDICALIST in March still more of a problem. E. J. B. Allen's departure to New Zealand, and the disorganisation consequent on this, was another militating factor.

It was found impossible to organise the League and get out the SYNDICALIST at the same time. This year, as last, it is being issued as a March-April number. From now onward we have two distinct departments, one for the League and one for the SYNDICALIST.

The assistant-secretary to the League is W. Nefydd Roberts, who is remembered for the bold stand he made a year or two back on behalf of the unemployed teachers. He is a born fighter. The sub-editor of the SYNDICALIST is the above-mentioned Norman Young, whose poems have appeared for some months back in our paper and elsewhere. He was, too, the editor of the *Link,* in which paper he saw that Syndicalism had fair play given to it.

I want everyone to know, too, that these recruits, with others, are giving their time and talent to the Syndicalist Movement for nothing. They are with us because their hearts have been with us since they first heard of Syndicalism through the "Don't Shoot" prosecutions. They are rebels desiring to make other rebels.

This reconstruction ensures a more settled working, and in future the SYNDICALIST will be out bang up to time, hotter and crisper than ever. See that it is spread broadcast.

I want to see that *Weekly Syndicalist* materialising. A monthly tends to become too academic. We want to hit hard and hit often.

The following is a list of subscriptions to the *Weekly Syndicalist.* We want some more :

	£	s.	d.
Previously acknowledged	75	13	10
Julian Leacock	0	5	0
Collection taken by G. B. on tour in S. Wales	2	0	0
Nelson (B.C.) Trades and Labour Council	0	2	6
W. H. Summers	0	1	0
Vancouver (B.C.) Syndicalist League	0	2	6
J. J. Smith	0	5	0
T. C. Hidden	0	3	10
Ex-Social-Democrat (down with the bureaucrats)	1	10	0
Collecting Sheet No. 3 (per B. Rose) : Rawding, Workingmen, 10s. ; Mr. Davis's Workingmen, 5s. ; B. Rose, 5s. ; M., 1s. ; J. Maclphsitz, 1s.	1	2	0
Collecting Sheet No. 4 (per D. Armstrong) : G. Wood, 2s. ; D. and O. Armstrong, 2s. ; Southall Branch, 6d. ; J. F. Tanner, 1s. ; A. H. Lewingdon, 1s.	0	5	6
Collecting Sheet No. 5 (per W. Harold Summers) : W. H. Summers, 6d. ; B. Shepherd, 3d. ; F. Bull, 3d. ; H. Smallone, 3d. ; A. E. Smith, 3d. ; W. S. C., 1s. ; W. A., 6d. ; Mrs. W. H. Summers, 3d.	0	3	6
Collecting Sheet No. 27 (per Georgina Healiss) : Georgina Healiss, 2s. 6d. ; George Healiss, 5s. ; Leonora Fair, 2s. 6d. ; C. Smitton, 2s.	0	12	0
The Syndicalist Tailoring Co.	0	7	6
	£82	9	2

As you will see there is a new subscriber to the fund, the Syndicalist Tailoring Company. Their advertisement appears elsewhere in this issue. I urge upon all who can do so to get their clothing made there, and so help to swell the fund.

GUY BOWMAN.

The Syndicalist
and Amalgamation News.

EDITED UNDER THE AUSPICES OF

The Industrial Syndicalist Education League

Offices:
4, MAUDE TERRACE, WALTHAMSTOW,
LONDON, E.

MONTHLY . ONE PENNY.

Post Paid Subscription:—
Great Britain or Abroad ... 12 months 1s. 6d.

Bundle Rates:—
1s. 6d. per. quire, Carriage Paid.
U.K.F. TERMS TO NEWSAGENTS.

The receipt of a Sample Copy is an invitation to Subscribe.

MARCH-APRIL, 1913.

THE CLASS STRUGGLE.

That mankind is economically divided into two classes, according to the method whereby they obtain a living, is becoming more generally recognised to-day.

Nevertheless, even by those to whom the "class struggle" is an accepted and proven fact, considerable difficulty arises as to just where the class line should be drawn, with much resulting confusion and consequent waste of energy.

This difficulty is one encountered in all branches of science, more or less, particularly at the point of contact, where the subject possesses traits found in both classes or species. An instance may be cited in that of the tomato, over which many a hot controversy has raged, as to whether it belonged to the fruit or the vegetable kingdom. In the division of the economic classes the same difficulty occurs, and that in regard to the small working business man.

The broad basis upon which the division is made is that a member of the working class, or a wage-slave, obtains the means of living through selling his own labour power, the ability to work—whether it be with a pick-and-shovel, a pen, or a monkey-wrench—for a certain amount of wages or salary. In the other class are those who obtain their living from profits received from money invested in some branch of industry or in land.

A hard and sharp division is here obtained—wages on one side and profits on the other; but in the case of the small business man and master-tradesman, whose livelihood is obtained partly from wages and partly from profits, the split occurs. He is part working-man and part capitalist, and consequently his interests are divided between the two classes. He is thus an unreliable quantity in the class struggle let him be ever so sincere and honest in his intentions.

As a working solution of the difficulty, I believe we should classify them thus : If they hire a worker, then they are capitalists ; if they do the work themselves, then they are workers. Or, again, we could classify them according to the methods by which the major portion of their livelihood is obtained ; which, we must admit, would not always be an easy matter to discuss. But to classify them according to their sentiments, as the political Socialists do, seems to me to render the class-struggle an absurdity.

While preaching the class-struggle, on platform and in press, Socialists yet admit into membership in their party members of the capitalist class, merely because they subscribe to their doctrines, and consequently much dissension occurs and a drifting away from the fundamental basis upon which the party was originally formed. For these people, be they ever so sincere and honest, have proven time and again by their actions their inability to see eye to eye with us on the problems which confront us daily in the workshop, and to act along lines which we consider to be to our material benefit.

That these people are intelligent and possess a much higher education than the average member of the rank and file is unquestioned, but they lack the practical class consciousness drilled into the workers in the daily struggle on the job, and their intelligence ends up in their dominating the party and misleading it along unprofitable lines.

This is one of the fundamental weaknesses of political parties, and one which renders them useless for the workers' purpose, irrespective of their intention towards the state.

The Socialists are thus not a *class* party, but a *humanitarian* party. This may be a very laudable ideal, but it is not a *class* one.

Either there is a class-struggle, or there isn't.

If there is—and all the facts go to prove it—then the only safe and sane method is

---

to fight it along class lines. Otherwise we will end in a cul-de-sac, and have to begin the whole thing over again.

It is here that Syndicalism, in opposition to the Socialist Party, is based upon the solid rock, operating solely through the workers themselves.

— W. GRAY.

WE AGREE.
STRAIGHT TALKS.

I.—"SABOTAGE AND BALDERDASH."

Justice cannot be obtained by peaceable and constitutional means.

In the workshop the working of capitalism can be impeded at every step by concerted plans.

We have heard of ca' canny.

We have heard of numerous accidents with machinery occurring at one time.

We have heard of the truth being told to customers.

We have heard of epidemics of straying luggage.

But all these things are wicked.

There is no harm in killing people with tinned diseased salmon.

There is no harm in killing people by lead-poisoning.

There is no harm in killing people for want of automatic couplings on railways.

Business is business.

II.—A REVOLUTION WANTED.

If you wish for a revolution you must consider how to move men.

The hope of a juster society must be put in their hearts.

It can be realised, if they determine to realise it.

(Not otherwise.)

The wealth of the world is greater to-day than ever before.

Men have been trying to fly during the whole period recorded by history, and have only just succeeded.

Things can be done which never before have been done.

The power of man to supply his needs is greater now than ever,

But the control of that power is given entirely to the few.

The many must get their fair share. This transfer of power is bound up with breaking the rights of property.

It is a revolution.

It cannot be accomplished by fine phrases and crosses made with a pencil.

Not entirely by constitutional and peaceable means.

SOLOMON II.
—From the *Daily Herald.*

WHEN?
By NORMAN YOUNG.

Our fathers stood in awe of unknown pow'rs,
    Of suns, and moons, and stars, and mighty things :
They knelt for help in terror-stricken hours,
    And gazed in fear on Death with outstretched wings.
They deemed divinity had touched their kings,
    And worshipped devils both of earth and shade ;
They came to Truth through weary wanderings :
    'Twas lack of learning made them so afraid.

But we, their slavish sons of latter days,
    Lift up our servile souls in hollow praise
Of mortals like ourselves—of underlings—
Too blind to conquer this sad state of ours,
Too deaf to hear the song that Freedom sings,
Too timorous to sack their blood-drenched tow'rs.
When shall we rise and for the robbed make room ?
When send gold-hungry tyrants to their doom ?

GOLDEN PRIVET.

Finest Stock in the World.
100,000 to choose from.

15in. to 18in., 3s. ; 18in. to 2ft., 4s. ; 2ft. to 2ft. 6in., 5s. ; 2ft. 6in. to 3ft., 6s. ; 3ft., 9s. per doz. Specimens from 2s. each.

All other Shrubs equally cheap.
Carriage paid on order of 10s.

F BAKER & SONS,
The Nurseries,
LOWER TOOTING and MERTON.
1 minute from Merton Tram Terminus.

RED RUBBER.
NO MORE PETITIONS.
By RUBBERITE.

(Continued from last month.)

V.

We must make our organisation grow; get everyone in the union. We must then formulate our list of grievances to be abolished, fines to be done away with, hours reduced, overtime stopped or reduced with increased pay, and a general rise in wages. A start should be made by a shop in Birmingham asking for the new scale. If the employers refuse, strike the shop in seven days ; if at the end of seven days the demands are not conceded, stop all the rubber workers in Birmingham. If then there is no remedy, call out all the rubber workers in the whole country, demanding concessions for every section. Such a method of increasing pressure would bring disruption into the employers ranks. They would be tempted to compel the firms to make concessions to avoid further demands. This policy of increased pressure caused by demanding concessions for every man, woman, and girl brought into the dispute would give the rubber workers a greater cohesion, since every grade would have something to gain by a victory. A start might be made with a demand for sixpence per hour for males over twenty-one years ; all girls over twenty should have at least 15s. per week. The employers can afford it, as there are very few rubber works that pay less than ten per cent. Labour should be the first charge, and if the employers cannot pay these moderate demands, let them shut up shop rather than starve the employees. Better to kill the works than kill the workers. With such a policy as this the workers could increase wages and reduce hours in double-quick time. Had the Midland rubber workers stuck to their organisation of some six years ago they would have been in a better position now. But better late than never ; begin now. There is a union that has been in existence for the past twenty years, but the workers have not availed themselves of it as they ought to have done. Whilst other industries have been gaining concessions, increases of wages, reductions of hours, the rubber workers have been standing still. It is time that they shook off their apathy and used the union as a lever to raise themselves out of the horrible quagmire of monotonous routine, and starvation wages. Let us fight for and win better conditions, so that in years to come we will look back on the spectre of the men who used to sift red antimony, and the "press-men" who pressed their souls as well as rubber at 4½d. and 5d. per hour, as being a relic of barbarous days. Let the rubber workers unite and fight, to live as men and women and not as mere machines. Join our union, and join all the unions together, so that the whole of the workers can win their emancipation from slavery.

TO ALL RUBBER WORKERS.

Would all rubber workers kindly ventilate their grievances at present obtaining in Rubber Works where he or she may be employed, giving particulars as to wages, hours of labour, conditions in general, whether any Trade Union is catering for their needs in the vicinity, so as to arrive at some definite plan of action, whereby the deplorable lack of unity may be overcome. The primary object is organisation, without which all efforts are wasted. Sweating predominates through the absence of any standardised rate of wages. Other trades are increasing in numbers and becoming more aggressive in character. Yet rubber plays an important part in every industry. We shall see to what extent sweating takes place. Weigh in. I need scarcely add all names and addresses will be held strictly confidential. All missives should be sent care of Guy Bowman, 4, Maude Terrace, Walthamstow, London, E.—Yours, &c.

RUBBERITE.

WHY SYNDICALISTS ORGANISE BY INDUSTRY.
By FRED BOWER.

Many members of the Working Class have agreed with us that our plan for industrial organisation is a good one. Then we have been asked the pertinent question, "Why should society be organised on the basis of industry?" Brief though this question is it is one that demands an adequate answer.

One does not need to be a student in order to realise that the most important matter in society is not its form of government, its general religion, nor yet its culture, but the conditions under which the necessities of life are produced. Lewis Morgan, in his monumental work, "Ancient Society," shows, with weighty evidence, the part that the production of wealth has played in human evolution. The satisfying of human requirements is the prime concern of society. Forms of society and forms of government have changed owing to the changed methods of wealth production.

Humanity was cradled in primitive communism ; it was the tribe that hunted, fished, fought, and lived in common. And as agriculture and the domestication of animals became known, that is, a new form of industry, so did the forms of tribal organisation change. The patriarchs, the heads of families, became the rulers, tribal communism gave way to consanguine communism — communism within the family.

With the increase of knowledge of agriculture tribes ceased to be migratory, village communities were established, and for years survived. With the growth of handicrafts, with inventions, trade guilds sprang up. Numerous villages, towns, and, later, the free cities federated, and as wealth increased, owing to new methods of production, a new civilisation grew. But owing to the fact that handicraft reigned supreme, that most trade was local, the tie uniting a given society was that of territory. Agriculture was still the main means of wealth production. The feudal system was the political expression.

When the ordinary citizens grew in wealth and power owing to the new methods of production and to their inter-city and international federations, the monarchs fought them. Under the pretext of either statecraft or religion, they ruined the guilds, robbed the communes and cities of their local power, created "nations" and ultimately "empires." When the old guilds were smashed industry was practically annihilated. Poverty reigned supreme amongst the "lower orders." The advent of machine production opened the way for a new social class. "Capitalism" began to evolve. With the application of steam to machinery and the growth and development of science, the balance of social power was handed to this new class, which was interested neither in agriculture nor handicrafts, but consisted, in the main, of moneylenders or traders.

The absolute monarchies were fought by this class, and the feudal monarchs and nobles who had killed the free federations of the people were transformed to limited monarchies and republics, and the representative system was inaugurated. The change of trade from being that of local supply of local wants, production for use under the guild system became national and international because of production for profit. Now men seldom know where the product of their labour will be ultimately sold and consumed. Empires have been created, colonial wars engaged in, new forms of government have been made, all owing to the

---

fresh methods of wealth production. And in all cases and in all times those who owned and controlled wealth production had social power. Civilisation has become international, men's needs are satisfied by the co-operation of others at the far corners of the earth ; the whole international working class has become a slave class to those who control the means of wealth production, and who thereby control governments.

Industry, wealth production, can easily be shown to be the chief agent of social progress or retrogression. Wealth production to-day has become a power for evil by reason of its monopoly by a comparative few. Men are no longer able to remain in their native village, town, or country ; local, social, and family ties are torn asunder owing to the internationalism of wealth production. All that remains of territorial connections is government. We are governed through our territorial connections, which are a relic of the feudal system, when land was the chief means of wealth production. We as workers can only win our emancipation from political class government and economic slavery when we seize control of the forces of production and abolish political authority. The capitalist methods of producing wealth have robbed us of local or national ties ; we have been made "fatherlandless rascals." We have more direct and immediate concern with our fellow workers in the various industries throughout the world than we have with the members of the capitalist class in our immediate district. Industry is international, the working class is international, and thus we are perforce compelled to have an international class patriotism which we call International Solidarity.

The emancipation of the working class in any one of the highly developed capitalist countries, particularly Europe, is unthinkable without the acquiescence or active aid of all. And as the Syndicalist movement grows, and as the workers become conscious of how political government is used to maintain and extend economic subjection, they cease to regard themselves as citizens of a country, and think of themselves as world-citizens of the industry in which they work.

Machinery has so simplified and sub-divided the different trades, causing crafts to disappear, that the only real unit is now the industry in which many crafts and part crafts are assembled. Trade divisions have disappeared in proportion, as machinery has developed, and fresh divisions of labour have sprung up with new industries.

The industrial division is the best for cohesion that can now be selected from a fighting or reconstructive view.

However, we base our conception of future society upon industry, because, in all societies and at all times, the methods of producing and distributing wealth have been the chief factor in determining the social and political organisation of society. Lewis Morgan, Thorold Rogers, and Paul Lafargue, all bear eloquent testimony to that fact.

We aim at establishing a society of free producers in a free community, and the abolition of territorial—that is, political government—in the sense in which it is understood to-day. Given freedom to produce and obtain the material necessities of life, men would instinctively seek freedom in other spheres of life. The man who is not an economic slave is hardly likely to remain one in any other sense.

Bread is Freedom ; Freedom, Bread.

RESOLUTION.

"Whereas, we are informed by Swedish labour organisations that three of our fellow-workers, ALGOT ROSBERG, ANTON NILSSON and ALFRED STERN, condemned to penal servitude for life, are still being kept in prison and are there being brutally maltreated ; and

"Whereas, we know that the act for which our aforementioned fellow-workers are made to suffer was the direct outcome of the manner in which the ruling class of Sweden conducted the struggle against the workers in the summer of 1908, and

"Whereas, the importation of foreign strike-breakers during those struggles was a flagrant provocation, apt to draw with it just such acts of reprisals as the one for which Rosberg, Nilsson, and Stern were condemned ; and

"Whereas these three fellow-workers, who are no criminals, but self-sacrificing martyrs to the cause of humanity, are now in prison for the fifth year ;

"Therefore, we the workers of ...., in meeting assembled to the number of ...., utterly condemn and protest against the further incarceration of these three men as a brutal act of class-vengeance, unworthy of a civilised people, and as an injustice and a standing insult to the workers of all countries ; and be it therefore

"Resolved, that we demand of you, as the King of Sweden, that Algot Rosberg, Anton Nilsson, and Alfred Stern be immediately released from prison ; and be it further

"Resolved, that we shall from this day on boycott all Swedish goods as well as all vessels carrying goods from and to Sweden and that we shall continue such boycott to the utmost of our power until the day we are informed by the same organised workers of Sweden that Rosberg, Nilsson, and Stern have been liberated."

....191..

THE CONGRESS OF THE AMERICAN FEDERATION OF LABOUR.

The most important fact of the Congress of the A.F. of L. that was held at Rochester, was the force of the growing activity of the Socialist minority. At the Congress of last year the Socialists did not receive more than 2,800 votes out of the total of 18,000. Gompers had made so many lively attacks that, after harmony had been secured, he made a formal declaration that he did not wish to dominate the Congress. This year all was changed. The Socialists were the aggressors, and they led a vigorous fight against Gompers. They put up a candidate against him, and presented a list of candidates for the committee against that of Gompers. Max Hayes, the Socialist candidate for Presidency, received 5,074, Gompers 10,974. And this time the Socialists declared plainly their object was to capture control of the Federation. If their increase of force follows itself at the same rate we can foresee them having a majority at the next Congress. But they are more numerous than the voting figures would indicate. First, because in all the unions now there are minorities of Socialists who are not represented at the Congress; second, because the system of representation favours the small Unions to the detriment of the large ones, and it is in the latter that the Socialists are most numerous.

Gompers and the Socialists.

Gompers himself is convinced of this, as is shown by the following incident. He told a few that when he saw the Socialists on the point of removing him, he would make a profession of Socialist faith, and by this means remain at the head of the Federation. Also, he eagerly seized the first opportunity to make the following statement.

I do not want to repeat to you that my opinions rest on principles. When the fundamental base of this organisation is changed you will find me the same. I shall not change. The opinions that I have now shall always be my opinions. If the time arrives for an essential modification of one method, I quit forthwith my position as President, but I shall always remain a member of my Union. I may become a modest member lost in the mass, but I shall never renounce my ideas.

During the Congress the Socialists did not leave a minute of respite to Gompers. They harassed him, and he has been so little used to such treatment, that he fell ill at the end of the Congress.

Syndicalism and Political Action.

The question of Industrial Unionism raised a great discussion. The Socialists submitted and developed the following proposition :

That, wherever practical, one organisation should have jurisdiction over an industry, and where, in the judgment of the men actually involved, it is not practical, then the committee recommends that they organise and federate in a department and work together in such a manner as to protect, as far as possible, the interests of all connecting branches.

This was defeated by 10,934 votes against 5,929 (the usual figure), and the Congress adopted a resolution approving of the existing state of affairs. Political Action also raised a lively debate. The Congress was divided into three groups upon this point.

1. The partisans of the tactics that consist of voting, outside all considerations of party, for the candidates that declare themselves most favourable to the Unionists.

2. The Socialists who considered the Socialist Party as being the political expression of the working class.

3. Those who consider that it would be profitable to create a Labour Party similar to that which exists in England.

The views of the first group prevailed, and the A.F. of L. continues to be politically neutral.

The A.F. of L. and the Unskilled.

Alarmed by the progress of " The Industrial Workers of the World " amongst the textile workers during the last few years, the leaders of the A.F. of L. have decided on a great effort to bring in the unskilled and non-qualified that the I.W.W. has successfully organised. A propaganda was made along these lines in the metal workers, the sawmills, and the slaughter-houses, of which the number is many millions.

A Socialist resolution aiming at making the election to the committee of the Federation by referendum was lost. The committee continues to be elected by the Congress. For the first time in the history of the A.F. of L. it was a Socialist who was nominated to represent the Federation at the English Trade Union Congress.

The number of members of the A.F. of L. is actually 1,770,145, an increase of only 8,210 on the figures of last year. Having given the state of spirit of the American workers, who feel more than ever the want of an active organisation, we must say that so small an increase is synonymous with stagnation.

The Tactics of the I.W.W.

The capture of the A.F. of L. by the Socialists, that appears to me next as inevitable, is an event of capital importance. The measure in which it can be used for profiting the workers' movement —and its present state is lamentable— depends, to a great extent, upon the attitude of the Syndicalists and those of the Socialists who, without being exactly Syndicalists, are very favourable to our method, and very sympathetic to our movement. Actually both of them are resolutely hostile to the A.F. of L., and abstain from participating in its work.

This policy is due above all to the existence of the I.W.W. The I.W.W. is organised on the conviction that the A.F. of L. cannot become revolutionary, and that it is necessary to build, outside of it, an entirely new organisation. Those of their members who are members at the same time of Unions affiliated to the A.F. of L.—many are in this case—consider these Unions as interloping organisations. All those who desire to see this disappear and leave the place free to the I.W.W. This attitude has annihilated their action in the A.F. of L. to such a point that, though they form a strong minority, they had not a single delegate at the Congress to explain and defend the principles of Syndicalism and speak of the General Strike, though the Socialists have been numerous.

On the question of political action, we have said with much reason that there was a thing on which they were all agreed : that it is alone political action that can save the workers' movement, and on that there was no divergence, except as to the form that action should take.

The irony of the situation is that the Socialists profit by the sentiments created by the Syndicalists, notably that of working-class solidarity and organisation by industries.

But if we put on one side the attitude of the Syndicalists towards the A. F. of L., we can easily conceive that the Socialists, when they have the majority, may transform the A.F. of L., thus rendering impossible of realisation the plan of the I.W.W. We may conjecture that they will destroy the power of the " Civic Federation," and that of the Catholic Church, substituting the idea of class for that of trade, abolishing high entrance fees in the Unions that are prohibitive; and seeking to organise the unskilled workers.

But a danger results from the tactics of the I.W.W. It is quite likely that the Socialists, once a majority in the A.F. of L., may turn their attention to the I.W.W., and attempt to capture that also, if they estimated that it is worth the trouble. As now, there is a strong minority—if not a majority—in the I.W.W. that have confidence in political action, and, as this element grows in the same proportion as the I.W.W., has given the lead in the intellectual development of the American workers—it will not be difficult. With the A.F. of L. and the I.W.W. in the hands of the Socialists, the Syndicalists would be obliged to keep quiet in the I.W.W., or leave again to form another organisation. But it is improbable that the last alternative is likely to be realised, for at this moment, amongst many of the Syndicalists, the sentiment is strong and growing ceaselessly that tactics followed by the I.W.W. are bad, and that endeavours should be made inside the A.F. of L.; that it is in the existing Unions that the Syndicalists must struggle without ceasing to accomplish the triumph of their methods. In fact, independent of the I.W.W. many propaganda leagues exist now throughout the land, and they propose to demonstrate the advantages of this method.

Amongst the I.W.W. members themselves are many symptoms of the gradual abandonment of the pretension of taking to themselves a sort of monopoly of the Labour movement, the old hostility of the A.F. of L. becomes fainter, and the demand each day more strong that the partisans of Direct Action should make their influence felt in the A.F. of L., and should struggle inside the existing organisations.

After all, the Socialists have proved that something may be done in the A.F. of L., and so there falls the greatest objection of the I.W.W., who pretended that nothing could be done.

As we see it, the situation is very complex, and we cannot make hypotheses on the ultimate development of the Labour movement. The next few years are years that will be marked in our history.

W. Z. FOSTER.

DOWN WITH THE SCABS!

OUR HEROES MUST BE SET FREE.

A STIRRING MANIFESTO FROM SWEDEN.

IT'S UP TO US, NOW!

A LETTER TO TOM MANN.

The following letter from Gustav Sjöström to Tom Mann speaks for itself :

" Kaptensgatan 25 Malmö, Sweden,
" March, 1913.

DEAR COMRADE,—

" Referring to the enclosed manifesto, directed to the workers of the world and which is to be spread broadcast all over the world, we take the liberty to particularly address ourselves to the English workers, and especially to the English transport workers.

" For that purpose we turn to you, Comrade Tom Mann, knowing that we can place the matter in no better hands.

" That we thus make a special appeal to the English workers does not in any manner imply that we wish to throw any responsibility upon the English working-class for the mass export of strike-breakers from England. We know full well that the blame is to be put on the capitalist system in which we live.

" But we have reason to believe that the workers of England shall be very willing to assist us in righting the wrong done by the Swedish and the English capitalist class in common. And the friendly co-operation of the English workers, and especially of the transport workers would be of the utmost importance to the world boycott of Swedish trade and commerce that we are compelled to resort to, due to the maritime and commercial importance of England. It may also be valuable as an object-lesson to would-be strike-breakers in the future.

" We trust that you, Comrade Mann, will cause our appeal to get the greatest possible publicity in the English-speaking world, and that you will see that it is brought before the greatest possible number of trade unions and other working-class organisations.

" We may add that we see in the proposed case of international action not only the possibility of obtaining the assistance needed on this occasion, but also a much-to-be-desired training in industrial solidarity in general.

" With kindest regards and fraternal greetings, we remain,

" Yours for International Solidarity and Action,

" G. SJOSTROM,
" For Sveriges Arbetares Central-organisation Solidaritet-Frihet.
" Mr. Tom Mann."

The manifesto mentioned in the above letter is here printed in full :

DO IT NOW!

What shall we do then? It will be an eternal disgrace to the British working-class if the three young stalwarts referred to above are allowed to languish many weeks longer in a capitalist prison. The conferences at Holborn and Manchester in November endorsed Direct Action as a means to Freedom. Here is a splendid opportunity for using the boycott to some purpose. Words never liberated anything yet. It is Action, and Action alone, that counts.

The accompanying resolution will be of no value if it remains a resolution. This is the destiny of most resolutions that are passed at our Little Bethels, where the faithful do congregate and do nothing else. Let us send our ultimatum to the King of Sweden by all means. The cumulative effect will mean a little. But the boycott of Swedish goods and Swedish ships is the thing. Remember that our Swedish comrades, as they themselves say, are willing to sacrifice themselves in this matter. Let us also do our part.

The working-class knows no barriers of nationality and race. What touches any worker touches the whole of the working-class. Perhaps it will be your turn next. We won the fight for Knox; we won the fight for Richardson. By solidarity and the boycott we can liberate Algot Rosberg, Anton Nilsson, and Alfred Stern. " If 'twere done when 'tis done, then 'twere well 'twere done quickly ! " Go to your Trade Union ! Get the resolution put ! And act !

The resolution referred to above will be found on page 2.

A CALL FOR INTERNATIONAL ACTION.

" Comrades and Fellow-workers !—

" We the workers of Sweden stand in dire need of the assistance of the workers of the whole world.

" It is not money we are asking for, but in the name of International Solidarity, we most urgently call upon the workers of every country to assist us in action.

" *We want you to help us open the prison doors for three of our comrades, Algot Rosberg, Anton Nilsson, and Alfred Stern.*

" These three fellow-workers, all of them young men in their twenties, are in prison for life, and—pardon having been denied them—it is evident to us that it is the purpose of our ruling class to allow them to perish behind the bars.

" And what is their crime?

" Let us tell it to you briefly.

" The summer of 1908 was a very turbulent period for the Swedish labour movement. Struggles were going on in various industries, the workers trying to wrest from their exploiters better conditions, and the latter trying by all means to down these efforts.

" Especially bitter was the struggle of the Longshoreman's unions. The men fought bravely and with splendid solidarity. The prospects of victory were great.

" But the Swedish employers, who always prate about their great love for our flag and our country, went into conspiracy with the International Shipping Federation, asking for help to crush the Swedish transportation workers.

" The International Shipping Federation hurried to the assistance of their Swedish fellow parasites by supplying them with English strike-breakers from their international corps of strike-breakers.

" About 1,200 of these wretches from the waterfronts of English cities were distributed in some of the principal ports of Sweden, among them the city of Malmö.

" Under the protection of police and military these vile strike-breakers took the bread out of the mouths of starving Swedish proletarians and their families, who were treated with the utmost brutality.

" The tension was at its pitch.

" Then on the night of the 12th of July, a bomb was exploded in the port of Malmö, in the vessel Amalthea, on board of which a number of English strike-breakers were being fed and housed.

" One of them was instantly killed, and seven others were more or less severely wounded.

" The bomb was not thrown in order to kill, but to scare. In fact, the English strike-breakers immediately demanded instantly to be taken out of the country.

" Our fellow-worker, Anton Nilsson, was the man who placed and lit the bomb, Algot Rosberg and Alfred Stern were his assistants.

" Anton Nilsson and Rosberg were condemned to death, but this sentence was commuted to penal servitude for life, a punishment which was also meted out to Stern.

" This happened in 1908.

" Nearly five years have consequently passed, and our comrades are still in prison !

" Three of the finest, noblest, and truest men the Swedish working-class movement has produced are thus suffering for an act sprung from the class-war, for a deed which was not committed for selfish purposes or with a view to private gain, but in a spirit of self sacrifice and class solidarity.

" What they undertook they did for the sake of their suffering fellow-men, and their deed was not of local significance only. It was an act that concerns the working-class of the whole world, in so far as our class rebels against slavery and oppression, and fights for economic emancipation.

" For this act our brave comrades are now being brutally beaten and maltreated in prison by the vindictive tools of our masters, and the prospects are that such treatment will continue until their hairs are grey or their bodies rest in the grave.

" Shall we allow this to continue?

" No, not if International Solidarity is anything but a mere phrase.

" We have started a powerful agitation for amnesty and for the liberation of these our comrades. We also intend, as far as our power goes, to apply the pressure of Direct Action.

" Still, we foresee that alone we shall not be able to open the prison doors for our beloved comrades. We the Swedish workers are not strongly enough organised on the economic field to be able to dictate to our masters. And it will be many years before we shall have succeeded in enlightening and organising our class for common action.

" But with International aid we can force the prison doors open.

Will you help us?

" What we ask of you requires no expense, no strenuous effort on your part. All we ask of you is that you immediately

Boycott all Swedish goods,

of whatever kind they may be, and that you

Boycott and " blockade " all vessels carrying goods from and to Sweden,

and that you do this so conscientiously and effectively as to completely strangle Swedish foreign trade and keep it dead until Rosberg, Nilsson, and Stern are again free men.

" This will be a staggering blow to our ruling class, and is sure to bring them on their knees, especially as we shall at the same time, by every conceivable means in our power, conduct the fight within our own borders.

" Naturally we understand that such a boycott is going to react most severely upon ourselves, but we stand ready to take those consequences.

" It is better to suffer unto death than to live with the shame of leaving our comrades to rot in prison.

" We also know that we speak for the majority of the Swedish working-class in asking you for this favour, in spite of all the protests and countermands that may come from self-seeking political leaders.

" Therefore, fellow-workers of the whole world, whenever you come across Swedish goods, do not buy them or handle them in any manner, be it discharging, loading, or transporting !

" Whenever you see the blue flag with the yellow cross steer clear of it ! It is the emblem of the Swedish master class. It stands for oppression, poverty, and misery for our class.

" The Swedish workers have no country, and recognise only two nations : the capitalist class and the working-class.

" Our flag is red—red as the sound blood that runs through the heart of every true working-man and working-woman on the face of the earth.

" Comrades and fellow-workers of the whole world !

" Heed our appeal !

" Remember our fellow-workers who are in prison for your cause and for ours !

" Help us to set them free !

BOYCOTT !   BOYCOTT !   BOYCOTT !

Central Organisation of Swedish workers,

pr " Gustav Sjöström, Otto Andersson."

The 'Amalgamation News' Page.

Notice.

All information respecting amalgamation news and Trade Union Activity, intended for publication on this page, must be sent to J. V. Wills, Secretary Amalgamation Committees' Federation, 10, Layard Road, Rotherhithe, London, S.E.

TO THE RANK AND FILE.

Prompted by the E.C., the General Union of the A.S.C. and J. have decided not to proceed with the question of Amalgamation as it would inflict injustice upon thousands of its members, and because it is impossible to carry out the scheme on account of the Trade Union Laws which protect the members' interests. In other words, the E.C. and General Council are the guardian angels watching over their flock, acting at the psychological moment and leading them from the danger zone.

In the same way that a non-unionist who believes in Unionism is waiting until everybody has a ticket, they are going to wait until a better scheme is formulated.

Why they have not seized the opportunities afforded them by attending the numerous conferences that have been held to make the scheme to their liking is not explained. One wonders why their objections which have cropped up at the ninth hour, and which " present insurmountable difficulties," were not brought before the conferences.

The chief objection is that the members residing in foreign countries will not be embraced in the scheme, and yet it was the A.S.C. and J. delegates who successfully moved that the date for the return of the voting papers should be extended until July 7, in order to allow time for the members residing abroad to ballot.

It proves that instead of this being a valid objection, it is a mean and plausible platitude.

It is now for the rank and file of the A.S.C. and J. to say whether they are going to submit to this domination from above. Surely there is sufficient intelligence and determination amongst the members to let those in office see that democracy shall prevail, and that they refuse to be treated like children who are unable to decide and control the welfare and future of the society!

There should be a warm time ahead for these autocrats. They should be taught to understand that the day has gone by when the unions can be run upon the ethics of a limited liability company and that their business is to carry out the instructions of the members instead of thwarting their desires and aspirations.

And so we hope the members will be aroused to their responsibility and take prompt and decisive action in demanding the right to vote upon probably what is the most important matter that has ever affected their organisation—a matter also that is vital to their emancipation

J. V. WILLS.

CREWE FOR AMALGAMATION.

On Thursday, February 6, a meeting of delegates from all branches of the Trades' Union movement was held in the Co-operative Lesser Hall, Crewe, under the auspices of the Trades Council. This meeting should have been addressed by J. V. Wills, of Rotherhithe, secretary of the Building Trades' Consolidation Committee, but, unfortunately, through a severe illness, he was unable to attend. We were able to secure the services of an able substitute in R. Coppock, organising delegate of the Operative Bricklayers' Society, Manchester. A good attendance of delegates heard Coppock do justice to his mission as he created a fine impression in their minds. After an hour's address and very little discussion the following resolution was carried unanimously :

Seeing the need for Amalgamation and Consolidation of Trades Unions, this joint meeting of the C.T.C. calls on all Branches of Trades Unions to pass a resolution asking their executive to do all in their power to bring about the closer unity of Societies.

On Saturday evening, February 8, a special general meeting of the Local Branch of the O.B.S. was addressed by Bro. Geo. Hicks, National Organiser of the Society, and a very enthusiastic evening was spent. Bro. Hicks on Amalgamation is a star artist.

H. HUSSEY.

BUILDING TRADE WORKERS FOR AMALGAMATION.

SUCCESSFUL DEMONSTRATION IN LIVERPOOL.

A large section of members of the building trades assembled at the Engineers' Hall, Mount Pleasant, Liverpool, on Sunday evening, February 9, to hear speeches on the necessity of amalgamation in the building trade.

Mr. Richardson (Painters) presided, and in opening the meeting remarked that it was their intention to consolidate the building industry into one standing Union, so that they would be enabled to meet the employer, who is already federated, on equal terms.

Mr. J. Hamilton (O.S.M.), in proposing the following resolution : " That this meeting of building trade workers, recognising the futility of sectional unionism to cope with the ever-increasing power of organised capitalism, pledges its heartiest support to the scheme for amalgamating all building trade workers into one industrial organisation," said that the Trades Unions of the building trade were the only Trade Union organisations which had something definite to lay before their members as the first step towards amalgamation on industrial union lines, and if they were successful they would be enabled to show other Unions in the same industries an example and lead them in the right direction for solidarity. As far as the scheme itself went, he thought it was a wise course in the inevitable industrial development. They were all workers whose interests were identical, and therefore it behoved them to give the scheme their support. Skilled labour was being supplanted by unskilled labour. Therefore they

Must Fight Unitedly

against the organised forces of capital.

Mr. F. Bower (O.S.M.), in seconding, stated that the nobility of labour was being more and more evidenced by events of recent date. Upon the workers rested the whole of society. What their forefathers were satisfied with was not sufficient for them. What they wanted to do was to bring all the workers on the one level ground. Even the hod-carrier must be brought on a level with the bricklayer and plasterer, to work with one common interest. If one section of the trade thought fit to look down upon another section then the fight was going to be a very laborious one. They must never despise a man because he had not had the opportunity of learning a trade. Labour at the present day was just wakening to her responsibility. He looked forward to the day when Liverpool would possess a Labour Hall of her own—(hear, hear)—and the same should apply to every large city in England.

Mr. G. Hicks (O.B.S., London), who delivered a rousing speech in support, said they wanted to amalgamate for the specific object of ending capitalism. Their object was not to make their Union a craft Union, but a class organisation. The working class must realise that they were all part and parcel of the industrial world, and all possessed one common grievance—the existence of the employer. " There never was a period," said Mr. Hicks, " when economic organisation was more necessary than to-day." They were undoubtedly the only important section of society, for they produced all the wealth, and therefore the interests of the employer and those of the workers were directly opposed to each other. Machinery was also entering into competition with skilled labour. At one time a man was master of his own house, possessed his own tools, and by that means produced the commodities of life for himself and his family ; but to-day, with the advent of machinery, that was impossible.

The Duty of the Trade Unions

now was to educate the worker into realising what his position was at the present time. That could be done very effectively on the industrial field, because all the economic questions of the day arose there, and could be dealt with more effectively. He had every faith in the strike, for he believed that that was the only weapon left to the workers. Intentions, at the present period of industrial unrest, were useless ; what they required was Direct Action. He believed that when the building industry was amalgamated they would succeed in bringing into the Union those who were still outside. In concluding, the speaker said that the small sectional strikes could be illustrated as being small clouds, which would eventually gather into one great mass and burst. This, he hoped, would correspond with the amalgamation of the building industry. (Applause.)

The resolution was passed unanimously.

A vote of condolence was passed with Jack Wills (Bermondsey), who should have been present, but was unable owing to a serious illness.

METAL, ENGINEERING, AND SHIP-BUILDING AMALGAMATION COMMITTEE.

The above Committee is still making headway. Our monthly meeting took place on February 8 at the Apple Tree and Mitre, and although there was not a big crowd much good work was done, those present manifesting great enthusiasm. The Secretary reported that lecturers had visited several T.U. branches and Trades Councils during the month, and requests for lecturers were still coming in. It was agreed to send a copy of our manifesto to all Engineering Branches, but before this can be done we must have some cash. Those who are doing the committee work have already dipped their hands down somewhat deeply, and I now appeal to all Engineers who see the need for amalgamation to assist us financially. The best way to do this is to get as many individual members as possible at a minimum sub. of 1d. per month.

There are 420,000 Trade Unionists in the Industry, and if ten per cent. of them paid 1d. per month we would have an income of £42 per week. And that is what I am after. We could then put a couple of organisers on the job. Then things would move. So see to it, you rebellious Engineers. Send to me for membership cards and be a collector in your branch and shop.

Negotiations are still proceeding between the Shipwrights and Boilermakers, and I hope ere long to report that they are amalgamated. There is also a revival of the agitation to link up the A.S.E. with the Boilermakers. We must specially propagate amongst the members of these unions. With these three linked up and called the Metal Workers' Union or the Metal and Engineering Workers' Union, with a membership of 250,000, we should have the nucleus for our Industrial Union. I particularly want to hear from Comrades in Birmingham, Derby, Southampton, Newcastle, Sheerness, Liverpool, Glasgow, and Portsmouth. There are great possibilities of committees being formed in these towns.

Don't forget our monthly meetings, second Saturday in the month, 7.30 p.m., at Apple Tree and Mitre, Cursitor Street, Chancery Lane, W.C.

W. F. WATSON, A.S.E., Hon. Sec.
26, Priory Road, Acton Green, W.

TAXI-DRIVERS' STRIKE.

To keep the strikers up to fighting pitch nightly meetings are being held in the various districts, which are addressed by different speakers, much educational work being done thereby. On Wednesday, February 12, W. F. Watson, A.S.E., hon. sec. of the Metal, Engineering, and Ship-building Amalgamation Committee, visited the Hammersmith strikers at the Windsor Castle, King Street, and gave them a lecture on " Amalgamation." He pointed out that it is essential that working-class organisation must proceed along parallel lines with the organisation of industry ; therefore, we must eliminate sectionalism and amalgamate on the lines of One Industry, One Union, One Card. Brother Watson also dwelt upon the insidious legislation recently introduced by the employers for the specific purpose of destroying our power, such as the Osborne Judgment, (blackleg) Labour Exchanges, Conciliation and Arbitration Boards, Insurance Act, and now we appear to be threatened with Compulsory Arbitration.

The lecturer then dealt with the difficulties, showing how they could be overcome. Chiefly the difficulties were financial, demarcation, skilled and unskilled in same Union, officialism, and autonomy to avoid over-centralisation, which entails bureaucracy.

The address was received with great enthusiasm, several intelligent questions being asked. The general impression is that the taxi-men, like nearly all Trade Unionist rebels, have learned the lesson of Class Solidarity, and when this dispute is ended one may rest assured that efforts will be made to link the taxi-men with the transport workers.

Provisional Committee for Amalgamation of the Building Industries Trade Unions into One Industrial Organisation.

BALANCE—SHEET

From January 18th, 1912, to December 31st, 1912, inclusive.

BY INCOME.

	£	s.	d.
Balance in hand, January 18, 1912	0	13	0
January 21.—By collection at General Meeting in Bricklayers' Hall	0	15	9
February 11.—Willesden Branch General Union Carpenters and Joiners	0	3	0
February 13.—London "City" Branch Amalgamated Painters	0	10	0
February 13.—Plymouth Branch Operative Bricklayers' Society	0	2	6
March 29.—District Committee House and Ship Painters	1	1	0
March 29.—Bro. Hamilton Operative Stone Masons' Society	0	1	0
April 23.—Walthamstow Operative Bricklayers' Society	0	5	0
April 30.—London Lodges Committee Operative Stone Masons	0	10	0
May 12.—Lewisham Branch United Operative Plumbers	0	3	6
May 12.—Income through sale of Postcard Photos of Committee	0	2	1
June 15.—Willesden Branch General Union Carpenters and Joiners	0	5	0
June 15.—Camden Town Branch Nat. Asso. Operative Plasterers	0	5	0
July 3.—London No. 4 Branch House and Ship Painters	0	5	6
July 15.—Willesden Green Branch General Union Carpenters and Joiners	0	10	0
July 20.—King's Cross Branch Operative Bricklayers' Society	0	5	0
July 26.—Brother Jordon General Labourers, from sale of No. 4 Leaflet	0	1	1
July 26.—Battersea Branch United Operative Plumbers	0	3	1
July 27.—Operative Bricklayers' Society, per Mr. John Batchelor	2	7	10
July 29.—Result of collection at Bricklayers' Hall, July 28	1	3	0
July 29.—No. 8 Branch United Order General Labourers	0	3	1
July 29.—Kensal Rise Branch General Union Carpenters and Joiners	0	5	0
August 12.—Bro. H. J. Adams Operative Bricklayers' Society	0	2	6
August 16.—Croydon Trades and Labour Council	0	2	10
August 16.—Battersea Branch House and Ship Painters, per Bro. J. Rogers	0	6	1
August 16.—Bro. Jordon, through No. 4 Leaflets	0	1	1
August 21.—London and Provincial Federation of Painters, from collection at meeting held August 17	0	10	0
August 23.—Holloway Division Nat. Asso. Operative Plasterers	0	10	0
August 25.—Collection at Painters' Meeting held in Bricklayers' Hall	1	3	4
August 26.—Income through sale of Postcard Photos	0	3	0
August 26.—Income from Diagrams, per J Wills	0	3	0
September 8.—Collection at Painters' Meeting, Bricklayers' Hall (Protest Meeting)	0	15	7
September 30.—Battersea Branch United Plumbers' Asso. (through Branch Levy)	1	4	0
October 7.—London District House and Ship Painters, collection at meeting, September 29	1	16	0
October 17.—Tottenham Branch Operative Bricklayers' Society	0	5	0
October 17.—Brentford Branch Operative Bricklayers' Society	0	5	0
October 22.—Willesden Green Branch Gen. Union Carpenters and Joiners	0	5	0
October 25.—Eastern Branch Electrical Trades Union	0	2	6
November 11.—London District Committee House and Ship Painters	2	2	0
November 11.—Willesden Green Branch Gen. Union Carpenters and Joiners	0	10	0
November 28.—Members of the Bricklayers' Society resident in Gowerton, South Wales	0	2	6
November 29.—Income from Diagrams of Prev. Com. for A.E.T.U.	0	1	0
December 29.—Kensal Rise Branch Gen. Union Carpenters and Joiners	0	5	0
	£21	10	1

BY EXPENDITURE.

	£	s.	d.
February 26.—Balance to Printer	0	13	8
March 12.—Part cost printing Protest Resolution in conjunction with P.C.A.E.T.U.	0	4	2
March 12.—Duplicate Letter Book	0	1	6
March 12.—Printing Leaflet No. 3	2	0	0
March 12.—Glazed Cloth and Wood for Banner re Prov. Committee's Photos	0	3	9½
July 24.—Printing Leaflet No. 4	2	9	0
August 9.—Amalgamation Diagrams	0	3	2
August 9.—Special Postage No. 4 Leaflet, Plumbers, Gen. U. Carp. and Joiners, Nat. Asso. Op. Plasterers, A.S.C. and J., and Gen. Office O.S.M.	2	0	6
August 26.—One Gross Photos, p.c. size	0	8	0
August 21.—Printing Handbills Painters' Protest Meeting, Aug. 25	0	7	6
September 9.—Postage No. 4 Leaflet, House and Ship Painters	0	12	0
October 9.—500 Letter Headings Memo Paper	0	5	6
November 7.—*Daily Herald* Advert	0	5	2
November 9.—50 Amal. Diagrams	0	1	6
November 30.—Advert. *Daily Herald*	0	5	3
November 20.—General Union Carp. and Joiners' Circular and Postage	1	4	0½
Travelling expenses for the year	0	3	10
By Post and Stationery	3	4	1
	£14	12	

	£	s.	d.
Income	21	10	1
Expenditure	14	12	7
Balance	£6	17	6

On behalf of the Committee,
GEORGE HICKS, Hon. Sec.

Examined and found correct :
H. PARISH,
T. S. BARRETT.

SYNDICALIST ACTIVITIES.

Tycroes.—Friday evening, January 31, Comrade Guy Bowman gave an address on "Syndicalism," at the above place, before a well-attended meeting, composed of slaves—slaves of the lamp—miners. Comrade Bowman explained Syndicalism in a very concise and practical manner, and we felt, and do still now, that his explanations have caused men to think, and we feel sure that the visit of Bowman to this place has been an inspiration, not only to those inside the Socialist movement, but also to those who are on the brink of awakening to their duty. In capitalist society the workers are the lower class, the capitalists are the upper class—because they are on our backs, if they were not on our backs they could not be above us. The workers have always been the lower class. In the ancient world, workers were abject slaves; in the middle ages, serfs; in modern times, wage-workers; and to become free men in Socialism is our next step of bondage, but that will never come. Every country waited for some Moses to lead them out of bondage, but that will never come. Every worker must fight the battle for Freedom his own self, that is, to become class-conscious, because freedom is not a gift, it is a thing to be fought for, and the sooner the better.
G. JONES.

"Edco" (Edmonton) Co-operative Men's Guild.—A large and representative meeting was held at Warmington House, 744, High Road, Tottenham, on February 6, when Brother Guy Bowman attended to give an address on "Syndicalism." This was given in his usual explicit manner. He explained how society was to be built up on the pillars of Industry, each Industry to be self-contained, and without the interference of external organisations, ignorant of the needs and desires of the industry involved. He outlined the threefold purpose of Syndicalism—viz. (1) To fight the masters for higher wages, shorter hours, and better conditions generally; (2) to fight the Revolution at the barricades when it becomes necessary; (3) to train the workers to manage the Industrial System after the Revolution. He dealt with the ineffectiveness of sectional strikes. He described the idea of the consultant Federation to ascertain and arrange production according to the community's needs. He advised Trade Unions to watch the action of the capitalist class, and to counteract such actions. He further dealt with the distributive side of the question, and showed how local administration by Trades or Industrial Councils would take the place of the present municipal bodies. He concluded his address by a trenchant attack upon Militarism. A short discussion followed. Brother H. Brown (Hackney T. and L. Council) raised the question of choice of Industry. Brother Temple (S.P.G.B.) claimed that the Paris Commune was not a class conscious revolution. Brother W. H. Legg (Hackney T. and L.C.) dealt with the economic objections to Syndicalism. A representative of the B.S.P. claimed that, with 500 Socialists in parliament, the People would be ready for Socialism, and the Capitalist System would be changed into a Socialist System. Another speaker claimed that Syndicalism would result in the minority bossing the majority. Guy Bowman replied to the discussion, and an instructive evening ended with thanks to the speaker from the chairman.
H. GILBERT.

Bromley T. and L.C.—Comrade Guy Bowman paid his first visit to Bromley on February 5, when we received our first instalment of Syndicalism. Syndicalism to most of us was, but a name, but after the very lucid and powerful address, delivered in the orator's own dramatic style, we can very plainly see there is more in Syndicalism than meets the eye. The ideal of a society based on federated industries, with connecting links through Trades Councils, seemed very simple and practicable, but there is a vast amount of educational work to be performed before it can become an accomplished fact. The lecturer's remarks re sabotage caused great amusement, but the very definite motive underlying it all made one think seriously. It is a great programme, and we can understand it was impossible to tackle all the various difficulties in one lecture, so we are looking forward to our comrade's next visit in March. That the workers must work out their own salvation is a fact we must all realise, and no one can deny that Syndicalism is a straight path to it, although a thorny one at present. In the discussion that followed, the chairman remarked that to him there seemed to be a missing link in the chain. That missing link was the non-unionist. "How was he to be dealt with?" Personally I think that is a point which requires special study. The lecturer's reply was by education and propaganda.
J. DAVIES.

Walworth B.S.P.—There was a good muster at the Walworth B.S.P. rooms on Sunday, February 16, to hear Guy Bowman expound "Syndicalism." He dealt in his usual breezy and virile manner with the three steps toward emancipation, (a) solidarity, (b) sabotage, giving the workers courage for revolt, and (c) revolution and the barricades. The examples which he quoted of acts of sabotage in France were eagerly gripped. In the discussion which followed, it was interesting to note that only feeble attempts were made to support political propaganda. One of the opposers of Syndicalism was to try underpropping by laying stress on the industrial side of the B.S.P. propaganda. But the fallacy that the army, navy and police are controlled by the political vote was much in evidence. As Bowman showed, the workers cannot control either army or navy until they are the dominant class, i.e., until they are stronger industrially than their bosses. We workers always like to take the line of least resistance, even when it leads us nowhere.
H. C. PUGH.

Worthing.—An able and detailed exposition of the principles of Syndicalism was given by Guy Bowman at Worthing, on Monday evening, February 17. The meeting was held under the auspices of the local I.L.P. There was an excellent attendance, including not a few Trade Unionists. Bowman began by emphasising the futility of parliamentary action. The capitalists would never allow the workers to peaceably dispossess them of the instruments of production. If the Socialists were to secure a parliamentary majority to-morrow, and were to attempt to carry out their programme, the capitalists would at once put the armed forces of the government into operation against them. After working for more than a quarter of a century the Socialists had reached the limits of effective propaganda. It now remained for the conscious

Industrial Syndicalist Education League

FIRST ANNUAL GENERAL MEETING, held on February 1st, 1913.

CONSTITUTION AGREED UPON.

At the Communist Club, Charlotte Street, W., on Saturday, February 1st, was held the first annual general meeting of the Industrial Syndicalist Education League. W. Nefydd Roberts, of the Teachers' Union, presided over a representative gathering of enthusiastic members and delegates.

The General Secretary, Guy Bowman, gave his report, which was adopted after an interesting discussion.

The balance-sheet was adopted, and a hearty vote of thanks was given to the General Secretary for his work in connection with the League.

The most interesting item of all was the adoption of a definite constitution. This was necessary owing to the increase in membership, both in the provinces and in London. The League, at its inception, was practically an affair of a few friends, and no need for definite rules was felt. However, as Syndicalism is essentially a rank-and-file movement, the members took affairs into their own hands by adopting an Object, Preamble, and Rules.

Tom Mann was re-elected President and Guy Bowman General Secretary of the League. W. Nefydd Roberts was elected Assistant Secretary and H. Pugh, Treasurer.

An Executive Committee of twelve were to be elected. The London portion of the Executive Committee were Messrs. B. Rose, J. F. Tanner, D. Armstrong, J. Walters, C. P. Robertson, and F. J. Passmore.

It was decided that six of the provincial Groups should be asked to elect their own representatives on the E.C.

It was agreed that "The Syndicalist" be designated as the official organ of the League, and that the constitution and a report of the annual general meeting should be printed in the next issue.

A vote of thanks and appreciation to the late Assistant Secretary, E. J. B. Allen, who has left for New Zealand, was carried, with a recommendation to the workers there.

The meeting was closed about 10.30 p.m., the members present feeling satisfied that good progress had been made up to that time, and that with the League definitely organised a wide field for increased activity was before them. Full of enthusiasm, they departed to their homes in London and the large provincial towns determined to make Syndicalism more of a force than ever it has been in this country. Below is the preamble and constitution as amended:

PREAMBLE.

History is the record of class struggles. Dominant to-day is the capitalist class, which can maintain its supremacy only so long as the working-class consents to produce wealth and sacrifice its ownership and control.

Being destitute of property, the Workers, in order to live, are compelled to sell their working power to the capitalists, who only employ them when a surplus can be made from their services—that is, the Workers are paid less in wages than the value of the wealth they produce.

For many years politicians of all creeds have regarded the Trade Unions merely as a means whereby they may reach parliament and obtain state offices. The path of politics is a delusion, because economic power precedes all other, and the Social Revolution can only be brought about by Direct Action on the Industrial Field. Syndicalism insists that through the Direct Activity of their own Members, the Unions must first seek to improve their economic conditions; then prepare themselves for the work of expropriating the owning class, and manage the Industrial system themselves after they have taken possession of it.

The Workers in the past sought to protect their interests by the formation of craft Unions, but with the development of machinery craft divisions and distinctions have been altered and modified, and in many cases have disappeared. These developments necessitate a corresponding change in the methods of the Unions, so that it will no longer possible, as hitherto, for some sections of the Workers to help in the defeat of another section by remaining in work when that section is on strike. This change can be wrought by organising according to industry (and with other industries) in order that a united body of Workers can face the employers.

Syndicalism declares that to obtain and retain the unity of the Workers as a class, Solidarity and Direct Action are the means to be adopted. Direct Action means those efforts taken by the Workers themselves against the employers and their state, through their own Organisations, without the aid of intermediaries of any description.

In order to spread the above principles, it is necessary to unite in a Propagandist body, which is neither a party nor a Trade Union, but which will be composed of associated groups of Revolutionary Trade Unionists and others drawn together for the purpose of educating themselves and their Fellow-Workers in the principles of Syndicalism. Such a body should not be composed of theorists, for it must not take the Workers away from the work they have to perform in their own Unions; on the contrary, it asks them to study their own case, thus doing for themselves that which the politicians glibly promise they will do for them but cannot.

Name.

Syndicalist Education League.

Object.

To carry on among Trade Unionists and Workers generally a campaign of education in the principles of SYNDICALISM—which is Revolutionary Unionism, since its immediate purpose is to conduct a scientific CLASS WAR against capitalism, such war having for its object the CAPTURE OF THE INDUSTRIAL SYSTEM and its management by the Workers themselves for the benefit of the whole community.

Composition.

The League shall be composed of Groups and Trade Union bodies and Individual members.

Membership.

The membership is open to any person who accepts the Preamble, Object, and Constitution, no matter what views may be held by that person regarding politics; but NO PERSON WHO DOES NOT DECLARE FOR NON-PARLIAMENTARY ACTION, and is not a bonâ-fide Trade Unionist, may share in the responsible work of administration of the League.

No one who will not become active in one or more of the following categories is expected to join:

1.—INVESTIGATING MEMBERS.—Those who are in a position to obtain inside information in regard to particular industries.

2.—LITERARY MEMBERS.—Those who have the time and ability to analyse and collate the information sent in by the investigators and observers, and to embody the results of the work in special articles for the Press and in pamphlets.

3.—DISTRIBUTING MEMBERS.—Those who want to see Syndicalist literature bought and read by the Working Class, and are therefore willing to go and sell it both in their workshops and at public meetings.

4.—SPEAKING MEMBERS.—Those who have the time and talent for public speaking, and are willing to place before public assemblies and Labour Bodies the conclusions reached by the investigators and writers.

5.—SUPPORTING MEMBERS.—Those who from all walks of life may be willing to assist work by their personal influence or money contributions—or both.

Entrance Fee.

Every intending member must fill in an application form, and send same to the General Secretary with a minimum sum of 1s. as an entrance fee; this sum to cover copy of rules, membership card, &c.

Groups.

Any six members of the League residing in a locality may form a Group, whose duty it shall be:

1.—To form or assist Amalgamation Committees for each Industry where necessary.

2.—To visit Trade Union Branches and other Working-Class Societies.

3.—To hold indoor and outdoor meetings in order to reach non-Unionists and get them to join the Unions, and to reach those Trade Unionists who for some reason or other do not attend their Branch Meetings.

4.—To endeavour to get Syndicalists elected upon all Trade Union bodies other than political office.

5.—To hold public meetings in halls where Unionists of all Trades may be brought together.

6.—To sell and distribute Syndicalist Literature wherever possible.

Individual Members.

Any persons who do not reside in a locality where a Group exists, or who do not wish to take part in the collective work of a Group, may remain individual members, and subscribe directly to headquarters.

Subscriptions.

All members of Groups shall subscribe 1d. per week to the headquarters to be paid to the Group Secretary, who shall forward the same to the head office at least once per month.

Subscriptions for local purposes to be fixed by the Groups themselves.

Affiliated Trade Unions, Trade Councils, and other Working-Class Organisations to pay 2d. per member per year.

Individual members shall pay a minimum subscription of 3d. per week, to be sent direct to the General Secretary.

Any member whose subscriptions are thirteen weeks in arrears shall be struck off the books, unless a satisfactory explanation be given.

Officials.

A Provisional Executive Committee shall be elected consisting of twelve members, and a President, a General Secretary, an Assistant Secretary, and a Treasurer. (*For the first year the P.E.C. shall be elected by the members present at the first G.M., February 1, 1913.*) After the first General Meeting the Executive and all officers shall be nominated and elected by a ballot vote of the League, taken as follows:

Nominations to be received by the General Secretary at least two months prior to the Annual General Meeting from Groups and affiliated bodies only.

General Secretary to issue ballot papers so that Secretaries of all Groups and affiliated bodies and also individual members shall receive them at least four weeks before the A.G.M.

Groups and affiliated bodies must convene special meetings to take the ballot, and only those present shall vote. A statement of all votes cast must be sent to the General Secretary at least ten days before the Annual General Meeting, where the result shall be declared. Votes to be counted by the General Secretary and the Executive Committee.

Individual members to forward their votes by post to the General Secretary.

No member of the E.C. shall hold office for two years in succession. One year shall elapse before a member is again eligible for election. Retiring members shall be available for consultation.

Six members shall be elected from the London area and six from the Provinces. The London members shall meet fortnightly, thus forming a permanent sub-committee. There shall be a meeting of the whole of the E.C. at least once every three months, at which meeting all matters relative to the internal affairs of the Organisation and its general business shall be considered. The members of the E.C. shall receive notice of each meeting of the E.C. at least seven clear days before the holding of each meeting, matter for agenda to be sent four clear days before the meeting, and agenda to be in hands of E.C. two clear days before each meeting, and all amendments and suggestions sent by provincial members unable to attend shall be considered.

The duties of the E.C. shall be to supervise the general work of the Organisation, initiate and maintain Propaganda, circulate literature, hold Local, National, and International Conferences on Syndicalism and Syndicalist proposals and activities that are calculated to spread Syndicalist principles.

The E.C. shall send all League notices, manifestoes, resolutions, &c., that are for publication to the organ of the League, the SYNDICALIST.

The General Secretary shall record the transactions of all E.C. meetings, shall draw up agendas for same and send to all E.C. members at least two clear days before E.C. meeting, shall send reports of E.C. meetings to provincial members of E.C. and to all Secretaries of Groups.

Organisers may be appointed by the E.C. if the financial position warrants it. The duties of the organisers shall be to spread the Propaganda of Syndicalism, circulate the official organ of the League and such other Syndicalist literature that may have been approved by the E.C., to obtain members and organise Groups of the League.

All Organisers and all other officials shall at all times be under the control of the E.C.

Group Officials.

Each Group shall appoint a Secretary whose duty it shall be: To receive contributions from members;

To receive all correspondence from headquarters or elsewhere, and lay same before the members of the Group;

To send a report of the Group's activities to the official organ of the League at least once a month;

To carry out the instructions of the Group.

Each group shall appoint a Literature Secretary, whose duty it shall be:

To receive and distribute copies of the official organ and other Syndicalist literature for sale amongst members of the Group and the general public;

To attend Trade Union and other working-class meetings, private and public, and push the sale of Syndicalist literature;

To supervise the work of the distributing members of his Group.

Temporary Rules for Matters Not Provided for at Present.

The E.C. shall have power to make rules on any matter not provided for in this Constitution. Such rules, however, shall be subject to revision at the Annual General Meeting.

Referendum.

Any three Groups may demand a referendum of the whole Organisation on any matter concerning the conduct of the E.C. or any official of the League, which referendum shall be taken by the General Secretary, and the result of any such referendum shall have the same effect as a resolution carried by the Annual General Meeting.

Annual General Meeting.

The A.G.M. shall be the supreme governing body of the Federation, and shall consist of delegates from each Group and Trade Union Body in the proportion of two for any number of members up to twenty, and one for every additional ten or fraction thereof, provided they are in good standing financially. No Group, &c., shall, however, send more than six delegates.

The A.G.M. to be held every year on the first Saturday in February.

All matter for the agenda of the A.G.M. to be in the hands of the General Secretary at least six weeks before the holding of the A.G.M. Agenda to be in hands of Groups, &c., at least four weeks, and final agenda at least three weeks, before the A.G.M.

COMRADES,
Now that the League is properly constituted, and that the rank and file determine absolutely the conduct and progress of the organisation, it is up to the Group secretaries to get to work, to make new members, organise meetings, sell literature, etc., and so get the workers stirring

SYNDICALIST ACTIVITIES.

minority to bring about the revolution. Socialists thought that this could be done by parliamentary methods. Syndicalists, on the contrary, were convinced that it was not going to be brought about without bloodshed and violence. Socialists insisted that the basis of the new form of society should be a centralised state, whereas Syndicalists, being opposed to a state of any kind, industrial as well as political, advocated the formation of self-contained sections of society, corresponding to the fourteen or fifteen great productive industries which existed to-day. In each industry the workers themselves would decide under what conditions they would work. They would not own, but they would control the industry. The function of each industrial group would be to find out the requirements of society and to regulate their output accordingly. The work of distribution in the Syndicalist Society would be performed by the Trades Councils, which would entirely supersede the existing municipal councils. A rigorous denunciation of militarism concluded an admirable address.

Several questions were answered, and a quantity of literature was sold.
R. CUTHBERT.

SYNDICALISM v. SOCIALISM.

DAVE ARMSTRONG v. FRIEND WEAVER.

We had a lively evening at Walworth on Wednesday, February 19, when Friend Weaver took on Armstrong in debate. As soon as the seconds were out of the ring, and the referee ready, Weaver opened his attack. He emphasised the fact that Kautsky laid down the necessity of a political revolution, preceding the social revolution. He was not in favour of Freedom. He wanted democratic administration of things, and accused the Syndicalists of not having made themselves acquainted with the principles of Social Democracy.

Armstrong, in replying, made it clear straightway that Force was the mid-wife which would deliver the new society out of the old. Majorities, he said, had never made history: it was always minorities. The revolutionary minority would, by their acts, develop revolutionary tendencies in the majority. True economic freedom meant, not "bossing"—not even by Social Democrat M.P.'s. We have no time to waste on parliament. It was the worker, as an individual, who would have to do things for himself.

Weaver asseverated in replying that emancipation could not be accomplished other than by political action. He said that every class struggle, whilst in the first place being economic, eventually became a political one. History was a history of class struggles, and also a history of political struggles. Political action was an essential means to emancipation. It was possible by this means to alter the sum total of the value of food, &c., taken by the working class; it was also possible to influence education.

Armstrong pointed out that politics divided the working class. Social Democrats, if they had done nothing else, had divided the workers into four political sects—the I.L.P., B.S.P., S.P.G.B., and the S.L.P. Where did this lead to? From day to day, hour to hour, the workers, as their own Marx had shown, were exploited and sweated in their industries. It was here, and here alone, that they could emancipate themselves. The Social Democrats were not revolutionary. They wanted to retain government. Their path led to state-ownership, which he was up against.

It was a fair, if warm fight, and five others besides the principals took part.
OLIVE STRONG.

Catford.—The room was full at the meeting of the Catford Clarion Club on March 9 to listen to a lecture on "Social Democracy." Owing to indisposition Guy Bowman lectured for an hour and, but from the enthusiasm accorded to Nefydd Roberts this did not militate against the meeting. In a fighting speech lasting about an hour "Bobs" put the Syndicalist position so convincingly as to carry the audience entirely with him. He showed how parliamentarism had led the workers up a cul-de-sac. The sending of men to a middle-class environment so put them out of contact with the workers as to cause them not to represent the workers at all. He held up to ridicule the Socialists of the docketing type who regard mankind as so many units to be classified out of existence.

His constructive criticism was as strong as his destructive. The workers' great need was to unite in militant industrial organisations. Sabotage, the Irritation Strike, and all other means to unite the workers in intelligent organisation were shown to be indispensable. The moral objection to these methods was well shown by reference to Lafargue's "My Right to be Lazy." The case was so strongly put that although the chairman specially appealed for opposition, it was not forthcoming. This should promise well for the linking up of our Catford friends with the I.S.E.L.
RICHARDSON.

Morris Hall, Clapham, Sunday, March 16, 1913.—To an appreciative audience of from fifty to sixty Guy Bowman lectured for an hour and fifty minutes. He said that he did not come to put before them a way out—a remedy for social ills. He was there to show them how those that produced the wealth of the country should have the product of their labour. The structure upon which Syndicalism would be built was dealt with at length. At present the state for ever pressed down upon the workers. Syndicalism would be built up by means of the industrial organisation of the workers. The upwards of fourteen industries under which these workers can be organised would be the pillars upon which this would be accomplished. This could only be brought about by the workers organising under capitalism and preparing for the revolution which would come in blood. The futility of the present organisation with political aims was well presented. He did not come to solicit their votes. He was not putting up for parliament. Guy Bowman or Tom Mann did not matter. What did matter were the principles that they advocated. The Trades Councils, as they at present exist, instead of doing any real work were engaged in aiding parliamentary candidatures. Very amusing was his description of the way in which these councils passed futile resolutions. The questions mainly dealt with the working under the new conditions. The ever-recurrent questions of the "Miners for the Miners" type were much in evidence. The meeting finished up with a fine summing up after the discussion.
H. G. PUGH.

THE HAYWOOD CASE.

By a referendum vote of 23,406 to
11,673 Wm. D. Haywood has been recalled
from the national executive committee of
the Socialist Party. Haywood, in a recent
speech, is alleged to have violated the following infamous constitutional provision
adopted by the Socialist Party at its last
convention :

"Any member of the party who opposes political action or advocates crime,
sabotage, or other methods of violence
as a weapon of the working-class in its
emancipation shall be expelled from membership in the party."

The recall of Haywood is the latest incident in the year's long quarrel between
the radical and conservative wings of the
S.P. So bitter has this quarrel become
that in all probability the recall was
effected for the deliberate purpose of
splitting the party and thus forcing the
radicals out of it. The plan will probably
succeed, hundreds of the radicals already
being so disgusted with the party that
they are avowedly remaining in it for the
sole purpose of disrupting it.

The fundamental question at issue is
political action versus Direct Action. To
this has been added another burning one
—the A.F. of L. versus the I.W.W.,
which has served to considerably intensify the quarrel. The conservatives advocate a maximum of political action and
a minimum of Direct Action. They endorse the conservative A.F. of L. The
radicals have a contempt for political reforms and put strong emphasis on Direct
Action. They endorse the revolutionary
I.W.W. Between these factions constant
war rages in the S.P. The radicals have
long tried to get the party to give up its
opportunism and to endorse industrial
unionism and the I.W.W., but to no
avail. The more numerous conservatives
continue to hold the party on a basis of
political reform and "neutrality" towards
all labour unions. Meanwhile they never
let slip an opportunity to help the A.F. of
L. or to knife the I.W.W. Hence the
quarrel that has reached such proportions
that astute Socialist politicians consider
the destruction of the party can be avoided
only by forcing the radicals out of it en
masse.

For "mud-slinging" the campaign
against Haywood has hardly ever been
equalled in the history of the United
States, even by capitalist politicians.
Practically all the big Socialist papers
turned their guns upon Haywood and un-
mercifully bombarded him with all kinds
of lies, accusations, misrepresentations,
&c., in a wholesale attempt to blacken his
character. One Socialist, Adolph Germer,
a prominent official of the United Mine
Workers, even accused Haywood of
having stolen funds from the Western
Federation of Miners when he was an
officer of that union. Haywood—probably through a growing contempt for
political action and the S.P.—made absolutely no defence whatever to the original
charges against him. Though repeatedly
asked to do so, he also refused to make
any statement whatever regarding his
attitude towards political action But
Germer's charges roused nim, and he has
challenged the officers of the Western
Federation of Miners (who are very probably the real instigators of the charges)
to bring the union's books before an impartial investigating committee for inspection. Just what will be the outcome of
the Haywood case is at this time difficult
to state. It is safe to state, however, that
the S.P. is facing one of the greatest
crises in its career.

WM. Z. FOSTER.

BOOK REVIEWS.

"Syndicalism and the Co-operative
Commonwealth (How we shall bring
about the Revolution)," by Emile Paland
and Emile Pouget ; translated by Charlotte and Frederic Charles (the New International Publishing Co., Oxford, England) ; cloth, 3s. 6d. net ; paper, 2s. 6d.
net.

This book by two men whose words will
have weight we have read with great
pleasure. Their way of presenting the
ideas, while not original, is greatly refreshing. It is pleasing to be transported
to the new conditions for awhile, to see
the work done, and our ideals accomplished. They not only theorise, however ; they show us the shocks that must
be met before this consummation. To
be prepared is half the battle.

MINING NOTES.

By " SYNDIC."

A Reaction.

The Minimum Wage strike has led to
a temporary reaction in South Wales.
The high hope, justly entertained, has
been disappointed. In the very hour of
victory the men saw the fruits given
away. Leaders almost unanimously advised the men to vote for a resumption of
work. In spite of advice from the militants the "rank and file" blindly followed
this advice. No one was more astounded
than the South Wales collier, when he
found England and Scotland voting
against a resumption of work. After
that vote was known, the men felt they
had been betrayed. Led to believe that
England and Scotland would vote almost
unanimously for resumption, Taffy found
himself in the position of a blackleg !
And then began the interminable sittings
of the Wages Board. After weary weeks
of waiting and arguing the men found
themselves completely dished. True, we
have an "award" under which men can
claim the minimum. But whoever does
so finds himself marked out for victimisation. Many men faced with this situation,
and full of bitter reflections on the result
of the strike, fell into the depths of despair.
Non-unionism increased to such an extent
that in some collieries more than half the
men were out of union. The employers
took full advantage of this. Speeding-up
and a hundred and one methods of pilfer-
ing wages were instituted. Harassed on
every hand, the men were faced with a
new difficulty. The Insurance Act made
some revision of that old evil, the
doctors' question, imperative. The
S.W.M.F. Executive suggested a scheme
which simply meant a further endowment of the doctors. It was that every
workman should submit to a reduction of
2d. in the pound from his wages. The
single men, already covered by a capita-
tion grant under the Insurance Act, were
to pay this and get for it—nothing. They
rebelled, and since they constitute fifty
per cent. of the men employed, there has
been a considerable rumpus.

A New Move.

All these factors have helped to retard
action here. With most of these difficulties solved, or on the way to solution,
we are now at liberty to deal with non-
unionism. The leaders believe in bludgeoning the men into line by force. We
have started a move to show the men
that if compulsion is used to form them
into a union, then they on their part must
insist that the Union is *worth* joining.
The various reforms which are needed to
effect this have been codified into a programme by the newly-formed *Trade
Union Reform League*, as it is provisionally named. A manifesto issued to Trade
Unionists in South Wales has been published under its auspices. This deals
with the reforms which are necessary to
make Trade Unions the effective fighting
weapons of the Working Class. We
hope to enlist in this body every militant
Unionist in South Wales. By mutual
help and counsel we hope to influence
profoundly the outlook of every Trade
Unionist. A Conference held at Swansea
on Easter Monday was open to representatives of any Trade Union in the Princi-
pality. Thus we are not catering for
miners alone, but aim at doing for South
Wales what the I.S.E.L. is doing for the
rest of Great Britain.

A propaganda will be conducted during
the coming summer, which will make the
Fat Man and the Labour Leader sit up.
Their unholy alliance will be duly and
thoroughly exposed. The necessary
administrative and organisational reforms
to enable the men themselves to control
their Unions will be put forward and debated at hundreds of meetings. A net-
work of branches will be established
throughout South Wales. These will be
composed of men who mean business and
are not afraid of work. Mainwaring,
Plebs Club, Tonypandy, will give any
information required. Also copies of the
manifesto can be obtained from him. All
interested please apply at once.

Anti-Militarism must also have its department. We may neglect this side, but
we find it does not neglect us. The
National Reserve, composed of ex-Service
men, is being pushed to the front. At one
colliery in the Rhondda over two hundred
men have been roped in. Officials interview the workmen, and if a man will not
"volunteer" to join they hint that his
job is not very secure. In reply to the
men's questions, they are told that they
will *not* be used during strikes. Quite
so ! at any rate not here ! They would
not be *reliable* enough ! But up in Scotland or London, who knows? When we
remember the soldiers stoking during the
railway strike in Ireland, we see they
might have quite other uses. Has the
government started to recruit a blackleg force, which will be used to break
strikes in the interest of Law and Order?
This movement is full of sinister possibilities, and needs to be watched and counter-
mined. Let us get to the work, Comrades
all !

The Syndicalist
and Amalgamation News

Edited under the :: auspices of the :: :: Industrial Syndicalist Education League. ::

President
TOM MANN

Secretary
GUY BOWMAN

VOL. II. NO. 5.   LONDON, DECEMBER, 1913.   MONTHLY, ONE PENNY.

AN ATTACK ON OUR-SELVES.

On the 26th September, 1912, in the *Labour Leader*, Mr. A. Fenner Brockway, answering arguments which Mr. Philip Snowden had not then spoken and attacking actions which Mr. Ramsay MacDonald (the friend of Mr. Asquith) had not then taken, said :

> Syndicalism has a message for the Socialist Movement. It emphasises the psychological value of the sense of battle. The mass of people will never become enthusiastic in response to a cold, reasoning appeal, nor will they give their energies with religious zeal to a cause which relies upon quiet and largely unobserved work in the House of Commons. We need a better understanding of psychology. We must strike the imagination of the people by raising bold issues and by not hesitating to take bold action. Above all, we must retain the fighting spirit.

In other words, a Labour Movement is an attempt to get people to live more complete lives, not, as you might frequently think, a preparation to enable them to pass some kind of academic examination. But I am not proposing to criticise those whom we disagree with, but to say something disagreeable to the readers of this paper, with whom I am in agreement. Why run another little paper? Can you really be so interesting that you will thereby catch a new public? Surely enough energy has already been wasted in the Labour Movement by well-intentioned but ill-informed, and often not sufficiently thorough, attempts at propaganda. It is no good running a paper which will not contain anything sufficiently striking to hold the attention of the indifferent.

We can't get on by praising one another's efforts in a little sect of mutual admirers. That would be quite contrary to the whole spirit of Syndicalism, which is trying to divest Socialism of all superfluous theory, and to drag people into efforts to free themselves by making them help in actions they never expected to participate in, rather than to argue them into accepting theories, which will not be of any great use to them. We are out not for an *ism* but for a rebellion.

Not that we can have action completely divorced from thought. There's some nonsense in an extreme "heart not head" attitude. The point is that if the future of a society of men and women is something that cannot be either prophesied in advance (as the Marxists keep prophesying it) nor planned out in advance by a few ingenious minds (as the Webbists keep planning it) but must arise from the force exerted by conflicting men and masses of men, then the great work is to set up the hope of an equal victory, where one class will not be free and experienced because another class is enslaved and tied to drudgery (even the change afforded by meal-times only exists on the pay-sheet and not in reality in the case of railway carmen and some shop assistants and of others who can be kept going continuously, so as to get more work out of them) :—I say the great work is to give people a hope for society as a whole, and such faith and passion as will set them in action, leaving them to think about the unforeseen detailed difficulties of the conflict, which, after all, is now only just beginning. People will think fast enough and better than they ever thought before when their passions are roused.

ARTHUR D. LEWIS.

AN OPEN LETTER TO THE W.S.P.U.

Mesdames,

As workers, like yourselves, in the honourable cause of revolt against slavery, we are moved to address to you the following well-intentioned words of warning and advice. Possibly you are aware, that there are few revolutionists left in this country who attach any importance to the vote, or to the system of so-called " representative " government, of which it is the professed symbol. The material objects of your agitation, therefore, do not recommend themselves to us as worthy of so much unselfish suffering and gallant sacrifice as yours.

Nevertheless, because of the high principles you have shown, and because of the daring disregard you have manifested for the sacred institution of property, we address to you the following message. Your organisation, we understand, is one of the richest in the world, and includes in its membership all classes of women from the plutocrat to the wage-slave. Yet, notwithstanding, you have failed to make any lasting impression or gain any permanent good-will among the millions of exploited women in this country, as you have failed to gain the vote by such acts of militancy as the burning of empty houses, the destruction of letter-boxes and their contents, and last, but not least, that single and really fine (but, we are afraid, unappreciated) sacrifice of Emily Wilding Davison.

We are going to tell you, mesdames of the Women's Social and Political Union, how you may get the vote, and at the same time how you may finally enlist on your behalf the sympathy and co-operation of the working men and women of this country, with whom and by whose help alone, we are convinced, will you achieve the ultimate freedom to which you and they aspire. We ask you to cease burning empty houses and destroying letters (those of the humble with those of the great), and suggest to you that more fitting objects of your militancy may be found in the hundreds and thousands of male (and female!) employers who live upon the sweated labour of members of your sex. We suggest that the finest propaganda you could ever do would be to make life a living hell to such exploiters, until they gave their employees a comparatively living wage.

The bodily prostitution of your sex on the streets of our cities is, we believe, one of the main planks in your propagandist platform. Has it never occurred to you to create a tumultuous public opinion on your side in the only fine and dramatic way possible—to go into the West-End, in a body thousands strong, and drive out with whips the thousands of men, procurer as well as plutocrat, whom you will find there nightly engaged in the bodily and mental ruin, not only of themselves, but of the unfortunates of your sex? It is in your power, we suggest, not only to administer a salutary lesson to these men, but also so to move popular indignation against this crime against the race as to force the Government to grant women the vote.

In conclusion, allow us to say that we shall be glad to see your sex get the vote, for the sooner you get it the sooner will you cast it away and return to militant methods in your struggle for freedom!

Yours sincerely,
THE SYNDICALIST.

OURSELVES AND THE REBELLION

The Syndicalist Congress has come and gone, and what with Jim Larkin, the Dublin strike, and Sir Edward Carson, the papers are full of the word Syndicalism. If we would believe our capitalist press, there is a very dangerous, anarchical, bomb-brandishing Syndicalist MOVEMENT in this country. It is time we realised and acknowledged that there is no Syndicalist movement at all. There is also no Socialist movement, and no Anarchist movement.

It might seem, then, that we are in a perilous condition ; that we are no nearer the revolution than before, for all our agitation and propaganda. But not so! We have said there is no Syndicalist or other social revolutionary movement, and it is time we admitted that movements, as movements, do not cut any ice. What heartens and encourages us in those moments of despair that come to us after reading the speech of some such statesman as Mr. J. H. Thomas, assistant secretary of the National Union of Railwaymen, is the fact of the growing revolt among the proletariat of this country against what we shall call Bossism (for lack of a better word), whether the Bossism of the Labour Fakir or of the capitalist.

We are going to say, here and now, that the revolution will not be the work of us or of any other " movement." It will be the work of the militant working-class, and the sooner we cease preaching to them and " leading " them, and get down from our platforms to work and kick with them inside their trade organisations, the sooner will they themselves bring to a head the rebellion which, even now, is manifesting itself in these islands.

THE NATIONALISATION SWINDLE.

The approach of the Nationalisation of Railways has had the somewhat ludicrous effect of making such shrewd observers as the learned young men of the " New Age " dance a frantic jig-step of mortification and alarm. They have even responded with an extremely well-written Open Letter to Railwaymen (which the " Daily Herald " has seen fit to reprint in its columns), warning the railwaymen that the intended nationalisation will postpone the possibility or practicability of Guild Socialism on the railways for some thirty years—the period in which the State proposes to buy out the present railway shareholder—and lapsing into some arrant nonsense about the increase in the National Debt, the interest on which, the " New Age " naively presumes, will be paid **DIRECTLY** out of the pockets of the railwaymen!

We are under no illusions as to the meaning of railway nationalisation. The sooner it comes, the sooner will the wage-slaves rid themselves of **THEIR** illusions concerning State Socialism and its tyranny. If the " New Age " really believes that the fact that the State bosses the railways is going to make a railway strike impossible, the " New Age " and its young men had better go and dig up a few live rail rebels—possibly they have not yet made their acquaintance!—and change their minds about it! From the railwayman's point of view, of course, we agree with the " New Age " that the State is going to be a thousand times harder employer than the railroad magnates of the present. At the same time, because its organisation and management are so much more cumbersome, and so much more machine-like, the State is going to make a bigger hash of things from both the public and the employees' point of view. And here is the loophole for the railwaymen, apart from the human certainty that if the rail bosses, with the State and the Armed Forces at their command, could not keep the men under, the State itself is not going to do it, militia or no militia!

WHY THE 'SYNDICALIST' REAPPEARS.

The SYNDICALIST is reappearing because it is needed. There is no other reason. No other reason could be strong enough to induce the Editor and his friends to shoulder the burden of a paper. The SYNDICALIST is needed for the shaping out amongst the working-class of a Syndicalist policy and philosophy. That is a thing that no other English paper is doing or has ever done, yet it is a thing that is essential to the progress of Syndicalism in Great Britain.

It is all very well for Lewis to say that we can never be interesting enough to create a new public. Probably we can't : but then we don't want to " hold the attention of the indifferent." The *Daily Herald* does that; other and lesser papers than the *Daily Herald* do that. But our business isn't to *make* rebels ; it is to influence those who already are rebels ; it is to form, within the larger mass of Syndicalist thought and feeling, a core of more highly developed, more matured, and definitely *Syndicalist* thought.

It is useless to say that this is not necessary. Guild Socialism, the revival of the Industrial Democracy of the Webbs, the sporadic appearances of the policy of the Socialist Labour Party, all give the lie to such a statement. Each of them is an effort to subdue, in the interests of State Socialism, that wave of feeling evoked by the earlier Syndicalist propaganda ; each is a " fake " movement trying to hustle the workers into the catacomb of a political society under the pretence of leading them to Industrial Freedom. In so far as they are sincere we wish them well ; but while they exist to deflect the current of real Syndicalism, the SYNDICALIST must exist to guide and shape the policy of the authentic, aggressive, practical Syndicalism of the working-class.

It is equally beside the mark to say that since Syndicalism is, above all, a real thing and not an idea, an impulse and not a system, therefore there is no need for the fashioning of a policy. This is simple muddle-headedness. Granted that the great work is to give men a hope for the future and an impulse of revolt for the present, does that minimise the need for a paper to transmute that hope and that impulse into definite schemes—plans for warfare and organisation? If the SYNDICALIST were not altogether in and of the Labour movement, there might be something in its criticism. But the SYNDICALIST is a working-class paper, and the appearance in its columns of a new idea or a new plan is the appearance of a new idea or a new plan amongst the working-class. As Lewis says, rightly enough, once they are stirred by passion people will think quickly enough and better than they ever thought before. But there must be some register of that better thinking ; there must be some well-built skeleton policy in existence before that better thinking can be effectively employed. " Spontaneous movements " and " creative crowds " are pretty phrases, but it is always a minority —a conscious minority—that does the business, and the concern of the SYNDICALIST is with that conscious minority. Let the *Herald* evoke the passion and the faith ; let us develop the judgment and the principles that shall direct that faith and passion. The creation of the impulse is essential, but so also is the creation of the means by which that impulse may be expressed.

But this can't be done so well by a monthly paper as it could by a weekly. Inevitably a monthly tends to become too academic; however well it may be edited it cannot reflect the conditions of the struggle vividly and swiftly enough. And Syndicalist policy is always a reflection of the conditions of the moment. So a weekly must come, and it is coming.

GUY BOWMAN.

The Syndicalist
and Amalgamation News.

EDITED UNDER THE AUSPICES OF

The Industrial Syndicalist Education League

Offices

4, MAUDE TERRACE, WALTHAMSTOW,
LONDON, E.

MONTHLY . ONE PENNY.

Post Paid Subscription—

Great Britain or Abroad .... 12 months 1s. 6d.

Bundle Rates—

1s. 6d. per qu're, Carriage Paid.

U.K.F. TERMS TO NEWSAGENTS.

The Receipt of a Sample Copy is an invitation to Subscribe.

DECEMBER, 1913.

JOHN TURNER ON THE DECLARATION OF PRINCIPLES.

Speaking at the meeting held on the evening of the last day of the International Syndicalist Conference, John Turner said that he could hardly express the delight he felt when he saw the declaration of principles that had been worked out by that Congress. Sometimes he had wondered whether the ideas of himself and those who agreed with him had made any progress; but no one reading that declaration could doubt they had. When he joined the Socialist movement thirty years ago it was the custom to celebrate the Paris Commune. He believed a working man or two had held office under the Paris Commune, and that fact used to be made the occasion of much talk as to the wonderful things that would happen if the working class came into power. He had never been able to follow the logic. He could never quite see how, by merely changing those who, through physical force, controlled more or less the social and economic destinies of any country, the economic and industrial conditions of the workers were to be simultaneously changed. He used to argue it out in a quiet way and get sat on. In those days it did not seem as if he could convince people. But events had gone on. During the thirty years we had seen at least one English colony where the working class had come into power, and where of course they had had to assume the responsibility which government always carried with it. He took this line of argument because the thing that marked the declaration and distinguished it from that of any other Socialist Congress was that it not only pilloried the capitalists but also the accompanying wrong and evil—namely, the state. (Applause.) If ever history remembered the Congress it would be because of that feature in the declaration of its principles. Turning then to Australia, the state he had referred to, they would see what was going to happen in older countries, where the opportunities for the workers were not yet so great because traditions and institutions kept the people back. When the Labour party came unexpectedly into power in the Commonwealth of Australia they were confronted with their own programme. An item in that programme was the nationalisation of the land without compensation. They went to the legal advisers of the Australian Government to know how it was possible to carry that out. Those advisers reported that if the Australian Government did nationalise the land without compensation it would not only have to fight the old country but France and Austria also, because big syndicates had been formed in those countries to hold Australian land. This had been done with the consent of previous Australian Governments, and the present Australian Government would be held responsible for the acts of its predecessors. At the next political Labour Conference in Australia that plank of their platform was quietly dropped and in its place appeared that lovely and euphonious political phrase, " Land Reform." (Laughter.) Then they would remember the railway strike in Australia, when the railway workers had the whole of the railways tied up. The railways of Australia were state owned, but the railway workers did not believe in being exploited even by the state. They struck, wicked men that

they were. What did the working-men Government of Australia do? Did they concede the reasonable demands of the railwaymen? Not a bit of it. Working men quickly acquire a middle-class soul when they get into power, and these working men with middle-class souls called a Cabinet meeting and did what any wealthy Australian Government would have done. They issued an order that if the railwaymen were not back at work in forty-eight hours they would forfeit their pension. The strike had been practically solid up to then, but within the forty-eight hours almost every man was back at his post, because the railwaymen knew that the Australian Government—working-men Government though it was —held them in the hollow of its hand and could punish every one of them by making him forfeit his pension. What did such things mean? They meant that the Australian Government, like the Government of any other country, new or old, was run by the money borrowed from the international capitalists, and the taxes of Australia went to pay the interest on that money. A working-men Government was just as much compelled to collect the money to pay this interest as any Liberal or Tory Government that might be. If those present appreciated these facts they would understand the logic which had made him and others. Anarchists. In the Trade Union movement they had taken up the Syndicalist position almost before the word itself was known; and those who knew him knew that he had worked in a quiet way in that movement, because it gave him an opportunity to express his ideas and opinions. He was sorry to say the rank and file of the Trade Unions were not with the Syndicalists. He was an official of a Trade Union—a position which he only wanted to hold so long as he could be of service to his fellows, and he knew that the members of the Trade Unions were not so advanced as many of the leaders of those bodies. If they were, the officials would change colour pretty quickly. Syndicalists had a great work of propaganda before them. For thirty years he and others had been striving in a quiet way, and they must not imagine that in three months, or three years, or even in thirty, they would see all they hoped to see. But they should not let that fact damp their enthusiasm. Let it determine them to be gritty and to go on. Their Congress had shown what a leap forward had been made by, at any rate a minority of the workers right throughout the world. (Applause.) It was minorities that always made for progress. Syndicalists should not imagine that the masses were with them, it was their work to bring them along; not only by talking, they must work hard. They must be willing to do the detail work of the Trade Unions, and they must show that theoretically they understood the position better than their fellows. If they did that, another thirty years might see the triumph of the principles enunciated that week. (Applause.)

First International Syndicalist Congress

HELD AT THE HOLBORN HALL, SEPTEMBER 27 to OCTOBER 2, 1913.

DECLARATION OF PRINCIPLES.

" That this Congress, recognising that the working class of every country suffers from capitalist slavery and State oppression, declares for the class struggle and international solidarity, and for the organisation of the workers into autonomous industrial Unions on a basis of free association.

" Strives for the immediate uplifting of the material and intellectual interests of the working class, and for the overthrow of the capitalist system and the State.

" Declares that the class struggle is a necessary result of private property in the means of production and distribution, and therefore declares for the socialisation of such property by constructing and developing our Trade Unions in such a way as to fit them for the administration of these means in the interest of the entire community.

" Recognises that, internationally, Trade Unions will only succeed when they cease to be divided by political and religious differences; declares that their fight is an economic fight, meaning thereby that they do not intend to reach their aim by trusting their cause to governing bodies or their members, but by using Direct Action, by the workers themselves relying on the strength of their economic organisations.

" And in consequence of these recognitions and declarations, the Congress appeals to the workers in all countries to organise in autonomous industrial Unions, and to unite themselves on the basis of international solidarity, in order finally to obtain their emancipation from capitalism and the State."

THE DECLARATION OF PRINCIPLES.

The above is the historic declaration of principles which was passed unanimously by the first International Syndicalist Congress. Previously there had been no international definition of Syndicalism. We had heard of Syndicalism in France, of Industrialism in America, and of the Industrial Democracy of Mr. and Mrs. Sidney Webb in England; exactly wherein these ideas agreed and wherein they differed was undefined. We hope those who have been asking what Syndicalism really means and stands for will now be satisfied.

HOW DID THE CONGRESS COME ABOUT?

The holding of the Congress was not the idea of an individual or a small group hastily carried into effect. It had been asked for by the Syndicalists of almost every country, resolutions to that effect being passed in more than one National Syndicalist Congress. But no one had ever taken the initiative and convened the Congress until the I.S.E.L. at the two conferences it held in November, 1912, at London and Manchester, passed the following resolutions:—

Whereas cases of international importance are getting every day more numerous, the work of the Trade Unionists of all countries should be co-ordinated, and an international policy decided upon;

Whereas war is the greatest calamity that could befall the international working-class movement, it is most urgent that common action should be decided upon by the workers of all countries;

This Conference calls upon the I.S.E.L. to convene an International Syndicalist Congress to be held in London as soon as possible.

At these conferences there were 254 delegates, appointed by 134 trade union branches and ten trade councils and representing altogether about 150,000 workers, and on the strength of these resolutions the I.S.E.L. went ahead with the preparations for the Congress. It sought first of all to get the support of those who were represented at the conferences referred to. It naturally thought that most of the societies there represented would support it by sending delegates; had they done so the small fee of ten shillings required with each delegate would have enabled it to cope with the expenses of calling the Congress. Unfortunately the anticipated support was not given. But he who risks nothing gains nothing; the invitations were sent out and the Congress was held. If the Congress has not

been the entire success we might have wished that fact is due to causes which are better not discussed here; had the I.S.E.L. stopped because of money considerations the Congress could not have been held at all. In any case, if the Congress had done nothing else than pass the Declaration of Principles printed above, that fact alone would have justified its convocation.

THE SYNDICALIST MOVEMENT.

Reports on the state of the Syndicalist movement in different countries were given by the delegates. Of these reports the best thought out and most interesting was that from Italy by Comrade De Ambris. It stated that the Syndicalist movement in Italy now comprises 103,000 workers. The German and Dutch reports were not only less interesting but less important; for the total number of Germans represented was only 9,500 and of Dutchmen 12,000. In the Belgian report we were told that in about a fortnight after the close of this Congress some revolutionary organisations there would be forming the Union Syndicaliste Belge.

THE INTERNATIONAL BUREAU.

There were on the agenda two distinct items, one demanding the establishment of an international bureau and the other the establishment of an international bulletin. A sub-committee amalgamated the two items and put them before the Congress as a single proposition. The establishment of a bureau was agreed to, and a great deal of discussion took place as to where it should be seated—in Paris or elsewhere. Naturally, most of the delegates wanted it established in la ville lumière, the centre of the intellectual life of Europe; but the Dutch and Germans favoured Holland. When the question came to be decided Alceste De Ambris, of Italy, pointed out that there were three methods whereby the vote might be taken: first, by the number of workers represented; second, by the number of delegates who voted; thirdly, by nationalities. De Ambris said that every one of these modes of voting had its advantages and its disadvantages; in this case he thought the best way would be by nationality. The Dutch and German delegates, however, who constituted one-third of the number of delegates present, although they did not represent more than 21,500 workers altogether, wanted the vote taken by

number of delegates voting, and this was done, whereas the Italians who had but three delegates represented 103,000.

ITEMS LEFT OVER.

Besides the matters it actually dealt with, the Congress was to have discussed, among other things, anti-militarism, the possibility of preventing international scabbing, emigration, the selection of an international language, and the religion and morals of the proletariat. To adequately deal with and dispose of so ambitious a programme would certainly have taxed the whole time and energies of the Congress. As it was, much more might have been done but for time-wasting squabbles which we hope may in future be avoided.

WAS THE CONGRESS A SUCCESS?

This question has been answered in the negative by almost everybody. For our part we repeat what we have said before, that it was justified by the declaration of principles which it evolved, while we regret exceedingly that, so much was left undiscussed on which an authoritative pronouncement of Syndicalist opinion would have been so important and valuable.

LA CRITIQUE EST FACILE MAIS L'ART EST DIFFICILE.

It is very easy for those who never do anything else to find fault with what has been achieved by other people. Many of the difficulties were due to this being a first Congress. Once a Congress is fairly established the task of organising it becomes far more easy. For one thing, its conveners have money at their disposal. Next, they have the addresses of everybody and are in communication with everybody. The conveners of this Congress were short of funds, and the addresses of most of the people with whom they wished to communicate were unknown to them. Matters like these explain any disappointment that may have been caused to some of our friends. Nevertheless, we can boast that something has been achieved that never was done before; and we have paved the way for further Congresses when, perhaps, some more intelligent, more capable, and more businesslike persons than ourselves will be able to bring about a magnificent success. At any rate, we hope so.

ANTICIPATIONS.

A writer in the *English Review* has called attention to the neglected fact that Joseph Mazzini, who, whatever one thinks of his political policies, principles, and actions, shines resplendent among modern celebrities as a man evincing sublime and unquestionable faith in the workers of all lands. For one who wrote fifty years ago, the following is a remarkable prediction of the present Syndicalist movement :

" The remedy for your present condition is the union of capital and labour in the same hands. When the entire fruit of labour shall be retained by Labour, the permanent causes of poverty will disappear from your midst. Your future lies in your emancipation from the exactions of capital, arbiter to-day of a production in which it has no actual share. You were *slaves* once, then *serfs*, then *wage-earners;* before long you shall be, if you will it, free producers and brothers in *Association—Associations* administered in a spirit of Republican brotherhood, by your own delegates, not subject to the despotism of the State and of a hierarchy arbitrarily constituted, and ignorant of your needs and aptitudes."

Comrade Rosmer, of *La Bataille Syndicaliste*, speaking on behalf of the C.G.T. of France at the I.S.E.L. Conference in London, spoke pertinently of Robert Owen. Indeed, it may be said that no one man so combined a theoretical and practical perception of the form of industrial organisation that would prove

stable, yield the greatest happiness to the workers, and quite supersede the system of vicious, soulless exploitation, as Robert Owen.

Saint Simon, who cannot possibly be omitted from a historic survey because of his passion for the rebuilding of the social life out of industry, managed to bring out all that was best in human endeavours. Comrade Rosmer opined that Syndicalism was only a Renaissance. He referred to the advocacy, in the early 'thirties, of the General Strike by the Grand National Consolidated Trades Union of Great Britain. It is a Renaissance, but it is a Renaissance which the thoroughly awakened and revolutionary nations of workers are finding to be the only possible next step to take. To us it is given to feel the spirit of it as we grip our tools and look around at our fellow-workers, our fellow-controllers of industry to be. In growing efficiency, in better and more agreeable comradeship, in greater patience, and in a fair reliance upon those we have chosen for office in our unions shall we enter upon the path of ultimate conquest.

Let us remember, too, that what Mazzini calls the terrible formula " Everyone for himself " is the direct fruit and policy of the capitalist, and must be replaced in our minds and hearts by the grand faith in each other and in our common work and purpose.

True, Mazzini had not freed himself from belief in popular state government as an auxiliary to industrial co-operation, but he was far before his time, and his eloquence rings true down to our day.

PROLETARIUS.

BE A MAN !

Young man : The lowest aim in your life is to be a good soldier. The " good soldier " never tries to distinguish right from wrong. He never thinks, never reasons; he only obeys. If he is ordered to fire on his fellow-citizens, on his friends, on his neighbours, he obeys without hesitation. If he is ordered to fire down a crowded street when the poor are clamouring for bread, he obeys and sees the grey hairs of age stained with red and the life tide gushing from the breast of woman, feels neither remorse nor sympathy. If he is ordered off as one of a firing squad to execute a hero or benefactor, he fires without hesitation, though he knows the bullet will pierce the noblest heart that ever beat in human breast.

A good soldier is a blind, heartless, soulless, murderous machine. He is not a man, he is not even a brute, for brutes only kill in self-defence. All that is human in him, all that is divine in him, all that constitutes a man, has been sworn away when he took the enlistment oath. His mind, his conscience, and his very soul are in the keeping of his officer.

No man can fall lower than a soldier— it is a depth beneath which we cannot go.

THE WEEKLY "SYNDICALIST."

Although through financial difficulties the monthly SYNDICALIST did not appear for six months, the following list of contributions towards the Weekly SYNDICALIST proves that the weekly is wanted, and that the time is not far off when it will be here :

	£	s.	d.
Previously acknowledged	82	9	2
David Coutts	0	17	6
Warrington B.S.P. (after a lecture delivered by Guy Bowman)	1	0	0
Lily Gair Wilkinson	12	0	0
Syndicalist Tailoring Co.	0	2	6
Frank Kendall	0	3	4
Joseph Dalby	5	0	0
Anna Lincoln	0	1	0
Sam Butterworth	1	0	0
Alice Dennis	0	5	0
J. R. Cripps	0	10	6
Huddersfield Friends (per Harold Francis)	0	11	3
Brighton I.L.P. collection (after a lecture delivered by Guy Bowman)	0	13	3
B. Gordon	0	1	7
	104	15	1

As announced before, we want the sum of £300 in order to bring the weekly out. So keep up your contributions if you want a Syndicalist fighting paper !

SYNDICALISM IN BIRMINGHAM.

Birmingham has ofttimes been described as "the hub of the universe." The Town Hall is begrimed with age, and the Municipal Buildings are in nowise mean, and in the Town Hall all sects and denominations expound their different creeds in this most imposing structure of Norwegian granite. The Council House is another palatial pile of masonry, to do ample justice to the city fathers; herein they may sit in comfort regulating the jurisdiction for the citizens.

There is the Bull Ring, where all the evils that inflict society are settled every week with consummate skill. Budding orators, with their magniloquent epigrammatic speeches, are still to be found there. The Bull Ring provides a haven for parties, where they can let loose their pent-up venom on unsuspecting heads.

There is Waterloo Street, locally known as "The Robbers' Wood," where lawyers are retained for the employers, asking to help more firmly the legal robbery of the workers. It is a quiet street, where silence is golden, and is still looked at askance with the workers. The Waterloo Street brethren supply a good sprinkling of our local governors, with their usual effrontery and characteristics. Birmingham manufactories are world-known.

The Syndicalists.

The Syndicalists are bobbing up, and their propaganda is surely making headway, for an ex-Lord Mayor referred to it as "pernicious," which is ample proof that our efforts are not wasted. The Trade Unions are in a process of augmentation; the flagrant inequality of the distribution of wealth has been forcibly brought home to the workers, and they are joining the Unions to get more.

Politics are in a state of dry rot. The workers are tired of spending time and money to municipalise industries and then having to fight the municipality for a living wage; they have learned that this is a roundabout way to gain even slight concessions.

Backward as the Birmingham workmen are, they are beginning to see the futility of it all. Aspiring political leaders are in a ferment at the stupendous change of thought. What is this pernicious doctrine that has wrought this change?

Political leaders would have us believe that the wrongs are political and not industrial. Birmingham has sent "the Seven" to the House of Commons time after time; yet, despite that, poverty, speeding up, and trustification of industries grows apace. The East toil and sweat for the West. The best things of life are for the few, not the many. The many produce, the few rob.

Politicians implore for a legal minimum wage, the lowest the workers can jog along on; whilst the Syndicalists demand the highest possible maximum that Labour can extract from nature.

Strikes have taken place within the last twelve months, thus clearly indicating the trend of events. The Birmingham Trades Council instituted an inquiry into the working conditions prevailing in various industries, which has proven that the most terrible cases of underpaid, overworked, physical degeneration takes place amongst its toiling thousands, shocking the most hardened.

Poverty is Rife.

The Birmingham Trades Council, having passed a resolution in favour of a 23s. per week minimum, found that there were thousands receiving even less than £1 per week, with the natural sequence of misery, destitution, prostitution, and emaciated women and bent men everywhere.

Syndicalism means self-reliance as against the delegation of politicians. Birmingham being an industrial town, this fact burns home. Discontent is rampant in all trades, showing the same activity everywhere. Each week sees some fresh rebellion from its toilers, the only surprising thing of which is the moderation of their demands.

The contented workman is a rarity, and from such ready material may be moulded that force which some day, by a supreme effort, will shape its own destiny by expropriating the capitalists, who for the nonce are omnipotent.

The Syndicalists are spreading their principles with unbounded zeal, their greatest opponents being the Socialists, surprising as this may seem. While the Socialists are the loudest in their denunciations of Syndicalism, they will oppose it without some even having taken the trouble to read what it really proposes. I have found many "comrades" like this.

Parliament has never given the slightest concession till forced. Parliamentary acts without a strong Trade Union movement to back them are useless. Those who own the implements of industry control the physical, moral, and social destiny of the people.

The employers are federating by industries crushing the workers under the Juggernaut wheels of industrialism, their ethical code being get rich quickly, beggar my neighbour, stereotype the workers as "hands," as per insurance (?) dodge.

Trade Unions which are mere benefit societies are in the "bow and arrow" stage of development, and their leaders, obsessed with the idea that the interests of Labour and Capital are identical, are past redemption.

Only workers know their own grievances, and therefore only workers can remedy them.

Selecting would-be M.P.'s is child's play in comparison with what could be done in Trade Union effort when intelligently used.

The Birmingham Trade Unions are getting ripe for federation, to work in unison. Firstly, for the betterment of the lowest paid and overworked; secondly, for the complete regeneration and transformation of society into one in which the wage system will be a thing unknown, except as a relic of barbarism, without even the security the barbarians enjoyed.

The Remedy.

Syndicalism means that the workers, manual and intellectual, shall own and control their own work (industry) in co-operation with other industries, organising and regulating with uniform preconcerted activity all that goes towards a fuller and happier life for all concerned. This can be done through the Trades Councils, which would be under the control of the Trade Unions, though having their own particular work regulated there.

Political subterfuges vanish into thin air. The state, with its gold-laced officials, would become impotent as such. Birmingham is destined to play an important part in this moving drama. The workers who now go to toil with a machine-like precision may one day use their power to raze the terrible inferno of Capitalism from the earth, becoming their own controllers, and helping to build one of the most beautiful edifices that was ever known, ushering in the Co-operative Commonwealth. Once free from the trammels of absurd politicians, the way may be long or short as the workers will it.

Every Trade Unionist should be a Syndicalist; every Syndicalist should be a Trade Unionist.

The Birmingham Trades Council has accepted the idea of a General Strike to prevent war. Cannot Birmingham Trade Unionists push forward an extension of that Direct Action against the Class War that is now taking place under their noses? "Birmingham's industries for Birmingham's workers" should be inscribed on their banners, with the goal clearly before them and all participating in the work of marching to their emancipation. The organised workers bent on organising their own work for the greatest possible benefit of all. Birmingham will then redeem its motto of "Forward"; it will then become a reality instead of a sham. Such is the propaganda of the Syndicalists, teaching the workers to rely solely upon their own resources.

P. C.

THE PAST OF SOCIAL DEMOCRACY

BY JACK RADCLIFFE.

Is Socialism dead? Frankly, I believe it is. Since "we all" have become Socialists, "Socialism" has come to mean anything one likes, which is as much as to say nothing at all.

Looking round upon the Socialist Movement, its most outstanding feature is its utter confusion, the hopeless chaos into which it has fallen. It is divided into four Parties—Parties *pour rire*, so far as their influence upon the political life of the country is concerned—the British Socialist Party, the Independent Labour Party, and those modern "tailors of Tooley Street," the Socialist Party of Great Britain and the Socialist Labour Party. The Fabian Society, in so far as it is anything more than a dilettante middle-class mutual admiration Society, is a useful ally of capitalism, making for the continuance of class government in a "servile state."

If one reads the periodical literature of these Parties, it becomes apparent that they hate each other even more than they profess to hate the capitalists. Thus, by their mutual antagonisms, they neutralise each other, and become an easy prey for their anti-Socialist opponents—or would be so, if the latter were not quite so intellectually feeble. Socialism, indeed, has been killed—by the Socialists.

If one goes back in thought to the classical days of the scientific Socialism of Marx and Engels, when our old Social Democratic Federation was young and vigorous, what a contrast is presented! Then we knew where we were. Then we had clear-cut issues and definitions presented to us, and which we, in turn, presented to others. But the fly in the ointment then—which has since caused the whole to stink—was the conception of political action. This was degenerated into mere parliamentarism which has quenched the fire of Revolutionary Socialism. Moreover, conditions have changed greatly in the last thirty years, a circumstance which our stalwart veterans do not seem able to realise.

Parliamentarism inevitably leads away from revolution and towards reform, away from a drastic change of economic system, and towards mere tinkering with effects, leaving their fundamental causes untouched.

It being impossible, as might have been expected, for uncompromising revolutionaries, who were out for the total abolition of capitalism and the wage system, to get into parliament, compromise was resorted to. This compromise could only be in one direction, towards the enemy's position and away from our own. Thus we got "Independent" Labourism with a laxity about Socialism, which has developed into a denial, by many who still call themselves Socialist, of the fundamental fact of the class-war, and a repudiation of revolutionary methods (vide J. Ramsay MacDonald's "Socialist Movement," &c.). This degeneration of the working-class movement becomes still worse as it shades off into mere Labourism, the only inspiration of which would seem to be an anæmic form of Nonconformist Christianism. Here we find it absolutely at the mercy of an utterly unscrupulous and hypocritical Liberalism which is able to fool the well-meaning sentimentalists, who are without the economic knowledge of the "materialistic" Socialists, to the top of their bent, and is always willing to buy over the self-seeking demagogues who have found, in these conditions of the labour movement, opportunities for their own personal advancement.

All this, it need hardly be said, is eminently satisfactory from the capitalist point of view.

When we turn to the British Socialist Party—of which we once had hopes—we find a degeneration of a somewhat different kind. It is (as has been said before) more in the nature of senile decay. The B.S.P. still professes to be revolutionary, but what it means by "revolution" is difficult to understand, seeing that every direct manifestation of the revolutionary spirit is immediately denounced by the leading exponents of B.S.P.'ism as "anarchism"; and, considering their constant and gross misrepresentations and abuse of Syndicalism, which is nothing more or less than the legitimate expression of those revolutionary ideas which the old S.D.F. inspired and which its successor the B.S.P. still claims to hold.

The B.S.P. "leaders" have only themselves to thank that the revolutionary spirit is expressing itself independently and apart, since they would not tolerate it within their organisation. Reading "the organ of Social Democracy" week by week, it is apparent that "the Social Democracy" is becoming more and more hidebound and reactionary as time goes on.

Apart from Syndicalism, the attitude of the organ aforesaid towards the militant women's movement is as disgraceful as that of the capitalist hooligan Press. We hold no brief for "Votes for Women." Indeed, we regret that so much energy and magnificent heroism should be thrown away on so worthless a cause. When the women get the vote, as they assuredly will, they will find it of no more use to them than it is to us men. It will not solve a single problem, but it will lead to a greater mass of such mischievous legislation as we have been cursed with of late years, the purpose and effect of which will be to curtail our liberties still further in the interests of a cunning and unscrupulous master-class.

Inasmuch as the suffrage movement is merely political and not economic, inasmuch as it does not aim at the overthrow of capitalism and the wage system, it will accomplish nothing towards the solution of those social evils, the existence of which most Suffragists recognise.

But the suffrage movement is exerting a fine educative influence on our girls and women. It is moulding the stuff of which the revolution will be made. By their militant tactics the Suffragists will assuredly gain their end. But to us it is somewhat ironical that they are by DIRECT ACTION bringing about a state of things under which they will be as impotent as the male "voting cattle" are now! From the day when the women get the vote will date the degeneration of the women's movement.

Nevertheless, the militant women are setting the men a fine example. If the men had the same courage, the same determination, and the same cohesion as the women have, we might hope to see the New Society in our own day and time. But, instead of sympathising with the militant women and trying to carry them further to something more vital and fundamental than the useless vote, and instead of endeavouring to inspire their own rank and file with the same rebellious ardour, our sluggish Socialist "leaders" join the Philistine chorus of sneering abuse and denunciation.

What will they do when the day is really at hand? Amuse themselves with competitions for the formation of "A Socialist Cabinet"? Nothing could be more strikingly significant than this. A list of representative Socialists is given in *Justice*, from which competitors are invited to "form a Cabinet." The list is a remarkable one and displays a humour no doubt unsuspected by its compiler. That it will cause the Philistine to jeer goes without saying; but it is far more calculated to move the serious, thinking Socialist to tears.

There we have it, and there we have illustrated to us in a plain, unmistakable way what is in the minds of most of these Socialists. Their great aim is parliament, and beyond parliament they cannot go. It has become an *idée fixe* with them. They dream of revolution "by act of parliament"! A Socialist Cabinet forsooth! Well, leave them to their tomfoolery; *we* have our work to do. They are "back numbers." Their Socialism is dead.

As for those silly little groups known as S.P.G.B. and S.L.P., they are our "sea-green incorruptibles," nourished on the pure milk of the doctrine; they do not count for anything serious, though they take themselves too seriously. Beyond a pretty talent for washing dirty linen in public their activities amount to nothing. So they may safely be left to afflict the air of street corners with all the wisdom they can extract from a few penny pamphlets on what is supposed to be "Marxian Socialism," which they do not understand. *Their* Socialism is dead.

Although Socialism is dead, strangled by the Socialists, THAT for which Socialism formerly stood is not dead. The revolutionary movement, of which Socialism was once truly part and parcel, goes forward. But it is finding other channels, other modes of expression, than arid parliamentarism. It refuses to be absorbed by the dry dust of Party politics. Its channels are over the industrial field, and the whole of organised labour is everywhere, consciously or unconsciously responding to its vivifying influence. Its modes of expression are in Direct Action. It has no use for parliaments or Cabinets. It will own, administer, and direct at first hand the common wealth in the common interests of all. Thus it will brook no "rulers," and it will need no "government." It will fructify in Communism, not Collectivism. And its name to-day is Syndicalism.

Socialism is dead!

THE BLACKLEG.
By JIM CONNELL.
(Author of "The Red Flag").

Air: "PADDIES EVERMORE."

There's a cuckoo* in our household
  And he terrifies our young,
For the habits of the traitor
  Have been often told and sung.
Though his feathers flutter softly
  There is murder in his heart,
And all down the toiling ages
  He has played the villain's part.

Chorus.—Oh! we hate the cruel tiger,
  And hyena, and jackal,
  But the false and dirty blackleg
  Is the vilest beast of all.

When we dress our brave battalions,
  And confront the Lords of Loot,
We behold the Scab desert us
  Ere the guns begin to shoot.
Just to gorge his greedy stomach,
  And to save his coward skin,
With salvation in the balance,
  He betrays his kith and kin.

Chorus.—Oh! we hate, &c.

You can tell him 'midst a thousand
  By his cringe and by his crawl,
For of dignity or courage
  He possesses none at all.
In the ale-shop he's a sponger,
  In the workshop he's a spy;
He's a liar and deceiver,
  With low cunning in his eye.

Chorus.—Oh! we hate, &c.

Let us flout him in the market;
  Let us "cut" him in the street;
Let us jeer him from all places
  Where the honest workers meet.†
When to greet his brazen features
  Every decent door is slammed,
We will leave him burst and broken
  To go down among the damned.

Chorus.—Oh! we hate, &c.‡

* "The young cuckoo, when hatched, immediately throws out of the nest all the legitimate occupants, the little murderer requiring all the insects its small foster-parents are able to provide for a small family."

"The cuckoo's note is so easily imitated that small boys are readily mistaken for one another—at a distance. Some human adults also resemble the cuckoo in other than vocal respects."—*Archbishop Mathew, of Ethelbert Lodge, Bromley, Kent, in "The Observer" of February* 16, 1913.

† The appearance of a blackleg in public constitutes a very appropriate occasion for practising the cuckoo's call.

‡ Supplies of this poem in leaflet form can be obtained by application to the Editor of the SYNDICALIST.

OPEN LETTER
TO THE
SCHOOLBOYS OF BRITAIN

Now, boys, you don't know me, but I want to be a chum to you. And I want to speak to you about Murder—I mean War. You know in your Sunday Schools you hear a Commandment which says "Thou shalt not kill." Of course that doesn't mean animals, because we have to kill sheep and cows and pigs and fish in order to live. But it means you must not kill men and women or boys and girls. Now, your teachers or ministers may want you to join the Cadets or Scouts or the Boys' Brigades. Then they order you to do this, that, and the other just as though you were a dog. Now, I want you to remember that you should take no orders from anybody but your father and mother. They are your best friends, and if one or both of them are dead I am very sorry, for I know how you must miss them, because I have lost my parents. Of course I am older than you in years, but I never want to forget that I was a boy.

Now, chums, I will tell you why I don't want you to join the Boys' Brigades, the Cadets, or the Scouts. It is because when you grow older the men whom your father works for will try to persuade you with pretty pictures of showy clothes to join the army. Immediately you join the army you are liable to be a murderer, because if a war starts you will have to go away to kill somebody. If you don't kill them you might get killed yourself; so it will be a case of you having to murder or be murdered. But that is not the worst. If your father or older brothers go on strike for more money, so that they can give mother more money for food and clothing for the household, then you may be ordered to shoot your own father or brother down. Anyhow, even if it is not your own relations, it will be somebody's father, or brother, or son; and other people love their children just as much as your father and mother love you. So, boys, I say again, don't join these Boys' Brigades, Scouts, or Cadets. I know you may think it looks swank to have a belt and cap on, but it is only done to cod you into thinking you are clever or brave, and when you get older they hope to have filled you with a desire to join the army and become a murderer. No, boys; the bravest men are the men like your dads, who brave the mighty ocean in all weathers if they are sailors, and go down into the dangerous bowels of the earth if they are miners, or work on high buildings or in unhealthy factories, etc. But our dads do this in order that we can live; whereas soldiers are kept alive without working in order to be ready to murder some men when the rich men of Britain want them to.

So don't join the army when you are older, for you may have to stick your bayonet into your father's or brother's stomach or shoot them dead when on strike. And although you may love them ever so much and would have to do this when you get your orders, or get murdered yourself. Read this again, hand it to your schoolmates, and some day when you get older you will be glad you took my advice.

So cheer up, chums, there's a better life ahead for us than there was for our dear old dads. And some day, when you get older like me, I hope you will be

A REBEL.

A
Remedy
for the
SWEATING SYSTEM!

Do you know that you can improve your conditions and those of your fellow-workers without any sacrifice? ∴ How! By supporting true Co-operation. By dealing at our Co-operative Stores, you strike at the great evil of sweating. We are not out for profit but to fight against poverty and starvation. Do not forget that these evils exist largely on account of the selfishness of those who possess the means of production and distribution, and remember to do your part by joining our Society at once. ∴

Buy C.W.S. (Co-operative productions) only, and be a true Co-operator. We stock the best Grocery & Drapery goods. Try our Teas at 1/4, 1/6, and 1/9, all full weight without the wrapper. ∴ ∴

The Hotel & Restaurant Employees'

Co-operative Society, Ltd.,

12, LITTLE NEWPORT ST.,
CHARING CROSS ROAD, W.C.

Large Hall (seating 250) To Let for Meetings, Concerts, &c. Special terms to Trade Unions.

Gustave Hervé

SINGLE COPIES can only be obtained for **3/6** post free (Library Edition) common 8vo, cloth gilt, or post free, **3/10**, from A. C. Fifield, 13, Clifford's Inn, London, E.C.

MY COUNTRY:
Right or Wrong.
By GUSTAVE HERVÉ.
Translated by Guy Bowman.

SPECIAL CHEAP EDITION.   STIFF COVERS.

Only to be obtained from societies, clubs, &c. No single copies sent out. Branches supplied at the following rates, cash with order:

1/- NET.

This cheap edition cannot be obtained from Mr. Fifield, but only of

GUY BOWMAN, Publisher, 4, Maude Terrace, Walthamstow, London, E.

6 for 5/3 ; 9 for 7/10 ; 12 for 9/6.

GOLDEN PRIVET.
Finest Stock in the World.
100,000 to choose from.

15in. to 18in., 3s. ; 18in. to 2ft., 4s. ; 2ft. to 2ft. 6in., 5s. ; 2ft. 6in. to 3ft., 6s. ; 3ft., 9s. per doz. Specimens from 2s. each.

All other Shrubs equally Cheap.

Carriage paid on order of 10s.

F. BAKER & SONS,
—— The Nurseries, ——
LOWER TOOTING and MERTON.
1 minute from Merton Tram Terminus.

C. J. SMITH,
8, St. James Street,
WALTHAMSTOW.

High-Class Pianos
from £12 12s. Cash.

OUR CELEBRATED PIANOS
— DEFY COMPETITION. —
Cash, or from 10s. monthly.

All Pianos Fully Warranted for 15 Years.

A WORKER'S NOTEBOOK.
By F. H. RO E.

FIERY CROSSES AND THINGS.

(From the *Manchester Evening News.*)

Neither the kindling nor the carrying of fiery crosses presents any insuperable difficulty—it is keeping the pesky things alight that makes the trouble. The somewhat melancholy spluttering out of the flaming symbol of the class war which Mr. Larkin brought from Dublin last week-end is a striking illustration of this fact. Not all the powers of sensationalism and excited sentiment could combine to keep the sorry business from fizzling out. Sunday's meeting in Manchester must have been a keen disappointment for people who attended in the hope of hearing oratorical hot stuff. The chastened tone of the gallant bearer of the fiery cross indicated that private conference prior to the meeting in the afternoon must have done something towards quenching the revolutionary ardour of the leaders, while the rambling and disjointed cackle from the platform quite extinguished the spirit of enthusiasm which it was designed originally to arouse. Perhaps the greatest mischief done by this "fiery cross" nonsense is that it has concentrated working-class interest upon individuals and distracted it in some measure from the Dublin workers and their sufferings. It has, perhaps, intensified the insolence and arrogance of the employers, not only in Dublin, but elsewhere. Unintelligent and immature platform stumping—no matter how loudly advertised by newspapers—has never had a much more advantageous effect.

Wednesday's Conference.

The decision of the Parliamentary Committee was inevitable, unless the members who compose it were all utterly demented. The proposition embodied in this crusade of rant was that a general strike should be called in Great Britain in sympathy with the Dublin strikers. The Committee, taking their cue from the Manchester meeting, have paused and rationally postponed their decision—for three weeks, they say. We know what this means. There will, of course, be no general strike—it would be the unkindest thing for the Dublin people if it were possible and were done. Everybody knows now that a general strike is a silly illusion and a thing impossible in practice. Partial and spasmodic transport strikes form the nearest approach in practice. The happy attribute of all firebrands is that they never last long. If you hold them long enough they inevitably burn the hands that hold them. It makes no difference if they are shaped like crosses, and cold water always settles them before they burn out, if it is timely applied. Syndicalism takes some curious views of industrial possibilities. There is an idea prevalent that a strike in Dublin can be won by making bad speeches in England, but it is quite a mistake.

The Right Course.

The Parliamentary Committee have taken the right course. To send all the help they can to the Dublin workers is a work that deserves—and will receive—all the whole-hearted support the British unions can give. It will hardly satisfy the "fiery cross" bearers; but, after all, they do not matter very much. Men who carry these flaming ensigns and howl for revolution one day, then tell us that "Home Rule" is of more consequence than winning the Dublin strike, are surely beneath considered criticism. It may interest some of these industrial bluff merchants to learn that the people most disappointed in their contemptible display are the revolutionists. It has given them another reminder that nobody really believes in violent revolution—not even themselves. When the apostle of syndicalism assures us that a purely political measure is more important than a great industrial movement—a movement which justifies by the gravity of its issues the raising of the "fiery cross" of the general strike, they must begin to harbour grave doubts as to where they are exactly. When the representative body of the British trade union movement turns on the cold-water hose, we realise that sanity still exists in the land.

To the Fiery Crusaders.

It does not matter so much whether the sympathetic general strike is good or bad in principle, economically sound or unsound in theory. The plain fact is that the British worker is not educated up—or down—to it. The Parliamentary Committee know this. They know that the revolutionary trade unionists are but a numerically contemptible minority, loud-mouthed and active possibly, capable of raising and even sustaining local agitations. But they know, too, that the mass of British trade unionists are absolutely disaffected towards the idea of syndicalism. It has been one of the deserved misfortunes of all the forms of revolutionary industrialism in this country that their advocacy has fallen to men who are simply vain-glorious and ill-balanced spouters. In this country they have never yet found a capable teacher. Imagine a man mouthing grandiloquently about industrial solidarity, fraternity, and brotherly love one moment and putting Home Rule for Ireland in front of industrialism the next. How the strongly organised workers of Belfast will be impelled to strike in sympathy with Dublin, and how eagerly they will respond to a "fiery cross" which is to lead them to battle for Home Rule! May it be suggested that men who say the first thing which comes to their tongues, obviously for the sake of making their voices heard, are not leaders worth following or even speakers worth hearing.

The Contemplated Crime.

What, in truth, is the reckless brutality that would have followed this "fiery cross" had it not been promptly pumped upon by common sense? A few salaried and well-fed agitators projecting the appalling design of calling a general cessation of work on the threshold of what is likely to be a severe and trying winter! Mr. Ben Tillett, always eager to go one better—or worse—in verbal violence than his contemporaries, opines that there will be no hope for the workers until they arm. I wonder where he will be on the great day upon which the massed legions of a class-conscious proletariat line up on the field of the industrial Armageddon. "He who would be free must himself strike the blow!" That will be a handy axiom wherewith to point the moral and adorn the tale of solidarity. Most people of that sort will be making encouraging speeches to the reserves on Tower Hill or some other place—where the fighting isn't. Everybody is to get a gun—except the marshals, who will direct the operations from a tactical position. I give due notice that I don't want a gun. I am going home the nearest way. The only democratic leader who ever got his head cracked in a revolutionary rising was John Burns. He supplied some of the blood on the first Bloody Sunday. It is generally conceded, in professional circles, that he set up a dangerous precedent, and no other leader of the struggling masses has ever done it since.

BOYCOTT
THE
INSURANCE CAPITALISTS

If you are insured, if you are about to insure, if you are not insured, it will be to your benefit to write for prospectus and full information of the

"SYNDIC INSURANCE BROKERAGE SOCIETY,"

who are in a position to give expert advice and to transact with the leading Friendly Societies (free from capitalistic control) all kinds of Insurances, for all readers of the "Syndicalist." Arrangements have been made whereby the whole of the commission will be placed to the fund for the "Weekly Syndicalist."

Life and Endowment Assurances are a speciality. We have the best tables. Immediate Full Benefit will be granted on all policies. Clients forward their premiums by post to us monthly, quarterly, or yearly.

No other, no fuss, and more money to the "Weekly Syndicalist."

WRITE NOW—AT ONCE—INFORMATION IS FREE.

Manager : Mr. F. C. HIDDEN, 51, Francis Avenue, Portsmouth.

Scott's Temperance Commercial Hotel,

9, Halliwell Street, Corporation Street
(Near Victoria Station).

MANCHESTER.

Bed and Breakfast from 2/6.   Boots extra.

J. SCOTT, Proprietor.

I. S. E. L.

Under the auspices of the above League, a series of

Lectures
AND
Debates

will be given every Sunday evening, at 7.30 p.m. prompt, from

December 7th, 1913, to April 5th, 1914, inclusive.

The Meetings will be held in the

CO-OPERATIVE HALL
12, LITTLE NEWPORT STREET,
Charing Cross Road, W.C.
(near the Hippodrome).

The First Lecture on

HOW TO SABOT THE LABOUR EXCHANGES

will be delivered by

A. G. BUCKENHAM
(Proletarian).

Don't forget Dec. 7th!
Tell your Friends!

Turn up at 7.15, as we want to start at 7.30 prompt.

PORTLAND STUDIO,
243, Kentish Town Road,
—— London, N.W. ——

ART PHOTOGRAPHY.

ALL MAKES BOUGHT. SOLD. HIRED. REPAIRED ETC.

THE TYPEWRITER PEOPLE
(LARKIN & LEWIS)

PADS FOR YOST MACHINES AT 6/6

1000 FACSIMILE CIRCULARS FROM 7/6

MINCING LANE HOUSE ARCADE

ASK FOR AVENUE 535

53 TO 69 EAST CHEAP LONDON E.C.

All the Profits

From your next order for Tailoring will go to the

"WEEKLY SYNDICALIST" FUND

If you place it with

THE SYNDICALIST TAILORING CO.,
174, GREAT TITCHFIELD STREET,
GREAT PORTLAND STREET, W.,

All the Benefits

Of West-End Cut and Finish and a Big Saving in Cost
WILL BE YOURS.

Suits to Measure	from 37/-
Chesterfield Overcoats ...	from 32/6

HELP YOURSELF TO THESE BENEFITS —— and you will —— the "WEEKLY SYNDICALIST" FUND

A Quarterly Balance-Sheet will be published.

1914

The Syndicalist
and Amalgamation News

Edited under the :: auspices of the :: :: Industrial Syndicalist Education League. ::

President
TOM MANN

Secretary
GUY BOWMAN

VOL. III. NO. 1. LONDON. JANUARY. 1914. MONTHLY. ONE PENNY.

OUR REBELLION.

THE GOSPEL OF HATRED THE ONLY GOSPEL OF HOPE.

It would be odd if putting a cross on a piece of paper against the name of a Socialist candidate made any great difference to society. At present we are in a society where a few people direct the lives of the many and rob them. To alter society by voting the few into Parliament, into the Cabinet, to become heads of parliamentary departments acting with permanent chiefs of Civil Service staffs managing nationalised industries, is to change names and to do nothing more. After you have done hard work of this kind the few still control the many.

Unless the worker learns to act for himself, driven on by his own proper feelings of rebellion against those who oppress, and of hatred for the self-satisfied robbers who forget the sources of their wealth, or, worse still, insult him with charity and kindliness and regulation of his life, he will always be the tool of others. The kind master and ruler is the most enslaving of all, because he is willing to look after his men and women at all times, when they are *not* at work for him as well as when they are.

The development of the workers' powers, so that they shall have confidence in themselves and feel able to lock out all bosses, managers, talking politicians, and every kind of non-producer, is the last thing the politician aims at. The political vote-catcher must offend no one.

The Gospel of Hatred is the only Gospel of Hope. Syndicalists believe in war on the members of the propertied class. Without it, the workers are not encouraged to act for themselves and by acting to increase their own powers.

Politicians like George Lansbury do not believe in it. Lansbury believes that "women and men of *all classes* . . . are awakening." He believes that "*people whose lives have been spent in luxury* . . . are understanding that conditions are wrong."

Syndicalists are opposed to such appeals to the rich. They would encourage the workers to distrust every theory which makes their freedom depend on persons or processes outside themselves and their own efforts.

A better society is not to be got either by sending someone to capture the state (and become incidentally a middle-class somebody with M.P. after his name and £400 a year in his bank, so long as he can catch enough votes) or by waiting for capitalism to evolve and society grow older.

Mr. Lapworth, the late editor of the *Daily Herald*, once told a meeting that:

"There is a rebel movement—a new rebellion. We are out not to teach a theory, but to disgust people with the degradation of the present system of society."

Just so. We are not anxious to teach a theory. Those who are forget that it is not cleverness or accurate argument that tells but force, moral and physical. I include moral force, because when we look to see what kind of men influence others and raise their determination up to the point of exerting physical force, we find it is men like Larkin—men who have personality and attractive power at least as much as brains.

Some parts of our work are being done for us by those who are not Syndicalists. The unreality of democracy becomes obvious. Even the workers whose hard lives keep them furthest from the facts begin to suspect that Asquith and Bonar Law and the *Express* and the *Mail* are so excited about Ulster because they do not want to see that some people are agitated about Dublin, and the starvation of those who will not consent to be dead tools in the hands of masters. The careers of politicians and leaders are obviously more interesting to themselves than the causes they so eloquently speak of on platforms. The Insurance Act, whether good or bad, obviously was never asked for or even foreseen by the electors, who are said to be represented by the Liberal Government. Programmes are always concocted above, at the centre, and not below, by the scattered and helpless rank-and-file members, who do obscure work. At the best, they are formulated by the managing idle, who agitate busily instead of going to the theatre. That there are things no politician dare say, for fear of losing all support from his party, Belloc and Chesterton have made clear. The observant note that once the Marconi contract was safely signed, the Marconi Company bought the Goldschmidt patent rights, although honest gentlemen had previously informed the country they were not workable. Such things, as well as the open sale of "honours" and the investment of party funds in railway shares, just when railway strikes are being considered by parliament, all help the ordinary man to feel sick of politics.

If much helps to discredit the bosses' conduct of the "national" business, few except the workers will do much to help the workers to conduct their own affairs properly. The development of the new society which will replace the old capitalist-governmental society is the business of the workers.

Trade Unions have to be made more effective fighting forces for winning increased wages, shorter hours, more security of employment, and rules of work less uncomfortable to the worker. There must also be made places where the worker is encouraged to see how he will work when masters have been abolished and to develop the powers he needs in order that he may himself supply both brains and hands in that day.

It is quite possible that new independent Industrial Trade Unions, with proper internal machinery for protecting local and craft interests and needs and opportunities for discussing technical difficulties will have to be formed. Possibly the existing Trade Unions are dying; perhaps opposing Unions are the best means of reviving them.

Committees or guilds of rebels within the old Unions may be needed to plan strikes and other forms of action that the present officials dislike.

ARTHUR D. LEWIS.

WORKERS' SONG.

By ANNA LINCOLN.

O ! ye who tend the meadows
And plant the waving corn !
O ! ye who work midst shadows
Of night until the morn !
Why laggard are ye, Brothers,
Your birthright to demand?
The right of self and others
To the fullness of the land !

CHORUS :

We want the land God gave us
As heritage for aye—
The land, and all its riches,
And naught shall say us nay !

O ! men in fiery furnace !
O ! men in dungeon mine !
O ! sisters at your weaving
Of fabrics smooth and fine !
Cease toiling, toiling ever ;
God never meant it so—
That death alone should sever
A life of work and woe !

CHORUS :

We want the land God gave us
As heritage for aye.
We workers mean to have it,
And naught shall say us nay !

O ! men of mighty England !
O ! mothers of its race !
Rise up and be rebellious
And take your rightful place
Its "might" is but your Labour—
Your ceaseless toil and sweat.
Come, join hands, ev'ry neighbour,
And let the foe be met !

CHORUS :

We want the land God gave us
As heritage for aye.
Our unity shall save us,
And NAUGHT shall say us nay !

IN CRITICISM OF CHRISTABEL.

SOME FATUOUS AND FUTILE FANCIES ON SEX-SLAVERY.

I think it is time to discuss in this paper the exact position of Miss Christabel Pankhurst, for I and others with me have the uneasy feeling that the whole problem of Votes for Women—a problem which but opens up the wider issues of complete social and economic freedom for women—is becoming more and more evidently the problem of Christabel.

Last month the SYNDICALIST in a very striking open letter to the W.S.P.U., dealt sufficiently with the problem of the vote, and showed, I think, how much further the revolutionary movement would have the women go, and how far wider and more ambitious are the principles of justice and freedom it entertains in connection with women. In the present article I want to express my feelings concerning what I will call the side-tracking, by a few sex-mad spinsters, of the whole feminine movement of revolt in the direction of a revolt against the male sex.

I am sorry to have to acknowledge that not a little truth was contained in the predictions of those Anti-Suffragists of some years ago who decried the women's revolt as a revolt against all those "fine institutions" of marriage and motherhood upon which our civilisation is built," &c., &c. A timely illustration comes to hand in the shape of a very amusing book on "The Hidden Scourge, and How to End It," by Christabel Pankhurst, being a reprint of those leading articles that have appeared in the *Suffragette* on the sex question.

The question of syphilis, or the "Hidden Scourge," as Christabel prefers to call it in her title (as a peace-offering to Conventionality !), has been very frankly discussed in the pages of the *Suffragette*, and more shrewdly and tolerantly in the *New Freewoman* for some time past, and we have no quarrel with Christabel's presentation of the case. With her conclusions, as summed up in the rather grandiose sub-title, "How to End It," we find ourselves at loggerheads. "The real cure of the great plague is a twofold one," she declares—"Votes for Women" (no smiles by request) " and *chastity for men !*"

There you have it, apart from the many wild and venomous adjectives Christabel employs in describing the conduct and character of that low animal, Man. "Chastity for men," she continues—" or in other words, their observance of the same moral standard *as is observed by women*—is . . . indispensable." I am no apologist for prostitution, or for sexual indulgence (the latter, quite frankly, needs no apologia, providing it occurs under conditions of freedom and equality for both parties), but I do wish to remark that men, notwithstanding an admittedly greater legal and social protection in this respect, do not succeed in being less chaste than women. Any woman who knows her sex and is willing to tell the truth will confirm that.

Again Christabel attempts to utter a trumpet note of challenge and defiance, but only manages to achieve about as imposing an attitude as that of a schoolgirl exhibiting her tongue behind the back of a teacher : "There can be no mating between the spiritually developed women of this new day and men who in thought or conduct with regard to sex matters are their inferiors. Therefore the birth-rate will fall lower yet."

Christabel's own conduct in sex-matters—though it is not hard to imagine it, from her general attitude towards men, and her ecstatic exaltation of women—does not concern or interest us here, but I cannot resist the remark that she will be convinced of her fatuity and futility, not by us mere men, but by the "wronged and outraged" members of her own sex. As a woman-writer in another feminist paper has said : "It is time Christabel turned from sex - slavery to wage-slavery !"

HOMO.

A STRIKE AGAINST RENT.

The East London Federation of the W.S.P.U. is working to bring about a "No Rent " strike for Votes for Women in the near future. This means that on a certain day it will be announced that no more rent will be paid until the Government agrees to give votes to women. As no arrears of rent will be paid after the strike is over, landlords should at once hurry up and demand Votes for Women before the strike begins.

"No Rent " strikers who obtain help from the Poor Law Guardians, says Sylvia Pankhurst, need not fear to have their relief stopped. Poor Law Guardians are not supposed to grant relief for payment of rent, but for food, firing, and clothes ; but the greatest safeguard against the possibility of the Guardians coming forward to help the landlords is that, should this be attempted, thousands of "No Rent " strikers will at once say that they mean to enter the workhouses if any threat of stopping relief is made. As the workhouses are unable to accommodate the thousands of strikers, their outdoor relief is quite safe.

"No Vote, No Rent " strikers need not fear eviction, for the landlords will not be able to put the brokers into the strikers' houses. The strike will not start until thousands are ready to join in, and the Government will not dare to allow thousands of evictions because, if thousands of families were to be sent out to tramp the streets without a roof to cover their heads, the Government knows that serious rioting would occur.

A couple of years ago the garment workers of Chicago in America were obliged to strike against rent, as well as against sweated employment, because they could not pay. There were many thousands of strikers, and only one family was evicted. As soon as the eviction had taken place the strikers went to the house where it had happened, tore off the doorstep, smashed the windows, and finally wrecked the building. No one was arrested ; no more evictions took place. There was only one eviction in Chicago. There will be no evictions in London when women begin the "No Rent " strike for the vote, for the People's Army will make the landlords too much afraid to turn anyone out. The landlords will also fear to put the brokers in, for the People's Army would rescue the furniture and carry it home in triumph if any such attempt should be made.

For generations the people of East London have been made to pay scandalously high rents on humiliating terms for miserable dwellings. The working women are now saying, " We shall be able to buy new clothes and enough food to eat out of the rent money when the strike begins." Poor people who own only a few houses and are without other means of subsistence will not be victimised. They will be allowed to apply to the "No Vote, No Rent " Strike Committee for a ticket entitling them to have their rent paid.

The Syndicalist
and Amalgamation News.

EDITED UNDER THE AUSPICES OF

The Industrial Syndicalist Education League

Offices—
4, MAUDE TERRACE, WALTHAMSTOW,
LONDON, E.

MONTHLY · ONE PENNY.

Post Paid Subscription—
Great Britain or Abroad ... 12 months 1s. 6d.

Bundle Rates—
1s. 6d. per quire, Carriage Paid.

U.K.F. TERMS TO NEWSAGENTS.

The Receipt of a Sample Copy is an invitation to Subscribe.

JANUARY, 1914.

IN FUTURE.

We have from time to time reprinted in this paper, from the *Manchester Evening News*, articles from the pen of Mr. Frank Rose, who is a well-known man in the labour world, and a member of the Amalgamated Society of Engineers.

Our object in reproducing Mr. Frank Rose's articles is not because we agree with him, or in order to indirectly show up the leaders of the late advanced movement, but because these movements which Mr. Rose condemns have been, and are being, carried on under the name of Syndicalism, whereas there is no particle of Syndicalism in them.

It has been said of the Dublin business that it was the first time the workers had shown such solidarity and determination in this country, and that for that reason alone it ought to be backed up. But this is not so at all. About twenty years ago, there occurred the great engineers' strike; it lasted six and a half months. There were about 60,000 affected, 27,000 of them being members of the A.S.E. The struggle was considered to be a splendid one, as it demonstrated loyalty to principle and devotion to the Trade Union cause in admirable fashion. The solidarity shown was not only national, but it became international, Germany alone contributing £14,575 and Australia £5,470. Yet the engineers, after a struggle that lasted nearly twice as long as the Dublin one, were beaten.

It was Mr. Frank Rose who, three years ago, debated with Tom Mann at Manchester on "Is Economic Organisation on the Lines of Industrial Unionism the Wisest and Best Method of Realising Socialism?" A verbatim report of that debate was published afterwards. Since, Mr. Frank Rose has had no kind words for us, as our readers may know, but is that a reason why his views, which are almost unique in the labour movement of this country, should not be put forward for the benefit of those who are out for the real advance of the working class.

Mr. Frank Rose's remarks and attacks on individuals may be somewhat bitter, but the question for us is whether there is any truth in them or not, and we believe that it is high time the true Syndicalists of this country should make up their minds as to how they are going to deal with the astounding fakirism which is to be found in the labour movement at the present time. As a matter of fact, one would have thought that with the events of the last three years, fakirism might be on a declining scale, but in truth there has never been as much fakirism in the labour movement of this country than there is to-day.

Is it not quite true that a good many people have posed as Syndicalists in this country and are not, nor have they ever been Syndicalists? Is it not also quite true that " the despicable rubbish they have prated has been a hotch-potch made up of scraps of Socialism, snippets of Anarchism, scrapings of old Trade Unionism, dregs of Liberal Labourism, clippings and shavings of every ' ism ' under the sun "?

Moreover, quite a host of other little movements have grown out of the Syndicalist oak. There is a faint revival of the Industrial Democracy of the Webbs and of American Industrial Unionism, which two were in existence before we came on the scene; but after that we were gratified with Guild Socialism, Daily Heraldism, and, lately, Larkinism. All of these simply amount to the " two arm " policy of the S.L.P. They are as many parasitic plants that have grown out of the Syndicalist oak and which will have to be dealt with by us as the mistletoe is dealt with by the Christmas pruner.

We have hitherto refrained from finding fault with anybody or criticising any manifestation of the Working Class, but surely the time has now arrived when we should definitely state our position and say what is Syndicalism and what is not; otherwise there would be no reason for our continued existence.

FRANK ROSE'S "WORKER'S NOTEBOOK."
Reprinted from the "Manchester Evening News."

"RANTING ABOUT 'SOLIDARITY' WHILE THEIR OVERT ACTS HAVE FRUSTRATED IT."

WHAT IS SYNDICALISM.
By F. H. ROSE.

There is a popular delusion extant to the effect that Syndicalism has received its death-blow at the hands of the special Trade Union Congress held this week in London. The plain truth is that Syndicalism has never been taught or expounded in this country at all. As a social ideal it is quite admissible and as well worth rational advocacy as any other dreamy vagary. Actually it means that all the workers are to be organised in separate industries, are to acquire the ownership and control of all the factors of wealth production and distribution, and conduct all industry in the common interest. Men and women have as much right to propagate this ideal and are as much entitled to respectful attention as any other section of propagandist. The thing itself may be right or wrong, but there is nothing inherently vicious in it. People who see, or think they see, sublime potentialities in human nature are always worth a place in the world. Nobody regards Tennyson as a fool or a rogue because he visualised a time when

—the common sense of most shall hold a fretful realm in awe
And the kindly earth shall slumber, lapt in universal law.

Meredith's "Old Chartist " sang:

I see a day when every pot shall boil
Harmonious, in one grand tea-garden.

The world's lore and literature are studded with the radiant inspirations of greater and diviner prophets who have hoped and dreamed of " the Kingdom of God upon earth."

Syndicalism in Britain.

In France, where Syndicalism struggles rather than flourishes, it is favoured with the benediction of anarchist communism, and its visionary but virtuous character is obvious. In Britain it has never existed at all, and, apart from the small body of British anarchists, not one living person has accepted its teaching or attempted to propagate it. The men like Mann, Lansbury, Tillett, and Larkin, who have posed as Syndicalists, are not and never have been Syndicalists. They have pirated the title and some of the technical jargon of Syndicalism, but that is not all or the worst. The despicable rubbish they have prated has been a hotch-potch made up of scraps of Socialism, snippets of anarchism, scrapings of old trade unionism, dregs of Liberal-Labourism, clippings and shavings of every " ism " under the sun. They have ranted about " solidarity " while their overt acts have frustrated it; they have chattered of " economic determinism " without knowing—or apparently caring—what it means; " the revolution," " the class war," and all the rest of the demagogue's repertory of stock gags and phrases have been spouted ad nauseam. But, boiled down to its nearest approach to simplicity, Syndicalism in Britain has resolved itself into " down tools, anywhere, anyhow, at any time, with cause or right or reason, or without either."

Industrial Unionism.

Mann, probably the most impudent of the whole conclave of bumptious charlatans, began by calling himself an Industrial Unionist. He was promptly and indignantly repudiated by every Industrial Unionist in this country. He then spoke of " Industrial Unionism or Industrial Syndicalism," clearly to suggest that these were two names for the same thing. Of course, he knew better—if he did not he was unqualified to speak at all. Industrial Unionism seeks the union of all workers in one organisation irrespective of industry or craft. As an ideal it is infinitely finer than Syndicalism. It may be no whit more practical or less visionary, but it is honest, and its advocates have at least set an example of unselfish and unmercenary sacrifice. That their voices have been drowned by those of the raucous stumpers of so-called Syndicalism is regrettable, because they were always worth hearing and reasoning with. My objection to true Syndicalism and to Industrial Unionism is not that I see anything wicked or malevolent in them, but that I regard them both as forms of impossiblism. My objection to the stuff that is paraded as Syndicalism in this country is to its shameless duplicity and immorality.

Manifestations.

We have already witnessed the passing of several notorieties as potential factors in the Labour movement. Touring in America is gayer and perhaps more profitable than agitating precariously at home.

This week we witness the passing of Larkin and his gang. He has lasted badly. Mann held the stage all through 1911; Grayson stood in for nearly a year before his extinction; Tillett has intermittent spasms of popularity yet; Lansbury, a poorer craftsman than either of those, held the limelight for fully three months. Larkin has burst within a month. Newspaper space may not be an infallible standard of public importance, but a celebrity who drops from seven columns verbatim to a ten-line summary in three weeks can hardly be said to be holding his own. When, however, the personalities are adequately suppressed, the marks they sometimes leave are more difficult to eliminate. There can be no doubt that this false and fraudulent campaign has given a strong stimulus to the strike mania which has affected the workers for the past three years. The idea that the strike is the only effective instrument for the purpose of industrial betterment has been sedulously preached, and the whole Trade Union world has been more or less under its influence.

Signs of Convalescence.

The Congress last week is stated to have quenched not only Larkin, but Larkinism. " Larkinism " appears to be another term for Syndicalism. In justice to true Syndicalists this must be stigmatised as a libel. It is a curiosity of the Congress that the men who have played the down tools and sympathetic game for rather more than it was ever worth were the loudest and most vehement in their denunciations of Larkin. They are always decrying Syndicalism and as consistently practising the distorted creed which passes under that name in England. The awakening to some rational sense of their own absurdity is but partial. Mr. James Thomas has just done, by the orders of his executive, what he and they should have done—and had the same opportunity of doing—a half-dozen times during the last three years. They had previously denounced railway strikes in sympathy one day and, finding their opposition unpopular, had sanctified the same strikes with official recognition and approval. In the case of the Great Western strike the proper and courageous course was tardily adopted. On the other hand, Mr. William Thorne goes straight from the Congress and threatens a sympathetic strike of tramwaymen to assist the Leeds gas-workers against the Leeds Corporation.

Syndicalists in Office.

A considerable number of newly-appointed officials of the unions are imbued with the crazy tenets of this bastard Syndicalism. In spite of all experience they cling to the absurd belief that employers are terrified by strikes and threats to strike. Let loose amongst the men, they are a distracting mischief; in conference with the employers, they are a constant menace. At a recent mixed conference in London between the representatives of workmen and employers in the engineering trade a typical instance of this kind was given. There has been a wages strike in one of the engineering sections. One recent acquisition to the officialism of the A.S.E. threatened the employers with a general strike in sympathy of all the trade if the employers refused to grant the demand of the striking section. One of the least pleasant results of this folly was a prompt repudiation of the fool by his colleagues. But it has to be borne in mind that to some extent these exhibitions are the reflex of some section of the rank and file.

The Moral of the Congress.

This week's special Congress is much more a repudiation of the man Larkin than a censure upon the incongruous mess which he and his friends call Larkinism and his professional rivals in the agitation market call Syndicalism. The personal note dominated the proceedings. There were yet few of us who mistakenly subordinated Larkin and his " ism "to considerations concerning his unhappy dupes in Dublin. I confess that I was ignoble enough to feel a solicitous interest in the trumpery detail of thousands of starving men, women, and children. It did not interest me profoundly to know that Larkin was a liar, that Havelock Wilson was a free labour agent in disguise, that Henderson was a traitor who sold Labour interests to the capitalist, or that the Congress delegates were non-elect. What I certainly know is that the Dublin strike should be settled. And if the terms offered by the employers are not as good as the strikers deserve and their friends might wish, they do involve the recognition of an organisation which the trade unions of this country have no cause to respect—and that is a great deal more than Larkin deserves.

CRITICISM & CONSTRUCTION

At the foot of the next column will be found a letter to the editor of the *Manchester Evening News*. The editor's sanction to its publication in full must not be regarded as a precedent to justify an expectation that all my critics will be similarly treated or even that Mr. Mason will be so treated again. But the letter differs from a great many I receive, both in its manner and its direction. It is not scurrilous, and it does not set up an arguable proposition. Its mistakes are due to obvious misunderstanding. The central charge is that I have " admitted that I would retain the use of the strike, but have never given any indication as to when it should be used." That is precisely what I have never done. For the past twelve years I have written in this and other newspapers and spoken from hundreds of public platforms against strikes in any form. I have never admitted that I would retain the use of the strike, or that I would allow either workers or capitalists to use it. The correlative charge, that I only criticise and do not construct an alternative, is surely thoughtless. I may not always have been precisely logical, but I have certainly been both patient and unswerving in an open advocacy of state compulsory arbitration as an alternative to the strike and lock-out. It is quite untrue that I " occasionally hint at fuller parliamentary representation plus Conciliation Boards " as a remedy.

Anything Better Than the Strike.

I prefer the settlement of industrial disputes by conciliation to their settlement by the strike or lock-out—that is all. I have written and spoken in favour of the adoption in this country of the Lemieux Act, only as a step towards the larger and truer method of compulsory arbitration. The Canadian method, though only conciliation in scope, has the sanction and authority of democratically made law to establish it. Will it surprise Mr. Mason to know that over 90 per cent. of the trade disputes in Canada are settled by the State Conciliation Courts without strikes and that the overwhelming proportion are settled in favour of Labour? In the Australasian Colonies we have the fuller measure of compulsory arbitration, a measure admittedly faulty in some respects, but its general results are such as to constitute a challenge which the strike and starve advocates in this country dare not take up. They can and do lie about it, and misrepresent it, and attempt to belittle it. All these matters have been elaborated in this column from time to time, and it comes rather as a surprise that a man of Mr. Mason's evident intelligence should mistake my meaning so completely as he appears to have done.

The " Broad Principle."

I am asked if I do not think it probable that, under any system of industrial adjustment, the ratio between wages and profits would, in nine cases out of ten, remain the same—that is to say, the rise in wages would be accompanied by a rise in prices. I do not. Prices would only rise to the extent of wage advances if there were no strikes at all. Now they rise to the extent of the wage advances, plus the cost of the strike, for every shred of authentic evidence demonstrates that capitalism charges the consumer with its total losses and not with part of them. Workers who have done me the honour of following this contribution consistently know that I have given frequent and detailed demonstrations of these facts; I may be excused for not repeating them for Mr. Mason's individual enlightenment. **We have seen that the Syndicalist strikes of the past three years have left the worker 1s. in the £ worse off, but that does not include a sum which cannot be far short of £50,000,000 which the workers have lost in funds and forfeited wages, and which the Treasury and Board of Trade returns clearly show has been safely pocketed by the employing classes. The evidence is as open to Mr. Mason as to me, and he will hardly expect me to work it all out for his special benefit.**

Begging the Question.

It seems to me to be sheer idleness to urge that the strike is the " only method the workers have of airing their grievances." It is the one infallible method of adding to their distresses. I should not write or even think harshly of the men who advocate the strike if I thought they were such dunces in economics as not to know this. It is because I am sure they do know that I am what Mr. Mason calls " unkind." I assure him that I mean all I have said about them and that I have not said quite all I

think yet. During no period of our history have strike and lock-out disturbances been so numerous, persistent, and extensive as during the past three years; during no period has the wealth of the employing classes swollen so prodigiously. Yet here is a man, presumably sane, who tells us in effect that the only way, to air the workers' grievances is to stuff more wealth into the already replete coffers of the wealthy. I should " have a little more sympathy for those who are trying to break their bonds " because I refuse to share the wickedness of helping the professional strike-mongers to bind them faster! Inferentially, Mr. Mason charges me with being an ex-trade unionist, ex-Labour man, and ex-Socialist. If he will eliminate that mendaciously prefix he will be nearer the truth, for I happen to be all three things which he alleges that I have ceased to be.

On the Defensive.

It is no part of my design to defend my opinions, my work, or my character. I am out to attack a monstrous wrong. I shall continue to denounce men who foment strikes in order to quarter themselves upon strike funds. I know of no meaner way of getting a living. It is because I have sympathy with those who are trying to break their bonds, Mr. Mason. I have as little respect for men who, though securely quartered as officials, engineer strikes for no better purpose than to gain public notoriety and advertisement. My critic need not look any further than Leeds to get specimens of the latter sort. I have not said worse of them than they can do. But that is not likely to silence me as long as I have a weapon to wield or a corner in which I can breathe. I know that the mass of the organised workers do not like strikes and do not want to engage in them. I know that most of the strikes of the last three years have been stimulated by small sections of men who call themselves Syndicalists, and that almost every one has been lost through the incapacity and vanity of the men who projected them. My fight is against the intolerable tyranny which adds poverty to poverty and heaps wrong upon wrong and meanwhile cants of love for the workers and assumes a hypocritical solicitude for the weak and oppressed, that calls upon credulous men to be heroes one day, and (as per Leeds) slinks away the next and leaves its dupes beaten and ashamed. That is why I am " unkind," Mr. Mason. If I have anything to repent it is that I have not more adequately deserved the accusation.

A Letter from a Critic.

To the Editor of the *Manchester Evening News.*

Sir,—A Notebook as a rule is a helpful thing. I respectfully suggest that the Worker's Notebook written up by Mr. Frank Rose is of little use to those whom it is intended to help—the workers. I venture to protest against the unkind and illogical attitude he assumes against those who are of different opinions to his own. Mr. Rose is entitled to his own rendering of the meaning of Syndicalism, but he ought to allow the same latitude to others. We do not see employers calling one another " bastard " Liberals and Tories. Tom Mann may be the " most impudent of all bumptious charlatans," and another person may be a " fool," but Mr. Rose has no need to make the sneer that it " does not interest him to know that Mr. Larkin is a 'liar,' Mr. Henderson a 'traitor,' &c. I can understand some men referring to the " passing of Larkin and his gang," and Messrs. Grayson, Mann, &c., but it seems strange from Mr. Rose, against whom it is alleged that he is an ex-Trade Unionist, ex-Labour man, and ex-Socialist.

I am a worker, and I recognise the futility of the strike as much as Mr. Rose, but I also recognise the futility of parliamentary representation and Conciliation Boards under existing circumstances. The strike, whilst it may be an obsolete weapon, is the only method by which the workers can air their grievances. Theoretically there is no difference between a non-unionist ventilating his grievance or refusing to work for an employer and a body of unionists going on strike. Mr. Rose admits that he would retain the use of the strike weapon, but he has never given any indication as to when it should be used. I think Disraeli said that it was the easiest thing in the world to make a criticism. It certainly is much harder to put forward a constructive policy. It is true that Mr. Rose occasionally hints that he would educate the worker up to having fuller parliamentary representation, plus Conciliation Boards. No sensible worker will doubt the necessity of the former, but it would be quite easy to prove that no more value can be placed upon it than upon the strike. As regards Conciliation Boards, I need not refer Mr. Rose to the recent withdrawals from one of the finest schemes ever put forward—the Brooklands Agreement, but I would like to deal with the broad principle involved in this recommendation. I ask whether it is not probable that in nine cases out of ten the ratio between the profits of the employer and the wages of the employé will remain the same—that is to say, the rise in wages will ultimately be accompanied by a rise in prices.

The two engine drivers who recently refused to touch " tainted " goods may have been very foolish, but it smacks of just as much heroism in the industrial war as the Balaclava charge did in actual warfare. If Mr. Rose would not be so cocksure about the success of his remedies he would, I feel sure, have a little more sympathy for those who are trying to break their bonds.

GEO. MASON.

THEIR VIEWS AND OUR REVIEWS.

REVOLUTIONARY SYNDICALISM.

By J. A. Estey, Ph.D. With an introduction by L. Lovell Price, M.A. P. S. King and Sons. 7s. 6d. net.

There is an extraordinarily silly passage in Mr. Price's introduction (on pages 20 and 21 of this book), which, while speaking of the alterations made in Marxism by reformist revisions, he appears to declare that at present persons " more valuable to society . . . receive larger rewards than those less urgently required," and that those Socialists have done well who have diluted their Socialism until it only means that " surpluses accruing to different members of society without exertion of their own should be taken by some means through taxation for the public gain." Does a Reader in Economic History in Oxford really think that men's pay corresponds in any sense to the value of their work? Some more intelligent professors of economics will tell him that, speaking roughly, it depends on supply and demand, and that the supply of those qualifying in professions which necessitate a long and expensive training is necessarily limited in a society where the wealth of parents is very unequal. Of course, butchers, bakers, and builders seem, to Mr. Price of very little value to himself and society, and he probably thinks some barristers, music-hall singers, and stockbrokers very valuable.

Mr. Price could learn something by reading parts of Estey's book carefully. Estey's book is a careful, though in places rather colourless, account of the labour movement in France. In presenting Syndicalist opinion in his own language, he sometimes makes it more Esteyan than Syndicalist. Thus he will get an effect by patching a bit of Sorel on a bit of Lagardella and presenting the whole as Syndicalist doctrine. Sorel very decidedly disbelieves in " evolution," though on page 93 Estey appears to think otherwise. But, then, Estey has a great love for the word " evolution." It is such a useful word for Conservatives that revolutionaries should avoid it; it justifies everyone's position and actions and persuades us that we, living human beings, form some mysterious concerns—called society, the state, and the government—which have " rights " and " developments " of their own. Whereas we and our ideas make and can alter and destroy them by our united efforts. Thus when the Puritans beheaded Charles I., the monarchy did not " evolve ": it temporarily ceased to be. Even if Charles II. was only a development of Charles I., his development was due to the altered desires of his subjects which checked his power.

Several sentences in Estey's book might serve as useful texts for English propagandists. Thus he says that the Federation of the Bourses du Travail believed that " the reforms which Labour demanded must be achieved, not through the electoral machinery but by the use of the direct pressure which the Syndicalists could bring to bear upon recalcitrant employers. With this opposition to political activity was coupled a strong antagonism to any form of centralisation. The Federation stood for freedom of action, for decentralisation, for local autonomy, for the principle of federalism, for Anarchism, as Proudhon understood the term, an anarchism of groups rather than an anarchism of individuals."

The reasons for the tendencies thus stated are not hard to find.

Unless the workers free themselves by their own efforts, they will not be free. Parliaments and committees are composed of important people, who leave the unimportant, vulgar masses helpless and with no work to do which will develop their own abilities and self-confidence. Every working man who feels unable to do his work without experts and masters to tell him what to do is a natural slave, and not merely a slave by accident.

But direction from a distant centre is direction by a little group of people in touch with one another, whom the rank and file cannot afford time and money enough to hold in control. The big Trade Union officials control the whole hierarchy of Trade Union officials and the rank and filer has no means of proving that the officials are not carrying out his wishes.

Officials and Members of Parliament are afraid of losing their positions and becoming nobodies again—obscure timber merchants or bricklayers or clerks. They consider votes.

These political prostitutes are also corrupted by the need to form strong parties and to get the help of these parties, in money and in other ways, at election times. If we knew who finances the Labour Party, it would throw light on its policy just as a little light has been thrown on Liberal doings by revelations concerning its party funds and the speculations of some of its prominent men. The Labour Party has rich supporters—some of these despise Socialism—and that may be a reason why the Labour Party does not make a fierce attack on the owners of capital. Then, too, the politician is corrupted from above by the controllers of governments, who have comfortable jobs for a Bell or Shackleton and can give our Ramsay a holiday in India.

Political parties, as Estey points out, are composed of individuals of every kind, capitalists and landlords living by property-owning, professional men and intellectuals. " However much such men may in theory support the emancipation of the labourers, it is not to be expected, the nature of the bourgeoisie being what it is, that when it comes to actual sacrifice they will allow those interests to be irretrievably damaged by what would happen if their theories were put in practice. . . . What have ' intellectuals ' in common with the proletariat? Nothing. They enter political parties, Socialist as well as any other, because politics is their hobby, their peculiar field, because they wish to advance their own selfish interests. If they form a part of a Socialist Party, it is because they hope thus to obtain the guidance of a proletarian movement, to impose upon it their authority and manipulate it to their own advantage. From such auxiliaries the labouring classes would have nothing whatever to gain. They would be submitted to a rigid discipline. . . . In short, their exploitation would continue."

Every parliamentarian is an Anti-Socialist because he has an immediate programme, a set of palliatives of the existing order. But an alternative programme to Socialism is an opposition programme. And all reforms that do not make for the confiscation of land and capital are Anti-Socialist. The class war and the abrupt substitution of a new society for the existing order are the distinctive characteristics of revolutionary Socialism, and when they are abandoned, Socialism has really changed into something else. Land and capital have either been seized by those who use them for producing or they have not.

In order to believe in the sudden decisive ending of Capitalism through the direct efforts of the workers themselves, it is not necessary to take the general strike quite literally. The general strike will take place when, moved by a sense of injustice and of their unnecessary sufferings, the workers offer such resistance to the working of the present system as to make it impossible. For there is no doubt but that a large mass of men cannot be forced to work when they are determined not to work properly. Such feelings may or may not show themselves precisely in the form of a strike.

Speaking of preparations for the future society, Estey explains:

" If workers can carry on the duties of factory-inspection which to-day are fulfilled by the agents of the state, they help to create a law in the factory which is not . . . capitalistic, . . . the beginning of new juridical relations which will be extended and universalised in the coming industrial era."

Estey's reasons for thinking the Syndicalist state impossible are interesting and well thought-out. He assumes that men as they now are will not be greatly altered by deliberate efforts to train themselves so as to be able to be free from bosses. He assumes that under Syndicalism authority and coercion will be as necessary as they are to-day. But the fact is, that unless the worker gets more capable and more united they will never succeed in defeating their present masters, and if they get more capable and more united they will succeed and masters will be superfluous.

ARTHUR D. LEWIS.

THOSE £300 FOR THE WEEKLY SYNDICALIST.

	£	s.	d.
Previously acknowledged	104	15	1
West Brompton N.U.R. (after a lecture delivered by Guy Bowman)	0	10	0
John Turner	0	5	0
	£105	10	1

As will be seen, the above fund has reached over one-third of what is wanted to start a weekly fighting paper. Several friends and supporters have promised comparatively large sums which they will pay in when the fund has reached one-half of the total. It is therefore up to you, comrades, to provide about another £45 if you want to enable us to express our opinion every week on current events. We have no doubt you will do so, but you ought to do it at once so that we might start next May.

THE NEW ORDER.

The New Order (3d.) and Eight " Tracts " (1d. each), dealing with parliament, land, money, labour, sex, education, hygiene, and religion. By W. Allan and Helen M. Macdonald. Questall Press, 12, Ormonde-terrace, Regent's Park, N.W.

Is this Syndicalism? If the worker should control his own industry, it may follow that he ought also to be liable for the science of society upon which such control can be founded.

The founder, whose theory has also been named Humanitism and Mellontism, started life as a farm labourer, afterwards becoming a worker in a machine factory, an accountant, a schoolmaster, a lawyer's clerk, a professor of agriculture, a journalist, an author, a tramp, &c., studying ardently on both hemispheres, and in different universities and colleges, all subjects which could throw light upon what he calls his " science of conduct," especially the sciences of food and hygiene.

The literature of the movement is contained in fourteen books, including pamphlets, but all that can be noticed here is the economic aspect and the pamphlets written by the author with his collaborator.

The material basis of the system is the area of land, and the hours of work thereon, needed to produce a " scientific ration " for an adult. After much inquiry and many experiments these turn out to average one-third of an acre and one hour a day. The question is then asked, Why should a man work ten hours daily when, by working one hour, he could produce a more substantial diet than he now consumes? Monopoly explains the reason why. The conclusion is that the product of this hour, if consumed by the producer would set him free, and then he could not be forced to spend any of these extra nine hours in working for masters. Naturally, there are men who cannot live on food alone, but there are also men who would be willing to work more than one hour daily, if freed from masters.

A suitable system of exchange is then introduced, a sort of double-entry bookkeeping, whereby the worker is assured that he gets the whole produce of his work, standardised as much as possible, or is free to exchange what portion he likes for work—outputs by others. This also avoids the necessity of placing every worker upon the land, or even of splitting up the land into plots allotted to each tiller or family. It is claimed that the more this scheme of exchange is in operation the less of existing money would be needed—a great consolation for all who hold that there is not now money enough to do the world's work.

In this scheme of organisation there can be no leaders—not even the founders themselves can lead. It should specially be welcomed by the unemployed, who could solve many of their periodical difficulties by getting the chance occasionally to work two or three hours daily upon the land.

MELLONTIST.

C. J. SMITH,
8, St. James Street,
WALTHAMSTOW.

High-Class Pianos
from £12 12s. Cash.

OUR CELEBRATED PIANOS — DEFY COMPETITION. — Cash, or from 10s. monthly.

All Pianos Fully Warranted for 15 Years.

HOW WE SHALL NOT MAKE THE REVOLUTION.

The appearance of another edition of the English translation of Pataud and Poujet's account of the creation of the Co-operative Commonwealth proves, at any rate, one thing. It proves that a fair number of copies of the book have been sold. But that it proves anything about the trend of working-class thought is not so sure.

To begin with, the price of the book* is such as to commend it more to the intellectual of the lower middle class than to the average workman. Then it is too neat and fanciful a piece of dreaming to commend itself to the man who is busy with the real business of Trade Union life. And thirdly, all the conditions of the story are too essentially French for the book to be of any great use to us who have English crowds and English labour organisations as the only raw materials to hand for the construction of a communist socety.

For practical use, in fact, there is precious little to choose between this twentieth century Utopia of Poujet and the sixteenth century Utopia of Sir Thomas More. For while Sir Thomas presents us with a finished and elaborate model of society and neglects to tell us how it was created, Poujet presents us with a roughly sketched and still evolving society and tells us frankly that it was evolved from a material that is not, so far, at our disposal.

That is to say the whole story of the book depends for probability upon the existence of a well-organised General Confederaton of Labour. Also the whole book depends for its proper understanding upon the reader knowing something of how the French Confederation of Labour is constituted and of the relations between the individual syndicates and the central body. Now we in England have not a Confederation of Labour. There is no popular talk of creating such a Confederation, and if, in spite of this, we had a Confederation of Labour the conditions of English social life would necessitate its working in a way very different to this revolution-making affair of Pataud's. Also we have not a public with any real acquaintance with the conditions of the French Syndicalism of which this book is a product.

Still, though the practical value of the book is very slight, there is a fine slapdash vigour about the story and the ideas. It is all so magnificently successful. Vast masses of men move across the stage; grey, threatening skies hang heavy over sullen, cowered soldiery; red suns and gusty winds " reflect the people's state of mind "; there is a little boycotting, a little sabotage, a little rioting, and the Capitalist State reels, falls, and smashes into pieces. And, out of chaos, brisk, happy, and new, steps the Syndicalist Republic. . . It is so fascinatingly easy; the illusion is so well kept up; even the most practical of us can be pardoned for feeling a little inspired, and asking himself, " Why not? "

But reading books like this and getting a nice glow of enthusiasm is a poor game; it's amusing, but it doesn't cut any ice.

This new edition, though, is rather a joyful thing to have in the house. The fresh drawings of Dyson's are much better than the old ones, and show the swing of his Titan's pencil at its best. Also the bibliography has been greatly enlarged, and is now somewhere near exhaustive. It recommends some non sense, of course, but it is valuable. The annoying quotations from Morris and " Jesus of Nazareth " are unfortunately still left at the beginning and end of the book—the absurdly affected Greek one amongst them. The Translator's note is, however, enlarged and made valuable by the additon of the Declaration of Principles drawn up at the First International Syndicalist Congress.

ALAN ADAIR.

* The New International Press, Oxford. 3s. 6d

THE FEDERATIONIST.

Official Organ of the General Federation of Trade Unions. December. No. 1. General Federation of Trade Unions, 54, Guildford-street, W.C.

So far as this new paper serves to cause trade unionists to ask why their organisations are not more successful, it will be doing admirable work, for which the Syndicalist will feel grateful. The first leader in this, its first number, is headed " Efficient Industrial Organisation," and declares that such questions as amalgamation of unions, the use of the strike, and the organisation of the internal management of unions " have got to be thoroughly dealt with."

So far, good. Other contents are less pleasing.

The General Federation of Trade Unions has certainly increased a common class feeling throughout the productive or working-class, and has caused a wider feeling of responsibility for men on strike anywhere, and in any trade, to be felt by trade unionists in crafts not immediately concerned by any particular dispute.

In the difficult situation created by the Insurance Act, the General Federation did try to get united action by the Trade Unions, in order to save the working of the Act from falling into the hands of the capitalist insurance companies. The Federation's policy may not have been the best policy, but it was better than the wriggling indecision of the bulk of the Trade Union officials.

No one could object to the General Federation's desire to secure the profits and directors' fees at present absorbed by life insurance companies if the work is seen to be merely what it is, a new scheme for slightly cheaper insurance, and if it in no way diverts or hinders the real work of Trade Unions. There are many advantages in manual workers getting to know that financial operations and business management are not horribly mysterious and difficult.

But the main purpose of the Trade Unions is not to imitate petty capitalist institutions for diminishing the evils of the present, but to fight for the downfall of this present order, and the construction of a new order in which those who build houses, grow food, make furniture, and transport goods from country to country in ships will not be at the mercy of glib and self-confident agents, brokers, and lawyers, whose business it is to gamble and invest in the results of useful processes in which they perform no useful part.

A. D. L.

THE NEWEST FABIANISM.

The World of Labour. By G. D. H. Cole, B.A. Bell. 5s. net.

This is one of those very dull books which stupefy you so much that you do not know whether they are good or not. But it discusses questions now requiring discussion. As, for instance, how, in an Industrial Union, will the special interests of individual crafts be protected and the subjects of special importance to them get discussed.

Cole's answers to questions may not always be right. He favours local strikes backed financially by the whole industry. Although he thinks our present-day Trade Union leaders asses, he believes in expert official control of strikes from a centre. He would retain unions of general labourers but, overcoming the idiotic jealousy which one trade union feels of another's successes, would have the members of a general union only stay in such a union until they can transfer to their own individual union.

As you would expect, the book takes up a middle-class, moderate indeterminate position, in that while Cole would like to see large powers transferred to the unions, he would not abolish the state. He is not an out-and-out Syndicalist, and has not the vigour of an out-and-outer. The mines, he thinks, are destined to be nationalised, and it is worth while for the miners to gain all they can by persuading the state to grant them good terms.

He does not expect political action to do more than industrial strength can force, but would use politics to second industrial force. He is against wages boards, except, perhaps, for sweated industries, because the wage the State fixes looks as if it were a just and proper wage, and, therefore, it tends to become a fixed maximum wage. The General Federation of Trades Unions needs strengthening, he says, in order that there may be a central fund for the support of all strikes approved by their central executives.

These fragments may be more stimulating than the whole arguments in the book, which, as I have suggested, as dished up by Cole himself, are somewhat indigestible.

A. DANIELS.

COMMENTS ON "SYNDICALISM AND THE TEACHER'S WORK."

Although we must always impress it upon teachers that their interests are identical with those of the manual workers in the class struggle, yet within this identity of interest there is a difference. In the new society we *must* have manual workers, and, so far as we can see, they must work in groups. William Morris, Blatchford, and other Utopian writers have dispensed with schools and teachers in their ideal Commonwealths. At any rate, even if we shall always have scholars who will impart their knowledge to those who wish to learn, the place of the ordinary class teacher can quite well be taken, when the average standard of education shall have become very much higher, by parent or friend. As, with regard to the future, the problem of the teacher is a special one, so now the war against capitalism must be carried on by the teacher in his own way, for he is not making dead things, but shaping living minds.

Having made these admissions, we may ask whether the teacher should not have some "ambition to control the educational system of the country." Mr. Sadler admits that the teachers ought to know the most about education, those teachers who now (in spite of doors "which have long been open") are paralysed in their work because of large classes and a tissue of 'regulations created by their ,'' superiors," and none the less embarrassing because changed so often. Why then are they not to control the educational system? Mr. Sadler is mildly sympathetic on the whole, but in the last paragraph, just when we expect his sympathy to issue in some definite proposal, he explains hurriedly that it really won't do, this Syndicalism business : "you know there are the rights of the nation, rights of parents . . . children . . . really haven't time to explain."

How any man can doubt that the teachers must, in the very nature of things, control their own affair, education, is a mystery. You can order a man to cut you a piece of wood of a certain breadth and length. He will do it for you. You can't order a man or a woman to perform certain tricks on a child's mind. The essential thing about an educator is that he should do his work freely, spontaneously. He is a kind of preacher as well as teacher, and, therefore, cannot "work to order." The dead weight of outside control is to the teacher what capitalistic exploitation is to the "worker." Mr. Sadler, after apologising for the inefficiency of administrators, says : "The whole question, however, deserves rather more attention on its psychological side, than it has hitherto received." Indeed it does ! And if you come to talk of psychology you will soon have to admit that to subject the teachers—who, *ex hypothesi*, must be free agents—to the insult of having to exercise their art, surrounded by the bureaucratic net, is a most unpsychological thing to do.

Again, what is the use of talking about the doors of the prison house having long been open? Small use that to the elementary teacher at any rate, for if he goes through that door he must take with him his class, and I doubt if even this wonderful doorway is wide enough to let through sixty children, packed in a solid mass. Mr. Sadler knows that "you must take the whole of the class along with you."

Why does not Mr. Sadler say exactly what power he wishes the nation or the parents to have in this affair of education? We must start with our fundamental notion of the freedom of the teacher, for how can he teach that which he does not wish to teach? But, then, there is the parent; there is the community. What are we to do about their interests? Now, the whole community evidently must have its say in the matter; it must lay down the general policy of national education in the same way as the whole community must tell the railwaymen what services are to be run, leaving the inner control entirely to the men themselves. Nor does it seem to us that you can entirely ignore the parent. It is true that the individual parent can be very stupid about his children ; very often he has the most short-sighted views about their welfare. Sometimes the teacher, even to-day, has to outwit the parent. Still, loop-holes must be left, and the parent given the right to withdraw his child from certain lessons.

Well, then, Mr. Sadler may say, what becomes of the "control of the teacher" now you have let the community and the parents into your little scheme? Our answer is try it and see. Just as every other group must receive its broad instructions from the community, so with the teachers. What, then, if a teacher cannot work freely within the lines laid down by the community? He will have to work independently of the main body of teachers. Any future scheme of society will have a place for such independent workers.

Mr. Sadler does not touch on the militant aspect of Syndicalism here and now, but as a matter of fact every keen teacher practises sabotage—he, cannot help it. He sabots the red-tapery of officialdom. He will have to sabot it more. He will have to decline to waste his time in filling up forms and cabalistic reports which have no meaning to anyone outside Bedlam. He must refuse to prostitute his art in the interests of a financial patriotism. He must see to it that he interprets the great writers and poets in their own way and not in the way that suits the "ethics" of capitalism.

For all this, the *Teachers' Register* may be valuable. It may result in the closing up of the ranks, in the giving a definite status to the secondary as well as to the elementary teacher. The former are now organised only to a small extent and can lay little claim to being called a "profession."

There are now hundreds of teachers—very far from calling themselves Socialists—who are waking up to their situation, are seeing that outside bureaucratic control is sapping their virtue, and is in itself an intolerable thing. Give them the ideal of "control" (after all, it is only self-respect and manly independence applied to a group instead of to an individual), and they will not only respond to it as an ideal for the future, but will find in it an inspiration to the fight of the moment.

JOSEPH DALBY.

THE COLD TRUTH ABOUT CANADA.

It may be a little interesting to acquaint our English fellow-workers of the general conditions that pervade the so-called prosperous atmosphere of this Golden West. If you had walked down one of our main streets yesterday, and caught a glimpse of the hungry, wan faces, the dejected, care-worn slaves peering hungrily at the half-filled cafés, and then turned your eyes toward a great plug-ugly policeman grasping a bunch of slaves and taking them to the jail on a charge of vagrancy, there to be tried and receive thirty days, I am under the impression you would gasp with horror until it fired you with a burning impetus to send broadcast the message : "Workers of the world, unite ; you have nothing to lose but your chains."

This winter has been a severe one for the slaves, and has provided a good harvest for the Salvation Army. The number of converts has been so great that they absolutely refused to save any more on the credit system, the poor, hungry toil-warped slaves being forced to beg, starve, and suffer incredible hardship. Yet, what sympathy have I with them? When we come forward and offer to them a solution to free them from the manacles of starvation, they walk like fools into the jails the degenerate minds have built, and how stupid to allow some bloated parasite to feast and wine off the things that they have produced.

It is a curious paradox, but still the fight is raging with all the ferocity of animal passion to teach the slaves their true position in Society, and we are doing it, believe me.

Slaves of the Rail.

As to the conditions that are general around here, I would like to picture to you the typical life of a railroad construction worker, for that is the usual occupation to which a slave in Canada has to resort.

All that a slave has here is what he carries on his back. That is, a pair of dirty, old, lousy blankets which serve as his home and possessions. In camp his bed-chamber is a double-decker—*i.e.*, a few boards constructed so that you may lay your worn-out bones on top over a few more huddled-up slaves. The Hotel à la carte of pork and beans—and beans and pork for a change—is admirably served in a tattered old tent with, at times, a few falls of snow to remind him it is winter, and after working a month, he is brought face to face with some mathematical problems as to why one dollar per— was stopped for hospital, five dollars for commissary, and about ten dollars for something that he should have had if he had not !

GOLDEN PRIVET.

Finest Stock in the World.
100,000 to choose from.

15in. to 18in., 3s. ; 18in. to 2ft., 4s. ; 2ft. to 2ft. 6in., 5s. ; 2ft. 6in. to 3ft., 6s. ; 3ft., 9s. per doz.   Specimens from 2s. each.

All other Shrubs equally Cheap.

Carriage paid on order of 10s.

F. BAKER & SONS,
— *The Nurseries,* —

LOWER TOOTING and MERTON.

1 minute from Merton Tram Terminus.

A

Remedy
for the
SWEATING SYSTEM !

Do you know that you can improve your conditions and those of your fellow-workers without any sacrifice ? How ! By supporting true Co-operation. By dealing at our Co-operative Stores, you strike at the great evil of sweating. We are not out for profit but to fight against poverty and starvation. Do not forget that these evils exist largely on account of the selfishness of those who possess the means of production and distribution, and remember to do your part by joining our Society at once. Buy C.W.S. (Co-operative productions) only, and be a true Co-operator. We stock the best Grocery & Drapery goods. Try our Teas at 1/4, 1/6, and 1/9, all full weight without the wrapper.

The Hotel & Restaurant Employees'

Co-operative Society, Ltd.,

12, LITTLE NEWPORT ST.,
CHARING CROSS ROAD, W.C.

Large Hall (seating 250) To Let for Meetings, Concerts, &c. Special terms to Trade Unions.

Emigrants, Keep Away !

The conditions here are bad, despite the attempt of the C.P. Rly. to try and flood the country with workers. If they only knew they would stay at home. There are thousands here looking for a master, and still the revolutionary fight is raging and growing enormously. This is a new local of about a year's existence, and we muster about 500, despite the despots forbidding free speech here. We are putting forward assiduously a new scheme whereby we can perfect a system of better organisation, which, roughly outlined, means that we are intending to concentrate all energy with a view to embracing the workers on the job, instead of wasting and sapping our vitality at the street-corner.

Kindly warn all emigrants through the medium of any influence as to the true conditions, and to keep away unless they are good rebels.—Yours for Industrial Freedom,

D. EVANS,
Secretary.

Local 79 I.W.W.,
134, 9th Avenue W.,
Calgary, Alberta,
Canada.
April 3, 1913.

The Syndicalist
and Amalgamation News

Edited under the :: auspices of the :: :: Industrial Syndicalist Education League. ::

President
TOM MANN

Secretary
GUY BOWMAN

VOL. III. NO. 2.   LONDON. FEBRUARY, 1914.   MONTHLY. ONE PENNY.

WHAT IS SYNDICALISM?

One of the most effective ways to neutralise an inconvenient movement is to patronise and pervert it. This has happened to Socialism until Socialism stands for anything one likes. Socialism to-day means anything — or nothing, and so has ceased to be any more a menace to the security of the plundering class.

The general theory of Socialism is sound enough, but the difficulty has always been one of the ways and means of bringing it about. This difficulty has been accentuated by the confusion of thought which prevails throughout the Socialist movement.

To provide these ways and means Syndicalism was forged, as a weapon is forged; not as a separate and antagonistic movement, but simply as an instrument. Having served its purpose in the warfare against the common enemy, capitalism; having enabled the Socialists to achieve their aim, Syndicalism would be laid aside, as one lays aside a sword after the battle.

This position and this purpose have been so carefully and precisely explained in "The Syndicalist" that only the hopelessly stupid or the deliberately dishonest could possibly misinterpret Syndicalism. "The Syndicalist" was issued regularly each month during 1912, part of 1913, and is now once again being issued regularly each month. Moreover, Syndicalism was defined with great care and in unmistakable terms by Guy Bowman in his pamphlet, "Syndicalism ; Its Basis and Ultimate Aim."

Syndicalism, in brief, consists in bringing about a certain kind of *industrial* organisation among those of the wage-workers who are sufficiently intelligent to be class-conscious. This organisation would enable these workers to succeed, even as a minority, where the whole labour movement signally fails, and is bound to fail, in the political field. The reason for this failure is that the political field is held by the plundering class, who will not permit it to be occupied by any really revolutionary members of the working-class.

But on the industrial field things are different. The workers are actually in possession there, if they only knew it. They have the whole machinery of production and distribution under their hands. Even a minority of Syndicalist workers in each industry could so order it that the plundering class who battens upon it and upon the workers in it would find precious little " batten " left there. And this without recourse to an actual strike.

How comes it, then, that' Syndicalism has been, and is, so bitterly opposed, even in such Socialist quarters as might have been expected to welcome it with open arms?

The reason is, we think, that the corrosion of parliamentary politics has so eaten into the souls of the leading exponents of Socialism that they are unable to understand or to conceive of anything else. And this despite the manifest failures of their hopeless policy!

Parliamentarism and the bureaucratic obsession which comes of it : these are the twin superstitions which must be dissipated if ever the working-class is to achieve emancipation.

JACK RADCLIFFE.

TRITE AND TRIPE.

A COLLECTION OF FAKES FOR MUGWUMPS ON THE MAKE.

Our policy hitherto has been to refrain from criticising other sections of what is called the "advanced" Labour movement. Fragments of Syndicalist ideas have, however, now been adopted by so many persons in the Socialist, Labour, and Trade Union movements that for the sake of clearness of thought it is necessary to examine them one by one.

INDUSTRIAL DEMOCRACY.

Some twenty years ago Mr. and Mrs. Sidney Webb wrote a book called "Industrial Democracy." There was nothing particularly original in that book, as might have been expected considering its source. The dry-as-dust bureaucratic minds of the Webbs produced the usual quantities of dust—such "rare and refreshing fruit" as is found by the shores of the Dead Sea. The Central Labour College, apparently, adopted the gospel of the Webbs. Hence anything like originality could not hope to grow in that barren place. The South Wales Miners' Federation and the National Union of Railwaymen support it and send students there. Here they have their minds moulded in accordance with the gospel of the Webbs and St. Marx. Then they are scattered over the country, just so many gramophone records preaching "Industrial Democracy," and using such words as " machinofacture " in order to try and make themselves important. TRADE Unions must be amalgamated into INDUSTRIAL Unions. Industrial Unions must combine to fight their battles. Vested interests of leaders prevent this consummation ; therefore : To hell with leaders. All of which is trite and—tripe, and none the less tripe because true. These outworn platitudes are preached by nobodies to those who do not take them seriously, nor care. As Frank Rose puts it, they have ranted about " Solidarity " while their overt acts have frustrated it, and they chatter about economics without knowing what it means.

As we have said of Social Democracy, Industrial Democracy means " the apotheosis of the weak, the exaltation of the defeated, the enthronement of the inefficient,and the survival of the unfittest."

And the Capitalist " fat man " looks on and laughs.

INDUSTRIAL UNIONISM.

As regards organisation, Industrial Unionism proposes the formation of brand-new Unions, of a kind diametrically opposed to the existing ones, whereas Syndicalism proposes to convert the existing ones. However, the formation of new Unions, or the use of the old ones for revolutionary purposes, may be considered rather as a question to be decided according to circumstances in each country than as a fundamental point distinguishing Industrial Unionism from Syndicalism.

Syndicalism was introduced after an extended propaganda of Industrial Unionism has been carried on. Most of the supporters came from the ranks of those who had been influenced by that previous propaganda, and Syndicalism was looked upon as being Industrial Unionism to be brought about by converting the existing Unions. This was perfectly true in a way, but was not all the truth.

Most of the advocates of Industrial Unionism see in the "One Big Union " idea the beginning and the end of their activities, and to this we Syndicalists object, and object seriously.

Whether intentionally or not, it is obvious that our Industrial Unionist friends have in their minds the creation of a centralised economic State, which from the very nature of its formation would speedily develop the attributes of a State—namely, the making of laws for its maintenance and providing moral and violent means in order to get those laws enforced.

Syndicalists stand for the freedom of the individual, and are therefore as much opposed to an Industrial State as to a Political State. Actually, we object to an Industrial State even more strenuously than we do a Political State ; for, under the second there are, at least, some people who are free, but under the first there would not be one man or woman left free.

There is a form of organisation which many Trade Unionists have adopted where they are well organised—namely, the shop committee—which is to us a most important matter, for through the establishment of shop-committees in each plant a still more localised form of autonomy can be obtained than even the autonomy of the local branch of the National Industrial Union would afford.

The establishment of autonomous workshops controlled through a shop committee means that the individual's initiative would have much greater possibilities of development. Thus, whilst we support the industrial form or organisation because of its possibilities for the growth of Solidarity, we also strive to make ample provision for individual freedom and initiative.

Industrial Unionism is the first item of the Syndicalist programme ; Direct Action as a weapon is another step towards the development of Freedom for the individual ; Sabotage is a direct affirmation of the individual's will, and we see our final hope in the free co-operation of individual workers controlling themselves from the autonomous workshop upwards. The necessary interconnection between trade and trade could be obtained by means of the Trades Council. We would have the local arrangements more important than any centre, because delegates at a centre always develop separate interests ; but if for the purpose of any special industry some central arrangement was necessary, then for that industrial purpose a central committee

could be formed ; in every case the local producers would be the important people, and any more distant committees at centres would be " regrettable necessities."

GUILD SOCIALISM.

Middle-class of the middle-class, with all the shortcomings (we had almost said " stupidities ") of the middle-classes writ large across it, " Guild Socialism " stands forth as the latest lucubration of the middle-class mind. It is a " cool steal " of the leading ideas of Syndicalism and a deliberate perversion of them.

We do not so much object to the term " guild " as applied to the various autonomous industries, linked together for the service of the common weal, such as is advocated by Syndicalism. But we do protest against the " State " idea which is associated with it in Guild Socialism.

Middle-class people, even when they become Socialists, cannot get rid of the idea that the working class is their " inferior " ; that the workers need to be " educated," drilled, disciplined, and generally nursed for a very long time before they will be able to walk by themselves. The very reverse is actually the truth. The average middle-class person, even if sentimentally a Socialist, knows no more about the real lives and thoughts and aspirations of the workers than of some obscure African tribe. It has been thrown against some of the Syndicalists that they are " middle-class " men. Well, by birth and early education, may be. But circumstances have " declassed " us, so that we are now wage-workers ; we are proletarians of the proletariat, and, realising this fact, we are class-conscious. Only one who has passed through the school of economic adversity is completely educated ; only he can come en rapport, as it were, with the " soul " of the wage-workers, of whom he is now one himself.

It is just the plain truth when we say that the ordinary wage-worker, of average intelligence, is better capable of taking care of himself than the half-educated middle-class man who wants to advise him. He knows how to make the wheels of the world go round.

DAILY HERALDISM.

The policy of the " Daily Herald " is to have no policy beyond " making rebels "—whatever that may mean. Rich women who rebel against want of a vote with which to protect their property join hands with anarchists.

We recognise that the " Daily Herald " has done good work of sorts, if only exposing the futility of parliamentarism, in flagellating those flabby human jelly-fish, the Labour Members, in showing up the pretentious humbug of Ramsay MacDonald, in stripping the mask of hypocrisy from the fat face of the Capitalist ogre. But, unfortunately, the " Daily Herald " is looked upon by most people, including the unintelligent among the Socialists, as a Syndicalist paper ; whereas the " Daily Herald " is nothing of the sort.

The controllers of the " Daily Herald," though they are continuously jeering and sneering at parliamentarianism, are, every one of them, from Lansbury downwards, passing through Ben Tillett and his pup Bob Williams, parliamentary candidates ; and if they have not yet been officially adopted in some constituency or other they are so in their own minds.

LARKINISM.

We have no doubt whatever of the absolute self-sacrificing sincerity of Jim Larkin. We admire his absolute singleness of purpose. But Larkin is a man of deep feeling and real sympathy, not of deep reasoning and real knowledge. Moreover, his mind is warped by clericalism.

Where the wealth is, there will the priests be also. So long as the wage-slaves of Dublin or anywhere else respect priests their servitude is hopeless.

Whatever Larkinism may be, it is not Syndicalism, because Larkin looks forward to an Irish Parliamentary Labour Party. Besides, we have always said that a strike that lasts more than a week is hopeless.

THE " TWO ARM " POLICY OF THE S.L.P.

Industrial Democracy, Industrial Unionism, Guild Socialism, Daily Heraldism, and other like " isms " all fall lamentably short both as ideals or as " practicable politics." They all advocate (with the exception of one section of the I.W.W'ers) the " two arm " policy, political (parliamentary) action joined with industrial organisation. This was the pet theory of the mummified Pope De Leon of America, and was imported in this country several years ago by the Socialist Labour Party. The Fabians, Guild Socialists, and Lansburyites would not, of course, dream of joining the S.L.P. They all laugh and jeer at it, and consider it a most negligible quantity. Yet their policy is exactly the same, but perhaps the S.L.P. would not dream of admitting them into their ranks, because it does not want fakirs.

Some of the advocates of the above " isms " fail to understand that by this linking of irreconcilable and mutually antagonistic methods they are frustrating the very objects they say they have in view. Others deliberately deceive because thy are " labour fakirs " on the hunt for soft jobs.

No politicians, no leaders, can ever win emancipation for the wage-workers. This can only be achieved by the workers themselves. This can only be achieved by the workers, and this is why Syndicalism is abused and maligned and misrepresented by the " mugwumps on the make."

WHERE THEY ARE SINCERE.

If a man who is, or wishes to be, a Member of Parliament assures you that it would be unwise to abandon the weapon of the vote, you are naturally inclined to consider his advice not quite impartial. It is votes for Parliament that give him a holiday in India or make him a somebody in Albert Hall demonstrations on Women's Suffrage. Labour politicians like power and prominence and intercourse with the rich and educated classes.

If they tell you that there is a Parliamentary Labour Party in South Africa, where martial law has been proclaimed in consequence of a strike, and where nine Labour speakers have been exiled, and that this proves how useful a Labour Party in Parliament is, you may be obliged to smile at the influence of personal interest on men's reasoning.

If women, while declaring that votes for women is the cure for every evil under the sun, forget to say that, in the opinion of many of the ardent advocates of women's suffrage, the tendency of the poor to attack the property of the rich is one of the greatest of evils, and that the propertied women's vote would be a great protection to her property. we may perhaps suspect that the women's suffrage movement is as insincere as other political movements.

On one subject only are we likely to see any sincere opinions in the Press of to-day. There is a hint of truthfulness in passages where we read of Botha and the iron politicians of South Africa *saving society*. Society, of course, is the present order of society, in which the fat and strong feed on the thin and weak.

Yes : men worship strength, and are really impressed when they see a man able to crush other men.

The future is hidden from us by a veil. But it is not necessary, or even probable, that the power of the workers should be shown by direct physical attack on the rich.

When they are conscious of the injustice of the world, of the lies with which the bestial lowness of commercialism is sanctified, the workers will be unable to live quiet lives of obedient drudgery. One man will go home unexpectedly and leave the rest of his gang disorganised ; another will secretly attack his machine and leave it crippled ; here a little group will plot how to madden their manager and make his life a burden ; there a whole crowd will be seized with slowness of movement—all these movements will be even worse to face than strikers, because the effects of a strike are calculable. Armed soldiers cannot make men do their work bearably well.

Remember this, workers, and prepare the minds of your fellows for the day of revenge.

The work will either be done by the workers for themselves or it will never be done at all.

ARTHUR D. LEWIS.

The Syndicalist
and Amalgamation News.

EDITED UNDER THE AUSPICES OF

The Industrial Syndicalist Education League

Offices—
4, MAUDE TERRACE, WALTHAMSTOW,
LONDON, E.

MONTHLY - ONE PENNY.

Post Paid Subscription—
Great Britain or Abroad ... 12 months 1s. 6d.

Bundle Rates—
1s. 6d. per quire, Carriage Paid.
U.K.F. TERMS TO NEWSAGENTS.

The Receipt of a Sample Copy is an invitation to Subscribe.

FEBRUARY, 1914.

INVINCIBLE IGNORANCE.

In another column we publish a letter from Mr. H. E. Langridge, of Australia, in which he informs us that from the creation of the world all great changes, such as the abolition of slavery and feudalism, have been due to political action.

But it is not true.

Consider the abolition of slavery in Europe. The mere fact that up to the time of Justinian the law restricted the power of masters by manumission to free their slaves, and that for a very long time the number of slaves diminished while the number of serfs increased, shows that a process was going on which the law at one time restrained, at another long after encouraged, but at no time created.

The abolition of the feudal system and of serfdom was a very gradual process, in which all historians select the Black Death as an important factor. This great pestilence left the lords of the manor with too much land for the diminished number of labourers; their revenues from land, at that time paid mainly in produce, diminished, while the cost of "free labour" increased. They were, therefore, forced to substitute pasturage of sheep, which required little labour, for the growth of crops, which required much. In order to do this they had to dispossess the serfs of their rights to the strips of land cultivated in common and redistributed every year.

It was without any change in the law that serfdom in England gradually ceased to exist.

When Mr. Langridge says "maximum wage abolished (after Black Plague)" he means maximum wage *fixed* in the Statute of Labourers. He is very silly to refer to this law at all, because it is an evidence of the powerlessness of parliament. Death, as we have said, by greatly lessening the number of labourers, raised wages. Parliament, enraged at this, tried to force them downwards by making it a crime, punishable by imprisonment, to ask for more than the earlier rates; but the law could not be enforced, and therefore, for a century, fresh laws had to be passed with a similar aim.

In more recent times, in France, the last remains of serfdom were abolished by the national assembly, a representative body. But why did they do it? *Because the peasants had by Direct Action burnt the castles of the nobles in order to destroy all records of the labour they had to give to their masters.*

This is very instructive. Nothing could more neatly illustrate our view of what parliaments do at times of great change. No one but a fool says that so long as parliament exists it will not at such times try to interfere.

But we say that such crises are produced outside parliament by the struggles between class and class.

When pressure is brought to bear on parliament, parliament is forced to act; and members of parliament forget whether they are Conservatives, Liberals, or Socialists.

Ordinary parliamentary reforms leave the few on top and the many slaving below.

Mr. Langridge must either be very ignorant or have a great faith in the ignorance of others, otherwise he could never have written his list of benefits due to political action.

But even if his list were as convincing as it is absurd, we should protest against too much influence being exerted by past history. History never repeats itself, and the question is not how men have struggled in the past but how we can most quickly get them to struggle for and win their freedom in the future. We are tired of arguments which begin "If the working class were more intelligent and would

vote only for Socialist candidates——" Even the scab knows that the idea at the bottom of trade unionism is the protection of the working class against the employing and propertied class; but at election times the majority of the electors are as much excited about Home Rule and about the peculiar wickedness of landlords and peers as they are by what concerns them.

Syndicalism acting through Trade Unionism unites the working class as a class having certain class interests. Politics unites into parties persons belonging to all classes but having certain opinions in common.

It is necessary with "damnable iteration" to repeat these simple facts owing to the invincible ignorance of our opponents.

AN INTERNATIONAL CONSPIRACY.

In the House of Lords Lord Murray has just made his confession. He, too, bought Marconis both for himself and as an investment for the Liberal Party.

We call attention to the fact in order to add the information that Lord Murray is not a Jew. Whatever the *New Witness* may think, not all knaves in Christendom are Jews. There are Protestants and Roman Catholics and Atheists among the capitalists.

Those who idealise the Catholic Church imagine it as standing on the side of the poor and struggling to restore a world of peasant proprietors and of small independent craftsmen owning their own tools.

The real Roman Catholic Church is always on the side of the rich. Remember Dublin!

The Duke of Norfolk and Lord Rothschild are hand in hand against the workers.

There is no Jewish conspiracy outside the imagination of certain Christians. The Jewish capitalist is too degenerate to conspire for any great aim. He is in a conspiracy against everyone and for his own gain, except when for the sake of that gain he has to protect the capitalist class.

But there is an international Catholic Church, always working against the worker.

We are opposed to all priests, including the Nonconformists, who nobbled the Labour Party, and the Atheists, who waste time in a depressing way by explaining what is not and has not happened.

It is impossible for most people who are acquainted with modern knowledge to accept the views of the universe taken by the established religions. Therefore the old religions must be swept away in order that the new faith which will inspire revolutionary action may arise.

But it will be a new faith inspiring new and bolder action.

We shall have more to say about the international power of the Roman Catholic Church and how it is used to crush the workers in future issues.

HOW LONG?

In England, where the envy of the world
　is earned,
They hold men's souls as less than com-
　mon dust;
For dust—in bulk—by commerce can be
　turned
To clinking gold. And the turners get
　—a crust!

In our " dear land "—the home of heroes'
　dreams—
The plagues of Hell are let loose
　unawares,
And Liberty as but a phantom seems
Who mocks us in our bitterest
　despairs.

In England, where the hosts of " holy "
　churches stand
And countless priests the Word of God
　proclaim,
The monster Greed and all his hideous
　band
Suck blood from England's helpless—
　and in God's Name!

Her pomp and splendour and her world-
　wide fame
Are built on silent MURDER, and the
　starved child's tears;
On toiling manhood's groans and toiling
　woman's shame;
And we cry " Long live Britannia ! "
　all the years!

Our saviours—who are fighting for the
　Truth—
They crucify and doom to prison cell.
One god has England—one that knows
　no ruth.
Bloody is its altar, and its rule is Hell.

How long shall England wallow in this
　mire?
When shall her people stand—a people
　free?
When be blotted out those words all writ
　in fire—
" England ! Thou are the land of
　Infamy ! "?

ANNA LINCOLN.

STATE OWNERSHIP AND THE WORKERS' LOT.

By JOHN LEWIS LINCOLN.

The movement towards the state ownership of the railways and the mines is a very serious mistake for the workers. The words state ownership mean, under capitalism, passing the management of these industries from private companies of dividend shareholders to government dividend stockholders. The *principle* of the management will be the same—the making of dividends, profits, out of the *workers*.

As are the shareholders now, so will the stockholders be the first and last consideration, and the highly-salaried official will be as highly salaried if he can sweat the workers in the stockholders' interests. Then, as now, the official will be paid for making dividends.

Postal Serfs.

This driving force operates in the state owned Post Office. Every conceivable means and excuse to force down the wages of the *workers* is used. The postal authorities take advantage of unemployment and necessity ruthlessly in the interests of their £4,000,000 a year profit. In every department they squeeze, and squeeze, and recover in fines from the workers all they can.

It is true that an advance in wages of £750,000 a year has just been made, but that is because the postal authorities have been face to face with the grave and serious discontent their " profit-making methods " has created. It is cheaper to give this advance, *and get it back by* new methods, than face the rapid desertion of their workers to other labour markets, the terrific loss an efficient postal strike would cause *them* and the business world. It is state owned and run in the interests of business far more than for the use of private citizens, who only get the advantages *given* to the business world.

The Army's Cheap Clothes.

The state-owned Army and Navy have a rank and file who are paid servants of the King. Their pay is very enticing, and causes thousands to desert other occupations for the service of their country. Does anybody smile? The great difficulty *really* is to get men at all, and only life's worst dregs of misfortune " take the shilling."

The expenses of the Army and the Navy have to be kept *down*. The *workers* are ground down to the least of subsistence possible.

The Army and the Navy are clothed and supplied with ammunition in government-managed clothing shops and arsenals.

The *workers* are here reduced to absolute *want*, to starvation pay. The women workers are so frightfully paid that the government management has almost made prostitution a necessity as a means of living.

There is the police force. I was in Birmingham when a strike of the police force was threatened and involved the city fathers (?) in an increased annual wages bill of £30,000, which enormous increase of one or two shillings a week for each man *of the rank and file* was to *ease* the *starvation* pay that is still given to them even now.

The expenses of policing have to be kept *down*. They are taken out of the *workers*.

State Slavery.

My title ought to be " State Ownership and the Workers' Little." It is into *this* that the railway men and the miners are being *led* by great and brilliant thinkers. State servants are completely under the control of the state authorities. Their wages fall because they dutifully obey. They are completely *slaves*. The rules and regulations provide directly or indirectly for insubordination. They must do what they are told, take what they are given in insolence and brutality and wages, and go where they are *drafted*, or leave their employment. The drafting of the workers means that they have no security of personal friendships, of home life, of intellectual and creative effort extending over a number of years or through a lifetime apart from their *work*.

The court-martial and the death penalty of the Army and Navy for insubordination has its equal in state-owned industry. You do your work in complete slavery or you leave the service—you lose your *work*. You are inside or outside. You have your starvation wages or you have starvation.

Such are the conditions of state owner-

ship under capitalism, as we *know* them, for the *workers*.

The Way Out.

Whether there is or there is not a soldiers' union or a Navy servicemen's union I have never heard. I should say not, because of the *direct* rules and regulations controlling *discipline* of the rank and file. Leaving the service is criminal—desertion and penalties touching the *person* complete the degradation and complete slavery of the Army and Navy man.

It will not be long before state-owned industry, *under* capitalism, will be so disciplined.

It has already had the *consent* of the Postal Union, numbering 37,000. They decided by ballot that they had no right to strike for better wages. It is not in their *masters'* rules and regulations.

It is already " in the air " that civil servants ought not to exercise the vote for the sake of discipline. The indirect " Obey, or go outside " of the Post Office is responsible for the discipline of the Postal Union in declaring they have no right to strike.

This is the *weakness* of the *individual*. The weakness of the individual is the *advantage* of those in power, whatever form the power may take. I may be, for example, a postman drawing an Army pension. The wages of my post are 21s. a week. My pension is 3s. a week compensation. The postal authorities give *me* 18s. a week and my pension brings it up to 21s. That is how one government department saves on another. " Obey, or go out " is the order to the individual.

Unite!

But *I* am a member of the Postal Union of 37,000 *men* who do *not* consent to this. I am the *whole* service, and I will *not* work on these terms.

I stop delivering letters. There are 37,000 of me. The whole service stops delivering letters. The whole business world is involved in terrific money loss, credit loss, and loss of business because of the *manifest* roguery of a State department.

The *public* says, " Pay the man his honest wages and get the postmen back to work. We can't go on. *We are ruined.*"

You have found a *death* penalty for the *master*. He has to submit to *discipline*.

I, as an individual, can lose my *weakness* by becoming an organised unit of 2,000,000 railway *workers*, 800,000 miners, an organised association of three, four, or seven million *workers*, who will *not* consent to the low wages and the dragooning of the *master* class under capitalism.

I have been pleased to see the masters *obey* the workers in reinstating servants wrongfully dismissed. The weakness of the individual has, so far, completely vanished.

The *penalty* was only threatened. The workers do not yet understand the *weakness* of business. The tumbling in of the masters after recent great strikes shows this weakness.

(*To be continued.*)

MORE BRASS.

A novel idea has occurred to the promoters of a scheme for a Sweepstake in connection with races for the Lincolnshire Handicap and the Derby.

A syndicate called the Turf Pool Syndicate, of Geneva, have put the sum of £1,250 to be handed over to any section of the Labour Movement that ten bonâ-fide Trade Unionists may recommend, and the following have been invited and accepted the invitation to recommend the allocation of the monies :—

Tom Mann, A.S.E.

A. A. Purcell, Furnishing Trades.

J. E. Gregory (late President L.T.C.).

J. Hopkins, Coalporters.

T. Bogie, Scottish Tailors.

Tom Higginson, Boilermakers.

Councillor W. B. Parker, L.S.C.

Geo. Carson, Glasgow Trades Council.

W. Goffrey, Bookbinders.

J. Macdonald, London Tailors.

Over and above this, the Syndicate, who from their published comments seem to be a straightforward firm, have invited the aforementioned to be present at the draw and satisfy themselves as to the genuineness of the concern, which has been accepted.

It will be interesting to note which section of the many deserving funds the £1,250 will benefit.

THE HOBO.
By LAURA PAYNE EMERSON.

The sun hung low o'er the mountain,
　Tinting each rugged crest,
And painting in golden glory
　The bending skies of the West;
When, dark like a speck on the landscape,
　With his blankets across his back,
Came a worn and weary hobo
　Down the dusty railroad track.

By the curve of the road at nightfall,
　Where the stars above glimmer and peep
Through a curtain of leaves and grasses,
　He laid him down to sleep;
And he thought as the song of the night
　bird
Soothed his tired and troubled mind :
There's room in the world, and plenty
　For all except me and my kind.

He slept, and lived in dreamland
　Where love spread her splendid wings,
And bore him from old surroundings
　To a better scheme of things.
He dwelt in a cosy cottage,
　With flowers blooming round the door,
Where all was wealth and gladness—
　There were no tramps, no poor.

A sweetheart wife beside him
　Made him of all men blest,
While the wee curly head of their darling
　Nestled close on his manly breast.
And there were great things to be doing ;
　The best that was in him he gave
To a world with no soldiers, no shackles,
　No prisons, no master, or slave.

O woe ! to a world whose workers
　Are cast like chaff to the wind—
When the lords cannot use them with
　profit—
Must go seeking, but cannot find.
O, cursed be the system for ever
　That robs human life of a home,
And sends young and old to the highway
　In quest of a living to roam.

O brother, out there by the roadside,
　O sister, outcast, in despair,
I am not fooled by false standards—
　I know very well why you're there.
'Twixt the millstones of life they have
　ground you ;
'Neath the Juggernaut, fainting, you lie,
Your blood turns the earth to crimson ;
　They are leaving you there to die.

But why will you die, ye toilers?
　You have the power and the might
To wrest from the cravens who hold them
Your bread, your freedom, your right.
O rise! in your infinite numbers;
　Unite on the sea and the land.
Let tyrants implore you for mercy.
Take the reins of the world in your hands.

THE SONG OF THE SCAB.

By "SCORPION."

Tune: "LADS IN NAVY BLUE."

Sing a song in praise of all the blacklegs.
Sing a song about the jolly scab,
He who helps us when the workers strike
And stops our game of grab.
Why always shout the praise of Tommy Atkins
And ne'er a word for scabs?
For when on strike
They do the thing we like
And drive our workmen back.
     Why in our glory do we tower?
     What is the secret of our power?

WORKERS' REPLY.

It is the scab, sir, the dirty scab, sir,
Which keeps the workers down.
Our old song, "Britannia Rules the
     Slaves" ("waves," beg pardon!),
We'll sing in every town.
It is the scab, sir, the dirty scab, sir,
Which keeps our wages down.
For he bludgeons us in bed (Dublin)
Till we're very nearly dead,
The lively little scabs in NAVY blue!

Sing a song in praise of LORANORDER,
     Sing a song how Botha broke the strike!
Such brave men we'll honour in the Press.
Such men as he we like!
Why should we run the mines with
     British labour
When blackmen are so cheap?
With Botha's help
We'll make the strikers yelp
And get the niggers back!
     Why in our glory do we tower?
     What is the secret of our power?

WORKERS' REPLY.

It is the burgher, the "loyal" burgher,
Who helps the fat man slay.
Our old song, "Britannia Rules the
     Slaves,"
We're going to sing to-day!
It is the burgher, the loyal burgher,
Who makes the railways pay.
For the railways must be run
By the help of scab and gun,
And the lively little scabs in KHARKI, too!

POLITICIANS & PROSTITUTES

I cannot think why the Women's Suffrage politicians are so perturbed by prostitution. A politician is a politician because he desires power; he is ambitious, and sees no less repulsive way of getting an easy life than by making popular statements on public platforms which he and other people, who are really in political circles, know must not be interpreted literally. He offers Tariff Reform or Socialism as easy cures for unemployment when he means they will increase somebody's profits or find Government jobs for a lot of people who have not secure incomes at present.

A prostitute is a prostitute because she is over-developed sexually at the age of sixteen or so, and has no more attractive life than that of prostitution open to her. The life has its disadvantages—precariousness, and the need to pretend affection where it is not felt. But the politician has to talk about the will of the people prevailing when he is quite determined it shall not.

There is far less deception about prostitution than about politics. The politician promises what he and his set never intend to give; his clothing of words conceals a very different body of performance. The prostitute really intends to give, but may not be able to retain all that expectation would suggest. It is not her fault that, since we cannot always be passionate, she must assume a desire when she has it not; but at least the tangible opportunity which she sold she faithfully puts before you.

With the politician it is the other way round. The nearer you get to tangible results the less he offers you.

To call prostitution "white slavery" is, of course, misleading. The shop-assistant is a slave in the same sense as the prostitute is. The male procurer, ponce, or bully is in most parts of the world an exceptional companion of the prostitute, and still more exceptionally does he coerce her in the slightest degree.

I must not let any personal experience of or temptation towards either illicit sexual intercourse or political power affect my judgment as to their relative harmfulness. Both do great harm. Why one should so much annoy those addicted to the other is not clear to me.

           A. WALTER DANIELLS.

OUR SUNDAY EVENINGS IN LONDON.

By ALAN ADAIR.

The Sunday evening meetings at Little Newport Street have not been altogether successful. Mind you, they have not been bad meetings : the discussions have all been worth having, and there have been first-rate speeches at some of them, but we have been late in getting started and the audiences were not as big as they ought to be. Of course, both lateness and small numbers are common ailments at all kinds of meetings, and good work may be done in spite of them; but we don't want to suffer from common ailments. We want our affairs to go with a swing; we mean to make them go with a swing, and so long as they don't go with a sufficient swing to give us a full hall every Sunday night we shall continue to say that our meetings are not altogether successful. Still, we must own that we have no right to complain; we have found new sympathisers, we have thrashed out debated questions of interest to all Syndicalists, and, finally, we have sold our literature and laid a good ground on which to build the success of the coming season.

For Discussion.

In one particular, perhaps, there has been a certain misunderstanding as to the purposes of the meetings. Last year the course of lectures that we had in the same hall was held for the purpose of explaining the nature of the Syndicalist proposals. Each lecturer represented the I.S.E.L., and each lecturer expressed the avowed opinions of the League. The meetings, in fact, were chiefly propagandist. But this year we are cruising on another tack; the propaganda is going on in other ways. These meetings are for discussion and criticism. We want the cloudy, unsettled element in our ideas to be cleared up in our debates; we want to find out the practical connection between Syndicalism and the things that are happening round about us. Syndicalism is always the reflection of the conditions of the moment, and to keep its reflections clear and accurate, it must be kept polished by criticism and discussion. So, though we hate needless talk and argument, we are frankly running these meetings for the sake of having conflicting points of view put before us. We are not a Church. We want our faults and limitations to be shown us, and our platform is put at the disposal of anyone who can interest us, whether he be a Syndicalist or not. But some of our friends do not see this.

Some Lectures.

For instance, when A. G. Buckenham came to address us on "The Relation of Free Trade to Syndicalism" there were one or two who said that, as Buckenham still believes in politics to a certain extent, therefore he was not qualified to take our platform. But, as a matter of fact, Buckenham's want of decision on the whole question of parliamentary action evoked one of the most vigorous, cut-and-thrust, slashing, dashing debates that we have had. If the speaker of the evening had taken the usual Syndicalist attitude the whole question might have remained untouched and some of us still have kept a sneaking trust in the ballot-box. As it is, no one who heard the speeches and is not deaf or a fool is likely to say that he still believes much in parliamentary action—unless, of course, he is a liar or one to whom the politicians give money.

When FRED W. DUNN spoke on "The New Unionism and the Old," much the same kind of thing happened. Some of the audience thought that Dunn was not sound in his ideas of a Syndicalist society, and consequently there was a discussion, in which the attitude of Syndicalism to the state was excellently developed.

Our View.

SILVIO CORIO, in his account of the Italian Syndicalist Movement, not only gave us a clear and accurate account of the Conference of the Italian Syndicalist Union, but managed very neatly to give a study of the Syndicalist attitude of mind in the way he answered the discussion.

GUY BOWMAN likewise in his lecture on "The Future of Syndicalism" put forward the characteristic Syndicalist point of view and had some interesting things to say on the problem of the foundation of new unions.

A. W. DAWSON, too, is a good Syndicalist, and though I did not hear his lecture he doubtless talked good Syndicalism, if not good morality, when he spoke on "Syndicalism and the Old Morality."

"How to Sabot the Labour Exchanges," the address with which A. G. Buckenham began the whole series, was also a perforation that no one could criticise as misrepresenting the I.S.E.L. ideas; on the contrary, it was a quite interesting study of something that all Trade Unionists must learn to reckon with, and certainly all good Syndicalists will agree with the lecturer's conclusion that the work of the Labour Exchanges is essentially work that the unions should do and in the near future must do for themselves.

The Future.

In the earlier part of the session there was a little too much of a hand-to-mouth existence about our meetings. That is to say, we only booked our lecturers from week to week, instead of fixing them up in advance. It was a mistake, and we have now remedied it by filling our calendar till the end of March. There are first-rate speakers coming, too. Miss Margaret Douglas is going to debate for us; W. F. Hay is coming from South Wales; John Syme will talk of a Police Union; Miss Talmedge and others equally interesting will praise, criticise, or condemn Syndicalism, and help us in the big, necessary business of finding out where we and those who share our views stand in relationship to the different wheels and pulleys in the complex social mechanism of our day. So let us have good audiences—the meetings will deserve them. We want to feel ourselves in touch with every phase of Syndicalist thought and feeling, and these meetings are the fittest rallying places for our friends and sympathisers. Come and let us fill our hall. Remember the time and place : Sunday, 7.30, the Co-operative Hall, Little Newport Street. It is THE meeting for all Syndicalists.

A MARTYR OF MILITARISM.

By LILY GAIR WILKINSON.

Maria Rygier is again in prison. Time after time she has been imprisoned. Last year in prison she came near to death. No sooner is she liberated than once more she defies the law by her writings and her public speeches, and once more the authorities think it well to get her out of the way.

Maria Rygier does not go to prison because women in Italy want to vote; she goes to prison because there are men and women in Italy who want freedom.

And this time?

This time it is because she wrote an article in defence of Masetti.

Augusto Masetti has been suffering the tortures of military régime in a criminal lunatic asylum for two years; they call him mad because he dared to shoot in the right direction.

Turned His Rifle.

When the Italian war in Tripoli began, this young man, who was a reservist, declared that he would not fight against the Turks. Since he was to be forced to kill, rather than go to Tripoli and murder harmless Arabs with whom he had no quarrel, he chose to turn his rifle against those who ordered him to become a murderer.

On October 30, 1911, Colonel Stroppa was addressing some reservists who were about to sail for Tripoli. He told them to have no pity on the barbarians and infidels whom they were going to fight, but to shoot them down for the glory of king and country. Crying "Down with war; long live Anarchism!" Masetti stepped from the ranks and shot the officer.

At that time Italy had been worked up by the jingo newspapers into a ferment of patriotism. The cry of "Assassin!" went up against Masetti, and most surely he would have been court-martialled and shot if the authorities had not feared an anti-militarist agitation. At such a time it would be serious to have a public trial at which anti-militarist ideals would be uttered. So Masetti was not tried. The rulers of Italy found, however, a simple way to revenge themselves against him. They had him declared mad, and they sent him (always without trial) to a criminal lunatic asylum. There is no worse hell on earth than military régime in a criminal lunatic asylum, and this young Italian hero has endured the agony of imprisonment in such a hell for the last two years.

And for writing in his defence Maria Rygier is again in prison.

There is urgent need to make these things known in this country and to join the Italian comrades in their agitation for the liberation of these prisoners. Anti-militarism in any country is the concern of workers in all countries.

Army Against Workers.

Already in England our rulers are preparing for Conscription. Already the army has been used against the workers in revolt.

We must understand the full meaning of these two facts, so that we may rouse ourselves to an anti-militarist campaign in this country. It is not a milk-and-water peace campaign that we need; not the maudlin hypocrisy of the peace-on-earth-and-goodwill type. No : what we need is the true anti-militarist propaganda of revolutionaries, which will carry the passion of revolution ever into the army and prepare men for actions as brave and as stern as the action of Masetti.

In this country, as in Italy, as everywhere, we have need of men like Augusto Masetti, within the army, who will, since weapons are put into their hands and they are forced to use them, know how to use them in the right way; and we have need outside the army of men and women who, like Maria Rygier, are fearless in their defence of such actions.

IN PRAISE OF POLITICS.

By H. E. LANGRIDGE.

(An open letter to the Trade Unionists of Australia per SYNDICALIST and 150 world's Labour, Trade Union, and Socialist papers.)

DEAR COMRADES,—

Mr. R. S. Ross's long letter in the last issue of our local Labour paper is not calculated to discourage you from devoting the requisite considerable proportion of your leisure energies in the parliamentary area, and consequently from the effort to exclude employers from your political party, so that it becomes a necessity to show the inseparableness of union and political action, that union action is only half industrial if it is not also political, and that political action is nearly entirely directly industrial in character; that political action, instead of being not direct, is the most DIRECT ACTION.

The following list of political achievements is, therefore, recorded, "lest we forget." (The writer would be glad of suggestions for improvement.)

DIRECT ACTION.

INDUSTRIAL LEGISLATION.
(Not including innumerable social enactments giving INDIRECT benefits.)

Past Centuries.—Slavery abolition, feudal abolition, choice of calling, choice of locality, choice of clothing, right to form union, apprenticeship laws, master and servants act, nationalisation (Army, Navy, police, roads, &c.).

Pay.—Maximum wage abolished (after Black Plague), wages a first claim, payment by goods abolished, pay on job or overtime, right to receive notice, limitation of attachment of wages, travel cost allowed, old-age pensions, maternity allowance, invalid pension, unemployment insurance, poll tax replaced by income tax, elementary schooling, school meals, technical education, &c.

Time.—Sunday cessation of work, government holidays, early closing, weekly half-holiday (uniform half-day); travelling time allowed, &c.

Conditions.—Child labour restriction, infant and under fourteen years of age, sanitary accommodation, accident safeguards, accident compensation, workmen's fares, mining on private property, &c.

Competition.—Expulsion of Chinese and other aliens, White Australia, invalidation of immigration agreements, employment pensions, &c.

Bargaining.—Compulsory conferences, industrial tribunals, agreements enforced, picketing permitted, lock-outs and strikes penalised, press gangs abolished, right to jobs and terms, per Government Shipping Office, &c.

Voice in Conference (Parliament).—Franchise, no plural voting, eligibility for election, payment of delegates (members of parliament), secret ballot, &c.

Administration.—Justice of the peaceships, officerships, policeships, ministerial positions (no magistrateships, judgeships, or governorships), &c.

Partial Abolition of Preference for Non-Unionists.

The Commonwealth Labour Party Triennial Conference functions politically for a real existing but crude ONE BIG UNION, in which Unionists and "mixed locals" (the political branches) act as a CLASS. It is born by and reared at the breast of Unionism. It can buy a DESTITUTE ALLOWANCE (invalid pension), or state Labour Parties can by minimum income bill, or free municipal bread and milk, remove the starvation deterrent, and thus allow all wage-earners to join their respective Union. It would throw all supply of labour into the hands of secretaries of respective Unons. The Union secretaries could then immediately solve the UNEMPLOYMENT problem; have former, &c., ELECTED; have employers' balance-sheets audited, and determine wages of superintendents for, and if desirable re-engage, working employer as captain of industry. Unions would subsequently consolidate establishments, so that they would be swiftly nationalised under purely democratically equal control.

Parents beget children, and how powerful is the influence of those children on the parents ! So with Destitute Allowance.

Don't forget that January 31 is latest date for Vic. Easter Conference proposals.

     27, Drummond Street, Carlton,
     Melbourne.

[For our reply to this letter, see "Invincible Ignorance" in another column

---

BOYCOTT
THE INSURANCE CAPITALISTS

If you are insured, if you are about to insure, if you are not insured, it will be to your benefit to write for prospectus and full information of the

"SYNDIC INSURANCE BROKERAGE SOCIETY,"

who are in a position to give expert advice and to transact with the leading Friendly Societies (free from capitalistic control) all kinds of Insurances, for all readers of the "Syndicalist." Arrangements have been made whereby the whole of the commission will be placed to the fund for the "Weekly Syndicalist."

Life and Endowment Assurances are a speciality. We have the best tables. Immediate Full Benefit will be granted on all policies.

Clients forward their premiums by post to us monthly, quarterly, or yearly.

No bother, no fuss, and more money to the "Weekly Syndicalist."

WRITE NOW—AT ONCE—INFORMATION IS FREE.

Manager : Mr. F. C. HIDDEN,
51, Francis Avenue,
Portsmouth.

Industrial Syndicalist Education League.

OBJECT.

To carry on among Trade Unionists and Workers generally a campaign of education in the principles of SYNDICALISM—which is Revolutionary Unionism, since its immediate purpose is to conduct a scientific CLASS WAR against capitalism, such war having for its object the CAPTURE OF THE INDUSTRIAL SYSTEM and its management by the Workers themselves for the benefit of the whole community.

MEMBERSHIP.

The membership is open to any person who accepts the above, no matter what views may be held by that person regarding politics; but NO PERSON WHO DOES NOT DECLARE FOR NON-PARLIAMENTARY ACTION, and is not a bonâ-fide Trade Unionist, may share in the responsible work of administration of the League.

OFFICIAL ORGAN.

"The Syndicalist," Monthly. Price 1d., post free 1½d. Yearly subscription, 1s. 6d. prepaid.—Published by Guy Bowman, 4, Maude Terrace, Walthamstow, London, E.

LITERATURE.

Latest Pamphlets out:
"Syndicalism: Its Basis, Methods, and Ultimate Aim," 1d., post free 1½d.
"The Case for Amalgamation," 1d., post free 1½d.
"The Logic of the Machine," 1d., post free 1½d.
Usual discount for quantities to Branches, Societies, &c.

Write for catalogue of further publications to Guy Bowman, 4, Maude Terrace, Walthamstow, London, E.

LECTURES.

Trades Councils, Trade Union Branches, Co-operative Societies, &c., &c., desirous of obtaining a lecturer on "Syndicalism" (no fees whatsoever, expenses only), should write to the General Secretary of the I.S.E.L., Guy Bowman, 4, Maude Terrace, Walthamstow, London, E.

GUY BOWMAN'S FIXTURES.

Feb. 22, Manchester; March 2, Walthamstow; March 4, Hackney; March 8, Anerley; March 12, York; March 13, Sheffield; March 16, Leeds; March 22, Huddersfield; March 29, Birmingham; April 1, Lambeth; April 5, Bury; April 19, Dulwich; April 26, Kingston.

SUNDAY EVENINGS IN LONDON.

A series of lectures and debates, under the auspices of the I.S.E.L., are given every Sunday evening, at 7.30, in the CO-OPERATIVE HALL, 12, Little Newport Street, Charing Cross Road (back of Hippodrome). All welcome. Questions and Discussion.

Printed and published by GUY BOWMAN, 4, Maude Terrace, Walthamstow, E.

The Syndicalist

and Amalgamation News.

Edited under the auspices of the Industrial Syndicalist Education League.

PRESIDENT :
TOM MANN.

SECRETARY :
GUY BOWMAN.

VOL. III.   NO. 3.   LONDON, JUNE, 1914.   MONTHLY, ONE PENNY.

"SOLIDARITY."

May Day and Other Demonstrations.

MEN OR EUNUCHS?

TRAMPS AND SUPER-TRAMPS.

Tramp! tramp!! tramp!!! Hark .o the ragged battalions marching! It is May Day, once the joyfullest festival in Merrie England ; to-day, the most drab, dismal, depressing, and damnable "holiday" in the calendar. Yet our Socialist and Labour papers yawp as though it were evidence that "the good time coming" is at hand! What is the matter with them? Are they sardonically humorous, or merely stupid?

Every year this fantastic parade takes place, and nothing happens. Every year the workers are persuaded to expose their starveling misery to the jeers of the cynical parasites and thieves, as they march Westward, past the clubs and mansions of their exploiters. With them march their "leaders," tramps and super-tramps together. The banners alone give some colour, some semblance of purpose to the business. Is it not a most dreadful exposure of the weakness, the impotence, of the Socialist and Labour Movements?

Arrived in Hyde Park, shepherded by those hired bullies of the master class, the police, the super-tramps make the usual speeches. Hearing them, we find that they have forgotten everything and learnt nothing. We do not like to think that all these orators are dishonest, but surely they must realise that the master class cares nothing for talk, and will give any promises so long as fulfilment is not expected. Deeds, not words, are necessary to stir the master class from its cynical inactivity in the matter of promises made to the Workers. Better that the master class should be forced into a policy of reaction and repression by deeds, than encouraged by empty noise to do nothing. But we fear that the May Day orators suffer from a diarrhœa of words, a disease which is fatal to any sort of strenuous activity!

The afflicted atmosphere having been agitated for the whole of one afternoon, the tramps sing "The Red Flag," cheer for the Social Revolution, and trudge back again to their kennels with another year of hopeless toil and penury before them. How long shall this wretched farce continue?

THEIR PREPOSTEROUS RESOLUTION.

"Universal Adult Suffrage, Payment of Election Expenses, Proportional Representation, Free Naturalisation for all foreigners after three years, continuous residence in Great Britain!"

Ye gods! It takes us back nearly eighty years! Our modern Labour (mis)Leaders have forgotten everything. Have they ever heard of the Chartists? Do they remember the six points of the Charter? Do they know that four out of those six points are now established?—with no results so far as the amelioration of the Workers' lot is concerned! Do they remember the "physical force men" among the Chartists, and how direct action did more to achieve such ends as were achieved than any "peaceful persuasion"? And—do they remember the betrayal of the Chartists by the politicians when more "moderate" councils prevailed?

We may believe that the demands made in the resolution may be granted—some time. We believe that even the initiative and the referendum may be established—some time. But will all these things lead to any alteration, let alone the destruction of the present system of capitalist exploitation and robbery? They will not and they can not.

We wonder if the typical Trade Union Leader understands the why and the wherefore of his Union. A Trade Union is proof of the existence of the Class War. It is evidence of the irreconcilable antagonism between capital and Labour. It makes clear those issues between the thieves and their victims which party-politics is designed to obscure. It should show the Wage-slave that to obtain even the recognition of his rights, he must fight in the last resort. War it is, and war it must be, to the bitter end. But not a war with mouths for guns and words for bullets. The master class knows this well. For this reason the masters select from the ranks of the Wage-workers the physically fittest, feed them, lodge them, and clothe them well, even if they do not pay them too well ; they call them "Police." What the ultimate function of the police is, even the Trade Union Leader knows. Behind the police are other Wage-slaves, perhaps not so well cared for, but not so badly off as the Wage-slave standard goes. If the batons of the police are not enough to slug the discontented Wage-slaves into subjection, the bayonets and bullets of the soldiers follow on.

This is the Class War, you Hyde Park Pifflers, as understood by the master class! Will you NEVER learn?

THE MUGWUMPS ON THE MAKE.

But is it doubtful whether the plundering classes care whether you learn or not. The pitiful display of May 1st is not one calculated to strike terror into them. Rather does it move them to shouts of derisive laughter. Half-fed, ill-clad, depressed, what could such a mob do, even if armed and knowing the use of arms? A few score of resolute, determined men, pledged to carry out the aggressive tactics of Syndicalism, would do more to shake the complacency and the security of the thieves than all these dejected demonstrators. There are such men, and one day they will be heard from.

And the speeches! All the worn and weary whiffling which we have suffered so long! Far better to make gramaphone records and turn them on annually. Such an arrangement would save the whifflers any greater effort than just winding up the machinery. The same old feeble jokes. The same old platitudes, insincerities, and conflicting theories and policies. All might be repeated with far less effort. The crowds would appreciate it just the same, seeing that they do not remember anything from one year to another. It would be possible vastly to improve the programme by wedging in between the speeches a few catchy music-hall songs. But there must be nothing, please, calculated to make the people think. That would never do. First of all it would not suit the Mugwumps on the Make, and secondly, it would not please the crowd. A Board of Censors, composed of Mugwumps, could arrange all that, to their own satisfaction and the satisfaction of the master class upon which they always have one eye lest they should give offence.

Saying this, we do not suggest that there are no earnest men among the anarchists or the various kinds of Socialists. But the very antagonism of these people's different policies makes them negligible. On the other hand, we are convinced that there are those whose business it is to obscure the issues ; to dupe the Wage-slaves into the belief that they are really doing something for them, and not merely seeking their own self-advancement.

These are the Mugwumps on the Make, the paid and trusted retainers of the master class.

"DEMANDING" ON BENDED KNEE.

The most humorous part of the whole business is the making of "demands." What the devil is the use of demanding anything from people whom you know damned well won't grant it unless it suits them? There are occasions when strong language is justified because necessary, and this is one of them. In these demands we can hear the whine of subserviency, and we note a certain weakening at the knee-joints of the demanders. The demand made, there it ends, and the thieves laugh, and proceed—not to grant it!

The master class knows that political "dem"ocracy—and social-democracy most of all—is a sham and a humbug. They know that they have the Wage-slaves under heel economically. They know that the opinion of the majority, even if ascertainable (which it is not), is of no value. They know that the "democratic majority" can be wangled any way they choose by the prostitute press. They know that the "democracy" can be worked up to a frenzy over anything that is not to the "democracy's" interest. The Boer War proved that, and a war-scare now would prove it again. It is proved in Ireland, where Ulster Wage-slaves are willing to fight over a cause which can benefit them no more than Home Rule can benefit Ireland as a whole. But would those same Ulster Wage-slaves be prepared to act in the same way in defence of their real interests, for the benefit of themselves, their wives and children, as against the robber classes of Ulster?

If every demand made by the Wage-slaves for better conditions of work and wages were backed up as might be found necessary, according to circumstances and conditions, the master class would realise that such demand was not "on bended knee."

HURRAH FOR SOLIDARITY !

The Resolution concludes with the advocacy of "the amalgamation of industries within each Union." Well and good, if such amalgamation means the forging of a weapon with which to face the amalgamated masters. But does it in this case, or will it under all conceivable conditions and circumstances? Of Trade Unions as they are, composed of men for the most part wholly class-UNconscious, possessing no ideal or ambition beyond a bob or two more a week, or an hour shorter working day, whose executive and officials are on excellent good terms with the bosses, we "hae oor doots."

The blacklegging of Unions of this kind upon each other is bad enough, we know. But would an amalgamation such as suggested, by stopping this, not stop industrial action altogether? With a Union consisting of amalgamated industries, there would be an endless increase of red tape, of which there is now too much in all conscience. Such a machine in the hands of officials of the usual type and temper, would be so cumbersome and unwieldy that, when occasion arose for it to move, the bosses would be insured ample time to prepare against its action.

Did the rank and file of the Union members intelligently understand the economic situation, were they class-conscious and aware of the meaning of the Class War and their own power, it would be another matter ; but, as things are at present, such an amalgamated industry would be a blind giant indeed.

Solidarity! Yes, we like the word. That is, if the Trade Union officials who use it really mean it in its true sense. But we know very well they do not. For them, "amalgamation" simply means a constitutional reform which will enable the Trade Union politicians, who (Liberal and Labour alike) are attached to the bosses' political party, to thrive in comfortable security

for years to come. It is intended, by this sort of amalgamation, to make industrial action more difficult, if not impossible.

No one has pointed this out more clearly than Frank Rose when he wrote : "They have ranted about 'solidarity' while their overt acts have frustrated it." The most dangerous men in the Labour Movement to-day are those who prate about "solidarity," when all the time they are after soft and secure jobs.

TO HELL WITH DEMONSTRATIONS !

Frankly, we are disgusted with the exhibition of humbug, chicanery, ignorance, and nincompoopery, which is always the outstanding characteristic of these demonstrations.

Our May Day demonstrators "re-asserted," at the outset, "their determination to emancipate themselves from wagedom." Magnificent! Surely, now, we should hear something resolute, something forcible. One cannot break the chains of slavery with a butter-knife, nor even by sending a Primitive Methodist to the House of Commons. Now we should hear the clarion call to action—to Revolution! "Hurrah! hurrah!! hurrah!!!" A rude little boy close by squeaked, "Pip! pip!!" His derision was more in order than he understood.

Following that grandiloquent declaration, there was a roaring as of sheep pretending to be lions. Their defiance of the enemy took the line of State charity, and State regulation of industry, such as the free maintenance of children in the National schools, abolition of the living-in system, and the like!

By all the gods, big and little, WHAT are we to make of these feeble footlers? Is it surprising that the master class and their prostitute press treat them with the supremest contempt?

No! It is not the majority that counts. The power to be reckoned with is the intelligent few who know and who understand, who are CLASS CONSCIOUS—the few who know how effectively to strike back in the Class War against their exploiters. The machinery of wealth production only works for the profit of the plunderers because the Workers do what they are expected to do. An intelligent two or three, among a group of their unintelligent fellows, can do almost as much as the whole lot together.

If the Iron Heel of capitalist oppression is ever to be thrust from off the breast of Labour, it will need Men to the task. These white-blooded, rabbit-gutted, spineless molluscs only invite bolder aggression from the plundering classes.

MEN VERSUS EUNUCHS.

Yes, we need Men! Strong men, brainy men, resolute men, men who fear neither god, man, devil, nor death ; men with all the attributes and powers of men. Where shall we find them among the Liberal-Labour "Leaders," where among the general run of Trade Union officials, where even among the Socialists of to-day? The most of those who lead the forces of Labour in the revolt against the classes of robbery and exploitation, are mere emasculated THINGS, neither men nor women. Would that they were even women, for the women to-day have far more virility than the men, however useless their cause.

Events in South Africa and in Ulster have shown that there are men, at least, among the master class. They have taught us lessons which, one would think, even a Labour Leader would not fail to learn. In the deportation of the Nine from Africa, in the drilling and arming of the Ulster dupes, in the refusal of army officers to obey their orders, we see how much constitution, law, order, and obedience mean to them, when these things go against their interests.

These events have shown to us another phase of "direct action," as understood by the master class. They know just how much, and how little, parliaments are worth. So long as parliaments serve their ends, well and good ; beyond that—Force! Let there be no mistake about it, you lamb-like lions of Labour. The capitalist beast will not be scared by oratory, nor will it be slain by demonstrations, resolutions, or demands, nor by bits of meaningless paper dropped into tin boxes, nor by all the Members you can contrive to send to parliament. Capitalism has no regard for religion, for morality, for patriotism, for constitution, for justice, or for law, if these things stand between it and its prey.

Though we hate the hypocrisy, the villainy, the low, brutal and unscrupulous cunning of the plundering classes, with a fierce and implacable hatred ; still we can respect them, in a measure, when they stand forth, armed, ruthless but courageous men, prepared to fight for their spoils.

Botha and Carson (types of the robber class) are Men. These Labour demonstrators are mere Eunuchs, neither men nor women.

But we have Men, too, as the enemy will find anon. Every day we are finding them, one here and one there. By and by, as they get into touch with one another, they will assert themselves. Then, we believe, the rank and file of the Wage-slaves, who stand now, uncertain, bemuddled by the bleating chorus around them, will follow the lead of these Men of their own class, to their final emancipation.

The Syndicalist

and AMALGAMATION NEWS.

EDITED UNDER THE AUSPICES OF
THE INDUSTRIAL SYNDICALIST
EDUCATION LEAGUE.

Offices—
4, MAUDE TERRACE, WALTHAMSTOW,
LONDON, E.

MONTHLY - - ONE PENNY.

Post Paid Subscription—
**Great Britain or Abroad.: 12 Months,
1s. 6d.**

Bundle Rates—
1s. 6d. per quire, Carriage Paid.
U.K.F. TERMS TO NEWSAGENTS.

**The Receipt of a Sample Copy is an
Invitation to Subscribe.**

JUNE, 1914.

SWANK AND SUPERSWANK.

The impotent futility of our political Labour Movement has been fearfully and wonderfully illustrated as a result of the South African deportations. We anticipated that the deported nine would be made the occasion of an expenditure of a good deal of " hot air," would be feted and fed, and would address sundry meetings. And then the whole business would fizzle out.

But the master stroke of Labour " statesmanship " and diplomacy came in the sending out of Tom Mann to fill the places of the deportees in South Africa. It was a thoroughly characteristic piece of absurdity. Tom Mann, who has been in everything by turns and stayed nowhere long, very naturally jumped at the chance of a pleasant little trip, involving no risks, and calling for no special expenditure of brain power. The authorities in South Africa had, no doubt, got Tom sized up pretty well, for they let him in without demur. Tom, of course, has justified their expectations, and is preaching " solidarity," which may mean anything or nothing as coming from him. We wonder what the South African Labour men think of it ? Judging from events, they seem better capable of looking after themselves than our Labour folk are of advising them. We do not suppose that their political successes during the recent elections will prove of any ultimate advantage to them. This lesson they will have to learn, as we are learning it. We think they will learn it rather more quickly.

But, to send Tom Mann to teach them ! If the workers of South Africa are anything like the men we think they are, they ought to resent it as an insult. If, on the other hand, they really want a " Jesus Christ " sent out to them, 8,000 miles away, then they are hopeless and not worth bothering about.

Why didn't our Labour people send Jim Larkin as well ? He would have been even more appropriate !

But the whole thing is but swank from beginning to end, in order that some people might get a job.

Larkin for East Fife ! The colossal intellect that conceived this idea deserves to be immortalised. That Larkin himself should not have seen the stupendous idiocy of the proposal was only natural. But that it should have had the tacit approval of the " Daily Herald "—even if it did not emanate therefrom—sets one furiously thinking.

We believe that there is a conspiracy afoot, both within and without, to discredit the parliamentary Labour Party. Not that we are in any way averse to this. The sooner parliamentary Labourism is made to stink in the nostrils of all serious and thoughtful men among the Working Class the sooner we shall begin to make some perceptible advance. When the workers cease from following the parliamentary will-o'-the-wisp and turn to the Syndicalist idea of Direct Action the revolution will be within view, and not before.

But this is not the intention of those who desire to make the parliamentary Labour Party even more ridiculous than it is now. Their purpose is to strengthen the position of the master class politically. Nothing would have been better calculated to do this than to put up Larkin against the Premier in East Fife.

We do not suppose that Larkin saw this, nor the rank and file of the " Daily Herald " League. But we have no doubt at all that the wire-pullers do.

For, after all, who and what is Larkin ? He rose to fame out of the Dublin labour troubles. He showed himself a courageous fighter, and there seems to be no doubt about his sincerity. But no one who has read his speeches, especially that which was reported verbatim and in full by the " Manchester Guardian," can fail to see that he has no real grasp of the situation. He is unable to focus his prospective, as the incident at Hull proved when he refused to speak with a divorced person as his chairman. Apart altogether from his general incoherence, this concrete fact exposed at once the manner in which his thinking is absolutely vitiated.

Behind Jim Larkin stands the black and sinister figure of the priest. This being so, he is utterly worthless as an effective fighter on behalf of Working Class emancipation. It has been said that the Hull incident was really a master stroke of diplomacy, in view of the fact that Larkin's Dublin followers are Roman Catholics. But we do not believe Larkin to be capable of any such master stroke. Neither do those who proposed that he should stand for East Fife against the Premier.

We have so far never doubted Larkin's earnestness and sincerity, but we have always considered him a man of great simplicity since the time of the first Syndicalist Conference in Manchester in 1910.

It will be recalled that the resolution before that Conference was for the formation of Syndicalist Education League to propagate the principles of Syndicalism throughout the British Isles.

Larkin asked the Conference to leave Ireland out of the resolution. He said " they had made enough hash of their own affairs—they must not interfere with Ireland." Exactly. Syndicalism would be the very last thing that the R.C. church would like to see in Ireland. It could not attach wires to it as it does to all political movements and organisations. Syndicalism could not be permeated by the Militia of Christ—which we shall have occasion to refer to again in the very near future.

Larkin on that occasion had somewhat to say about " political earwigs," and now he looks like becoming one of those interesting insects himself. We were to leave Ireland out of it. Very well, then, why cannot Larkin leave England and Scotland out of it, and stick to his Ireland ? Why is he touring this country under the auspices of the " Daily Herald " ?

We know that our Labour " statesmen " and " political earwigs " have made enough hash of their own affairs but we hardly think that Mr. James Larkin is the heaven-born genius who shall set them straight.

What swank !

No, this is super-swank.

By the way, we wonder if Larkin knows anything about the Militia of Christ ?

REJOICE, O WORKERS !

By Lewis Lincoln.

Rejoice with me, O Workers !
That Justice softly calls
To Liberty from thraldom,
To Freedom's spacious halls.
Rejoice, rejoice, O Workers !
Re-echo ! heart and voice,
The new-born call of " Welcome "
That Justice chants. Rejoice !

The way is steep and heavy ;
The struggle long and stern ;
Justice whispers still, " Reward ! "
While hearts with sorrow burn.
From aye to overlasting
Has Right been held in chain ;
Resolve for Justice, Workers !
Great tyranny's disdain.

The task is great that meets you :
Your flag you shall unfurl,
And take your place where Freedom
Knows no enslaved churl.
Work on, work well, work bravely,
And TAKE each trench and wall,
Until you stand all Freemen
In the halls of Freedom's Hall.

Rejoice, rejoice, O Workers !
THE WORK is to your hand.
'Tis Justice calls to Freedom,
And gives to you the land.
The task is great before you ;
To it with hand and voice ;
And while you work for JUSTICE,
In her " Reward " rejoice !

THE COMING TERROR.

By RAGNER REDBEARD.

The unqualified glorification of " Modern Science " is strongly to be denounced. There is evil in Modern Science, much evil, and profound illusion. It is another false redeemer, a new betrayal. Eventually all this will be found out. Woe and torment and terror are lurking in its train. It is a creeping monster, a hideous coiling dragon, but, half hidden as yet, behind dark and unlifted veils.

Some day " the Scientist," popularly acclaimed as a wonderful Saviour, will climb into governmental authority, and become the most remorseless and implacable of tyrants—all-seeing, all-hearing, all-knowing Jehovah—an organic terror as it were, more frightful to live under than ever was " the Holy Church " in the heyday of its undivided and untrammelled regulative might.

What is a " Scientist " anyhow but a priest—the priest of a new idolatry as deceptive and absurd as that of Benares or Jerusalem or Rome.

The gospel of human perfectability, or of human purification, either by " Laws," or by " Scientific Regulation," is just as much of a delusion as the gospel of " salvation by the blood of the lamb."

The conventional evangels of public hygiene and medicine of industrial adjustment or of artificial sex-selection (Eugenics), are quite as great a hoax as the now discredited gospels of praying and voting.

In fact, " Modern Science " is a huge superstition, a sort of popular sorcery—a bewitchment. There is no truth or beneficence in it whatever—as time will tell.

Once permit a body of scientific mandarins to get the upper hand in Society, and they would be enabled—in the name of the Public Good—to wield positively infernal powers for the enslavement and exploitation of the entire human race, or for the perpetration of frightful crimes to satiate personal ambition, lust, or experiment.

All the highly centralised enginery of oppressive state-craft, industrialism, religion, and tax gathering would be at their imperial command, supplemented by weird psychic, aerial, or magnetic devices (or disease bacteria) of diabolical destructive ingenuity and of practically omniscient coercive force.

Even with present knowledge a supreme junta of scientific Super-men could probably poison the very air we breathe, extinguish armies by pressing a button, or maybe annihilate entire communities as it were with an Olympian nod.

Under the Reign of Science, the most ruthless and most cold-blooded of all monsters would be Lord of the World. No one individual could stand up against such crushing and stupendous and " Godlike " powers. Anyone who even dared to think in opposition to " the Law " could be slain with a waft of lightning, or trussed upon an operating table (behind impregnable police walls) and emasculated ; or the virile cells of his brain removed as a priestly sacrifice to the Science Idol.

The frightful atrocities perpetrated on helpless millions by the evil priests of Ancient Egypt, Babylon, Atlantis, and prehistoric antiquity, could and would be all revived and renewed under pretentious disguises and fair sounding names—for every scientist is a potential Torquemada.

Think this out for yourself. Don't be hypnotised all your days by the treacherous avatars of current philosophy and literature. Have a mind of your own. Put two and two together and calculate with your own brain from your own particular angle. Don't believe what everybody believes. Don't take things too much for granted. Beware of all Hierarchies of Science, Church, or State.

When new men with new ideals obtain limitless sway, what always happens ? Do they not become at once tyrants and robbers and enemies of mankind ?

What would take place, therefore, were the fanatic Edisons and Saleebys, the Galtons and Maxims, the Huxleys and Burbans, of to-morrow to seat themselves on the throne of the mighty ?

If they planned to crush, exploit, torment, exterminate an entire population (in order to carry out some " Scientific " purpose), who would dare to challenge them or question their injunctions ?

Woe unto mankind, I say, woe unto all mankind when the priests of Modern Science are lords on high. " Modern Science " crowned and sceptred, armed to the teeth, directing irresistible and mystic forces, controlling the brain powers of nations, and in possession of vast treasures, would be the most diabolical despotism this earth has ever known.

The Roots of Empire.

By Ap. Hughes.

Foreword.

Lycurgus, real or imaginary, left the people he had guided, and started on a journey into the unknown. His spirit still hovers over the failures of the peoples of Europe. The restless soul has been moved to expression by contemplation of those failures. Moving and brooding along the streets and amongst the peoples of the eastern end of this great city it could not but be greatly agitated. At the flag-waving and tub-thumping before and amongst the children on the King's birthday it so far lost control as to give vent to articulate speech. The result is the following interesting document.

Treasure Houses.

I did myself before a building of ugly appearance. The three stories thereof pushed themselves up through the smoke of the factories around. The foremost part of this day had I spent in the temples where are stored great treasures of the nation. The gallery named Tate and the museum of Victoria and Albert. Of the latter names I could not find record that they had in any wise added to the freedom or real greatness of the people. Two others I did find better named, and all did contain vast treasures richly housed.

Housing of Greater Treasures.

Then did it enter my mind to see in whatwise the young of the nation were housed and prepared. Having in mind how the lesser treasures were harboured, surely, thought I, these people will harbour their great treasures so much the more wisely. Think, then, of my amaze when I was led through streets the like of which I never had before seen. The houses were of brick, dirty, and of no beauty of architecture. No sign of a tree did I note, but only houses, houses, houses. Being greatly tired with this sight, I did ask my guide if it were not possible for to get to a school but only through such a place. I had but lately said this when I found myself before the building I have already pointed out.

The Palace of Pedagogy.

From this building there came to me certain sounds as of children's voices—not merry and glad, as one would expect, but giving vent to certain sayings as if under compulsion. After much weariness of climbing steps we at last did attain unto a large chamber. No beautiful balconies did I espy, neither were there pillars of marble upholding the roof. Seated at the end of his chamber was a man who at our approach arose wearily. My guide made him aware of my intentions, and I did go to work forthwith.

The Greatest Empire.

Entering a room which was nigh unto this chamber I did find myself in the presence of the inhabitants of the great building. Although not a large room, quite a number of boys were there gathered. But what touched me nearly was what was going forward. The teacher (for so he was called) spake of an empire both rich and great. Then told me how men, by killing and taking and conquering, did make this empire big. The men of this empire were all free—no slave could breathe therein. Indeed, no such empire had before been seen or known. At this was I greatly rejoiced—at last had I discovered that country for which I sought. Taking up that from which they also read, I did again note those expressions the which I had heard by word of mouth. 'Twas said* : " We are very proud that there are no slaves in any part of the world which belongs to us. We often say that no slave can breathe on British soil."

The next tells us of the brave merchants in the Indies : " The soldiers were but few, and when the merchants found that they were in such danger they rushed on board some ships in the river. They took with them as much of their wealth as they could carry away, and then left the soldiers in the fort to meet the foe."

This is about the people who produce the wealth—those ragged and starved phopue we had seen on our way hither : " Now, the workers in the mills who mind the machines have shorter hours and better wages. The rooms have plenty of light and air. And after work they have spare time to improve their minds and to enjoy themselves."

It was with a great effort that I contained myself until the children had escaped, that I might know the whereabouts of this empire and which road would lead thereto.

The Promised Land.

Thus wise did I address myself :
" Sage, good sir ! I have heard you speak of an empire which is blessed with such freedom and greatness that I do at once determine to make my way thither. Tell me, therefore, along which road I must proceed."

Teacher (looking over his spectacles in wonder) : " My dear man, just use your eyes and you will see this place. This is the country I described. It is indeed the most extensive empire, and we live under the most unfettered freedom that the world has ever known. It contains also that stability which the Romans and Greeks lacked, for it is founded on the church. If you will attend to-morrow you will see how Britons, and Britons alone, can commemorate such greatness."

I was so astonished that I was beside myself. " What ! " I screamed, " this dirty, ugly, and rotten city the greatest in the world ? I pity the world. These half-clothed, half-fed, and brutish slaves the freest people ? God save the people ! " With this I went out, determined, however, to finish my researches on the morrow.

April 19th— The Great Day of Empire.

When I arrived next day I found the boys and girls were marshalled out of the great building with what they did call a playground. In the stead of green grass sown with daisies was a hard, grey pavement. No extent of view could be seen except on two sides. Here, however, did appear to the eye, instead of hills and trees and an open stretch of sky, piles of bricks named houses, lines and lines of chimneys, and a grey, smoky sky. The faces that were turned towards me were some beautiful faces, some that had been rosy faces, but all marred by that look the which is only seen amongst those that have been hungry and cold. The covering of many was funny to see. One boy near me had no sleeves to his coat, and his bare legs poked through cloth of peculiar shape. The teacher did tell me of one boy that had been " sewn up for the winter." A few of the boys were there with bare legs. Altogether they did differ greatly from the boys and girls which I knew aforetime in my country.

Flag Worship.

Then did commence what to me was very peculiar and also funny if it was not so sad. These children, with their pinched faces and ragged clothes, did salute and bow to what to me seemed far all the world like a piece of coloured cloth. They sang the while they did salute and bow : " We salute thee and we pray, God, to bless our land to-day." Not much of their land did I see that they knew, and of little object did it seem to me to worship a piece of coloured cloth. More to my mind would it have been if they could be healthy, well clad, and well fed. But I complain before I finish.

This do, and thou shalt live.

Then a man rose who was indeed not of these parts. He had health, he did not hunger, he had on good clothes although of peculiar shape. This man, then, again gave them to know of the empire. Its richness and greatness and freedom were again put before them. They were to work hard and serve their masters well, and they then might be successful as he was. They must not grumble, however, but be satisfied with the state that the good men pleased to call them to. I got tired of listening to the same thing for so long that I vastly amused myself by watching two boys before me play a game they named " odds and evens."

When this man did at last stop they all joined in singing what they pleased to call a national anthem. The words, however, were a laudation of a personage called a king, and did not speak of the nation at all. I was wakened by a man at my elbow who did actually request me to take off my hat. This was the last stone in the bucket of my anger, and it did overflow. I could not forbear but strike the man for a cringing varlet. He was left wondering who had so struck him.

FAT AND HIS MULE.

By JACK RADCLIFFE.

The other day I had business with Fat at his private house. He dwells in a huge and beautiful mansion, standing in its own wide grounds, walled in and aloof from the common herd like you and me. He has motor cars and flunkeys, art treasures of inestimable value—and much too much more to catalogue. Also, I saw Mrs. Fat, arrayed in garments of price ; and the little Fats playing with expensive toys.

Now, this particular Fat never did a day's useful work in his life, and what is more, he never, never will.

Seeing and knowing all this, I marvelled exceedingly at the great generosity of the workers who built the house and the motor cars, who lodge and feed, clothe and tend, Mr. and Mrs. Fat and the little Fats. And all for nothing !

As I returned home, on top of a tram car, I ruminated on this wise : How far is Fat justified ? It seemed to me, in the end, that he is fully justified by the tacit consent of the Workers.

Yes ! brother Wage-slave, it is "up to you." So long as you, or the majority of you, are content to swink and sweat for a pittance, whilst the bulk of your produce goes to swell the belly of Fat, Fat is justified. The fittest (or the fattest) survive, and their fitness is proven by the fact that they do survive, that they are on top and stay there.

Fat's beast of burden is You, brother Wage-slave ; collectively, you are the " Working Mule." When the Mule won't go, or starts kicking, he is cajoled with such sweet and luscious carrots as old age pensions, blackleg labour exchanges, fraudulent insurance acts, and the like. Or his attention is diverted by a German war bogey, or some such queer performance as is going on in Ireland. Alternatively, he is walloped by police, or pricked behind by the bayonets of soldiers, all recruited (Oh, the rich humour of Fat !) from his own class. If he is still obstinate, he is shot, and be damned to him.

Such, however, is the utter contempt of Fat for his Mule that he has given the Mule, to all appearances, such political power as, if used, would dislodge Fat with a dull thud.

But will this political power be used by the Mule ? Fat knows very well that it will not. And why ? Because of the fact, demonstrated throughout history, that political power is always in the hands of the class, or classes, who control, the revenues. This may appear academic, but it is true. So long as the ECONOMIC CONDITIONS of industrial capitalism remain, Fat is secure, no matter what the political forms may be.

So long as you can be " doped " with religious, political, and patriotic superstitions, so that you lose class-consciousness, it does not matter whether you have political power or not. If you have the power, you will not be able to think clearly enough to use it aright. Fat will always be able to outwit you.

If you should wake up in sufficient numbers, and begin to think clearly, become class-conscious, still it will not matter whether you have political power or not. Fat will then use force, " direct action " (as he always does in the last resort) to repress you, and you will have to use " direct action " to unseat him, or go under again. There is no other way. Fat knows this well enough, but, unfortunately, the Mule does not—as yet.

Thus Fat pats his belly and smiles, sitting complacently on his Mule. And, so far, Fat is justified in his fatness.

But there are signs that the Mule is beginning to wake up. There is a wicked twinkle in his eye. He shakes his ears now and again, to the great indignation of the flies (species : LIBERALIS-LABORIS FAKIRIUM, REX PATRIOTICUM, SOCIALISMUS PARLIAMENTARIENSIS, HYPOCRITICUS NON-CONFORMICA, SANCTIMONIA ECCLESIASTICUS, and some others of lesser importance), whose continual buzzing has so long confused his poor brain.

When the Mule does make up, he will spit that bit out of his mouth. Then Fat will lose control and drop. This will mean the Revolution. And the Mule will rise up a MAN.

May we live to see it !

Syndicalism for Clerks.

By " REMUS,"

Member of the National Executive N.U.C.

THE AVERAGE CLERK'S MENTALITY.

As one of that vast army of non-producers—the clerical workers—I have been particularly struck with the fact that neither at working-class demonstrations nor in articles written for the specific benefit of the Working Class are clerks mentioned, and have come to the conclusion that this is due to the apathy of the average clerk towards, and his aloofness from, any progressive movement.

The average member of the clerical world appears to view organisation as something beneath his " dignity," and suitable only for what he pleases to call the " ordinary working man " ; though why he should look upon those engaged in manual labour only as working men is beyond comprehension, although the fact remains.

It is probably owing to the fact that the clerk is, in the majority of cases, in closer personal contact with his employer ; and this close association having a deleterious effect upon his mind, he readily assimilates their views.

Many employers encourage their clerks to believe that they are specially favoured by confiding minor details of their businesses in them, which confidence induces a false sense of security, and deludes them into the belief that there is no need for their combining with their fellows in order to obtain better conditions, and to combat encroachments on their liberty.

These things lead to a marked absence of that spirit of independence so necessary to enable the clerk to obtain emancipation from the servile state into which he has drifted, and from which he can emerge only by joining forces with the whole of his fellow workers.

Another favourite dodge of the employing class, so soon as they find one of their clerical workers with a more sensible outlook upon life than his fellows, and who is taking an interest in trying to induce them to organise in order that they may improve their conditions, is to dangle before him " better prospects," " higher wages," " advancement of position," etc., promises which in many cases the clerk readily seizes upon ; only to find that, after he has given up his work on behalf of his fellows, and has no longer the power of an organisation behind his back, the employer fails to fulfil his promises, and the clerk, left to his own resources, has to bow to the inevitable.

He is then in a worse position than before—despised by his fellow workers, whom he has forsaken at the instance of those who have no interest in his welfare ; and looked upon with contempt by his employer that he should be so easily induced to betray his principles.

HIS INDIVIDUAL IMPOTENCE.

This kind of clerk must be brought to realise that it is not those, in the majority of cases, who have ability, and are loyal to their fellows, who are elevated to positions of " trust " and to supervisory posts ; but rather those whom the employer can rely upon to serve his purpose, and who will betray and bully those whom he is set to supervise.

He is expected to see that the work of an office is carried out in as economical a manner as possible, and cannot therefore reasonably be expected to advance the claims of those under him to higher wages and less hours of working ; for, if he did so, and was found to have much sympathy with them, his employer would, I venture to suggest, have little further use for him. The grabbing at these proverbial " bunches of carrots," together with snobbishness, false pride, and an imagined superiority over the manual worker are the greatest drawbacks to the welfare of the clerical worker, and until he arouses himself from the state of somnolence in which he has so long remained, his position will become more and more precarious, and he will be looked upon with scorn by those of his fellow workers who are endeavouring to improve their conditions, and to obtain lasting benefits for themselves and their comrades in adversity.

It is with the object of trying to arouse the clerical worker to a sense of his individual impotence, and to show him what we Syndicalists are convinced is the only method by which he, together with his fellow workers, can obtain emancipation, and achieve that great consummation, " The World for the Workers," in which shirkers will have no place, that this pamphlet is written.

INDIGNITIES HE HAS TO PUT UP WITH.

The clerk to-day suffers indignities which those he choses to look down upon would not long tolerate, and, instead of occupying the position of dignity he would have us believe, is in a state of degradation.

The writer knows of firms where the clerks are " timed " when performing natural functions, in one case being allowed only ten minutes per day for that purpose—and finding trouble if they dare to exceed that allowance. Then again, an enormous amount of unpaid overtime is worked by those in the clerical world, and, although it may be argued by some that holidays are paid for, on examination it will be found that the overtime worked fully compensates for the holidays granted.

Often insult is added by an allowance for tea, which amounts to, on an average, about sixpence per day—for which the clerk is expected to work two hours extra.

Work this out, and you have the value placed upon the clerk's spare time by the employing class !

In some cases, however, he is not even valued at so high a rate as this, but is allowed tea on a graduated scale, ranging from threepence to fivepence per day, according to the amount of overtime worked ; and, lest the clerk should place too high a value on himself, he has to advance the tea-money till the end of the week, when, if his time is satisfactory the money is refunded ; but, if he has on any evening placed a little higher value on his time, and left the premises a few minutes earlier than the time specified, the money for that night is forfeited.

He is expected to suffer these and numerous other indignities in silence, and should he dare to protest is told that, if he is not satisfied, he can find another situation, as there are plenty of men outside who will gladly take his job at less wages than he is getting.

This is, unfortunately, in the majority of cases, too true ; the specialisation of work under the various systems now in vogue in practically all the large industries, and the consequent creation of posts requiring little knowledge or ability, making it an easy matter to find men who, with a little tuition, are able to fill the average clerk's place.

THE ENCROACHMENT OF MACHINERY.

These present indignities and dangers to the welfare of the clerical worker are not, however, the only ones he has to contend with. The gradual but certain encroachment of machinery into the domain of the clerk is a menace to his whole future, unless he profits by the lesson taught to the manual worker by the introduction of machinery into the factories and workshops, and turns the machinery to his own advantage. The majority of clerks have not seen, or perhaps heard of, the wonderful pieces of machinery which will, sooner or later, displace a considerable number of their class, and swell the already large number of unemployed ; thereby increasing the competition for vacant situations, and reducing wages.

A recent case, which came under the writer's notice recently, goes to prove this contention. At a large firm in the Midlands two machines were introduced for the purpose of invoicing the goods—which machines are operated by two young girls, who are able to do the work hitherto performed by FOUR invoice clerks ; and this is only one of a large number of cases which can be cited as showing the dangers which confront clerks in the near future through the introduction of machinery.

We have seen some of the indignities and hardships of clerical life ; now let us consider the surest way to combat these and other evils, and to obtain better conditions, increased wages, and all those things which go towards making life what it should be—a joy and a pleasure ; instead of a sordid monotony, as it is at present for the Working Class.

OLD-FASHIONED TRADE UNIONISM.

Some of us who are clerical workers have already realised that it is only by organised effort that we can achieve these objects, and have banded ourselves in the National Union of Clerks, which is a Trade Union fighting for the betterment of clerks generally, with, it must be admitted, a certain amount of success.

Trade Unionism, however, although it has achieved a degree of success, cannot, by virtue of its constitution, secure any lasting benefits to the workers ; and Trade Unions are to-day, and in their present form, a source of weakness to the Labour Movement.

" Why, then, did the writer join a Trade Union ? " I hear some one ask. To him I would reply, " Because the Trade Union form of organisation is the only one at present existing industrially ; and, believing in the organisation of the workers, I joined the N.U.C. as catering for the section of the Working Class to which I belong."

Trade Unionism presupposes the continued existence of the capitalist class, and its chief objects are to fight for better wages, shorter hours of working, and better conditions while at work ; and also to protect its members against unscrupulous employers.

By its division of the workers into various sections or trades—each short-sightedly trying to defend the interests of its own members, with no regard to the interests of the members of other sectional unions—it tends to cripple the whole movement.

Trade Unionism sends the workers in sections to fight the employing class, who artfully use the power of the great mass of workers who are, for the time, at peace with them, to crush the section of workers in revolt. This occurred in the London Dock Strike of 1912, when the men, to the lasting disgrace of the Labour Movement, were defeated ; but in the great Transport Strike of 1911, when the whole of the men in the industry withdrew their labour, the men won the fight.

Another great drawback to the fighting power of Trade Unions is the making of agreements.

An employer will make an agreement with the members of one Trade Union to terminate on a certain date, and with another Union to terminate on a different date, the dates being as far apart as possible, thus making it practically impossible for the whole of the workers to act unitedly. When one section takes action in order to remedy some grievance that may arise, the others—fearful of breaking their agreement—remain at work, thus assisting to defeat their fellow unionists, simply because they are not members of the same union, and, consequently, are bound by a different agreement.

This causes the " blacklegging " by the members of one Union on the members of another, and shows the folly of sectionalism.

These agreements are often made during a bad period of trade, and, consequently, the wages fixed by the agreement are based upon a low figure ; and, when a period of good trade arrives, the workers find themselves unable to demand a rise of wages, because they are bound by an agreement not to ask for any alteration in their wages for a period usually of from three to five years.

(To be continued.)

Clerical Militarism.

By ARTHUR D. LEWIS.

The " upper " classes naturally contain an undue proportion of men of a cruel disposition who like killing and violence for their own sakes. It is the man of prey who rises in our exploiting order of society. Hence well-bred men encourage as far as possible any sport or training in which there is either actually or as a make-believe any degree of what Veblen calls " emulative ferocity." The boy scouts, church brigades, school sports and athletics all have an element of this kind.

We gladly admit that at a certain age the aggressive instincts develop quite properly, and that a love of fighting and of adventure in a boy AS A TEMPORARY PROMINENT CHARACTERISTIC is not a bad thing. The idea of scouting after enemies, of ambushes, avoiding Red Indians, piratical fighting, and so on is not at all unhealthy in a boy. The element of make-believe is consciously present at that age. But the aim of the clericalist-militarist is to train play into earnest.

A grown man chiefly interested in excelling others in physical feats is a brute. And the clergy, lords, and right honourables who encourage all this marching and mock-fighting have their own purpose. They are not anxious to free the Workers from the rule of the shirkers. It is impressed on all these scouts and brigaders that discipline—that is to say, strict obedience to officers derived from the " upper " classes—is going to be their main duty. " Discipline " is the first and last object of the whole of this clerical-militarist drilling.

Among the servile class, obedience is a man's chief duty. The safest outlet for the common man's need for emotional activity is to be found in ferocity combined with obedience : that is the master-class argument. " Let them fight our battles insofar as it is not content merely to do our work," say they.

Every respectable person encourages the Working Class in amusements that divert their mind from rebellion against their slavery.

The churches, theoretically on the side of peace, always egg on all the combatants whenever there is a war. War, but not class-war, is always compatible with a christian's conduct in this imperfect world of sin.

The Syndicalist
and Amalgamation News.

Edited under the auspices of the Industrial Syndicalist Education League.

PRESIDENT :
TOM MANN.

SECRETARY :
GUY BOWMAN.

VOL. III.　NO. 4.　　　LONDON, JULY, 1914.　　　MONTHLY, ONE PENNY.

STRAIGHT TALKS.

Fifty Points Against Parliament.

By Solomon II.

CONTENTS.

FIFTY POINTS AGAINST PARLIAMENT.

I.
The Will of the People.

The Insurance Act may be a good Act or a bad Act ; that we are not for the moment concerned to argue about.

But whoever heard it argued about or agitated on, before it was brought into parliament ?

Is it not in itself enough to prove that parliament, which pretends to represent the will of the people, does not represent the will of the people ?

For it shows that parliament supplies important laws, which the people had never dreamt of.

Democratic parliamentary government is not democratic.

II.
Democratic Government.

Democratic parliamentary government is not democratic.

One man votes Liberal because he is a Free Trader, another because his father was a Liberal, a third because he is a Nonconformist.

And the result is that parliament passes the Insurance Act.

III.
The M.P.

The election of a representative to parliament obviously takes him away from working-class surroundings and puts him in Westminster.

Your member of parliament lives like a member of parliament.

He cannot live on a pound a week.

He does not want to live on a pound a week.

He lives in London, and possibly takes holidays in India or the colonies.

Because he is an M.P., the papers print what he says and pay for it.

The member of parliament loses the feelings of a working man, who is embittered at the life which is squeezed out of him without his ever knowing what life is.

The member of parliament is one of the governing class.

And the people whom he is said to represent remain in the governed class.

IV.
The Governing Class.

A member of parliament is one of the governing classes ; his position is quite different from that of common working-men.

Parliament does not increase the capacity and confidence of the workers ; it teaches them to obey orders.

Parliament is one of the institutions by which the few control the many.

V.
Who Gets Elected ?

It is the idle, educated, and rich who are most likely to get elected to parliament.

The rich, idle, and educated do not want to " represent " the poor, uneducated, and working class.

Men first degrade their fellows and then hate them for being degraded.

VI.
Why was it Invented ?

Parliament was instituted to protect the property-owners.

This is suggested by the old cry, revived by the women, of " No vote, no tax," or " No taxation without representation."

Ownership of property is power, and the vote reflects that power. Elected representatives can peaceably adjust the powers of the property-owners, when their interests clash.

Parliament is noted for peaceable bargaining and compromise.

Parliament is not noted for confiscation and direct opposition.

Parliament is " a conciliation board."

" Like all conciliation boards, it seeks to hide the class struggle, the direct opposition between those who live by owning and those who live by working."*

Early parliaments frankly disregarded the unpropertied many. They were composed only of the propertied.

* W. F. Hay, in THE SYNDICALIST for February, 1914.

VII.
The Voters.

The first reason why political action tends to hinder the class struggle, and is therefore unsuitable for a policy of uncompromising confiscation is that the political candidate appeals to MEN OF ALL CLASSES ; he does not urge the workers to attack the robbers.

His cry is : " Why can you not ALL vote for me ? "

He wants votes from men with different interests.

The parliamentary candidate is elected by a motley crowd, after he has expressed opinions and given pledges on a motley lot of subjects.

VIII.
A Motley Crowd.

Elected by a motley crowd, whose favour he needs for re-election, a member of parliament forms part of a motley party.

Such a party is faced by other parties with equally vague intentions.

Such a body must be ill-suited for spreading a dogmatic revolutionary doctrine, highly objectionable to the rich, from whom it is proposed to take their source of income.

IX.
It Does Not Frighten.

The parliamentary candidate makes himself as agreeable as he can to everyone.

He does not frighten the capitalists.

They know a few fiery speeches mean no harm to them.

Speeches are only words.

X.
Kick Them.

Revolutions, confiscations of property, great changes, are not brought about by parliament.

Parliament may register them, may try to modify or check them, but it does not create them.

The M.P. says : " I am powerless, because there is in public opinion, no rioting, no agitation to drive me on."

He asks to be kicked.

It does not matter to you whether you kick a Conservative or a Socialist.

Both alike will act if you kick them.

Why not kick them with riots and unexpected strikes, and not both to elect your man ?

What does it matter to you whom you kick ?

XI.
Agreed !

The majority of the politicians, who belong to the Liberal, Conservative, and Nationalist Irish party are, it is universally admitted, agreed on the most important matters.

They believe in protecting property and keeping the working-class in subjection.

They discuss what they differ about, not what they agree about.

They fight elections only on what they differ about.

The consequence is that at election times, people are interested in subjects which do not vitally influence their position.

Thus both in Free Trade and Protected countries there is poverty and insecurity of employment.

In " prohibition " and " drinking " countries there is poverty, unemployment (and incidentally drink !).

Whether the Church is established or disestablished, there are rich and poor.

Whether you have a big navy or a little, there are slums and rich men's houses.

Politicians do not let elections be fought on issues that would prevent the few from riding on the backs of the many.

The rich purse-holders who control all the parties are careful to discuss anything that does not matter at election times.

XII.
The Concentrated Few.

Forty millions of people cannot express an opinion.

They cannot get into touch with one another.

Even if you institute the Referendum and the initiative (the most thorough reforms in the direction of making parliament more democratic) it will be a few men with money who will decide what every elector is to be asked to put on the parliamentary programme or finally to pass into law.

Because forty million people cannot express their views, they are at the mercy of political bosses who decide what programmes shall be discussed and who put forward candidates for the elections.

Candidates with money, with a rich trade union behind them, or safe men whom the political bosses have allowed to become prominent, because they have them on a string, will always be favoured.

XIII.
The Few Decide.

Six hundred and seventy men are so many that they cannot arrange business together.

The six hundred and seventy men have the most part of their parliamentary work done for them by three or four important men in the Cabinet of a dozen or so.

These few men decide what is to be discussed most of the time.

Government at the centre must be government by the manageable little group.

And the little powerful group in the big body of politicals never consists of the most unbendable men of principle ; it consists of schemers and solid lawyers and " spell-binders," or men who can lure the silly public.

There are fundamental difficulties, which not even the Referendum or Initiative could overcome. The scattered many cannot find out their own views ; it is the few in close touch with one another who control.

XIV.
The Cabinet.

A few men in the Cabinet control the political programmes.

At a general election candidates not chosen by the people start discussing issues decided on by the little group of Cabinet and ex-Cabinet ministers, who control the government and the opposition.

Every class is rent across by opinions on nonsensical issues.

Classes are not united to fight for their class interests.

The workers are not united as workers to fight the owners, but broken up into Free Traders and Protectionists, Nonconformists and Churchmen, teetotallers and drinkers, Unionists and Home Rulers, Imperialists and Little Englanders, and according to a host of other opinions, on which we have opinions, irrespective of class.

The robber-class of capitalists goes on pocketing rent and interest.

(Whereas we want no politics, no religion, no morals, no philosophy, no conceptions of history to stand in the way of the whole working-class uniting against their common enemy, capital owned privately and causing exploitation, you are wage-earners fighting for your rights, and everything else is a minor matter.)

XV.
The Few Act First.

It is the conscious and heroic minority who set the despairing multitude into action.

It is not by the silly excitements of elections, and by rotten arguments and by equally rotten evasions of argument, that men are wrought up to great efforts.

It is by inspiring deeds, the inspiring deeds of the defiant few.

The few not stopping to ask the opinions of the many, but acting in their interests.

XVI.
If You Nationalise.

If you proceed to interfere with industry by means of parliament, parliament will naturally take more power for itself.

It will be more likely to nationalise or municipalise industries, than to transfer power to the trade unions.

A parliament of propertied men will nationalise industries in order to get the price it wants for its shares, if there is the faintest danger of anyone else nationalising them on terms more favourable to the workers.

But state capitalism is very like private capitalism.

The names are changed, not the relative position of classes.

Government stockholders replace shareholders.

The manager under any other name will act the same.

The wages paid depend on what the workers can extort.

Workers in a closely united Union can get better terms from the state or from private employers.

Ask the women who work for government clothing factories whether the government ever pays low wages.

Did the telephone employees gain greatly when the telephones were taken over by the state ?

The crown is not a kindly landlord.

XVII.
As a Sounding-board.

Parliament is a bad sounding-board and not a good platform for revolutionary speeches.

It is controlled by those who will always keep revolutionary discussions out of order.

The programme to be discussed is mainly arranged by a few ministers.

Parliament expels revolutionaries and besides the Labour Party consists of respectable men.

XVIII.
Intrigues.

Many of those who move in political circles do not believe in democracy : they believe that the intriguing few can force a measure on the careless and ignorant, many but misrepresenting it on platforms.

The intriguing few say that Tariff reform means work for it, or the Insurance Act means ninepence for fourpence, or Socialism is the care for every ill, but their cries are only intended for popular consumption.

The experts know that one kind of a tariff will make a few trades better off ; that the Insurance Act means fourpence a week off your wages for the worst possible system of slovenly doctoring and that Socialism is a difficult process.

But the men who like carrying out this kind of work are a mean crowd.

The success of their party, the obtaining of posts and the retaining of help at the next general election (it would not do to get isolated by too much independence) influence them.

The few who are suitable for political success are a vile few.

XIX.
Ignorant and afraid.

When it approaches realities of work and wages, parliament is ignorant and afraid.

The big employer or the trade union general secretary see all the details of working life through the eyes of other people.

Statistics and diagrams replace feeling and experience.

XX.

Any parliament is a parliament of expert talkers professing to control expert officials, who tell the workers what to do.

The expert civil service commisioners and officials in reality frequently control their parliamentary chiefs.

These Chairmen of Impartial Boards, Managers of Exchanges, Secretaries, soon undeceive the worker who expects to get any improvement of position out of an act of parliament.

XXI.
The House of Talk.

Parliament is a house of dull talk.

But man expresses little himself in talk.

Men will not give way because they are not able to answer arguments.

It is force that overcomes opposition.

It is power that alters society

Not talk.

(Continued in Next Issue).

The Syndicalist
and AMALGAMATION NEWS.

EDITED UNDER THE AUSPICES OF

THE INDUSTRIAL SYNDICALIST EDUCATION LEAGUE.

Offices—

4, MAUDE TERRACE, WALTHAMSTOW, LONDON, E.

MONTHLY - - ONE PENNY.

Post Paid Subscription—

Great Britain or Abroad: 12 Months, 1s. 6d.

Bundle Rates—

1s. 6d. per quire, Carriage Paid.

U.K.F. TERMS TO NEWSAGENTS.

The Receipt of a Sample Copy is an Invitation to Subscribe.

JULY, 1914.

THE BOYS' BRIGADE.

General Baden-Powell, founder of the Boy Scout movement, writes in " The Scout " :—

" I was glad, the other day, to see so many Boy Scouts at the memorial service in St. Paul's Cathedral to Sir William Smith, the founder of the Boys' Brigade.

" Many thousands of boys have reason to thank that great man for having got a good start in life.

" He began the Boys' Brigade in Glasgow in 1883 with only thirty boys, and it has since spread all over the empire, until it now numbers over 70,000 in the United Kingdom, and 120,000 with the Overseas branches.

" The Church Lads' Brigade were afterwards started on similar lines. And, more recently, the Boy Scouts have come into existence.

" All these big brotherhoods of boys, though they wear different uniforms and do different kinds of work and drill from each other, all work to the same end, which is to give boys a good time and to make better men of them ; so we are all friends, and do not sneer at the others because they do not happen to be the same as ourselves. It would be small and snobbish to do that. We are more like different branches in an army—there are cavalry, artillery, infantry, airmen, and others ; they have different duties from each other, and they wear different uniforms, but they are all working to the same end, namely, the good of their country and their king, and they are all good friends and comrades.

" And so I hope it is with the Scouts and other brigades of boys—especially since the whole idea of this army of boys was started by the one man—Sir William Smith."

The great defect of our schools, according to all types of educational reformers, is that the classes are so large that regimentation has to take the place of any personal interest of teacher and pupil in each other. But Sunday school teachers, instead of recognising that millions of children are not being helped in school, and must be neglected in the homes of over-worked and over-worried parents, are all for MORE DISCIPLINE, when they find the children wild on Sundays. The Boys' Brigade declares : " Discipline should be the first consideration." This brigade combines military drill for boys under 17 with Bible classes in connection with churches and " other responsible Christian " bodies. Gymnastics and foreign mission work go hand in hand. Its object is the " advancement of Christ's kingdom among boys, and the promotion of habits of obedience." The patron of the Boys' Brigade is his majesty King George V. Not a word is said about the possibility of a Christian's duty to rebel, or of loyalty to the people.

Every moral and physical means is used to keep the lower orders blindly obedient to superiors, automatically responsive to the intentions of the possessing class. No doubt many of the officers are gentlemen of an unintelligent piety, who obey their own vague instincts without knowing what they are doing. They do not see the secret purpose of this inappropriate combination of military organisation with instruction on the life of Christ.

Syndicalism for Clerks.
By " REMUS,"
Member of the National Executive N.U.C.

II.—CONTINUED FROM LAST ISSUE.

I have written enough to show that trade, or sectional unionism, is of little use in the great fight for Freedom.

It attempts to pit small portions of the Working Class against not only the enemy, but against the remainder of its own class, and by so doing is doomed to failure.

NEW-FASHIONED INDUSTRIAL UNION.

What, then, is the remedy for all the evils with which we, as clerks, together with all other sections of workers, are surrounded—insanitary offices and workshops, long hours of working, unpaid overtime, and a hundred and one others under the present system ?

We must learn that we all have interests in common—skilled and unskilled, manual and clerical worker, and that if we develop our combined power, and act unitedly, we cannot fail to obtain complete emancipation, and secure to the Working Class all those things which go towards making life full and free.

Instead of the old motto of the sectional Unions, " Each for himself and the devil take the hindmost," we must inscribe on our banners the revolutionary motto, " An injury to one is an injury to all " !

The first thing to do in order to realise this object is to form revolutionary organisations for the express purpose of securing to the workers the whole of the fruits of their labour.

And by revolutionary we do not necessarily mean that we are out for riot and bloodshed, as many would have the workers believe ; although it may be that the objects we are out for will not altogether be attained by " kid-glove " methods.

Further, the formation of these revolutionary organisations does not mean that we are to break up our existing Trade Unions right away, and form new organisations ; but that we must endeavour to transform our present Unions, remodelling them on a scientific basis, in order that they may be thoroughly efficient fighting machines.

The first step we must take in the formation of these organisations is to convince the members of the unions that it is only by joining forces with the whole of their fellow workers in an industry that any hope of progress can be held.

Clerks, instead of holding the narrow views outlined in the early part of this pamphlet, must be brought to realise that their interests are identical with those of the manual workers, and must do all in their power to assist in the formation of these larger Unions ; they must hold out the hand of fellowship to their fellows in adversity, and so help to banish that suspicion in which members of the clerical world are (in many cases justifiably, it must be admitted) held.

It will thus be seen that clerks, instead of remaining permanently organised in a sectional union, must eventually become members of the larger amalgamations catering for the whole of the workers in an industry ; and this remark applies with equal force to all other sections of workers.

ADVANTAGES TO BE GAINED.

It will not require much imagination to enable the clerical worker to realise the advantages to be gained by him through this amalgamation with the manual workers, and to see that the unscrupulous employer, when faced with the power of the whole of the workers in the industry, will think twice before he endeavours to inflict any injustice upon his clerks !

For their part, the clerical portion of the Unions would be of immense value to the Unions as a whole, and the manual workers would gain considerably by the amalgamation, once the clerk became conscious of his duty to his fellows.

By virtue of their positions, clerks have, in the majority of cases, access to the correspondence of their employers, and, consequently, have a better opportunity of keeping an eye on the various moves of those individuals.

It will be readily seen, therefore, what a valuable help the clerk could be in such an organisation as we have outlined.

Other mutual advantages will quickly occur to anyone with the least bit of imagination, but sufficient has, I think, been written to show the undoubted benefits to be derived from the amalgamation of the various trade unions in an industry into one large organisation.

There then arises the question of those clerks who are engaged in one industry for a time, and then move into another industry ; and some arrangement will have to be made in order to facilitate their transfer from one organisation to another.

The simplest way, and the one I would advocate, of dealing with this problem, would be for the whole of the organisations to adopt an uniform TRADE contribution, to be based on the amount required to cover the purely trade purposes, viz. :—Strike, Victimisation, Educational, and Progaganda Funds, leaving the purely friendly section benefits, such as sick, death, etc., to be fixed as the members chose, consummate, of course, with actuarial soundness.

This arrangement would enable the whole of the members of the different organisations to have an uniform card, which, on being shown fully paid up, would entitle them to be transferred to any of the unions.

OFFICIALS AND PARASITES.

It will be found that the greatest obstacles in the way of these proposals are the paid officials of the various trade unions of to-day, whose main objects is to retain their jobs, and to put themselves to as little trouble as possible.

No small group of persons, however, must be allowed to stand in the way of progress, and, if it becomes necessary to clear these place-seekers out of the way, we can either pension them off (in cases where they have been valued workers for their present organisations), or, what reason is there that they should not rejoin their colleagues in the office, mill, or workshop—and earn their living as heretofore ?

So much for officialdom ?

Now, having shown the method of organisation for those clerks and others who are engaged in the various industries, there remains that army of clerical workers who are engaged in what we may term the " parasitical professions," such as the law, bank, stockbrokers, merchants, etc., clerks, to be dealt with.

The reason we call them " parasitical professions " is because they, like parasites, live on others.

Of course, they are necessary under the present rotten system of society, in order to bolster up the exploitation of the workers.

For instance, the only need there is for lawyers is to explain the law, which they themselves have made.

The only use there is for the stockbroker is as an intermediary between one set of capitalists and another ; while the only use there is for the merchants is to act as a medium between the manufacturer and the consumer, thereby adding another profit on to the cost of commodities, and a further burden on the workers.

In a sane system of society, these people would have no place ; but, until that time arrives, provision for those they employ has to be made in our scheme of reorganisation.

I would suggest that during the transition stages, and in order to protect their interests, the clerks engaged in these trades become organised in a general Clerical Union, which would have as its members those clerical workers who are not engaged in any of the staple industries.

Of course, after the transition stages were passed, and the new order of society founded, these clerks would be transferred into one or other of the industries, and found useful work, where they could perform duties which would benefit the whole of the, then, working community.

I would strongly appeal to this class of clerical worker, which is perhaps the most snobbish of the whole class (due in some measure to the fact that he rarely comes into contact with a " workman " during his daily round), to study this great question of organisation, from which he has for so long held aloof—join hands with his fellows, before he finds himself ground out of existence between the workers and the capitalists. He may think himself safe, and that the day is afar off ; but let him read the writing on the wall, and he will not feel so smug and complacent !

We have seen from the foregoing some of the hardships and indignities of clerical life ; we have seen that the old fashioned, sectional Trade Unionism cannot obtain for them complete emancipation ; and we have seen the first step to be taken in the formation of the revolutionary fighting organisations, which will eventually capture the means of Life, and so pave the way to that time when clerks, along with the other workers, will be able to enjoy all the beauties and the joys of a full, free, and healthy existence !

I will now proceed with the methods it is proposed to adopt in order to make capitalism unprofitable, thereby abolishing the wage system, with its attendant evils—poverty, crime, and prostitution—and take possession of the means of life.

DIRECT ACTION.

Under the present wage system, the Working Class are, in order to live, compelled to secure the permission of the capitalists, simply because these own the means of life.

It is therefore obvious that we, the workers, must obtain possession of the various industries, and control them in our own interests, for until that is done no hope can be held for our complete emancipation. The only way in which we can accomplish this is by Direct Action, which has been practiced time after time with sufficient success to justify its advocacy by Syndicalists.

It is no novelty !

Our forefathers, again and again, were persecuted and imprisoned for daring to assert their rights to combine in order to protect themselves against the rapacity and cruelty of their employers, but in spite of that, they persisted in their use of Direct Action, determined to carry out their objects, whether with legal sanction or not, and in the end parliament was compelled to legalise Trade Unionism.

We must follow their example, and if we decide that certain actions are in the interests of the workers, we must carry them out determinedly, letting no obstacle stand in the way of progress.

We need not consider the legality or otherwise of our course of action, but only whether it is right and necessary that we should adopt it as a method to be used in the cause of Freedom, and, having so decided, to act accordingly

By so doing we can relegate to the scrap-heap all those laws which are detrimental to our interests as workers (just as the ruling class ignores those laws which are on the statute, but are detrimental to their interests as profit-mongers), thereby rendering impotent the efforts of the powers that be, who frame the laws simply to enable them to protect and retain possession of their wealth and property, and keep the workers in a state of servility.

Of the various forms of Direct Action the Syndicalists propose to use, perhaps the more important ones are the Partial Strike, Sabotage, and the General Strike.

By the aid of the Partial Strike we can carry on a guerilla warfare, harassing the enemy, winning concessions, and protecting ourselves against the continual attacks of the employing class ; and, although not one of the weapons to be used in the final overthrow of capitalism, its value is great during the time we are preparing for the final coup !

As showing the success of the Partial Strike, we have only to instance the cases of Driver Knox and Guard Richardson, and the Lightning Strikes of the bakers and hotel waiters in London.

(To be continued.)

LIBERTY AND THE GREAT LIBERTARIANS.
By Charles T. Sprading.
(The Golden Press, 6/- nett).

[Reviewed by Jack Wood.]

This is an epoch-making book. A fearless, trenchant, new and complete anthology of Libertarian philosophy in opposition to all that is authoritarian in church and state. From Christian and agnostic, from atheism and science, he has called the brains of the ages. Fearless and of wonderful value in that he presents Herbert Spencer's deleted chapter in full, " The right to ignore the state," left out of " Socal Statics " after the 1850 edition.

Mary Wollstone craft's " Rights of Women " (still the Magna Charta of women struggling to be free) was an epoch-making book and lives. So was William Godwin's " Political Justice." Thomas Paine's " Crisis," " Common Sense," and " The Rights of Man " shook conventionality and authoritarianism to their very basic roots. Robert Burns, poet and prophet, with his spiritual-economic insight, and Voltaire, dealt death-blows on the claims of authority and government, not only in Scotland and France, but world wide, and their momentum is increasing.

In " Liberty and the Great Libertarians " we find a compilation, an arsenal of ammunition, never before, as a whole, presented to the world. For students and thinkers its value cannot be over estimated. In current literature it stands unique. It will hold its own. Life, reality, on its every page. Just as " Progress and Poverty," by Henry George, the " Fabian Essays " later, and later still Blatchford's " Merrie England " took the peoples by storm and compelled attention, so this latest anthology of Libertarians will find its way on to the shelves, and into the minds and consciences of an awakening world. Hence, I say, read it. To quote the old book for what it is worth, " A wayfaring man, though a fool, may run and read " it. It's a new signpost pointing the road to Freedom, to the Co-operative Commonwealth, where the unit shall be of more value than the state as now understood.

The comprehensiveness of the work of Sprading is proven by the full index at back of the book, which adds to its value. No more weary searching in the libraries for " authorities on our side," or for humanity—they are here in a nutshell, a five years' work of love for Freedom.

Quoting from the book, Max Muller says : " All truth is safe, and nothing else is safe ; and he who keeps back the truth, or withholds it from men, from motives of expediency is either a coward or a criminal, or both."

" Liberty and the Great Libertarians " presents statements of great thinkers which the conventional, superstition-ridden world deems it wise to conceal from the common or general mind. From Edmund Burke to Kropotkin, from Dr. John Clifford, of Westbourne Park Chapel, London, back to John Milton, we hear the clarion call for equal liberty. Voluntary, not begged nor vouchsafed. What does Dr. Clifford say ? " All our liberties are due to men who, when their conscience has compelled them, have broken the laws of the land." And John Milton (earning blindness as his wages in defence of liberty) : " Give me liberty to know, to utter, and to argue freely, according to conscience."

The book contains thirty-two chapters on leading thinkers, each headed with succinct biography. The preface and introduction by Sprading are void of acrimony. At a glance we shake mental hands with Max Stirner (The Ego and his Own), Hobbes of " Leviathan " renown, Wilhelm Von Humboldt, Edward Carpenter, Oscar Wilde, Ferrer (Modern School), Spinoza (the ejected), Shelley, William

LIBERTY AND THE GREAT LIBERTARIANS.

By Charles T. Sprading.

(CONTINUED FROM PAGE 2).

Morris, Huxley, Ellen Key, Renan, Goldsmith, Thoreau, Debs, Shaw, Tolstoy, John Stuart Mill, Darrow, Beecher, Theodore Parker, Alfred Russell Wallace, Ingersoll, Bradlaugh.

So herein, preachers, lawyers, socialists, anarchists, students, and agitators of varied hue will find a book as pregnant with potent truths as the sky is begemmed with stars.

Colton in his celebrated " L " well wrote : " Works of true merit are seldom very popular in their own day ; for knowledge is on the march, and men of genius are the videttes that are in advance of their comrades. They are not with them, but before them ; not in the camp, but beyond it." So this book. It contends that society will thrive without the state, and, as Kropotkin puts it, we seek " a confederation of citizens, not a flock of subjects."

Bakunin is coming to the front. He was left " high and dry," not shipwrecked ; and the Syndicalist and Industrial activities of the present hour, world-wide, are his living monument.

From the modernity of Wm. Marion Reedy to the transcendtalism of Ralph Waldo Emerson ; from the fiery invective of Byron (Lord by accident) to the weird ultra genius of Edgar Allan Poe ; from Swinburne's " Songs before Sunrise " to the fervor of Altgeld ; from the keen Mathematician William Kingdom Clifford to the serious comicalities of Mr. Dooley ; from the Florentine Barnum of the middle ages—Machiavelli—to the politically-bought John Morley—they all voice equal liberty and the aspirations of the " Great Libertarians " as produced in this last contribution under consideration.

Believing with Victor Hugo that ' The future is with Voltaire, and not with the church ; the future is with the book, and not with the sword ; the future is with life, and not with death," we opine that " Liberty and the Great Libertarians " is, and will be, a beacon light, a help, towards not only the emancipation of a class but of the human race.

TIGER.

By Witter Bynner. (P. J. Rider, 1s. net.)

[Reviewed by Arthur D. Lewis.]

This is a brief drama of New York life.

Whatever may be the case in New York, in London it is seldom necessary to trap girls into brothels with pretence of marriage.

" Tiger " does show some understanding of the fact that women may prefer prostitution to being servants or shop assistants at low wages. This is something to be thankful for at a time when so much nonsense is being spread about by the women suffragists, which would cause you to suppose that it is man the male that is all to blame, and not at all the master and mistress class because they keep wages low and the conditions of life monotonous and uninspiring.

The " situation " presented—a father finding his own daughter when he is looking for a prostitute—resembles one used by Maupassant in a story. Though not treated adequately here, it does not entirely lose its natural force.

It is a good thing to find a publisher and author willing to force the public to look again at facts, even if I cannot agree with American critics that it is " a tabloid masterpiece," or " a perfect bit of work," or even " stronger than a year of sermons." But it is worth reading.

War.--What For ?

By FRANK ANSTEY.

The men who want war are the men who make a profit out of it. The trust constructed by the international firms that make war material for all the nations of the world is as powerful as the Steel Trust of America. The total capital of the firms within the trust is over £70,000,000, and behind it stand massed the great banks of the world.

Within the trust are Krupps, Vickers, Armstrong's, Cammel Laird and Co., Chilworth's, B.S.A., Harvey Steel Co., Nobel's Dynamite, Odero of Genoa, Orlando of Leghorn, Aufocklagan of Hamburg, Hagen of Cologne, the United Steel Co., Harland and Wolff, Whitworths, El Hispanio Construccion, United Carbide Co., Whitehead and Co., and fifty other armament or ammunition makers of various nationalities.

In short, all the great British, German, French, Italian, Russian, Spanish, and American firms are in it. The Deutsche Bank, Deutsche Vereins Bank, Hanoversche Bank, Moulet Bank of Switzerland, Bayles and Kembell's Bank of New York, Union Bank of Scotland, and the National Provincial Bank of England all directly hold shares in the trust, while many others in all countries are controlled by the directors of the trust or their agents.

Of the men connected with the War Trust, either as debenture trustees in absorbed companies or as directors in one or other of the working trustified corporations, there are high dignitaries of the church, powerful politicians, army and navy officers and great magnates of the world of money.

Profits of Patriotism.

In Great Britain the following Conservative ex-Ministers derive profit from the War Trust :—Lord Balfour of Burleigh, Earl Grey, and the Right Hon. A. Lyttleton. Among the present English Liberal ministry are Runciman, Hobhouse, and Ure, Lord High Chamberlain Baron Sandhurst, British Ambassador, C. M. McDonell, and president of the Board of Trade, T. A. Pease, of Pease and Co., pig iron contractors to the Admiralty.

Amongst army and navy officers connected with the trust are Admirals Charles Beresford, Digby Morant, Archibald Douglas, Edmund Freemantle, and Vice-Admirals Reginald Bacon and Charles Ottley. Amongst the more prominent army officers are Generals Brackenbury and Andrew Noble, Major-Generals Nicholson and Micklen, and a host of majors, colonels and captains. They all draw profits from companies supplying war material to the enemy.

The following dignitaries of the church also make a profit out of blood and enhance their incomes from the millions of money spent on war material :—Bishops of Adelaide, Chester, Hexham, Kensington, Newport, and Newcastle ; also Archdeacons Campbell, Clarke, Richardson, Seagrave, and Watkins.

The International Combine.

All these British militarists, politicians, and churchmen are related, per medium of the War Trust, with militarists, politicians, and churchmen in other countries. They know no divisions of race or creed. They constitute an international band of profit-mongers, banded together to stimulate national fears and secure expenditure on war material, out of which these harpies make profit and augment their fortunes.

Amongst this international brotherhood of war material makers competition has no existence. When a war scare has been worked up in Germany, France, Australia, or any other country, the trust decides which firms shall tender, and at what prices they shall tender. The firm or firms to get the work put in their price—the others are so far above the agreed-on price that their tendering is only a farce. Many firms inside the trust have been closed, and the work concentrated. The closed firms are consoled with trust debentures, upon which they draw profits, as if their firms were in profit-going order.

Fakirs and their Fakes.

In order to work up war scares, the War Trust owns or subsidises newspapers in all countries. The newspaper press as an all-powerful instrument for creating popular alarms is used by the War Trust for the purpose of increasing their business and their profits. The higher the war scare develops in any country the greater the number of orders for guns and munitions of war.

The process of working on the feelings of a community so as to provoke orders for guns, etc., was recently put before the German parliament by Liebknecht. He produced letters and telegrams and pay dockets and proved the case of the Franco-German war scare of 1912 up to the hilt.

In France and Germany newspapers were bought or subsidised by the trust, and the object of that purchase or support became transparent when the journals began to publish sensational reports of the military activity of the " enemy." In France the public were told that Germany was arming, and that its objective was France. In Germany the public were told that France was arming, and that its objective was Germany. The readers in both countries digested the sensational intelligence with consternation ; they got uneasy, their patriotism was aroused. The German wanted guns to protect the Faderland and the Frenchman shouted for guns to protect La Belle France. As a consequence, orders for munitions of war poured into the war material manufacturers from the governments of both countries.

The Bogey Man.

In both countries a bogey was invoked to exploit French and German patriotism, and the result came back in immense profits to the war scare mongers. What appeared to the outside world as a struggle of rival patriotisms was the sordid conspiracy of great capitalists, who knew no country, and whose only object was to use nationalities for their own enrichment, even if it meant the extermination of the nation of which they professed to be loyal and loving subjects.

What was true of the Franco-German scare is true of the Germo-British scare, and of the Japanese invasion scare, the last now admitted to have been a fake for imperial purposes. Japan had got to the end of its capacity as a good consumer of war material ; Australia is raked in to make up the sales. Sometimes the take gets beyond control, and an actual crisis is precipitated. War material is consumed and human lives, but the profits of the trust go soaring up, and the people who are left alive are cursed with the burden arising from the wastage of war.

* * * *

The trust controls papers not only in France and Germany, but in England and Scotland, to make up periodical war scares. Amongst the British newspapers known to be owned by the trust are the London " Daily Telegraph," Sheffield "Daily Telegraph," Liverpool " Daily Post," Dundee " Advertiser," " People's Journal," and " People's Friend." Those subsidised to assist or to accept articles written by agents of the trust are countable by scores.

The Power behind the Curtain.

The trust builds ships, equips arsenals, manufactures artillery, supplies rifles and ammunition for every country on earth. They are interested in war, as out of it comes their profits. If two nations can be stimulated to war the trust supplies both parties with the means of mutual destruction, and extracts profits from both. Which wins is of no importance. The primary object is that orders shall come rolling in and profits go mounting up. When one party to the fight has exhausted its financial resources, the war comes to an end, and those combatants are free from the war scare fake for a generation. The trust turns to fresh fields and pastures new. Russia has been out of the running as a scarecrow for many years. There are no signs of its reappearance. The Japanese invasion fake is off. The only effective existing scarecrow is Germany, and how it is going to be got to work in Australia nobody seems to know.

* * * *

If to-day the entire outlay upon armaments could be placed upon the shoulders of the panic-mongers, invasion scares would soon cease.

* * * *

The Struggle.

But the task of the international arbitrationists is rendered doubly difficult by the enormous influence of the manufacturing classes interested in the use of war material. They are powerful in money and in social influence, and are in close touch with the powers that move in political and diplomatic circles. They are supported by the military and naval officials, who fear the passing of their occupation. They also are interested in seeing the expenditure go upward, and, as the " Age " said the other day, " If they had their way, ample preparations for defence in Australia would mean ten or twelve millions per year." It is exactly against these influences that a democracy must inevitably be at war. The cost of peace becomes as terrifying as actual war. Men live perpetually on their fears, and the useful possibilities of life are sapped and destroyed.

The moneyed capitalist class interested in the sale of material, and the military section interested in the maintenance of an exclusive caste, are astute enough to trade upon the racial pride and upon the sentimental traditions of the multitude. To this pride and those traditions they address themselves, whether from press or platform, whether to German or British, and by these means nations are kept apart, industries crippled, multitudes kept poor, that a non-productive class may be created, and the makers of war material grow richer and more powerful.

It is not for these things that the Labour Movement came into existence. This is not the way to " defend civilisation." The Labour Movement functioned to make war upon hunger, disease, dirt, destitution, ignorance, unemployment, and slums, not upon imaginary enemies—enemies that no man can tell you who they are or what they are. It functioned to create wealth widely diffused amongst the people, not to extract it from the processes of industry, that it might be wasted on bogeys and concocted terrors.

SITTINGS OF EGGS.

TOPICAL YARNS.

By Arthur D. Lewis.

THE SALVATION ARMY.

The greatest of all the Clerical Militarist organisations has been holding an expensive congress in the Strand, at which it has entertained delegates shipped from Africa, Borneo, and other distant places. I refer, of course, to the Salvation Army. This is the most autocratically governed of all " armies." The first old " General " was no believer in the possible inspiration of other people. He was such an autocrat that he sacrificed two of his own children to his claims to rigid obedience to himself. " Loyalty to the General " is to-day emphasised in the " Army."

The army is a big trading concern, and acts as a detective agency, tea-dealer, insurance company, emigration agency, paper-sorter, wood-chopper, rag-sorter, and builder, and makes a payment, at the expense of the charitable public, to its shareholders.

Abroad, its beneficial (?) work as evangelising agent is combined, after the fashion of other missionaries, with teaching the natives to work for the profit of others.

" Boothism " is the essence of the worst features of the worst kind of religion. It persistently uses fear of Hell as its great weapon. It worships a dead Bible.

The best defence of it that can be made is that it provides a religion for the almost feeble-minded.

This clericalist Salvation Army is blessed by king, prince, minister, and president because it keeps the people safely in a religion which pays no heed to anything except the Soul ; it teaches them a religion of silly, illiterate songs, of intoxicating noise, stimulating rhythm, impassioned confessions, testimonies, hallelujah's, praise God's, and amens.

Salvation Army religion is a symptom of the terrible ignorance of a large part of the population. The Salvation Army provides quack remedies for prostitution, unemployment, and drink. It depresses wages, by paying men in kind, when they have dropped out of work and are helpless because they have no tools, and paying them below the standard rates for wood-chopping and building. The capital for these purposes is given by the charitable, and therefore the army can get contracts which no one else can afford to take.

The army does not succeed with its " redemptive " work ; it enlists the born dissenting types of pietists, and has no effect on the lost drunkard and helpless submerged.

The army obtains money under false pretences from people who do not know which of its numerous tasks their contributions will be used for.

Roman Catholic Hypocrisy.

The hypocrisy of the Roman Catholic Church is seen in its attitude towards artificial preventitives of conception. No questions are asked at confessions, and no warnings offered to rich and educated persons. But the working-class, that mainly suffers from a high birth-rate, is left ignorant, or taught that all children came from God, and all interference to prevent births highly immoral. How cruel to pay no heed to the probable fate of the God-given children ! Here, once again, religion and conventional morality are opposed to kindness. If child follows child at the shortest interval, they must be born weak, and suffer neglect from their mother, who is harassed by so many helpless little children, needing so much watching. Often they die. What useless suffering caused by the holy church !

News from France.

The fall of the French ministry directly concerns us. Our own armaments are needed in order to retain the friendship of our friends abroad, as well as to keep attractive " backward " countries exposed to the gaze and grasp of our friends at home, our native stock-brokers, and financiers. Just as we are told we must increase our armaments because Germany, our foe, does so, so we are told, if the Three Years' Law is maintained, we must increase them in order to reciprocate the " great sacrifices " made by our friends, France and Russia, and to retain the advantages of being associated with them. And why does France need to arm ? Not so much because the enormous armaments of Germany might meet her " face to face " on the frontier, as because there is so much " peaceful penetration " to be done in savage and backward countries.. The modern profiteer does not want to conquer the fields of Alsace ; he wants to conquer fields for investment in Morocco. Modern diplomacy (backed up by modern armies) is a protection of the interest of the various national usurers. Every financier has the support of his government, which he in turn supports as long as it gives him something in return. The French are more controlled by financiers, who have interests in Algiers and Morocco, than by sentimentalists who do not do business with Alsace.

The Syndicalist
and Amalgamation News.

Edited under the auspices of the Industrial Syndicalist Education League.

PRESIDENT : TOM MANN.

SECRETARY : GUY BOWMAN.

VOL. III.　NO. 5.　　　LONDON, AUGUST, 1914.　　　MONTHLY, ONE PENNY.

Topical Yarns.

Militarism---God and Mammon---Prize-Fights.

By Arthur D. Lewis.

The Boy Scouts Again.

" If you don't like it from the business point of view, look at it from the Christian and patriotic point of view," says Sir Robert Baden-Powell, appealing to a Manchester audience for funds for his Boy Scouts, and showing a good knowledge of the intelligence and consistency of an English audience. The old gibes about people believing on Sundays and when the organ plays, what they do not for a minute take seriously on business-like Mondays, are amply justified. A thing may be very pretty or heaven-deserving from a Christian point of view, but not at all likely to turn out well from a business point of view. This seems to confirm an old text about it not being possible to serve God and Mammon ; but however inconsistent God and Mammon-worship are, we can evidently alternate one with the other.

* * * *

Medical Referees.

Mr. James Burnet, M.D., in the " Medical World " (a paper advocating a state medical service) has been dealing with some groups of people who malinger. Strangely enough, these criminals are casual labourers, old soldiers, charwomen, and people of that ill-paid kind. By malingering under the Insurance Act they can get 7s. 6d. a week. But a good man can tell if their tale is true or false. A man came to Mr. Burnet complaining of " severe lumbago," which (he said) prevented him from stooping. " I examined his back very carefully, but no inducement on my part would make him stoop. . . . Then, as if a happy thought had struck me, I said to him quite suddenly, ' I am sure you must have something wrong with your left ankle ; you might take off your boot, please.' At once, forgetting his ' severe lumbago,' he bent forward and unlaced his boot ! " This, evidently marks the discovery of a new profession. " It would certainly pay the National Insurance Commissioners, or rather the societies at present which administer the sickness benefits, to appoint medical referees. . . . But these men must be well paid. . . . The appointments should be given to men on their merits, to men who have had the necessary experience. They should be paid at the rate of £750 a year to commence with, rising by annual increments to £1,000. These figures represent the minimum salary, and they should be pensionable after a definite term of years." Is this a serious or a satirical suggestion ?

* * * *

Mr. J. M. Robertson, M.P.'s Taste.

Of course, there is a certain amount of nonsense talked about literature, although the classes that read no good novels and poetry would learn much about life and human motives if they did. Mr. J. M. Robertson was once a bold Atheist and a determined defender of the rights of subject nations ruled by British officials ; he had an eye and a pen for grievances in Egypt, South Africa, and India. He specialised in opposition to Imperialism, until the Liberal party, recognising his ability, and anxious to avoid all this able criticism of its foreign and colonial policy, gave him a paid post on the Board of Trade ; since then, his game being won, he naturally is as docile publicly as Mr. Masterman. In a recent book on " Elizabethan Literature," Mr. Robertson perorates by specially praising these three lines from Cleopatra's speech before suicide :—

" Give me my robe, put on my crown ;
I have
Immortal longings in me ; now no more
The juice of Egypt's grape shall moist
this lip."

But, really, why should a woman about to die say, " I shall drink no more Egyptian wine " ; unless, indeed, she had been exceptionally fond of drinking ? The little men will praise in famous and great authors their faults. But, then, an insincere political speech-maker would like the resonant nonsense of the stage.

* * *

Recent Prize Fights.

If only the workers would take the war between the classes as seriously as they do the prize-fights between Bombardier Wells and Colin Bell, Carpentier and Gunboat Smith, or Welch and Ritchie ! At present the class-war is largely one-sided. The propertied never forget their interests and unite as a class whenever expedient. The worker often snobbishly admires his enemies. The organisation of our society is so large and complicated that men seem to suffer from the working of an automatic machine, in which no one seems to blame. This is one cause of the despicable patience with which the workers suffer. Of course, too, being always ordered about, they feel incapable of acting without orders. If their position is to alter, they must increase their power of planning their own work and facing responsibilities. The stupidity of the working class is easily explained—boxed in over-crowded rooms, in some cases never in a bedroom alone, even when at school sandwiching school-work with wage-earning work and with helping mother, without any encouragement to think, they are not likely to be very intelligent ; but their stupidity blocks the way to a change in society. Only a stupid class would prefer to retain the " half-time " school system of Lancashire.

* * * *

Booing a Princess.

England is losing the qualities which made it what it was. On July 8th the Princess Royal was booed. It seems that some dirty bricklayers and stonemasons presumed to imitate doctors and barristers ; no one was to lay bricks who did not uphold their ideas of professional honour ; just as if a bricklayer has any need for protecting himself against those who would undersell him, as a doctor, of course, must kick against heretical manipulators of stiff joints, or an Inn of Court refuse to let men competent in the law but with wrong political views act as barristers. The Princess, laying a foundation-stone on a blackleg basis of scab's brickwork, was howled at. Can it be that his majesty the King, with all his heroes and his footmen and guards, will ever fail to be greeted with bared heads and loud hurrahs by a fool people, who never ask : " What is he in himself and what has he actually done ? " All this is one of the results of Sunday cinema shows ; for, as the Rev. H. J. Waldron says in " T.P.'s Weekly " :—" The abolition of reverence for Sunday and religion must inevitably carry with it the abolition of reverence for many other things, such as property and authority, etc." But it is hardly respectful to work the Royal Family in as part of " etc."

* * * *

Liberal Love for the Labourer.

Those who read the newspapers carefully will remember that for the past five years or so (these facts of ancient history are not clearly in the minds of people with anything to do) there has been, off and on, a great Liberal land campaign. It may be wanted at a general election. There was once a land song, but the people are still landless. Anyhow, from time to time orators are let loose to denounce feudalism and dukes ; they unchain their indignation at the long hours and low wages of country labourers ; they build houses at the cost of a few millions, and untie their sympathy with cases of over-crowding, leaky roofs, a contaminated water supply, and other charms of the sweet English countryside, as it is seen by the wretched nonentities who make it productive. Of late the labourers, instead of waiting for Lloyd George's great law to help them, have starved themselves by striking in order to try to coerce the farmers to give them a little of what every loyal Liberal says they ought to have. But independent action of this kind must not be encouraged. The hypocritical " Daily Chronicle," relating how Trade Unionism has spread in Wiltshire, and how demands have been presented for better wages and hours, and how, in consequence, one active Trade Unionist has been sacked, goes on to say : " Whatever the merits of the case in question, the fact remains that representatives of the union yesterday went to London and received sanction from headquarters for a general strike." After all their sympathy with landless labourers, they are ready to say : "Whatever the merits of the case, the fact remains."

LOOK HERE.

" Weekly Syndicalist "

FUND.

£300

Wanted.

Already Subscribed	£109	5	7
To be Subscribed	£190	14	5
Total - £300	0	0

BUCK UP !

Re " M.P. Vulgaris."

The Natural History of the Politician.

By Jack Radcliffe.

The natural history of the various parasitical pests which infest the social organism has yet to be written. There is, it is true, a vast mass of data which has been collected by various investigators. But unfortunately these seldom bring to their studies that true scientific spirit which is necessary for a clear understanding of the objects observed.

Politicans Professionalis.

It is thus my endeavour to present to my intelligent, learned, and more or less gentle readers a short monograph dealing with the natural history of that genus or family of social parasites known as the *Politicans professionalis*, or professional politician.

P. professionalis is divided into the following species :—*P. conservatorum* (sub-species, *Ulsterius Carsonii* ; *P. liberalis-unionistes* ; *P. liberalis-laboritis fakirium* ; and *P. socialismus parliamentariensis* (sub-species, *Homerulea Redmondii*).

The nits from which these parasites are hatched are widely distributed. Those of *P. conservatorum* and *P. liberalis-unionistes* are usually the younger sons of the aristocracy, wealthy capitalists and commercial men, bankers, lawyers, and military or naval officers. Their distribution over these classes is irregular. *P. liberalis-fakirium* is usually found among trade union officials, and also among certain nonconformist Bible-punchers, who turn the little Bethels into centres of political propaganda. *P. socialismus* originates from those bodies known as the Independent Labour Party and the British Socialist Party.

Shading-off Process.

This general classification should not be interpreted too strictly, as the species tend to shade off, one into the other, in the order given, so gradually that it is sometimes impossible accurately to place certain individuals who partake partly of the nature of one and partly of another. Moreover, they are all more or less protean. That is to say, they may actually change from one to another, according to circumstances and their own interests. Thus, to use popular language (instead of scientific terms), the parliamentary socialist tends to become a liberal-labour fakir, who, in turn, may pass by degrees into the liberal unionist, and this last again may pass over to the conservative. The reverse process, except as between conservatives and liberals, is seldom if ever observed.

Trimming His Sails.

A nit having been hatched by the party caucus, or committee of selection, appears next in the larval, grub, or maggot stage. He is then known as " the candidate." This is the most interesting period at which to observe the wriggling creature. He is remarkable for the quantity and variety of the promises he is prepared to make to the electorate, and also for the number of lies he is prepared to tell about his political opponents and about himself. He is, in fact, ready to make use of any statement, evasion, subterfuge, or shift—he will, so to speak, trim his sails to any passing breeze—in order to obtain the votes upon which his further development depends. This applies with equal force to each and all of the species enumerated. The possession of brains, character, and conscientiousness is a serious drawback for the evolution of the grub into the mature form. It is, however, seldom that a candidate possessing these qualities is selected.

The Fully-Developed Parasite.

The efforts of the rival candidates and their supporters provide a roaring farce for the amusement of the gods and such men as can see the humour of it, and is called a " parliamentary campaign." This culminates in the " election " when one or more of the grubs (according to the nature of the constituency) is " returned." He is now the fully-developed parasite, known as a " member of parliament." He proceeds to the nest or hive of his kind, known as the House of Commons, where he sheds more or less completely every one of the principles he had previously professed. His function from now onward is to assist the wealthy classes, who own the country and its resources, in ruling, governing, and keeping in a proper state of subjection those very people whose votes have placed him in this position. This functioning, however, is natural in the higher species. *P. conservatorum* and *P. liberalis*, and from these nothing else is expected.

The Fakir.

But *P. liberalis-laboris fakirium* and *P. socialismus* are expected by some simple-minded persons to behave otherwise. It is difficult to understand why these should prove any exception to the rule, and indeed they do not. In order to prevent any aberrations on their part, however, a sum of £400 per annum is provided for each, and in addition prospects are held out to them of positions carrying still higher rates of pay. There are cases on record, it is true, of odd individuals of these species endeavouring to act up to their previously expressed promises and principles. But they are always boycotted by their fellows, or are driven forth from the hive.

The purpose in life of the political parasites is to safeguard and protect the interests of the wealthy classes, and to fasten more securely upon the community the domination of its capitalistic exploiters. Their main activity is to obscure every true, popular issue in a cloud of words, varied by the skilful manipulation of " red herrings " (such as tariff reform, free trade, the Welsh disestablishment bill, home rule, and the Ulster agitation), and by the promotion of such " reforms " as are calculated to lead their working class victims into the belief that they are being benefited, when all the time they are being reduced to a more absolute and certain state of servitude.

The Senile Variety.

There is another variety of political parasites, whose genesis and evolution are somewhat different. I allude to those found in that section of the parliamentary hive known as the House of Lords. They belong exclusively to *P. conservatorum* and *P. liberalis*, and their function is the same as of those who are found in the House of Commons under the same classifications.

When the Working Class realises the true nature and vicious functioning of these parasites they will stop their development by destroying the system which gives rise to them.

The Syndicalist

and AMALGAMATION NEWS.

EDITED UNDER THE AUSPICES OF

THE INDUSTRIAL SYNDICALIST EDUCATION LEAGUE.

Offices—

4, MAUDE TERRACE, WALTHAMSTOW, LONDON, E.

MONTHLY · · ONE PENNY.

Post Paid Subscription—

Great Britain or Abroad: 12 Months, 1s. 6d.

Bundle Rates—

1s. 6d. per quire, Carriage Paid.

U.K.F. TERMS TO NEWSAGENTS.

The Receipt of a Sample Copy is an Invitation to Subscribe.

AUGUST, 1914.

OUR STUDENTS' COLUMN.

Though our space is very limited, we will print each month one or more essays from comrades now in the movement. But we do not want articles on theory. We prefer information on the employers' organisations and methods. We wish to give every encouragement to those who desire to assist us if they will bear the above points in mind.

Is Political Action any use to the Working Class?

By R.D.

I had first entitled this article " Is Political Action Played Out ? " and then I remembered how I had heard some parliamentarian Socialists say : " If the actions of parliament do not affect us, then we can afford to leave it alone." So I thought I would alter it to " Is Political Action any Use to the Working Class ? "

Let us as workers examine our position in society. We gain our livelihood in the industrial arena ; whether it be field, factory, or workshop does not matter. So long as we labour for wages we know that our labour is exploited for profit by the other class. It matters not what political creed we may hold. The exploiting class have just as little regard for the Tory workman as for the Revolutionary parliamentarian Socialist (whatever that may be). He realises that as long as they keep quietly producing profits for him, they are quite harmless, even though they call themselves rebels. The great factor of our subjection is not a political one at all, it is solely an economic one, and it is to gain the economic control over our own lives and welfare that we ought to be seeking. The political party that happens to be in power at any time is simply the marionette of the economic control at that time. Surely it is well known that the great financiers, as the Rothschilds, Astors, etc., have far greater power in controlling present society than such pigmies as Asquith, Lloyd George, and Ramsay MacDonald, who are simply danced about by the economic pressure on their various strings. It is economic power that controls political parties, the same economic power that controls us in the factories, etc. To say that you are a political rebel causes no qualms to the exploiter. But attempt to question his economic power and control, and say you will control your own industrial welfare ; then watch the enemy. He would run blubbering to his parliament as a little child to its mother, saying : let me have all the force of law and order against this class who want to control their own welfare. And he would get all that he asked for, because he pulls the strings of parliament. The same would apply with a B.S.P. government, because they would simply be the reflex and pawns of a B.S.P. society, and any section of thought that may rise up in differentiation to theirs would have to be crushed, and the only way to crush an uprising on the economic field is by force.

Now, then, let us just see how this parliamentarism acts in regard to the proletarian class. We have had it in operation sufficiently long to be able to form some ideas of its working. We will leave the antique Liberalism and Toryism out of it, and say we become interested in the great progressive time of the Keir Hardies, John Burnses, David Shackletons (chance every one may have forgot him), about ten years ago, when these parliamentary stalwarts were going to legislate us out of our economic bondage. Ten years is a fair slice of a man's life, and what do we find has taken place with respect to the great advancement of Labour on the political field. Two of the previously mentioned stalwarts have gone bag and baggage over to the side with economic power, whilst the only fame I can recollect in the case of the other one is such literature as " Can a Man be a Christian on a Pound a Week ? " and the " Queenie Gerald Flat Case."

However, we find that a certain section of proletariat parliamentarians are not disheartened. They come along and mount the rostrums, styling themselves as the only particular brand of political party which has any hope for the worker. All else is illusion, etc., etc. " The present Labour Party that was going to do wonders for you is only after all a body of fakirs. We are the real rebels who are going to turn parliament inside out and legislate your emancipation." Yet they often say " You must emancipate yourself."

What a contradiction ! It is an insult to the term " rebel " to be seeking election to the House of Commons. The revolt of the people will not take place in the House of Commons. It will take place on the industrial field, and that is where all rebels are required and ought to be. What reason is there to believe that men of the type of Bill Gee, Victor Grayson, and George Lansbury, with ten years of parliamentary atmosphere and £400 a year, would be any better than the average member of the Labour Party ? The retort may be : " Send them and see " ; which is tantamount to another well-known phrase not attributed to a political rebel : " I think we have sent them and NOT seen."

How do heterodoxy and rebelling inside our legislative chamber operate. We will take the case of Victor Grayson as a modern type of rebellious M.P. When the House was discussing a grant of £30,000 to Lord Cromer, he got up and opposed, and attempted to draw the attention of the members to the lamentable conditions prevailing within a stone's throw of that House. He was told he was out of order and to sit down, and eventually was removed and suspended. His political rebelling was at an end. Therefore, I should say that we cannot afford to waste valuable time and money in fighting government ! We must centralise our efforts for emancipation on the industrial field, by any methods. If the rank and file in any industry think that sabotage would be profitable to them in fighting the unscrupulous enemy, then let them use it. In my opinion, however, we shall have to concentrate our efforts upon the general strike, which is the greatest weapon for showing the power we possess. At the same time, sections of trade unions must concentrate their efforts solely upon endeavouring to gain the control for themselves of the industries they work in. I believe that to work on these lines is the quickest and surest way of achieving Socialism. The tactics may be styled under any name you like. But they are the methods that I stand by, and political action sinks into absolute oblivion in comparison.

ABERDEEN.

By J. Edward Morgan

Famed hamlet of the Northern Hills,
　　Sweet Aberdeen.
Thou drivest me from drink to pills,
　　Fair Aberdeen.
But yesterday a nameless thing,
To-day e'en kings their tribute bring,
For thy foul stench is on the wing—
　　Blest Aberdeen.

We've prattled much of love and law,
　　Great Aberdeen.
And slaves have bent the knee in awe,
　　Oh, Aberdeen !
But thou hast nailed that ancient lie
With " Might is Right " and clubs on high,
While overlords on earth reply :
　　Brave Aberdeen !

In dream prophetic this I see,
　　Cursed Aberdeen !
Thou hell-belched brat of Tyranny,
　　Doomed Aberdeen !
I see the avenging gods repair ;
I see their wrathful torches flare,
To purge thy stench from earth and air,
　　Damned Aberdeen !

Thou castrate, cockroach, bludgeoned imp,
　　" Brave Aberdeen " ;
Whoremongers' bastard, pissmire pimp,
　　Foul Aberdeen !
'Twould steep my soul in bubbling bliss,
To grab you as you belch and hiss,
And drown you in a pot of —— tea—
　　Dear Aberdeen !

FREE LOVE.

The Social Significance of the Modern Drama.

BY EMMA GOLDMAN.

Boston : R. G. Badger, 1 dollar, net

Reviewed by A. Daniels.

Emma Goldman, who gives summaries of the more propagandist plays of Ibsen, Stindberg, Endermann, Hauptmann, Wedekind, Maeterlinck, Restand, Brieux, Shaw, Galsworthy, Houghton, Sowerby, Yeats, Lenox, Robinson, T. G. Murray, Tolstoy, Tchekhof, Gorki, and Andreyev, counts duty a curse that fetters the spirit of man, and the marriage institution a degradation.

But some feeling of duty will always exist while it at all hurts us to hurt others. The immorality which says, " I do not care a damn about other people's feelings," or, in more vulgar language, " I can't help your troubles," is beyond most of us.

I think there is some stupidity in those who, like Emma Goldman and Bernard Shaw, do not see that however hard it is to live faithfully as man and wife, the monogamic ideal of marriage does so appeal to our emotional nature that men and women are seriously unhappy in trying to destroy it.

A man may give himself pleasure by satisfying an instinct and yet be unhappy. For in order to be happy you must satisfy both your conscious mind and your unconscious self ; both your inner and your outer being.

The plans which these advanced men set forth for the reform of marriage they cannot expect to be carried out for a long time. And, meantime, what effects are they likely to have on ordinary, unenterprising people with narrow opportunities ? I believe bad effects.

The alteration needed in marriage is one which will reject the grossly material view of Christianity, in which marriage, though a sacrament, is yet a mere license to do what were better left undone, and in which all idea of companionship is neglected. Inability to enter into useful communication with each other should be the best reason for divorce ; not mere physical infidelity, which may be a thing of little meaning.

Conventionalities and stupidities do not sum up the present ideal of marriage and the family.

It must, however, be admitted that men frequently, and women occasionally, cannot meet anyone who understands their best intentions.

Intellectual revolutionaries are generally too hopeful with regard to what can be done to produce a harmony of sexual needs, and not hopeful enough with regard to what may be done to produce a harmony between our conflicting material needs, by abolishing ownership almost entirely. Our sexual instincts vary so much that mating is hard. Sexual instincts, like other instincts, are largely out of accord with utility. Evolutionists declare they were produced to suit surroundings which we have left.

Chiefly on the Crowd's Thinking.

" Le Syndicalisme Europeen," by Paul Louis. Félix Alcan. Paris. 3 fr. 50.

A carefully written account of trade unionism in Germany, England, Belgium, the Netherlands, Switzerland, Italy, Austria-Hungary, Denmark, Sweden, and Norway. It gives accounts of the industrial condition of each country, the number of trade unionists in it, and the history of their legal position and policy.

Syndicalism in France, by Louis Levine, Ph.D., being the second revised edition of " The Labour Movement in France." P. S. King & Son. 7s. 6d. net (cloth).

This is the second edition of an admittedly first-class book on the French labour movement, full of facts but a bit academic. It is too late to say much more, but I will quote a sentence or two which corrects a common error with regard to the attitude towards politics of those who believe in direct attitude : " The direct method of forcing the state to yield to the demands of the working man consists in exerting external pressure on the public authorities. Agitation in the press, public meetings, manifestations, demonstrations, and the like are the only effective means of making the government reckon with the will of the working class. By direct pressure on the government the working men may obtain reforms of immediate value to themselves. Only such reforms, gained and upheld by force, are real. All other reforms are but a dead letter and a means of deceiving the working men." In other words, as long as parliament exists it will interfere in important matters. But it is not an originating force. It does not create, it obeys. Therefore, it is better to kick it than to try to put " your " representative into it—to kick it with every possible threat and show of strength.

ARE YOU A STAMP LICKER?

If so, you are drawing TIGHTER the net of legislation which is gradually leading back to

Serfdom, Slavery, and Inquisition.

By Margaret Douglas.

In our campaign against the Insurance Act we are sometimes asked why we do not concentrate our whole energy on the emancipation of the workers instead of attacking one piece of fraudulent and oppressive legislation, and I should like to reply to that question in THE SYNDICALIST at greater length than is possible at the street corner.

My reply is that the Act is a new obstacle thrown across the road to freedom—an obstacle that is growing larger and more formidable every day that it remains in force, and one that must be pushed aside or beaten down before further advance is possible.

History is the record of the gradual emancipation of the worker from slavery, through serfdom, to legally established freedom and equality as between man and man. Of course it is quite easy to be sarcastic or laugh about this nominal equality of the wage-earner and the capitalist, but it *was something gained* ; it marked a real and necessary stage in the advance, and, having established his theoretic claim to freedom, the worker found himself at the beginning of the twentieth century free to face the great problem of economic emancipation.

The Ticketed and the Free.

Just at this moment the Insurance Act drops on his head, bringing its rare fruit, its sunshine into cottage windows, and sweeping the mists from the valleys of Wales—the Insurance Act, which has re-established the inequality of man, which has robbed the workers of the little freedom they had won, and which seeks to keep them in permanent subjection and control.

In the first place, class distinction is once more established by law ; the community is divided into two classes —the ticketed and the free. The wage-earners may not work, or live, without their licences ; the well-to-do are free. In effect, the card is a new barrier raised between the classes, a perpetual reminder to the worker that he is different, inferior, and exists only by permission of those who, free themselves, issue the licence which serves as his passport to work and wages.

Improvident Wretches !

The moral effect of this new barrier may not at first seem serious, but watch its subsequent developments. The card system is set up by Part I. of the Act in somewhat formal fashion but under Part II. the new bureaucrats get to work in earnest. The two and a half million men and women who come under this section are compelled to report themselves at the Labour Exchanges, where elaborate records are compiled as to their activities, appearance, trade union enthusiasm, or zeal in the cause of free labour ! Having persuaded the workers to submit to this inquisition in the noble cause of social reform, the state then proceeds to dictate the terms on which the " benefits " shall be received. Are you impertinent to your foreman ? For shame ! No benefit for six weeks. Do you presume to decline the pleasant job we offer (100 miles from your home, perhaps) ? No benefit for you. Do you dare to take risks like other human beings and throw up a hard, ill-paid job on the chance of bettering yourself ? Improvident wretch ! No benefit for six weeks. If you go on strike there is no benefit. The Labour Party approve of this, so of course it must be right. But it is not so easy to see why they allowed the clause which deprives the locked-out worker of any claim to benefit unless they wish, through him, to put pressure on would-be strikers.

For Obedient and Docile Serfs.

While investigating the worker's " claim " to the benefit he has bought with his own money, the officials ask his late employer for information about him, and all the time they are collecting the material which will enable them to supply employers with exactly the kind of labour they require—a hundred dangerous Syndicalists, or sixty non-union navvies —and all the time a spirit of servility and dependence is being fostered in the workers. The knowledge that they can only get their money back on terms dictated by the state will insensibly tend to make men inclined to fall in with those terms. At this moment there are thousands of pounds invested in government securities which have been taken week by week from the wages of the men in the building trade. Had this money been in the Post Office savings bank or in the union coffers it would have been very useful to the wives and children during the present dispute ; but it is safely stored out of harm's way, and the builders' men must learn that benefits are only for the obedient and docile serfs of the industrial state.

A Detective Agency.

The inquisition of the Insurance Act can be judged by the following form which was sent a few days ago to an employer of my acquaintance :

NATIONAL INSURANCE ACT—
UNEMPLOYMENT INSURANCE.

Court of Referees.　Metropolitan.

Case No. ....
Appellant's Name ....
Book No. ....
Employed from .... to ....
Occupation ....
Foreman on Job ....

QUESTION.　　　ANSWER.

1. Was the workman discharged because he did not sign on 24/1/14 the agreement drawn up by the London Master Builders, or

2. Was he discharged for slackness of work ?
　　If for slackness of work, please state :

(a) Was the slackness due to the fact that his work depended on other men who were discharged for refusing to sign the agreement, or

(b) Would he have been discharged on this date in any case ?

This is the kind of legislation the Labour Party ask for and were actually praising in the House of Commons a week or so back when one of their number proposed a resolution asking for more !

Drawing Tighter the Net of Inquisition.

" Forget the drawbacks ; think of the benefits," is the cry of those responsible for the imposition of the Act, and I should like to examine these benefits and consider the Act as a measure of health insurance another time. To-day I will only state that better benefits might have been given for less money in other and simpler ways had the politicians been earnest in their desire to help the poor and sick. The present Act is an experiment in *registration as a means of control*, and the fact that on March 3rd Mr. John Burns informed a grateful Labour Party that he hoped to extend Part II. of the Act to further classes of industry during the present year proves that the experience of its working has justified the expectations of its framers.

The only essential feature of the present Act is the card or licence, and it is this card that the Insurance Tax Resisters seek to abolish or destroy. If we do not succeed the card will be used as the basis of all sorts of future legislation of a compulsory character, imposing further restrictions on the liberty of the workers, drawing tighter the net of inquisition and control until the wage-earner is bound hand and foot, a serf in fact and in name.

STRAIGHT TALKS.

Fifty Points Against Parliament.

By Solomon II.

II.—Continued from Last Issue.

XXII.

Corrupt.

The politician is corrupted from above by his leaders' power of bringing him into prominence : he may be asked to speak or passed over. When arrangements are made with the Government that the debate shall close at such a time after one speaker has put the labour point of view, he may or may not be the speaker.

A little show of independance increases your value : it throws dust in the eyes of the public : but never let your teeth back up your bark.

From above, corruption comes in the form of paid posts, titles, and help in elections.

From below, the politician is corrupted by bargaining for votes.

In the mass, he is corrupted by wealth's control of party funds.

And individually by his own income and advancement.

XXIII.

Its Tone.

The traditions of the House of Commons are the traditions of leisured and educated gentlemen.

Who would not prefer them to the traditions of rough, ignorant working-men ?

Put your working-man in parliament and he tries to improve himself by imitating the gentlemen around him.

He forgets the fury of those who knew their life's blood is being drunk by refined ladies and gentlemen.

XXIV.

No Temper.

Experience shows that parliamentary parties are never revolutionary.

Not one Socialist party but has been a disappointment.

In some countries a show of force is preserved so long as Socialist members are persecuted, imprisoned and denied the rights of others. It soon ceases after they are treated civilly.

Note how Millerand, Jaures and Viviani, correspond to Burns, Ramsay MacDonald and Richard Bell.

Political Socialism inevitably deteriorates into reformism.

XXV.

Leave it to us.

The voter is told to vote and then to wait until the M.P. can find an opportunity to do something for him.

Parliamentary action soothes. It demands patience.

Whereas strikes, for example, resemble war in that they abound with painful incidents.

They produce fury, resentment, determination to revenge, to gain more, to crush, to make an end of the enemy.

XXVI.

Recent Events.

Disclosures about sales of honours, about the investment of party funds in concerns dependent on coming legislation (railways and Marconi's), Marconi's purchase of Goldschmidt's patent after the government contract had been signed (although Goldschmidt's rights were said to be valueless before), the paid posts given to men who "blocked" awkward motions and who did other dirty jobs for their masters :—these are all things that have helped to discredit parliament.

XXVII.

Be a drudge.

The politician says :—" Vote for me and trust in me."

Do the drudgery, not the brainwork.

Because you are not in parliament where statesmen arrange the future of the country.

You must not carp at us : you do not understand the exigences of the parliamentary situation.

If we seem to run away, there is a good reason for our action.

Parliament encourages the workers to continue to be fools and hands, instead of being complete human beings.

XXVIII.

A Game.

Parliament is like a cricket match : one side fields while the other bats.

If there were no opposition there would be no game.

No sensible person takes games quite seriously.

XXIX.

All Politicians are Liars.

XXX.

No Certainty about the Law.

Employers take advantage of laws intended for the workers' benefit.

They lengthen hours, discharge men, take on women, or introduce labour-saving machinery in order not to lose by what the law dictates.

The direct fight of men against masters is more straightforward than any parliamentary struggle.

At the end of each conflict it is clearer who has won.

XXXI.

Sacrifices for the Cause.

In political life there are many people who have " made great sacrifices for the cause."

They do this by giving up some trade they do not like, and instead—making speeches on platforms, editing newspapers, taking charge of elections, and doing other work which they do like.

Jobs ought to be found for some of these people.

Some are " prospective parliamentary candidates " ; others are taken over by the government—Labour Exchanges and the Insurance Act absorbed a host.

All these paid persons have to prove that the work they do is very useful to the workers.

Labour Exchanges and the Insurance Act are very valuable, say those who get fat salaries out of working them.

XXXII.

Reform.

The purpose of reform is to keep things as they are by repairing the parts which are endangering the whole.

The purpose of reform is to improve the worker as a means for making profit for the employer.

A parliament composed of men of all classes is necessarily compromising and reformist.

The purpose of revolution is to take away the power of the rich and leisured class, and to distribute power and liberty equally.

XXXIII.

Parliament and the Trade Unions.

The tone of parliament is established by the parasitic class—the class that lives, not by producing, but by gambling in the marketing of what others produce ; financiers, monopolists, and spreaders of false news.

They are the people who will be abolished in the coming society.

Trade Unions consist of those who do the necessary work of the world.

The present Trade Unions are very imperfect, but they do contain the permanently necessary class.

Why should we try to convert to our uses what is fundamentally the organ of our enemies, and neglect what is fundamentally our own ?

XXXIV.

The Great Leaders of Parties.

Westminster is far from most of the workers.

The heroes and villains on its stage are, of course, the unreal creations of journalists' imaginations.

How can most of the people judge clearly what is done at Westminster ?

The great leaders of parties are made by beards, eye-glasses, newspaper lies, and the work of unknown men who coach them.

XXXV.

Our Snobs.

Men with us are admired according to their power of making money.

A man is not admired for himself, but for his property.

Therefore our state is not democratic, but oligarchic : we are not really ruled by the many, but by the rich few.

The rich are able to gain the favour of the many.

The rich are fully represented in parliament ; their ideals are vile, and they corrupt all who come within the region in which what they admire is considered good.

The many admire the rich and vote for them.

They lick the hand that robs them.

XXXVI.

The Class-War.

We want to get the class-war into the centre of the stage of attention.

Reasons have been given why parliament does not do this.

The more parliament is regarded as a House of Pretence the more probable it will be that the class-war idea will become important in the minds of the people.

XXXVII.

Parliament Controls Ignorantly.

When parliament acts it tries to increase its own power and the power of the kind and humble state.

But listen to this opinion on the control of a learned profession by amateurs in that profession :—

" The control of a medical service should be entirely medical : no one but a medical man can possibly judge of the value of medical work, and until this fact is recognized by the nation . . . the position of medical officers under local health authorities, boards of guardians, county councils, etc. [will] be unsatisfactory."*

If doctors understand their trade better than outsiders, so do dockers, shipwrights, fishermen, and miners.

*" The Medical World," Nov. 13th, 1913, p. 585.

XXXVIII.

Parliament Tickets and Dockets.

Parliament naturally seeks to keep power in its own hands.

At the most it delegates power, keeping final control of it at the centre.

More and more we drift towards a centralised government controlled in Whitehall offices.

Labour exchanges, insurance benefits, old-age pensions, and development funds are all controlled at central London offices by high officials who take no notice of your complaints or opinions.

More and more, men are ticketed and traceable, and can be punished if they do not please the State, in which the rich are powerful.

The insurance card is a pass-port : it gives information to employers.

And this is inevitable : if you use parliament it will get the state to intervene : the parliamentarians will not give away powers they might retain.

Parliament would make trade unions into machines for carrying out its laws, and break their spirit and their power of fighting masters.

XXXIX.

State Servants.

When parliament is asked to help the worker, it helps in ways that increase the power of parliament. Hence its love of industries run by state departments.

State servants are servants of the public, the community ; their steady work protects the lives of babes, of widows, the poor, and the aged.

They would be peculiarly selfish if they struck.

In Australia, in 1903, when a strike took place on the railways, the Government introduced an Anti-Strike Bill.

In Hungary and France, the state has stopped strikes by using its power of calling on men as military reservists to do their work on the railways or suffer severe penalties.

In Victoria, in consequence of a strike, the law of 1906 forbids all persons in the public service from taking any part in political work, except secretly recording their own votes.

XL.

The Heroic Few.

Individuality is very rare.

What does it matter what the many think ?

It is the heroic few who lead them.

The few by their actions create new worlds, new hopes, new possibilities.

Not the many, who can be duped into a polling station, there to put a cross with a pencil against a name.

Society cannot be altered without a great effort.

XLI.

Vague Abstractions.

The idea of the state, of government, of law, leads people astray.

These are vague abstractions.

Society is the result of the desires and capacities of the people who build it up.

Property exists because of the ideas of labourers and judges, of policemen, shopkeepers, and chemists.

To change society, you must change the ideas and capacities of individuals.

There is not such a thing as a state apart from the persons in it.

The state does not bring about changes, it can only register them.

XLII.

The Conscience of the Nation.

Such majesty surrounds parliament that what it does is inevitably to some extent justified.

But parliament in reality represents the class which compose it—rich men and corrupted poor men, made to share the ideas of the propertied by contact with them.

When parliament sets a standard of wages and conditions—and sets as low a standard as it dares, seeing the degree of discontent then existing among the workers—it is the community, the sacred public, the important consumers, that have spoken.

Not the vulgar herd that makes the necessities of life, and on whom all the superfluities and refinements depend.

XLIII.

Courage Needed.

Parliament, being a vote-catching machine, is timid, opportunist, and unprincipled.

To get a revolution you need courage, directness, fixed principles, and passion.

XLIV.

Two Theories.

There are two theories of society.

Some say men are by nature slaves and masters of slaves, though it is true that some who are naturally slaves are born to be masters, and some are born slaves who should be masters.

Those who believe this say the people have no eye for one naturally suitable for mastership : they elect flatterers and deceivers : government by voting is absurd.

Others believe in levelling, and think that the qualities of all are worth developing : they see value in that which the mob possesses, but which the peculiar heroes do not possess.

They complain that democracy is a sham, and that representatives never represent.

XLV.

Politics Confuses.

When a political proposal is brought forward it is soon sicklied over with doubts and difficulties.

Are those who propose it sincere ? Will the benefits it promises be neutralised by disadvantages, intentionally imposed by opponents of the measure, or unintentionally arising from the workings of selfish commercialism, and will one man's gain be balanced by another's loss ?

This is not what we want. We want a great vision and a passionate desire to spur the worker on to violent efforts.

Without this, nothing great can be achieved.

The Class-War and the Working-Class victory are simple issues. Politics confuses.

XLVI.

Cut Down the Tree.

We preach a Class-War and marshall the Workers against the property-owners.

Parliament is necessarily peaceable. It follows one will-o'-the-wisp after another.

We would cut down the evil tree of poverty at the root, not train and lop its branches until it presents a weird shape.

XLVII.

Action and Opinion.

Many a man who thinks he is a Conservative or a Liberal when you talk of politics is on the right side in a direct conflict between Capital and Labour.

He agrees with strikers' actions and assaults on blacklegs, while he cannot agree with their " politics."

We want the workers to unite in attacking the power of property by every possible means ; we do not so much care whether or not they agree about theories.

XLVIII.

Politics and Trade Unionism.

When discussing things in general or the latest political cry, a man will talk nonsense.

The same man will often talk sense about his own trade.

He knows something about his own trade : it is real to him. He knows what he wants in connection with it.

He talks empty words about politics. Politics are unreal, while trade organizations deal with realities.

XLIX.

The Party Machines.

On Nov. 22nd, 1913, Lloyd George told a deputation that unpopular measures could be passed by the Party Machine.

The Last.

The Working-Class has to take the means of production, the land and factories, and to lock out the master-class.

If they cannot do it, it will never be done for them.

Nothing but a show of power will ever make the owners yield.

The workers must show their power, not how easily they are duped, as they show when they trust in lying politicians.

If orders could fight the battle for them, the subservience and sense of helplessness of the workers would be left unaltered.

Parliament is powerless, unless outside parliament there is power to support it.

But if you have the power to do what you want, what need also to elect delegates to parliament ?

Has it seemed in South Africa and Ulster as if armies and authorities necessarily obey mere laws and constitutions ?

Armies may be loyal to officers, and officers to their class and prejudices.

Men can be deported by force, law or no law.

What you can do, you need no parliament to do for you.

Trades Councils News.

From our Correspondents.

Newport (Mon.).—By 37 votes to 14 the Trades Council of Newport (Mon.) voted against a proposal to ask the Town Council to take a poll of the citizens to see if they wanted Sunday trams. A correspondent tells us :—" The Labour Movement in this town has been blotted out by these seekers of chapel votes, and of having the honour of attending church with the new made mayor every November. This crowd turned almost frantic on Friday last, June 12th, when one delegate moved to protest against spending a couple of hundred pounds on decorations for a visit of a member of the royal unemployed, on visiting the new dock next month to do the people the honour of performing the opening ceremony. O, Guy, you should have seen them, they were all Republicans in a moment, and the resolution of protest was carried almost unanimously. These are the chaps, who a fortnight ago were afraid to trust the people, and take a poll of the town in reference to Sunday cars. Marvellous chaps ! "

Huddersfield.—Here the Trades and Labour Council has made more than one discussion about cutting out the " Labour," and only admitting Trade Unions, organised for industrial purposes. Mr. Crowe, who moved one of the resolutions, said " it was ridiculous that an employer should be enabled to be a delegate to that Council, as was the case with Mr. Riley. The masters, whether they were Socialists or anything else, had to get their living out of the workers, and that being so, it was imperative that no master should be allowed on a Trades Council."

The resolution was defeated, but all the same, Trades Councils, which are destined to be the means by which local crafts will come into association with one another for the supply of the local needs, have purposes so much more important than any connected with the game of politics, played at polling booths at intervals of years, that resolutions of this kind will recur all over the place. The time will come when it will be seen that industrial problems can only be solved industrially, and not by means of charity or politics. The party game is to such an extent played by loyal followers, who never decide anything by their own thinking, but leave everything to the members of parliament, who are presumed to be in a better position to judge, that we must use new methods, which will not leave all the thinking and deciding to so few people.

Liverpool.—The Fund Committee dealing with the money subscribed to help those who lost relatives on whom they were wholly or partly dependent in the " Empress of Ireland " disaster, has refused to allow any representatives of the Trades Council (and consequently of the workers' unions) to serve on it. The funds are being administered so as to cause great dissatisfaction. The sums offered are insufficient, and the relatives have been grossly insulted by members of the committee, who visit their houses for purposes of investigation. The whole concern seems to have dropped into the hands of the doctrine-ridden, inhuman pedants who belong to the Charity Organisation Society—people whose instincts and feelings are not strong enough to enlighten their brains to the absurd narrowness of their economic theories. The General President of the National Union of Ship Stewards, Mr. Cotter, is one of the nominees whom the Lord Mayor of Liverpool refuses to admit to the committee.

Portsmouth.—There is a very important Trades Council in this place, containing an affiliation of some 60 branches, representing an aggregate of about 10,000 members. The secretary, Mr. H. G. Harris, is a railway man, who urges the members to read the " Daily Citizen " every day. In his annual report for last year he tells his readers, in connection with the South African troubles, that " the utter barrenness of the Syndicalist position has been ruthlessly exposed." Mr. Roberts, the chairman, is believed to be a Nonconformist, and though a very charming man, one can easily imagine the shock he must have sustained when he heard Guy Bowman address the Council's delegates a little while ago. Anyhow, when some members proposed and seconded a vote of thanks to the Syndicalist speaker, Mr. Roberts refused to put it, and said he hoped that in future the Council would devote its time to more useful business.

Syndicalism for Clerks.

By "REMUS,"

Member of the National Executive N.U.C.

III.—Continued from Last Issue.

SABOTAGE.

Sabotage is one of the chief weapons to be used in the attack on the capitalist state, and it has the advantage of not requiring the active co-operation of the whole of the workers in an industry to ensure its successful application.

A militant minority in the Unions can, by adopting the various forms of Sabotage, demoralize an industry, and by so doing, compel the " timid " majority to share in the benefits obtained ; and while perhaps this is not altogether as we would desire, yet it prevents the majority from hindering progress.

Another advantage of Sabotage is that it can be practiced while the workers are drawing the sinews of war, in the shape of wages—thus hitting the enemy doubly, and not having to rely upon Trade Union funds. The capitalist class are practicing this method in its most dangerous forms every day, with disastrous results to the community.

The adulteration of food, the brewing of beer from corn leaves and chemicals, the making of sweets with vaseline, boots with paper soles, boilers with inferior metals and weak spots—these, and a thousand and one methods of adulteration and swindling, are sapping the vitals of the nation, and with the object of—what ?

Simply with the object of increasing their banking accounts. Capitalist Sabotage is inspired by the greed of gold ; whereas the Sabotage advocated by the Syndicalists is inspired by altruistic motives, having for its only object the emancipation of the workers.

It is directed against the greed and avarice of the capitalist class, and practices which would injure the general public are tabooed.

It is not wise, when writing on this subject, to divulge your plans to the enemy ; but to illustrate one of the more peaceful, and at the same time very effective, forms of Sabotage, I will give an example. This is what is called the ca' canny method, meaning the restriction of output.

Practiced on an extensive scale, and by sufficient numbers, the workers could, by this method, compel the employing class to engage more workers in the offices and workshops in order to cope with the work—thereby reducing the army of unemployed without, assisting to raise wages all round, and shortening the hours of labour. They would thus be serving a twofold purpose, by reducing the margin of profit and partially solving the unemployed problem.

Numerous other forms of Sabotage will readily occur to my readers, but enough has been written to show the efficacy of the method, and to whet their appetite for more information regarding this form of Direct Action.

THE GENERAL STRIKE.

We now come to the General Strike, which is the form of Direct Action which will be used in order to accomplish the final overthrow of the capitalist system ; and very little imagination is necessary to enable one to picture the result of a general policy of " down tools," combined with militant action.

In order to bring about the General Strike it will not be necessary to secure the co-operation of the whole of the workers in the initial stages.

As I have shown in that portion of this pamphlet dealing with Sabotage, it is possible for a militant minority in the Unions, by practising various forms of Sabotage intelligently, to completely demoralise industry, and make impossible the continuance of capitalist profit-making.

The capitalists, finding that the smooth working of their industries is no longer possible, will probably retaliate by a vast " lock-out," thus closing the source of income—in the shape of wages—to the workers ; who will then be compelled to act in a drastic manner, there being three alternatives open to them.

They can starve ! They can go back to work for the capitalist class on worse terms and in greater degradation than they have hitherto known ; or they can take possession of the means of Life, and run and control them in their own interests !

Which alternative will they choose ?

Will it be starvation, slavery, or Freedom ?

The fight for Freedom, and the taking possession of the various industries, will be no drawing-room affair, as I have said previously, but will only be achieved by militant and insurrectionist methods.

The capitalist class will defend by all the means in their power their possessions, as has been clearly demonstrated in Dublin, South Africa, and elsewhere ; and it is for the workers to make suitable preparations for the attack on, and the capture of, those possessions.

AFTER THE GENERAL STRIKE.

Having accomplished the General Strike, and thereby the overthrow of the capitalist system, we will see how it is proposed to manage and run the industries so that the whole of the community may obtain the fullest possible benefit from their labours ; and here we shall see why the State, as it is understood to-day, will cease to exist.

Of the perfectly logical assumption that the workers in an industry know more about the working of the industry than do those outside, the control of each industry should be vested in a committee consisting of delegates appointed by the various sections of workers in an industry, each section having equal representation on these committees.

These delegates would not be appointed by reason of their possessing an engaging personality, great oratorical ability, or an ability to " boss " and speed up their fellows, as is so often the case under the present system ; but by examination, having proven themselves to be possessed of more knowledge and ability for the positions than their fellow-workers. These industrial committees would have complete autonomy on all matters concerning the industry alone, being only answerable to the workers in the industry.

Take, for example, the Boot and Shoe-Making Industry, and suppose that a machine was invented capable of turning out footwear in larger quantities and with less labour than hitherto.

The question of the installation of those machines would be a matter of figures, and would be decided by the members of the industry, no outsiders being allowed to interfere in matters of this description. This autonomy would extend downwards to each section of the workers in the various industries, they understanding the needs and requirements of their trade better than would those of another trade in the industries.

Thus, the clerical workers would have autonomy as to what method of keeping records, etc., should be adopted, while other sections would have autonomy in all matters affecting them directly.

Each industry would regulate its output according to the demands made upon it by the whole of the community.

Take, again, for example, the Boot and Shoe-Making Industry.

The requirements of the community in footwear could easily be ascertained by a simple process of arithmetic, basing the figures on so many pairs of boots, etc., for each individual per year.

The industry would then prepare for the supply of footwear required, regulating the hours of labour accordingly ; and the same process would obtain throughout the whole of the industries.

LOCAL COMMITTEES.

In regard to local matters, affecting the welfare of the inhabitants of a town or village, these would be regulated by a committee similar to our present Trades Councils, and composed of delegates from the various industries, who would be appointed by the workers in each industry, according to their proven ability in administrative matters, and by examination ; not by virtue of their influence, or influence used on their behalf, as is so often the case under the present system.

These local committees would also adjust matters between the industries in a locality, and arbitrate generally on local affairs.

Then we come to the National Administrative Committees, which, I would suggest, should be composed of delegates appointed by the local committees, the appointments being made by virtue of their having passed a searching examination in administration, and because of their knowledge in matters of national import, and their proven ability on the local bodies.

These National Committees would deal with matters of national importance and arbitrate on matters that may arise between localities.

They would have no dictatorial powers as to whether certain action should be taken from time to time by certain industries, or localities ; these matters being decided by the workers themselves.

If an industry or a locality decided that certain action was desirable and necessary to their particular interests, they would be free to act, without outside interference.

It will thus be seen that Syndicalism offers no careers to unscrupulous, place-seeking individuals ; hence the bitter opposition of many of our so-called " leaders " to its advocacy.

Sufficient has been written, I think, to give my readers some idea as to what the proposals of the Syndicalists really are, and to stimulate them into a further study of the subject.

AN APPEAL.

I would appeal to those who are convinced that the present system is unjust, and that the new form of organisation is necessary, and that the old-fashioned Trade Unionism is of little use in the great struggle for Freedom, to put their brains and their energy into an attempt to convert others to their way of thinking ; and by education and enthusiasm inspire them to greater deeds than they have hitherto known.

Only by our own efforts, standing firmly together, can we ever achieve that great consummation, " The World for the Workers," and enjoy to the full a free and happy life, wherein no one who works, or is unable to work through physical or mental disability shall go unfed, unclothed, or uncared for.

It is to this end that the aim of the Syndicalists is directed, and if through reading this pamphlet some of my readers are converted to these ideals and desires, my little effort will not have been in vain.

I cannot conclude better than by quoting the lines of Goethe :

" We are not here to play, to dream, to drift,
We have hard work to do, and loads to lift ;
SHUN NOT THE STRUGGLE—FACE IT—'tis God's gift ! "

(Concluded.)

THE BLACK INTERNATIONAL.

By F. Tarrida del Marmol.

Labour in its struggle for emancipation must perforce encounter and vanquish numerous enemies. The capitalist, the landlord, the state, the army, and the priest are all so many foes who have to be destroyed.

Perhaps of them all, the priest is the most formidable. He is certainly the oldest. In the shape of the Catholic Church he has managed to keep his organisation together through three distinct historical periods. Sorely battered by the bourgeois revolution, shorn of much of its wealth and power, Catholicism ever looks forward (or backward) to a restoration of the state of things which prevailed previous to the French Revolution. And herein lies a danger to the working-class movement. Catholic writers, in many cases, criticise capitalism, and seem to be in agreement with some of the attacks made on the present order by Syndicalists, Socialists, and Anarchists. But if the reader will analyse the writings of Mr. Belloc, for instance, he will find that in reality what Catholics complain of in capitalism is that precisely it engenders Freethought, Trade Unions, Socialism, Syndicalism, Anarchism, and other menaces to social peace.

Another danger is that the proletariat has decided to treat religion as a private matter. The Socialists, for electoral reasons, and the Syndicalists because they wish to unite the workers on the basis of their economic interests, have adopted a neutrality towards the churches, to which Catholicism has responded by furious attacks on organised Labour, the organisation of Catholic Unions which function as blackleg supplying agencies, etc. Recent events at Dublin are calculated to make the supporters of mentality a little uneasy.

But what I wish to point out here is that the Vatican is an international centre of conspiracy against the people. In our time Persia, Turkey, China, and Portugal have overturned some of the political barriers to their evolution. I have no desire to exaggerate the benefits of merely political freedom. But, after all, the Labour Movement flourishes better in a constitutional atmosphere than in a despotic regime. Portuguese Syndicalism was born with the Republic just as Trade Unionism was born of capitalism. It is for us to go onwards, but not to allow Catholic scribes to induce us with their sophistries to turn back.

And let us take note that in every one of the four cases I have mentioned, all the forces of international reaction have been let loose against the countries named. And this reaction has in every case been headed by Catholics. In the case of Portugal they have actually been successful in misleading some Anarchists and Syndicalists. Such is the hatred that the Catholic church feels towards liberty that even where apparently it stands to gain by a new regime it fights bitterly against it. Take the case of Ireland. Irish Home Rule will undoubtedly settle the national issue, and allow many Irish workers to think more of their class interests. And the increased political freedom will be favourable to Labour. Therefore Catholicism, regardless of its present predominance in Ireland, fights against Home Rule. The Duke of Norfolk, and with him 31 out of the 33 Roman Catholic peers, Lord Edmond Talbot, Major Archer-Shee, and Mr. Rowland Hunt, in their hatred of liberty, line up side by side with fanatical Orangemen whose cry is " To Hell with the Pope." And what about the curious attitude of such Catholic " democrats " as Scurr, Belloc, and the brothers Chesterton ?

Let Labour men be on their guard against the church. Wherever Catholicism flourishes, the propagandists of working-class ideas find a barrier. And that barrier had to be overthrown. In the words of Voltaire " Ecrasez l'infame."
